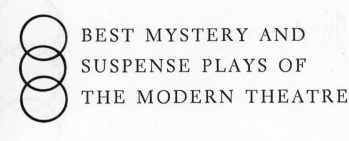

BEST MYSTERY AND SUSPENSE PLAYS OF THE MODERN THEATRE

BOOKS AND PLAYS BY STANLEY RICHARDS

BOOKS: BEST MYSTERY AND SUSPENSE PLAYS OF THE MODERN THEATRE
BEST PLAYS OF THE SIXTIES
MODERN SHORT COMEDIES FROM BROADWAY AND LONDON
BEST SHORT PLAYS OF THE WORLD THEATRE: 1958–1967
THE BEST SHORT PLAYS 1971
THE BEST SHORT PLAYS 1970
THE BEST SHORT PLAYS 1969
THE BEST SHORT PLAYS 1968
CANADA ON STAGE

PLAYS: THROUGH A GLASS, DARKLY
AUGUST HEAT
SUN DECK
TUNNEL OF LOVE
JOURNEY TO BAHIA
O DISTANT LAND
MOOD PIECE
MR. BELL'S CREATION
THE PROUD AGE
ONCE TO EVERY BOY
HALF-HOUR, PLEASE
KNOW YOUR NEIGHBOR
GIN AND BITTERNESS
THE HILLS OF BATAAN
DISTRICT OF COLUMBIA

BEST MYSTERY AND SUSPENSE PLAYS OF THE MODERN THEATRE

Edited with an introductory note and prefaces to the plays
by *STANLEY RICHARDS*

Illustrated with photographs from the original productions

DODD, MEAD & COMPANY • NEW YORK

NOTE: All plays contained in this volume are fully protected under the Copyright Laws of the United States of America, the British Empire, including the Dominion of Canada, and all other countries of the International Copyright Union and the Universal Copyright Convention. Permission to reproduce, wholly or in part, by any method, must be obtained from the copyright owners or their agents. (See Caution notices at the beginning of each play.)

FOR KAY E. RADTKE
AND MARGARET NORTON

CONTENTS

CONTENTS

AN INTRODUCTORY NOTE

It is erroneous to deny the mystery and suspense play its rightful place in the history of drama just as it is presumptuous to classify it as a second-class theatre citizen. Perhaps the vast commercial success of a number of the genre has overshadowed the significant fact that many were warmly endorsed by the most erudite and the crustiest of critics. For example, six of the plays in this collection were named as one of the "ten best" of their respective seasons and Agatha Christie's *Witness for the Prosecution* received the esteemed New York Drama Critics' Circle Award as best foreign play of 1954–55. As far as audience receptivity is concerned, the thriller's stage longevity is noteworthy. In New York alone, nine of the plays—*Sleuth* had just opened at the time of this writing—represented in this volume tallied more than 5,000 performances in their original productions. What went beyond—with countless revivals, road, stock and amateur performances—only God and the plays' copyright holders can determine.

There always are among us those self-appointed élitists who automatically associate mass public acceptance with inferiority of taste and product. Yet, while the critics may offer their blessings, it is the public who must offer its patronage in order for a play to survive. The fact that the plays found within these pages enjoyed enormous audience popularity on stage and in various metamorphoses in other media has proven unequivocally that they have fulfilled one of the theatre's major functions, which is to entertain.

Although the origin of modern comedy generally is attributed to France, that resourceful nation also had a hand in creating melodrama. It all began with Guilbert de Pixérécourt (1773–1844) who became known as *"le père du mélodrame."* A prolific French dramatist who created more than fifty melodramas during his lifetime, he also was singularly honored by a constant pilferage of his works. Many of his plays, or, at least, their substance, soon crossed the channel to England, and in 1802 his *Coelina: ou l'Enfant du Mystère* (historically regarded as the first genuine melodrama) was produced by Kemble at Covent Garden in a free translation by Thomas Holcroft (1745–1809) called *Tale of Mystery*. Thus, the form officially came into the English-language theatre. It may be added at this point that the medieval mystery plays have no connection with what we regard today as "mysteries." They were religious dramas based on the Holy Mysteries of the Bible, hence their early designation as "mystery plays."

Melodrama continued its triumphant course right into the twentieth century led by William Gillette's 1899 adaptation of Sir Arthur Conan Doyle's *Sherlock Holmes* stories. Although it was a success of major proportions—Gillette revived it frequently until 1931 when he gave the play its farewell tour—Sir Arthur's son, Adrian, wrote to this editor: "We regret that as we do not have a high opinion of this play we do not wish it to be published." A paradoxical and startling comment, to say the least, for Gillette's dramatization never became obsolete and undoubtedly poured a fortune in royalties into the coffers of the Conan Doyle estate for more than half a century.

With *Sherlock Holmes*, melodrama began to take on gradual refinements and there was less of the blood and thunder of the earliest days. (One of the stage directions in Holcroft's piece deserves to be quoted: "Amid terrible lightning, thunder, hail, rain, and suitable music, the fugitive villain enters pursued, as it were, by heaven and earth.") In the mid-thirties, after all those bodies had fallen out of innumerable stage closets and clutching hands had receded to the dark and dreadful passages concealed by mysterious mobile wall panels, melodrama turned a new and most welcome corner. It developed into the psychological thriller, a change from the direct to the indirect, where hair-raising effects were subordinated to the greater validity of situation and characterization.

Even the most invidious of stage villains found himself imbued with some recognizable human characteristics. In short, characters who populated the contemporary mystery and suspense play—and the latter description is somewhat redundant for *every* type of play must have an element of suspense, otherwise there would be little point in sticking around for the final curtain—had progressed from formularized figures to individuals, no matter how hellish or lethal their bent. No longer was it all a matter of twists and turns of plot: characterization had become as essential to the form as it was to all types of drama. Even in *Dracula*, the oldest work represented in this collection and, undeniably, one that flaunts the old heraldry, there still is an exceptionally conceived character, Count Dracula, and he is the foremost reason why the play, in spite of its outmoded gimmickry, has endured.

Action, of course, had not been neglected for though characters set a play's wheels in motion, it is the action that keeps them spinning. As Sir Max Beerbohm once stated: "The drama is, after all, essentially a vehicle for action. For drama, as the Greeks quite frankly called it, is essentially, or at least mainly, a thing to cause the excitement of pity and awe, or of terror, or of laughter . . . where the characters are saying and doing things in your very presence. The theatre, I would say, is a place for thrills."

And now the moment has come for the editor to vanish through an artfully concealed panel in his studio and permit the plays to get on with their *raison d'être*.

Overture and beginners, please!

STANLEY RICHARDS

Witness for the Prosecution

AGATHA CHRISTIE

Agatha Christie

It could hardly be more fitting than to open this collection with a work by Agatha Christie, the *grande dame* of mystery and suspense. Fifty years after she revolutionized detective fiction with her first published novel, *The Mysterious Affair at Styles*—which introduced her immortal character Hercule Poirot to the world—Mrs. Christie remains supreme in her realm. Her eighty or so books, translated into many languages, have enjoyed worldwide sales of 350 million copies. Yet, with all consideration to her reputation as mystery novelist, it must be acknowledged that Mrs. Christie is a formidable figure in the theatre as well. Since 1928, when *Alibi*, the Michael Morton dramatization of her classic *The Murder of Roger Ackroyd*, ran for 250 performances at the Prince of Wales Theatre in London, Mrs. Christie has been represented on stage by at least eighteen plays that either she herself has written or have been adapted by others from her stories. Her theatre pieces, and approximately fifteen motion pictures culled from her works amply justify the observation of the distinguished British critic, Ivor Brown: "Nowadays we live, not only as readers, but as play and filmgoers, in a whirl of Christie criminology."

Based on her short story of similar title, *Witness for the Prosecution* is regarded by connoisseurs as her finest hour in the theatre. It is a first-rate courtroom drama with a tightly woven plot that keeps tension and suspense mounting until the sensational double twist that brings down the curtain. "You can never trust Mrs. Christie to have finished until the curtain is irrevocably down," according to W. A. Darlington, "for she has a miraculous faculty for constructing puzzles which seem to have one solution and turn out to have another equally plausible." Mrs. Christie does not only complicate clues: she creates convincing and colorful characters and her duplication of the Old Bailey courtroom is populated by some of her most intriguing stage people.

Witness for the Prosecution originally opened on October 28, 1953, at the Winter Garden Theatre, London, and ran for 458 performances. The New York première took place on December 16, 1954, at Henry Miller's Theatre. Brooks Atkinson of *The New York Times* termed the thriller "one of the best" of its genre; so, apparently, did theatregoers who patronized it for 644 performances. At season's end, it received the 1954–55 New York Drama Critics' Circle Award as the year's best foreign play. It was a signal honor, for never before or since has the accolade been bestowed upon a mystery or suspense drama. Not to be outdone in the honors department, Billy Wilder's 1958 film version of *Witness for the Prosecution*, which starred Charles Laughton, Marlene Dietrich, and Tyrone Power, won four Academy Award nominations.

Achieving honors and setting records come as readily to Mrs. Christie as does her fluency in lethal fancies. During one period, 1953–54, she became England's first distaff playwright to have three offerings running concurrently in the West End: *Witness for the Prosecution; Spider's Web;* and *The Mousetrap.*

That, however, was merely Mrs. Christie's foothold on theatrical records for, in due time, *The Mousetrap*, which opened on November 25, 1952, went on to become the longest-running play in London's theatre history. As of this writing, it is entering its nineteenth year and has played over 7,400 performances. Before its legendary opening, Mrs. Christie regarded it as "a well-constructed little play that might well run for six months or so." Her producer, Peter Saunders, was somewhat more optimistic: he prophesied an engagement of about fourteen months. That was in 1952. Since then both author and management have evaded any predictions about its final count, for the end is not remotely in sight.

Agatha Christie's other plays include: *Ten Little Indians; Verdict; Hidden Horizon; Towards Zero; The Hollow; The Unexpected Guest; Rule of Three; Appointment With Death; Black Coffee; Go Back for Murder;* and *Love From a Stranger,* which she dramatized with Frank Vosper, an eminent British actor who mysteriously disappeared at sea while sailing home after appearing in the play on the Broadway stage.

To enumerate all of her novels and short stories published between 1920 and 1970, when she celebrated her eightieth birthday with the publication of her eightieth book, *Passenger to Frankfurt*, would require considerable space. A listing, however, is available in an appreciation and bibliography of her work: *Agatha Christie, Mistress of Mystery* by G. C. Ramsey.

Born Agatha Mary Clarissa Miller in 1890 at Torquay in Devonshire, the English countryside that has served as the setting for many of her stories, in her youth she studied piano and voice in Paris, and with the encouragement of her mother and the novelist-dramatist Eden Phillpotts, a Devon neighbor, wrote what she has described as "stories of unrelieved gloom, where most of the characters died." Considering her later professional authorship, that is hardly surprising, for as Ivor Brown so aptly put it: "Has any writer ever had a greater corpus of corpse-ridden books and plays? Mrs. Christie is incapable of seeing two or three living persons gathered together without imagining a fourth who has ceased to live."

In 1914, she married Archibald Christie, and although the marriage was dissolved fourteen years later, she professionally retained the Christie name. Her second husband is the noted archaeologist Sir Max Mallowan, whom she married in 1930, and she often has served as his assistant on expeditions in the Middle East. The couple maintain two residences, a home near Oxford and an estate in Devonshire.

A fellow of the Royal Society of Literature, Agatha Christie, in 1971, was created a Dame of the Order of the British Empire by Queen Elizabeth II.

Witness for the Prosecution was first produced by Peter Saunders at the Winter Garden Theatre, London, on October 28, 1953. The cast was as follows:

GRETA, typist to Sir Wilfrid	*Rosalie Westwater*
CARTER, Sir Wilfrid's Chief Clerk	*Walter Horsbrugh*
MR. MAYHEW, a solicitor	*Milton Rosmer*
LEONARD VOLE	*Derek Blomfield*
SIR WILFRID ROBARTS, Q.C.	*David Horne*
INSPECTOR HEARNE	*David Raven*
PLAIN-CLOTHES DETECTIVE	*Kenn Kennedy*
ROMAINE	*Patricia Jessel*
CLERK OF THE COURT	*Philip Holles*
MR. JUSTICE WAINWRIGHT	*Percy Marmont*
ALDERMAN	*Walter Horsbrugh*
MR. MYERS, Q.C.	*D. A. Clarke-Smith*
COURT USHER	*Nicolas Tannar*
COURT STENOGRAPHER	*John Bryning*
WARDER	*Denzil Ellis*
THE JUDGE'S CLERK	*Muir Little*
1ST BARRISTER	*George Dudley*
2ND BARRISTER	*Jack Bulloch*
3RD BARRISTER	*Lionel Gadsden*
4TH BARRISTER	*John Farries Moss*
5TH BARRISTER	*Richard Coke*
6TH BARRISTER	*Agnes Fraser*
1ST MEMBER OF THE JURY	*Lauderdale Beckett*
2ND MEMBER OF THE JURY	*Iris Fraser Foss*
3RD MEMBER OF THE JURY	*Kenn Kennedy*
A POLICEMAN	*David Homewood*
DR. WYATT, a police surgeon	*Graham Stuart*
JANET MACKENZIE	*Jean Stuart*
MR. CLEGG, a laboratory assistant	*Peter Franklin*
THE OTHER WOMAN	*Rosemary Wallace*

Directed by	Wallace Douglas
Décor by	Michael Weight

Witness for the Prosecution was first presented in the United States at Henry Miller's Theatre, New York, on December 16, 1954, by Gilbert Miller and Peter Saunders. The cast was as follows:

CARTER	*Gordon Nelson*
GRETA	*Mary Barclay*
SIR WILFRID ROBARTS, Q.C.	*Francis L. Sullivan*
MR. MAYHEW	*Robin Craven*
LEONARD VOLE	*Gene Lyons*
INSPECTOR HEARNE	*Claude Horton*
PLAIN-CLOTHES DETECTIVE	*Ralph Leonard*
ROMAINE	*Patricia Jessel*
THIRD JUROR	*Dolores Rashid*
SECOND JUROR	*Andrew George*
FOREMAN OF THE JURY	*Jack Bittner*
COURT USHER	*Arthur Oshlag*
CLERK OF THE COURT	*Ronald Dawson*
MR. MYERS, Q.C.	*Ernest Clark*
MR. JUSTICE WAINWRIGHT	*Horace Braham*
ALDERMAN	*R. Cobden-Smith*
JUDGE'S CLERK	*Harold Webster*
COURT STENOGRAPHER	*W. H. Thomas*
WARDER	*Ralph Roberts*
BARRISTER	*Henry Craig Neslo*
BARRISTER	*Brace Conning*
BARRISTER	*Ruth Greene*
BARRISTER	*Albert Richards*
BARRISTER	*Franklyn Monroe*
BARRISTER	*Sam Kramer*
POLICEMAN	*Bryan Herbert*
DR. WYATT	*Guy Spaull*
JANET MACKENZIE	*Una O'Connor*
MR. CLEGG	*Michael McAloney*
THE OTHER WOMAN	*Dawn Steinkamp*

Directed by	Robert Lewis
Designed by	Raymond Sovey
Costumes supervised by	Kathryn Miller

ACT ONE

The Chambers of Sir Wilfrid Robarts, Q.C., in London. Late afternoon.

ACT TWO

The Central Criminal Court, London—better known as The Old Bailey. Six weeks later. Morning.

ACT THREE

SCENE 1: *The Chambers of Sir Wilfrid Robarts, Q.C. The same evening.*

SCENE 2: *The Old Bailey. The next morning.*

TIME: *The present.*

ACT ONE

The Chambers of SIR WILFRID ROBARTS, Q.C.

The scene is SIR WILFRID's *private office. It is a narrow room with the door left and a window right. The window has a deep built-in window seat and overlooks a tall plain brick wall. There is a fireplace center of the back wall, flanked by bookcases filled with heavy legal volumes. There is a desk right center with a swivel chair right of it and a leather-covered upright chair left of it. A second upright chair stands against the bookcases left of the fireplace. In the corner up right is a tall reading desk, and in the corner up left are some coat hooks attached to the wall. At night the room is lit by electric candle-lamp wall brackets right and left of the fireplace and an angle-poise lamp on the desk. The light switch is below the door left. There is a bell push left of the fireplace. The desk has a telephone on it and is littered with legal documents. There are the usual deedboxes and there is a litter of documents on the window seat.*

When the curtain rises it is afternoon and there is sunshine streaming in through the window. The office is empty. GRETA, SIR WILFRID's *typist, enters immediately. She is an adenoidal girl with a good opinion of herself. She crosses to the fireplace, doing a "square dance" step, and takes a paper from a box-file on the mantelpiece.* CARTER, *the Chief Clerk, enters. He carries some letters.* GRETA *turns, sees* CARTER, *crosses and quietly exits.* CARTER *goes to the desk and puts the letters on it. The telephone rings.* CARTER *lifts the receiver.*

CARTER: [*Into the telephone*] Sir Wilfrid Robarts' Chambers . . . Oh, it's you, Charles . . . No, Sir Wilfrid's in Court . . . Won't be back just yet . . . Yes, Shuttleworth Case . . . What—with Myers for the prosecution and Banter trying it? . . . He's been giving judgment for close on two hours already . . . No, not an earthly this evening. We're full up. Can give you an appointment tomorrow . . . No, couldn't possibly. I'm expecting Mayhew, of Mayhew and Brinskill, you know, any minute now . . . Well, so long. [*He replaces the receiver and sorts the documents on the desk*]

[GRETA *enters. She is painting her nails*]

GRETA: Shall I make the tea, Mr. Carter?

CARTER: [*Looking at his watch*] It's hardly time yet, Greta.

GRETA: It is by my watch.

CARTER: Then your watch is wrong.

GRETA: I put it right by the radio.

CARTER: Then the radio must be wrong.

GRETA: [*Shocked*] Oh, not the radio, Mr. Carter. That *couldn't* be wrong.

CARTER: This watch was my father's. It never gains nor loses. They don't make watches like that nowadays. [*He shakes his head, then suddenly changes his manner and picks up one of the typewritten papers*] Really, your typing. Always mistakes. [*He crosses to* GRETA] You've left out a word.

GRETA: Oh, well—just one word. Anyone might do that.

CARTER: The word you have left out is the word *not*. The omission of it entirely alters the sense.

GRETA: Oh, does it? That's rather funny when you come to think of it. [*She giggles*]

CARTER: It is not in the least funny. [*He tears the letter in half and hands the pieces to her*] Do it again. You may remember I told you last week about the celebrated case of Bryant and Horsfall. Case of a will and a trust fund, and entirely owing to a piece of careless copying by a clerk . . .

GRETA: [*Interrupting*] The wrong wife got the money, I remember.

CARTER: A woman divorced fifteen years previously. Absolutely contrary to the intention of the testator, as his lordship himself admitted. But the wording had to stand. They couldn't do anything about it. [*He crosses to the desk*]

GRETA: I think *that's* rather funny, too. [*She giggles*]

CARTER: Counsel's Chambers are no place to be funny in. The Law, Greta, is a serious business and should be treated accordingly.

GRETA: You wouldn't think so—to hear some of the jokes judges make.

CARTER: That kind of joke is the prerogative of the Bench.

GRETA: And I'm always reading in the paper about "laughter in Court."

CARTER: If that's not caused by one of the judge's remarks you'll find he'll soon threaten to have the Court cleared.

GRETA: [*Starting for the door*] Mean old thing. [*She turns back*] Do you know what I read the other day, Mr. Carter? [*Sententiously*] "The Law's an Ass." I'm not being rude. It's a quotation.

CARTER: [*Coldly*] A quotation of a facetious nature. Not meant to be taken seriously. [*He looks at his watch*] You can make the tea— [*He pauses, waiting for the exact second*]—now, Greta.

GRETA: [*Gladly*] Oh, thank you, Mr. Carter. [*She crosses quickly to the door*]

CARTER: Mr. Mayhew, of Mayhew and Brinskill, will be here shortly. A Mr. Leonard Vole is also expected. They may come together or separately.

GRETA: [*Excitedly*] Leonard Vole? [*She crosses back to the desk*] Why, that's the name—it was in the paper . . .

CARTER: [*Repressively*] The tea, Greta.

GRETA: Asked to communicate with the police as he might be able to give them useful information.

CARTER: [*Raising his voice*] *Tea!*

GRETA: It was only last . . . [CARTER *glowers at* GRETA] The tea, Mr. Carter.

[GRETA, *abashed but unsatisfied, exits.* CARTER *continues his arrangement of the papers, muttering to himself*]

CARTER: These girls. Sensational—inaccurate—I don't know what the Temple's coming to. [*He examines a typewritten document, makes an angry sound, picks up a pen and makes a correction*]

[GRETA *enters*]

GRETA: [*Announcing*] Mr. Mayhew.

[MR. MAYHEW *and* LEONARD VOLE *enter.* MAYHEW *is a typical middle-aged solicitor, shrewd and rather dry and precise in manner.* LEONARD *is a likable, friendly young man, about twenty-seven. He is looking faintly worried.* MAYHEW *carries a brief case*]

MAYHEW: [*Giving his hat to* GRETA] Sit down, Mr. Vole. [*He puts his brief case on the desk*] Good afternoon, Carter.

[GRETA *takes* LEONARD'S *hat and hangs both on the pegs above the door. She then exits, staring at* LEONARD *over her shoulder*]

CARTER: Good afternoon, Mr. Mayhew. Sir Wilfrid shouldn't be long, sir, although you never can tell with Mr. Justice Banter. I'll go straight over to the Robing Room and tell him that you're here with . . . [*He hesitates*]

MAYHEW: With Mr. Leonard Vole. Thank you, Carter. I'm afraid our appointment was at rather short notice. But in this case time is—er—rather urgent. [*As* CARTER *crosses to the door*] How's the lumbago?

CARTER: [*Turning*] I only feel it when the wind is in the East. Thank you for remembering, Mr. Mayhew.

[CARTER *exits hurriedly.* MAYHEW *sits left of the desk.* LEONARD *prowls uneasily*]

MAYHEW: Sit down, Mr. Vole.

LEONARD: Thanks—I'd rather walk about. I—this sort of thing makes you feel a bit jumpy.

MAYHEW: Yes, yes, very probably . . .

[GRETA *enters. She speaks to* MAYHEW, *but stares with fascinated interest at* LEONARD]

GRETA: Would you care for a cup of tea, Mr. Mayhew? I've just made it.

LEONARD: [*Appreciatively*] Thanks. I don't mind if I . . .

MAYHEW: [*Interrupting; decisively*] No, thank you.

LEONARD: [*To* GRETA] Sorry. [*He smiles at her. She smiles back at him and exits. There is a pause. Then, abruptly and with a rather likable air of bewilderment*] What I mean is, I can't believe it's *me* this is happening to. I keep thinking—perhaps it's all a dream and I'll wake up presently.

MAYHEW: Yes, I suppose one might feel like that.

LEONARD: What I mean is—well, it seems so silly.

MAYHEW: [*Sharply*] Silly, Mr. Vole?

LEONARD: Well, yes. I mean I've always been a friendly sort of chap —get on with people and all that. I mean, I'm not the sort of fellow that does—well, anything violent. [*He pauses*] But I suppose it will be—all right, won't it? I mean you don't get convicted for things you haven't done in this country, do you?

MAYHEW: Our English judicial system is, in my opinion, the finest in the world.

LEONARD: [*Not much comforted*] Of course there was that case of— what was his name—Adolf Beck. I read about it only the other day. After he'd been in prison for years, they found out it was another chap called Smith. They gave him a free pardon then. That's a thing that seems odd to me—giving you a "pardon" for something you haven't done.

MAYHEW: It is the necessary legal term.

LEONARD: Well, it doesn't seem right to me.

MAYHEW: The important thing was that Beck was set at liberty.

LEONARD: Yes, it was all right for him. But if it had been murder now —if it had been murder it would have been too late. He would have been hanged.

MAYHEW: [*Dry but kindly*] Now, Mr. Vole, there is really no need to take a—er—morbid point of view.

LEONARD: [*Rather pathetically*] I'm sorry, sir. But you see, in a way, I'm rather getting the wind up.

MAYHEW: Well, try and keep calm. Sir Wilfrid Robarts will be here presently and I want you to tell your story to him exactly as you told it to me.

LEONARD: Yes, sir.

MAYHEW: But meantime perhaps we might fill out a little more of the detail—er—background. You are at present, I understand, out of a job?

LEONARD: [*Embarrassed*] Yes, but I've got a few pounds put by. It's not much, but if you can see your way . . .

MAYHEW: [*Upset*] Oh, I'm not thinking of—er—legal fees. It's just the—er—pictures I'm trying to get clear. Your surroundings and —er—circumstances. How long have you been unemployed?

[LEONARD *answers everything readily, with an engaging friendliness*]

LEONARD: About a couple of months.

MAYHEW: What were you doing before that?

LEONARD: I was in a motor servicing firm—kind of mechanic, that's what I was.

MAYHEW: How long had you worked there?

LEONARD: Oh, about three months.

MAYHEW: [*Sharply*] Were you discharged?

LEONARD: No, I quit. Had words with the foreman. Proper old b—— [*He breaks off*] That is, he was a mean sort of chap, always picking on you.

MAYHEW: Hm! And before that?

LEONARD: I worked in a petrol station, but things got a bit awkward and I left.

MAYHEW: Awkward? In what way?

LEONARD: [*Embarrassed*] Well—the boss's daughter—she was only a kid, but she took a—well, a sort of fancy to me—and there was nothing there shouldn't have been between us, but the old man got a bit fed up and said I'd better go. He was quite nice about it and gave me a good chit. [*He suddenly grins*] Before *that*, I was selling egg beaters on commission.

MAYHEW: Indeed.

LEONARD: [*Boyishly*] And a rotten job they were, too. I could have invented a better egg beater myself. [*Catching* MAYHEW'*s mood*] You're thinking I'm a bit of a drifter, sir. It's true in a way—but I'm not really like that. Doing my army service unsettled me a bit —that and being abroad. I was in Germany. It was fine there. That's where I met my wife. She's an actress. Since I've come back to this country I can't seem somehow to settle down properly. I don't know really just what I want to do—I like working on cars best and thinking out new gadgets for them. That's interesting, that is. And you see . . .

> [SIR WILFRID ROBARTS, Q.C., *enters. He is followed on by* CARTER. SIR WILFRID *is wearing his* Q.C.'s *jacket and bands and carries his wig and gown.* CARTER *carries* SIR WILFRID's *ordinary jacket and bow tie*]

SIR WILFRID: Hullo, John.

MAYHEW: [*Rising*] Ah, Wilfrid.

SIR WILFRID: [*Handing the wig and gown to* CARTER] Carter told you I was in Court? Banter really surpassed himself. [*He looks at* LEONARD] And this is Mr.—er—Vole?

MAYHEW: This is Leonard Vole.

LEONARD: How do you do, sir?

SIR WILFRID: How do you do, Vole? Won't you sit down?

> [LEONARD *sits left of the desk*]

How's the family, John? [*He crosses to* CARTER, *who assists* SIR WILFRID *to change his jacket and remove his bands*]

MAYHEW: Molly's got a touch of this twenty-four hour flu.

SIR WILFRID: Too bad!

MAYHEW: Yes, damnable. Did you win your case, Wilfrid?

SIR WILFRID: Yes, I'm glad to say.

MAYHEW: It always gives you satisfaction to beat Myers, doesn't it?

SIR WILFRID: It gives me satisfaction to beat anyone.

MAYHEW: But especially Myers.

SIR WILFRID: [*Taking the bow tie from* CARTER] Especially Myers. [*He crosses to the mirror*] He's an irritating—gentleman. [*He puts on his bow tie*] He always seems to bring out the worst in me.

MAYHEW: That would appear to be mutual. You irritate him because you hardly ever let him finish a sentence.

> [CARTER *exits, taking the wig, gown, jacket and bands with him*]

SIR WILFRID: He irritates me because of that mannerism of his. It's this—[*He clears his throat and adjusts an imaginary wig*] that drives me to distraction, and he will call me Ro-barts—Ro-barts. But he's a very able advocate, if only he'd remember not to ask leading questions when he knows damn well he shouldn't. But let's get down to business.

MAYHEW: Yes. I brought Vole here, because I am anxious for you to hear his story exactly as he told it to me. [*He takes some typewritten papers from his brief case*] There is some urgency in the matter, it seems. [*He hands the papers to* SIR WILFRID]

SIR WILFRID: Oh?

LEONARD: My wife thinks I'm going to be arrested. [*He looks embarrassed*] She's much cleverer than I am—so she may be right.

SIR WILFRID: Arrested for what?

LEONARD: [*Still more embarrassed*] Well—for murder.

[SIR WILFRID *perches himself on a corner of the desk*]

MAYHEW: It's the case of Miss Emily French. You've probably seen the reports in the Press? [SIR WILFRID *nods*] She was a maiden lady, living alone but for an elderly housekeeper, in a house at Hampstead. On the night of October the fourteenth her housekeeper returned at eleven o'clock to find that apparently the place had been broken into, and that her mistress had been coshed on the back of the head and killed. [*To* LEONARD] That is right?

LEONARD: That's right. It's quite an ordinary sort of thing to happen nowadays. And then, the other day, the papers said that the police were anxious to interview a Mr. Leonard Vole, who had visited Miss French earlier on the evening in question, as they thought he might be able to give them useful information. So of course I went along to the police station and they asked me a lot of questions.

SIR WILFRID: [*Sharply*] Did they caution you?

LEONARD: [*Vaguely*] I don't quite know. I mean they said would I like to make a statement and they'd write it down, and it might be used in court. Is that cautioning me?

[SIR WILFRID *exchanges a glance with* MAYHEW, *and speaks more to him than to* LEONARD]

SIR WILFRID: [*Rising*] Oh well, can't be helped now.

LEONARD: Anyway, it sounded damned silly to me. I told them all I could and they were very polite and seemed quite satisfied and all that. When I got home and told Romaine about it—my wife that is—well, she got the wind up. She seemed to think that they —well—that they'd got hold of the idea that *I* might have done it.

[SIR WILFRID *moves the chair near the fireplace to center for* MAYHEW, *who sits*]

So I thought perhaps I ought to get hold of a solicitor—[*To* MAYHEW] so I came along to you. I thought you'd be able to tell me what I ought to do about it. [*He looks anxiously from one to the other*]

SIR WILFRID: You knew Miss French well?

[LEONARD *rises, but* SIR WILFRID *motions him to sit*]

LEONARD: Oh, yes, she'd been frightfully kind to me. Actually it was a bit of a bore sometimes—she positively fussed over me, but she meant it very well, and when I saw in the paper that she'd been killed I was awfully upset, because, you see, I'd really got fond of her.

MAYHEW: Tell Sir Wilfrid, just as you told me, how it was you came to make Miss French's acquaintance.

LEONARD: [*Turning obediently to* SIR WILFRID] Well, it was one day in Oxford Street. I saw an old lady crossing the road carrying a lot of parcels and in the middle of the street she dropped them, tried to get hold of them again and found a bus was almost on top of her. Just managed to get to the curb safely. Well, I recovered her parcels from the street, wiped some of the mud off them as best I could, tied up one again that had burst open with string and generally soothed the old dear down. You know the sort of thing.

SIR WILFRID: And she was grateful?

LEONARD: Oh, yes, she seemed very grateful. Thanked me a lot and all that. Anyone would think I'd saved her life instead of her parcels.

SIR WILFRID: There was actually no question of your having saved her life? [*He takes a packet of cigarettes from the desk drawer*]

LEONARD: Oh, no. Nothing heroic. I never expected to see her again.

SIR WILFRID: Cigarette?

LEONARD: No, thanks, sir, never do. But by an extraordinary coincidence, two days later I happened to be sitting behind her in the theatre. She looked round and recognized me and we began to talk, and in the end she asked me to come and see her.

SIR WILFRID: And you went?

LEONARD: Yes. She'd urged me to name a day specially and it seemed rather churlish to refuse. So I said I'd go on the following Saturday.

SIR WILFRID: And you went to her house at . . . [He looks at one of the papers]

MAYHEW: Hampstead.

LEONARD: Yes.

SIR WILFRID: What did you know about her when you first went to the house?

LEONARD: Well, nothing really but what she'd told me, that she lived alone and hadn't very many friends. Something of that kind.

SIR WILFRID: She lived with only a housekeeper?

LEONARD: That's right. She had eight cats, though. Eight of them. The house was beautifully furnished and all that, but it smelt a bit of cat.

SIR WILFRID: Had you reason to believe she was well off?

LEONARD: Well, she talked as though she was.

SIR WILFRID: And you yourself?

LEONARD: [Cheerfully] Oh, I'm practically stony broke and have been for a long time.

SIR WILFRID: Unfortunate.

LEONARD: Yes, it is rather. Oh, you mean people will say I was sucking up to her for her money?

SIR WILFRID: [Disarmed] I shouldn't have put it quite like that, but in essence, yes, that is possibly what people might say.

LEONARD: It isn't really true, you know. As a matter of fact, I was sorry for her. I thought she was lonely. I was brought up by an old aunt, my Aunt Betsy, and I like old ladies.

SIR WILFRID: You say old ladies. Do you know what age Miss French was?

LEONARD: Well, I didn't know, but I read it in the paper after she was murdered. She was fifty-six.

SIR WILFRID: Fifty-six. You consider that old, Mr. Vole, but I should doubt if Miss Emily French considered herself old.

LEONARD: But you can't call it a chicken, can you?

SIR WILFRID: [Sitting right of desk] Well, let us get on. You went to see Miss French fairly frequently?

LEONARD: Yes, I should say once, twice a week perhaps.

SIR WILFRID: Did you take your wife with you?

LEONARD: [Slightly embarrassed] No, no, I didn't.

SIR WILFRID: Why didn't you?

LEONARD: Well—well, frankly, I don't think it would have gone down very well if I had.

SIR WILFRID: Do you mean with your wife or with Miss French?

LEONARD: Oh, with Miss French. [He hesitates]

MAYHEW: Go on, go on.

LEONARD: You see, she got rather fond of me.

SIR WILFRID: You mean, she fell in love with you?

LEONARD: [Horrified] Oh, good Lord no, nothing of that kind. Just sort of pampered me and spoiled me, that sort of thing.

SIR WILFRID: [After a short pause] You see, Mr. Vole, I have no doubt part of the police case against you, if there is a case against you which as yet we have no definite reason to suppose, will be why did you, young, good-looking, married, devote so much of your time to an elderly woman with whom you could hardly have very much in common?

LEONARD: [Gloomily] Yes, I know they'll say I was after her for her money. And in a way perhaps that's true. But only in a way.

SIR WILFRID: [Slightly disarmed] Well, at least you're frank, Mr. Vole. Can you explain a little more clearly?

LEONARD: [Rising and moving to the fireplace] Well, she made no secret of the fact that she was rolling in money. As I told you, Romaine and I—that's my wife—are pretty hard up. I'll admit that I did hope that if I was really in a tight place she'd lend me some money. I'm being honest about it.

SIR WILFRID: Did you ask her for a loan?

LEONARD: No, I didn't. I mean, things weren't desperate. [He be-

comes suddenly rather more serious as though he realized the grav-
ity of that] Of course I can see—it does look rather bad for me.
[He resumes his seat]

SIR WILFRID: Miss French knew you were a married man?

LEONARD: Oh, yes.

SIR WILFRID: But she didn't suggest that you should bring your wife
to see her?

LEONARD: *[Slightly embarrassed]* No. She—well, she seemed to take
it for granted my wife and I didn't get on.

SIR WILFRID: Did you deliberately give her that impression?

LEONARD: No, I didn't. Indeed I didn't. But she seemed to—well,
assume it, and I thought perhaps if I kept dragging Romaine into
it she'd, well, lose interest in me. I didn't want exactly to cadge
money from her, but I'd invented a gadget for a car—a really good
idea it is—and if I could have persuaded her to finance that, well,
I mean it would have been *her* money, and it might have brought
her in a lot. Oh, it's very difficult to explain—but I wasn't spong-
ing on her, Sir Wilfrid, really I wasn't.

SIR WILFRID: What sums of money did you obtain at any time from
Miss French?

LEONARD: None. None at all.

SIR WILFRID: Tell me something about the housekeeper.

LEONARD: Janet MacKenzie? She was a regular old tyrant, you know,
Janet was. Fairly bullied poor Miss French. Looked after her very
well and all that, but the poor old dear couldn't call her soul her
own when Janet was about. *[Thoughtfully]* Janet didn't like me
at all.

SIR WILFRID: Why didn't she like you?

LEONARD: Oh, jealous, I expect. I don't think she liked my helping
Miss French with her business affairs.

SIR WILFRID: Oh, so you helped Miss French with her business affairs?

LEONARD: Yes. She was worried about some of her investments and
things, and she found it a bit difficult to fill up forms and all that
sort of thing. Yes, I helped her with a lot of things like that.

SIR WILFRID: Now, Mr. Vole, I'm going to ask you a very serious question. And it's one to which it's vital I should have a truthful answer. You were in low water financially, you had the handling of

this lady's affairs. Now did you at any time convert to your own use the securities that you handled? [LEONARD *is about to repudiate this hotly*] Now, wait a minute, Mr. Vole, before you answer. Because, you see, there are two points of view. Either we can make a feature of your probity and honesty or, if you swindled the woman in any way, then we must take the line that you had no motive for murder, since you had already a profitable source of income. You can see that there are advantages in either point of view. What I want is the truth. Take your time if you like before you reply.

LEONARD: I assure you, Sir Wilfrid, that I played dead straight and you won't find anything to the contrary. Dead straight.

SIR WILFRID: Thank you, Mr. Vole. You relieve my mind very much. I pay you the compliment of believing that you are far too intelligent to lie over such a vital matter. And we now come to October the . . . [*He hesitates*]

MAYHEW: The fourteenth.

SIR WILFRID: Fourteenth. [*He rises*] Did Miss French ask you to go and see her that night?

LEONARD: No, she didn't, as a matter of fact. But I'd come across a new kind of gadget and I thought she'd like it. So I slipped up there that evening and got there about a quarter to eight. It was Janet MacKenzie's night out and I knew she'd be alone and might be rather lonely.

SIR WILFRID: It was Janet MacKenzie's night out and you knew that fact.

LEONARD: [*Cheerfully*] Oh yes, I knew Janet always went out on a Friday.

SIR WILFRID: That's not quite so good.

LEONARD: Why not? It seems very natural that I should choose that evening to go and see her.

SIR WILFRID: Please go on, Mr. Vole.

LEONARD: Well, I got there at a quarter to eight. She'd finished her supper but I had a cup of coffee with her and we played a game of Double Demon. Then at nine o'clock I said good night to her and went home.

MAYHEW: You told me the housekeeper said she came home that evening earlier than usual.

LEONARD: Yes, the police told me she came back for something she'd forgotten and she heard—or she says she heard—somebody talking with Miss French. Well, whoever it was, it wasn't me.

SIR WILFRID: Can you prove that, Mr. Vole?

LEONARD: Yes, of course I can prove it. I was at home again with my wife by then. That's what the police kept asking me. Where I was at nine thirty. Well, I mean some days one wouldn't know where one was. As it happens, I can remember quite well that I'd gone straight home to Romaine and we hadn't gone out again.

SIR WILFRED: You live in a flat?

LEONARD: Yes. We've got a tiny maisonette over a shop behind Euston Station.

SIR WILFRID: Did anybody see you returning to the flat?

LEONARD: I don't suppose so. Why should they?

SIR WILFRID: It might be an advantage if they had.

LEONARD: But surely you don't think—I mean if she were really killed at half past nine my wife's evidence is all I need, isn't it?

[SIR WILFRID *and* MAYHEW *look at each other*]

MAYHEW: And your wife will say definitely that you were at home at that time?

LEONARD: Of course she will.

MAYHEW: [*Rising and moving to the fireplace*] You are very fond of your wife and your wife is very fond of you?

LEONARD: [*His face softening*] Romaine is absolutely devoted to me. She's the most devoted wife any man could have.

MAYHEW: I see. You are happily married.

LEONARD: Couldn't be happier. Romaine's wonderful, absolutely wonderful. I'd like you to know her, Mr. Mayhew.

[*There is a knock at the door*]

SIR WILFRID: [*Calling*] Come in.

[GRETA *enters. She carries an evening paper*]

GRETA: The evening paper, Sir Wilfrid. [*She points to a paragraph as she hands the paper to him*]

SIR WILFRID: Thank you, Greta.

GRETA: Would you like a cup of tea, sir?

SIR WILFRID: No, thank you. Oh, would you like a cup, Vole?

LEONARD: No, thank you, sir.

SIR WILFRID: No, thank you, Greta.

[GRETA *exits*]

MAYHEW: I think it would be advisable for us to have a meeting with your wife.

LEONARD: You mean have a regular round-table conference?

[SIR WILFRID *sits right of the desk*]

MAYHEW: I wonder, Mr. Vole, if you are taking this business quite seriously enough?

LEONARD: [*Nervously*] I am. I am, really, but it seems—well, I mean it seems so much like a bad dream. I mean that it should be happening to me. Murder. It's a thing you read about in books or newspapers, but you can't believe it's a thing that could ever happen to you, or touch you in any way. I suppose that's why I keep trying to make a joke of it, but it isn't a joke, really.

MAYHEW: No, I'm afraid it's not a joke.

LEONARD: But I mean it's all right, isn't it? Because I mean if they think Miss French was killed at half past nine and I was at home with Romaine . . .

MAYHEW: How did you go home? By bus or underground?

LEONARD: I walked. It took me about twenty-five minutes, but it was a fine night—a bit windy.

MAYHEW: Did you see anyone you knew on the way?

LEONARD: No, but does it matter? I mean Romaine . . .

SIR WILFRID: The evidence of a devoted wife unsupported by any other evidence may not be completely convincing, Mr. Vole.

LEONARD: You mean, they'd think Romaine would tell a lie on my account?

SIR WILFRID: It has been known, Mr. Vole.

LEONARD: Oh, I'm sure she would, too, only in this case I mean she won't be telling a lie. I mean it really is so. You do believe me, don't you?

SIR WILFRID: Yes, I believe you, Mr. Vole, but it's not me you will have to convince. You are aware, are you not, that Miss French left a will leaving you all her money?

LEONARD: [*Absolutely flabbergasted*] Left all her money to me? You're joking!

[MAYHEW *resumes his seat*]

SIR WILFRID: I'm not joking. It's in tonight's evening paper.

[*He hands the paper across the desk.* LEONARD *reads the paragraph*]

LEONARD: Well, I can hardly believe it.

SIR WILFRID: You knew nothing about it?

LEONARD: Absolutely nothing. She never said a word. [*He hands the paper to* MAYHEW]

MAYHEW: You're quite sure of that, Mr. Vole?

LEONARD: Absolutely sure. I'm very grateful to her—yet in a way I rather wish now that she hadn't. I mean it—it's a bit unfortunate as things are, isn't it, sir?

SIR WILFRID: It supplies you with a very adequate motive. That is, if you knew about it, which you say you didn't. Miss French never talked to you about making a will?

LEONARD: She said to Janet once, "You're afraid I shall make my will again," but that was nothing to do with me. I mean, it was just a bit of a dust-up between them. [*His manner changes*] Do you really think they're going to arrest me?

SIR WILFRID: I think you must prepare yourself, Mr. Vole, for that eventuality.

LEONARD: [*Rising*] You—you will do the best you can for me, won't you, sir?

SIR WILFRID: [*With friendliness*] You may rest assured, my dear Mr. Vole, that I will do everything in my power to help you. Don't worry. Leave everything in my hands.

LEONARD: You'll look after Romaine, won't you? I mean, she'll be in an awful state—it will be terrible for her.

SIR WILFRID: Don't worry, my boy. Don't worry.

LEONARD: [*Resuming his seat; to* MAYHEW] Then the money side, too. That worries me. I've got a few quid, but it's not much. Perhaps I oughtn't to have asked you to do anything for me.

MAYHEW: I think we shall be able to put up adequate defense. The Court provides for these cases, you know.

LEONARD: [*Rising and moving above the desk*] I can't believe it. I can't believe that I, Leonard Vole, may be standing in a dock saying "Not guilty." People staring at me. [*He shakes himself as though it were a bad dream, then turns to* MAYHEW] I can't see why they don't think it was a burglar. I mean, apparently the window was forced and smashed and a lot of things were strewn around, so the papers said. [*He resumes his seat*] I mean, it seems much more probable.

MAYHEW: The police must have some good reason for not thinking that it was a burglary.

LEONARD: Well, it seems to me . . .

[CARTER *enters*]

SIR WILFRID: Yes, Carter?

CARTER: Excuse me, sir, there are two gentlemen here asking to see Mr. Vole.

SIR WILFRID: The police?

CARTER: Yes, sir.

[MAYHEW *rises*]

SIR WILFRID: [*Rising and crossing to the door*] All right, John, I'll go and talk to them.

[SIR WILFRID *exits and* CARTER *follows him off*]

LEONARD: My God! Is this—it?

MAYHEW: I'm afraid it may be, my boy. Now take it easy. Don't lose heart. [*He pats* LEONARD *on the shoulder*] Make no further statement—leave it all to us. [*He replaces his chair near the fireplace*]

LEONARD: But how did they know I'm here?

MAYHEW: It seems probable that they have had a man watching you.

LEONARD: [*Still unable to believe it*] Then they really do suspect me.

[SIR WILFRID, DETECTIVE INSPECTOR HEARNE *and a plain-*

clothes DETECTIVE *enter. The* INSPECTOR *is a tall, good-looking officer*]

INSPECTOR: [*As he enters; to* SIR WILFRID] I'm sorry to trouble you, sir.
SIR WILFRID: This is Mr. Vole.

[LEONARD *rises*]

INSPECTOR: [*Crossing to* LEONARD] Is your name Leonard Vole?
LEONARD: Yes.
INSPECTOR: I am Detective Inspector Hearne. I have here a warrant for your arrest on the charge of murdering Emily French on October fourteenth last. I must warn you that anything you say may be taken down and used in evidence.
LEONARD: O.K. [*He looks nervously at* SIR WILFRID, *then crosses and takes his hat from the coat hook*] I'm ready.
MAYHEW: Good afternoon, Inspector Hearne. My name is Mayhew. I am representing Mr. Vole.
INSPECTOR: Good afternoon, Mr. Mayhew. That's quite all right. We'll take him along and charge him now. [LEONARD *and the* DETECTIVE *exit*] Very seasonable weather we're having just now. Quite a nip of frost last night. We'll be seeing you later, sir, I expect. [*He crosses to the door*] Hope we haven't inconvenienced you, Sir Wilfrid.
SIR WILFRID: I am never inconvenienced. [*The* INSPECTOR *laughs politely and exits. He closes the door*] I must say, John, that that young man is in a worse mess than he seems to think.
MAYHEW: He certainly is. How does he strike you?
SIR WILFRID: Extraordinarily naïve. Yet in some ways quite shrewd. Intelligent, I should say. But he certainly doesn't realize the danger of his position.
MAYHEW: Do you think he did it?
SIR WILFRID: I've no idea. On the whole, I should say *not*. [*Sharply*] You agree?
MAYHEW: [*Taking his pipe from his pocket*] I agree.

[SIR WILFRID *takes the tobacco jar from the mantelpiece and hands it to* MAYHEW, *who fills his pipe*]

SIR WILFRID: Oh, well, he seems to have impressed both of us favorably. I can't think why. I never heard a weaker story. God knows what we're going to do with it. The only evidence in his favor seems to be his wife's—and who's going to believe a wife?

MAYHEW: [*With dry humor*] It has been known to happen.

SIR WILFRID: She's a foreigner, too. Nine out of the twelve in a jury box believe a foreigner is lying anyway. She'll be emotional and upset, and won't understand what the prosecuting counsel says to her. Still, we shall have to interview her. You'll see, she'll have hysterics all over my Chambers.

MAYHEW: Perhaps you'd prefer not to accept the brief.

SIR WILFRID: Who says I won't accept it? Just because I point out that the boy has an absolute tomfool story to tell.

MAYHEW: [*Handing the tobacco jar to* SIR WILFRID] But a true one.

SIR WILFRID: [*Replacing the jar on the mantelpiece*] It must be a true one. It couldn't be so idiotic if it wasn't true. Put all the facts down in black and white and the whole thing is utterly damning. [MAYHEW *feels in his pockets for matches*] And yet, when you talk to the boy, and he blurts out these damning facts, you realize that the whole thing could happen just as he said. Damn it, I had the equivalent of an Aunt Betsy myself. I loved her dearly.

MAYHEW: He's got a good personality, I think. Sympathetic.

SIR WILFRID: [*Taking a matchbox from his pocket and handing it to* MAYHEW] Yes, he ought to go down well with the jury. That cuts no ice with the judge, though. And he's the simple sort of chap who may get rattled easily in the box. [MAYHEW *finds that the box is empty and throws it in the wastepaper basket*] A lot depends on this girl. [*There is a knock at the door. He calls*] Come in.

[GRETA *enters. She is excited and a little scared. She closes the door*]

SIR WILFRID: Yes, Greta, what is it?

GRETA: [*In a whisper*] Mrs. Leonard Vole is here.

MAYHEW: Mrs. Vole.

SIR WILFRID: Come here. You saw that young man? He's been arrested for murder.

GRETA: [*Crossing to* SIR WILFRID] I know. Isn't it exciting?

SIR WILFRID: Do you think he did it?

GRETA: Oh no, sir, I'm sure he didn't.

SIR WILFRID: Oh, why not?

GRETA: He's far too nice.

SIR WILFRID: [*To* MAYHEW] That makes three of us. [*To* GRETA] Bring Mrs. Vole in. [GRETA *exits*] And we're probably three credulous fools—taken in by a young man with a pleasing personality.

[CARTER *enters and stands to one side*]

CARTER: [*Announcing*] Mrs. Vole.

[ROMAINE *enters. She is a foreign woman of great personality, but very quiet. Her voice has a strangely ironic inflection*]

MAYHEW: My dear Mrs. Vole.

[*He goes toward her with a great air of sympathy, but is slightly rebuffed by her personality.* CARTER *exits, closing the door behind him*]

ROMAINE: Ah! You are Mr. Mayhew.

MAYHEW: Yes. This is Sir Wilfrid Robarts, who has agreed to handle your husband's case for him.

ROMAINE: How do you do, Sir Wilfrid?

SIR WILFRID: How do you do?

ROMAINE: I have just come from your office, Mr. Mayhew. They told me you were here with my husband.

SIR WILFRID: Quite, quite.

ROMAINE: Just as I arrived I thought I saw Leonard getting into a car. There were two men with him.

SIR WILFRID: Now, my dear Mrs. Vole, you must not upset yourself. [ROMAINE *is not in the least upset. He is slightly disconcerted*] Won't you sit down, here?

ROMAINE: Thank you. [*She sits in the chair left of the desk*]

SIR WILFRID: There is nothing to be alarmed about as yet, and you must not give way.

ROMAINE: [*After a pause*] Oh, no, I shall not give way.

SIR WILFRID: Then let me tell you that, as perhaps you already suspect, your husband has just been arrested.

ROMAINE: For the murder of Miss Emily French?

SIR WILFRID: I'm afraid so, yes. But please don't be upset.

ROMAINE: You keep saying that, Sir Wilfrid, but I am not upset.

SIR WILFRID: No. No, I see you have great fortitude.

ROMAINE: You can call it that if you like.

SIR WILFRID: The great thing is to be calm and to tackle all this sensibly.

ROMAINE: That suits me very well. But you must not hide anything from me, Sir Wilfrid. You must not try and spare me. I want to know everything. [*With a slightly different inflection*] I want to know—the worst.

SIR WILFRID: Splendid. Splendid. That's the right way to tackle things. Now, dear lady, we're not going to give way to alarm or despondency, we're going to look at things in a sensible and straightforward manner. [*He sits right of the desk*] Your husband became friendly with Miss French about six weeks ago. You were —er—aware of that friendship?

ROMAINE: He told me that he had rescued an old lady and her parcels one day in the middle of a crowded street. He told me that she had asked him to go and see her.

SIR WILFRID: All very natural, I think. And your husband did go and see her.

ROMAINE: Yes.

SIR WILFRID: And they became great friends.

ROMAINE: Evidently.

SIR WILFRID: There was no question of your accompanying your husband on any occasion?

ROMAINE: Leonard thought it better not.

SIR WILFRID: [*Shooting a keen glance at her*] He thought it better not. Yes. Just between ourselves, why did he think it better not?

ROMAINE: He thought Miss French would prefer it that way.

SIR WILFRID: [*A little nervously and sliding off the subject*] Yes, yes, quite. Well, we can go into that some other time. Your husband, then, became friends with Miss French, he did her various little services, she was a lonely old woman with time on her hands and she found your husband's companionship congenial to her.

ROMAINE: Leonard can be very charming.

SIR WILFRID: Yes, I'm sure he can. He felt, no doubt, it was a kindly action on his part to go and cheer up the old lady.

ROMAINE: I daresay.

SIR WILFRID: You yourself did not object at all to your husband's friendship with this old lady?

ROMAINE: I do not think I objected, no.

SIR WILFRID: You have, of course, perfect trust in your husband, Mrs. Vole. Knowing him as well as you do . . .

ROMAINE: Yes, I know Leonard very well.

SIR WILFRID: I can't tell you how much I admire your calm and your courage, Mrs. Vole. Knowing as I do how devoted you are to him . . .

ROMAINE: So you know how devoted I am to him?

SIR WILFRID: Of course.

ROMAINE: But excuse me, I am a foreigner. I do not always know your English terms. But is there not a saying about knowing something of your own knowledge? You do not know that I am devoted to Leonard, of your own knowledge, do you, Sir Wilfrid? [*She smiles*]

SIR WILFRID: [*Slightly disconcerted*] No, no, that is of course true. But your husband told me.

ROMAINE: Leonard told you how devoted I was to him?

SIR WILFRID: Indeed, he spoke of your devotion in the most moving terms.

ROMAINE: Men, I often think, are very stupid.

SIR WILFRID: I beg your pardon?

ROMAINE: It does not matter. Please go on.

SIR WILFRID: [*Rising*] This Miss French was a woman of some considerable wealth. She had no near relations. Like many eccentric elderly ladies she was fond of making wills. She had made several wills in her lifetime. Shortly after meeting your husband she made a fresh will. After some small bequests she left the whole of her fortune to your husband.

ROMAINE: Yes.

SIR WILFRID: You know that?

ROMAINE: I read it in the paper this evening.

SIR WILFRID: Quite, quite. Before reading it in the paper, you had no idea of the fact? Your husband had no idea of it?

ROMAINE: [*After a pause*] Is that what he told you?

SIR WILFRID: Yes. You don't suggest anything different?

ROMAINE: No. Oh, no. I do not suggest anything.

SIR WILFRID: [*Sitting*] There seems to be no doubt that Miss French looked upon your husband rather in the light of a son, or perhaps a very favorite nephew.

ROMAINE: [*With distinct irony*] You think Miss French looked upon Leonard as a son?

SIR WILFRID: [*Flustered*] Yes, I think so. Definitely I think so. I think that could be regarded as quite natural, quite normal under the circumstances.

ROMAINE: What hypocrites you are in this country.

[MAYHEW *sits on the chair near the fireplace*]

SIR WILFRID: My dear Mrs. Vole!

ROMAINE: I shock you? I am so sorry.

SIR WILFRID: Of course, of course. You have a continental way of looking at these things. But I assure you, dear Mrs. Vole, that is *not* the line to take. It would be most unwise to suggest in any way that Miss French had—er—any—er—feelings for Leonard Vole other than those of a—of a mother or—shall we say—an aunt.

ROMAINE: Oh, by all means let us say an aunt, if you think it best.

SIR WILFRID: One has to think of the effect on the jury of all these things, Mrs. Vole.

ROMAINE: Yes. I also wish to do that. I have been thinking of that a good deal.

SIR WILFRID: Quite so. We must work together. Now we come to the evening of October fourteenth. That is just over a week ago. You remember that evening?

ROMAINE: I remember it very well.

SIR WILFRID: Leonard Vole called on Miss French that evening. The housekeeper, Janet MacKenzie, was out. Mr. Vole played a game of Double Demon with Miss French and finally took leave of her about nine o'clock. He returned home on foot, he tells me, arriving at approximately twenty-five minutes past nine.

[*He looks interrogatively at her.* ROMAINE *rises and moves to the fireplace.* SIR WILFRID *and* MAYHEW *rise*]

ROMAINE: [*Without expression; thoughtfully*] Twenty-five past nine.

SIR WILFRID: At half past nine the housekeeper returned to the house to get something she had forgotten. Passing the sitting room door she heard Miss French's voice in conversation with a man. She assumed that the man with Miss French was Leonard Vole, and Inspector Hearne says that it is this statement of hers which has led to your husband's arrest. Mr. Vole, however, tells me that he has an absolute alibi for that time, since he was at home with you at nine thirty. [*There is a pause.* ROMAINE *does not speak although* SIR WILFRID *looks at her*] That is so, is it not? He was with you at nine thirty?

[SIR WILFRID *and* MAYHEW *look at* ROMAINE]

ROMAINE: That is what Leonard says? That he was home with me at nine thirty?

SIR WILFRID: [*Sharply*] Isn't it true?

[*There is a long silence*]

ROMAINE: [*Moving back to her chair; presently*] But of course. [*She sits*]

[SIR WILFRID *sighs with relief and resumes his seat*]

SIR WILFRID: Possibly the police have already questioned you on that point?

ROMAINE: Oh, yes, they came to see me yesterday evening.

SIR WILFRID: And you said . . . ?

ROMAINE: [*As though repeating something that she has learned by rote*] I said Leonard came in at nine twenty-five that night and did not go out again.

MAYHEW: [*A little uneasily*] You said . . . ? Oh!

ROMAINE: That was right, was it not?

SIR WILFRID: What do you mean by that, Mrs. Vole?

ROMAINE: [*Sweetly*] That is what Leonard wants me to say, is it not?

SIR WILFRID: It's the truth. You said so just now.

ROMAINE: I have to understand—to be sure. If I say, yes, it is so, Leonard was with me in the flat at nine thirty—will they acquit him? [SIR WILFRID *and* MAYHEW *are puzzled by* ROMAINE's *manner*] Will they let him go?

MAYHEW: If you are both speaking the truth then they will—er—have to acquit him.

ROMAINE: But when I said—that—to the police, I do not think they believed me. [*She is not distressed; instead she seems faintly satisfied*]

SIR WILFRID: What makes you think they did not believe you?

ROMAINE: [*With sudden malice*] Perhaps I did not say it very well?

[SIR WILFRID *and* MAYHEW *exchange glances.* MAYHEW *resumes his seat.* ROMAINE's *cool, impudent glance meets* SIR WILFRID's. *There is definite antagonism between them*]

SIR WILFRID: [*Changing his manner*] You know, Mrs. Vole, I don't quite understand your attitude in all this.

ROMAINE: So you don't understand? Well, perhaps it is difficult.

SIR WILFRID: Perhaps your husband's position is not quite clear to you?

ROMAINE: I have already said that I want to understand fully just how black the case against—my husband is. I say to the police, Leonard was at home with me at nine thirty—and they do not believe me. But perhaps there is someone who saw him leave Miss French's house, or who saw him in the street on his way home?

[*She looks sharply and rather slyly from one to the other.* SIR WILFRID *looks inquiringly at* MAYHEW]

MAYHEW: [*Reluctantly*] Your husband cannot think of, or remember, anything helpful of that kind.

ROMAINE: So it will be only his word—and mine. [*With intensity*] And mine. [*She rises abruptly*] Thank you, that is what I wanted to know.

MAYHEW: But, Mrs. Vole, please don't go. There is a lot more to be discussed.

ROMAINE: Not by me.

SIR WILFRID: Why not, Mrs. Vole?

ROMAINE: I shall have to swear, shall I not, to speak the truth and all the truth and nothing but the truth?

[*She seems amused*]

SIR WILFRID: That is the oath you take.

ROMAINE: [*Now openly mocking*] And suppose that then, when you ask me—[*She imitates a man's voice*] "When did Leonard Vole come home that night?" I should say . . .

SIR WILFRID: Well?

ROMAINE: There are so many things I could say.

SIR WILFRID: Mrs. Vole, do you love your husband?

ROMAINE: [*Shifting her mocking glance to* MAYHEW] Leonard says I do.

MAYHEW: Leonard Vole believes so.

ROMAINE: But Leonard is not very clever.

SIR WILFRID: You are aware, Mrs. Vole, that you cannot by law be called to give testimony damaging to your husband?

ROMAINE: How very convenient.

SIR WILFRID: And your husband can . . .

ROMAINE: [*Interrupting*] He is not my husband.

SIR WILFRID: What?

ROMAINE: Leonard Vole is not my husband. He went through a form of marriage with me in Berlin. He got me out of the Russian zone and brought me to this country. I did not tell him, but I had a husband living at the time.

SIR WILFRID: He got you out of the Russian sector and safely to this country? You should be very grateful to him. [*Sharply*] Are you?

ROMAINE: One can get tired of gratitude.

SIR WILFRID: Has Leonard Vole ever injured you in any way?

ROMAINE: [*Scornfully*] Leonard? Injured me? He worships the ground I walk on.

SIR WILFRID: And you?

[*Again there is a duel of eyes between them, then she laughs and turns away*]

ROMAINE: You want to know too much. [*She crosses to the door*]

MAYHEW: I think we must be quite clear about this. Your statements have been somewhat ambiguous. What exactly happened on the evening of October fourteenth?

ROMAINE: [*In a monotonous voice*] Leonard came in at twenty-five minutes past nine and did not go out again. I have given him an alibi, have I not?

SIR WILFRID: [*Rising*] You have. [*He crosses to her*] Mrs. Vole . . . [*He catches her eye and pauses*]

ROMAINE: Yes?

SIR WILFRID: You're a very remarkable woman, Mrs. Vole.

ROMAINE: And you are satisfied, I hope?

[ROMAINE *exits*]

SIR WILFRID: I'm damned if I'm satisfied.

MAYHEW: Nor I.

SIR WILFRID: She's up to something, that woman—but what? I don't like it, John.

MAYHEW: She certainly hasn't had hysterics all over the place.

SIR WILFRID: Cool as a cucumber.

MAYHEW: What's going to happen if we put her into the witness box?

SIR WILFRID: God knows!

MAYHEW: The prosecution would break her down in no time, especially if it were Myers.

SIR WILFRID: If it's not the Attorney General, it probably will be.

MAYHEW: Then what's your line of attack?

SIR WILFRID: The usual. Keep interrupting—as many objections as possible.

MAYHEW: What beats me is that young Vole is convinced of her devotion.

SIR WILFRID: Don't put your trust in that. Any woman can fool a man if she wants to and if he's in love with her.

MAYHEW: He's in love with her all right. And trusts her completely.

SIR WILFRID: More fool he. Never trust a woman.

CURTAIN

ACT TWO

*The Central Criminal Court, London—better known as
The Old Bailey. Six weeks later. Morning.*

*The section of the courtroom seen has a tall rostrum, the
bench, running from down right to up center. On it are
the armchairs and desks for the* JUDGE, *his* CLERK *and the*
ALDERMAN. *Access to the bench is by a door in the up right
corner and by steps up right from the floor of the court.
On the wall over the* JUDGE's *chair are the Royal Arms and
the Sword of Justice. Below the bench are small desks and
chairs for the* CLERK OF THE COURT *and the* COURT STENOG-
RAPHER. *There is a small stool right of the desks for the*
USHER. *The witness box is immediately below the up center end of the bench. Up center is a door leading to the
Barristers' Robing Room and up left center are glass-
paneled double doors leading to a corridor and other parts
of the building. Between the doors are two pews for the*
BARRISTERS. *Below the pews is a table with three chairs and
a stool. The dock is left and is entered by a door in the
left wall and a gate in the upstage rail. There are chairs
in the dock for* LEONARD *and the* WARDER. *The jury box is
down right, only the back of the three end seats being
visible to the audience.*

When the curtain rises, the Court has opened. The JUDGE,
MR. JUSTICE WAINWRIGHT, *is seated center of the bench.
The* JUDGE's CLERK *is seated right of him and the* ALDER-
MAN *is seated left of the* JUDGE. *The* CLERK OF THE COURT
and the STENOGRAPHER *are in their seats below the bench.*
MR. MYERS, Q.C., *for the Prosecution, is seated right of
the front row of Barristers with his* ASSISTANT *left of him.*

SIR WILFRID, *for the Defense, is seated left of the front row of Barristers with his* ASSISTANT *right of him. Four* BARRISTERS, *one a woman, are seated in the back row of the Barristers' seats.* LEONARD *is standing in the dock with the* WARDER *beside him.* DR. WYATT *is seated on the stool right of the table. The* INSPECTOR *is seated on the chair above the right end of the table.* MAYHEW *is seated left of the table. A* POLICEMAN *stands at the double doors. Three* MEMBERS OF THE JURY *are seen, the first a man, the* FOREMAN, *the second a* WOMAN *and the third a* MAN. *The* USHER *is administering the oath to the* WOMAN JUROR *who is standing.*

WOMAN JUROR: [*Holding the Bible and oath card*] . . . lady the Queen and the prisoner at the Bar whom I shall have in charge, and a true verdict give according to the evidence.

    [*She hands the Bible and oath card to the* USHER, *then sits. The* USHER *gives the Bible and oath card to the* FOREMAN]

FOREMAN: [*Rising*] I swear by Almighty God that I will well and truly try and true deliverance make between our sovereign lady the Queen and the prisoner at the Bar whom I shall have in charge, and a true verdict give according to the evidence.

    [*He hands the Bible and oath card to the* USHER, *then sits. The* USHER *puts the Bible and card on the ledge of the jury box, then sits on his stool*]

CLERK: [*Rising*] Leonard Vole, you are charged on indictment for that you on the fourteenth day of October in the County of London murdered Emily Jane French. How say you, Leonard Vole, are you guilty or not guilty?

LEONARD: Not guilty.

CLERK: Members of the Jury, the prisoner stands indicted for that he on the fourteenth day of October murdered Emily Jane French. To this indictment he has pleaded not guilty, and it is your charge to say, having heard the evidence, whether he be guilty or not.

[*He motions to* LEONARD *to sit, then resumes his own seat.* LEONARD *and the* WARDER *sit.* MYERS *rises*]

JUDGE: One moment, Mr. Myers. [MYERS *bows to the* JUDGE *and resumes his seat. He turns to the jury*] Members of the Jury, the proper time for me to sum up the evidence to you, and instruct you as to the law, is after you have heard all the evidence. But because there has been a considerable amount of publicity about this case in the Press, I would just like to say this to you now. By the oath which each of you has just taken you swore to try this case on the evidence. That means on the evidence that you are now going to hear and see. It does not mean that you are to consider also anything you have heard or read before taking your oaths. You must shut out from your minds everything except what will take place in this Court. You must not let anything else influence your minds in favor of or against the prisoner. I am quite sure that you will do your duty conscientiously in the way that I have indicated. Yes, Mr. Myers.

[MYERS *rises, clears his throat and adjusts his wig in the manner taken off by* SIR WILFRID *in the previous scene*]

MYERS: May it please you, my lord. Members of the Jury, I appear in this case with my learned friend Mr. Barton for the prosecution, and my learned friends Sir Wilfrid Robarts and Mr. Brogan-Moore appear for the defense. This is a case of murder. The facts are simple and up to a certain point are not in dispute. You will hear how the prisoner, a young and, you may think, a not unattractive man, made the acquaintance of Miss Emily French, a woman of fifty-six. How he was treated by her with kindness and even with affection. The nature of that affection you will have to decide for yourselves. Dr. Wyatt will tell you that in his opinion death occurred at some time between nine thirty and ten on the night of the fourteenth of October last. You will hear the evidence of Janet MacKenzie, who was Miss French's faithful and devoted housekeeper. The fourteenth of October—it was a Friday—was Janet MacKenzie's night out, but on this occasion she happened to return for a few minutes at nine twenty-five. She let herself in with a key and upon going upstairs to her room she passed the door of the sitting room. She will tell you that in the sitting room she heard the voices of Miss French and of the prisoner, Leonard Vole.

LEONARD: [Rising] That's not true. It wasn't me.

[The WARDER restrains LEONARD and makes him resume his seat]

MYERS: Janet MacKenzie was surprised, since as far as she knew, Miss French had not expected Leonard Vole to call that evening. However, she went out again and when she returned finally at eleven she found Miss Emily French murdered, the room in disorder, a window smashed and the curtains blowing wildly. Horror stricken, Janet MacKenzie immediately rang up the police. I should tell you that the prisoner was arrested on the twentieth of October. It is the case for the prosecution that Miss Emily Jane French was murdered between nine thirty and ten p.m. on the evening of the fourteenth of October, by a blow from a cosh and that the blow was struck by the prisoner. I will now call Inspector Hearne.

[The INSPECTOR rises. He holds a file of papers which he refers to often during the scene. He hands a typewritten sheet to the CLERK and another to the STENOGRAPHER. He then enters the witness box. The CLERK hands the sheet to the JUDGE. The USHER rises and stands by the witness box. The INSPECTOR picks up the oath card and Bible from the ledge of the box]

INSPECTOR: I swear by Almighty God that the evidence that I shall give shall be the truth, the whole truth and nothing but the truth. Robert Hearne, Detective Inspector, Criminal Investigation Department, New Scotland Yard.

[He puts the Bible and oath card on the ledge of the box. The USHER sits on his stool]

MYERS: Now, Inspector Hearne, on the evening of the fourteenth of October last were you on duty when you received an emergency call?

INSPECTOR: Yes, sir.

MYERS: What did you do?

INSPECTOR: With Sergeant Randell I proceeded to twenty-three Ashburn Grove. I was admitted to the house and established that the occupant, whom I later ascertained was Miss Emily French, was dead. She was lying on her face, and had received severe injuries to the back of her head. An attempt had been made to force one of the windows with some implement that might have been a chisel. The window had been broken near the catch. There was glass strewn about the floor, and I also later found fragments of glass on the ground outside the window.

MYERS: Is there any particular significance in finding glass both inside and outside the window?

INSPECTOR: The glass outside was not consistent with the window having been forced from outside.

MYERS: You mean that if it had been forced from the inside there had been an attempt to make it look as though it had been done from the outside?

SIR WILFRID: [Rising] I object. My learned friend is putting words into the witness's mouth. He really must observe the rules of evidence. [He resumes his seat]

MYERS: [To the INSPECTOR] You have been engaged on several cases of burglary and housebreaking?

INSPECTOR: Yes, sir.

MYERS: And in your experience when a window is forced from the outside, where is the glass?

INSPECTOR: On the inside.

MYERS: In any other case where the windows have been forced from the outside, have you found glass on the outside of the window some distance below, on the ground?

INSPECTOR: No.

MYERS: No. Will you go on?

INSPECTOR: A search was made, photographs were taken, the place was fingerprinted.

MYERS: What fingerprints did you discover?

INSPECTOR: Those of Miss Emily French herself, those of Janet Mac-

Kenzie and some which proved later to be those of the prisoner, Leonard Vole.

MYERS: No others?

INSPECTOR: No others.

MYERS: Did you subsequently have an interview with Mr. Leonard Vole?

INSPECTOR: Yes, sir. Janet MacKenzie was not able to give me his address, but as a result of a broadcast and a newspaper appeal, Mr. Leonard Vole came and saw me.

MYERS: And on October the twentieth, when arrested, what did the prisoner say?

INSPECTOR: He replied, "O.K. I'm ready."

MYERS: Now, Inspector, you say the room had the appearance of a robbery having been committed?

SIR WILFRID: [*Rising*] That is just what the Inspector did not say. [*To the* JUDGE] If your lordship remembers, that was a suggestion made by my friend—and quite improperly made—to which I objected.

JUDGE: You are quite right, Sir Wilfrid. [MYERS *sits*] At the same time, I'm not sure that the Inspector is not entitled to give evidence of any facts which might tend to prove that the disorder of the room was not the work of a person who broke in from outside for the purpose of robbery.

SIR WILFRID: My lord, may I respectfully agree with what your lordship has said. Facts, yes. But not the mere expression of opinion without even the facts on which it is based. [*He sits*]

MYERS: [*Rising*] Perhaps, my lord, if I phrased my question in this way my friend would be satisfied. Inspector, could you say from what you saw whether there had or had not been a bona fide breaking in from outside the house?

SIR WILFRID: [*Rising*] My lord, I really must continue my objection. My learned friend is again seeking to obtain an opinion from this witness. [*He sits*]

JUDGE: Yes, Mr. Myers, I think you will have to do a little better than that.

MYERS: Inspector, did you find anything inconsistent with a breaking in from outside?

INSPECTOR: Only the glass, sir.

MYERS: Nothing else?

INSPECTOR: No, sir, there was nothing else.

JUDGE: We all seem to have drawn a blank there, Mr. Myers.

MYERS: Was Miss French wearing jewelry of any value?

INSPECTOR: She was wearing a diamond brooch, two diamond rings, value of about nine hundred pounds.

MYERS: And these were left untouched?

INSPECTOR: Yes, sir.

MYERS: Was in fact anything taken?

INSPECTOR: According to Janet MacKenzie, nothing was missing.

MYERS: In your experience, when anyone breaks into a house do they leave without taking anything?

INSPECTOR: Not unless they're interrupted, sir.

MYERS: But in this case it does not seem as if the burglar *was* interrupted.

INSPECTOR: No, sir.

MYERS: Do you produce a jacket, Inspector?

INSPECTOR: Yes, sir.

[*The* USHER *rises, crosses to the table, picks up the jacket and hands it to the* INSPECTOR]

MYERS: Is that it?

INSPECTOR: Yes, sir.

[*He returns the jacket to the* USHER. *The* USHER *replaces the jacket on the table*]

MYERS: From where did you get it?

INSPECTOR: I found it at the prisoner's flat some time after he was arrested, and later handed it to Mr. Clegg at the lab, to test for possible bloodstains.

MYERS: Lastly, Inspector, do you produce the will of Miss French?

[*The* USHER *picks up the will from the table and hands it to the* INSPECTOR]

INSPECTOR: I do, sir.

MYERS: Dated October the eighth?

INSPECTOR: Yes, sir.

[*He returns the will to the* USHER. *The* USHER *replaces the will on the table, and resumes his seat*]

MYERS: After certain bequests, the residue is left to the prisoner?

INSPECTOR: That's right, sir.

MYERS: And what is the net value of that estate?

INSPECTOR: It will be, as far as can be ascertained at the moment, about eighty-five thousand pounds.

[MYERS *resumes his seat.* SIR WILFRID *rises*]

SIR WILFRID: You say that the only fingerprints you found in the room were those of Miss French herself, the prisoner Leonard Vole and Janet MacKenzie. In your experience, when a burglar breaks in does he usually leave fingerprints or does he wear gloves?

INSPECTOR: He wears gloves.

SIR WILFRID: Invariably?

INSPECTOR: Almost invariably.

SIR WILFRID: So the absence of fingerprints in a case of robbery would hardly surprise you?

INSPECTOR: No, sir.

SIR WILFRID: Now, these chisel marks on the window. Were they on the inside or the outside of the casement?

INSPECTOR: On the outside, sir.

SIR WILFRID: Isn't that consistent—and only consistent—with a breaking in from the outside?

INSPECTOR: He could have gone out of the house afterwards to have done that, sir, or he could have made those marks from the inside.

SIR WILFRID: From the inside, Inspector? Now how could he have possibly done that?

INSPECTOR: There are two windows together there. Both are casements, and with their catches adjacent. It would have been easy for anyone in the room to open one window, lean out, and force the catch of the other.

SIR WILFRID: Tell me, did you find any chisel near the premises, or at the prisoner's flat?

INSPECTOR: Yes, sir. At the prisoner's flat.

SIR WILFRID: Oh?

INSPECTOR: But it didn't fit the marks on the window.

SIR WILFRID: It was a windy night, was it not, on October fourteenth?

INSPECTOR: I really can't remember, sir. [He refers to his notes]

SIR WILFRID: According to my learned friend, Janet MacKenzie said that the curtains were blowing. Perhaps you noticed that fact yourself?

INSPECTOR: Well, yes, sir, they did blow about.

SIR WILFRID: Indicating that it was a windy night. I suggest that if a burglar had forced the window from the outside and then swung it back, some of the loose glass might easily have fallen down *outside* the window, the window having been blown back violently by the wind. That is possible, is it not?

INSPECTOR: Yes, sir.

SIR WILFRID: Crimes of violence, as we all have been unhappily aware, have been much on the increase lately. You would agree to that, would you not?

INSPECTOR: It's been a little above normal, sir.

SIR WILFRID: Let us take the case that some young thugs had broken in, who meant to attack Miss French and steal; it is possible that if one of them coshed her and found that she was dead, they might give way to panic and leave without taking anything? Or they might even have been looking for money and would be afraid to touch anything in the nature of jewelry?

MYERS: [Rising] I submit that it is impossible for Inspector Hearne to guess at what went on in the minds of some *entirely* hypothetical young criminals who may not even exist. [He sits]

SIR WILFRID: The prisoner came forward of his own accord and gave his statement quite willingly?

INSPECTOR: That is so.

SIR WILFRID: Is it the case that at all times the prisoner has protested his innocence?

INSPECTOR: Yes, sir.

SIR WILFRID: [Indicating the knife on the table] Inspector Hearne, will you kindly examine that knife? [The USHER rises, picks up the *knife and hands it to the* INSPECTOR] You have seen that knife before?

INSPECTOR: I may have.

SIR WILFRID: This is the knife taken from the kitchen table in Leonard Vole's flat and which was brought to your attention by the prisoner's wife on the occasion of your first interview with her.

MYERS: [*Rising*] My lord, to save the time of the Court, may I say that we accept this knife as being a knife in the possession of Leonard Vole and shown to the Inspector by Mrs. Vole.

[*He sits*]

SIR WILFRID: That is correct, Inspector?

INSPECTOR: Yes, sir.

SIR WILFRID: It is what is known, I believe, as a French vegetable knife?

INSPECTOR: I believe so, sir.

SIR WILFRID: Just test the edge of the knife with your finger—carefully. [*The* INSPECTOR *tests the knife edge*] You agree that the cutting edge and the point are razor sharp?

INSPECTOR: Yes, sir.

SIR WILFRID: And if you were cutting—say, ham—carving it, that is, and your hand slipped with this knife, it would be capable of inflicting a very nasty cut, and one which would bleed profusely?

MYERS: [*Rising*] I object. That is a matter of opinion, and medical opinion at that.

[*He sits. The* USHER *takes the knife from the* INSPECTOR, *puts it on the table, and resumes his seat*]

SIR WILFRID: I withdraw the question. I will ask you instead, Inspector, if the prisoner, when questioned by you as to the stains on the sleeve of his jacket, drew your attention to a recently healed scar on his wrist, and stated that it had been caused by a household knife when he was slicing ham?

INSPECTOR: That is what he said.

SIR WILFRID: And you were told the same thing by the prisoner's wife?

INSPECTOR: The first time. Afterwards . . .

SIR WILFRID: [*Sharply*] A simple yes or no, please. Did the prisoner's wife show you this knife, and tell you that her husband had cut his wrist with it slicing ham?

INSPECTOR: Yes, she did.

[SIR WILFRID *resumes his seat*]

MYERS: [*Rising*] What first drew your attention to that jacket, Inspector?

INSPECTOR: The sleeve appeared to have been recently washed.

MYERS: And you were told this story about an accident with a kitchen knife?

INSPECTOR: Yes, sir.

MYERS: And your attention was drawn to a scar on the prisoner's wrist?

INSPECTOR: Yes, sir.

MYERS: Granted that that scar was made by this particular knife, there was nothing to show whether it was an accident or done deliberately?

SIR WILFRID: [*Rising*] Really, my lord, if my learned friend is going to answer his own questions, the presence of the witness seems to be superfluous. [*He sits*]

MYERS: [*Resignedly*] I withdraw the question. Thank you, Inspector.

[*The* INSPECTOR *stands down, and exits up left. The* POLICEMAN *closes the door behind him*]

MYERS: Dr. Wyatt.

[DR. WYATT *rises and enters the box. He carries some notes. The* USHER *rises, hands the Bible to him and holds up the oath card*]

WYATT: I swear by Almighty God that the evidence that I shall give shall be the truth, the whole truth and nothing but the truth.

[*The* USHER *puts the Bible and oath card on the ledge of the witness box and resumes his seat*]

MYERS: You are Dr. Wyatt?

WYATT: Yes.

MYERS: You are a police surgeon attached to the Hampstead Division?

WYATT: Yes.

MYERS: Dr. Wyatt, will you kindly tell the Jury what you know regarding the death of Miss Emily French?

WYATT: [*Reading from his notes*] At eleven p.m. on October fourteenth, I saw the dead body of the woman who subsequently proved to be Miss French. By examination of the body I was of the opinion that the death had resulted from a blow on the head, delivered from an object such as a cosh. Death would have been practically instantaneous. From the temperature of the body and other factors, I placed the time of death at not less than an hour previously and not more than, say, an hour and a half. That is to say between the hours of nine thirty and ten p.m.

MYERS: Had Miss French struggled with her adversary at all?

WYATT: There was no evidence that she had done so. I should say, on the contrary, that she had been taken quite unprepared.

[MYERS *resumes his seat*]

SIR WILFRID: [*Rising*] Doctor, where exactly on the head had this blow been struck? There was only one blow, was there not?

WYATT: Only one. On the left side at the asterion.

SIR WILFRID: I beg your pardon? Where?

WYATT: The asterion. The junction of the parietal, occipital and temple bones.

SIR WILFRID: Oh, yes. And in layman's language, where is that?

WYATT: Behind the left ear.

SIR WILFRID: Would that indicate that the blow had been struck by a left-handed person?

WYATT: It's difficult to say. The blow appeared to have been struck directly from behind, because the bruising ran perpendicularly. I should say it is really impossible to say whether it was delivered by a right- or left-handed man.

SIR WILFRID: We don't know yet that it was a *man*, Doctor. But will you agree, from the position of the blow, that if anything it is more likely to have been delivered by a left-handed person?

WYATT: That is possibly so. But I would prefer to say that it is uncertain.

SIR WILFRID: At the moment the blow was struck, would blood have been likely to have got onto the hand or arm that struck the blow?

WYATT: Yes, certainly.

SIR WILFRID: And only on that hand or arm?

WYATT: Probably only on that hand and arm, but it's difficult to be dogmatic.

SIR WILFRID: Quite so, Dr. Wyatt. Now, would great strength have been needed to strike such a blow?

WYATT: No. From the position of the wound no great strength would have been needed.

SIR WILFRID: It would not necessarily be a man who had struck the blow. A woman could have done so equally well?

WYATT: Certainly.

SIR WILFRID: Thank you. [*He sits*]

MYERS: [*Rising*] Thank you, Doctor. [*To the* USHER] Call Janet MacKenzie.

[WYATT *stands down, and exits up left. The* POLICEMAN *opens the door. The* USHER *rises and crosses to center*]

USHER: Janet MacKenzie.

POLICEMAN: [*Calling*] Janet MacKenzie.

[JANET MACKENZIE *enters up left. She is a tall, dour-looking Scotswoman. Her face is set in a grim line. Whenever she looks at* LEONARD, *she does so with loathing. The* POLICEMAN *closes the door.* JANET *crosses and enters the witness box. The* USHER *stands beside the witness box.* JANET *picks up the Bible in her left hand*]

USHER: Other hand, please.

[*He holds out the oath card.* JANET *puts the Bible into her right hand*]

JANET: I swear by Almighty God that the evidence that I shall give shall be the truth, the whole truth and nothing but the truth.

[*She hands the Bible to the* USHER. *The* USHER *puts the*

Bible and oath card on the ledge of the witness box, and resumes his seat]

MYERS: Your name is Janet MacKenzie?

JANET: Aye—that's my name.

MYERS: You were companion housekeeper to the late Miss Emily French?

JANET: I was her housekeeper. I've no opinion of companions, poor feckless bodies, afraid to do a bit of honest domestic work.

MYERS: Quite so, quite so, I meant only that you were held in esteem and affection by Miss French, and were on friendly terms together. Not quite those of mistress and servant.

JANET: [*To the* JUDGE] Twenty years I've been with her and looked after her. She knew me and she trusted me, and many's the time I've prevented her doing a foolish action!

JUDGE: Miss MacKenzie, would you please address your remarks to the Jury.

MYERS: What sort of a person was Miss French?

JANET: She was a warmhearted body—too warmhearted at times, I'm thinking. A wee bit impulsive too. There was times when she'd have no sense at all. She was easily flattered, you see.

MYERS: When did you first see the prisoner, Leonard Vole?

JANET: He came to the house, I mind, at the end of August.

MYERS: How often did he come to the house?

JANET: To begin with once a week, but later it was oftener. Two and even three times he'd come. He'd sit there flattering her, telling her how young she looked and noticing any new clothes she was wearing.

MYERS: [*Rather hastily*] Quite, quite. Now will you tell the Jury in your own words, Miss MacKenzie, about the events of October the fourteenth.

JANET: It was a Friday and my night out. I was going round to see some friends of mine in Glenister Road, which is not above three minutes' walk. I left the house at half past seven. I'd promised to take my friend the pattern of a knitted cardigan that she'd admired. When I got there I found I'd left it behind, so after supper I said I'd slip back and get it as it was a fine night and no distance.

I got back to the house at twenty-five past nine. I let myself in
with my key and went upstairs to my room. As I passed the sitting
room door I heard the prisoner in there talking to Miss French.

MYERS: You were sure it was the prisoner you heard?

JANET: Aye, I know his voice well enough. With him calling so often.
An agreeable voice it was, I'll not say it wasn't. Talking and laughing they were. But it was no business of mine so I went up and
fetched the pattern, came down and let myself out and went back
to my friend.

MYERS: Now I want these times very exact. You say that you re-
entered the house at twenty-five past nine.

JANET: Aye. It was just after twenty past nine when I left Glenister
Road.

MYERS: How do you know that, Miss MacKenzie?

JANET: By the clock on my friend's mantelpiece, and I compared it
with my watch and the time was the same.

MYERS: You say it takes three or four minutes to walk to the house,
so that you entered the house at twenty-five minutes past nine,
and you were there . . .

JANET: I was there under ten minutes. It took me a few minutes to
search for the pattern as I wasna' sure where I'd left it.

MYERS: And what did you do next?

JANET: I went back to my friend in Glenister Road. She was delighted with the pattern, simply delighted. I stayed there until
twenty to eleven, then I said good night to them and came home.
I went into the sitting room then to see if the mistress wanted
anything before she went to bed.

MYERS: What did you see?

JANET: She was there on the floor, poor body, her head beaten in.
And all the drawers of the bureau out on the ground, everything
tossed hither and thither, the broken vase on the floor and the
curtains flying in the wind.

MYERS: What did you do?

JANET: I rang the police.

MYERS: Did you really think that a burglary had occurred?

SIR WILFRID: [Jumping up] Really, my lord, I must protest. [He sits]

JUDGE: I will not allow that question to be answered, Mr. Myers. It should not have been put to the witness.

MYERS: Then let me ask you this, Miss MacKenzie. What did you do after you had telephoned the police?

JANET: I searched the house.

MYERS: What for?

JANET: For an intruder.

MYERS: Did you find one?

JANET: I did not. Nor any signs of disturbance save in the sitting room.

MYERS: How much did you know about the prisoner, Leonard Vole?

JANET: I knew that he needed money.

MYERS: Did he ask Miss French for money?

JANET: He was too clever for that.

MYERS: Did he help Miss French with her business affairs—with her income tax returns, for instance?

JANET: Aye—not that there was any need of it.

MYERS: What do you mean by not any need of it?

JANET: Miss French had a good, clear head for business.

MYERS: Were you aware of what arrangements Miss French had made for the disposal of her money in the event of her death?

JANET: She'd make a will as the fancy took her. She was a rich woman and she had a lot of money to leave and no near relatives. "It must go where it can do the most good," she would say. Once it was to orphans she left it, and once to an old people's home, and another time a dispensary for cats and dogs, but it always came to the same in the end. She'd quarrel with the people and then she'd come home and tear up the will and make a new one.

MYERS: Do you know when she made her last will?

JANET: She made it on October the eighth. I heard her speaking to Mr. Stokes, the lawyer. Saying he was to come tomorrow, she was making a new will. He was there at the time—the prisoner, I mean, kind of protesting, saying, "No, no." [LEONARD *hastily scribbles a note*] And the mistress said, "But I want to, my dear boy. I want to. Remember that day I was nearly run over by a bus. It might happen any time."

[LEONARD *leans over the dock and hands the note to* MAY-HEW *who passes it to* SIR WILFRID]

MYERS: Do you know when your mistress made a will previous to that one?

JANET: In the spring it was.

MYERS: Were you aware, Miss MacKenzie, that Leonard Vole was a married man?

JANET: No, indeed. Neither was the mistress.

SIR WILFRID: [*Rising*] I object. What Miss French knew or did not know is pure conjecture on Janet MacKenzie's part. [*He sits*]

MYERS: Let us put it this way. You formed the opinion that Miss French thought Leonard Vole a single man? Have you any facts to support that opinion?

JANET: There was the books she ordered from the library. There was the *Life of Baroness Burdett Coutts* and one about Disraeli and his wife. Both of them about women who'd married men years younger than themselves. I knew what she was thinking.

JUDGE: I'm afraid we cannot admit that.

JANET: Why?

JUDGE: Members of the Jury, it is possible for a woman to read the life of Disraeli without contemplating marriage with a man younger than herself.

MYERS: Did Mr. Vole ever mention a wife?

JANET: Never.

MYERS: Thank you. [*He sits*]

[SIR WILFRID *rises*]

SIR WILFRID: [*Gently and kindly*] I think we all appreciate how very devoted to your mistress you were.

JANET: Aye—I was.

SIR WILFRID: You had great influence over her?

JANET: Aye—maybe.

SIR WILFRID: In the last will Miss French made—that is to say the one made last spring, Miss French left almost the whole of her fortune to you. Were you aware of that fact?

JANET: She told me so. "All crooks, these charities," she said. "Expenses here and expenses there and the money not going to the object you give it for. I've left it to you, Janet, and you can do what you think's right and good with it."

SIR WILFRID: That was an expression of great trust on her part. In her present will, I understand, she has merely left you an annuity. The principal beneficiary is the prisoner, Leonard Vole.

JANET: It will be wicked injustice if he ever touches a penny of that money.

SIR WILFRID: Miss French, you say, had not many friends and acquaintances. Now why was that?

JANET: She didn't go out much.

SIR WILFRID: When Miss French struck up this friendship with Leonard Vole it made you very sore and angry, didn't it?

JANET: I didn't like seeing my dear lady imposed upon.

SIR WILFRID: But you have admitted that Mr. Vole did not impose upon her. Perhaps you mean that you didn't like to see someone else supplanting you as an influence on Miss French?

JANET: She leaned on him a good deal. Far more than was safe, I thought.

SIR WILFRID: Far more than you personally liked?

JANET: Of course. I've said so. But it was of her good I was thinking.

SIR WILFRID: So the prisoner had a great influence over Miss French, and she had a great affection for him?

JANET: That was what it had come to.

SIR WILFRID: So that if the prisoner had ever asked her for money, she would almost certainly have given him some, would she not?

JANET: I have not said that.

SIR WILFRID: But he never received any money from her?

JANET: That may not have been for want of trying.

SIR WILFRID: Returning to the night of October the fourteenth, you say you heard the prisoner and Miss French talking together. What did you hear them say?

JANET: I didn't hear what they actually said.

SIR WILFRID: You mean you only heard the voices—the murmur of voices?

JANET: They were laughing.

SIR WILFRID: You heard a man's voice and a woman's and they were laughing. Is that right?

JANET: Aye.

SIR WILFRID: I suggest that is exactly what you did hear. A man's voice and a woman's voice laughing. You didn't hear what was said. What makes you say that the man's voice was Leonard Vole's?

JANET: I know his voice well enough.

SIR WILFRID: The door was closed, was it not?

JANET: Aye. It was closed.

SIR WILFRID: You heard a murmur of voices through a closed door and you swear that one of the voices was that of Leonard Vole. I suggest that that is mere prejudice on your part.

JANET: It was Leonard Vole.

SIR WILFRID: As I understand it you passed the door twice, once going to your room, and once going out?

JANET: That is so.

SIR WILFRID: You were no doubt in a hurry to get your pattern and return to your friend?

JANET: I was in no particular hurry. I had the whole evening.

SIR WILFRID: What I am suggesting is that on both occasions you walked quickly past that door.

JANET: I was there long enough to hear what I heard.

SIR WILFRID: Come, Miss MacKenzie, I'm sure you don't wish to suggest to the Jury that you were eavesdropping.

JANET: I was doing no such thing. I've better things to do with my time.

SIR WILFRID: Exactly. You are registered, of course, under the National Health Insurance?

JANET: That's so. Four and sixpence I have to pay out every week. It's a terrible lot of money for a working woman to pay.

SIR WILFRID: Yes, yes, many people feel that. I think, Miss MacKenzie, that you recently applied for a national hearing apparatus?

JANET: Six months ago I applied for it and not got it yet.

SIR WILFRID: So your hearing isn't very good, is that right? [He lowers his voice] When I say to you, Miss MacKenzie, that you could not possibly recognize a voice through a closed door, what do you answer? [*He pauses*] Can you tell me what I said?

JANET: I can no' hear anyone if they mumble.

SIR WILFRID: In fact you didn't hear what I said, although I am only a few feet from you in an open court. Yet you say that behind a closed door with two people talking in an ordinary conversational tone, you definitely recognized the voice of Leonard Vole as you swept past that door on two occasions.

JANET: It was him, I tell you. It was him.

SIR WILFRID: What you mean is you want it to be him. You have a preconceived notion.

JANET: Who else could it have been?

SIR WILFRID: Exactly. Who else could it have been? That was the way your mind worked. Now tell me, Miss MacKenzie, was Miss French sometimes lonely all by herself in the evening?

JANET: No, she was not lonely. She had books from the library.

SIR WILFRID: She listened to the wireless, perhaps?

JANET: Aye, she listened to the wireless.

SIR WILFRID: She was fond of a talk on it, perhaps, or of a good play?

JANET: Yes, she liked a good play.

SIR WILFRID: Wasn't it possible that on that evening when you returned home and passed the door, that what you really heard was the wireless switched on and a man and woman's voice, and laughter? There was a play called *Lover's Leap* on the wireless that night.

JANET: It was not the wireless.

SIR WILFRID: Oh, why not?

JANET: The wireless was away being repaired that week.

SIR WILFRID: [*Slightly taken aback*] It must have upset you very much, Miss MacKenzie, if you really thought Miss French intended to marry the prisoner.

JANET: Naturally it would upset me. It was a *daft* thing to do.

SIR WILFRID: For one thing, *if* Miss French had married the prisoner it's quite possible, isn't it, that he might have persuaded her to dismiss you.

JANET: She'd never have done that, after all these years.

SIR WILFRID: But you never know what anyone will do, do you? Not if they're strongly influenced by anyone.

JANET: He would have used his influence, oh yes, he would have done his best to make her get rid of me.

SIR WILFRID: I see. You felt the prisoner was a very real menace to your present way of life at the time.

JANET: He'd have changed everything.

SIR WILFRID: Yes, very upsetting. No wonder you feel so bitterly against the prisoner. [*He sits*]

MYERS: [*Rising*] My learned friend has been at great pains to extract from you an admission of vindictiveness toward the prisoner . . .

SIR WILFRID: [*Without rising, and audibly for the benefit of the Jury*] A painless extraction—quite painless.

MYERS: [*Ignoring him*] Did you really believe your mistress might have married the prisoner?

JANET: Indeed I did. I've just said so.

MYERS: Yes, indeed you have. In your view had the prisoner such an influence over Miss French that he could have persuaded her to dismiss you?

JANET: I'd like to have seen him try. He'd not have succeeded.

MYERS: Had the prisoner ever shown any dislike of you in any way?

JANET: No, he had his manners.

MYERS: Just one more question. You say you recognized Leonard Vole's voice through that closed door. Will you tell the Jury how you knew it was his?

JANET: You know a person's voice without hearing exactly what they are saying.

MYERS: Thank you, Miss MacKenzie.

JANET: [*To the* JUDGE] Good morning. [*She stands down and crosses to the door up left*]

MYERS: Call Thomas Clegg.

[*The* POLICEMAN *opens the door*]

USHER: [*Rising and crossing to center*] Thomas Clegg.

POLICEMAN: [*Calling*] Thomas Clegg.

[JANET *exits.* THOMAS CLEGG *enters up left. He carries a notebook. The* POLICEMAN *closes the door. The* USHER *moves to the witness box and picks up the Bible and oath card.* CLEGG *enters the witness box and takes the Bible from the* USHER]

CLEGG: [*Saying the oath by heart*] I swear by Almighty God that the evidence that I shall give shall be the truth, the whole truth and nothing but the truth.

[*He puts the Bible on the ledge of the witness box. The* USHER *puts the oath card on the ledge of the witness box, and resumes his seat*]

MYERS: You are Thomas Clegg?

CLEGG: Yes, sir.

MYERS: You are an assistant in the forensic laboratory at New Scotland Yard?

CLEGG: I am.

MYERS: [*Indicating the jacket on the table*] Do you recognize that coat?

[*The* USHER *rises, crosses to the table and picks up the jacket*]

CLEGG: Yes. It was given to me by Inspector Hearne and tested by me for traces of blood.

[*The* USHER *hands the coat up to* CLEGG *who brushes it aside. The* USHER *replaces the jacket on the table, and resumes his seat*]

MYERS: Will you tell me your findings?

CLEGG: The coat sleeves had been washed, though not properly pressed afterwards, but by certain tests I am able to state that there are traces of blood on the cuffs.

MYERS: Is this blood of a special group or type?

CLEGG: Yes. [*He refers to his notebook*] It is of the type O.

MYERS: Were you also given a sample of blood to test?

CLEGG: I was given a sample labeled "Blood of Miss Emily French." The blood group was of the same type—O.

[MYERS *resumes his seat*]

SIR WILFRID: [*Rising*] You say there were traces of blood on both cuffs?

CLEGG: That is right.

SIR WILFRID: I suggest that there were traces of blood on only one cuff—the left one.

CLEGG: [*Looking at his notebook*] Yes. I am sorry, I made a mistake. It was only the left cuff.

SIR WILFRID: And it was only the left sleeve that had been washed?

CLEGG: Yes, that is so.

SIR WILFRID: Are you aware that the prisoner had told the police that he had cut his wrist, and that that blood was on the cuff of this coat?

CLEGG: So I understand.

[SIR WILFRID *takes a certificate from his* ASSISTANT]

SIR WILFRID: I have here a certificate stating that Leonard Vole is a blood donor at the North London Hospital, and that his blood group is O. That is the same blood group, is it not?

CLEGG: Yes.

SIR WILFRID: So the blood might equally well have come from a cut on the prisoner's wrist?

CLEGG: That is so.

[SIR WILFRID *resumes his seat*]

MYERS: [*Rising*] Blood group O is a very common one, is it not?

CLEGG: O? Oh, yes. At least forty-two per cent of people are in blood group O.

MYERS: Call Romaine Heilger.

[CLEGG *stands down and crosses to the door up left*]

USHER: [*Rising and crossing to center*] Romaine Heilger.

[*The* POLICEMAN *opens the door*]

POLICEMAN: [*Calling*] Romaine Heilger.

[CLEGG *exits.* ROMAINE *enters up left. There is a general buzz of conversation in the Court as she crosses to the witness box. The* POLICEMAN *closes the door. The* USHER *moves to the witness box and picks up the Bible and oath card]*

USHER: Silence!

[*He hands the Bible to* ROMAINE *and holds up the card*]

ROMAINE: I swear by Almighty God that the evidence that I shall give shall be the truth, the whole truth and nothing but the truth.

[*The* USHER *replaces the Bible and oath card on the ledge of the witness box, and resumes his seat*]

MYERS: Your name is Romaine Heilger?

ROMAINE: Yes.

MYERS: You have been living as the wife of the prisoner, Leonard Vole?

ROMAINE: Yes.

MYERS: Are you actually his wife?

ROMAINE: I went through a form of marriage with him in Berlin. My former husband is still alive, so the marriage is not . . . [*She breaks off*]

MYERS: Not valid.

SIR WILFRID: [*Rising*] My lord, I have the most serious objection to this witness giving evidence at all. We have the undeniable fact of marriage between this witness and the prisoner, and no proof whatsoever of this so-called previous marriage.

MYERS: If my friend had not abandoned his customary patience, and had waited for one more question, your lordship would have been spared this further interruption.

[SIR WILFRID *resumes his seat*]

MYERS: [*Picking up a document*] Mrs. Heilger, is this a certificate of a marriage between yourself and Otto Gerthe Heilger on the eighteenth of April, nineteen forty-six, in Leipzig?

[*The* USHER *rises, takes the certificate from* MYERS *and takes it to* ROMAINE]

ROMAINE: It is.

JUDGE: I should like to see that certificate. [*The* USHER *gives the certificate to the* CLERK, *who hands it to the* JUDGE] It will be exhibit number four, I think.

MYERS: I believe it will be, my lord.

JUDGE: [*After examining the document*] I think, Sir Wilfrid, this witness is competent to give evidence.

[*He hands the certificate to the* CLERK. *The* CLERK *gives the certificate to the* USHER, *who hands it to* MAYHEW. *The* USHER *then resumes his seat.* MAYHEW *shows the certificate to* SIR WILFRID]

MYERS: In any event, Mrs. Heilger, are you willing to give evidence against the man you have been calling your husband?

ROMAINE: I'm quite willing.

[LEONARD *rises, followed by the* WARDER]

LEONARD: Romaine! What are you doing here?—what are you saying?

JUDGE: I must have silence. As your counsel will tell you, Vole, you will very shortly have an opportunity of speaking in your own defense.

[LEONARD *and the* WARDER *resume their seats*]

MYERS: [*To* ROMAINE] Will you tell me in your own words what happened on the evening of October the fourteenth.

ROMAINE: I was at home all the evening.

MYERS: And Leonard Vole?

ROMAINE: Leonard went out at half past seven.

MYERS: When did he return?

ROMAINE: At ten minutes past ten.

[LEONARD *rises, followed by the* WARDER]

LEONARD: That's not true. You know it's not true. It was about twenty-five past nine when I came home. [MAYHEW *rises, turns to* LEONARD *and whispers to him to be quiet*] Who's been making you say this? I don't understand! [*He shrinks back and puts his hands to his face. Half whispering*] I—I don't understand. [*He resumes his seat*]

[MAYHEW *and the* WARDER *sit*]

MYERS: Leonard Vole returned, you say, at ten minutes past ten? And what happened next?

ROMAINE: He was breathing hard, very excited. He threw off his coat and examined the sleeves. Then he told me to wash the cuffs. They had blood on them.

MYERS: Did he speak about the blood?

ROMAINE: He said, "Dammit, there's blood on them."

MYERS: What did you say?

ROMAINE: I said, "What have you done?"

MYERS: What did the prisoner say to that?

ROMAINE: He said, "I've killed her."

LEONARD: [*Rising; frenzied*] It's not true, I tell you! It's not true!

[*The* WARDER *rises and restrains* LEONARD]

JUDGE: Please control yourself.

LEONARD: Not a word of this is true.

[*He resumes his seat. The* WARDER *remains standing*]

JUDGE: [*To* ROMAINE] You know what you're saying, Mrs. Heilger?

ROMAINE: I am to speak the truth, am I not?

MYERS: The prisoner said, "I have killed her." Did you know to whom he referred?

ROMAINE: Yes, I knew. It was the old woman he had been going to see so often.

MYERS: What happened next?

ROMAINE: He told me that I was to say he had been at home with me all that evening, especially he said I was to say he was at home at half past nine. I said to him, "Do the police know you've killed her?" And he said, "No, they will think it's a burglary. But anyway, remember I was at home with you at half past nine."

MYERS: And you were subsequently interrogated by the police?

ROMAINE: Yes.

MYERS: Did they ask you if Leonard Vole was at home with you at half past nine?

ROMAINE: Yes.

MYERS: What did you answer to that?

ROMAINE: I said that he was.

MYERS: But you have changed your story now. Why?

ROMAINE: [*With sudden passion*] Because it is murder. I cannot go on lying to save him. I am grateful to him, yes. He married me and brought me to this country. What he has asked me to do always I have done it because I was grateful.

MYERS: Because you loved him?

ROMAINE: No, I never loved him.

LEONARD: Romaine!

ROMAINE: I never loved him.

MYERS: You were grateful to the prisoner. He brought you to this country. He asked you to give him an alibi and at first you consented, but later you felt that what he had asked you to do was wrong?

ROMAINE: Yes, that is it exactly.

MYERS: Why did you feel it was wrong?

ROMAINE: When it is murder. I cannot come into Court and lie and say that he was there with me at the time it was done. I cannot do it. I cannot *do* it.

MYERS: So what did you do?

ROMAINE: I did not know what to do. I do not know your country and I am afraid of the police. So I write a letter to my ambassador, and I say that I do not wish to tell any more lies. I wish to speak the truth.

MYERS: That *is* the truth—that Leonard Vole returned that night at ten minutes past ten. That he had blood on the sleeves of his coat, that he said to you, "I have killed her." That is the truth before God?

ROMAINE: That is the truth.

[MYERS *resumes his seat*]

SIR WILFRID: [*Rising*] When the prisoner went through this form of marriage with you, was he aware that your first husband was still alive?

ROMAINE: No.

SIR WILFRID: He acted in good faith?

ROMAINE: Yes.

SIR WILFRID: And you were very grateful to him?

ROMAINE: I was grateful to him, yes.

SIR WILFRID: You've shown your gratitude by coming here and testifying against him.

ROMAINE: I have to speak the truth.

SIR WILFRID: [Savagely] Is it the truth?

ROMAINE: Yes.

SIR WILFRID: I suggest to you that on the night of October the fourteenth Leonard Vole was at home with you at nine thirty, the time that the murder was committed. I suggest to you that this whole story of yours is a wicked fabrication, that you have for some reason a grudge against the prisoner, and that this is your way of expressing it.

ROMAINE: No.

SIR WILFRID: You realize that you are on oath?

ROMAINE: Yes.

SIR WILFRID: I warn you, Mrs. Heilger, that if you care nothing for the prisoner, be careful on your own account. The penalty for perjury is heavy.

MYERS: [Rising and interposing] Really, my lord. I don't know whether these theatrical outbursts are for the benefit of the Jury, but I do most respectfully submit that there is nothing to suggest that this witness has spoken anything but the truth.

JUDGE: Mr. Myers. This is a capital charge, and within the bounds of reason I would like the defense to have every latitude. Yes, Sir Wilfrid.

[MYERS resumes his seat]

SIR WILFRID: Now then. You have said—that there was blood on both cuffs?

ROMAINE: Yes.

SIR WILFRID: Both cuffs?

ROMAINE: I have told you, that is what Leonard said.

SIR WILFRID: No, Mrs. Heilger, you said, "He told me to wash the cuffs. They had blood on them."

JUDGE: That is precisely my note, Sir Wilfrid.

SIR WILFRID: Thank you, my lord. [To ROMAINE] What you were saying is that you had washed both cuffs.

MYERS: [Rising] It is my friend's turn to be inaccurate now, my lord. Nowhere has this witness said she washed both cuffs, or indeed that she washed even one. [He sits]

SIR WILFRID: My friend is right. Well, Mrs. Heilger, did you wash the sleeves?

ROMAINE: I remember now. It was only one sleeve that I washed.

SIR WILFRID: Thank you. Perhaps your memory as to other parts of your story is equally untrustworthy. I think your original story to the police was that the blood on the jacket came from a cut caused while carving ham?

ROMAINE: I said so, yes. But it was not true.

SIR WILFRID: Why did you lie?

ROMAINE: I said what Leonard told me to say.

SIR WILFRID: Even going so far as to produce the actual knife with which he was cutting the ham?

ROMAINE: When Leonard found he had blood on him, he cut himself to make it seem the blood was his.

LEONARD: [Rising] I never did.

SIR WILFRID: [Silencing LEONARD] Please, please. [LEONARD resumes his seat. To ROMAINE] So you admit that your original story to the police was all lies? You seem to be a very good liar.

ROMAINE: Leonard told me what to say.

SIR WILFRID: The question is whether you were lying then or whether you are lying now. If you were really appalled at murder having been committed, you could have told the truth to the police when they first questioned you.

ROMAINE: I was afraid of Leonard.

SIR WILFRID: [Gesturing toward the woeful figure of LEONARD] You were afraid of Leonard Vole—afraid of the man whose heart and spirit you've just broken. I think the Jury will know which of you to believe. [He sits]

MYERS: [*Rising*] Romaine Heilger. I ask you once more, is the evidence you have given the truth, the whole truth and nothing but the truth?

ROMAINE: It is.

MYERS: My lord, that is the case for the prosecution. [*He sits*]

> [ROMAINE *stands down and crosses to the door up left. The* POLICEMAN *opens the door*]

LEONARD: [*As* ROMAINE *passes him*] Romaine!

USHER: [*Rising*] Silence!

> [ROMAINE *exits. The* POLICEMAN *closes the door. The* USHER *resumes his seat*]

JUDGE: Sir Wilfrid.

SIR WILFRID: [*Rising*] My lord, members of the Jury, I will not submit to you, as I might, that there is no case for the prisoner to answer. There *is* a case. A case of very strong circumstantial evidence. You have heard the police and other expert witnesses. They have given fair, impartial evidence as is their duty. Against them I have nothing to say. On the other hand, you have heard Janet MacKenzie and the woman who calls herself Romaine Vole. Can you believe that their testimony is not warped? Janet MacKenzie —cut out of her rich mistress's will because her position was usurped, quite unwittingly, by this unfortunate boy. [*He pauses*] Romaine Vole—Heilger—whatever she calls herself, who trapped him into marriage, whilst concealing from him the fact that she was married already. That woman owes him more than she can ever repay. She used him to save her from political persecution. But she admits no love for him. He has served his purpose. I will ask you to be very careful how you believe her testimony, the testimony of a woman who, for all we know, has been brought up to believe the pernicious doctrine that lying is a weapon to be used to serve one's own ends. Members of the Jury, I call the prisoner, Leonard Vole.

> [*The* USHER *rises and crosses to the witness box.* LEONARD *rises, and goes into the witness box. The* WARDER *follows*

LEONARD *and stands behind him. The* USHER *picks up the
Bible, hands it to* LEONARD *and holds up the oath card*]

LEONARD: I swear by Almighty God that the evidence that I shall
give shall be the truth, the whole truth and nothing but the truth.

[*He puts the Bible on the ledge of the witness box. The*
USHER *replaces the oath card on the ledge of the witness
box, and sits*]

SIR WILFRID: Now, Mr. Vole, we have heard of your friendship with
Miss Emily French. Now I want you to tell us how often you
visited her.

LEONARD: Frequently.

SIR WILFRID: Why was that?

LEONARD: Well, she was awfully nice to me and I got fond of her.
She was like my Aunt Betsy.

SIR WILFRID: That was an aunt who brought you up?

LEONARD: Yes. She was a dear. Miss French reminded me of her.

SIR WILFRID: You've heard Janet MacKenzie say Miss French thought
you were a single man, and that there was some question of marrying you. Is there any truth in this?

LEONARD: Of course not. It's an absurd idea.

SIR WILFRID: Miss French knew that you were married?

LEONARD: Yes.

SIR WILFRID: So there was no question of marriage between you?

LEONARD: Of course not. I've told you, she treated me as though she
was an indulgent aunt. Almost like a mother.

SIR WILFRID: And in return you did everything for her that you could.

LEONARD: [*Simply*] I was very fond of her.

SIR WILFRID: Will you tell the Jury in your own words exactly what
happened on the night of October the fourteenth?

LEONARD: Well, I'd come across a kind of cat brush—a new thing in
that line—and I thought it would please her. So I took it along
that evening. I'd nothing else to do.

SIR WILFRID: What time was that?

LEONARD: Just before eight I got there. I gave her the cat brush. She
was pleased. We tried it out on one of the cats and it was a suc-

cess. Then we played a game of Double Demon—Miss French was very fond of Double Demon—and after that I left.

SIR WILFRID: Yes, but did you not . . .

JUDGE: Sir Wilfrid, I don't understand this piece of evidence at all. What is a cat brush?

LEONARD: It's a brush for brushing cats.

JUDGE: Oh!

LEONARD: A sort of brush and comb combined. Miss French kept cats—eight of them she had, and the house smelt a bit . . .

SIR WILFRID: Yes, yes.

LEONARD: I thought the brush might be useful.

SIR WILFRID: Did you see Janet MacKenzie?

LEONARD: No. Miss French let me in herself.

SIR WILFRID: Did you know Janet MacKenzie was out?

LEONARD: Well, I didn't think about it.

SIR WILFRID: At what time did you leave?

LEONARD: Just before nine. I walked home.

SIR WILFRID: How long did that take you?

LEONARD: Oh, I should say about twenty minutes to half an hour.

SIR WILFRID: So that you reached home . . . ?

LEONARD: I reached home at twenty-five minutes past nine.

SIR WILFRID: And your wife—I will call her your wife—was at home then?

LEONARD: Yes, of course she was. I—I think she must have gone mad. I . . .

SIR WILFRID: Never mind that now. Just go on with your story. Did you wash your coat when you got in?

LEONARD: No, of course I didn't.

SIR WILFRID: Who did wash your coat?

LEONARD: Romaine did, the next morning. She said it had got blood on it from a cut on my wrist.

SIR WILFRID: A cut on your wrist?

LEONARD: Yes. Here. [He holds out his arm and shows his wrist] You can still see the mark.

SIR WILFRID: When was the first you heard of the murder?

LEONARD: I read about it in the evening paper the next day.

SIR WILFRID: And what did you feel?

LEONARD: I was stunned. I could hardly believe it. I was very upset too. The papers said it was a burglary. I never dreamed of anything else.

SIR WILFRID: And what happened next?

LEONARD: I read that the police were anxious to interview me, so of course I went along to the police station.

SIR WILFRID: You went along to the police station and made a statement?

LEONARD: Yes.

SIR WILFRID: You were not nervous? Reluctant to do so?

LEONARD: No, of course not. I wanted to help in any way possible.

SIR WILFRID: Did you ever receive any money from Miss French?

LEONARD: No.

SIR WILFRID: Were you aware that she had made a will in your favor?

LEONARD: She said she was ringing up her lawyers and going to make a new will. I asked her if she often made new wills and she said, "From time to time."

SIR WILFRID: Did you know what the terms of this new will were to be?

LEONARD: I swear I didn't.

SIR WILFRID: Had she ever suggested to you that she might leave you anything at all in her will?

LEONARD: No.

SIR WILFRID: You have heard the evidence that your wife—or the woman whom you considered as your wife—has given in Court.

LEONARD: Yes—I heard. I can't understand—I . . .

SIR WILFRID: [Checking him] I realize, Mr. Vole, that you are very upset, but I want to ask you to put aside all emotion and to answer the question plainly and simply. Was what that witness said true or untrue?

LEONARD: No, of course it wasn't true.

SIR WILFRID: You arrived home at nine twenty-five that night, and had supper with your wife?

LEONARD: Yes.

SIR WILFRID: Did you go out again?

LEONARD: No.

SIR WILFRID: Are you right- or left-handed?

LEONARD: Right-handed.

SIR WILFRID: I'm going to ask you just one more question, Mr. Vole. *Did you kill* Emily French?

LEONARD: *No, I did not.*

[SIR WILFRID *sits*]

MYERS: [*Rising*] Have you ever tried to get money out of anybody?

LEONARD: No.

MYERS: How soon in your acquaintance with Miss French did you learn that she was a very wealthy woman?

LEONARD: Well, I didn't know she *was* rich when I first went to see her.

MYERS: But, having gained that knowledge, you decided to cultivate her acquaintance further?

LEONARD: I suppose that's what it looks like. But I really liked her, you know. Money had nothing to do with it.

MYERS: You would have continued to visit her, no matter how poor she'd been?

LEONARD: Yes, I would.

MYERS: You yourself are in poor circumstances?

LEONARD: You know I am.

MYERS: Kindly answer the question, yes or no.

JUDGE: You must answer the question, yes or no.

LEONARD: Yes.

MYERS: What salary do you earn?

LEONARD: Well, as a matter of fact I haven't got a job at the moment. Haven't had one for some time.

MYERS: You were recently discharged from your position?

LEONARD: No, I wasn't—I quit.

MYERS: At the time of your arrest how much money had you in the bank?

LEONARD: Well, actually only a few pounds. I was expecting some money in, in a week or two.

MYERS: How much?

LEONARD: Not very much.

MYERS: I put it to you, you were pretty desperate for money?

LEONARD: Not desperate. I—well, I felt a bit worried.

MYERS: You were worried about money, you met a wealthy woman and you courted her acquaintance assiduously.

LEONARD: You make it sound all twisted. I tell you I liked her.

MYERS: We have heard that Miss French used to consult you on her income tax returns.

LEONARD: Yes, she did. You know what those forms are. You can't make head or tail of them—or she couldn't.

MYERS: Janet MacKenzie has told us that Miss French was a very good business woman, well able to deal with her own affairs.

LEONARD: Well, that's not what she said to me. She said those forms worried her terribly.

MYERS: In filling up her income tax forms for her you no doubt learned the exact amount of her income?

LEONARD: No.

MYERS: No?

LEONARD: Well—I mean naturally, yes.

MYERS: Yes, very convenient. How was it, Mr. Vole, that you never took your wife to see Miss French?

LEONARD: I don't know. It just didn't seem to crop up.

MYERS: You say Miss French knew you were married?

LEONARD: Yes.

MYERS: Yet she never asked you to bring your wife with you to the house?

LEONARD: No.

MYERS: Why not?

LEONARD: Oh, I don't know. She didn't like women, I don't think.

MYERS: She preferred, shall we say, personable young men? And you didn't insist on bringing your wife?

LEONARD: No, of course I didn't. You see, she knew my wife was a foreigner and she—oh, I don't know, she seemed to think we didn't get on.

MYERS: That was the impression you gave her?

LEONARD: No, I didn't. She—well, I think it was wishful thinking on her part.

MYERS: You mean she was infatuated with you?

LEONARD: No, she wasn't infatuated, but she, oh, it's like mothers are sometimes with a son.

MYERS: How?

LEONARD: They don't want him to like a girl or get engaged or anything of that kind.

MYERS: You hoped, didn't you, for some monetary advantage from your friendship with Miss French?

LEONARD: Not in the way you mean.

MYERS: Not in the way I mean? You seem to know what I mean better than I know myself. In what way then did you hope for monetary advantage? [He pauses] I repeat, in what way did you hope for monetary advantage?

LEONARD: You see, there's a thing I've invented. A kind of windscreen wiper that works in snow. I was looking for someone to finance that and I thought perhaps Miss French would. But that wasn't the only reason I went to see her. I tell you I liked her.

MYERS: Yes, yes, we've heard that very often, haven't we—how much you liked her.

LEONARD: [Sulkily] Well, it's true.

MYERS: I believe, Mr. Vole, that about a week before Miss French's death, you were making inquiries of a travel agency for particulars of foreign cruises.

LEONARD: Supposing I did—it isn't a crime, is it?

MYERS: Not at all. Many people go for cruises when they can pay for it. But you couldn't pay for it, could you, Mr. Vole?

LEONARD: I was hard up. I told you so.

MYERS: And yet you came into this particular travel agency—with a blonde—a strawberry blonde—I understand—and . . .

JUDGE: A strawberry blonde, Mr. Myers?

MYERS: A term for a lady with reddish fair hair, my lord.

JUDGE: I thought I knew all about blondes, but a strawberry blonde . . . Go on, Mr. Myers.

MYERS: [To LEONARD] Well?

LEONARD: My wife isn't a blonde and it was only a bit of fun, anyway.

MYERS: You admit that you asked for particulars, not of cheap trips, but of the most expensive and luxurious cruises. How did you expect to pay for such a thing?

LEONARD: I didn't.

MYERS: I suggest that you knew that in a week's time you would have inherited a large sum of money from a trusting elderly lady.

LEONARD: I didn't know anything of the kind. I just was feeling fed up—and there were the posters in the window—palm trees and coconuts and blue seas, and I went in and asked. The clerk gave me a sort of supercilious look—I *was* a bit shabby—but it riled me. And so I put on a bit of an act—[*He suddenly grins as though enjoying remembrance of the scene*] and began asking for the swankiest tours there were—all *de luxe* and a cabin on the boat deck.

MYERS: You really expect the Jury to believe that?

LEONARD: I don't expect anyone to believe anything. But that's the way it was. It was make-believe and childish if you like—but it was fun and I enjoyed it. [*He looks suddenly pathetic*] I wasn't thinking of killing anybody or of inheriting money.

MYERS: So it was just a remarkable coincidence that Miss French should be killed, leaving you her heir, only a few days later.

LEONARD: I've told you—I didn't kill her.

MYERS: Your story is that on the night of the fourteenth, you left Miss French's house at four minutes to nine, that you walked home and you arrived there at twenty-five minutes past nine, and stayed there the rest of the evening.

LEONARD: Yes.

MYERS: You have heard the woman Romaine Heilger rebut that story in Court. You have heard her say that you came in not at *twenty-five minutes* past nine but at *ten minutes past ten.*

LEONARD: It's not true!

MYERS: That your clothes were bloodstained, that you definitely admitted to her that you had killed Miss French.

LEONARD: It's not true, I tell you. Not one word of it is true!

MYERS: Can you suggest any reason why this young woman, who has been passing as your wife, should deliberately give the evidence she has given if it were not true?

LEONARD: No, I can't. That's the awful thing. There's no reason at all. I think she must have gone mad.

MYERS: You think she must have gone mad? She seemed extremely sane, and self-possessed. But insanity is the only reason you can suggest.

LEONARD: I don't understand it. Oh, God, what's happened—what's changed her?

MYERS: Very effective, I'm sure. But in this Court we deal with facts. And the fact is, Mr. Vole, that we have only your word for it that you left Emily French's house at the time you say you did, and that you arrived home at five and twenty minutes past nine, and that you did not go out again.

LEONARD: [*Wildly*] Someone must have seen me—in the street—or going into the house.

MYERS: One would certainly think so—but the only person who did see you come home that night says it was at ten minutes past ten. And that person says that you had blood on your clothes.

LEONARD: I cut my wrist.

MYERS: A very easy thing to do in case any questions should arise.

LEONARD: [*Breaking down*] You twist everything. You twist every-thing, I say! You make me sound like a different kind of person from what I am.

MYERS: You cut your wrist deliberately.

LEONARD: No, I didn't! I didn't do anything, but you make it all sound as though I did. I can hear it myself.

MYERS: You came home at ten past ten.

LEONARD: No, I didn't. You've *got* to believe me. You've got to *believe* me!

MYERS: You killed Emily French.

LEONARD: I didn't do it.

> [*The lights fade quickly, leaving two spots on* LEONARD *and* MYERS. *These fade too as he finishes speaking and the curtain falls*]

I didn't kill her! I've never killed anybody! Oh, God! It's a night-mare. It's some awful, evil dream.

CURTAIN

ACT THREE

SCENE 1

The Chambers of SIR WILFRID ROBARTS, Q.C. *The same evening.*

When the curtain rises, the stage is empty and in darkness. The window curtains are open. GRETA *enters immediately and holds the door open.* MAYHEW *and* SIR WILFRID *enter.* MAYHEW *carries his brief case.*

GRETA: Good evening, Sir Wilfrid. It's a nasty night, sir.

[GRETA *exits, closing the door behind her*]

SIR WILFRID: Damned fog! [*He switches on the wall brackets and crosses to the window*]

MAYHEW: It's a beast of an evening. [*He removes his hat and overcoat and hangs them on the pegs*]

SIR WILFRID: [*Closing the window curtains*] Is there no justice? We come out of a stuffy courtroom gasping for fresh air, and what do we find? [*He switches on the desk lamp*] Fog!

MAYHEW: It's not as thick as the fog we're in over Mrs. Heilger's antics. [*He crosses to the desk and puts down his case*]

SIR WILFRID: That damned woman. From the very first moment I clapped eyes on her, I scented trouble. I knew she was up to something. A thoroughly vindictive piece of goods and much too deep for that simple young fool in the dock. But what's *her* game, John? What's she up to? Tell me that.

MAYHEW: Presumably, it would seem, to get young Leonard Vole convicted of murder.

SIR WILFRID: But why? Look what he's done for her.

MAYHEW: He's probably done too much for her.

SIR WILFRID: And she despises him for it. That's likely enough. Ungrateful beasts, women. But why be vindictive? After all, if she was bored with him, all she had to do was walk out. There doesn't seem to be any financial reason for her to remain with him.

[GRETA *enters and crosses to the desk. She carries a tray with two cups of tea*]

GRETA: I've brought you your tea, Sir Wilfrid, and a cup for Mr. Mayhew, too. [*She puts one cup on each side of the desk*]

SIR WILFRID: [*Sitting near the fireplace*] Tea? Strong drink is what we need.

GRETA: Oh, you know you like your tea really, sir. How did it go today?

SIR WILFRID: Badly.

GRETA: Oh, no, sir. Oh, I do hope not. Because he didn't do it. I'm sure he didn't do it. [*She crosses to the door*]

SIR WILFRID: You're still sure he didn't do it. [*He looks thoughtfully at her*] Now why's that?

GRETA: [*Confidently*] Because he's not the sort. He's *nice*, if you know what I mean—ever so nice. He'd never go coshing an old lady on the head. But you'll get him off, won't you, sir?

SIR WILFRID: I'll—get—him—off.

[GRETA *exits*]

SIR WILFRID: [*Rises; almost to himself*] God knows how. Only one woman on the jury—pity—evidently the women like him—can't think why—he's not particularly—[*He crosses to the desk*] good looking. Perhaps he's got something that arouses the maternal instinct. Women want to mother him.

MAYHEW: Whereas Mrs. Heilger—is *not* the maternal type.

SIR WILFRID: [*Picking up his tea*] No, she's the passionate sort. Hot blooded behind that cool self-control. The kind that would knife a man if he double-crossed her. God, how I'd like to break her down. Show up her lies. Show *her* up for what she is.

MAYHEW: [*Taking his pipe from his pocket*] Forgive me, Wilfrid, but aren't you letting this case become a personal duel between you and her? [*He moves to the fireplace, takes a pipe cleaner from the jar on the mantelpiece and cleans his pipe*]

SIR WILFRID: Am I? Perhaps I am. But she's an evil woman, John. I'm convinced of that. And a young man's life depends on the outcome of that duel.

MAYHEW: [*Thoughtfully*] I don't think the Jury liked her.

SIR WILFRID: No, you're right there, John. I don't think they did. To begin with, she's a foreigner, and they distrust foreigners. Then she's not married to the fellow—she's more or less admitting to committing bigamy. [MAYHEW *tosses the pipe cleaner into the fireplace*] None of that goes down well. And at the end if it all, she's not sticking to her man when he's down. We don't like that in this country.

MAYHEW: That's all to the good.

SIR WILFRID: Yes, but it isn't enough. There's no corroboration of his statements whatsoever. [*He puts his tea on the desk*] He admits being with Miss French that evening, his fingerprints are all over the place, we haven't managed to find anybody who saw him on the way home, and there's the altogether damning matter of the will. [*He stands above the desk*] That travel agency business doesn't help. The woman makes a will in his favor and immediately he goes inquiring about luxury cruises. Couldn't be more unfortunate.

MAYHEW: I agree. And his explanation was hardly convincing.

SIR WILFRID: [*With a sudden complete change of manner and becoming very human*] And yet, you know, John, my wife does it.

MAYHEW: Does what?

SIR WILFRID: [*Smiling indulgently*] Gets travel agencies to make out itineraries for extensive foreign tours. For both of us. [*He takes the tobacco jar from the mantelpiece and puts it on the desk*]

MAYHEW: Thank you, Wilfrid. [*He sits and fills his pipe*]

SIR WILFRID: She'll work it all out to the last detail and bemoan the fact that the boat misses a connection at Bermuda. She'll say to me that we could save time by flying but that we wouldn't see anything of the country, and—[*He sits*] what do I think? And I say, "It's all the same to me, my dear. Arrange it as you like." We both know that it's a kind of game, and we'll end up with the same old thing—staying at home.

MAYHEW: Ah, now with *my* wife, it's houses.

SIR WILFRID: Houses?

MAYHEW: Orders to view. Sometimes I think that there's hardly a house in England that's ever been up for sale that my wife hasn't been over. She plans how to apportion the rooms, and works out any structural alterations that will be necessary. She even plans the curtains and the covers and the general color scheme.

> [*He rises, puts the tobacco jar on the mantelpiece and feels in his pocket for matches.* SIR WILFRID *and* MAYHEW *look at each other and smile indulgently*]

SIR WILFRID: H'm—well . . . [*He becomes the Q.C. again*] The fantasies of our wives aren't evidence, worse luck. But it helps one to understand why young Vole went asking for cruise literature.

MAYHEW: Pipe dreams.

SIR WILFRID: [*Taking a matchbox from the desk drawer*] There you are, John. [*He puts the box on the desk*]

MAYHEW: [*Crossing to the desk and picking up the matchbox*] Thank you, Wilfrid.

SIR WILFRID: I think we've had a certain amount of luck with Janet MacKenzie.

MAYHEW: Bias, you mean?

SIR WILFRID: That's right. Overdoing her prejudice.

MAYHEW: [*Sitting*] That was a very telling point of yours about her deafness.

SIR WILFRID: Yes, yes, we got her there. But she got her own back over the wireless.

> [MAYHEW *finds that the matchbox is empty, throws it in the wastepaper basket and puts his pipe in his pocket*]

SIR WILFRID: Not smoking, John?

MAYHEW: No, not just now.

SIR WILFRID: John, what really happened that night? Was it robbery with violence after all? The police have to admit that it might have been.

MAYHEW: But they don't really think so and they don't often make a mistake. That inspector is quite convinced that it *was* an inside job—that that window was tampered with from the inside.

SIR WILFRID: [*Rising and crossing below the desk*] Well, he may be wrong.

MAYHEW: I wonder.

SIR WILFRID: But if so, who was the man Janet MacKenzie heard talking to Miss French at nine thirty? Seems to me there are two answers to that.

MAYHEW: The answers being . . . ?

SIR WILFRID: First that she made the whole thing up, when she saw that the police weren't satisfied about its being a burglary.

MAYHEW: [*Shocked*] Surely she wouldn't do a thing like that?

SIR WILFRID: Well, what did she hear, then? Don't tell me it was a burglar chatting amicably with Miss French—[*He takes his handkerchief from his pocket*] before he coshed her on the head, you old clown.

[*He coshes* MAYHEW *with the handkerchief*]

MAYHEW: That certainly seems unlikely.

SIR WILFRID: I don't think that that rather grim old woman would stick at making up a thing like that. I don't think she'd stick at anything, you know. No—[*Significantly*] I don't think—she'd stick —at—*anything*.

MAYHEW: [*Horrified*] Good Lord! Do you mean . . . ?

[CARTER *enters and closes the door behind him*]

CARTER: Excuse me, Sir Wilfrid. A young woman is asking to see you. She says it has to do with the case of Leonard Vole.

SIR WILFRID: [*Unimpressed*] Mental?

CARTER: Oh, no, Sir Wilfrid. I can always recognize that type.

SIR WILFRID: [*Moving above the desk and picking up the teacups*] What sort of a young woman?

CARTER: [*Taking the cups from* SIR WILFRID] Rather a common young woman, sir, with a free way of talking.

SIR WILFRID: And what does she want?

CARTER: [*Quoting somewhat distastefully*] She says she "knows something that might do the prisoner a bit of good."

SIR WILFRID: [*With a sigh*] Highly unlikely. Bring her in. [CARTER *exits, taking the cups with him*] What do you think, John?

MAYHEW: Oh, well, we can't afford to leave any stone unturned.

> [CARTER *enters and ushers in a* WOMAN. *She appears to be aged almost thirty-five and is flamboyantly but cheaply dressed. Blonde hair falls over one side of her face. She is violently and crudely made up. She carries a shabby handbag.* MAYHEW *rises*]

CARTER: The young lady.

> [CARTER *exits*]

WOMAN: [*Looking sharply from* SIR WILFRID *to* MAYHEW] Here, what's this? Two o' yer? I'm not talking to two of yer. [*She turns to go*]

SIR WILFRID: This is Mr. Mayhew. He is Leonard Vole's solicitor. I am Sir Wilfrid Robarts, Counsel for the Defense.

WOMAN: [*Peering at* SIR WILFRID] So you are, dear. Didn't recognize you without your wig. Lovely you all look in them wigs.

> [MAYHEW *gives* SIR WILFRID *a nudge, then stands above the desk*]

WOMAN: Havin' a bit of a confab, are you? Well, maybe I can help you if you make it worth my while.

SIR WILFRID: You know, Miss—er . . .

WOMAN: [*Sitting*] No need for names. If I did give you a name, it mightn't be the right one, might it?

SIR WILFRID: As you please. You realize you are in duty bound to come forward to give any evidence that may be in your possession.

WOMAN: Aw, come off it! I didn't say I knew anything, did I? I've *got* something. That's more to the point.

MAYHEW: What is it you have got, madam?

WOMAN: Aye-aye! I was in court today. I watched that—that trollop give her evidence. So high and mighty about it too. She's a wicked one. A Jezebel, that's what she is.

SIR WILFRID: Quite so. But as to this special information you have . . .

WOMAN: [*Cunningly*] Ah, but what's in it for me? It's valuable, what I've got. A hundred quid, that's what I want.

MAYHEW: I'm afraid we could not countenance anything of that character, but perhaps if you tell us a little more about what you have to offer . . .

WOMAN: You don't buy unless you get a butcher's, is that it?

SIR WILFRID: A butcher's?

WOMAN: A butcher's 'ook—look.

SIR WILFRID: Oh, yes—yes.

WOMAN: I've got the goods on her all right. [*She opens her handbag*] It's letters, that's what it is. Letters.

SIR WILFRID: Letters written by Romaine Vole to the prisoner?

WOMAN: [*Laughing coarsely*] To the prisoner? Don't make me laugh. Poor ruddy prisoner, he's been took in by her all right. [*She winks*] I've got something to *sell*, dear, and don't you forget it.

MAYHEW: [*Smoothly*] If you will let us see these letters, we shall be able to advise you as to how pertinent they are.

WOMAN: Putting it in your own language, aren't you? Well, as I say, I don't expect you to buy without seeing. But fair's fair. If those letters will do the trick, if they'll get the boy off, and put that foreign bitch where she belongs, well, it's a hundred quid for me. Right?

MAYHEW: [*Taking his wallet from his pocket and extracting ten pounds*] If these letters contain information that is useful to the defense—to help your expenses in coming here—I am prepared to offer you ten pounds.

WOMAN: [*Almost screaming*] Ten bloody quid for letters like these! Think again.

SIR WILFRID: [*Crossing to* MAYHEW *and taking the wallet from him*] If you have a letter there that will help to prove my client's innocence, twenty pounds would I think not be an unreasonable sum for your expenses.

> [*He crosses to the desk, takes ten pounds from the wallet, returns the empty wallet to* MAYHEW, *and takes the first ten pounds from him*]

WOMAN: Fifty quid and it's a bargain. That's if you're satisfied with the letters.

SIR WILFRID: Twenty pounds.

[*He puts the notes on the desk. The* WOMAN *watches him and wets her lips. It is too much for her*]

WOMAN: All right, blast you. 'Ere, take 'em. Quite a packet of 'em. [*She takes the letters from her handbag*] The top one's the one will do the trick.

[*She puts the letters on the desk, then moves to pick up the money.* SIR WILFRID *is too quick for the* WOMAN *and picks up the money. The* WOMAN *quickly retrieves the letters*]

SIR WILFRID: Just a moment. I suppose this is her handwriting?

WOMAN: It's her handwriting all right. She wrote 'em. It's all fair and square.

SIR WILFRID: We have only your word for that.

MAYHEW: Just a moment. I have a letter from Mrs. Vole—not here, but at my office.

SIR WILFRID: Well, madam, it looks as though we'll have to trust you—[*He hands her the notes*] for the moment.

[*He takes the letters from her, smoothes them out and begins to read. The* WOMAN *slowly counts the notes, carefully watching the others meanwhile.* MAYHEW *moves to* SIR WILFRID *and peers at the letters. The* WOMAN *rises and crosses toward the door*]

SIR WILFRID: [*To* MAYHEW] It's incredible. Quite incredible.

MAYHEW: [*Reading over his shoulder*] The cold-blooded vindictiveness.

SIR WILFRID: [*To the* WOMAN] How did you get hold of these?

WOMAN: That'd be telling.

SIR WILFRID: What have you got against Romaine Vole?

[*The* WOMAN *crosses back to the desk, suddenly and dramatically turns her head, swings the desk lamp so that it flows on to her face on the side that has been turned away from the audience, pushing her hair back as she does so, revealing that her cheek is all slashed, scarred and disfigured.* SIR WILFRID *starts back with an ejaculation*]

WOMAN: See that?

SIR WILFRID: Did *she* do that to you?

WOMAN: Not her. The chap I was going with. Going with him steady, I was too. He was a bit younger than me, but he was fond of me and I loved him. Then she came along. She took a fancy to him and she got him away from me. She started to see him on the sly and then one day he cleared out. I knew where he'd gone. I went after him and I found them together. [*She sits*] I told 'er what I thought of 'er and 'e set on me. In with one of the razor gangs, he was. He cut my face up proper. "There," he says, "no man'll ever look at you now."

SIR WILFRID: Did you go to the police about it?

WOMAN: Me? Not likely. 'Sides it wasn't 'is fault. Not really. It was hers, all hers. Getting him away from me, turning 'im against me. But I waited my time. I followed 'er about and watched 'er. I know some of the things she's bin up to. I know where the bloke lives who she goes to see on the sly sometimes. That's how I got hold of them letters. So now you know the whole story, mister. [*She rises, thrusts her face forward and pushes her hair aside*] Want to kiss me? [SIR WILFRID *shrinks back*] I don't blame yer.

SIR WILFRID: I'm deeply sorry, deeply sorry. Got a fiver, John? [MAYHEW *shows his empty wallet. He takes his wallet from his pocket and extracts a five-pound note*] Er—we'll make it another five pounds.

WOMAN: [*Grabbing the note*] 'Oldin' out on me, were yer? Willin' to go up another five quid. [*She advances on* SIR WILFRID. *He backs toward* MAYHEW] Ah, I knew I was being too soft with you. Those letters are the goods, aren't they?

SIR WILFRID: They will, I think, be very useful. [*He turns to* MAYHEW *and holds out a letter*] Here, John, have a butcher's at this one.

[*The* WOMAN *slips quickly out of the door*]

MAYHEW: We'll have a handwriting expert on these for safety's sake, and he can give evidence if necessary.

SIR WILFRID: We shall require this man's surname and his address.

MAYHEW: [*Looking around*] Hullo, where has she gone? She mustn't leave without giving us further particulars.

[SIR WILFRID *exits hurriedly*]

SIR WILFRID: [*Off; calling*] Carter! Carter!

CARTER: [*Off*] Yes, Sir Wilfrid?

SIR WILFRID: [*Off*] Carter, where did that young woman go?

CARTER: [*Off*] She went straight out, sir.

SIR WILFRID: [*Off*] Well, you shouldn't have let her go. Send Greta after her.

CARTER: [*Off*] Very good, Sir Wilfrid.

[SIR WILFRID *returns*]

MAYHEW: She's gone?

SIR WILFRID: Yes, I've sent Greta after her, but there's not a hope in this fog. Damn! We must have this man's surname and address.

MAYHEW: We won't get it. She thought things out too carefully. Wouldn't give us her name, and slipped out like an eel as soon as she saw us busy with the letters. She daren't risk having to appear in the witness box. Look what the man did to her last time.

SIR WILFRID: [*Without conviction*] She'd have protection.

MAYHEW: Would she? For how long? He'd get her in the end, or his pals would. She's already risked something coming here. She doesn't want to bring the man into it. It's Romaine Heilger she's after.

SIR WILFRID: And what a beauty our Romaine is. But we've got something to go on at last. Now, as to procedure . . .

CURTAIN

SCENE 2

The Old Bailey. The next morning.

When the curtain rises, the Court is awaiting the entry of the JUDGE. LEONARD *and the* WARDER *are seated in the dock. Two* BARRISTERS *are seated at the left end of the back row of Barristers' seats.* SIR WILFRID *and his* ASSISTANT *are in their places.* MAYHEW *is standing at the table talking to* SIR WILFRID. *The* CLERK OF THE COURT, *the* JUDGE'S

CLERK *and the* STENOGRAPHER *are in their places. The three visible* MEMBERS OF THE JURY *are seated. The* POLICEMAN *is at the doors up left. The* USHER *is standing at the top of the steps up right center.* MYERS, *his* ASSISTANT *and two* BARRISTERS *enter up center.* MYERS *crosses to* SIR WILFRID *and starts talking angrily. The* ASSISTANT *and the* BARRISTERS *take their seats. There are three knocks on the* JUDGE's *door. The* USHER *comes down the steps.*

USHER: Stand up. [ALL *stand. The* JUDGE *and* ALDERMAN *enter by the* JUDGE's *door and take their seats*] All persons who have anything further to do before my lady the Queen's justices of Oyer and Terminer and general gaol delivery for the jurisdiction of the Central Criminal Court draw near and give your attendance. God Save the Queen.

[*The* JUDGE *bows to the Court and* ALL *take their seats. The* USHER *sits on the stool*]

SIR WILFRID: [*Rising*] My lord, since this was adjourned, certain evidence of a rather startling character has come into my hands. This evidence is such that I am taking it upon myself to ask your lordship's permission to have the last witness for the prosecution, Romaine Heilger, recalled.

[*The* CLERK *rises and whispers to the* JUDGE]

JUDGE: When exactly, Sir Wilfrid, did this evidence come to your knowledge?

[*The* CLERK *sits*]

SIR WILFRID: It was brought to me after the Court was adjourned last night.

MYERS: [*Rising*] My lord, I must object to my learned friend's request. The case for the prosecution is closed and . . .

[SIR WILFRID *sits*]

JUDGE: Mr. Myers, I had not intended to rule on this question without first observing the customary formality of inviting your observations on the matter. Yes, Sir Wilfrid?

[MYERS *sits*]

SIR WILFRID: [*Rising*] My lord, in a case where evidence vital to the prisoner comes into possession of his legal advisers at any time before the jury have returned their verdict, I contend that such evidence is not only admissible, but desirable. Happily there is clear authority to support my proposition, to be found in the case of the King against Stillman, reported in nineteen twenty-six *Appeal Cases* at page four-six-three. [*He opens a law volume in front of him*]

JUDGE: You needn't trouble to cite the authority, Sir Wilfrid, I am quite familiar with it. I should like to hear the prosecution. Now, Mr. Myers.

[SIR WILFRID *sits*]

MYERS: [*Rising*] In my respectful submission, my lord, the course my friend proposes is, save in exceptional circumstances, quite unprecedented. And what, may I ask, is this startling new evidence of which Sir Wilfrid speaks?

SIR WILFRID: [*Rising*] Letters, my lord. Letters from Romaine Heilger.

JUDGE: I should like to see these letters to which you refer, Sir Wilfrid.

[SIR WILFRID *and* MYERS *sit. The* USHER *rises, crosses to* SIR WILFRID, *collects the letters, passes them to the* CLERK, *who hands them to the* JUDGE. *The* JUDGE *studies the letters. The* USHER *resumes his seat*]

MYERS: [*Rising*] My friend was good enough to tell me only as we came into Court that he intended to make this submission, so that I have had no opportunity to examine the authorities. But I seem to remember a case in, I think, nineteen thirty, the King against Porter, I believe . . .

JUDGE: No, Mr. Myers, the King against Potter, and it was reported in nineteen thirty-one. I appeared for the prosecution.

MYERS: And if my memory serves me well, your lordship's similar objection was sustained.

JUDGE: Your memory for once serves you ill, Mr. Myers. My objection then was overruled by Mr. Justice Swindon—as yours is now, by me.

[MYERS *sits*]

SIR WILFRID: [*Rising*] Call Romaine Heilger.

[*The* USHER *rises and moves down center*]

USHER: Romaine Heilger.

[*The* POLICEMAN *opens the door*]

POLICEMAN: [*Calling*] Romaine Heilger.

JUDGE: If these letters are authentic it raises very serious issues.

[*He hands the letters to the* CLERK. *The* CLERK *hands the letters to the* USHER *who returns them to* SIR WILFRID. *During the slight wait that ensues,* LEONARD *is very agitated. He speaks to the* WARDER *then puts his hands to his face. The* USHER *sits on the stool.* MAYHEW *rises, speaks to* LEONARD *and calms him down.* LEONARD *shakes his head and looks upset and worried.* ROMAINE *enters up left, crosses, and enters the witness box. The* POLICEMAN *closes the door*]

SIR WILFRID: Mrs. Heilger, you appreciate that you are still on your oath?

ROMAINE: Yes.

JUDGE: Romaine Heilger, you are recalled to this box so that Sir Wilfrid may ask you further questions.

SIR WILFRID: Mrs. Heilger, do you know a certain man whose Christian name is Max?

[ROMAINE *starts violently at the mention of the name*]

ROMAINE: I don't know what you mean.

SIR WILFRID: [*Pleasantly*] And yet it's a very simple question. Do you or do you not know a man called Max?

ROMAINE: Certainly not.

SIR WILFRID: You're quite sure of that?

ROMAINE: I've never known anyone called Max. Never.

SIR WILFRID: And yet I believe it's a fairly common Christian name, or contraction of a name, in your country. You mean that you have never known anyone of that name?

ROMAINE: [*Doubtfully*] Oh, in Germany—yes—perhaps, I do not remember. It is a long time ago.

SIR WILFRID: I shall not ask you to throw your mind back such a long way as that. A few weeks will suffice. Let us say—[*He picks up one of the letters and unfolds it, making rather a parade of it*] the seventeenth of October last.

ROMAINE: [*Startled*] What have you got there?

SIR WILFRID: A letter.

ROMAINE: I don't know what you're talking about.

SIR WILFRID: I'm talking about a letter. A letter written on the seventeenth of October. You remember that date, perhaps.

ROMAINE: Not particularly, why?

SIR WILFRID: I suggest that on that day, you wrote a certain letter—a letter addressed to a man called Max.

ROMAINE: I did nothing of the kind. These are lies that you are telling. I don't know what you mean.

SIR WILFRID: That letter was one of a series written to the same man over a considerable period of time.

ROMAINE: [*Agitated*] Lies—all lies!

SIR WILFRID: You would seem to have been on—[*Significantly*] intimate terms with this man.

LEONARD: [*Rising*] How dare you say a thing like that? [*The* WARDER *rises and attempts to restrain* LEONARD. *He waves the* WARDER *aside*] It isn't true!

JUDGE: The prisoner in his own interest will remain silent.

[LEONARD *and the* WARDER *resume their seats*]

SIR WILFRID: I am not concerned with the general trend of this correspondence. I am only interested in one particular letter. [*He reads*] "My beloved Max. An extraordinary thing has happened. I believe all our difficulties may be ended . . ."

ROMAINE: [*Interrupting in a frenzy*] It's a lie—I never wrote it! How did you get hold of that letter? Who gave it to you?

SIR WILFRID: How the letter came into my possession is irrelevant.

ROMAINE: You stole it. You are a thief as well as a liar. Or did some woman give it to you? Yes, I am right, am I not?

JUDGE: Kindly confine yourself to answering Counsel's questions.

ROMAINE: But I will not listen.

JUDGE: Proceed, Sir Wilfrid.

SIR WILFRID: So far you have only heard the opening phrases of the letter. Am I to understand that you definitely deny writing it?

ROMAINE: Of course I never wrote it. It is a forgery. It is an outrage that I should be forced to listen to a pack of lies—lies made up by a jealous woman.

SIR WILFRID: I suggest it is *you* who have lied. You have lied flagrantly and persistently in this Court and upon oath. And the reason *why* you have lied is made clear by—[*He taps the letter*] this letter—written down by you in black and white.

ROMAINE: You are crazy. Why should I write down a lot of nonsense?

SIR WILFRID: Because a way had opened before you to freedom—and in planning to take that way, the fact that an innocent man would be sent to his death meant nothing to you. You have even included that final deadly touch of how you yourself managed accidentally to wound Leonard Vole with a ham knife.

ROMAINE: [*Carried away with fury*] I never wrote that! I wrote that he did it himself cutting the ham . . .

[*Her voice dies away. All eyes in Court turn on her*]

SIR WILFRID: [*Triumphantly*] So you know what is in the letter—before I have read it.

ROMAINE: [*Casting aside all restraint*] Damn you! Damn you! Damn you!

LEONARD: [*Shouting*] Leave her alone! Don't bully her!

ROMAINE: [*Looking wildly around*] Let me get out of here—let me go!

[*She comes out of the witness box. The* USHER *rises and restrains* ROMAINE]

JUDGE: Usher, give the witness a chair.

[ROMAINE *sinks onto the stool, sobs hysterically and buries her face in her hands. The* USHER *sits*]

JUDGE: Sir Wilfrid, will you now read the letter aloud so that the Jury can hear it.

SIR WILFRID: [*Reading*] "My beloved Max. An extraordinary thing has happened. I believe all our difficulties may be ended. I can come to you without any fear of endangering the valuable work you are doing in this country. The old lady I told you about has been murdered and I think Leonard is suspected. He was there earlier that night and his fingerprints will be all over the place. Nine thirty seems to be the time. Leonard was home by then, but his alibi depends on me—on *me*. Supposing I say he came home much later and that he had blood on his clothes—he did have blood on his sleeve, because he cut his wrist at supper, so you see it would all fit in. I can even say he told me he killed her. Oh, Max, beloved! Tell me I can go ahead—it would be so wonderful to be free from playing the part of a loving, grateful wife. I know the Cause and the Party comes first, but if Leonard was convicted of murder, I could come to you safely and we could be together for always. Your adoring Romaine."

JUDGE: Romaine Heilger, will you go back into the witness box? [ROMAINE *rises and enters the witness box*] You have heard that letter read. What have you to say?

ROMAINE: [*Frozen in defeat*] Nothing.

LEONARD: Romaine, tell him you didn't write it! *I* know you didn't write it.

ROMAINE: [*Turning and fairly spitting out the words*] Of course I wrote it.

SIR WILFRID: That, my lord, concludes the case for the defense.

JUDGE: Sir Wilfrid, have you any evidence as to whom these letters were addressed?

SIR WILFRID: My lord, they came into my possession anonymously, and there has been as yet no time to ascertain any further facts. It would seem likely that he came to this country illegally and is engaged on some subversive operations here . . .

ROMAINE: You will never find out who he is—never. I don't care what you do to me. You shall never know.

JUDGE: Do you wish to re-examine, Mr. Myers?

[SIR WILFRID *sits*]

MYERS: [*Rising rather unhappily*] Really, my lord, I find it somewhat difficult in view of these startling developments. [*To* ROMAINE] Mrs. Heilger, you are, I think, of a highly nervous temperament. Being a foreigner you may not quite realize the responsibilities that lie upon you when you take the oath in an English court of law. If you have been intimidated into admitting something that is not true, if you wrote a letter under stress or in some spirit of make-believe, do not hesitate to say so now.

ROMAINE: Must you go on and on torturing me? I wrote the letter. Now let me go.

MYERS: My lord, I submit that this witness is in such a state of agitation that she hardly knows what she is saying or admitting.

JUDGE: You may remember, Mr. Myers, that Sir Wilfrid cautioned the witness at the time of her previous statement and impressed upon her the sacred nature of the oath she had taken. [MYERS *sits*] Mrs. Heilger, I wish to warn you that this is not the end of the matter. In this country you cannot commit perjury without being brought to account for it, and I may tell you that I have no doubt proceedings for perjury will shortly be taken against you. The sentence for perjury can be severe. You may stand down.

[ROMAINE *stands down. The* POLICEMAN *opens the door.* ROMAINE *crosses and exits. The* POLICEMAN *closes the door*]

JUDGE: Sir Wilfrid, will you now address the Jury on behalf of the defense?

SIR WILFRID: [*Rising*] Members of the Jury, when truth is clearly evident it speaks for itself. No words of mine I'm sure can add to the impression made upon you by the straightforward story which the prisoner has told, and by the very wicked attempt to incriminate him, evidence of which you have just witnessed . . .

[*As* SIR WILFRID *speaks the lights dim to blackout. After a few seconds the lights come up. The* JURY *are out but are just re-entering the box*]

CLERK: [*Rising*] Vole, stand up. [LEONARD *rises*] Members of the
Jury, are you all agreed upon your verdict?

FOREMAN: [*Standing*] We are.

CLERK: Do you find the prisoner, Leonard Vole, guilty or not guilty?

FOREMAN: Not guilty, my lord.

> [*A buzz of approbation goes round the court*]

USHER: [*Rising*] Silence!

JUDGE: Leonard Vole, you have been found not guilty of the murder
of Emily French on October fourteenth. You are hereby discharged
and are free to leave the Court.

> [*He rises.* ALL *rise. The* JUDGE *bows to the Court and exits
> up right, followed by the* ALDERMAN *and the* JUDGE'S
> CLERK]

USHER: All persons who have anything further to do before my lady
the Queen's justices of Oyer and Terminer and general gaol delivery for the jursidiction of the Central Criminal Court may de-
part hence and give your attendance here again tomorrow morning
at ten thirty o'clock. God Save The Queen.

> [*The* USHER, *the* JURY *and the* STENOGRAPHER *exit down
> right. The* BARRISTERS, ASSISTANTS *and the* CLERK OF THE
> COURT *exit up center. The* WARDER *and the* POLICEMAN
> *exit up left.* LEONARD *leaves the dock and crosses to*
> MAYHEW]

MAYHEW: Congratulations, my boy!

LEONARD: I can't thank you enough.

MAYHEW: [*Tactfully indicating* SIR WILFRID] This is the man you've
got to thank.

> [LEONARD *crosses to meet* SIR WILFRID, *but comes face to
> face with* MYERS, *who glares at him, and exits up center*]

LEONARD: [*Turning to* SIR WILFRID] Thank you, sir. [*His tone is less
spontaneous than it was to* MAYHEW. *He dislikes* SIR WILFRID *it
seems*] You—you've got me out of a very nasty mess.

SIR WILFRID: Nasty mess! Do you hear that, John? Your troubles are over now, my boy.

MAYHEW: But it was a near thing, you know.

LEONARD: [*Unwillingly*] Yes, I suppose it was.

SIR WILFRID: If we hadn't been able to break that woman down . . .

LEONARD: Did you have to go for her the way you did? It was terrible the way she went to pieces. I can't believe . . .

SIR WILFRID: [*With all the force of his personality*] Look here, Vole, you're not the first young man I've known who's been so crazy over a woman that he's been blinded to what she's really like. That woman did her level best to put a rope round your neck.

MAYHEW: And don't you forget it.

LEONARD: Yes, but why? I can't see why. She's always seemed so devoted. I could have sworn she loved me—and yet all the time she was going with this other fellow. [*He shakes his head*] It's unbelievable—there's something there I don't understand.

[*The* WARDER *enters up left*]

WARDER: Just two or three minutes more, sir. We'll slip you out to a car by the side entrance.

LEONARD: Is there still a crowd?

[ROMAINE, *escorted by the* POLICEMAN, *enters up left*]

POLICEMAN: [*In the doorway*] Better wait in here, ma'am. The crowd's in a nasty mood. I'd let them disperse before you try to leave.

ROMAINE: Thank you.

[*The* POLICEMAN *and the* WARDER *exit.* ROMAINE *crosses toward* LEONARD]

SIR WILFRID: [*Intercepting* ROMAINE] No, you don't.

ROMAINE: [*Amused*] Are you protecting Leonard from me? Really, there's no need.

SIR WILFRID: You've done enough harm.

ROMAINE: Mayn't I even congratulate Leonard on being free?

SIR WILFRID: No thanks to you.

ROMAINE: And rich.

LEONARD: [*Uncertainly*] Rich?

MAYHEW: Yes, I think, Mr. Vole, that you will certainly inherit a great deal of money.

LEONARD: [*Boyishly*] Money doesn't seem to mean so much after what I've been through. Romaine, I can't understand . . .

ROMAINE: [*Smoothly*] Leonard, I can explain.

SIR WILFRID: No!

> [SIR WILFRID *and* ROMAINE *look at each other like antagonists*]

ROMAINE: Tell me, do those words the Judge said mean that I shall—go to prison?

SIR WILFRID: You will quite certainly be charged with perjury and tried for it. You will probably go to prison.

LEONARD: [*Awkwardly*] I'm sure that—that everything will come right. Romaine, don't worry.

MAYHEW: Will you never see sense, Vole? Now we must consider practicalities—this matter of probate.

> [MAYHEW *draws* LEONARD *aside, where they murmur together.* SIR WILFRID *and* ROMAINE *remain, measuring each other*]

SIR WILFRID: It may interest you to know that I took your measure the first time we met. I made up my mind then to beat you at your little game, and by God I've done it. I've got him off—in spite of you.

ROMAINE: In *spite*—of me.

SIR WILFRID: You don't deny, do you, that you did your best to hang him?

ROMAINE: Would they have believed me if I had said that he was at home with me that night, and did not go out? Would they?

SIR WILFRID: [*Slightly uncomfortable*] Why not?

ROMAINE: Because they would have said to themselves: this woman loves this man—she would say or do anything for him. They would have had sympathy with me, yes. But they would not have *believed* me.

SIR WILFRID: If you'd been speaking the truth they would.

ROMAINE: I wonder. [*She pauses*] I did not want their sympathy—I wanted them to dislike me, to mistrust me, to be convinced that I was a liar. And then, when my lies were broken down—then they believed . . . [*In the Cockney accent of the* WOMAN *who visited* SIR WILFRID *at his office*] So now you know the whole story, mister —like to kiss me?

SIR WILFRID: [*Thunderstruck*] My God!

ROMAINE: [*As herself*] Yes, the woman with the letters. I wrote those letters. I brought them to you. I was that woman. It wasn't *you* who won freedom for Leonard. It was *I*. And because of it I shall go to prison. [*Her eyes close*] But at the end of it Leonard and I will be together again. Happy—loving each other.

SIR WILFRID: [*Moved*] My dear . . . But couldn't you trust me? We believe, you know, that our British system of justice upholds the truth. We'd have got him off.

ROMAINE: I couldn't risk it. [*Slowly*] You see, you *thought* he was innocent . . .

SIR WILFRID: [*With quick appreciation*] And you *knew* he was innocent. I understand.

ROMAINE: But you do not understand at all. *I* knew he was *guilty*.

[SIR WILFRID *is thunderstruck*]

SIR WILFRID: But aren't you afraid?

ROMAINE: Afraid?

SIR WILFRID: Of linking your life with a murderer's.

ROMAINE: You don't understand—we love each other.

SIR WILFRID: The first time I met you I said you were a very remarkable woman—I see no reason to change my opinion.

[SIR WILFRID *crosses and exists up center*]

WARDER: [*Off*] It's no good going in there, miss. It's all over.

[*There is a commotion off up left and then a* GIRL *comes running on. She is a very young strawberry blonde with a crude, obvious appeal. She rushes through the Q.C.'s bench and down to* LEONARD]

GIRL: Len, darling, you're free. [*She embraces him*] Isn't it wonderful?

They're trying to keep me out. Darling, it's been awful. I've been nearly crazy.

ROMAINE: [*With sudden violent harshness*] Leonard—who—is—this girl?

GIRL: [*To* ROMAINE; *defiantly*] I'm Len's girl. I know all about *you*. You're not his wife. Never have been. You're years older than him, and you just got hold of him—and you've done your best to hang him. But that's all over now. [*She turns to* LEONARD] We'll go abroad like you said on one of your cruises—to all those grand places. We'll have a wonderful time.

ROMAINE: Is—this—true? Is she your girl, Leonard?

> [LEONARD *hesitates, then decides that the situation must be accepted*]

LEONARD: Yes, she is.

ROMAINE: After all I've done for you . . . What can *she* do for you that can compare with that?

LEONARD: [*Flinging off all disguise of manner, and showing coarse brutality*] She's fifteen years younger than you are. [*He laughs.* ROMAINE *flinches as though struck. Menacingly*] I've got the money. I've been acquitted, and I can't be tried again, so don't go shooting off your mouth, or you'll just get *yourself* hanged as an accessory after the fact.

> [LEONARD *turns to the* GIRL *and embraces her.* ROMAINE *picks up the knife from the table*]

ROMAINE: [*Throwing her head back in sudden dignity*] No, that will not happen. I shall not be tried as an accessory after the fact. I shall not be tried for perjury. I shall be tried for murder—[*She stabs* LEONARD *in the back*] the murder of the only man I ever loved.

> [LEONARD *drops. The* GIRL *screams.* MAYHEW *bends over* LEONARD, *feels his pulse and shakes his head.* ROMAINE *looks up at the* JUDGE's *seat*]

Guilty, my lord.

CURTAIN

Dial "M" for Murder

FREDERICK KNOTT

Frederick Knott

Dial "M" for Murder, unquestionably one of the most internationally performed suspense plays of the mid-century, came to the theatre by a circuitous route. After devoting fully eighteen months to its completion, Frederick Knott submitted his play to a number of London managements, prominent and otherwise, but he unvaryingly met with defeat in his attempts to gain a production. Disillusioned but undaunted, he finally consented to its presentation on British television. It received an excellent press, enthralled several million viewers, and even more significantly, caught the perspicacious eye of producer James P. Sherwood, who detected its theatrical potentials. Under his auspices, the play finally reached its destination, a West End stage, on the evening of June 19, 1952. Praised as "one of the most brilliant and ingenious thrillers London has seen in decades," Dial "M" for Murder ran for 425 performances at the Westminster Theatre and also achieved the historic honor of being the first television production to be adapted for the British theatre.

With Maurice Evans, in one of his infrequent appearances in a contemporary role, at the helm of a splendid company, the play opened at the Plymouth Theatre, New York, on October 29, 1952, and again incited chills and cheers. In his coverage for The New York Times, Brooks Atkinson summarized the event as "remarkably good theatre, tingling with excitement." The critical verdict was unanimous: Dial "M" for Murder had provided "more melodramatic excitement than Broadway had experienced in years; a constantly absorbing play which holds your attention like a vise." And it did, for 552 performances.

Within a few years, Dial "M" for Murder had successfully played in twenty-seven countries and in eighteen languages. There was one rather rude exception: the suspense drama had dialed a wrong number in Moscow. The well-known Pushkin Drama Theatre (Moscow) and the Leningrad Comedy Theatre had been presenting a Russian translation of the play under the title *Telephone Call*, and it had aroused considerable interest on the part of the Soviet theatregoing public. That is, it did until the Communist party newspaper *Pravda* lowered the boom on the thriller by condemning it as "profoundly alien to Soviet morals." Undampened by the official Soviet chill, the play nonetheless continued to be performed in various satellite countries with no perceptible damage to hierarchically established morals.

A master at plot construction, Frederick Knott has reversed the procedure of most suspense plays. In *Dial "M" for Murder* the excitement does not arise from trying to solve a murder. The audience, from the outset, knows who instigates the plan, sees the plot fail, and the would-be assassin himself killed. Rather, the tension grows from the attempts to break down the culprit's seemingly perfect alibi so that an innocent person can be saved from execution. It is one of the theatre's most adroit and ingenious tales of blackmail, murder, and sleuthing, and its popularity with theatrical companies continues unabatedly to this day. Ironically, Alfred Hitchcock's 1954 film version of the play (with Ray Milland, Grace Kelly, and Robert Cummings) has become one of the staples of television's late shows, thus restoring Mr. Knott's work to its original presentational media.

Frederick Knott was born in Hankow, China, where his father taught science at Griffith College. He went to England for his education and attended Cambridge University. He made his first visit to America in 1937 as captain of the Oxford-Cambridge tennis team, which played Harvard and Yale. From 1939 to 1946, he served in the British Army, winding up his military career as a major. After being demobilized, Mr. Knott did some film-script writing, but it wasn't until his first play, *Dial "M" for Murder*, emerged from the television screen to the stage of the Westminster Theatre that he enjoyed total success as a writer.

His second play, *Wait Until Dark*, was presented in New York in 1966. Directed by Arthur Penn and with Lee Remick in the role of a blind young woman who outwits a trio of smalltime criminals, it lasted for 373 performances. Although it did not achieve the substantial success of *Dial "M" for Murder*, it reaffirmed the fact that Frederick Knott was a master craftsman in the realm of modern melodrama.

Dial "M" for Murder was first presented on the stage by James P. Sherwood at the Westminster Theatre, London, on June 19, 1952. The cast was as follows:

SHEILA WENDICE	*Jane Baxter*
MAX HALLIDAY	*Alan MacNaughtan*
TONY WENDICE	*Emrys Jones*
CAPTAIN LESGATE	*Olaf Pooley*
INSPECTOR HUBBARD	*Andrew Cruickshank*

Directed by	John Fernald
Setting by	Paul Mayo

Dial "M" for Murder was first presented in the United States at the Plymouth Theatre, New York, on October 29, 1952, by James P. Sherwood. The cast was as follows:

MARGOT WENDICE	*Gusti Huber*
MAX HALLIDAY	*Richard Derr*
TONY WENDICE	*Maurice Evans*
CAPTAIN LESGATE	*Anthony Dawson*
INSPECTOR HUBBARD	*John Williams*
THOMPSON	*Porter Van Zandt*

Directed by	Reginald Denham
Setting and Lighting by	Peter Larkin
Costumes by	Noel Taylor

SCENE: *The living room of the Wendices' flat in London.*

ACT ONE

SCENE 1: *A Friday evening in September.*
SCENE 2: *An hour later.*

ACT TWO

SCENE 1: *Saturday evening.*
SCENE 2: *Later that night.*
SCENE 3: *Sunday morning.*

ACT THREE

A few months later. Early afternoon.

ACT ONE

SCENE 1

The living room of the Wendices' flat in London.

It is about 6:20 P.M. on a Friday in September.

This is the ground floor apartment of a large house which has been converted into apartments. On the right are French windows which look out on to Charrington Gardens. There is a small terrace immediately outside. The heavy full-length curtains are at present drawn open. Inside the windows are shutters. These are folded back into the wall and are hardly noticeable. The fireplace is down left. On the wall above the mantelpiece is a mirror. Up left is a door leading to the bedroom; at the back two steps lead up into a small hall. Right of the hall is the kitchen. Back center of the hall is the entrance door to the flat (hall door). It has a Yale-type lock. When this door is open we can see through into a narrow passage outside which leads left to the street door. Back of the passage is a staircase leading up (from left to right) to the apartment above. The stairs pass the hall doorway at about the fifth step. Inside the hall door and to the left is a coat rack. At the back on the extreme right there are shelves with books in the top and bottles and drinking glasses on the bottom shelf. Underneath this bookshelf is a cupboard. In the wall on the extreme left there are corresponding shelves. Inside this are TONY's silver tennis trophies, a tennis racket is on the top shelf and on each side of the shelves, on the walls, are tennis photographs. In the extreme right upstage corner is a standard lamp. Right center is a flat table-desk on which there is a telephone and address book and a desk diary. The desk chair has its back to the windows. Below the desk is a wastepaper basket. Left center is a sofa. Right of this is a stool. Behind sofa is an oblong table on which there is a silver cigarette case and a vase of flowers. Down left is a chair and behind this chair is a small wall table with a wicker mending basket filled with stockings, scissors, etc. Below the sofa is a low, round coffee table.

There is a chandelier over the center of the room and two wall brackets in the left wall above the fireplace. Both of these are controlled by light switches inside and on the right of the hall door. The standard lamp is switched on and off at the standard lamp itself.

At present no lights are on, it still being daylight outside, but the light begins to fade during the first scene between MAX *and* MARGOT.

The fire is burning brightly and the hall door is closed.

As the curtain rises, MARGOT *is handing* MAX *a drink. She suddenly hears something in the passage outside and opens and peeps through the hall door for a moment. Then she closes the hall door and turns to* MAX.

MARGOT: [*A little worried*] For a moment I thought it was Tony. I'm sorry I interrupted you. What were we talking about . . . ?

MAX: I was just telling you that I murdered exactly fifty-two people since I saw you last.

MARGOT: [*With a laugh, picking up her drink. Sits on couch*] Oh, yes—one a week. How *did* you do it?

MAX: Every way I could think of. I electrocuted some in their baths, locked others in the garage with the motor running or pushed them through windows and over cliffs. Other weeks I preferred to poison, shoot, strangle, stab, slug or suffocate.

MARGOT: Just according to how you felt?

MAX: When you write for that kind of television you don't have time to feel anything.

MARGOT: Where do you get all your ideas from?

MAX: Oh—newspaper stories—police files—bad dreams—other writers . . .

MARGOT: You once told me you'd never write anything that wasn't original.

MAX: Huh—you try being original fifty-two times a year!

MARGOT: Suppose you just dry up and can't think of anything?

MAX: If it comes to that I just use my three hats.

MARGOT: What do you mean?

MAX: I've got three old hats marked: Who kills who, How, and Why.

MARGOT: Which is what? I mean what's Why?

MAX: Why is the motive for killing. You've got to have a motive, you know. There are only five important ones. Fear—jealousy—money—revenge—and protecting someone you love. I just write them down on pieces of paper and pick one out of the Why hat.

MARGOT: Sounds rather like sorting the week's washing.

MAX: It's about as artistic as that. But better paid. It's no more frustrating than writing plays that aren't produced or novels that aren't published. . . . And don't forget this: It all goes to prove that WITO makes teeth bright—white and *bite!* Makes amends and keeps your friends.

MARGOT: [*Laughs*] Let's have your glass, Max.

MAX: No . . . I'm all right, thanks.

MARGOT: I could hardly believe it when I heard your voice. At first I thought you were phoning from New York.

MAX: Yes, I thought you were shouting a little louder than necessary. As a matter of fact I was just around the corner. [*A pause, anxiously*] Was it all right . . . my phoning like that?

MARGOT: Yes, of course.

MAX: Was that—Tony who answered?

MARGOT: Yes, it was. [*An awkward pause*] I do hope he isn't going to be too late. Poor darling. He always gets caught when we're going to the theater. [*Pause*] So you're not here on a holiday—this time?

MAX: No, not this time. I came over to write some short TV films. After that I think I'll finally knock off for a year and write that novel. I've got to write it some day.

MARGOT: Another crime story?

MAX: I have to stick to crime—it's my stock in trade. But there's no reason why a murder story can't be as good as anything else. And I think I could write a good one if I took the time. I thought of a pretty fair gimmick on the plane coming over. There's a pair of twins—identical—one lives in Paris and the other in New York—all of a sudden they both decide to . . .

[MARGOT *has been growing anxious and loses interest in all this*]

MARGOT: [*Interrupting*] Max, before Tony comes I ought to explain something.

MAX: Yes?

MARGOT: I didn't tell him anything about us.

MAX: Oh.

MARGOT: When you rang up yesterday, I just said that you were a television writer I'd met when he was in America.

MAX: Well, that's true enough.

MARGOT: I said I'd met you again just before you went back to New York and you promised to look us up if you ever came back.

MAX: I see.

MARGOT: Max, I know you think it's silly, but when you get to know Tony, you'll understand why.

MAX: Margot, I'd like to get one thing straight. [*Rises, sits on arm of couch*] Things are o.k. now between you and Tony?

MARGOT: They couldn't be better. [*Rather intensely*] And I want to keep them that way.

MAX: [*Nods*] I'm very glad—at least I guess I will be when I get used to the idea.

MARGOT: [*Gratefully*] Thank you, Max.

MAX: [*Lightly*] I couldn't do this for anyone else, you know.

MARGOT: There's something else, Max.

MAX: Yes?

MARGOT: I wasn't going to tell you but . . .

MAX: Come on, let's have it . . .

MARGOT: Well, you remember those letters you wrote me?

MAX: Of course.

MARGOT: After I read them I burnt them. I thought it best. All except one. You probably know the one I mean.

MAX: I can guess. I never should have written it.

MARGOT: I know. But I loved it just the same. I used to carry it round wherever I went. Then one day Tony and I were going to spend the weekend with some friends in the country. While we were waiting on the platform I noticed my handbag was missing . . . and the letter was inside.

MAX: I see. . . . Where was this?

MARGOT: Victoria Station. I thought I must have left it in the restaurant but when I went to look for it, it had gone.

MAX: You never found it?

MARGOT: I recovered the handbag about two weeks later from the lost and found. But the letter wasn't there. [*Pause*] Then a week after, I received a note. It told me what I had to do to get the letter back.

MAX: Go on.

MARGOT: I was to draw fifty pounds from my bank in five-pound notes, then change them for used one-pound notes. It said that if I went to the police or told anyone else—he would show the letter to my husband.

MAX: May I see it? [MARGOT *exits into bedroom.* MAX *gets up and paces uneasily around the room. He takes a cigarette from the silver box and lights it. Then* MARGOT *enters holding two white envelopes. She hands one of these to* MAX *who takes out the note and examines it*] Printed—all capitals. Anyone could have done this.

[MARGOT *hands him another envelope*]

MARGOT: Then—two days later—I got this one.

[MAX *takes out the second note*]

MAX: [*Glancing at the postmarks*] Both mailed in Brixton. [*Reading*] "Tie up money in a package and mail to John S. King, 23 Newport Street, Brixton, S.W.9. You will get your letter by return." Well, of all the . . .

MARGOT: That's a little shop. People use it as a forwarding address.

MAX: Did you mail the money?

MARGOT: Yes, but the letter was never returned. . . . So after waiting two weeks I went there. They said they'd never heard of a man by that name, and the parcel was still there. It had never been opened.

MAX: Well, I suppose that's something. [MAX *puts the notes back in the envelopes and puts them into his wallet*] May I keep these?

MARGOT: [*Hesitates*] Yes. . . . If you like.

MAX: You didn't tell Tony?

MARGOT: No, I didn't tell anyone. [*Pause*] I can't understand why the man didn't collect the money.

MAX: He was probably in jail by that time. [*Pause*] You never heard from him again?

MARGOT: No.

MAX: Well, let me know if you do. I'll find him and fix him so he can't read, let alone write. [*Pause*] Is that why you asked me to stop writing?

MARGOT: Yes. I was in an awful panic. I imagined that every letter you wrote me would be opened and read by someone.

MAX: Why didn't you tell me?

MARGOT: You couldn't have done anything. You would probably have made me tell Tony and the police. As it was only fifty pounds I thought I'd pay up and have done with it.

MAX: Margot, are you ever going to tell Tony—about us?

MARGOT: [*Horrified*] No. I couldn't possibly tell him. Not now.

MAX: Why not? Don't you think we'd all get on better in the end if . . .

MARGOT: Please, Max, I know Tony—you don't.

MAX: You don't have to tell me. Just the thought of meeting him makes me, shall we say, uncomfortable.

MARGOT: Oh, you'll get on fine. He's changed a lot this last year. . . . Now, he's a model husband. [*Slowly and thoughtfully*] In fact, it was exactly a year ago that it happened.

MAX: What happened?

MARGOT: Tony suddenly grew up. He seemed to change overnight from a rather selfish little person into a perfectly reasonable grownup. You remember that night—I came to say good-bye?

MAX: How could I forget? Tony had gone off to play in a tennis tournament.

MARGOT: He did—but he came back. I'm not much good at writing about things like this, so I didn't try. But when I left you that night I came back here. I sat down on the sofa and had a good cry. Then I fell asleep. When I woke up he was standing in the hall with all his bags and tennis rackets. He just said that he had decided to give up tennis for good and settle down.

MAX: Just like that?

[MARGOT *gets up. Takes* MAX's *glass and hers to drink bar and mixes drinks*]

MARGOT: Just like that. Of course I didn't believe him at first. I'd got so used to tagging around after him wherever he went, I could see no end to it. But he meant it all right. He went out the very *next* day and got himself a job. [A *church clock chimes*] What were we doing—exactly a year ago?

MAX: I was putting the mushrooms into the spaghetti. I nearly turned round and said, "I can't go through with this. Let's find Tony and have it out with him."

MARGOT: I felt that way, too. I wanted so much to say something— and all I could do was to stand there—quite uselessly—with a drip on the end of my nose. What did you do when I'd gone?

MAX: I walked along the Embankment and stared at the Chelsea gas works.

MARGOT: [*With a laugh*] Were you thinking about the gas works— or me?

MAX: Neither. I was writing a story. I always do when I'm miserable.

MARGOT: A sad story?

MAX: A triumphant story—my hero was an eminent writer coming from America with his pockets full of money ready to snatch his lady love from the arms of her jealous husband.

MARGOT: [*Smiling*] Only to find that husband and wife were very happy, thank you.

MAX: And that he was very glad to know it.

MARGOT: [*Handing* MAX *his glass*] Max, let's drink to—the way things turn out.

MAX: [*Raising glass to* MARGOT] Way things turn . . .

> [*But before they can drink, there is the sound of a key in the door. They both turn toward it, as if it had interrupted their toast.* TONY *enters. He is thirty-four and has an easy charm. His mind is always active and he usually seems very sure of himself*]

MARGOT: Oh, there you are. . . . We thought you were never coming. . . . What have you been up to?

TONY: Sorry, darling. The boss blew in just as I was leaving.

> [*As* TONY *takes off his overcoat and hangs it up,* MAX *stands a little awkwardly, facing hall*]

MARGOT: Tony, this is Max Halliday.

TONY: Hullo, Max.

MAX: [*Shaking hands*] Tony . . .

TONY: I'm terribly sorry to be so late. Has Margot been looking after you all right? How's your drink?

MARGOT: We've been drinking ourselves silly waiting for you.

TONY: [*Mixing himself a drink*] Well, how do you like it over here, Max?

MAX: Fine.

TONY: Is this your first visit to London?

MAX: Uh—no—I was here a year ago for a vacation.

TONY: Oh, yes, that's right. Margot told me. You write for the radio, don't you?

MAX: Television—for my sins.

TONY: Ah, yes. Television, poor fellow. Are you staying long?

MAX: I'm not sure. I've some writing to do. When that's finished I'd like to stay a while longer and do some traveling.

TONY: That's a good idea. But don't spend all your time in museums and cathedrals. Once you've seen one, you've seen the lot, if you ask me. Do you fish?

MAX: No, I'm afraid I don't.

TONY: Pity. If you did I'd suggest you went up to Scotland for the . . .

MARGOT: He doesn't fish, darling.

TONY: No, he doesn't. I guess that's that. Well, if you want showing around any time just let us know. [*To* MARGOT] Darling, we could take Max to the Tower of London.

MAX: I'm afraid I've already been there.

TONY: Oh, what a shame! I've always wanted to go to the Tower. But seriously, Max, if there's anything we can do any time . . .

MAX: Thank you, Tony. I'll remember that.

MARGOT: Darling, it's getting late. Did you reserve the table?

TONY: Yes. Seven o'clock.

MARGOT: [*Jumping up*] Well, come on then. [*Moving toward bedroom*] Get your coats on.

TONY: Oh, darling. Slight alteration in plans.

MARGOT: [*Turning*] Now don't say you can't go.

TONY: [*With a shrug*] I'm afraid so. Old man Burgess is flying to Brussels on Sunday and we all have to get our monthly reports in by tomorrow.

MARGOT: Oh, no! Can't you do it when you get back tonight?

TONY: 'Fraid not. It will take hours. I shall have to fake half of it.

MARGOT: Can you join us after the theater? We might go somewhere.

TONY: Give me a ring in the intermission. If I'm inspired I might make it . . .

MARGOT: Do try. I'll just get my things, Max.

[MARGOT *exits to bedroom*]

TONY: [*Handing tickets to* MAX] Here are the tickets, Max.

MAX: Thanks.

TONY: I'm afraid this is extremely rude of me.

MAX: Not at all. I'm sorry you can't come, though.

TONY: You must come to dinner one night.

MAX: Thanks, I'd like to.

TONY: I say—are you doing anything tomorrow night?

MAX: Saturday? I don't think so.

TONY: [*Delighted*] That's perfect. How would you like to come to a stag party—just down the road?

MAX: [*Puzzled*] A stag party?

TONY: Yes. Some American boys have been playing tennis all over the Continent and we're giving them a sort of farewell dinner.

MAX: But I'm no tennis player.

TONY: That doesn't matter. You know New York and all that. [MARGOT *enters from bedroom. She wears overcoat and carries handbag*] Darling. Max is coming to the party tomorrow night.

MARGOT: Oh, good. [*To* MAX] You'd better drop in here first and have a drink.

TONY: That's the idea.

MARGOT: [*To* TONY] By the way, aren't you dressing?

TONY: Dinner jackets—yes. [*To* MAX] Is that all right?

MAX: Well, no. My trunk was supposed to arrive today, but I'm afraid it's not here yet.

TONY: [*Worried*] Oh. [*Pause*] You could rent one, of course.

MARGOT: Don't be silly. Darling, it isn't that important.

TONY: Just a minute. I've got an idea.

[TONY *exits quickly into bedroom leaving door open*]

MARGOT: Now we really are going to be late.

MAX: Shall I try and get a taxi?

MARGOT: No. We can usually pick one up. [*Glancing at bedroom*] Tony, we must go.

[TONY *returns with dinner jacket*]

TONY: Hold it a second. Just try this on, Max.

MARGOT: What on earth?

TONY: It's only my old single-breasted but it might do.

[*As* MAX *takes off coat reluctantly*]

MAX: Look—if dressing is as important as all this—let's forget it, shall we?

TONY: Nonsense.

[TONY *helps* MAX *on with dinner jacket*]

MARGOT: That dreadful old thing—it reeks of moth balls.

MAX: Well, they say that writers will do anything for a square meal.

TONY: Oh, it does look a little meager, doesn't it?

[MAX *gestures, indicating that dinner jacket is too small.*

MARGOT *helps* MAX *off with dinner jacket and* TONY *helps him on with coat*]

MARGOT: I refuse to let you send Max out looking like a scarecrow. Surely he can go as he is.

[*Throws dinner jacket to* TONY]

MAX: Anyway, my stuff will be here by tomorrow. Let's hope that it is.

MARGOT: Come on, Max, let's go before he tries on the pants.

[MARGOT *and* MAX *exit.* TONY *stands in open doorway and watches them go*]

TONY: Enjoy yourselves. Hey, Max!

MAX: [*Offstage*] Yes?

TONY: Try and sell the odd ticket and have a drink on the proceeds. Good-bye—have a good time.

[TONY *closes the door. Turns bracket lights off and crosses to curtains. He closes curtains, switches on standard lamp and turns to telephone. After staring at the phone for a few seconds he picks it up and dials. After a pause* LESGATE's *voice can be heard in the phone receiver*]

LESGATE: Hullo.

TONY: Hullo? Hampstead 2837?

LESGATE: Yes.

TONY: Could I speak to Captain Lesgate, please?

LESGATE: Speaking.

TONY: Oh, good evening. You don't know me; my name's Fisher. . . . I understand you have a car for sale.

LESGATE: An American car.

TONY: That's right; I saw it at your garage. How much are you asking?

LESGATE: Eleven hundred.

TONY: Eleven hundred! I see. It certainly looks just the job for me but I don't like the price much.

LESGATE: I didn't like it when I bought it.

TONY: [*With a laugh*] Now when can we meet?

LESGATE: How about tomorrow afternoon?

TONY: I don't think I can manage that. [*Pause*] No, I can't. And I'm going to Liverpool on Sunday. I was rather hoping . . . I say, I suppose you couldn't come round to my flat tonight?

LESGATE: Where is it?

TONY: Maida Vale—I'd call on you only—I've twisted my knee rather badly.

LESGATE: Oh, I'm sorry. What's your address?

TONY: 61a Charrington Gardens.

LESGATE: Harrington . . .

TONY: No—Charrington.

LESGATE: Charrington . . .

TONY: That's right. Turn left at the underground. It's about two minutes' walk.

LESGATE: I'll be there in about an hour.

TONY: About an hour? That's extremely good of you. [*Anxiously*] By the way, will you be bringing the car?

LESGATE: I'm afraid I can't tonight because it's . . .

TONY: [*Relieved*] That doesn't matter. I had a good look at it. Perhaps you would bring the registration book and any necessary papers.

LESGATE: Of course.

TONY: I don't see why we shouldn't settle the whole thing here and now—provided you drop the price sufficiently.

LESGATE: I'm afraid that's quite out of the question.

TONY: Huh! We'll see what a couple of drinks can do.

LESGATE: [*Amused*] Huh, huh, huh.

TONY: Huh, huh, huh. Well—good-bye.

LESGATE: Good-bye.

[*Hangs up*]

TONY: [*Hangs up*] Captain Lesgate!

CURTAIN

SCENE 2

*The Same. One hour later. The room is softly lit by the
standard lamp and brackets. A pair of white cotton gloves
lies on the stool.*

As the curtain rises, TONY *enters from the bedroom carrying an old leather suitcase which he places carefully against
the wall left of drink cupboard. Then he turns and surveys
the room. He looks at the cotton gloves for a moment,
then goes and picks them up and lays them neatly on the
left arm of the sofa. He considers the effect and is satisfied.
He then starts for the bedroom. The doorbell rings and
interrupts him. He turns and deliberately assumes a painful limp. He opens the hall door.* LESGATE *stands outside
wearing an overcoat.*

LESGATE: Mr. Fisher?
TONY: Yes. Captain Lesgate?
LESGATE: Yes.
TONY: Do come in. This is very good of you. Let me have your coat.
     [*He takes it and hangs it up*] Have any difficulty finding your way?
LESGATE: None at all.

          [*They enter the room*]

TONY: Do sit down.
LESGATE: Thank you.
TONY: Now, how about a drink?

          [TONY *limps to the drink cabinet.* LESGATE *watches him
          curiously for a few moments*]

LESGATE: I can't help thinking I've seen you before somewhere.
TONY: [*Looking up sharply*] Funny you should say that. The moment
     I opened the door I . . . [*He stops suddenly*] Wait a minute . . .
     Lesgate? You're not Lesgate—Swann! C. J. Swann—or was it
     C. A.?

LESGATE: C. A. . . . you've a better memory than I have . . . Fisher? When did we meet?

TONY: Weren't you at Cambridge?

LESGATE: Yes.

TONY: Must be twenty years ago. You wouldn't remember me. . . . I only came your last year.

LESGATE: Well! What a coincidence!

[*They shake hands*]

TONY: [*Going to drink cupboard*] This calls for a special drink. I was planning to palm you off with an indifferent port. Let's see what what we have here. [*Holding up the brandy*] How about this?

LESGATE: Perfect. [*Sits on sofa*] By the way—how did you know my car was for sale?

[TONY *pours brandy into two glasses before answering*]

TONY: Your garage told me.

LESGATE: That's odd. I don't think I mentioned it to anyone there.

TONY: I was stopping for a fill-up. I told them I was looking for an American car and they gave me your phone number. I say, it is for sale, isn't it?

LESGATE: [*Laughing*] Well, of course.

TONY: Good. But I refuse to discuss the price until you've had at least three brandies.

[TONY *hands* LESGATE *his glass*]

LESGATE: [*Taking it*] I warn you. I drive a hard bargain, drunk or sober.

TONY: So do I.

[*They laugh*]

LESGATE: You know, I think I must have seen you since we left Cambridge.

TONY: Ever been to Wimbledon?

LESGATE: That's it—Wendice—Tony Wendice . . . [*Bewildered*] Then what's all this about Fisher?

TONY: [*With a teasing glance*] What's all this about Lesgate? [LES-
GATE *looks embarrassed*] Do you like a cigar?

LESGATE: [*Taking out pipe*] I'll stick to this pipe, if you don't mind.
[TONY *hesitates for a split second as if this throws him a
little, then, turning away*]

TONY: That's one habit you've changed.

LESGATE: Oh?

[TONY *goes to wall and takes down a framed photograph
of a group of young men at dinner*]

TONY: I remember at college you always used to smoke rather expensive cigars. Wait a minute, I think I have a picture of you.
[*Showing the photograph to* LESGATE] Yes, look, here's an old
photo of you at a reunion dinner. . . . There you are on the right
with the biggest cigar in the business.

LESGATE: [*Amused*] Huh! That was the first and last reunion I ever
went to. What a murderous thug I look.

TONY: [*Even more amused*] Yes—you do rather. Of course, I always
remember you because of the College Ball. [*Pause*] You were the
treasurer, weren't you?

LESGATE: Honorary treasurer. I used to organize the beastly things.

TONY: Yes. Some of the ticket money was stolen, wasn't it?

[TONY *sits on sofa*]

LESGATE: That's right. Nearly a hundred pounds. I'd left it in a cash
box in my study. In the morning, it had gone. Still makes me sweat
to think of it.

TONY: It was the college porter, of course.

LESGATE: Yes, poor old Alfred. He never could back a winner. They
found the cash box in his back garden. . . .

TONY: . . . But not the money.

[LESGATE *hands the picture back to* TONY]

LESGATE: Good lord, twenty years ago!

TONY: What are you doing nowadays?

[*Pause*]

LESGATE: I deal in property. [*Changing the subject*] I don't follow tennis very closely. Did you play at Wimbledon this year?

TONY: No. I've given up tennis or rather tennis gave me up. One has to earn a living sometime, and I'd had a pretty good run for my money. I went round the world three times.

LESGATE: I suppose you were treated like a film star?

TONY: Film stars get paid.

LESGATE: There is that.

TONY: Of course I managed to save a bit on expenses. In seven years I put away just over a thousand pounds. Not much compared with your film stars!

LESGATE: What are you doing now? Making up for lost time?

TONY: I sell sports equipment. Not very lucrative but it gives me plenty of spare time.

LESGATE: [*Looking round the room*] Well, I'm here to tell you you manage to run a very comfortable place.

TONY: [*Modestly*] My wife has some money of her own. Otherwise I should hardly feel like blowing a thousand pounds on your car.

LESGATE: Eleven hundred. Yes, people with capital don't realize how lucky they are. I'm already resigned to living on what I can earn.

[*Pause*]

TONY: [*Thoughtfully*] Of course, you can still marry for money.

[*Pause*]

LESGATE: Yes, I suppose some people make a business of that.

TONY: [*Quietly*] I know I did.

[*Pause*]

LESGATE: [*With a laugh*] You mean the girl you fell in love with happened to have some money of her own.

TONY: No. [*Pause*] I always intended to marry for money. I had to. Whilst I was in first-class tennis I met wealthy people all over the world—I was somebody—while my wind lasted! I decided to snap up the first chance I got. I nearly married a tubby Boston deb with five million dollars; it got as far as pictures in the papers and then she threw me over for an heir to a chain of grocery stores. Funny how they stick together. I finally settled for a good deal less—a lot more easily. My wife had been a fan of mine for some time.

[*Pause*]

LESGATE: Well—that's putting it pretty bluntly.

TONY: Have I shocked you?

LESGATE: No, I always admire a man who knows what he wants.

TONY: To know what you want *to pay for*—that's the thing. Everything has its price. People fail because they want to buy cheap. I've learnt to pay a big price for anything I really want. . . . I usually get it.

LESGATE: Yes, I'm sure you do. [*Looking at his wrist watch*] I haven't a great deal of time . . .

TONY: I was telling you about my wife. She got her money from her late aunt, who got it from her late husband, who got it from his first wife. Of course, a large chunk gets lopped off every time somebody dies but quite a bit has managed to filter through.

LESGATE: [*Joking*] You say you married for money. Why do you think she married you?

TONY: [*Quite simply*] I was a tennis star. She would never have married a commercial salesman.

LESGATE: But you've given up tennis. She hasn't left you.

[*Pause*]

TONY: She nearly did.

[TONY *starts to get up rather painfully*]

LESGATE: [*Rising*] Let me, Wendice. You've got a groggy knee.

TONY: Oh, thanks, old boy. Let's have that bottle over here, shall we?

LESGATE: Good idea.

[LESGATE *collects brandy from desk; he pours brandy into* TONY's *glass and then into his own.* TONY *watches him all the time*]

TONY: Would you like to hear about it?

LESGATE: Hear what?

TONY: About my wife—how she nearly left me.

LESGATE: It's your privilege—you're the host.

TONY: Oh, thanks. To be frank, I think you might help. Just man to man advice, you know.

LESGATE: I'm at your service.

[LESGATE *puts bottle down on round table and sits down*]

TONY: After we were married I played in the various championships and Margot tagged along. I think she found it all a bit much. Hospitality—outside this country—can be pretty exhausting. When we got back she tried to persuade me to give up tennis and play husband instead. [*Rises*] In the end, we compromised. I went alone to America for the grass court season and returned after the National Championships. I soon realized that a lot had happened while I was away. For one thing—she wasn't in love with me any more. There were phone calls that would end abruptly if I happened to walk in. And there was an old school friend she used to visit from time to time. Then one day we had a row; I wanted to play in a covered court tournament and as usual she didn't want me to go. I was in the bedroom—the phone rang. It all sounded pretty urgent. After that she seemed rather keen that I should play in that tournament after all, so I packed my kit into the car and drove off. [*Pause*] I parked the car two streets away and walked back on my tracks. Ten minutes later she came out of this house and took a taxi. I took another. [*Pause*] Her old school friend lived in a studio in Chelsea. I could see them through the studio window as he cooked spaghetti over a gas ring. They didn't say much. They just looked very natural together. Funny how you can tell when people are in love. Then I started to walk. I began to wonder what would happen if she left me. I'd have to find some way of earning a living to begin with. Suddenly I realized how much I'd grown to depend on her. All these expensive tastes I'd acquired while I was at the top—and now big tennis had finished with me—and so, apparently, had my wife. I can't ever remember being so scared. I dropped into a pub and had a few drinks. As I sat in the corner I thought of all sorts of things. . . . I thought of three different ways of killing him. I even thought of killing her. That seemed a far more sensible idea—and just as I was working out how I could do it—I suddenly saw something which completely changed my mind. [*Pause*] I didn't go to that tournament after all. When I got back she was sitting exactly where you are now. I told her I'd decided to give up tennis and look after her instead.

[*Pause*]

LESGATE: Well?

TONY: [*Sharp change of mood*] As things turned out—I needn't have got so worked up after all. Apparently that spaghetti evening had been a sort of fond farewell. The boy friend had been called back to New York.

LESGATE: An American?

TONY: Yes. There were long letters from there. . . . They usually arrived on Thursdays. She burnt all of them except one. That one she used to transfer from handbag to handbag. It was always with her. That letter became an obsession with me. I *had* to find out what was in it—and finally—I did. That letter made very interesting reading.

LESGATE: You mean you stole it?

TONY: Yes. I even wrote her two anonymous notes offering to sell it back.

LESGATE: Why?

TONY: I was hoping *that* would make her come and tell me all about him—but it didn't—so I kept the letter.

[TONY *takes out wallet, and lets the letter fall out of it onto sofa.* LESGATE *picks it up and examines envelope*]

LESGATE: Why are you telling *me* all this?

TONY: Because you're the only person I can trust. [LESGATE *puts the letter back in wallet and* TONY *snaps wallet shut*] Anyway, that did it. It must have put the fear of God into them because the letters stopped—and we lived happily ever after. [*Changes tone*] Funny to think that just a year ago I was sitting in that Knightsbridge pub—actually planning to murder her—and I might have done it if I hadn't seen something that changed my mind.

LESGATE: [*Tapping pipe on ash tray on table back of sofa*] Well. [*Tap—tap—tap*] What did you see? [*Tap—tap*]

TONY: [*Quietly*] I saw you.

[*Long pause*]

LESGATE: [*Turning round slowly to* TONY] What was so odd about that?

TONY: The coincidence. You see only a week before I'd been to a reunion dinner and the fellows had been talking about you. How you'd been court-martialed during the war—a year in prison! That was news. Mind you, at college we'd always said old Swann would end up in jail—that cash box, I suppose.

LESGATE: What about it?

TONY: [*With a laugh*] My dear fellow, everybody knew you took that money. Poor old Alfred.

LESGATE: [*Rising*] Well, thanks for the drink. Interesting hearing about your matrimonial affairs, I'm sure. [*Moving to hall*] I take it you won't be wanting that car after all?

TONY: Don't you want me to tell you why I brought you here?

LESGATE: Yes, I think you'd better.

[*During his following speech,* TONY *gets up from the sofa. He has dropped his limp. He takes out his handkerchief, wipes fingerprints off the reunion photograph and returns it to wall. Then he carefully wipes ash tray, part of table and the brandy bottle. He crosses behind desk—takes ash tray and dumps ashes into fireplace—again wipes with handkerchief. He crosses to* LESGATE *and gets his glass, wipes it and puts it on coffee table*]

TONY: It was when I saw you in the pub that it happened. Suddenly everything became quite clear. Only a few months before, Margot and I had made our wills—quite short affairs leaving everything we had to each other in case of accidents. Hers worked out at just over ninety thousand pounds. Investments, mostly—all too easy to get at. And that was dangerous as they'd be bound to suspect me. I'd need an alibi—a very good one—and then I saw you. I'd often

wondered what happened to people when they came out of prison
—people like you, I mean. Can they get jobs? Do old friends rally
round? Suppose they'd never had any friends. I was so curious
to know that I followed you. I followed you home that night and—
would you mind passing your glass? Thank you, thank you so much
—and I've been following you ever since.

LESGATE: Why?

TONY: I was hoping that, sooner or later, I might—catch you at something and be able to . . .

LESGATE: Blackmail me?

TONY: Influence you. After a few weeks I got to know your routine
which made it a lot easier.

LESGATE: Rather dull work.

TONY: To begin with, yes. But you know how it is—you take up a
hobby and the more you get to know of it the more fascinating it
becomes. You became quite fascinating. In fact, there were times
when I felt that you—almost belonged to me.

LESGATE: That must have been fascinating.

TONY: You always went dog-racing on Mondays and Thursdays. I
even took it up myself—just to be near you. You'd changed your
name to Adams.

LESGATE: Yes, I got bored with Swann. Any crime in that?

TONY: No, none at all. And you used to go to a little private club
in Soho. It had an odd name . . . [Remembering] The Kettle of
Fish, that's it. The police closed it down recently, I believe—someone was caught taking drugs or something.

LESGATE: [Casually] I never heard about that. I went there to eat.
There's no crime in that either.

TONY: None whatever. In fact, there was nothing really illegal about
you. I got quite discouraged, and then one day you disappeared
from your lodgings, so I phoned your landlady. I said, "Mr. Adams
owed me five pounds." . . . Apparently that was nothing. Mr.
Adams owed her six weeks' rent and her best lodger fifty-five
pounds! And Mr. Adams had always been such a nice gentleman.
That's what seemed to upset her most.

LESGATE: Yes, that's what always upsets them most.

[LESGATE *strolls to round table and reaches for the brandy bottle*]

TONY: I say, old boy, if you want another drink, do you mind putting on these gloves? [LESGATE *glances at the gloves on the arm of the sofa but does not pick them up*] Thanks. Now, where were we? Oh, yes, I'd lost you and then I found you one day at the dog-racing and tailed you home to your new lodgings in Belsize Park. There Mr. Adams became Mr. Wilson. Mr. Wilson left Belsize Park last July owing fifteen weeks' rent and somewhat richer for his brief encounter with a . . . Miss Wallace. You used to go out with Miss Wallace on Wednesdays and Sundays. She certainly was in love with you, wasn't she? I suppose she thought you were growing that handsome mustache to please her. Poor Miss Wallace.

LESGATE: This is all most interesting. Do go on.

TONY: July—August—September . . . Apartment one two seven Carlisle Court . . . Occupant . . . A Mrs. Van Dorn. Her late husband left her two hotels and a large apartment house—furnished. What a base to operate from, Captain Lesgate! The only trouble is, she does rather enjoy being courted, and she is so very expensive. Perhaps that's why you've been trying to sell her car for over a month.

LESGATE: Mrs. Van Dorn asked me to sell it for her.

TONY: I know. I called her up just before you arrived here. She only wanted eight hundred.

[*Pause.* LESGATE *remains perfectly still*]

LESGATE: [*Casually*] Where's the nearest police station?

TONY: Opposite the church. Two minutes' walk.

LESGATE: Suppose I walk there now?

TONY: What would you tell them?

LESGATE: Everything.

TONY: Everything? All about Mr. Adams and Mr. Wilson?

LESGATE: I shall simply tell them you are trying to blackmail me into . . .

TONY: Into?

LESGATE: Murdering your wife.

[*Pause*]

TONY: I almost wish you would. When she heard that we'd have the best laugh of our lives.

LESGATE: Aren't you forgetting something?

TONY: Am I?

LESGATE: You've told me a few things tonight.

TONY; What of it?

LESGATE: Suppose I tell them how you followed her to that studio in Chelsea—how you watched them cooking spaghetti and all that rubbish. Wouldn't that ring a bell?

TONY: It certainly would. They'd assume you followed her there yourself.

LESGATE: Me? Why should I?

TONY: Why should you steal her handbag? Why should you write her all those blackmail notes? Can you prove that you didn't? You certainly can't prove that I did. It will be a straight case of your word against mine.

LESGATE: [Amused] Huh, that ought to puzzle them. What could you say?

TONY: I shall say that you came here tonight—half-drunk—and tried to borrow money on the strength that we were at college together. When I refused you said something about a letter belonging to my wife. As far as I could make out you were offering to sell it to me. I gave you what money I had and you gave me the letter. It has your fingerprints on it. Remember? [Takes wallet out of pocket and shows it to him] Then you said if I went to the police you'd tell some crazy story about my wanting you to murder my wife. But before we go any further, old boy—do consider the inconvenience. You see, I'm quite well known . . . and there would be pictures of you as well. Sooner or later a deputation of lodgers and landladies would come forward to testify to your character. And someone is almost certain to have seen you with Miss Wallace. [Pause] You were always careful not to be seen around with her— I noticed. You usually met in out-of-the-way places where no one would recognize you—like that little tea shop in Pimlico.

LESGATE: That was her idea, not mine.

TONY: Yes, it was a bit crummy, wasn't it? Hardly a place to take Mrs. Van Dorn. By the way, does Mrs. Van Dorn know about—Mr.

Adams—and Mr. Wilson . . . and Miss Wallace? You were planning to marry Mrs. Van Dorn, weren't you?

LESGATE: Smart, aren't you?

TONY: Not really, I've just had time to think things out—putting myself in your position. That's why I know you're going to agree.

LESGATE: What makes you *think* I'll agree?

TONY: For the same reason that a donkey with a stick behind him and
a carrot in front goes forwards and not backwards.

[*Long pause*]

LESGATE: Tell me about the carrot.

[*Long pause.* TONY *looks straight at* LESGATE]

TONY: One thousand pounds in cash.

[*Long pause.* LESGATE *looks up at* TONY *and their eyes
meet*]

LESGATE: For a murder?

TONY: For a few minutes' work. That's all it is. And no risk. I guar-
antee. That ought to appeal to you. You've been skating on very
thin ice.

LESGATE: [*With a great effort to appear amused*] I don't know what
you're talking about . . .

TONY: You should know. It was in all the papers. A middle-aged
woman found dead due to an overdose of cocaine. Appeared as
though she'd been taking the stuff for quite a time—but no one
knows where she got it. . . . But we know—don't we? Poor Miss
Wallace! [*This bites* LESGATE *and there is a long silence. Changing
his tone*] Yes, you should take a long holiday abroad. Surely a
honeymoon with Mrs. Van Dorn would be preferable to ten years'
detention at Dartmoor. My thousand pounds should see you safely
married to her. You'll find it makes such a difference to have some
money in the family.

LESGATE: [*Amused and sarcastic*] This thousand pounds—where is
it?

TONY: [*Quite serious*] It's in a small attaché case in a checkroom.

[*Pause*]

LESGATE: Where?

TONY: Somewhere in London. Of course, we don't meet again. As soon as you've—delivered the goods, I shall mail you the checkroom ticket and the key to the case. [TONY *opens drawer in desk and, using his handkerchief, takes out a bundle of one-pound notes. He throws this across the room so that it lands on the sofa*] You can take this hundred pounds on account.

[LESGATE *looks down at the money but doesn't touch it*]

LESGATE: [*Still skeptical*] The police would only have to trace one of those notes back to you and they'd hang us from the same rope.

TONY: They won't. For a whole year I've been cashing an extra twenty pounds a week. Always in fivers. I then change them for these at my leisure.

LESGATE: [*Rises, crosses to desk*] Let's see your bank statement.

TONY: By all means. [TONY *opens desk drawer and takes out his bank statement. He holds it open for* LESGATE *to see.* LESGATE *puts out his hands to touch it*] Don't touch!

LESGATE: Turn back a page. [TONY *turns back the page*] Your balance has dropped by over a thousand pounds in the year. Suppose the police ask you about that?

TONY: [*With a smile*] I go dog-racing twice a week.

LESGATE: They'll check with your bookmaker . . .

TONY: Like you—I always bet on the Tote . . . [*Pause*] Satisfied?

[*Long pause.* LESGATE *is standing right of desk with back to windows.* TONY *faces him from other side of desk*]

LESGATE: When would this take place?

TONY: Tomorrow night.

LESGATE: Tomorrow! Not a chance. I've got to think this over.

TONY: It's got to be tomorrow. I've arranged things that way.

LESGATE: Where?

TONY: Approximately where you're standing now.

[LESGATE *reacts to this. After a considerable pause*]

LESGATE: [*Quietly*] How?

TONY: Tomorrow evening, Halliday—that's the American boy friend —and I will go out to a stag party just down the road. She will stay here. She'll go to bed early and listen to Saturday Night Theater on the radio. She always does when I'm out. At exactly twenty-three minutes to eleven you will enter the house by the street door. [*Moving to hall*] You'll find the key of this door under the stair carpet—here.

> [TONY *opens the hall door and leaves it wide open. He looks around to see that no one is watching and then points to one of the stairs which is clearly visible through the open door. He then comes in and closes the hall door*]

LESGATE: The fifth step.

TONY: That's the one. Go straight to the window and hide behind the curtains. [*Pause*] At exactly twenty minutes to eleven, I shall go to the telephone in the hotel to call my boss. I shall dial the wrong number—this number. That's all I shall do. [*Pause*] When the phone rings you'll see the lights go on under the bedroom door. When she opens it the light will stream across the room, so don't move until she answers the phone. [*Pause*] There must be as little noise as possible. [*Pause*] When you've finished, pick up the phone and give me a soft whistle. Then hang up. Don't speak, whatever you do. I shan't say a word. When I hear your whistle I shall hang up and redial—the *correct* number this time—I shall then speak to my boss as if nothing has happened and return to the party.

LESGATE: [*Looking round*] What happens then? Go on!

> [TONY *picks up leather suitcase*]

TONY: You'll find this suitcase here. It will contain some clothes of mine for the cleaners. Open it and tip the clothes out onto the floor. [TONY *picks up the suitcase. He carries it back of couch to fireplace and puts it on the floor. He points to trophies on mantelpiece*] Then fill it with the cigarette box and some of these cups. Close the lid but don't snap the locks. [*Pause*] Then leave it here —just as it is now.

LESGATE: As if I left in a hurry?

TONY: That's the idea. Now—the window. If it's locked, unlock it and leave it open. [*Pause*] Then go out exactly the same way as you came in.

LESGATE: [*Indicating hall door*] By that door?

TONY: Yes—and here's the most important thing—as you go out, return the key to the place where you found it.

LESGATE: Under the stair carpet?

TONY: Yes.

[LESGATE *looks round the room, puzzled*]

LESGATE: Exactly what is supposed to have happened?

TONY: They'll assume you entered by the window. You thought the apartment was empty so you took the suitcase and went to work. She heard something and switched on her light. You saw the light go on under the door and hid behind the curtains. When she came in here you attacked her before she could scream. When you realized you'd actually killed her, you panicked and bolted into the garden leaving your loot behind.

LESGATE: [*Rises*] Just a minute . . . I'm supposed to have entered by the windows. What if they had been locked?

TONY: It wouldn't matter. You see, she often takes a walk round the garden before she goes to bed and she usually forgets to lock up when she gets back. That's what I shall tell the police.

LESGATE: But she may say that . . .

[*Pause*]

TONY: She isn't going to say anything—is she?

[*Pause, while* LESGATE *sees the logic of this*]

LESGATE: Is there any reason why I shouldn't leave by the garden?

TONY: Yes. You'd have to climb an iron gate. If anyone saw you, you might be followed.

LESGATE: [*Turning to hall door*] All right. I leave the flat—put the key back under the stair carpet, and go out by the street door. Suppose the street door's locked—how should I get in in the first place?

TONY: The street door's never locked.

LESGATE: When will you get back?

TONY: About twelve. I shall bring Halliday back for a nightcap—so we shall find her together. And we shall have been together since we left her—and there's my alibi.

[LESGATE *looks round the room trying to visualize things. He moves slowly to hall door, opens it a few inches and peeps toward stairs. After a few seconds he closes it and turns to* TONY]

LESGATE: You've forgotten something.

TONY: What?

LESGATE: When you return with—what's his name?—Halliday, how will you get into the apartment?

TONY: I shall let myself in.

LESGATE: But your key will be under the stair carpet. He's bound to see you take it out. That will give the whole show away.

[*During* TONY's *speech,* TONY *goes to door, wipes fingerprints off door handles, etc. Then crosses to desk and wipes desk and desk chair*]

TONY: No, it won't be my key under the carpet. It will be hers. I shall take it from her handbag and hide it out there, just before I leave the flat. She won't be going out so she won't miss it. When I return with Halliday I'll use my own key to let us in. Then, while he's searching the garden or something, I'll take her key from under the stair carpet and return it to her handbag before the police arrive.

LESGATE: How many keys are there to that door?

TONY: Just hers and mine.

[*The telephone rings.* TONY *hesitates, uncertain whether he should answer it. Then he goes to far side of desk so that he stands facing* LESGATE *with his back to the window. He picks up telephone. As soon as* TONY *answers phone,* LESGATE *picks up cotton gloves from arm of sofa and puts them on. He then moves around the room as follows: He opens the bedroom door and peers inside. He switches on bedroom light and, leaving door wide open, crosses to light switch and switches it off then crosses and switches off standard lamp so that room is now lit only by the light from the bedroom. He crosses behind* TONY *to curtains and peers behind them. He draws the curtains aside. He unlocks the window, opens it and peers into the garden. He then opens and closes the window twice as if testing for a creak. He locks window and draws curtains shut. He switches on standard lamp and other lights and crosses to bedroom, switches off light and closes the door. He then strolls to sofa and stares down at the bundle of notes. He is doing this as* TONY *hangs up and looks across at him*]

[*Telephone conversation—*TONY *and* MARGOT. *Her voice can be heard through receiver and she is gay and very happy*]

TONY: Maida Vale 0401.

MARGOT: Tony, it's me.

TONY: [*Delighted*] Hullo, darling! How's it going?

MARGOT: [*With great enthusiasm*] Wonderfully! It's really a dreadful play—and we're enjoying every minute.

TONY: Oh—I'm sorry—I mean I'm glad.

MARGOT: How are you?

TONY: Very sleepy. [*Yawns*] I've just made myself some coffee to try and keep awake. Oh, darling, just a minute, I think there's someone at the door. [*To* LESGATE, *muffling telephone*] Careful, you can be seen from the bedroom window. [*To* MARGOT] Sorry, darling, false alarm.

MARGOT: You will join us, won't you?

TONY: I'm afraid not—I hardly seem to have started.

MARGOT: [*Really disappointed*] Oh, Tony! It never does work out, does it?

TONY: Oh, we'll manage it one day.

MARGOT: I say, darling . . .

TONY: Yes?

MARGOT: It seems awfully mean but—would you mind if Max and I went somewhere afterwards? You see . . .

TONY: Of course I don't mind. What do you want to do—dance?

MARGOT: Ummm!

TONY: Take him to Gerry's.

MARGOT: How do we get in?

TONY: Just mention my name. I don't know about the band but the food's good.

MARGOT: What are you doing about food?

TONY: Oh, I opened a tin of that luncheon meat.

MARGOT: Oh, you poor darling.

TONY: By the way, Maureen rang up just after you left. Wants us to go to dinner on Wednesday. You've got something down in your diary but I can't read your writing. [*He peers at the desk diary*] Looks like Al—Bentall. Who's he? Another of your boy friends?

MARGOT: Albert Hall, you idiot!

TONY: Oh, the Albert Hall, of course. I'm so glad we can't go to Maureen's—she's such a filthy cook . . .

MARGOT: There's the bell—I must fly.

TONY: All right. 'Bye, sweet—enjoy yourself. [*Looks across at* LESGATE] Well?

[LESGATE *picks up the notes and whisks them like a pack of cards*]

LESGATE: [*Quietly—with a nod*] It's a deal.

[As LESGATE *puts the notes in his inside pocket:*]

CURTAIN

ACT TWO

The same. Saturday evening. The room is lit by the over-head lights and brackets. It is dark outside, the curtains are not drawn. The fire is burning brightly. The leather suitcase stands, as before, by the drink cabinet. MARGOT and MAX are sitting on the sofa. She is showing him an album of press clippings. There are other clippings and folded newspapers on the round table in front of them. TONY is at drink shelf mixing drinks. TONY and MAX wear dinner jackets. MARGOT is not wearing evening dress. As the curtain rises they are all laughing.

TONY: . . . After that, he lost concentration and didn't win another game.

MARGOT: [*To* TONY] Where's the picture of the Maharajah?

TONY: [*Moving behind sofa, hands drink to* MAX] It's somewhere among those loose ones. [MARGOT *searches among clippings on round table.* TONY *goes and stands with back to fire. To* MARGOT] Darling. When are you going to finish pasting in those press clippings?

MARGOT: I shall find time—one of these days. [*Unfolding piece of newspaper*] Oh, here we are. [*Showing it to* MAX] There's the Maharajah. Isn't he dreamy?

TONY: He had four Rolls Royces and enough jewels to sink a battle-ship, but all he really wanted was to play at Wimbledon.

[MARGOT *collects clippings from round table*]

MARGOT: The poor darling. He was so short-sighted he could hardly see the end of his racket—let alone the ball.

MAX: [*Turning pages of album*] You ought to write a book about all this.

[MAX *hands album to* MARGOT. *She puts the clippings inside it and lays it on the round table*]

MARGOT: Why don't you two collaborate? A detective novel with a tennis background.

TONY: Murder on the center court . . . How about it, Max? Will you provide me with the perfect murder?

MAX: Nothing I'd like better.

TONY: How do you start to write a detective story?

MAX: Forget the detection and concentrate on crime. The crime's the thing. Imagine you're going to steal something, or murder somebody.

TONY: Is that what you do? Hmm! Interesting.

MAX: I always just put myself in the criminal's shoes and keep saying: "Well, what do I do next?"

MARGOT: [*To* MAX] Do you really believe in the perfect murder?

[*Pause*]

MAX: Absolutely—on paper. And I think I could plan one better than most people—but I doubt if I could carry it out.

TONY: Why not?

[TONY *rises and moves to fireplace*]

MAX: Because in stories things turn out as the author plans them to. . . . In real life they don't—always. [*He catches* MARGOT's *eye and they give each other a little smile*] I imagine my murders would be rather like my bridge. . . . I'd make some damned stupid mistake and never realize it until I found that everyone was looking at me.

[TONY *laughs and glances round at the clock*]

TONY: I think we'd better drink up, Max.

[*He finishes drink and crosses back of couch to drink shelf*]

MAX: All right, sir.

[*He rises*]

MARGOT: [*To* MAX] Are you doing anything tomorrow?

MAX: No. I don't think so.

MARGOT: [*To* TONY] Why don't we all drive down to Windsor for lunch?

TONY: Good idea. [*To* MAX] Come along early. At least—not too early. We may be nursing a hangover.

[TONY *crosses to stool*]

MAX: About eleven?

TONY: [*To* MAX] That'll do fine. [*To* MARGOT *as he moves to hall*] By the way, darling, did I lend you my latchkey? I can't find it anywhere.

MARGOT: [*Getting up*] I may have them both in my handbag. I'll just look.

[MARGOT *exits to bedroom.* MAX *goes to hall to get his overcoat.* TONY *goes to French windows. He unlocks and opens a window and peers outside*]

TONY: Raining pretty hard. I think I could lend you an old raincoat, if that's any good.

MAX: [*Taking down overcoat*] This will do. It isn't far, is it?

TONY: No—just around the corner.

[TONY *glances round at* MAX *to see if he is looking but he is putting on his overcoat and has his back to* TONY. TONY *deliberately opens one window a few inches, draws the curtains across the windows.* MARGOT *enters from the bedroom carrying a handbag. She opens it and takes out a zip purse. Out of this she takes a latchkey*]

MARGOT: I've only got one here. Are you sure yours isn't in your overcoat?

TONY: Yes, I've looked there. Could you lend me yours?

MARGOT: [*Holding key in hand*] Well, that's a bit awkward.

TONY: [*Turning to* MARGOT] Why?

MARGOT: I may want to go out.

[*Pause*]

TONY: Tonight?

MARGOT: Yes. I thought I might go to a movie or something.

TONY: But—aren't you going to listen to the radio—Saturday Night Theater?

MARGOT: [*Sitting on right end of sofa*] No, it's a thriller. I don't like thrillers when I'm alone.

TONY: [*Casually*] I see.

[*He goes and picks up raincoat on hall chair*]

MARGOT: In any case I'll be back before you so I can let you in.

TONY: [*Putting on raincoat*] We won't be back till after midnight. You may be asleep by then.

[*He crosses to desk, taking gloves from raincoat pocket to put them on*]

MAX: [*To* MARGOT] You can always leave your key under the proverbial mat.

[TONY *drops his key out of one of his gloves onto desk*]

TONY: [*Picking it up*] All right, chaps. Had it here in my glove all the time.

[*Puts key back in raincoat pocket*]

MARGOT: That settles that.

[*She returns her key to her zip purse. She puts purse back in handbag, closes it and leaves it on oblong table*]

TONY: What movie are you going to?

MARGOT: The Classic, I expect.

TONY: Will you get in? Saturday night.

MARGOT: I can always try. Now, don't make me stay in. You know how I hate doing nothing.

TONY: Nothing? But there're hundreds of things you can do. Have you written to Peggy about last weekend? And what about these clippings? It's an ideal opportunity.

MARGOT: Well, I like that! You two go gallivanting while I have to stay in and do those boring clippings.

[TONY *suddenly goes sullen*]

TONY: Oh, very well then, we won't go.

[*He moves left above couch removing raincoat*]

MARGOT: [*Astonished*] What do you mean?

TONY: Well, it's quite obvious you don't want us to go out tonight—
so we won't. We'll stay here with you. What shall we do—play
cards?

[*Puts raincoat on chair*]

MARGOT: Now, Tony darling . . .

[*She rises and goes to front of coffee table*]

TONY: [*Going to phone*] I'd better phone the Grendon and tell them
we're not coming.

[MARGOT *stops* TONY *going to the phone*]

MARGOT: Tony, please. Don't let's be childish about this. I'll do your
old press clippings.

TONY: You don't have to if you don't want to.

MARGOT: But I *do* want to. [*She picks up press clippings album*]
Have we any paste?

TONY: There's some in the desk, I think.

MARGOT: Good. [*Takes album to desk*] And some scissors. In the
mending basket. [TONY *goes to mending basket. He opens it, looks
underneath a pair of* MARGOT's *stockings and takes out a long pair
of scissors.* MARGOT, *taking out empty paste tube from desk drawer*]
Oh, look . . . the paste tube is empty. [*Exasperated*] It would be.
[TONY *stares at the empty paste tube which* MARGOT *is holding*]
Never mind. Mrs. Lucas is bound to have some.

TONY: Who's she?

MARGOT: She lives just across the road. I'll drop around later. [TONY
can't hide his annoyance. MARGOT *reaches for scissors*] Thank you,
darling.

[TONY *passes her scissors*]

MAX: Why not make some? All you need is some flour and starch.

TONY: Good idea. Do you know how to do it, Max?

MAX: [*Moving to kitchen*] In two shakes.

[MAX *exits to kitchen*]

TONY: Good old Max! [*To* MARGOT] I'm sorry, darling. Was I very unreasonable?

MARGOT: [*Moving to* TONY] No, I don't mind. I tell you what . . . I'll paste these in tonight and you put up that extra shelf in the kitchen . . . As you promised.

TONY: First thing tomorrow. Promise.

[*He kisses her*]

MAX: [*Calling from kitchen*] Where's the starch?

MARGOT: I'll show you.

[MARGOT *exits to kitchen. We can hear them talking through the open door.* TONY *looks at oblong table. He glances quickly toward kitchen and then moves to* MARGOT's *handbag and opens it. He takes out purse, zips it open and takes out key and puts it on table. He then zips the purse shut, returns it to handbag and closes bag, leaving it in exactly the same position as before. He picks up key and goes and opens hall door, leaving it wide open. He then looks along passage and to the landing above, then he lifts the stair carpet and places the key underneath. As he does this* MARGOT *gives a little peal of laughter from the kitchen.* TONY *turns back, a little startled; as he strolls back into the room,* MARGOT *enters from the kitchen with a cup and spoon.* MAX *follows her. As she is entering:*]

It looks like vichysoisse without the chives.

MAX: If it starts to get thick, add a little water—and keep stirring.

[MARGOT *puts down cup on desk and starts to arrange the newspapers and clippings.* TONY *and* MAX *stand in hall*]

TONY: Keep the fire in for us, darling.

[*He gets coat from chair*]

MARGOT: I will.

TONY: Oh, and it's just possible old man Burgess will phone tonight. If he does, tell him I'm at the Grendon. It may be rather important.

MARGOT: What's the number?

TONY: It's in the book.

MARGOT: All right. Well, look after each other.

MAX: We will. Good night, Margot.

MARGOT: 'Night, Max. [To TONY] You'll run Max home in the car afterwards, won't you, darling?

TONY: Of course. We'll drop in here first for a nightcap. Sure you won't be up?

MARGOT: I shall be fast asleep. And I *don't* want to be disturbed.

TONY: Then we'll be as quiet as mice. [TONY *kisses* MARGOT] Good night, darling.

MARGOT: Good night.

TONY: Come on, Max.

> [*They exit.* MARGOT *switches on lamp, turns on radio. Then she turns off chandelier and brackets. She turns to her work. She looks resigned to it. She unfolds a piece of newspaper, picks up scissors, starts cutting. Music swells to:*]

CURTAIN

SCENE 2

The same. Later that night. MARGOT *has finished pasting in* TONY's *press clippings and has left the album lying open on the desk. By the album lie some pieces of newspaper and the scissors. The wastepaper basket is overflowing with cut pieces of newspaper.*

When the curtain rises the room is lit only by the light from the fire which is still burning well. After a few seconds the hall door opens, but only about two inches, as if someone was listening.

Another few seconds and LESGATE *enters. He stands in*

the doorway perfectly still—listening. He wears a raincoat and kid gloves but no hat. He closes the door without a sound except for the final click as it locks. As he crosses silently he takes off his scarf and ties two knots in it.

NOTE: *This scarf must have tassel ends, to emphasize, later, that it is a scarf and must be silk and tan colored so that* MARGOT *could mistake it for a stocking.*

LESGATE *crosses to French windows. The phone rings. He quickly hides behind curtains.*

After some time the light goes on under the bedroom door and MARGOT *enters from the bedroom. She leaves the door wide open and the light is thrown across the room.* MARGOT *puts on a dressing gown as she crosses to the telephone.*

She goes to the far side of the desk and answers the phone with her back turned to the window.

MARGOT: Hullo . . . [*She listens for several seconds, then louder*] Hullo!

[MARGOT *does not notice* LESGATE *as he comes from behind the curtains. His gloved hands hold each end of the silk scarf in which two knots have been tied.* MARGOT *has had the phone in her left hand. She puts phone hand down and jiggles the receiver with her right. Just as she is jiggling the receiver* LESGATE *attacks her, throwing the scarf over her head and drawing it back sharply against her throat. With a strangled gurgle she drops the phone.* LESGATE *holds her back against his body but* MARGOT's *hands catch hold of the scarf and try to tear it away. They struggle for a moment, then* LESGATE *winds the scarf, with his left hand, right around her neck and at the same time she turns round so that she faces him with the scarf crossed at the back of her neck. He pushes her against the end of the desk and forces her down until she is bent right back along the top of the desk with her head downstage. In his efforts to tighten the scarf he leans right over her so that his body almost touches hers.* MARGOT's *right hand leaves the scarf and waves over the end of the desk, groping for the scissors. She grabs them and strikes with one of the points into* LESGATE's *back.* LESGATE *slumps over her and then very slowly rolls over the left side of the desk landing on his back with a strangled grunt.* MARGOT *continues to lie back over the desk, completely exhausted. Then she manages to get to her feet, all the time fighting for breath. She tears the scarf away from her throat but it remains looped around her shoulders. She grabs the telephone. At first she has difficulty in speaking. A sharp "Hullo" from* TONY *can be heard from the receiver*]

TONY: Hullo!

MARGOT: [*In short gasps*] Get the police—quickly—police!

TONY: Margot.

MARGOT: Who's that?

TONY: Darling, it's me . . .

MARGOT: Oh, thank God—Tony, come back at once!

TONY: What's the matter?

MARGOT: [*Panicking*] I can't explain now. Come quickly—*please!*

TONY: [*Angrily*] Darling, pull yourself together. . . . What is it?

MARGOT: [*Recovering slightly*] A man—attacked me . . . tried to strangle me . . .

TONY: Has he gone?

MARGOT: No—he's dead . . . he's dead . . . [*A long pause*] Tony—Tony! Are you still there?

TONY: [*Frozen*] Margot!

MARGOT: Yes?

TONY: Now, listen very carefully.

MARGOT: Yes, I'm listening.

TONY: Don't touch anything! I'll be with you in a minute.

MARGOT: No, I won't.

TONY: Don't touch anything and don't speak to *anybody*—until I get back.

MARGOT: All right. I won't touch anything.

TONY: You promise?

MARGOT: [*In angry panic*] Yes, I promise—only please be quick!

> [*She begins to sob with fright as she replaces the phone. She staggers to window and opens it, goes outside. After several seconds she returns, having left scarf outside. The windows remain open. As she reaches desk and sees the body, she starts to door, stops and collapses on hall chair, sobs, then exits into bedroom and locks door. Chimes are heard from church clock outside. Sound of street door opening. Running footsteps. Sound of key in lock, door opens.* TONY *switches on wall bracket lights only. He takes in situation, stares at body, then at handbag and back to body, then he takes key out of door, puts it in raincoat pocket. He closes door quietly. He turns on standard lamp. He crosses to* LESGATE *and starts to turn body one way, then rolls him over toward the window. He sees scissors that are sticking in his back. He glances at hands for blood and then glances at bedroom door. Searches for key in* LESGATE'S *pockets. He can't find it. Sound of bedroom door unlocking.* TONY *rises and* MARGOT *comes rushing into his arms*]

MARGOT: Oh, Tony, Tony, Tony . . .

TONY: It's all right—it'll be all right. What happened?

> [MARGOT *suddenly throws her arms round him and clings like a frightened child.* TONY *lifts her head slightly so he can see her throat*]

MARGOT: He got something around my throat—it felt like a stocking.

TONY: Are you sure? Let me see. [*He touches her throat gently and she turns her head away quickly*] I'd better call a doctor.

MARGOT: [*Shocked at the thought*] But he's dead.

TONY: I know. When he fell he must have driven those scissors right through himself.

MARGOT: [*Turning away*] Horrible! Can't you . . . ?

TONY: Yes—right away. [TONY *exits quickly into bedroom.* MARGOT *suddenly puts her hand to her head. She turns and looks round the room. She sees her handbag on the sofa table, opens it, and fishes around inside.* TONY *enters from the bedroom carrying a blanket. When he sees what* MARGOT *is doing he stops dead and stares at her in horror*] What are you doing?

MARGOT: [*Taking out a bottle of aspirin*] Will you get me some water, please?

> [MARGOT *drops the handbag onto the table.* TONY *fills a glass with water from the drink cabinet and hands it to* MARGOT *who swallows some aspirin and takes a drink.* TONY *throws the blanket over* LESGATE]

TONY: [*Quietly*] That's better.

> [*He covers the body*]

MARGOT: Shut the window, please.

TONY: No—we mustn't touch anything until the police arrive. [*Looking at open window*] He must have broken in. [*Looking around room*] I wonder what he was after? [*Looking at bookcase*] Those cups, I expect.

MARGOT: When will the police get here?

TONY: [*Startled*] Have you called them already?

MARGOT: No. You told me not to speak to anyone. Hadn't you better call them now?

TONY: [*Pause*] Yes, in a minute.

MARGOT: [*Moving to bedroom*] I'll get dressed.

TONY: Why?

MARGOT: They'll want to see me.

TONY: They're not going to see you.

MARGOT: But they'll have to ask me questions.

TONY: They can wait until tomorrow. I'll tell them all they want to know.

> [*As* TONY *is speaking he keeps looking around the desk, searching for something.* MARGOT *moves to bedroom door and then turns*]

MARGOT: Tony.

TONY: Yes?

MARGOT: Why did you phone me?

[TONY *stares back at her for at least three seconds before answering*]

TONY: What? Er—sorry—I'll tell you about that later. I just thought of something. You said he used a stocking . . .

MARGOT: I think it was a stocking—or a scarf. Isn't it there?

TONY: [*Looking around*] No. But I expect they'll find it. Now you get back to bed. I'll phone them right away.

[*He goes over to* LESGATE. *Searches for key, finds it in raincoat pocket. Sighs with relief. Goes back to oblong table and returns key carefully to zip purse and closes handbag. Sighs with relief again. Returns to body and covers it with blanket. Then goes to phone and dials.* MARGOT *appears in bedroom door*]

MARGOT: Where's Max, Tony?

TONY: I told him to go straight home. . . . Hullo, Operator—give me the Maida Vale Police quickly . . .

MARGOT: Did you tell him?

TONY: No. I wasn't sure what had happened, so I just said I was feeling rotten . . . Darling . . . go back to bed and . . .

[MARGOT *closes her door*]

POLICE: [*Offstage, heard through receiver*] Maida Vale Police.

TONY: Police? There's been a ghastly accident.

POLICE: Yes, sir?

TONY: A man has been killed.

POLICE: Your name, sir?

TONY: Wendice.

POLICE: [*Spelling*] D I double S . . . ?

TONY: No. D I C E.

POLICE: Your address, sir?

TONY: 61a Charrington Gardens. It's the ground-floor apartment.

POLICE: When was this 'ere accident?

TONY: About ten minutes ago. He broke in and attacked my wife . . .

POLICE: A burglar?

TONY: [*Impatiently*] Yes. I'll explain everything when you get here. How long will that take?

POLICE: About two minutes.

TONY: Two minutes.

POLICE: Don't touch anything, will you, sir?

TONY: No. We won't touch anything. Good-bye.

> [*He hangs up and looks around the room. Finally he goes to open window and steps out. Stoops down and picks something up. Comes back into room. He is holding each end of* LESGATE'*s scarf with the two knots. Strolls thoughtfully to mending basket, searches in it and finds a stocking. He holds up scarf and stocking, comparing them. Then he drops stocking on stool and hides scarf in his pocket. He then kneels down beside* LESGATE *and takes out his wallet*]

MARGOT: [*Off, sharply*] Tony!

TONY: [*Calling back*] All right, darling. Won't be a minute.

> [TONY *takes letter (* MAX'*s) out of his wallet and is about to put it in* LESGATE'*s pocket as:*]

CURTAIN

SCENE 3

The same. Sunday morning. About 11 A.M.

The curtains are drawn open and it is bright and sunny outside. The wastepaper basket has been emptied. LESGATE'*s body has been removed but the blanket, folded once, still lies over "the spot" to hide bloodstains.*

The fire is out and has not been touched since last night. The dirty breakfast things lie on the coffee table. MARGOT *is still very nervous. She stands center as curtain rises.*

MARGOT: More coffee?

TONY: [*Off*] No, thank you.

[*He enters from bedroom tying tie, goes to front of fire-place*]

MARGOT: We'd better call Max—[*Quietly*]—and tell him.

TONY: I have. He's on his way over.

MARGOT: [*Trying to cheer up*] Did he like the party last night?

TONY: He certainly did. Made a remarkably good speech, except that he would keep referring to us as Limies. [*He laughs*] Oh, yes, he's all there, is Max . . . Where did you dig him up?

[*Pause*]

MARGOT: I—met him at Peggy's once—and then I met him again just before he went back to New York.

TONY: [*Lightly*] Oh, yes—so you told me.

[*Pause*]

MARGOT: Tony, why did you . . . ? ⎫
TONY: By the way, I . . .   ⎬ *Together*
                                        ⎭

TONY: Sorry.

MARGOT: No, go on.

TONY: I've closed the shutters in the bedroom, that's all.

MARGOT: [*Anxiously*] Why?

TONY: People have started to go out for their Sunday papers. We now have a collection of refined snoopers.

MARGOT: How awful! Is it in the papers already?

TONY: I don't think so—not yet. But news travels fast. [*Pause*] What were you going to say?

MARGOT: I—can't remember—it's gone for the moment.

[*The phone rings.* MARGOT *gives a nervous start.* TONY *answers it*]

TONY: Hullo.

REPORTER: [*Offstage, heard through receiver*] Mrs. Wendice, please.

TONY: This is Mr. Wendice.

REPORTER: Oh, good morning, sir. I'm with the C. & S. News Service. Might I see Mrs. Wendice for a few minutes?

TONY: I'm afraid my wife can't see anyone just now—not for a day or two.

REPORTER: Oh. Was she hurt in any way?

TONY: No. She's all right now.

REPORTER: I just want one or two photographs.

TONY: [*Suddenly annoyed*] Well, how would you feel? I'm sorry—good-bye.

[TONY *rings off*]

MARGOT: Who was that?

TONY: Just a reporter—wanted to take some photographs of you.

MARGOT: I suppose we shall get a lot of that.

TONY: Not for long. As soon as the inquest's over they'll forget all about it. . . . So will you.

MARGOT: When will it be?

TONY: The inquest? Tomorrow or Tuesday—I should think.

MARGOT: [*Nervously*] What will happen?

TONY: Nothing to worry about. The coroner will probably give you a pat on the back for putting up such a good show.

MARGOT: For killing a man?

TONY: Now don't start getting ideas about that. It was him or you. As the police surgeon said, it was lucky those scissors were on the desk.

MARGOT: I hope I don't have to see that doctor again.

TONY: No, he hadn't much bedside manner, had he?

MARGOT: Why were the police so long last night?

TONY: Were they? I didn't notice. I'm afraid I dropped off to sleep very quickly.

MARGOT: I know you did. They stayed for hours. Cars seemed to be coming and going all night.

TONY: I only saw the sergeant. Nice chap. He seemed to have it all under control.

MARGOT: At one time I thought they must be turning all the furniture round.

TONY: [*Looking around the room*] Well, they haven't made much mess. They've even emptied the wastepaper basket. That was thoughtful of them.

MARGOT: Someone kept flashing a light under the bedroom door.

TONY: Taking photographs, probably.

MARGOT: About two o'clock I couldn't stand it any longer. I got up and came in here.

TONY: [*Surprised*] You came in here? What for?

MARGOT: To ask them when they expected to finish. But when I saw them I—couldn't say anything. Two men were on the floor with a tape measure. Another was outside. He kept opening and shutting the window. They all stopped what they were doing and looked at me. I felt such a fool. [*Slowly*] And on the desk—were a pair of shoes. . . . His, I suppose. [*Putting hand to head*] It was horrible!

[TONY *has remembered something*]

TONY: Darling—before I forget—the sergeant wanted to know why you didn't phone the police immediately.

MARGOT: [*Flustered*] But how could I? You were on the phone.

TONY: I know, but . . .

MARGOT: [*Agitated*] You distinctly told me not to speak to anyone until you got here.

TONY: I know, darling. But I told him a slightly different story.

MARGOT: Why?

TONY: I said that you didn't call the police because you naturally assumed that I would phone them from the hotel.

[*Pause*]

MARGOT: Why did you say that?

TONY: Because—it was the perfectly logical explanation—and he accepted it. You see, if they got the idea that we had delayed reporting it—even for a few minutes—they might get nosy and start asking a lot of questions and . . .

MARGOT: So you want me to say the same thing?

TONY: I think so. [*Doorbell rings*] Just in case it comes up again. I expect that's Max. Let him in, will you, darling? I'll just get rid of these.

[TONY *exits into kitchen with tray of dishes.* MARGOT *goes to hall door and opens it.* DETECTIVE INSPECTOR HUBBARD *is standing in the passage outside*]

HUBBARD: [*Removing hat*] Good morning, madam.

MARGOT: Oh! Good morning.

HUBBARD: Mrs. Wendice?

MARGOT: Yes.

HUBBARD: I'm a police officer. [*Pause*] May I come in?

MARGOT: Of course. [*Nervously*] Excuse me, I'll tell my husband you're here.

HUBBARD: Thank you.

> [MARGOT *exits to kitchen.* HUBBARD *looks around for a place to hang his hat. He sees pegs by the door and hangs it up. He then strolls into the room and looks the place over, getting his bearings. He glances deliberately from the blanket to the window, to the telephone, to the bedroom door. He then looks around until he sees the mending basket.* TONY *and* MARGOT *enter*]

TONY: Good morning.

HUBBARD: Good morning, sir. I'm Chief Inspector Hubbard. I'm in charge of the Criminal Investigation of this division.

TONY: I think I gave your sergeant all the necessary information.

HUBBARD: Yes, I've seen his report, of course, but there are a few things I'd like to get first hand. I gather my sergeant only saw you for a few moments, Mrs. Wendice? [*Turning suddenly to* MARGOT] Mrs. Wendice?

MARGOT: Yes . . . I . . .

TONY: My wife was suffering from considerable shock.

HUBBARD: [*Sympathetically*] Yes, that was a very nasty experience you had. [*Turning to bedroom door*] Mind if I take a look around?

TONY: Go ahead. The bedroom and bathroom are through here. . . .

> [TONY *follows* HUBBARD *into the bedroom.* MARGOT *starts to follow them, then hangs back. She is now very nervous. She looks at the blanket on the floor and stares at it for a moment. Then she goes to the cigarette box on the coffee table, opens it, takes out a cigarette, fingers it and then puts it back again.* HUBBARD *and* TONY *enter from bedroom*]

HUBBARD: Well, he certainly didn't get in by the bathroom.

TONY: And the kitchen has bars on the window. [TONY *opens the kitchen door.* HUBBARD *glances in for a moment and then comes back into the room*] We assume he must have come in through these windows.

HUBBARD: Hmmm. I understand that you weren't here when this happened, sir?

TONY: No. I was at a dinner party at the Grendon Hotel.

HUBBARD: Just down the road?

TONY: Yes. By a curious coincidence I was actually phoning my wife when she was attacked.

HUBBARD: So I gather. Can you tell me exactly what time it was?

TONY: I—I'm not sure.

HUBBARD: Did you notice—Mrs. Wendice?

MARGOT: No, I didn't.

HUBBARD: You phoned the police at three minutes to eleven, sir.

TONY: Let me see—in that case it must have been—about a quarter to eleven. By the way—won't you sit down, Inspector?

[TONY *waves* HUBBARD *to the sofa.* TONY *brings the stool to sofa and sits*]

HUBBARD: Thank you.

MARGOT: Have you any idea who he was?

HUBBARD: Yes. At least we've discovered where he lived. There still seems to be some confusion as to his real name.

MARGOT: Oh?

HUBBARD: He appeared to have several. [*Suddenly, looking at* MARGOT] Had you ever seen him before?

MARGOT: [*Bewildered*] Why—no. Of course not. [HUBBARD *takes out his notebook and produces two snapshots of different sizes. He hands them to* MARGOT, *one by one, and watches her very closely as she glances at them and hands them back*] Oh, is this—him?

HUBBARD: Yes. You don't recognize him?

MARGOT: No. I—I never saw him.

HUBBARD: Didn't you even—catch a glimpse of his face?

MARGOT: No. You see, he attacked me from behind and it was dark. I hardly saw him at all.

HUBBARD: [*Pleasantly*] But before I showed you those photographs, you said you'd never seen him before. [*A pause; he watches her face*] How could you know that—if you never saw his face last night?

[*Pause*]

MARGOT: I don't quite understand . . .

TONY: Inspector, my wife simply meant that, as far as she knew, she had never seen him before.

HUBBARD: [*To* MARGOT] Was that what you meant?

MARGOT: [*Nervously, returns photos*] Yes—I'm sorry.

HUBBARD: How about you, sir? Ever seen him before?

> [HUBBARD *hands* TONY *one of the photographs.* TONY *looks and hands it back*]

TONY: No. [HUBBARD *hands him the other.* TONY *looks at it*] No . . . [*He hands it back*] At least . . . [*Taking another look*]

HUBBARD: Yes?

TONY: [*Amazed*] It's very like someone I was at college with—the mustache makes quite a difference.

HUBBARD: What was his name?

TONY: Now you're asking. . . . It's over twenty years since I left.

HUBBARD: Was it Lesgate?

TONY: No.

HUBBARD: Wilson?

TONY: No.

HUBBARD: Swann?

TONY: No . . . Swann? Wait a minute—Swann . . . Yes, that's it. [*Crosses back of couch, gets photo off wall and brings it to* HUBBARD] Look, here's an old photo taken at a reunion dinner. We were at the same college. There he is—it's unbelievable!

HUBBARD: Did you know him well?

TONY: No. He was senior to me.

HUBBARD: Have you met him since then?

TONY: No—at least—come to think of it, I did see him—quite recently [*Pause*] but not to speak to.

HUBBARD: When was that?

TONY: About six months ago. It was at a railway station. . . . Waterloo, I think. I remember noticing how little he'd changed.

HUBBARD: Had he a mustache then?

TONY: [*Pauses for thought, then hands photo back to* HUBBARD] No.

[HUBBARD *makes a note of this. Then he turns to* MARGOT]

HUBBARD: [*Getting up*] Mrs. Wendice, would you show me exactly what happened last night?

MARGOT: Tony, do I have to?

TONY: Afraid so, darling.

[TONY *helps her up. As she talks,* MARGOT *crosses to bedroom and then back of couch to center and then to phone*]

MARGOT: I was in bed when the phone rang. I got up and came in here.

HUBBARD: Did you switch this light on?

MARGOT: No.

HUBBARD: Just show me exactly where you were standing.

[MARGOT *stands as she did, with back half-turned to window*]

MARGOT: I stood here. I picked up the phone.

HUBBARD: Are you sure you had your back to the window like that?

MARGOT: Yes.

HUBBARD: But why?

MARGOT: [*Bewildered*] Why not?

[HUBBARD *stands at left of desk facing window*]

HUBBARD: Why go around the desk? I should have picked it up from this side.

[HUBBARD *picks up the phone with right hand and then replaces it*]

TONY: Surely my wife can remember . . .

HUBBARD: Just a moment, sir.

MARGOT: But I always answer the phone from here.

HUBBARD: Why?

MARGOT: So that if I want to write anything down—I can hold the phone in my left hand.

[*She places her left hand on the phone*]

HUBBARD: I see. All right—go on.

MARGOT: I picked up the phone. Then he must have come from behind the curtain and attacked me. He got something round my neck . . .

HUBBARD: Something? What do you mean by "something"?

MARGOT: I think it was a stocking.

HUBBARD: I see. What happened then?

MARGOT: He pushed me over the desk. I remember distinctly feeling for the scissors . . .

HUBBARD: Where were those scissors usually kept?

MARGOT: [*Pointing*] In that mending basket. I'd forgotten to put them away.

HUBBARD: Now what makes you think he came from behind those curtains?

MARGOT: Where else could he have been?

HUBBARD: The curtains were drawn, I suppose?

MARGOT: Yes, they were.

HUBBARD: Did you draw them yourself?

TONY: [*A little weary of all this*] I drew them, Inspector—before I went out.

HUBBARD: Did you lock the window at the same time?

TONY: Yes.

HUBBARD: Are you quite sure of that, sir?

TONY: Perfectly sure. I always lock up when I draw the curtains.

HUBBARD: Then how do you suppose he got into this room?

TONY: We assumed—that he broke in.

HUBBARD: There's no sign of a break-in. The lock's quite undamaged.

TONY: But he must have done. When I got back that window was wide open. At least . . . Margot, are you sure you didn't go out into the garden last night and forget to lock up afterwards?

MARGOT: I did go out for a moment. After—after he attacked me.

I wanted to get some air. I pushed the window open and stood
on the terrace outside.

HUBBARD: Did you call for help?

MARGOT: I'd just spoken to my husband on the telephone.

HUBBARD: You say you pushed the window open. Are you sure you
didn't unlock it first?

MARGOT: Yes. Quite sure.

HUBBARD: Was it already open?

MARGOT: I—I—don't remember.

[*Pause*]

HUBBARD: Mrs. Wendice, why didn't you ring the police immediately
this happened?

[TONY *catches* MARGOT's *eye and she looks at him for a
moment*]

MARGOT: [*Trying to remember what* TONY *told her*] I was trying to
get through—to the police when I discovered that my husband
was on the line. [*Pause*] I naturally thought he would call the
police—from the hotel—before he came here.

[*Pause.* TONY *looks relieved*]

HUBBARD: [*Quietly*] Didn't it occur to you to call—for a doctor?

MARGOT: No.

HUBBARD: Why ever not?

MARGOT: He was—dead.

HUBBARD: [*Quietly*] How did you know that?

MARGOT: I—it was obvious.

HUBBARD: Did you feel his pulse?

MARGOT: No—of course I didn't. Anyone would have realized he was
dead. . . . One look at those staring eyes . . .

HUBBARD: So you did see his face, after all?

MARGOT: [*Losing control*] I saw his eyes. I can't remember his face!

TONY: Inspector, my wife has obviously never seen this man before.
And if he didn't get in by those windows—how did he get in?

[HUBBARD *strolls across to hall door*]

HUBBARD: [*Slowly*] As a matter of fact we're quite certain he came in by this door.

> [HUBBARD *opens it a few inches and closes it with a click. Then he looks across at* TONY]

MARGOT: [*Quietly*] But it was locked.

TONY: Margot, did you open this door at all—and forget to close it after we'd gone?

MARGOT: No.

HUBBARD: How many keys are there to this door?

MARGOT: Only two. Mine was in my handbag and [*To* TONY] you had yours with you.

TONY: That's right.

HUBBARD: Has the caretaker got a key?

MARGOT: No.

HUBBARD: [*To* MARGOT] Do you employ a charwoman?

MARGOT: Yes, but she hasn't got one either. I'm always in when she comes.

TONY: What makes you think he came in that way?

HUBBARD: [*Quite simply*] His shoes.

TONY: His shoes?

> [HUBBARD *crosses to window*]

HUBBARD: The ground was soaking wet last night. If he'd come in by the garden he'd have left marks all over the carpet. [*Pause*] He didn't leave any because he wiped his shoes on the front door mat.

TONY: How can you tell?

HUBBARD: It's a fairly new mat and some of its fibers came off on his shoes . . .

TONY: But surely . . .

HUBBARD: And there was a small tar stain on the mat and some of the fibers show that as well. There's no question about it.

TONY: [*Suddenly*] Wait a minute, I think I've got it. [*To* MARGOT] You remember when your bag was stolen?

MARGOT: Yes.

TONY: Wasn't your key inside?

MARGOT: Yes, but it was still there when—I got it back.

HUBBARD: [*Interested*] Just a moment. I'd like to hear about this. What sort of bag?

TONY: A handbag, Inspector. My wife lost it at Victoria Station.

MARGOT: I got it back from the lost and found office about two weeks later.

HUBBARD: Was anything missing?

MARGOT: All the money had gone.

HUBBARD: Anything else?

[MARGOT *seems uncertain what to say*]

MARGOT: No.

HUBBARD: [*Casually*] No papers—or letters?

MARGOT: No.

HUBBARD: [*With sudden emphasis*] Are you quite sure about that?

MARGOT: [*Determined*] Yes.

HUBBARD: And your latchkey was in your handbag when you lost it?

MARGOT: Yes, but it was still there when it was returned.

TONY: Whoever stole that money could have had the key copied.

HUBBARD: Where was the bag found eventually?

MARGOT: At Victoria Station.

TONY: But not until several days later. By which time he could have had a duplicate made and returned the original to the bag.

HUBBARD: Before you go any further with this—how did he get in through the street door?

TONY: The street door's always unlocked.

HUBBARD: I see. He could have had your key copied. And he could have used it to open this door—but of course, he didn't.

TONY: Why not?

HUBBARD: Because if he had—the key would still have been on him when he died. But no key was found when we went through his pockets.

[*Pause*]

TONY: I see. Well—we seem to be back where we started.

HUBBARD: Not quite. [*Pause*] You said you saw this man at Waterloo Station?

TONY: Yes.

HUBBARD: Are you sure it wasn't—Victoria?

[TONY *thinks for a moment*]

TONY: It may have been. [*Turning to* MARGOT *excitedly*] When did you lose the bag? Wasn't it that weekend when we went to Peggy's? Yes, it was. It was Victoria. I remember now. He was sitting in the restaurant when I saw him.

HUBBARD: [*To* MARGOT] And was that where you left your handbag?

TONY: Yes, it was. [*To* MARGOT] You were with me, of course—didn't I say something about—there's someone I was at college with?

MARGOT: I don't remember.

[TONY *looks at* HUBBARD *who looks at* MARGOT]

HUBBARD: It looks as if he may have had something to do with that handbag, after all. The next thing is to get all this down on paper. I'd like you both to make an official statement before the inquest. [*Pause*] My office is only a few minutes from here. Perhaps you could come now?

[*The doorbell rings*]

TONY: Excuse me.

[TONY *opens hall door and* MAX *enters*]

MAX: Hello, Tony. [MAX *goes to* MARGOT *and then notices* HUBBARD] Margot . . .

TONY: Max, this is Inspector Hubbard. This is Mr. Halliday, Inspector. He was with me last night.

MAX: [*Bewildered*] How do you do?

HUBBARD: Mr. Halliday, as you were with Mr. Wendice last night, you may be able to help us here. Did you notice what time it was when he went to the phone?

[MAX *thinks for a moment*]

MAX: Yes—it was about twenty to eleven.

HUBBARD: [*Making note*] How did you come to notice that?

MAX: Well, when Mr. Wendice got up from the table I thought for a moment we were leaving the party, so I looked at my watch.

HUBBARD: Thank you, sir. You see, it was when Mrs. Wendice came in here to answer his call that she was attacked.

MAX: You mean [*To* TONY] you were phoning Margot . . . ?

TONY: Yes.

MAX: But I don't get this. I asked you if we were leaving and you said you were just going out to phone . . . your boss . . .

MARGOT: [*Sitting up*] Tony, I know what I was going to ask you. Why did you phone me last night?

[*All turn on* TONY]

HUBBARD: [*Crossing to* TONY] Now, just a moment. Before I lose the thread of this. At about twenty to eleven you left your party to phone your boss?

TONY: Yes. I used the pay phone in the lobby.

HUBBARD: Now, how long were you on the phone to your boss before you called your wife?

TONY: [*Smugly*] As a matter of fact I never did speak to him. I couldn't remember his number—so I rang my wife to ask her to look it up in the address book on the desk.

MARGOT: You mean you hauled me out of bed just to give you his phone number?

TONY: I had to. [*To* HUBBARD] My boss was flying to Brussels this morning and I wanted to remind him of something. It was rather important.

HUBBARD: Wasn't there a telephone directory in the hotel?

TONY: [*Calmly*] Yes, but he was at home—his home number isn't listed.

HUBBARD: So you never called him, after all?

TONY: No. Naturally when I heard what had happened here—I forgot all about it.

HUBBARD: I see. [*To* MAX] Mr. Halliday, Mr. and Mrs. Wendice are coming to my office now to make their statements. [*Taking out notebook*] Would you give me your address, sir? I may want to get in touch with you.

[TONY *goes out by hall door*]

MAX: Certainly.

MARGOT: I'll get my coat.

[*She exits into bedroom*]

MAX: I'm staying at the Carfax Hotel. . . .

HUBBARD: [*Handing* MAX *notebook and pencil*] Just write it down there, will you? Telephone number as well. [*Watching* MAX *write*] Ever been over here before, sir?

[MAX *doesn't see the catch in this*]

MAX: [*Writing*] Yes, about a year ago.

HUBBARD: Umhm.

[MAX *hands notebook to* HUBBARD *who glances at address and returns it to his pocket.* TONY *enters by hall door*]

TONY: Inspector, there's a devil of a crowd outside. Can't you send them away?

HUBBARD: They'll come back faster than they go, sir. I was going to suggest we left by the garden. Isn't there a gate at the far end?

TONY: Yes, but it may still be locked. I'll just see.

[TONY *unlocks window and exits into garden.* HUBBARD *waits till he has gone and then turns to* MAX]

HUBBARD: [*Confidentially*] How much does he know—about you and Mrs. Wendice?

MAX: [*Startled*] What are you talking about?

HUBBARD: You wrote a letter to Mrs. Wendice—from New York. [MAX *only stares at* HUBBARD] It was found in the dead man's inside pocket. I didn't mention it because I wasn't sure how much Mr. Wendice knew. Have you any idea how it got there?

MAX: No.

[MARGOT *enters from bedroom. She is wearing an over-coat and carries her handbag*]

MARGOT: Where's Tony?

MAX: He's just gone into the garden.

HUBBARD: Mrs. Wendice. When you lost your handbag, did you lose a letter as well?

[MARGOT *looks quickly at* MAX]

MARGOT: No.

MAX: Margot, it was found in this man's pocket.

HUBBARD: You did lose it—didn't you?

[*Pause*]

MARGOT: Yes, I did.

HUBBARD: I asked you that before, didn't I?

MARGOT: Yes—but you see—my husband didn't know about it.

HUBBARD: This man was blackmailing you, wasn't he?

[*No reply*]

MAX: It's no good, Margot. Tony will have to know about it now.

[MAX *takes out his wallet.* MARGOT *stares at him horrified*]

MARGOT: No!

MAX: It's the only thing to do. Inspector, after Mrs. Wendice lost my letter she received these two notes.

[MAX *hands the two blackmail notes to* HUBBARD *who reads them*]

HUBBARD: [*Glancing at postmarks*] Last February. [*To* MARGOT] How many times have you seen this man?

MARGOT: [*Angrily*] I've never seen him!

HUBBARD: [*To* MAX, *briskly*] Mr. Halliday, I'd like you to come along with us.

MAX: Yes, of course.

HUBBARD: Mrs. Wendice, when you come to make your statement there may be other police officers present. I shall warn you first that anything you say will be taken down and may be used in evidence. Now, never mind what you've told me so far. We'll forget all about that. From now on tell us exactly what you know about this man and exactly what happened last night. If you try and conceal anything at all it may put you in a very serious position.

MARGOT: I wish you'd explain what you mean by all this.

HUBBARD: I will. You admit that you killed this man. [*Enter* TONY] You say you did it in self-defense. Unfortunately, there were no witnesses, so we've only your word for that.

TONY: But I heard it all—over the telephone, Inspector.

HUBBARD: [*Turning to* TONY] What exactly did you hear, Mr. Wendice?

TONY: I heard—well, I heard a series of gasps.

HUBBARD: Did you hear anything to indicate that a struggle was going on?

TONY: Well, what I heard was perfectly consistent with what my wife told me.

HUBBARD: So all you really know of the matter is what your wife told you, isn't it? [*To* MARGOT] You suggest that this man came to burgle your flat, but there's no evidence of that. There is evidence, however, that he was blackmailing you.

TONY: Blackmail?

MAX: It's true, Tony.

HUBBARD: You suggest that he came in by the window—and we know he came in by that door.

MARGOT: [*Frantically*] But he can't have got in that way. That door was locked and there are only two keys. [*Fumbling in her handbag*] My husband had his with him and mine was in my handbag . . . [*Takes out her latchkey and holds it up*] Here!

[*There is a pause*]

HUBBARD: [*Quietly*] You could have let him in.

[*Pause*]

TONY: You're not suggesting that she let him in herself?

HUBBARD: At present, that appears to be the only way he could have entered.

MARGOT: Don't you even believe I was attacked? [*Puts her hand to her throat*] How do you think I got these bruises on my throat?

HUBBARD: You could have caused those bruises yourself. A silk stock-

ing was found outside the window. It had two knots tied in it.
Does that mean anything to you?

MARGOT: I suppose that must have been the stocking he used.

[*Pause*]

HUBBARD: We found the twin stocking wrapped in newspaper at the
bottom of the wastepaper basket. Can you explain why your at-
tacker should do that?

MARGOT: No.

HUBBARD: Those stockings were yours, weren't they?

MARGOT: [*Horrified*] No!

HUBBARD: We know they were. One of the heels had been darned
with some silk that didn't quite match. We found a reel of that
silk in your mending basket.

[MARGOT *rushes to mending basket and searches inside*]

MARGOT: [*Thoroughly frightened*] Tony, there was a pair of stockings in here!

[TONY *goes to desk, picks up phone and dials frantically*]

TONY: I've heard of police deliberately planting clues to make sure
of a conviction. I just didn't realize they did it in this country.

MARGOT: [*Running across to* TONY] His men were in here for hours
last night. They could easily have taken those stockings out and
done anything with them.

TONY: Of course they did. And they wiped his shoes on the door mat
as well.

[MARGOT *turns to* MAX]

ROGER: [*Offstage, heard through receiver*] Hullo.

TONY: [*Into phone*] Hullo, Roger. Thank God you're in. Tony
Wendice, here. Now listen, Roger—we had a burglary last night.
And Margot was attacked.

ROGER: Margot! Was she hurt?

TONY: No, she's all right, but the man was killed. The police are here
now. And don't laugh—but they're suggesting that Margot killed
him intentionally. . . .

HUBBARD: [*Interrupting*] I wouldn't say that if I were you.

ROGER: Well! That's a good one!

TONY: It's funny, isn't it? Now, can you come round at once? To the Maida Vale Police Station. . . .

ROGER: Be there right away.

TONY: Thanks, old boy. Good-bye. [TONY *rings off and crosses to* MARGOT] It's all right, darling, Roger's going to meet us at the police station.

HUBBARD: Mr. Wendice, I should advise you. . . .

TONY: Our lawyer will give us all the advice we need, thank you.

> [TONY *and* MARGOT *start to exit.* MAX *sees handbag on sofa*]

MAX: Here's your bag, Margot.

> [TONY *opens French window*]

MARGOT: Oh, thank you, Max.

> [*She takes bag, looks around the room, thoroughly bewildered. She turns and exits by French window.* MAX *follows her out.* HUBBARD *is about to exit, then turns to* TONY]

HUBBARD: You are coming, sir?

TONY: But of course, Inspector.

HUBBARD: [*Mumbling, half to himself*] Mm—I see—yes—I just wondered . . .

> [HUBBARD *exits.* TONY *gives a brief glance around the room. He is now in complete control of the situation. He puts his hands in his pockets and follows* HUBBARD *out*]

CURTAIN

ACT THREE

The same. A few months later. Early afternoon.

The furniture has been rearranged. Curtains open but shutters have been fastened. No light except sharp rays through shutters. On the desk are a bottle of whiskey and a glass. The wastepaper basket is overflowing with odd junk and crumpled newspapers. Next to this there is a paper carrier containing groceries. A bed has been brought into the room with its head up-center. It has not been made properly for several days. Against the fireplace is the sofa. Odd clothing and robe are thrown over sofa. On the floor is TONY's *leather suitcase with the lid open, half packed. The electric portable fire has been plugged in and stands between sofa and bed. When the curtain rises the room is in darkness. Footsteps are heard in the passage outside and a key turns in the hall door.* TONY *enters. He wears a raincoat, and carries a small blue fiber attaché case.* TONY *switches on the lights. He takes key out of door and puts it in raincoat pocket, then takes coat off. He puts coat on chair in hall. Closes door. He puts attaché case on bed, looks at watch, then crosses to table. He turns on radio. He returns to attaché case and unlocks it. He takes out a wad of pound notes, puts it in pocket and relocks case. Radio fades in. He looks up at the set and listens intently.*

ANNOUNCER: . . . The main obstacles were the export of fruit and vegetables. Agreement has now been reached that the export quotas originally asked for be lowered by twelve and a half per cent. [*Pause*] The Home Secretary has written to the lawyers of Mrs. Margot Wendice to say that he has decided that there are not sufficient grounds to justify his recommending a reprieve. At the Old Bailey last November, Mrs. Wendice was found guilty of the murder of Charles Alexander Swann and was sentenced to death. [*Pause*] The official forecast is that there will be bright periods and showers in all districts today. Frost is expected again tonight, especially in the South. [*Phone rings*] The time is now eleven minutes past one and that is the end of the news . . .

[TONY *switches off radio and crosses to phone*]

TONY: [*Into phone*] Hullo!

PENDLETON: [*Offstage, heard through receiver*] Mr. Wendice?

TONY: Yes?

PENDLETON: Pendleton here.

TONY: Oh, good afternoon.

PENDLETON: Have you decided about the letters?

TONY: Yes—I'll be quite frank with you—the cost of the defense has been very high. I shall have to ask for five hundred pounds.

PENDLETON: Five hundred! But I'm only asking for her letters . . .

TONY: That's all very well—how would you like your wife's letters read by millions of people?

PENDLETON: I'm prepared to offer three fifty . . .

TONY: No, I'm sorry. I've quite made up my mind.

PENDLETON: Could you give me a little time to think this over?

TONY: By all means, think it over—only I'm going away the day after tomorrow. [*The door buzzer.* TONY *glances anxiously at the door. Quietly*] Excuse me. I shall have to ring you back.

[*He rings off. Goes to door and opens it.* MAX *stands in the passage outside. He wears neither coat nor hat. They stare at each other for a moment or two*]

MAX: Hello, Tony.

TONY: Hullo, Max.

MAX: May I come in?

TONY: Of course, you're quite a stranger.

MAX: [*Entering*] I'm sorry I haven't been around before. I wasn't sure how you felt—after . . .

TONY: That's all right. It's rather chilly in here. I'll switch on . . .

[TONY *stops short as he sees attaché case on bed*] I'll switch on the fire. Let's find somewhere for you to sit. [*Covers attaché case with clothes*] I've hardly seen anyone for weeks. I'm getting quite used to it. I've had to move in here because everybody stops in the street and peers in at the bedroom window. When the appeal failed they started climbing into the garden. You can't blame them, I suppose—it's cheaper than the zoo and far more topical.

MAX: I—had to come—in case there was anything . . .

[TONY *takes a typed letter from his pocket and hands it to* MAX]

TONY: [*Quietly*] I'm afraid it's settled, Max. Our lawyer received this from the Home Secretary this morning.

[MAX *reads letter and hands it back to* TONY]

MAX: You mustn't give up trying. It's not over yet.

TONY: I'm afraid it is. [*At bed*] We've done all we can. I went to the prison this morning to—say good-bye, but she wouldn't see me. I was rather glad—she never did like good-byes. [*Pause, simply*] I shan't see her again.

MAX: Tony. I take it you'd do anything—to save her life?

TONY: [*Surprised*] Of course.

MAX: Even if it meant going to prison for several years?

TONY: [*After a pause*] I'd do absolutely anything.

MAX: I think you can—I'm certain. [*Slowly*] If you tell the police *exactly* the right story.

TONY: The right story?

MAX: Listen, Tony. [*Sits on bed*] I've been working this out for weeks. Just in case it came to this. It may be her only chance.

TONY: Let's have it.

MAX: You'll have to tell the police that you hired Swann to murder her.

[*Long pause.* TONY *can only stare at* MAX]

TONY: [*Rises*] What are you talking about?

MAX: It's all right, Tony—I've been writing this stuff for years. I know what I'm doing. Margot was convicted because no one would believe her story. Prosecution made out that she was telling one lie after another—and the jury believed him. But what did his case amount to? Only three things. My letter—her stocking, and the idea that, because no key was found on Swann, she must have let him in herself. [*Pause*] Now Swann is dead. You can tell any story you like about him. You can say that you did know him. That you'd met him, and worked out the whole thing together. Now the blackmail. Swann was only suspected of blackmail for two reasons. Because my letter was found in his pocket and because you saw him the day Margot's bag was stolen.

TONY: Well?

MAX: You can now tell the police that you never saw him at Victoria. That the whole thing was an invention of yours to try and connect him with the letter.

TONY: But the letter was found in his pocket.

MAX: Because you put it there.

TONY: [*Pause*] You mean I should pretend that I stole her handbag?

MAX: Sure. You could have.

TONY: But why?

MAX: Because you wanted to find out who was writing to her. When you read my letter you were so mad you decided to teach her a lesson.

TONY: But I can't say that I wrote those blackmail notes.

MAX: Why not? No one can prove that you didn't.

[TONY *thinks it over*]

TONY: All right. I stole her bag and blackmailed her. What else?

MAX: You kept my letter and planted it on Swann after he'd been killed.

TONY: Wait a minute—when could I have done that?

MAX: After you got back from the party and before the police arrived. At the same time you took one of Margot's stockings from the mending basket and substituted it for whatever Swann had used.

[TONY *thinks it over*]

TONY: Max, I know you're trying to help but—can you imagine anyone believing this?

MAX: You've got to make them believe it.

TONY: But I wouldn't know what to say. You'd have to come with me.

MAX: No. I couldn't do that. They know the sort of stuff I write. If they suspected we'd talked this out they wouldn't even listen. They mustn't know I've been here.

TONY: Max! It's ridiculous. Why should I want anyone to murder Margot?

MAX: Oh, one of the stock motives. Had Margot made a will?

[*Pause*]

TONY: I—yes, I believe she had.

MAX: Are you the main beneficiary?

TONY: I suppose so.

MAX: Well, there you are.

TONY: But thousands of husbands and wives leave money to each other, without murdering each other. The police wouldn't believe a word of it! They'd take it for exactly what it is. A husband desperately trying to save his wife.

MAX: [*Rises*] Well, it's worth a try. They can't hang you for planning a murder that never came off. Face it. The most you'd get would be a few years in prison.

TONY: Thanks very much.

MAX: . . . And you'd have saved her life. That doesn't seem too big a price.

TONY: That's fine coming from you, Max. Her life might not be in danger at all if it hadn't been for you. It was because of your—association with her that she lost the sympathy of the jury. Don't get me wrong, Max. If there was the slightest chance of this coming off—of course I'd do it. But it's got to be convincing. How—how could I have persuaded Swann to do a thing like this?

MAX: You'd have to say you offered him money.

TONY: What money? I haven't got any.

[*Pause*]

MAX: You would have Margot's money.

TONY: It would be months before I could lay my hands on that. And people don't commit murder on credit. No, we'll have to think up something better than that . . .

MAX: [*Fighting to concentrate*] All right—we will. There is an answer and we've got to find it. [*Pause*] How much time have we got?

TONY: [*As if he can hardly say it*] It's tomorrow morning . . .

[*Door buzzer. Offstage door slams. Footsteps*]

MAX: Ssssssh!

[*They stop and listen. They look at each other.* TONY *goes to open the door.* MAX *snaps his fingers to attract* TONY's *attention. He motions* TONY *to wait and crosses quietly and exits into kitchen. When* TONY *opens the hall door* INSPECTOR HUBBARD *is standing in the passage outside. He carries a raincoat over his arm and a briefcase*]

TONY: Oh—hullo, Inspector. [HUBBARD *enters and* TONY *closes the door. Anxiously*] Is it—about my wife?

HUBBARD: [*Sympathetically*] Er—no, sir. I'm afraid not.

TONY: [*Surprised*] What is it, then?

[HUBBARD *hangs his briefcase on the same chair as* TONY's *raincoat and then hangs up his hat and raincoat on coat rack*]

HUBBARD: I'm making enquiries in connection with a robbery that took place about three weeks ago.

TONY: Can't this wait a few days?

HUBBARD: [*Sincerely*] Of course, sir, I'm very conscious of your position. If I may—I would like to say how deeply sorry I am that things . . .

TONY: [*Curtly*] Yes, Inspector—all right. How can I help you?

HUBBARD: The cashier of a factory in Ledbury Street was attacked in his office and two men made off with several hundred pounds— mostly in pound notes.

TONY: What's all this got to do with me?

HUBBARD: In cases like this, all police divisions are asked to keep a lookout for anyone spending large sums of money.

[*He pauses as if expecting Tony to say something*]

TONY: I see.

HUBBARD: I was wondering if you had sold anything recently—for cash.

TONY: Why?

HUBBARD: My sergeant happened to be making enquiries at Wales' garage the other day. [*Pause*] It appears that you settled an account there recently for—[*Glancing at notebook*]—just over sixty pounds.

TONY: [*Casually*] Yes. I happened to have quite a lot on me at the time so I paid cash.

HUBBARD: I see. Had you just drawn this money from your bank?

[*Pause*]

TONY: [*On his guard*] Have you been to my bank, Inspector?

HUBBARD: [*With a smile*] As a matter of fact, I have. They wouldn't help me. Bank statements are always jealously guarded. [*Good-naturedly*] Where'd yer get it, sir?

TONY: Is that any of your business?

HUBBARD: If it was stolen money—yes, sir. It is my business. [*Taking out his pipe and holding it up*] Do you mind if I smoke?

TONY: Go ahead. [*With a laugh*] Do you really think I've been receiving stolen money?

HUBBARD: Until you tell me where you got it—I shan't know what to think—shall I? [HUBBARD *feels around in his pockets and then goes to hall and takes a tobacco pouch from one of the pockets of his raincoat*] You see, if you got that money from someone you didn't know—well, that might be the very person we're looking for. Hullo! [*He stoops down and appears to pick up something from the carpet just beneath his raincoat*] Is this yours, sir?

[*He holds up a latchkey*]

TONY: [*Moving nearer*] What is it?

HUBBARD: [*Casually*] Somebody's latchkey. It was lying on the floor—just here.

[TONY *crosses to hall and feels in the pockets of his rain-*

coat. From one of them he takes out his latchkey and holds it up]

TONY: No. I've got mine here.

[*At the same time* HUBBARD *opens hall door and tries to fit the other key into the lock*]

HUBBARD: No. It's not yours. [TONY *puts his key back into his raincoat pocket*] It may be mine, then. [*Feeling in pockets of his raincoat*] Yes, it is. It must have dropped out of my pocket. There's a small hole here. [*He walks a few paces back into the room, looking at key in his hand. Continuing as he goes*] That's the trouble with those keys—they're all alike. [*He puts key carefully into his side pocket*] I'm sorry, sir, you were saying . . . ?

[TONY *is at a loss*]

TONY: I—I don't think I was . . .

HUBBARD: [*At right of bed*] Oh, yes—about that money—I'd be grateful if you'd tell me where you got it. After all, a hundred pounds is quite a lot to carry around.

TONY: You said sixty a moment ago.

HUBBARD: Did I? Er—yes—my sergeant decided to dig a little deeper before he put in his report. [*Pulling at his pipe*] He said you'd also paid—a bill at your tailor's and another—for wines and spirits.

TONY: I'm sorry he went to all that trouble. If he'd come straight to me, I could have explained it at once. I simply won rather a large sum at dog-racing.

HUBBARD: Over a hundred pounds?

[TONY *glances anxiously toward the kitchen door*]

TONY: [*Quietly*] Yes, over a hundred pounds. It has been done before, you know.

[*Sits*]

HUBBARD: I see. [*Smiling*] Why didn't you tell me this straight away, sir?

TONY: [*Coldly*] Because I'm a little ashamed to be caught going to dog-racing when my wife is under sentence of death.

HUBBARD: [*Sympathetically*] I know how it is, sir. Helps to take your mind off things. [*Moving to hall*] Well, that answers everything, doesn't it? I'm sorry to have had to bother you at this time.

TONY: [*Going to open hall door*] Not at all.

[HUBBARD *takes his hat off the peg and then turns to* TONY]

HUBBARD: [*Casually*] Oh, there is just one other thing, sir. Have you a small blue attaché case?

[TONY *is obviously shaken by this. He does not reply for several seconds*]

TONY: Don't say you've found it already?

[HUBBARD *strolls back into the room*]

HUBBARD: Why? Have you lost it?

TONY: Yes. I was going to report it this afternoon. I think I left it in a taxi. How did you know about that attaché case, Inspector?

[HUBBARD *watches* TONY *closely, takes out pad and pencil. The door of the kitchen opens a little, but neither* TONY *nor* HUBBARD *notices it*]

HUBBARD: The wine shop mentioned that you had it when you paid your bill. So my sergeant checked back on your garage and your tailor. They both remembered you having it with you when you paid them.

TONY: Yes. I use it instead of a briefcase.

HUBBARD: [*Going to hall door*] Well, these taxi-men are pretty good at turning things in. I hope you'll find it all right. [*Enter* MAX] Oh! Mr. Halliday.

[MAX *stands there staring curiously at* TONY]

MAX: [*Quietly*] Before you go, Inspector—I think Mr. Wendice has something to tell you.

HUBBARD: Oh, has he?

[HUBBARD *turns to* TONY. TONY *stares at* MAX. MAX *goes to sofa and looks under some of* TONY's *clothes*]

MAX: Where did you put it, Tony?

TONY: [*At bed*] What's come over you?

MAX: [*Crossing to bed*] When I was in here just now there was a small attaché case. I can't remember just where I saw it but . . . [MAX *lifts* TONY's *dressing gown and reveals the case. He carries it to desk and tries to open it but it is locked. Quietly*] Got the key, Tony?

TONY: Have you gone mad?

[MAX *takes metal ice pick from drinks tray*]

MAX: Very well. If there's no key we'll have to open it some other way.

HUBBARD: [*To* MAX] Just a moment, sir. [*To* TONY, *sharply*] Why did you say you left this in a taxi?

TONY: I thought I had. [MAX *is busily working on the lock*] Don't be a fool, Max. I've got the key somewhere. [*Searching in pockets*] I don't know what all the fuss is about. . . . [MAX *suddenly fixes point of poker behind the lock and gives a twist*] Max, you . . .

MAX: It's all right, Tony, I'll buy you a new one.

[MAX *opens case and takes out an evening paper and six bundles of one-pound notes. He lays them on the desk.* MAX *stacks them on the desk, one by one.* HUBBARD *throws hat onto bed, crosses to desk and examines the money*]

HUBBARD: Must be over five hundred pounds here. [*Turning to* TONY] Where did you get it?

MAX: I can tell you *why* he got it. That money was to have been paid to a man named Swann—after he had murdered Mrs. Wendice in this room. As you know, there was—an accident—so it wasn't necessary to pay Swann, after all. Obviously he couldn't produce all this without questions being asked—so he lived on it. He's been living on it ever since the twenty-eighth of September.

HUBBARD: [*To* TONY] Well, Mr. Wendice?

MAX: Just now you said you'd do anything to save Margot. What's made you change your mind?

TONY: [*To* HUBBARD] Before you came, Inspector, he was trying to persuade me to go to the police and tell the most fantastic story you ever heard. Apparently I bribed Swann to murder my wife so that—correct me if I go wrong, Max—so that I could inherit all her money. And that isn't all. You remember that letter of Mr. Halliday's? Well, it wasn't Swann who stole it. I did! And I wrote those two blackmail notes. And I kept Mr. Halliday's letter and planted it on the body. . . .

MAX: [To HUBBARD] And that stocking which was found . . .

TONY: Oh, yes—the stocking. Perhaps I'd better tell this. It may sound more like a confession. I substituted . . . [To MAX] Is that the right word? I substituted one of my wife's stockings for—er— the other one—you follow me, don't you? Er—what else, Max?

[MAX *goes to hall door and opens it*]

MAX: [To HUBBARD] He told Swann he would hide his key somewhere out here. [*He looks up and feels along the ledge above and outside the door*] Probably on this ledge. Swann let himself in, then hid behind the curtains. Then Wendice phoned from the hotel and brought her . . .

[TONY *sits*]

HUBBARD: Just a minute. If Swann had used Mr. Wendice's key—it would still have been on him when he died. Besides, how did Mr. Wendice get in when he returned from the hotel?

[*Pause*]

MAX: [*Thinking it out as he goes*] She could have let him in—and he could have taken his key out of Swann's pocket before the police arrived.

HUBBARD: But he let himself in with his own key. That was established at the trial—don't you remember?

[MAX *appears defeated by this*]

TONY: Come on, Max—your move.

[MAX *goes to hall door and looks up again at the ledge outside. As he speaks he demonstrates*]

MAX: [*Slowly, but not overemphasized*] Swann could have taken the key from here—unlocked the door—and then returned it to the ledge before he went in.

HUBBARD: [*Interrupting*] All right, Mr. Halliday. This is all very interesting, but it isn't getting me any nearer what I came to find out.

MAX: [*Frantic*] But this is a matter of life and death! What else matters?

HUBBARD: What matters to me is where Mr. Wendice got this money, that's all I want to know.

[MAX *closes the door and crosses quickly to desk*]

MAX: We'll soon find out how long he's had it.

[MAX *starts to go through top drawer*]

TONY: Now, what's the matter?

[MAX *takes out a checkbook and examines the stubs*]

MAX: [*Excitedly showing checkbook to* HUBBARD] There you are, Inspector. The last check he wrote was on the twenty-seventh of September. That was the day before this happened. I tell you he's been living off it ever since. [HUBBARD *looks through the checkbook stubs*] Here's his bank statement.

[MAX *opens drawer and takes out the black folder. He opens it on the desk and examines the entries*]

HUBBARD: [*Looking at bank statement*] He hasn't drawn any large sums from his bank. Nothing over—fifty-three pounds.

[HUBBARD *drops folder on desk.* MAX *picks it up and examines it*]

MAX: But just look at these, Inspector—nearly every week—thirty-five pounds—forty—thirty-five—forty-five . . . He could have saved it up.

TONY: Of course—I may have been planning all this for years!

MAX: [*Threatening*] Where did you get it?

TONY: Are you sure you want to know? [*To* MAX, *grimly*] I warn you, Max, you won't like it.

MAX: Come on.

TONY: Very well—you asked for it. [*Pause*] When she called me back from the party that night I found her kneeling beside Swann and going through his pockets. She kept saying he had something of hers—but she couldn't find it. She was almost hysterical. That's why I wouldn't let the police question her. In the state she was in she would have told every lie under the sun. The next morning she showed me that money—just like it is now—all in one-pound notes. She said, "If anything happens to me—don't let them find this." [*Pause*] After she was arrested I took the money in that case to Charing Cross Station and left it in the checkroom. Whenever I needed money I took it out and left it in some other checkroom. I knew that if you found it she wouldn't stand a chance. You see, she was just about to give it to him when she killed him instead.

MAX: Do you expect anyone to believe this?

TONY: I've really no idea. What about it, Inspector?

[*Pause*]

HUBBARD: Hmmmmmmmm? [*At desk*] Well, it certainly seems to fit in with the verdict at the trial.

MAX: [*Frantic*] You mean you're not even going to check up on this? She's being hanged tomorrow.

[TONY *goes to bed*]

HUBBARD: [*Wearily*] All this has been out of my hands for months. There's been a trial and an appeal . . .

MAX: Of course, it wouldn't do you much good, would it? You'd have to admit you arrested the wrong person.

TONY: I think you ought to go.

MAX: You bet I'll go. [*Goes to hall*] But you've made one mistake. [*Pause*] What will happen when Margot hears about all this?

[*Pause*]

TONY: She'll deny it, of course.

MAX: And perhaps she'll change her will. [*This gets under* TONY's skin. MAX *opens hall door. He looks straight at* TONY. *Slowly*] You'll have done it all for nothing.

> [MAX *exits. From now on* HUBBARD *speaks to* TONY *very gently, almost as if he was a child.* TONY *turns to* HUBBARD]

TONY: Suppose I had told that story of his. Would anyone have believed me?

HUBBARD: Not a chance, sir. Before nearly every execution someone comes forward like this. This must have been very distressing for you—coming as it did.

> [TONY *sits*]

TONY: Do you think they'll let him see her? I—I don't want her upset just . . .

HUBBARD: Have a word with your lawyer. He might be able to prevent it. [*Nodding at money on desk*] And I should get all that money into the bank before someone pinches it.

TONY: Thank you—I think I will.

HUBBARD: [*Taking down hat from peg*] By the way, I was asked to tell you—there are a few things belonging to Mrs. Wendice at the police station.

TONY: What sort of things?

> [*During these next few speeches,* HUBBARD *takes down his own raincoat and changes it for* TONY's *on the hall chair.* TONY *has his back turned and does not notice*]

HUBBARD: Just some books—and a handbag, I believe. They'd like you to come and collect them sometime.

TONY: You mean—after tomorrow?

HUBBARD: Yes—or today, if you like. Just ask the desk sergeant— he knows all about it. [HUBBARD *picks up his briefcase and* TONY's *raincoat and puts the latter over his arm. Crosses to* TONY *and puts out his hand*] Well, good-bye Mr. Wendice. I don't suppose we shall meet again.

TONY: [*Shaking hands*] Good-bye, Inspector—and thank you.

> [HUBBARD *exits.* TONY *waits till he hears the door slam.*

Then he crosses to desk and pours whiskey into a glass and drinks it. He picks up one of the bundles of notes and whisks it like a pack of cards. He picks up attaché case, examines lock, throws it on bed and looks around the room. He picks up the paper carrier bag, tips contents on desk, fills bag with bundles of notes, covers them with newspaper. He crosses to bed, leans across it and switches off electric fire. He then crosses to hall with paper bag and takes HUBBARD's *raincoat and throws it over his arm. He switches off light and exits. Sound of footsteps and street door opening and slamming. The pink glow of electric fire dies slowly. There is a sound of key in lock. The hall door opens and* HUBBARD *enters. He switches on pencil torch and looks around the room. He looks at key and then pockets it carefully. He throws his briefcase and raincoat on the bed and crosses to the desk. He picks up the phone and dials a number]*

POLICE: [*Offstage, heard through receiver*] Hullo.

HUBBARD: Maida Vale Police? Chief Inspector here. Give me Sergeant O'Brien quick.

[*Pause*]

O'BRIEN: O'Brien.

HUBBARD: Hubbard . . . Look, I've got back in again. Start the ball rolling.

O'BRIEN: Yes, sir.

[HUBBARD *rings off. He looks around the desk until he finds* TONY's *bank statement and starts to examine it again. There is a crash of broken glass from behind shutters.* HUBBARD *puts out torch and moves silently into the kitchen. Someone opens the French windows but the shutters bar his way. A knife is inserted through the crack where the shutters meet and the bar which holds them together is lifted off its pin. Shutters fly open, letting daylight into the room.* MAX *enters. He immediately goes to desk and starts searching for something.* HUBBARD *appears from kitchen]*

HUBBARD: What are you up to? [MAX *looks up, startled]* What's the idea?

MAX: Where's his bank statement?

HUBBARD: Never mind about that. You've got to get out of here—quick.

MAX: [*Raising his voice*] Have you got it?

HUBBARD: Ssssssh! Not so loud.

MAX: But don't you see . . .

HUBBARD: [*Savagely, but in half-whisper*] Shut up! [*Almost frantic*] If you want to save Mrs. Wendice, keep quiet and let me handle this.

MAX: You?

> [*Sound of street door opening, footsteps.* HUBBARD *raises his hand to keep* MAX *quiet and then points to door]*

HUBBARD: Sssssssssh! [*They both stand motionless watching the door. Sound of someone trying to insert key into lock. Then silence for a moment. Door buzzer rings twice.* HUBBARD *raises his hand to restrain any movement from* MAX. *Footsteps move away. Sound of street door shutting.* HUBBARD *breathes a sigh of relief. He opens bedroom door and peers toward the street]* Whew! You nearly ditched us then. I should have locked you up.

MAX: What in the hell is all this?

HUBBARD: [*Letting off steam*] They talk about flatfooted policemen! May the saints protect us from the gifted amateur! [*He crosses to the open window and looks out into the garden for several seconds. Quietly*] You'd better prepare yourself for a surprise, Mr. Halliday.

> [HUBBARD *continues to stare outside and then suddenly backs into the room waving* MAX *away from the window. After several seconds* MARGOT *appears, followed by* THOMP-SON, *a police constable in uniform.* MARGOT *is dressed in the same clothes she was wearing at the end of Act Two, and she carries the same handbag. She stops in the win-*

dow as she sees the two men. Her appearance should in-
dicate that she has been through a great deal during the
last two or three months]

MARGOT: Hullo, Max. [MAX *goes to her*] Where's Tony?

MAX: He—he's gone out.

MARGOT: When will he be back?

HUBBARD: [*His manner is official and brisk*] We're not sure. All right,
Thompson. [THOMPSON *exits*. HUBBARD *turns to* MARGOT] Was it
you who rang just now?

MARGOT: Yes. [*Surprised*] Why didn't you let me in?

HUBBARD: You've got a key. Why didn't you use it?

MARGOT: I did. But it didn't fit the lock.

HUBBARD: And you know why—don't you?

MARGOT: No, I don't. [*Pause*] Has the lock been changed?

HUBBARD: May I have your bag? [*Goes to bed.* MARGOT *gives up her
handbag.* HUBBARD *opens it, undoes the zip purse and takes out
the key. He holds it up*] You knew this wasn't your key, didn't
you?

MARGOT: No.

[HUBBARD *picks up the attaché case from the bed. He
shows it to her*]

HUBBARD: Your husband has explained this, you know. You can tell
us all about it now.

[MARGOT *stares at it.* HUBBARD *watches her face*]

MARGOT: [*Bewildered*] What is it? Why am I . . . ? I don't understand.

[HUBBARD *looks at her steadily for a moment*]

HUBBARD: No. I don't believe you do. [*Kindly*] Come and sit down,
Mrs. Wendice.

[MARGOT *crosses to sofa and sits down.* HUBBARD *puts key
and purse back into handbag*]

MAX: What's going on here?

[HUBBARD *goes to desk and looks out of window*]

HUBBARD: [*Shouting into garden*] Thompson!

THOMPSON: [*From garden*] Sir.

[THOMPSON *enters*]

HUBBARD: Take this handbag to the police station.

THOMPSON: Yes, sir.

[THOMPSON *slips his arm through the straps of the hand-bag and exits*]

HUBBARD: Wait a minute, you clot. You can't go down the street like that. [HUBBARD *takes his briefcase from desk and exits into garden*] Put it in this.

MAX: Margot, what is this? Why are you here?

MARGOT: [*As if in a dream*] I don't know. [*Slowly*] About an hour ago the warden came to see me. He just said I was to be taken home. Two detectives drove me here. They parked just around the corner. Then that policeman came up and said I could go. But I couldn't get this door open. When I left the policeman was still outside and he brought me around by the garden. [*Getting up*] Where's Tony? He was supposed to visit me this morning but they said he couldn't come. Has anything happened to him?

MAX: No—nothing. [HUBBARD *enters from garden. He closes the window, locks it and closes shutters. Then he goes to hall and switches on light*] Inspector, do you think you could tell us what you're up to?

HUBBARD: Mrs. Wendice, what I've got to tell you may come as a shock.

MARGOT: Yes?

HUBBARD: We strongly suspect that your husband had planned to murder you.

[MARGOT *stares at* HUBBARD *for a moment and then turns to* MAX]

MAX: He's right, Margot. He arranged for Swann to come here that night and kill you.

[MARGOT *shows no sign of emotion*]

MARGOT: How long have you known this?

HUBBARD: [*Surprised*] Did you suspect it yourself?

MARGOT: [*Working it out in her mind*] No—never—and yet . . . [*She looks around the room for several seconds then turns suddenly to* MAX] What's the matter with me, Max? I don't seem able to feel anything. Shouldn't I break down or something?

MAX: It's delayed action, that's all. In a couple of days you're going to have one hellava breakdown. [*Puts an arm around her. To* HUBBARD] When did you find out?

HUBBARD: The first clue came quite by accident. We discovered that your husband had been spending large numbers of pound notes all over the place. It ran into over three hundred pounds and it appeared to have started about the time you were arrested. Now, I had to find out where he got this money and how. Then I remembered that, after you were arrested, we searched this flat and I saw a copy of his bank statement in that desk. So yesterday afternoon, I went to the prison and asked to see your handbag, and while I was doing this I managed to lift your latchkey. Highly irregular, of course, but my blood was up. Then, this morning when your husband was out, I came here to look at his bank statements. [*Pause*] I never saw it because I never got through that door. . . . You see, the key I had taken from your handbag didn't fit the lock. [*Three loud knocks on the ceiling above. They all look up and* HUBBARD *rushes to the hall and switches off lights*] Don't make a sound. [*Sound of a street door opening and shutting. Footsteps move along passage to hall door and stop. Long pause and then footsteps move away. Street door opens and slams. After a few moments* HUBBARD *goes and opens the hall door. Calling up*] Williams.

WILLIAMS: [*From upstairs*] Sir!

HUBBARD: Who was it?

WILLIAMS: Wendice, sir.

HUBBARD: Which way did he go?

WILLIAMS: Hold on. [*Pause*] Toward the police station, sir.

HUBBARD: Good. [HUBBARD *closes hall door and switches on lights.*

Crosses to telephone] That was a near one. [*Picks up phone and dials a number*] Maida Vale Police?

o'brien: [*Offstage, on phone*] Yes, sir. O'Brien.

hubbard: Hubbard here . . . Look, O'Brien, he's found out about his raincoat. . . . He just came back and couldn't get in. I think he's on his way to the station now. Has Thompson arrived with the handbag?

o'brien: Yes, sir.

hubbard: Good. Now, look—give Wendice those books and the handbag and make sure he sees the key. . . . Better make him check the contents and sign for it. If he wants his own key and raincoat . . . er, tell him I've gone to Glasgow.

o'brien: Yes, sir.

hubbard: Any questions?

o'brien: No questions.

hubbard: Right . . . Call me back when he leaves the station. . . . [*During the phone call* max *moves slowly to hall door and opens it. He looks up thoughtfully at the ledge above the door, then stares down at the spot where Swann died and then back to the ledge. He feels along it with his fingers and looks puzzled. To* max, *as he rings off*] Well, Mr. Halliday, have you got it?

max: [*Puzzled*] I don't think so. [*Slowly*] Where is Mrs. Wendice's key?

> [hubbard *goes through open door into passage. He takes her key from under the stair carpet and holds it up. Then he replaces it exactly in the same place*]

hubbard: It took me just half an hour to find it.

max: But if it was there—why didn't Wendice use it just now?

hubbard: He didn't use it because he doesn't realize it's there. He still thinks it's in his wife's handbag. You see, you were very nearly right. [*To* margot] He told Swann that he would leave your key under the stair carpet, Mrs. Wendice, and told him to return it to the same place when he left. But as Swann was killed he naturally assumed that your key would still be in one of Swann's pockets. That was his little mistake. Because Swann had done exactly what you suggested, Mr. Halliday. [*Going through the motions*] He unlocked the door—and then returned the key *before* he came in. . . .

MAX: And it's been out there ever since! And the key Wendice took out of Swann's pocket and returned to her handbag was . . .

HUBBARD: Swann's own latchkey! Mind you, even I didn't guess that at once. At first I thought your husband must have changed the lock. It had always surprised me that no key was found on Swann's body. After all, most men carry a latchkey about with them. Then I had a brainwave. I took the key that was in your handbag to Mrs. Van Dorn's and unlocked the door of her flat. Then I borrowed her telephone and called Scotland Yard.

MARGOT: Why did you bring me back here?

HUBBARD: Because you were the only other person who could possibly have left that key outside. I had to find out if you knew it was there.

MARGOT: Suppose I had known?

HUBBARD: [*With a smile*] You didn't!

MARGOT: [*Suddenly*] Max!

MAX: Yes, darling?

MARGOT: I think I'm going to have that breakdown right now!

[MARGOT *turns her head into* MAX's *shoulder and begins to cry softly.* MAX *puts his arms around her. Phone rings*]

HUBBARD: O'Brien?

O'BRIEN: Yes, sir. He's just left the station.

HUBBARD: Right! [*Rings off. To* MARGOT *and* MAX *as he crosses to hall door*] Try and hang on a little longer. [*Opens door and calls up*] Williams!

WILLIAMS: [*Upstairs*] Sir!

HUBBARD: He's just left the station. . . . Give me a thump if he comes this way.

WILLIAMS: [*From upstairs*] Right, sir.

[HUBBARD *closes door and makes sure it is locked properly*]

MARGOT: [*To* MAX] Handkerchief.

[MAX *produces his handkerchief and* MARGOT *wipes her eyes and gives her nose a good blow*]

MAX: [*To* HUBBARD] What happens now?

HUBBARD: Sooner or later he'll come back here. As I've pinched his key, he'll have to try the one in the handbag. When that doesn't fit he'll realize his mistake, put two and two together and look under the stair carpet.

MAX: But . . . if he doesn't do that—all this is pure guess work. We can't prove a thing.

HUBBARD: That's perfectly true. [*Slowly, with emphasis, pointing to hall door*] But once he opens that door—we shall know everything.

[*Pause*]

MAX: What will you do then?

HUBBARD: I'm to phone the Home Secretary personally. He's standing by for my call now.

MAX: And Mrs. Wendice?

HUBBARD: Will have nothing else to fear . . .

[*There are three thumps on the ceiling.* MAX *and* MARGOT *stand up.* HUBBARD *switches off the lights and stands by the telephone facing hall. Long silence*]

MAX: [*Gently*] All right, Margot?

MARGOT: [*In a whisper*] Yes—I'm all right.

[MAX *puts his arms around* MARGOT]

HUBBARD: [*Softly*] Quiet, now, you two. [*There is another long silence and then the sound of the street door opening and shutting. Footsteps to hall door. Pause. Sound of key in lock. It doesn't fit. Long pause. Footsteps moving back to front door. Slam.* MAX *gives a start. He opens bedroom door and peeps through. In whisper:*] Careful!

MAX: He's going round by the garden. He'll see the broken glass.

HUBBARD: Ssssh!

[*Pause*]

MAX: [*In a low whisper*] He's coming back.

HUBBARD: He's remembered.

> [*Long pause.* MAX *closes bedroom door silently and returns to* MARGOT. *Sound of street door opening and footsteps along passage to hall door. Silence for a few seconds. . . . Then sound of key in door. The door opens and* TONY *enters. He is carrying* HUBBARD'S *raincoat,* MARGOT'S *handbag and some books. He stands silhouetted in the doorway and stares at the key in the door. Then he takes it out thoughtfully and stares back at the fifth step of the staircase, and then looks back at the key in his hand. Then he switches on the light and with his back to the audience closes the door shut, then turns and walks into the room. After several paces he sees* MARGOT *and* MAX, *stares at* MARGOT *for a long moment and then drops the books and the handbag to the ground. Then he turns and sees* HUBBARD. *Suddenly he throws away his raincoat and rushes to the hall door in a panic. He opens the hall door but a* DETECTIVE *in plain clothes moves in from the left and blocks his way.* TONY *turns back into the room and stares at* MARGOT. MARGOT *turns her head away from* TONY *and toward* MAX. HUBBARD *looks* TONY *up and down for a moment, then moves very slowly to the telephone and dials a number*]

CURTAIN

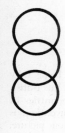

Sleuth

ANTHONY SHAFFER

Anthony Shaffer

On the evening of February 12, 1970, Anthony Shaffer was best known to Londoners as a television writer, an occasional novelist, and perhaps most of all as the twin brother of one of Britain's leading modern dramatists, Peter Shaffer. By the end of that same evening, however, Anthony Shaffer had vanquished his secondary status; when the curtain rang down at the St. Martin's on the final moment of *Sleuth*, his initial West End play, there was unequivocal evidence that an outstanding new dramatist had emerged from the wings. Here indeed was a playwright of major resources whose ingenious plotting was complemented by an impressive hand at creating singular characters and honing dialogue to its wittiest, most chillingly effective, "where laughter and the scent of horror are intriguingly harnessed together."

Mr. Shaffer's first-night triumph was promulgated in the British press by a series of dazzling notices. Felix Barker of the London *Evening News* hailed *Sleuth* as "the most ingenious detective play we have seen for years." Harold Hobson, the dean of English theatre critics, proclaimed in *The Sunday Times*: "Anthony Shaffer's *Sleuth* is an outstanding example of the thriller considered as a fine art. . . . It treats the conventional detective story with a Peacockian Gothic mockery, with a baroque juxtaposition of exotic phrases, an amused frenzy of alliteration, a cool mastery of impermissible insult: and simultaneously it is both exciting and endlessly surprising. *Sleuth* is a play to see, to be astonished by, and to brood over."

Described by *Variety* as "a smart, gripping and civilized murder yarn which also is a slick parody of the popular type of detective whodunit novel of the thirties," *Sleuth* became an instantaneous London success, breaking all box-office records at the half-century-old St. Martin's Theatre. Fourteen foreign productions soon followed, and on November 12, 1970, the play had its New York première at the Music Box Theatre, with the original stars, Anthony Quayle and Keith Baxter, repeating their widely acclaimed performances as, respectively, Andrew Wyke and Milo Tindle. According to the press, the three other cast members either performed their tasks "admirably" or had "missed their cues." Since their stage existence is handled by the author in a very special way and is an integral component of the play's unique design, the editor must herewith abstain from further comment.

The Shaffer twins were born in Liverpool, England, on May 15, 1926. Their first nine years were spent, as Peter has described it, in "a nice, middle-class neighborhood," and then their father, who was in real estate, moved the family of five (a third son, Brian, was born in 1929) to London in 1935. At the outbreak of World War II, to ensure the children's safety and to accommodate the sudden decentralization of the father's real-estate business, there followed a whole series of moves, terminated by the enrollment of Anthony and Peter at St. Paul's, a highly regarded public school "with a fine academic reputation, comparable to Eton but with none of that English public school snobbery." Their studies were interrupted in 1944 when, instead of being drafted into the armed forces, the brothers were conscripted for service as coal miners. After a grueling tour of duty in the mines of Kent and Yorkshire, they were released and Anthony, as well as Peter, entered Cambridge University.

Anthony came down from Cambridge (where he was editor of the university magazine, *Granta*) in 1950. He then became a barrister, but the lure of writing persisted. After several years of poring over legal briefs and documents, he decided to enter journalism and started writing commercials and documentaries and, for a while, had his own advertising agency.

It was during this period that Anthony Shaffer also began to write plays, principally for television, and collaborated with Peter on a mystery novel, *How Doth the Little Crocodile?* which was published in England under the pseudonym "Peter Anthony." Later, when the novel was issued in the United States, it appeared under their individual names and was followed by a second collaborative suspense effort: *Withered Murder.*

Although genuine recognition and acclaim as a playwright came more than a decade later to Anthony than it did to Peter, the careers of the Shaffer twins have provided some striking parallels. Peter's initial West End play, *Five Finger Exercise*, produced in 1958, became an immediate success in London and abroad and established him as a dramatist of the first rank. It ran in the West End for 607 performances and brought forth a citation as the year's "best play by a new playwright," in a poll of London newspaper reviewers. In 1970, Anthony sprang to international success and prominence with *his* first West End play, *Sleuth*, which earned for *him* a citation as the year's "most promising playwright," in *Variety*'s annual poll of London theatre critics. And as a further parallel, Peter's newest play, *The Battle of Shrivings*, preceded the West End première of Anthony's *Sleuth* by exactly one week.

In addition to maintaining a creative eye on the worldwide fortunes of *Sleuth*, Mr. Shaffer (who is married to former model Carolyn Soley and has two young daughters) has been busy as a screen writer. His first endeavor, *Fourbush and the Penguins*, recently was filmed on location in the Antarctic. He also has completed the screenplays for *Play with a Gypsy* (an intellectual thriller); *Masada*, scheduled for production in Israel; and *Black Comedy*, the cinematic version of Peter's celebrated stage play.

Shortly after *Sleuth* settled into its long and prosperous West End run, Michael Billington, in his coverage for *Plays and Players* magazine, observed: "To find a thriller that is both funny and adroit is rare enough to make any self-respecting critic chew his homburg with ecstasy. . . . In fact, *Sleuth* is so agreeably expert that it leaves one wondering why the stage-thriller has virtually disappeared."

An indisputable truth, the latter, for until now it was left to a diminishing handful of skillful creators to perpetuate this exacting and highly intricate form of drama. Yet, as Shakespeare sagely once set down, "there's a time for all things," and perhaps the advent of Anthony Shaffer at this crucial moment in theatre history will come as a restorative balm to the stage thriller, a dramatic form that has intrigued, captivated, and entertained playgoers for more than a century.

Sleuth was first produced by Michael White at the St. Martin's Theatre, London, on February 12, 1970. The cast was as follows:

ANDREW WYKE	*Anthony Quayle*
MILO TINDLE	*Keith Baxter*
INSPECTOR DOPPLER	*Stanley Rushton*
DETECTIVE SERGEANT TARRANT	*Robin Mayfield*
POLICE CONSTABLE HIGGS	*Liam McNulty*
Directed by	Clifford Williams
Designed by	Carl Toms
Lighting by	Francis Reid

Sleuth had its New York première on November 12, 1970, at the Music Box Theatre, under the auspices of Helen Bonfils, Morton Gottlieb, and Michael White. The cast was as follows:

ANDREW WYKE	*Anthony Quayle*
MILO TINDLE	*Keith Baxter*
INSPECTOR DOPPLER	*Philip Farrar*
DETECTIVE SERGEANT TARRANT	*Harold K. Newman*
POLICE CONSTABLE HIGGS	*Roger Purnell*

Directed by	Clifford Williams
Designed by	Carl Toms
Lighting by	William Ritman

SCENE: *Andrew Wyke's country home in Wiltshire, England.*

ACT ONE

A summer evening.

ACT TWO

Two days later.

ACT ONE

The living room of Andrew Wyke's Norman Manor House in Wiltshire, England. It is stone flagged, and a tall window runs the height of the back wall. It is divided laterally by a minstrels gallery which, in turn, is approached by a winding staircase. A wardrobe, stage left, and a grandfather clock, and bureau stage right stand on the gallery. Upstage right is the hallway leading to the unseen front door. Upstage left a corridor leads into another part of the house. Standing in this corridor is a large basket hamper. Games of all kinds adorn the room, ranging in complexity from chess, draughts and checkers, to early dice and card games and even earlier blocking games like Senat and Nine Men Morris. Sitting by the window, under the gallery, is a life-size figure of a "Laughing Sailor."

A summer evening. ANDREW WYKE, *is sitting at his desk, typing. He is a strongly built, tall, fleshy man of fifty-seven, gone slightly to seed. His fair hair carries on it the suspicion that chemical aid has been invoked to keep the gray at bay. His face, sourly amused and shadowed with evaded self-knowledge, is beginning to reflect the absence of constant, arduous employment. He wears a smoking jacket and black tie.*

The clock strikes eight o'clock. ANDREW *turns to look at clock, finishes typing, takes the page from the typewriter and begins to read.*

ANDREW: "Since you appear to know so much, Lord Merridew, sir," said the Inspector humbly, "I wonder if you could explain just how the murderer managed to leave the body of his victim in the middle of the tennis court, and effect his escape without leaving any tracks behind him in the red dust. Frankly, sir, we in the Police Force are just plain baffled. There seems no way he could have done it, short of black magic." St. John Lord Merridew, the great detective, rose majestically, his huge Father Christmas face glowing with mischievous delight. Slowly he brushed the crumbs of seedy cake from the folds of his pendulous waistcoat. "The police may be baffled, Inspector," he boomed, "but Merridew is not. It's all a question of a little research and a little ratiocination. Thirty years ago, the murderer, Doctor Grayson, was a distinguished member of the *Ballets Russes*, dancing under the name of Oleg Graysinski. The years may have altered his appearance, but his old skill had not deserted him. He carried the body out to the center of the tennis court, walking on his points along the white tape which divides the service boxes. From there he threw it five feet into the court, toward the base line, where it was found, and then, with a neatly executed fouetté, faced about and returned the way he had come, thus leaving no traces. There, Inspector, that is Merridew's solution."

[*He picks up his drink*]

Splendid! Absolutely splendid! Merridew loses none of his cunning, I'm glad to say. He's as neat *and* as gaudy as ever he was.

[*The doorbell rings.* ANDREW *finishes his drink slowly, then exits to hallway*]

ANDREW: [*Offstage, in hall*] Oh, hullo. Good evening. Milo Tindle? is it?

MILO: [*Offstage, in hall*] Yes. Mr. Wyke?

ANDREW: Yes. Do come in, won't you?

MILO: Thank you.

[*The front door is heard to close.* ANDREW *walks back into the room followed by* MILO TINDLE. *He is about thirty-five, slim, dark-haired and of medium height. He has a sharp, sallow face alive with a faintly Mediterranean wariness. Everything about him is neat, from his exactly parted hair to the squared-off white handkerchief in the breast pocket of his blue mohair suit*]

ANDREW: Let me take your coat.

[ANDREW *hangs coat on coatrack*]

Did you find the entrance to the lane all right?

MILO: Yes.

[MILO *walks about surveying room*]

ANDREW: Well done. Most people go straight past it. It's very nice of you to come.

MILO: Not at all. I found your note when I got down from London this afternoon.

ANDREW: Oh good. I pushed it through your letter box.

MILO: Er . . . What's this? [*He indicates the figure of the "Laughing Sailor"*]

ANDREW: Oh, that's Jolly Jack Tar the Jovial Sailor. He and I have a very good relationship. I make the jokes and he laughs. [*He moves the sailor's head manually*] You see, ha-ha-ha! Now let me get you a drink. [*He crosses to drinks table*] What will you have? Scotch, gin, vodka?

MILO: Scotch.

ANDREW: How do you like it? Soda, water, ice?

MILO: Just ice. And what's this?

[MILO *has crossed to a table on which there is a large game*]

ANDREW: Oh, that's a game.

MILO: A child's game? [*He picks up one of the pieces*]

ANDREW: It's anything but childish, I can assure you. I've been studying it for months, and I'm still only a novice. It's called Senat, played by the ancient Egyptians. It's an early blocking game, not unlike our own Nine Men Morris. Would you mind putting that back where you found it? It's taken me a long time to get it there. How are you settling in at Laundry Cottage?

MILO: Very well.

ANDREW: Using it for weekends, that sort of thing?

MILO: Yes, that's the sort of thing.

ANDREW: It's a charming little place. Well, cheers.

MILO: Cheers.

ANDREW: Now do come and sit down. Forgive me if I just tidy up a bit. I've just reached the denouement of my new book. "The Body On the Tennis Court." Tell me, would you agree that the detective story is the normal recreation of noble minds?

MILO: Who said that?

ANDREW: Oh, I'm quoting Philip Guedalla. A biographer of the thirties. The golden age when every cabinet minister had a thriller by his bedside, and all the detectives were titled. Before your time, I expect.

MILO: Perhaps it would have been truer to say that noble minds were the normal recreation of detective story writers.

ANDREW: Yes. Good point. You know, even in these days I still set my own work among the gentry. And a great number of people enjoy it, in spite of the Welfare State.

MILO: I'm surprised they haven't done any of your stuff on television.

ANDREW: Oh, God forbid!

MILO: Well, they're always doing crime stories.

ANDREW: What—you mean those ghastly things where the police race around in cars and call all the suspects chummy?

MILO: Yes. That's the kind of thing.

ANDREW: Oh, no. That's not my line of country at all. That is detective fact, not detective fiction.

MILO: And of course as such is of much less interest to noble minds.

ANDREW: Yes, yes, you've put it in a nutshell, my dear Milo, if I may so address you.

MILO: Of course.

ANDREW: Thank you, we need to be friendly. Now do sit down and let me get you another drink. I'm one up on you already.

> [MILO *starts to sit in chair below staircase.* ANDREW *moves to drinks table*]

I understand you want to marry my wife.

> [A *pause.* MILO *is disconcerted by the directness of the question*]

You'll forgive me raising the matter, but as Marguerite is away for a few days, she's up in the North you know, visiting some relatives . . .

MILO: Is she?

ANDREW: Yes, so I thought it an appropriate time for a little chat.

MILO: Yes.

ANDREW: Well, is it true?

MILO: Well . . . Well, yes, with your permission of course.

ANDREW: Oh, yes, of course. [*He crosses to* MILO *with his drink*] Zere, put zat behind your necktie.

MILO: Cheers.

ANDREW: Prost. [*He stands in front of fireplace*] Yes, I'm glad to see you're not like so many young men these days, seem to think they can do anything they like without asking anyone's permission.

MILO: Certainly not.

ANDREW: Good. I'm pleased to hear it. I know you won't object then if I ask you a few questions about your parents and so on.

MILO: My mother was born in Hereford, a farmer's daughter. My father is an Italian who came to this country in the thirties.

ANDREW: Jewish?

MILO: Half, on his mother's side, that for the Fascists was the important side. The male, they felt, didn't transmit the disease so virulently.

ANDREW: [*Tut-tutting*] Dreadful business, dreadful.

MILO: Of course I'm not at all religious myself, I'm an agnostic.

ANDREW: [*Crosses to center of room*] My dear boy, you don't have to explain to me. We're all liberals here. I have no prejudice against Jews, or even half-Jews. Why some of my best friends are half-Jews . . . Mind you, I hope you have no objections to any children that you and my wife may have being brought up Church of England?

MILO: None whatsoever if that's what Marguerite wants.

ANDREW: You haven't discussed it yet?

MILO: Not yet, it doesn't seem to have cropped up.

ANDREW: Well, I suppose in some ways that's rather a relief. But if you take my advice you'll opt for C. of E. It's so much simpler. A couple of hours on Christmas Eve and Good Friday and you've seen the whole thing off nicely. And if you throw in Remembrance

Sunday, they give you the Good Christian medal with oak leaf cluster.

MILO: It's the same with a lot of Jews. My father used to say, "Most people only talk to their really old friends two or three times a year. Why should God be angry if He gets the same treatment?"

ANDREW: [*Insincerely*] Very amusing. Your father? Was his name Tindle? It doesn't sound very Italian.

MILO: His name was Tindolini. But if you had a name like that in England in those days you had to make "a-da-nice cream." He was a watchmaker and so he changed it.

ANDREW: Was he a successful man?

MILO: No. His business failed. He went back to Italy. I send him money from time to time and go and visit him and get a little sun or skiing, depending, of course, on the season.

ANDREW: Ah!

MILO: It's not that I'm disloyal to Britain, you understand. It's just that the Cairngorms and Minehead don't offer the same attractions.

ANDREW: And you? What do you do?

MILO: I'm in the Travel business. I have my own agency in Dulwich.

ANDREW: Tindle's Travels, eh? I see, and where do you live?

MILO: I live above the office.

ANDREW: In Dulwich?

MILO: Yes, I rent the whole house. It's really most convenient, and . . . and it's most attractive, too. It's Georgian.

ANDREW: H'm, I'm sure it's perfectly delightful, but I doubt whether an eighteenth-century architectural gem in Dulwich whispers quite the same magic to Marguerite as it does to you.

MILO: She adores old houses. She can't wait to live there.

ANDREW: I understood she was *already* living there—at least for a couple of nights a week. I'm not mistaken, am I?

[MILO *shrugs in embarrassment*]

And surely your motive in renting the cottage down here was to increase the incidence of this hebdomadal coupling?

MILO: I came to be near the woman I love. It is a great pain for us to be apart. You wouldn't understand.

ANDREW: Possibly. But I understand Marguerite well enough to know that she does not adore old houses. She's lived here quite a time, and between them the rising damp and the deathwatch beetle have put the boot into her good and proper. She's only got to see a mullioned window and it brings her out in lumps.

MILO: [Hotly] Perhaps it wasn't the house so much as the person she had to share it with!

ANDREW: Now, now. I thought you were well brought up. Surely you know it's very rude to make personal remarks.

MILO: I'm sorry. You were disparaging my lover.

ANDREW: On the contrary, I was reminiscing about my wife.

MILO: It comes to the same thing.

ANDREW: Things mostly do, you know. I'll wager that within a year, it's *you* who will be doing the disparaging, and I who will be doing the rhapsodizing, having quite forgotten how intolerably tiresome, vain, spendthrift, self-indulgent and generally bloody crafty she *really* is.

MILO: If you don't love Marguerite, you don't have to abuse her!

ANDREW: Never speak ill of the deadly, eh?

MILO: Now look here . . .

ANDREW: If I choose to say that my wife converses like a child of six, cooks like a Brightlingsea landlady, and makes love like a coelacanth, I shall.

MILO: That's just about enough . . .

ANDREW: And I certainly don't need her lover's permission to do so either! In fact, the only thing I need to know from you is, can you *afford* to take her off my hands?

MILO: Afford to . . .

ANDREW: Afford to support her in the style to which she *wasn't* accustomed before she met me, but now is.

MILO: [Gestures around the room] She won't need all this when *we're* married. It'll be a different life—a life of love and simplicity. Now go ahead—sneer at that! It's almost a national sport in this country—sneering at love.

ANDREW: I don't have to sneer at it. I simply don't *believe* you. For Marguerite, love is the fawning of a willing lap dog, and simplicity, a square-cut ten-carat diamond from Van Cleef and Arpels.

[MILO *rises and goes to drinks table to put down glass*]

MILO: I don't know what I'm doing here. With a little effort, I'm sure you could find a much more appreciative audience!

ANDREW: Oh, now, Milo. You disappoint me. Rising to your feet like that and *bridling*.

MILO: [*Abashed*] I wasn't bridling. I was *protesting*.

ANDREW: It looked like a good old-fashioned Hedy Lamarr bridle to me.

MILO: [*Turning to* ANDREW] Who?

ANDREW: Oh, very good! Very good! Why don't you just sit down and we'll talk about something that matters desperately to both of us.

MILO: Marguerite?

ANDREW: Money! Have you got any?

MILO: Well, I'm not a millionaire, but I've got the lease on the house and some capital equipment, and the turnover in the business this year has been growing every month. By this time next year, I . . .

ANDREW: This year, next year, sometime never. What you're saying in fact is that at present you're skint.

MILO: I'll survive.

ANDREW: I'm sure you will, but survival is not the point. Presumably, when you're married to Marguerite you'll want a fast car, a little place in the sun, and a couple of mistresses.

MILO: Why "presumably?" Just because you need those things.

ANDREW: Certainly I do. And so does every right-thinking, insecure, deceitful man. The point is *how* to get them. [*He moves to drinks table*]

MILO: I'm sure you do all right. [*He crosses to fireplace*]

ANDREW: Me? Oh NO. Just this fading mansion, the slowest Lagonda in Wiltshire, and only one mistress, I'm afraid.

MILO: Tēa? The Finnish lady who runs the Sauna Bath at Swindon.

ANDREW: Oh, so you know about her, do you?

MILO: Marguerite and I have no secrets from each other.

ANDREW: Not even mine, it seems. [*Mock mystical*] Tēa is a Karelian Goddess. Her mother was Ilma, supreme divinity of the air; her father was Jumala, the great Creator. Her golden hair smells of pine, and her cobalt eyes are the secret forest pools of Finlandia.

MILO: I hear she's a scrubbed blonde with all the sex appeal of chilled Dettol.

ANDREW: [*With dignity*] There are those who believe that cleanliness is next to sexiness. And if I were you, I wouldn't pay much attention to what Marguerite says. You can take it from me that Tēa's an engaging little trollop, and she suits me mightily. Mind you, she takes a bit of keeping up with, it's a good thing I'm pretty much of an Olympic sexual athlete.

MILO: I suppose these days you're concentrating on the sprints rather than the long distance stuff.

ANDREW: Not so, dear boy. [*He sits*] I'm in the pink of condition. I could copulate for England at any distance.

MILO: Well, they do say, in Olympic circles, that the point is to take part, rather than to win, so I suppose there's hope for us all. Are you going to marry her?

ANDREW: Marry a Goddess? I wouldn't presume. I might get turned into a birch tree for my audacity. Oh, no, I simply want to live with her.

MILO: So what's stopping you?

ANDREW: Basically the firm of Prurient and Pry Ltd., whom you and Marguerite have seen fit to employ. Don't look so innocent. Those Woodbine-stained private detectives who've been camping outside Tēa's flat for the last week.

MILO: [*Crossing to center of room*] So you spotted them?

ANDREW: A Bantu with glaucoma couldn't have missed them. No one can read the *Evening News* for four hours in a Messerschmitt bubble car, and expect to remain undetected.

MILO: Sorry about that. It was Marguerite's idea.

ANDREW: Who else's? Who paid?

MILO: I did.

ANDREW: I wonder you could afford it.

MILO: It was an insurance policy against you changing your mind about divorcing Marguerite.

ANDREW: My dear boy, let us have no misunderstanding. I've nothing against you marrying Marguerite. There's nothing I want more than to see you two tucked up together. But it's got to be a fixture. I want to be rid of her for life, not just a two-week Tindle Tour,

economy class. No, you listen to me. You don't know her like I do.
You think you do, but you don't. The real truth of the matter is
that if you fail her, by which I mean canceling the account at Har-
rods, or shortchanging her on winter in Jamaica, she'll be back to
me in a jiffy mewing for support—and guilty wife or no, she may
be entitled to get it.

MILO: Don't be so bloody pathetic. Winter in Jamaica? I'm not going
to take her for winter in Jamaica. You're worrying unnecessarily.
Once Marguerite is married to me she'll never think of returning
to you. Never. And don't worry about my being able to look after
her either.

ANDREW: I see. You mean as soon as you and she are married, Marguerite will joyously exchange Cartiers for the Co-op?

MILO: So she's used to luxury. Whose fault is that?

ANDREW: It's not a fault if you can afford it. But can you? Knowing
you to be hard up has she shown any sign of mending her ways in
these last idyllic three months? When did she last turn down
Bolinger for the blandishments of Babycham? Or reject crêpes
suzette in favor of roly-poly? No, no I'm not joking, how much has
this brief liaison cost you so far? Five hundred pounds? Eight
hundred pounds? One thousand pounds? And that father of yours
in Italy, when did you last send him any money? You see why I'm
concerned. I tell you. She'll ruin you. To coin a phrase, in two
years you'll be a used gourd. And what's more, a used gourd with a
sizable overdraft.

MILO: We've often talked about money. I've told her we spend too
much.

ANDREW: And she takes no notice?

MILO: [Low] None.

ANDREW: A silvery laugh? A coquettish turn of the head?

MILO: Something like that.

ANDREW: Exactly. Well, it's to solve this little problem that I have
invited you here tonight. This, as they say, is where the plot
thickens.

MILO: Ah!

ANDREW: I'll get you another drink. [He crosses to drinks table. In
"Listen with Mother" style] Are you sitting comfortably? Then

I'll begin. Once upon a time there was an Englishman called Andrew Wyke who, in common with most of his countrymen, was
virtually castrated by taxation. To avoid total emasculation, his
accountants advised him, just before the last devaluation, to put
a considerable part of his money, some 135,000 pounds, into jewelry. His wife, of course, was delighted.

MILO: You made her a present of it?

ANDREW: Absolutely not. It's still mine, as well she knows. But we
felt she might as well wear it, as bank it. After all, it's fully insured.

MILO: I see what you mean by the plot thickening. It usually does
when insurance is mentioned.

ANDREW: I'm glad you follow me so readily. I want you to steal that
jewelry.

MILO: [Astounded] What?

ANDREW: Tonight, for choice. Marguerite is out of the house. It's an
admirable opportunity.

MILO: You must be joking.

ANDREW: You would know it if I were.

MILO: [Playing for time] But . . . But what about the servants?

ANDREW: I've sent Mr. and Mrs. Hawkins to Weston-super-Mare for
a forty-eight-hour paddle. They won't be back till Sunday night.
So, the house is empty.

MILO: I see.

ANDREW: What do you say?

MILO: It sounds criminal.

ANDREW: Of course it's criminal. All good money-making schemes in
England have got to be these days. The jewelry, when it's not in
the bank, lives in the safe under the stairs. It's there now. All you
have to do is steal them, and sell them abroad and live happily ever
after with Marguerite. All I have to do is to claim the insurance
money and live happily ever after with Téa. [Pause] Well, in my
case perhaps, not ever after, but at least until I get fed up with a
cuisine based on the elk.

MILO: Is that what you asked me over to hear? A scummy little plot
to defraud the insurance company?

ANDREW: I'm sorry you find the plot scummy. I thought it was nicely
clear and simple.

MILO: Nicely obvious and clearly unworkable. Supposing I do as you say and take the jewels. If I sell them under my own name I'll be picked up just as soon as you report their loss. If I sell them to a fence, always supposing I could find one, I'd get a fraction of their value.

ANDREW: Not with the fences I know.

MILO: [Derisory] What fences would you know?

ANDREW: I know some of the finest fences in Europe. Prudent yet prodigal. I met them some years ago while researching "The Deadly Affair of the Druce Diamond."

MILO: Never read it.

ANDREW: Pity, it was an absolute fizzer—sold a hundred thousand copies. Anyway, on your behalf I have already contacted a certain gentleman in Amsterdam. He will treat you very well; you won't get full value of the jewels but you will get two-thirds, say ninety thousand pounds, and you'll get it in cash.

MILO: Why should this man be so generous?

ANDREW: Because he will have what fences never have—title to the jewels. I will see to it that in addition to the jewels, you also steal the receipts I got for them. All you have to do is hand them over together. Now what does my insurance company discover when it swings into action, antennae pulsing with suspicion? It discovers that someone impersonating Andrew Wyke sold the jewels for ninety thousand pounds cash. They've still got to pay me. Hard cheese. Think it over. Take your time. There's no hurry.

[A pause. MILO considers the proposition. ANDREW walks away from MILO, humming lightly to himself. He stops by a roll-a-penny wall game and plays it to a successful con-clusion. MILO paces up and down, indecisive. He suddenly turns and faces ANDREW]

MILO: Look, I know this sounds stupid, but . . . but well, have you had any experience—I mean, have you ever actually committed a crime before?

ANDREW: Only in the mind's eye, so to speak. For the purpose of my books. St. John Lord Merridew would have a pretty lean time of it if I didn't give him any crime to solve.

MILO: Who?

ANDREW: My detective, St. John Lord Merridew. Known to millions all over the civilized world. "An ambulatory tun of port with the face of Father Christmas." That's how I describe him. "A classical scholar with a taste for good pipes and bad puns, but with a nose for smelling out evil, superior to anything, in the force."

MILO: Oh, yes, the police are always stupid in your kind of story, aren't they? They never solve anything. Only an amateur sleuth ever knows what's happening. But that is detective fiction. This is fact.

ANDREW: I am aware of the difference, Milo. I also know that insurance investigators are sharp as razors, and that's why, as they say in the athenaeum, everything's got to be done kosher and according to cocker.

MILO: I'm just saying there's a difference between writing and real life, that's all. And there's another thing. How do I know this thing isn't one big frame-up?

ANDREW: Frame-up?

MILO: Yes. That you really hate my association with your wife, and would give five years of Olympian sexual athleticism to see me in jail. Once I'm clear of the house, an anonymous phone call to the police . . .

ANDREW: And be stuck with Marguerite for another bickering eternity? Bodystockings on the breakfast tray, false eyelashes in the washbasin, the bottles, the lotions, the unguents, the oils, the tribal record player and that ceaseless vapid yak. Oh, yes, I could shop you to the police, nothing easier, but whatever for? Still, it's for you to evaluate, old boy.

MILO: Well, I . . . I, er . . .

ANDREW: If you don't trust me . . .

MILO: Oh, I trust you, but . . .

ANDREW: It's a very simple proposition. You have an expensive woman and no money. It seems to me if you want to keep Marguerite there is only one thing you can do—you must steal those jewels.

MILO: Why don't *you* steal them and simply hand them over to me?

ANDREW: I should have thought that was obvious. The burglary has to look real. The house has actually to be broken into.

MILO: Well, why don't *you* break into it?

ANDREW: [*Brooklyn accent*] Hey, Milo baby, will you do me a favor. Leave this to me, huh? You know what I mean? Crime is my speciality. I've got such a great plan and I've got it all worked out to the last detail. You're the star, I'm just the producer.

MILO: Ninety thousand pounds?

ANDREW: Ninety thousand pounds tax free. In cash. It would take a lot of Tindle Tours to make that kind of money.

MILO: All right, I'll do it. Where shall I break in?

[MILO *rushes for the stairs*]

ANDREW: Hold your horses. Now the first thing you've got to do is disguise yourself.

MILO: What on earth for?

ANDREW: Supposing someone saw you climbing in.

MILO: Who? You're not overlooked.

ANDREW: Who knows? A dallying couple. A passing sheep rapist. And, dear boy, remember the clues we're to leave for the police and the insurance company. We don't want your footsteps in the flower beds, or your coat button snagged on the window sill. Oh, no, you *must* be disguised!

MILO: All right, what do you suggest?

ANDREW: [*He crosses to corridor and brings back a large hamper*] As Marguerite has assuredly told you, in younger days we were always dressing up in this house. What with amateur dramatics and masquerades and costume balls, there was virtually no end to the concealment of identity.

MILO: She's never mentioned it.

ANDREW: No . . . ? [*A touch wistful*] Well, it was all some years ago. [*Briskly*] Anyway, let's see what we've got. [*He opens basket and holds up the pieces of the burglar suit, one by one*] Item. A face mask, a flat cap, a striped jersey and bag marked Swag.

MILO: I thought the idea was that I was *not* to be taken as a burglar?

ANDREW: Fashions have changed, you know.

MILO: Not quickly enough. It's asking for trouble.

[ANDREW *puts the costume back and brings out a Ku Klux Klan outfit*]

ANDREW: Ku Klux Klan invade country home. Fiery cross, flames on Salisbury plain. Police baffled.

MILO: Isn't it a trifle conspicuous for Wiltshire?

ANDREW: Yes, you may be right! [*Holds up a monk's costume*] Here is one of my favorites. How about Father Lightfingers?

MILO: Oh, for God's sake . . .

[MILO *shakes his head decisively*]

ANDREW: Oh, come on. Let's make this a Gothic folly. [*Edgar Lustgarten voice*] Perhaps we shall never know the identity of the cowled figure seen haunting the grounds of the Manor House on the night of the terrible murder. Even today, some locals claim to hear the agonized screams of the victim echoing around the chimney pots.

MILO: Murder? Anguished screams of the victim? What are you talking about? It's a simple robbery we're staging here, that's all.

[*An uneasy pause*]

ANDREW: [*Normal voice*] Quite right, Milo. I was carried away for a moment. I'm not sure I wasn't going to add a crucified countess entombed in her bedroom, guarded by a man eating sparrow hawk.

MILO: Look here, Andrew, you probably think this is one huge joke. But it's my freedom you're playing with.

ANDREW: I'm merely trying to bring a little romance into modern crime, and incidentally into your life.

MILO: Marguerite will bring all the romance into my life I need, thank you all the same.

ANDREW: Marguerite romantic? Marguerite couldn't have got Johann Strauss to waltz!

MILO: Look, Andrew, these are great costumes, but haven't you just got an old pair of wellies, a raincoat, and a sock that I can pull over my head?

ANDREW: Old pair of wellies and a sock? How dreary! That's the whole trouble with crime today. No imagination. I mean, you tell me, does your heart beat any faster when you hear that a lorry load of cigarettes has been knocked off in the Walworth Road?

MILO: Not particularly.

ANDREW: Well, of course not. Or that a ninety-three-year-old night watchman has had his silly interfering old skull split open with a lead pipe?

MILO: Of course not.

ANDREW: Well then, what's the matter with you? Where's your spunk? Let's give our crime the true sparkle of the thirties, a little amateur aristocratic quirkiness. Think of all that wonderful material! There's the ice-dagger, the poison that leaves no trace, the Regie cigarette stubbed in the ash tray, charred violet notepaper in the grate, Dusenberg tire marks in the driveway, the gramophone record simulating conversation, the clutching hand from behind the arras, sinister Orientals, twin brothers from Australia— "Hi there, cobber, hi there, blue"—where were you on the night of the thirteenth? I swear I didn't do it, Inspector, I'm innocent I tell you, innocent . . .

MILO: God, you've gone off like a firecracker!

ANDREW: And why not? We're on the brink of a great crime. Don't you feel the need to give your old archenemy, Inspector Plodder of the Yard, a run for his money? And you're the *star*, you're the *who-what-dun-it!*

MILO: Well, what about this? [*He holds up courtier's costume*]

ANDREW: Ah! Monsieur Beaucaire. He's very good. Lots of beauty spots and wig powder to let fall all over the place. Or what about this? Little Bo Peep?

> [ANDREW *sings "Little Bo Peep" and dances about holding up the costume*]

MILO: No.

ANDREW: Why not?

MILO: I haven't got the figure for it.

ANDREW: Are you quite sure? An indifferent figure shouldn't materially affect the execution of this crime.

MILO: Quite sure.

ANDREW: Well, you are choosey, aren't you? There's not a great deal left. [*He pulls out a clown's costume. Large pantaloons, waiter's dicky, tail coat*] We'll have to settle for "Joey."

MILO: Wow!

ANDREW: Can't you see it all, the tinsel, the glitter, the lights, the liberty horses, the roar of the crowd, and Milo, all the kiddies love you.

MILO: [*Happily*] All right! It seems the costume most appropriate to this scheme.

ANDREW: Well, give me your coat. I'll hang it up for you. We don't want the police to find any fibers of this beautiful suit.

> [MILO *takes off his jacket and gives it to* ANDREW]

Oh, and the shirt and trousers too.

MILO: What?

ANDREW: Oh, yes, you know how clever they are in those laboratories of theirs. That's it. Don't be shy. Into your smalls. Oh, I know a well-brought-up boy when I see one. Folds his pants at night.

> [MILO *gives him his carefully folded trousers.* ANDREW *runs up the stairs, and with a sudden violent gesture, roughly throws the suit into the wardrobe, while* MILO *takes off his shirt and tie and shoes*]

MILO: Shirt and shoes.

> [MILO *holds up his shirt, shoes, and tie*]

ANDREW: Very good, sir. The Quick Clean Valet Service always at your disposal, sir. [*He pushes them into the wardrobe, then watches* MILO *changing with great satisfaction. Softly*] Give a clown your finger and he'll take your hand.

MILO: What was that?

ANDREW: Just an old English proverb I was thinking of.

> [MILO *sings to himself* "On With the Motley" *and ends it with* "Ninety-thousand pounds tax free, in cash" *as he dresses*]

MILO: Ecco, Milo!

ANDREW: Bravissimo! Now all you need are the boots.

[MILO *pulls a huge pair of boots from the basket*]

MILO: Hey, I could go skiing on these when I go to Italy!

ANDREW: "The clown is such a happy chap,
His nose is painted red,
His trousers baggy as can be,
A topper on his head.
He jumps around the circus ring,
And juggles for his bread,
Then comes the day he tries a trick,
And drops down . . ."

Come on do us a trick.

MILO: What sort of trick?

ANDREW: Oh, I don't know. Trip up—fall on your arse.

MILO: Certainly not, I don't think that's a very good idea.

ANDREW: Well, what about a bit of juggling then.

[ANDREW *takes two oranges from the drinks table and throws them to* MILO. *He then produces an umbrella from the basket and throws it to* MILO *who opens it and runs around the room and finally trips up on his boots*]

MILO: Christ!

ANDREW: Sorry, dear boy. But you know the rule of the circus. If at first you don't succeed . . .

MILO: Give up. Can we get on with this charade, please!

ANDREW: Of course. Yours to command. [*He opens swag bag*] Here are the tools of your trade. One glass cutter to break in with; a piece of putty for holding on to the cut piece of glass so it doesn't clatter onto the floor and awake the ravenous Doberman pinscher you suspect lurks inside; and a stethoscope.

MILO: A stethoscope?

ANDREW: Safe breakers for the use of. The theory is you tried to pick the lock by listening to the tumblers, failed, and then employed gelignite.

MILO: [*Alarmed*] Gelignite?

ANDREW: Yes. Leave that to me. Now how about some bizarre touch

—say a signed photograph of Grock left impaled on a splinter of glass.

MILO: A signed photograph of Grock! [*Angry*] Why don't you take a full page ad in *The Times* and tell them what we're doing!

ANDREW: I was only trying to lighten Inspector Plodder's day for him . . . If you don't like the idea . . .

MILO: [*Earnestly*] There's no such animal as Inspector Plodder outside of books. It'll be Inspector Early Bird, or Superintendent No Stone Unturned. You can bet your bottom dollar on that. I can't walk in this costume. These boots are ridiculous. [*He stumbles and starts to take them off*]

ANDREW: Keep them on. Can't you see it all. Wiltshire paralyzed. The West Country in a ferment. Where will Big Boot strike next?

MILO: But . . .

ANDREW: [*Reasonably*] All these boots will tell the police is that a true professional realized the flower beds would carry footprints, and decided to disguise his own perhaps a trifle eccentrically. Now are you ready? Got everything? Glass cutter? Putty?

ANDREW: ⎱ The mask!
MILO: ⎰

[ANDREW *takes top hat and mask from basket*]

ANDREW: Good. Now go through that door, round the house and across the lawn. To your right you will discover a shed. In it is a ladder. Bring the ladder back and stand it against the house so you can climb up to the gallery.

MILO: Will you come out and hold it steady?

ANDREW: Certainly not. I don't want *my* footprints in the flower beds.

MILO: I'm not very good at heights.

ANDREW: Improvise. Place one foot above the other. It's called climbing.

MILO: O.K.

ANDREW: Good luck.

[MILO *bows and goes through the hall door.* ANDREW *takes a length of flex and black box with gelignite, black tape,*

and detonator from desk drawer. After a few minutes MILO
appears at window]

ANDREW: For Christ's sake, can't you keep those bloody boots off my
Busy Lizzies!

[MILO *disappears and presently reappears with the ladder
which he places against the window and starts to climb.*
ANDREW *sits with his back to the window and reacts to
the noises he hears. As he attaches the detonator to the
flex he speaks in an old woman's voice*]

Puss, Puss, Puss, do you hear a noise, Puss? Was that a step on
the stairs? No, it was just the wind. You know, Puss, I sometimes
think there's a curse on this house. But you shouldn't pay any
attention to me. I'm just a silly old woman who is afraid of her
own shadow.

[*Noise of glass cutter scoring window*]

What was that, Puss? Someone's prowling in the grounds. We're
all going to be murdered in our beds. No, no, the front door's
locked, and the window's too high, no one can get into our snug
little home.

[MILO *drops pane of glass*]

ANDREW: [*Rises, exasperated*] What *are* you doing now?
MILO: I dropped the glass.

[ANDREW *groans theatrically. After a further struggle* MILO
*succeeds in climbing in through the window, onto the
gallery*]

Whew! What do I do with the putty? [*He indicates the putty*]
ANDREW: Leave it where it is.
MILO: I can lose this at any rate. [*He puts mask on bureau*] Now
for the safe!
ANDREW: No. Not straight away. You're not meant to know where
they are. Search around. Go into the bedroom. Disturb a few
things. Throw some clothes on the floor—Marguerite's for choice
. . . That's it.

[MILO *goes into the bedroom and returns with a pile of women's clothes which he puts neatly on the floor*]

ANDREW: [*Rushes up to gallery*] Don't pack 'em. Ravage 'em. Don't you know how burglars leave a place? [*He takes a flying kick at the pile of his wife's clothes, sending them flying all over the room*] Now try the wardrobe. Rumple the contents a little. Actually that's enough. Those shirts were made for me by Baget & Grub, chemise makers to monarchs.

MILO: [*Throws the shirts out with relish*] Got to be thorough. It would be suspicious if the burglar played favorites.

[ANDREW's *socks and underwear follow, cascading out all over the gallery*]

ANDREW: Oh, it's a martyrdom. [*Shouting*] Will you stop that, Milo, and rifle that bureau immediately!

[*Reluctantly,* MILO *crosses to the bureau and tries a drawer*]

MILO: It's locked.

ANDREW: Of course it's bloody locked! Use your jimmy on it.

MILO: I haven't got a jimmy. You didn't give me one.

ANDREW: [*Exasperated*] Well, we'd better go and find one, hadn't we?

[*They tramp downstairs*]

Honestly, Milo, you are the soppiest night interloper I've ever met. I can't think what Marguerite sees in you.

MILO: The sympathy and kindness of a kindred spirit, actually.

ANDREW: It's like a Bengali tiger lying down with a Bush Baby.

MILO: I know we're a damn sight happier than you are with your ice maiden.

ANDREW: You probably take it more seriously, that's all.

MILO: You have to be serious if you want to be in love.

ANDREW: You have to be serious about crime if you want to *afford* to be in love. Now get cracking on that bureau.

[MILO *climbs the stairs. He starts work on the bureau with the jimmy. After a pause, the drawer yields and he opens it]*

MILO: There is a set of false teeth. They look like a man's.
ANDREW: [*Furious*] Put them back at once.
MILO: Sorry. Your spares?
ANDREW: [*Pause*] Come down at once.

> [MILO *comes down the stairs and crosses to* ANDREW *who has plugged the flex into a light switch*]

Keep your feet off the flex. Right, stand by for count down five-four-three-two-one. Contact!

> [*Noise of explosion and puff of smoke from safe*]

MILO: There she blows. Ah! It's hot.
ANDREW: You've got gloves on! Get in there!

> [MILO *rummages in the safe and finds a large jewel box. He examines it carefully, occasionally shaking it gently*]

What the hell are you shaking it for? It's a jewel box, not a maraca.
MILO: I thought it might have some secret catch on it. It's locked, you see.
ANDREW: Well, smash it open. Jesus! You've all the killer instinct of a twenty-year-old Sealyham.

> [MILO *attacks the box with his jimmy*]

MILO: It's such a pretty box—it seems such a waste.

> [*The box opens to reveal its precious contents.* MILO *stands entranced, letting the jewels flash and sparkle through his fingers*]

Dear God!
ANDREW: Ah! Moses looks upon the promised land.

> [MILO *sits at base of stairs*]

MILO: They're very beautiful. Look at this ruby necklace!
ANDREW: That we got on our honeymoon.
MILO: It's fantastic.

ANDREW: I never cared for it myself. I always thought it made Marguerite look like a blood sacrifice.

MILO: I'd like my father to be here now. Poor blighter, he had no idea what it was all about . . . sitting there every night hunched up over those watches like a little old gnome, squinting his eyesight away, and for what—to give me an education at a second-rate public school. I suppose he thought he had to do it—that he owed it to me and the brave new Anglo-Saxon world he'd adopted. Poor old bugger.

ANDREW: Here, put them in your pocket for a start. I'll get you the receipts in a moment. Now! This is the fun bit. It's the moment when the householder, his attention attracted by a noise upstairs, surprises his burglar. In the ensuing struggle, the house is sacked.

MILO: Why is it necessary for you to surprise me at all?

ANDREW: Because if I've seen you at close quarters, I can always describe you to the police . . .

[MILO *reacts as if hit*]

MILO: Now look here . . .

ANDREW: . . . Wrongly. [INSPECTOR's *voice*] Did you manage to get a good look at the intruder's face, sir? [*Normal voice*] Yes, Inspector, I did. It may just have been a trick of the light, but his face didn't look wholly human. If you can imagine a kind of prognathic stoat, fringed about with lilac colored hair, and seemingly covered with a sort of boot polish. . . .

MILO: [*Patiently*] I understand. How much sacking do you want done?

ANDREW: A decent bit, I think, a few chairs on their backs, some china ornaments put to the sword. You know—convincing but not Carthaginian.

[MILO *carefully turns a chair over and leans a small table against the sofa. He takes a china ornament and stands it upright on the floor.* ANDREW *watches impatiently*]

Surely you don't call that convincing?

[ANDREW *throws over another table, spills the contents of a drawer, and turns books out of his book case*]

That's better. Let the encyclopedias fly like autumn leaves . . . I never liked saltglaze. [*He drops a china ornament to the floor where it breaks*] I can't think why Marguerite is devoted to it.

[*The two men survey the room*]

It still doesn't look right. Come on. Let's see what accident does to artifice.

[ANDREW *seizes* MILO *and wrestles him round the room, overturning things as they go.* MILO, *apart from being the shorter, is much hampered by his big boots and floppy clown's clothing, so that* ANDREW *is able to pummel him severely*]

MILO: You're bigger than I am. It's not fair.
ANDREW: Nonsense. You're the underdog, aren't you? You've got the support of the crowd.
MILO: A good big 'un will always lick a good little 'un.
ANDREW: The bigger they are the harder they fall.

[MILO *receives a particularly hard blow*]

MILO: Here, steady on, old man!
ANDREW: They never come back. [*He pushes* MILO *over the fender into the fireplace*]
MILO: Christ! That hurt!

[ANDREW *helps him up*]

ANDREW: Come on, back into the ring. Don't despair. This fight is fixed. It's about now that I take a dive. This is where you lay me out cold.
MILO: What? For real?
ANDREW: Naturally. When the police come I must be able to show them a real bump.

[MILO *smiles weakly*]

I thought you'd like this bit.

[MILO *tentatively moves toward a lamp*]

MILO: What shall I use?

ANDREW: Not my opaline, if you don't mind.

[MILO *picks up the brass poker*]

MILO: This is it. The poker, the original blunt instrument. [*He beats logs viciously*]

ANDREW: [*Eyes the poker apprehensively*] Steady on, Milo. Don't get carried away.

MILO: Well, I'm doing my best.

ANDREW: We are not talking about a murder weapon. We are discussing an object from which I receive, in the classic formula, a glancing blow which renders me temporarily unconscious.

MILO: Such as?

ANDREW: Well, I don't know exactly. Why don't you use your imagination? Ask yourself what those fathers of the scientific detective story—R. Austin Freeman or Arthur B. Reeve—would have come up with.

MILO: Huh?

ANDREW: You know. *The Red Thumb Mark*, 1907. *The Silent Bullet*, 1912.

[MILO *still looks blank*]

Oh, do try . . . I know, perhaps we could think of a device which will raise a lump but not damage the cranium.

MILO: [*Trapped into joining in*] How about a bee sting projected into the scalp with a blowpipe?

ANDREW: Do you have such sting, pipe, or bee?

MILO: Well . . . no.

ANDREW: No. Still, seven out of ten for trying. I know, you can always tie me up and gag me and leave me to be found by the cleaning woman. [*Charlady's voice*] Lawks, Mr. Wyke, what are you doing all trussed up like a turkey cock? [*He mimes being tied up and gagged and tying to get the charlady to untie him*] Mmmmmmmmmmmmmm . . . Mmmmmmmmmmmm . . . Mmmmmmmmmmmm . . . [*Charlady's voice*] Trying out something for one of them creepy books of yours, are you, sir? Well, don't mind me. I won't disturb you. I'll just get on with the dusting.

MILO: [*Patiently*] If I don't knock you out, how do I manage to tie you up?

ANDREW: [*Normal voice*] That's a very good question. I know. You could hold a gun on me.

MILO: We professional burglars don't like firearms much.

ANDREW: But, as you're a rank amateur you can conquer your scruples. [*He produces a gun from the desk drawer*] Here. How about this? Don't you think its wicked-looking blue barrel is just the thing?

MILO: Is it loaded?

ANDREW: Naturally. What use would it be otherwise? Perhaps it should go off in the struggle.

MILO: Why?

ANDREW: It would add credence to my story of your holding a gun on me. Hearing a noise and fearing burglars, I took my revolver and went to investigate. You attacked me. In the struggle it went off. Being an old fraidy-cat householder, I allowed brutish you to take possession of it. You then held it on me while you tied me up. Right?

MILO: I suppose so.

ANDREW: Uninventive but believable. Now then, what to sacrifice? What do you say to the demolition of that gaudy Swansea puzzle jug? The gloriously witty idea is that when you tip it up the liquid pours out of a hole in the back, and not through the spout.

MILO: A bit obvious, really.

ANDREW: Exactly! Obvious and ugly. Let us expose its shortcomings. [*He draws a bead on it, then lowers the gun*] On the other hand, the crème brulé coloring lends it an attractive solidity I should miss. Now how about that giant Staffordshire mug with the inscription on it? What does it say?

MILO: [*Moves a little toward it and reads it aloud*] "In the real cabinet of friendship everyone helped his neighbor and said to his brother, be of good cheer."

ANDREW: Proletarian pomposity!

[ANDREW *suddenly raises his gun and fires, shattering the jug.* MILO *turns in surprise, as he realizes the bullet must have passed reasonably close to his head*]

You might have said good shot.

MILO: Good shot.

ANDREW: [*Insouciant*] It's nothing. [*He looks around him. His eye falls on a china figurine poised on the banister rail above him. He takes aim*] Down with all imperialistic, deviationist, reactionary Dresden shepherdesses! [*He shoots and the Dresden shepherdess flies into pieces*]

MILO: Bravo!

ANDREW: What fun this is! Did you ever know Charlie Begby?

MILO: I don't think so.

ANDREW: Terribly funny fellow. I once saw him bag three brace of duck with one shot. The only trouble was they were china ducks on his auntie's drawing room wall. I said, "You can't do that, it's the closed season." [*He presses button on desk and the sailor laughs*] I told you he always laughs at my jokes.

[MILO *laughs.* ANDREW's *mood changes abruptly*]

It's not really all that funny. There's an open season on some creatures all the year round. [*He turns the gun on* MILO] Seducers and wife stealers for example.

MILO: [*Nervous*] Only in Italian opera, surely.

ANDREW: [*Hard*] You should know. It's your country of origin, is it not?

MILO: No. I was actually born here in England.

ANDREW: Were you now! Dear old cradle-of-the-parliamentary-system-who-screws-my-wife-merits-a-large-pink-gin-England?

MILO: Sense-of-humor-fair-trial-England, I mean.

ANDREW: That's the way a foreigner talks. In private he thinks, filthy wet country, ugly red cold men who don't know how to treat women.

MILO: What's brought all this on? What are you doing with that gun?

ANDREW: Pretty obviously pointing it at you.

MILO: For God's sake, why?

ANDREW: [*Slowly*] Because I'm going to kill you.

MILO: You're going to . . . [*Laughs nervously*] Oh Jesus! I suppose this is some sort of game.

ANDREW: Yes. We've been playing it all evening. It's called "You're going to die and no one will suspect murder."

[*A pause.* MILO *considers his position*]

MILO: You mean all this steal my wife's jewels stuff was just a . . .

ANDREW: Of course! I invited you here to set up the circumstances of your own death. The break-in, the disguise, the jewels in your pocket, the householder aroused, the gun going off in the struggle and then the final fatal shot. I might even get a commendation from the police, for "having a go."

MILO: For God's sake, Andrew, knock it off!

ANDREW: Can you find a flaw in it?

MILO: [*Beginning to feel desperate*] Marguerite! They'll trace the connection between me and Marguerite. They'll know that's why you did it.

ANDREW: I am quite entitled to tackle a man wearing a mask plundering my house in the middle of the night. How was *I* expected to know who you were? Oh no, the law will have every sympathy with me. Property has always been more highly regarded than people in England. Even Marguerite will assume you were just an adventurer who only loved her for her jewels—a petty sneak thief who found larceny less burdensome than marriage. You really are a dead duck, aren't you? Not a moral or romantic attitude left.

MILO: I believe you *are* serious.

ANDREW: I'm not afraid of killing you, if that's what you mean.

MILO: You've got to be. Mortally afraid for your soul.

ANDREW: I didn't think the Jews believed in hell.

MILO: We believe in not playing games with life.

ANDREW: Ha! Wit in the face of adversity. You've learnt *something* from the English. Here's another thing. All right, a sporting chance. Why don't you run for it?

MILO: And give you the chance to shoot me down in cold blood?

ANDREW: Hot blood, you mean. I'm going to shoot you down in cold blood anyway.

[MILO *tries to run but falls over his boots*]

MILO: Look, stop pointing that gun at me . . . I hate guns . . . please . . . this is sick.

ANDREW: You should be flattered by the honor I'm doing you—to take your life light-heartedly—to make you the center piece of an arranged bit of fun. To put it another way, your death will recreate a noble mind.

MILO: This is where I came in.

ANDREW: And where you go out, I'm afraid! The only question to be decided is where the police shall find you. Sprawled over the desk like countless colonels in countless studies? Or propped up in the log basket like a rag doll? Which do you think? Early Agatha Christie or early Nicholas Blake?

MILO: For Christ's sake, Andrew, this is not a detective story, this is real life. You are talking of doing a real murder. Of killing a real man—don't you understand?

ANDREW: Perhaps I shouldn't do it with a gun at all. Perhaps I should shove the ham knife into you, and leave you face down in the middle of the room—[*Melodramatic voice*]—your blood staining the flagstones a deep carmine.

MILO: [*Shudders*] Oh, God!

ANDREW: Or best of all, how about a real 1930's murder weapon —the mashie niblick? I've got one in my golf bag.

[*He fetches the golf club from the hall.* MILO *dives for the telephone but is too late*]

You would be discovered in the fireplace, I think, in a fair old mess. [*Dramatic voice*] The body lay on its back, its limbs grotesquely splayed like a broken puppet. The whole head had been pulped as if by some superhuman force. "My God," breathed the Inspector, paling. "You'd better get a tarpaulin, Thompson . . . Excuse me, sir, but was all this violence strictly necessary?" "I'm sorry, Inspector. It was when I saw him handling my wife's nightdresses. I must have completely lost control of myself." [*He throws down the golf club*] No. I think the scene the police find is simply this. After the fight you flee up the stairs, back to your ladder. I catch you on the landing and in the renewed struggle I shoot you. Nothing succeeds like simplicity, don't you agree, Milo? Now then, some of my own fingerprints on my own revolver. [*He takes glove off and holds the gun in his naked hand*] On your feet, up!

[ANDREW *forces* MILO *to mount the stairs by shoving the gun in his back.* MILO *gives a sudden spasmodic shudder*]

Did you know that Charles I put on two shirts the morning of his execution? "If I tremble with cold," he said, "my enemies will say it was from fear; I will not expose myself to such reproaches." You must also attempt dignity as you mount the steps to the scaffold.

[MILO *demurs and sinks to his knees near the top step*]

MILO: [*Terrified and pleading*] But why, Andrew? Why?

ANDREW: Don't snivel. You can't think it'll gain you mercy.

MILO: I must know why!

ANDREW: I'm amazed you have to ask. But since you do, it's perfectly simple. I hate you. I hate your smarmy, good-looking Latin face and your easy manner. I'll bet you're easy in a ski lodge, and easy on a yacht, and easy on a beach. I'll bet you a pound to a penny, that you wear a gold charm round your neck, and that your chest is hairy and in summer matted with sun oil. I hate you because you are a mock humble, jeweled, shot cufflinked sponger, a world is my oyster-er, a seducer of stupid women, and a king among marshmallow snakes. I hate you because you are a culling spick. A wop—a not one-of-me. Come, little man, did you really believe I would give up my wife and jewels to you? That I would make myself *that* ridiculous.

MILO: Why not? You're not in love with her.

ANDREW: She's mine whether I love her or not. I found her, I've kept her. I am familiar with her. And once, she was in love with me.

MILO: And now she's in love with me, and the dog in the manger won't let go. [*He tries to attack him*] The mad dog in the manger who should be put down for everyone's sake!

ANDREW: [*Deadly*] And you are a young man, dressed as a clown about to be murdered. Put the mask on, Milo.

[A *pause*]

MILO: No, please.

[ANDREW *reaches up and lifts the clown mask off the banister where* MILO *had previously hung it*]

ANDREW: Put it on!

[MILO *takes the mask and fumbles it onto his face*]

Excellent. Farewell Punchinello!

[ANDREW *lifts the pistol to* MILO's *head.* MILO *is shaking with fear*]

MILO: [*High falsetto*] Please . . . !

[ANDREW *slowly pulls the trigger.* MILO *falls backwards down the stairs and lies still.* ANDREW *walks past him, pausing to peer closely to see whether there is any sign of life. He lifts the lolling head and lets it thump back, carelessly, onto the stairs. Satisfied that he has done his work well, he straightens up, and smiles to himself*]

ANDREW: Game and set, I believe.

SLOW CURTAIN

ACT TWO

Two days later.

The curtain rises to the sound of the slow movement of Beethoven's Seventh Symphony which is playing on a record player. ANDREW *enters from kitchen with a tray containing a large pot of caviar, toast, wedge of lemon, a bottle of champagne and glass. He puts tray on desk and stands conducting the music. The movement comes to an end.* ANDREW *crosses to record player and turns over the record. He returns to desk and starts to eat. The telephone rings.*

ANDREW: Hullo . . . Yes, Hawkins, where are you? What? Well you should have checked the times of the trains . . . I've had to get my own supper for the third time running . . . Yes, yes, I daresay, but you know how helpless I am without you and Mrs. H. Man cannot live on baked beans alone, you know . . . All right . . . All right, tomorrow morning. But first thing, mind you.

[ANDREW *continues eating for some minutes. The front doorbell rings. After a slight pause,* ANDREW *goes to answer it*]

DOPPLER: [*Offstage, in hall*] Good evening, sir.

ANDREW: [*Offstage, in hall*] Evening.

DOPPLER: Mr. Wyke.

ANDREW: Yes?

DOPPLER: My name is Inspector Doppler, sir. Detective Inspector Doppler. Of the Wiltshire County Constabulary. I'm sorry to be calling so late. May I have a few words with you on a very important matter?

[ANDREW *enters, followed by* INSPECTOR DOPPLER, *a heavily*

*built, tallish man of about fifty. His hair is balding, and he
wears cheap round spectacles on his fleshy nose, above a
graying moustache. His clothes—dark rumpled suit, under
a half-open light-colored mackintosh—occasion no surprise, nor does his porkpie hat]*

ANDREW: The Wiltshire County Constabulary you say? [*Turning off
music*] Come in. Always pleased to see the police.

DOPPLER: Can't say the same about everyone, sir. Most people seem
to have what you might call an allergy to us.

ANDREW: Would you join me in a brandy, Inspector? Or are you going to tell me you don't drink on duty?

DOPPLER: Oh, no, sir. I *always* drink on duty. I can't afford to in my
own time.

[DOPPLER *sits center*]

ANDREW: [*Handing the* INSPECTOR *a brandy*] Well, what can I do for
you, Inspector?

DOPPLER: I'm investigating a disappearance, sir.

ANDREW: Disappearance?

DOPPLER: Yes, sir. Of a Mr. Milo Tindle. Do you know him, sir?

ANDREW: Yes, that's the chap who's taken Laundry Cottage.

DOPPLER: He walked out of his cottage on Friday night and hasn't
been seen since.

ANDREW: Great Scott!

DOPPLER: Do you know this gentleman well, sir?

ANDREW: Vaguely. He came to the house once or twice. How can I
help you?

DOPPLER: When did you last see Mr. Tindle, sir?

ANDREW: Oh, months ago. I can't exactly remember. As I told you,
he wasn't a close friend; rather more an acquaintance.

DOPPLER: Really, sir? That doesn't quite accord with our information. In fact, he told Jack Benn, the licensee of the White Lion
he was coming to see you, two nights ago.

ANDREW: Publicans are notorious opponents of exactitude, Inspector.
Vinous gossip is their stock in trade. In particular, I've always
found that Jack Benn's observations need constant correction.

DOPPLER: Really, sir? I was wondering if you could correct something else for me.

ANDREW: What's that?

DOPPLER: The impression gained by a man who happened to be passing your house two nights ago that a fierce struggle was taking place in here.

ANDREW: Does it look like it?

DOPPLER: And that shots were fired?

ANDREW: [*Uncertainly*] Shots?

DOPPLER: Three, our man thinks.

ANDREW: A car backfiring?

DOPPLER: No, sir. These were shots. From a gun. Our man is positive.

ANDREW: May I ask why you took two days to call round and ask me about all this?

DOPPLER: Well, sir, things take longer to check out than you think. We like to be certain of our facts before troubling a gentleman like yourself.

ANDREW: Facts? What facts?

DOPPLER: After our informant reported the incident, we did a spot of checking in the village, and as I say Mr. Benn was very helpful.

ANDREW: There's an upright citizen, then.

DOPPLER: Quite so, sir.

ANDREW: If there were more like him . . .

DOPPLER: He told us that Mr. Tindle popped into the pub Friday evening for a quick one, and said he was just on his way up to you. Well, what with him being a newcomer to these parts and all, we thought we'd better have a word with him, and see if he could throw any light on the subject. But as I previously indicated he seems to have disappeared, sir.

ANDREW: But what's that got to do with me?

DOPPLER: He wasn't at his cottage all of Saturday, nor all today. We must have called half a dozen times.

ANDREW: By Jove, Merridew would have been proud of you! Now Inspector, if that's all you have to say . . .

DOPPLER: When we stepped inside Mr. Tindle's cottage to make sure he'd come to no harm, we found this note, sir. [*Reading*] "Urgent

we talk. Come Friday night eight o'clock. Wyke." May I ask
whether this is your handwriting, sir?

> [DOPPLER *shows him the note.* ANDREW *tries to retain it,
> but* DOPPLER *takes it back*]

ANDREW: [*Trapped*] Yes. It's mine all right.

DOPPLER: So Mr. Tindle *was* here?

ANDREW: Yes. The Potman spoke sooth.

DOPPLER: Perhaps you wouldn't mind answering my original question
now, sir.

ANDREW: Which one?

DOPPLER: Was there a struggle here two nights ago?

ANDREW: In a manner of speaking, yes. It was a game we were playing.

DOPPLER: A game? What kind of game?

ANDREW: It's rather difficult to explain. It's called Burglary.

DOPPLER: Please don't joke, sir.

ANDREW: Isn't it about time you told me I don't know the serious-
ness of my own position?

DOPPLER: A man comes here, there is a fight. Shots are heard. He disappears. What would you make of that if you were me?

ANDREW: An open-and-shut case. But things are not always what
they seem, Inspector. My man, Merridew, once proved by a pho-
netic misspelling the forgery of a document allegedly written by a
deaf mute.

DOPPLER: I'm waiting for an explanation.

ANDREW: Tindle arrived at eight and left about an hour and a half
later. I haven't seen him since.

DOPPLER: And nor has anyone else, sir.

ANDREW: This is absurd. Are you suggesting that I killed Tindle?

DOPPLER: Killed Tindle, sir? I never mentioned kill.

ANDREW: Oh, really! You can't pull that old one on me. [*Mimicking*
INSPECTOR'S *voice*] Garrotted, sir? Might I ask how you knew that
her ladyship was garrotted? [*Normal voice*] Surely *you* told me so,
Inspector. [INSPECTOR'S *voice*] No, sir. I never mentioned it!

DOPPLER: I'm sorry you find us so comic, sir. On the whole, what we
do is necessary.

ANDREW: "You're just doing your job," that's the overworked phrase, isn't it?

DOPPLER: Possibly, sir. Your wife and Mr. Tindle have been associating closely for some time.

ANDREW: Oh, so you know about that, do you? I suppose you can't keep anything quiet in a small village.

DOPPLER: Perfectly true, sir.

ANDREW: You aren't suggesting a crime passionel, I hope, Inspector —not over Marguerite? It would be like knifing somebody for a tablespoonful of Co-operative white blancmange.

DOPPLER: I'm very partial to blancmange, sir. I find it a great standby.

ANDREW: [Oratorically] "All of you had either means, motive or opportunity," said Inspector Doppler as he thoughtfully digested another spoonful of his favorite pud. "But only one of you had all three."

DOPPLER: Exactly so, sir! That person is you.

ANDREW: Forgive me, Inspector, I suppose I'd better tell you what happened.

DOPPLER: Yes.

ANDREW: Want a bribe to believe it?

DOPPLER: I'll have another drink.

ANDREW: As you seem to know, Tindle was having an affair with my wife. Now, I'm one of that rare breed of men who genuinely don't mind losing gracefully to a gent who's playing by the same rules. But to be worsted by a flash crypto-Italian lover, who mistakes my boredom for impotence and my provocative energy for narcissism is too much. It's like starting every game thirty down, and the umpire against you.

DOPPLER: You mean you couldn't bring yourself to accept the situation, sir. Is that what you're saying?

ANDREW: I think what infuriated me most was the things he said about me—things that Marguerite repeated to me. I mean, no man likes to listen to the other man's witticisms when he's trying to choke down his late night Ovaltine.

DOPPLER: What sort of things, sir?

ANDREW: Oh, you know, smarmy, deceitful things which any lover can make about any husband. It's just too easy for them with a captive audience groggy on rediscovered youth and penis envy. [*Pause*] It's not really playing the game.

DOPPLER: You seem to regard marriage as a game, sir.

ANDREW: Not marriage, Inspector. *Sex.* Sex is the game with marriage the penalty. Round the board we jog toward each futile anniversary. Pass go. Collect two hundred rows, two hundred silences, two hundred scars in the deep places. It's just as well that I don't lack for amorous adventure. Finlandia provides.

DOPPLER: Are you trying to tell me that because of your indifference to your wife, you had no motive for killing Mr. Tindle?

ANDREW: I'm simply saying that in common with most men I want to have my cookie and ignore it. That's rather witty!

DOPPLER: Well, sir. I must say you're very frank.

ANDREW: Disarmingly so, I hope.

DOPPLER: Please go on.

ANDREW: As I say. I thought I'd teach Mr. Tindle a lesson for his presumption. In a curious way, some of his remarks which Marguerite repeated to me led me to believe that he was worth taking a little trouble with—even perhaps worth getting to know. Well, the shortest way to a man's heart is humiliation. You soon find out what he's made of.

DOPPLER: So you invited him here and humiliated him?

ANDREW: I did indeed! I took a leaf out of the book of certain eighteenth-century secret societies. They knew to a nicety how to determine whether someone was worthy to be included amongst their number and also how to humiliate him in the process. I refer of course to the initiation ceremony.

DOPPLER: Would it be something like bullying a new boy at school?

ANDREW: Not unlike, but the victim had the choice of refusal. When Count Cagliostro, the noted magician, sought admission to one such society, he was asked whether he was prepared to die for it, if need be. He said he was. He was then sentenced to death, blindfolded and a pistol containing powder but no shot placed against his temple and discharged.

DOPPLER: And you did this to Mr. Tindle?

ANDREW: More or less. I invited Milo here and suggested to him that as my wife had expensive tastes and he was virtually a pauper, the only course open for him was to steal some valuable jewels which I had in the safe.

DOPPLER: And he agreed to this?

ANDREW: With alacrity. I persuaded him to get out of his clothes and to dress as Grock, in which ludicrous disguise he broke into the house and blew open the safe. He then pocketed the jewels, struggled convincingly round this room and was about to make off, when I turned nasty and revealed the purpose of the evening. This, of course, was that I had maneuvered him into a position whereby pretending to mistake him for a burglar, I could, as the outraged householder, legitimately shoot him as he raced away up the stairs. By the time the police arrived I would be standing in my night attire innocent, bewildered and aggrieved. And as you well know, Inspector, there's no liar in Britain, however unconvincing, more likely to be believed than an owner-occupier standing with his hair ruffled in front of his own fireplace, wearing striped Viyella pajamas under a camel Jaeger dressing gown.

DOPPLER: What was Mr. Tindle's reaction to all this?

ANDREW: It was electrifying! He swallowed my story hook, line and sinker. He fell on his knees, pleaded for his life, but I was implacable. I put the gun against his head and shot him with a *blank* cartridge. He fainted dead away. It was most gratifying.

DOPPLER: Gratifying or not, sir, Mr. Tindle must have been put in fear for his life. Such action invites a grave charge of assault.

ANDREW: Well, I suppose that's marginally better than the murder charge you were contemplating a few minutes ago.

DOPPLER: I still am contemplating it, sir.

ANDREW: Oh, come now, Inspector. I've told you what happened. After a few minutes, Mr. Tindle recovered his senses, realized shrewdly that he wasn't dead after all and went off home.

DOPPLER: [*Shaking his head in disbelief*] Just like that?

ANDREW: Well, he needed a glass or two of cognac to get the parts working. I mean, wouldn't you?

DOPPLER: I doubt whether I would have survived completely undamaged, sir. The whole thing sounds like the most irresponsible trick.

ANDREW: Irresponsible? It was quite the contrary. I was upholding the sanctity of marriage. That's more than most people are prepared to do these days. By this action I was clearly stating "Marriage isn't dead. It's alive and well and living in Wiltshire."

DOPPLER: Tell me, did Mr. Tindle say anything when he left?

ANDREW: No. He seemed speechless. [*Laughs*] He just lurched off.

DOPPLER: I'm sorry you appear to find all this so funny, Mr. Wyke. We may not take quite the same attitude.

ANDREW: Look, why don't you see this from my point of view? In a sense, Milo *was* a burglar. He was stealing my wife.

DOPPLER: So you tortured him?

ANDREW: [*Exploding*] Don't you see. It was a *game!*

DOPPLER: A game?

ANDREW: A bloody game, yes!

DOPPLER: It sounds rather sad, sir—like a child not growing up.

ANDREW: What's so sad about a child playing, eh!

DOPPLER: Nothing, sir—*if* you're a child.

ANDREW: Let me tell you, Inspector. I have played games of such complexity that Jung and Einstein would have been honored to have been asked to participate in them. Games of construction and games of destruction. Games of hazard, and games of callidity. Games of deductive logic, inductive logic, semantics, color association, mathematics, hypnosis and prestidigitation. I have achieved leaps of the mind and leaps of the Psyche unknown in ordinary human relationships. And I've had a great deal of not wholly innocent fun.

DOPPLER: And now, sir, you have achieved murder.

ANDREW: No!

DOPPLER: I believe so, sir.

ANDREW: No!!

DOPPLER: Would you mind if I looked around?

ANDREW: Go ahead. Crawl about the floor on hands and knees. Get your envelope out and imprison hairs. Gather ye blunt instruments while ye may.

[DOPPLER *rises and starts to examine the room*]

ANDREW: [*Slowly*] I ask myself, if I wanted to conceal Milo . . .

[DOPPLER *shakes the sailor on his passage round the room*]

... where would I put him? In the cellar? ... Too traditional! In the water tank? ... Too poisonous! In the linen chest? ... Too aromatic! In the furnace? ... Too residual! In the herbaceous border? ... Too ossiferous! In the ...

DOPPLER: Excuse me, sir, but these holes in the wall here and here. They look like bullet holes.

ANDREW: [*Slowly*] Quite right, Inspector. So they are.

DOPPLER: I understood you to say, sir, that you used a blank.

ANDREW: Two live bullets to set up the trick. One blank to complete it. I had to persuade Tindle I was in earnest. After all, there's really no point in playing a game unless you play it to the hilt.

DOPPLER: I see, sir. One blank. I'd like you to show me where Mr. Tindle was when you killed him.

ANDREW: Pretended to kill him, you mean.

DOPPLER: Quite so, sir. Show me, please, exactly where he was when the bullet hit him.

ANDREW: You do realize of course, there wasn't a real bullet.

DOPPLER: [*Skeptically*] Very well, sir. Show me where he was when the blank cartridge was fired.

[ANDREW *mounts the stairs followed by the* INSPECTOR]

ANDREW: He was standing, kneeling, crouching about here. He fainted and fell down the stairs. Bang!

[DOPPLER *passes* ANDREW]

DOPPLER: I see. About here you say, sir?

ANDREW: Toward me. Come on. Come on. Stop.

DOPPLER: Were you close to Mr. Tindle when you fired the gun?

ANDREW: Very. I was standing over him in fact, with the gun pressed against his head. The actual feel of the gun coupled with the noise of the explosion was what did the trick.

[DOPPLER *scrutinizes the staircase*]

Could I interest you in a magnifying glass?

[DOPPLER *bends down to examine the staircase, then the*

banisters, suddenly he rubs a finger on them, and straightens up, wiping them on his handkerchief]

DOPPLER: Joke blood, sir?

ANDREW: [*Nervous*] I'm not quite sure I follow, Inspector.

DOPPLER: This here on the banisters. It's dried blood.

ANDREW: Blood? Where?

DOPPLER: Here in the angle of the banister—

[*Warily,* ANDREW *crosses to the stairs. He examines the banisters and slowly straightens up. His expression is confused and fearful]*

Don't touch it, sir! Oh, look sir, here's some more. Someone's been rubbing at the carpet. Do you see, sir? There, deep in the pile, that's blood, sir. Oh! It's still damp. Could you explain how it got there, sir?

ANDREW: I have no idea, Milo . . . er . . . he was a little burnt . . . You must believe me!

DOPPLER: Why should I, sir?

ANDREW: But it's impossible, it was only a game.

DOPPLER: A game, sir? With real bullets and real blood?

ANDREW: [*Gabbling*] There's the hole cut in the pane of glass with the diamond cutter . . . and there are the marks of the ladder on the sill outside . . . and if you look down you'll see the imprint of the other end of the ladder and of size twenty-eight shoes or whatever they were, still there in the flower bed and this is the bureau that he broke open . . .

[DOPPLER *descends the stairs]*

DOPPLER: [*Hard*] Thank you, sir, but I don't require a conducted tour. Over the years my eyes have been adequately trained to see things for themselves.

ANDREW: I'm sure they have, Inspector. I only meant to point out facts which would help substantiate my story. And that's the safe we blew open . . .

DOPPLER: Where are the jewels now, sir?

ANDREW: I put them in the bank yesterday.

DOPPLER: On a Saturday?

ANDREW: Yes, Inspector, on a Saturday. I went to Salisbury and I put them in the night safe. I felt they'd be better off there. I mean, anyone could break in and steal them.

DOPPLER: How provident, sir.

ANDREW: And look down the corridor, you'll see the dressing-up basket . . .

[DOPPLER *turns away and looks out of the window, over the garden*]

DOPPLER: You didn't point out that mound of earth in the garden, did you, sir?

[ANDREW *joins* DOPPLER *at the window*]

ANDREW: Mound of earth? What mound of earth?

DOPPLER: Over there—by the far wall. Under the yew tree. Would you say it had been freshly dug, sir?

ANDREW: [*Shouting*] How the hell should I know! It's probably something the gardener's doing. A new flower bed I think he said.

DOPPLER: A flower bed under a yew tree, sir?

ANDREW: [*Shouting*] I've already told you I don't know! Why don't you ask him yourself? He's probably out there somewhere, maundering around on his moleskinned knees, aching for an opportunity to slander his employer.

DOPPLER: Funny, sir. I've always found gardeners make excellent witnesses. Slow, methodical, positive.

ANDREW: Inspector, I've had just about enough of this farce! Go and dig the damned thing up, if you want to.

DOPPLER: Oh, we shall, sir. Don't worry.

ANDREW: [*Persuasive*] Look, do you really think that I'd bury Tindle in the garden, and leave all that newly turned earth for everyone to find?

DOPPLER: If you weren't expecting us, sir, yes. In a couple of weeks, with some bulbs or a little grass seed, it would be difficult to tell it had ever been disturbed. We in the police know just how fond murderers are of their back gardens, sir.

ANDREW: [*Attempts a laugh*] You're nearer a killer's heart in a garden than anywhere else on earth, eh?

DOPPLER: Except a bedroom, sir. I think you'll find that's still favorite. [*He starts rummaging in the wardrobe*] Tch! Tch! Tch! What a way to keep clothes! All screwed up at the back of your wardrobe. Why should you do that, I wonder? [*He holds up* MILO's *shirt*] That's an interesting monogram. I.W. No, I've got it the wrong way up—M.T.

ANDREW: Let me see that.

DOPPLER: [*Reading*] Made by Owen & Smith of Percy Street. 16.8.69 for Mr. Milo Tindle. Tell me something, sir.

> [ANDREW *seizes the shirt and stares at it in horror, unable to speak.* DOPPLER *holds up* MILO's *jacket and carefully reads the name in the inside pocket*]

When Mr. Tindle lurched off, as you put it, did he lurch naked?

ANDREW: [*In great distress*] Believe me, Inspector. I have no idea how those clothes got there.

DOPPLER: Didn't you tell me that Mr. Tindle stripped off here the other night to disguise himself as a clown?

ANDREW: Yes, that's right.

DOPPLER: Another part of the humiliation process, I suppose?

ANDREW: But he changed back before he left. I mean, you can't really see him walking through the village dressed as a clown, can you?

DOPPLER: No, sir, I can't. Which makes the appearance of his clothes here all the more significant.

ANDREW: It's all so difficult . . .

DOPPLER: On the contrary, sir, I think it's all very simple. I think you started this as a game, exactly as you say you did, in order to play a diabolical trick on Mr. Tindle but that it went wrong. Your third shot was not a blank as you had supposed, but was in fact a live bullet which killed Mr. Tindle stone dead, spattering his blood on the banisters in the process. When you realized what you'd done, you panicked and simply buried him in the garden. It was silly of you not to wash the blood properly off the banisters and burn his clothes, though.

ANDREW: I swear Tindle left here alive.

DOPPLER: I don't believe it.

ANDREW: I didn't murder him.

DOPPLER: I accept that. As I said, I think it happened by accident. We'll be quite content with a charge of manslaughter.

ANDREW: [Shouting] I did not kill him! He left here alive.

DOPPLER: If you will pardon a flippancy, sir, you had better tell that to the judge.

ANDREW: Look. There's one way of settling this. If you think Tindle is in the garden, go and dig him up.

DOPPLER: Don't need to find him, sir. Recent decisions have relieved the prosecution of producing the corpus delicti. If Mr. Tindle is not under the newly turned earth, it will merely go to indicate that in your panic you first thought of putting him there, then changed your mind and buried him somewhere else.

ANDREW: Where?

DOPPLER: Does it matter? Spook Spinney! Flasher's Heath! It's all the same to us. He'll turn up sooner or later—discovered by some adulterous salesman, or rutting boy scout. And if he doesn't, it scarcely matters, there's so much circumstantial evidence against you. Come along, it's time to go.

ANDREW: [A cry] No!

DOPPLER: I'm afraid I must insist, sir! There's a police car outside.

ANDREW: [Louder] You may have a fleet of police cars out there. I'm not going!

DOPPLER: Now let's have no trouble, sir. Please don't make it difficult.

ANDREW: [Wildly] I must see a lawyer. It's my right!

[ANDREW backs away. DOPPLER makes to seize him, there is a scuffle]

DOPPLER: We can make a call from the station, sir. We wouldn't want to do anything unconstitutional. Come on, sir. Don't despair. At the most you'll only get seven years!

ANDREW: [Horrified] Seven years!

DOPPLER: Seven years to regret playing silly games that go wrong.

ANDREW: [Bitterly] It didn't go wrong. It went absolutely right. You've trapped me somehow.

DOPPLER: Yes, sir. You see, we real life detectives aren't as stupid as we are sometimes portrayed by writers like yourself. We may not have our pipes, or orchid houses, our shovel hats or deer-stalkers, but we tend to be reasonably effective for all that.

ANDREW: Who the hell are you?

DOPPLER: Detective Inspector Doppler, sir, spelt as in C. Doppler, 1803-1853, whose principle it was that when the source of any wave movement is approached, the frequency appears greater than it would to an observer moving away. It is also not unconnected with Doppler meaning double in German—hence Doppleganger or double image. And of course, for those whose minds run to these things, it is virtually an anagram of the word Plodder. Inspector Plodder becomes Inspector Doppler, if you see what I mean, sir!

ANDREW: [A shriek] Milo!

MILO: [Normal voice] The same.

> [MILO peels off his disguise which apart from elaborate face and hair make-up—wig, false nose, glasses, cheek padding and moustache—also includes a great deal of body padding, and elevator shoes, which have had the effect of making him taller than ANDREW, where in reality he is a fraction shorter]

ANDREW: You shit!

MILO: Just so.

ANDREW: You platinum-plated, copper-bottomed, dyed-in-the-wool, all-time knockdown dragout, champion bastard Milo!

MILO: Thanks.

ANDREW: You weasel! You cozening coypu!

MILO: Obliged.

ANDREW: You mendacious bollock of Satan. Milo! You triple-dealing turd!

MILO: In your debt.

ANDREW: Mind you, I'm not saying it wasn't well done. It was— brilliant.

MILO: Thank you.

ANDREW: Have a drink, my dear fellow?

MILO: Let me wash first. I'm covered in make-up and spirit gum.

[ANDREW *shakily pours himself a whiskey*]

ANDREW: Just down the corridor. Cheers!

MILO: Good health.

[MILO *exits to bathroom as* ANDREW *gulps down his drink*]

ANDREW: Yes, I must say, Milo, I congratulate you. It was first class. You really had me going there for a moment.

MILO: [*Quizzically*] For a moment?

ANDREW: For a long moment, I concede. Of course, I had my suspicions toward the end. Flasher's Heath indeed! That was going a bit far.

MILO: I was giving you one of your English sporting chances.

ANDREW: What did you think of *my* performance? The anguish of an innocent man trapped by circumstantial evidence.

MILO: Undignified—if it was a performance.

[MILO *returns, picks up his clothes and goes upstairs to the wardrobe where he dresses in his own clothes*]

ANDREW: Of course it was, and it had to be undignified to be convincing. As I say, I had my suspicions.

MILO: Indeed? How cleverly you kept them to yourself.

ANDREW: And how well you executed it. I loved your Inspector Doppler. His relentless courtesy, his chilly rusticity, his yeoman beadiness.

MILO: [DOPPLER *voice*] I'm glad you view the trifling masquerade in that light, sir.

ANDREW: I suppose you slipped in here yesterday when I was over in Salisbury?

MILO: Yes, I waited to see you leave.

ANDREW: And dumped the clothes in the wardrobe, and sprinkled a little sacrificial blood on the banisters.

MILO: Exactly. But it wasn't my blood you will be relieved to hear. It was obtained from a pig's liver.

ANDREW: Ugh! Perhaps you will do me the favor of wiping it off in a minute. I don't wish to fertilize the woodworm.

MILO: Question. Where would you find homosexual woodworms?

ANDREW: What?

MILO: In a tallboy.

[ANDREW *grimaces*]

[*Then, sharply*] I'd like that drink now.

ANDREW: Yes, of course. [*He goes to drinks table and pours a brandy for* MILO] You deserve it.

MILO: [*Sits on chair under staircase*] You know, I haven't congratulated you on your game yet. You brought it off with great élan.

ANDREW: Did you think so? Oh good! Good! I must say I was rather delighted with it myself. Tell me . . . did you really think that your last moment on earth had come?

MILO: Yes.

ANDREW: You're not angry, are you?

MILO: Anger is a meaningless word in this context.

ANDREW: I've already tried to explain it to you. I wanted to get to know you—to see if you were, as I suspected, my sort of person.

MILO: A games-playing sort of person?

ANDREW: Exactly.

MILO: And am I?

ANDREW: Most certainly. There's no doubt about it.

MILO: And what exactly is a games-playing person?

ANDREW: He's the complete man—a man of reason and imagination; of potent passions and bright fancies. He's joyous and unrepenting. His weapons are the openness of a child and the cunning of a pike and with them he faces out the black terrors of life. For me personally, he is a man who dares to live his life without the crutch of domestic tension. You see, at bottom, I'm rather a solitary man. An arrangement of clouds, the secret mystery of landscape, a game of intrigue and revelation, mean more to me than people—even the ones I'm supposed to be in love with. I've never met a woman to whom the claims of intellect were as absolute as they are to me. For a long time I was reticent about all this, knowing that most people would mistake my adroit heart for one of polished stone.

But it doesn't worry me any longer. I'm out in the open. I've turned my whole life into one great work of happy invention.

MILO: And you think I'm like this?

ANDREW: Yes, I do.

MILO: You're wrong.

ANDREW: I'm not. Look at the way you chose to get back at me—by playing Inspector Doppler.

MILO: That was just the need for revenge. Every Italian knows about that.

ANDREW: Rubbish. You could have revenged yourself in one of many crude Mafiosi ways—cutting off the gardener's hands, for example, or staking the cleaning woman out on the gravel, or even I suppose, as a last resort, scratched loutish words on the bonnet of my Lagonda. But no, you had to resort to a game.

MILO: I like to pay back in kind.

ANDREW: And is honor satisfied? Is it one set all?

MILO: [*Hard*] By no means. Your game was superior to mine. I merely teased you for a few minutes with the thought of prison. [*Low*] You virtually terrified me to death.

ANDREW: My dear fellow . . .

MILO: [*Slowly, thinking it out*] And that changes you profoundly. Once you've given yourself to death, actually faced the fact that the coat sleeve button, the banister, the nail on your fourth finger, are the last things you're going to see ever—and then *heard* the sound of your own death—things cannot be the same again. I feel I've been tempered by madness. I stand outside and see myself for the first time without responsibility.

ANDREW: [*Nervous*] That's shock, my dear chap. It'll pass. Here, have another drink.

> [ANDREW *reaches for the glass.* MILO *jerks away. He is in great distress*]

How cold you are. Milo, my dear fellow, I didn't realize how absolutely cold . . .

MILO: So that my only duty is to even our score. That's imperative. As you would put it "I'm three games up in the second set, having lost the first, six love." That's right, isn't it? That's about how you see it? I should hate to cheat.

ANDREW: You're being too modest, Milo. In my scoring it's one set all.

MILO: Oh, no, I can't accept that. You see, to the ends of playing the game and drawing honorably level, I *have* killed someone.

ANDREW: Killed someone?

MILO: Murdered someone. Committed murder.

ANDREW: You're not serious.

MILO: Yes.

ANDREW: What is this? Some new murder game?

MILO: Yes. But it has a difference. Both the game and the murder are real. There's absolutely no point in another pretense murder game, is there?

ANDREW: [*Soothing*] No, none. But I don't like to take advantage of you in this emotional state.

MILO: [*Shouting*] It can't wait!

ANDREW: [*Soothing*] All right. All right. Let's play your game. Who did you kill?

MILO: Your girl friend, Tëa . . .

ANDREW: You killed Tëa?

MILO: [*A little giggle*] She whose cobalt eyes were the secret forest pools of Finlandia. I closed them.

ANDREW: You . . .

MILO: I strangled her—right here on this rug I strangled her and . . . I had her first.

ANDREW: You raped and str . . .

MILO: No. Not rape. She wanted it.

ANDREW: You're lying. You can't take me in with a crude game like this. [*With braggadocio*] Honestly, Milo. You're in the big league now. I gave you credit for better sport than this.

MILO: You'll have all the sport you can stomach in a moment, Andrew. That I promise you.

ANDREW: Really, Milo, I think it would be better if . . .

MILO: When I was here yesterday, planting the blood and clothes for my Inspector Doppler scene, Tëa stopped by. I strangled her.

She was under that freshly dug mound of earth in the garden that so took Doppler's fancy.

ANDREW: Was? You mean she's not there now?

MILO: No. I moved her.

ANDREW: [Derisory] You moved her? Where to? Flasher's Heath I suppose.

MILO: Something like that. It was too easy leaving her here . . . Too easy for the game you are going to play against the clock before the police arrive.

ANDREW: The police?

MILO: Yes. You see, about an hour ago I 'phoned them up and asked them to meet me here at ten o'clock tonight. They should be here in about ten minutes.

ANDREW: [Sarcastic] Yes, yes. I'm sure they will be. Led, no doubt, by intrepid downy Inspector Doppler.

MILO: Oh, no. It'll be a real policeman, have no fear of that. Detective Sergeant Tarrant his name is. I told him a lot about you, Andrew. I said that I knew you to be a man obsessed with games-playing and murder considered as a fine art. Your life's great ambition, I said, of which you'd often spoken, was to commit an actual real life murder, hide the body somewhere where it couldn't be traced to you and then leave clues linking you with the crime, strewn about your house in the certain knowledge that the pedestrian and simple-minded police wouldn't recognize them for what they were.

ANDREW: Obsessed with games-playing and murder considered as a fine art! That's rather ingenious of you, Milo. But it won't work. Please sir, Andrew Wyke can't rest until he's committed a real murder which is going to make fools out of all you coppers. Honestly! Tell that to the average desk sergeant and you'll find yourself strapped straight into the giggle jacket.

MILO: Not so in fact, I told them that if they didn't believe me, one look at your bookcase and the furnishings of your house would confirm what I said about your obsessions.

ANDREW: [Slow] Go on.

MILO: I also told them that two days ago your girl friend had come to my house in great distress saying you suspected she was having affairs with other men and had threatened to kill her.

ANDREW: The police believed all that?

MILO: After some demur, yes.

ANDREW: The fuzz are watching too much T.V.

MILO: You mustn't resent imagination in public office, Andrew. Of course, I went on I had no proof that any harm had actually been done to her, but I thought I had better report the matter, particularly as I had just received an excited phone call from you, Andrew, saying you were all set to achieve your life's great ambition.

ANDREW: My dear boy, I quite appreciate you have been captivated by the spirit of games-playing and the need, as you see it, to get even, but frankly you are trying too hard to be a big boy, too soon. [*He goes to the telephone and dials*] Hullo, Joyce, this is Andrew. May I speak to Tẽa . . . she what? . . . when was this? Where . . . ? Oh, my God!

[*He replaces the receiver and takes a drink straight from the bottle.* MILO *is very excited*]

MILO: I told you. I killed her yesterday. Now sweat for your life. You have a little over eight minutes before the law arrives. It's your giant brain against their plodding ones. Concealed in this room are two incriminating clues. And as a final expression of your contempt for the police you hid the murder weapon itself. Do you follow me so far?

ANDREW: [*Admiringly*] You bastard!

MILO: No judgments please. Three objects. Those you don't find, be sure the police will. I should add that they're all in plain view, though I have somewhat camouflaged them to make the whole thing more fun. The first object is a crystal bracelet.

ANDREW: Not . . .

MILO: Yes, I tore it off her wrist . . . off you go. It's inscribed "From Andrew to Tẽa, a propitiatory offering to a Karelian Goddess."

ANDREW: All right! All right! I know how it's inscribed.

[ANDREW *takes off his jacket and starts his search*]

MILO: Would you like some help?

ANDREW: Yes, damn you!

MILO: Tch! Tch! . . . "For any man with half an eye. What stands

before him may espy; But optics sharp it needs I ween, To see
what is not to be seen."

ANDREW: [*Furious*] You said everything was in plain view.

MILO: Well, it's paradoxical old me, isn't it?

ANDREW: I'll get my own back for this . . . don't worry. That I
promise you! I'll roast you for this . . . I'll make you so sorry you
ever . . .

MILO: Six minutes.

ANDREW: [*Slowly, to himself*] I must think . . . I must think . . .
It's in plain view, yet not to be seen. H'm . . . there's a visual
trick involved.

[ANDREW *searches the room*]

MILO: A propitiatory offering, eh! What was it you had to propitiate
for, I ask myself?

ANDREW: None of your bloody business!

MILO: Just for being yourself, I suppose. Just for being cold, torturing,
Andrew Wyke. Poor Téa, I wonder if all her jewelry was inscribed
with apologies for your bullyboy behavior.

ANDREW: That's a cheap jibe.

MILO: Mind you, at least you gave her some. Marguerite just had the
use of them.

ANDREW: I see what you're doing. You're trying to distract me . . .
But you won't succeed . . . I'll solve your puzzle . . . Let me
think . . . Optics sharp it needs to see what is not to be seen . . .
with the naked eye? It's microscopic! You only see a fraction of
it. That's it!

[ANDREW *picks up the microscope and uses it*]

MILO: You won't need the Sherlock Holmes kit, Andrew. The
bracelet is full-sized and in full view. Though the detective angle
is not a bad one. I wonder how your man, Merry*dick*, would have
gone about the search.

ANDREW: [*Furious*] Merrydew! St. John Lord Merrydew!

MILO: Perhaps he'd have clambered up on to that desk to look at
the plinth, hauling his great tun of port belly after him.

[ANDREW *climbs up on his desk to inspect the plinth*]

Or perhaps he'd have gone straight to the chimney and shoved his fat Father Christmas face right up it.

[ANDREW *runs to the chimney and climbs inside it*]

"My God!" cried the noble Lord, puking on his pipe and indulging his famed taste for bad puns. "This is hardly a *sootable* place for a gentleman!"

[ANDREW *emerges from the chimney*]

ANDREW: I won't listen to you. I must think . . . What are the properties of crystal? It's hard . . . It's brilliant . . . It's transparent.

MILO: You're getting warm, Andrew.

ANDREW: You look through it and you don't see it. Now the only place to conceal a transparent thing, so as to make it invisible yet keep it in plain view, is in another transparent thing like . . .

[ANDREW *inspects various glass objects including* MILO's *drink which he is holding conspicuously. Finally he crosses to the ornamental tank, downstage right, and lifts out the bracelet*]

ANDREW: Suddenly it's all as clear as crystal. I don't need to destroy this, do I? She could have left this here anytime.

MILO: True, it was only planted so that the police could read the inscription. At least they'd know that your relationship with Téa hadn't always been a happy one.

ANDREW: Very subtle. What next?

MILO: The next object is much more damning. The clue is a riddle, which goes as follows:

"Two brothers we are,
    Great burdens we bear,
On which we are bitterly pressed.
    The truth is to say,
    We are full all the day,
And empty when we go to rest."

ANDREW: Oh, I know that . . . don't tell me . . . full all the day, empty when we go to rest . . . it's a . . . it's a pair of shoes!

MILO: Very good. In this case, one right, high-heeled shoe. Size six. The other, I need hardly add, is on Tēa's body.

ANDREW: Oh, my God! Poor Tēa.

[ANDREW *searches the room*]

MILO: Poor Tēa, eh? Well, that's a bit better. It's the first sign of sorrow you've shown since you heard of her death.

ANDREW: It's not true! You think I don't care about Tēa, don't you? But I must save myself.

MILO: You're loving it. You're in a high state of brilliance and excitement. The thought that you are playing a game for your life is practically giving you an orgasm. It's pitiable.

ANDREW: Hold your filthy tongue! What you see before you is someone using a mighty control to keep terror in check, while he tries to solve a particularly sadistic and morbid puzzle. It's a triumph of the mind over atavism!

[ANDREW *searches under the stairs and in the bookshelves and pipe racks, then the sailor's foot and finally finds the shoe in a brightly decorated cornucopia attached to the stage left column*]

Ah! What have we here?

MILO: Very good! Sorry it's so messy. It's only earth from Tēa's first grave in your garden.

[ANDREW *burns the shoe in the stove*]

ANDREW: Now there's one thing left, isn't there? The murder weapon, that's what you said. Now you strangled her here. What with? Let's see . . . a rope . . . a belt . . . a scarf . . .

MILO: It bit into her neck very deeply, Andrew. I had to pry it loose.

ANDREW: You sadistic bloody wop!

MILO: I hope I didn't hear that correctly . . . It would be foolish to antagonize me at this stage. Because as you're certain to need a lot more help, I would hate to have to give you an oblique, Florentine sort of one, sewn with treachery and double-dealing.

ANDREW: [*Controlling himself*] All right! All right!

MILO: As Don Quixote in common with a great number of chaps remarked, "*No es Oro todo que reluce.*"

ANDREW: But the other chaps, of course, didn't say it in Spanish, did they?

MILO: Well, at least you know it was Spanish, even if you can't speak it. I suppose that's what is meant by a general education in England.

ANDREW: God, you're pretty damned insufferable, Milo.

MILO: I've learnt it. Let's try you on a little Latin. Every gentleman knows Latin. I'm sure you're acquainted with the Winchester College Hall Book of 1401?

ANDREW: [*Sarcastic*] Naturally. As a matter of fact I've got the paperback by my bedside.

MILO: [*Bland*] Then you will remember an entry by Alanus De Insulis—"*Non teneas nurum totum quod splendet ut aurum.*"

ANDREW: [*Sarcastic*] I'm afraid I can't have got that far yet.

MILO: Pity . . . I suppose I could put it another way. "*Que tout n'est pas or qu'on voit luire.*" The French, of course, is thirteenth century.

ANDREW: Say it again, slowly.

MILO: All-that-glitters . . .

ANDREW: All that glitters isn't gold . . . Why didn't you say that in the first place . . .

[MILO *whistles a scale*]

Golden notes? . . . Golden whistle? . . . Golden cord? . . . Golden cord! You strangled her with a golden cord and put it round the bellpull.

[ANDREW *runs to the bellpull, examines it, but finds nothing*]

No, you didn't.

[MILO *whistles "Anything Goes"*]

Anything goes. In olden d . . . In olden days a . . . glimpse of stocking. It's in the spin dryer!

[ANDREW *rushes off down corridor to kitchen*]

MILO: Cold, cold. It's in this room, remember.

ANDREW: [*Returning*] Where do you put stockings? On legs, golden legs . . . [*He examines the golden legs of the fender, then a chair*]

MILO: [*Sings*] "In olden days a glimpse of stocking was looked on as something shocking . . ." I thought I heard something.

[MILO *exits to hallway. A moment later, he returns*]

MILO: Yes, Andrew, it's the police. They're coming up the drive.

ANDREW: [*Desperate*] Keep them out! Give me one more minute!

MILO: A glimpse of stocking, remember.

[MILO *exits to hallway*]

MILO: [*Offstage*] Good evening. Detective Sergeant Tarrant?

TARRANT: [*Offstage*] Yes, sir. This is Constable Higgs.

MILO: Good evening, Constable.

HIGGS: Good evening, sir.

[*The grandfather clock strikes ten*]

ANDREW: Olden days . . . A glimpse . . . Now you see it, now you don't! Of course, the clock.

[*He rushes to clock and finds stocking*]

MILO: [*Off*] Nice of you to be so prompt. I apologize for keeping you waiting out there for a moment. The front door's a bit stiff.

TARRANT: [*Off*] That's all right, sir. We're used to waiting.

MILO: Won't you hang your coats up? It's a bit warm inside.

TARRANT: Thank you, sir. I expect we'll be here a little time.

[ANDREW *puts stocking into fire*]

MILO: [*Off*] Here, Constable. Let me take your helmet.

HIGGS: Thank you, sir. If it's all the same to you, I think I'll keep it with me, but I'll take my coat off.

[*Door slams offstage*]

MILO: [*Off*] Come in, gentlemen. May I introduce Mr. Andrew

Wyke. Andrew, may I introduce Detective Sergeant Tarrant and Constable Higgs.

ANDREW: [*Calls*] Come in, gentlemen, come in.

[*A pause. No one enters*]

MILO: [*Off*] Or perhaps I should say Inspector Plodder and Constable Freshface. Thank you, Sergeant. We won't be needing you after all.

TARRANT: That's all right, sir. Better to be safe than sorry, that's what I say. Good night, sir.

MILO: Good night, Sergeant. Good night, Constable. Good night, sir.

[MILO *returns from hallway.* ANDREW *sinks on the settee, shattered*]

MILO: Aren't you going to ask about Tēa? She did call here yesterday looking for you when I was here setting the Doppler scene. I told her about the trick you had played on me with the gun. She wasn't a bit surprised. She knows only too well the kind of games you play—the kind of humiliation you enjoy inflicting on people. I said I wanted to play a game to get even with you, and I asked her to help me. I asked her to lend me a stocking, a shoe, and a bracelet. She collaborated with enthusiasm. So did her flat-mate, Joyce. Would you like to telephone her, she'll talk to you now? Of course you don't really have much to say to her, do you? She's not really your mistress. She told me you and she hadn't slept together for over a year. She told me you were practically impotent— not at all, in fact, the selector's choice for the next Olympics.

[ANDREW *hides his head as* MILO *starts up the stairs*]

ANDREW: Where are you going?

MILO: To collect Marguerite's fur coat.

ANDREW: She's not coming back?

MILO: No. Among other things she said she was fed up with living in Hamleys.

ANDREW: Hamleys?

MILO: It's a toy shop in Regent Street.

ANDREW: Milo.

MILO: Yes?

ANDREW: Don't go. Don't waste it all on Marguerite. She doesn't appreciate you like I do. You and I are evenly matched. We know what it is to play a game and that's so rare. Two people coming together who have the courage to spend the little time of light between the eternal darkness—joking.

MILO: Do you mean live here?

ANDREW: Yes.

MILO: [Scornfully] Is it legal in private between two consenting games-players?

ANDREW: Please . . . I just want someone to play with.

MILO: No.

ANDREW: Please.

MILO: No. Most people want someone to *live* with. But you have no life to give anyone—only the tricks and the shadows of long ago. Take a look at yourself, Andrew, and ask yourself a few simple questions about your attachment to the English detective story. Perhaps you might come to realize that the only place you can inhabit is a dead world—a country-house world where peers and colonels die in their studies; where butlers steal the port, and pert parlormaids cringe, weeping malapropisms behind green baize doors. It's a world of coldness and class hatred, and two-dimensional characters who are not expected to communicate; it's a world where only the amateurs win, and where foreigners are automatically figures of fun. To be *puzzled* is all. Forgive me for taking Marguerite to a life where people try to *understand*. To put it shortly, the detective story is the normal recreation of snobbish, outdated, life-hating, ignoble minds. I'll get that fur coat now. I presume it *is* Marguerite's, unless, that is, you've taken to transvestism as a substitute for nonperformance.

> [MILO *disappears into the bedroom.* ANDREW *sits on below, crushed and humiliated. After a minute, he rises and starts wearily across the room. Suddenly he stops as a thought enters his mind*]

ANDREW: [*To himself*] The coat! . . . The fur coat . . . of course . . . I've got him! [*He brightens visibly—a man who realizes sud-*

denly that he can rescue a victory out of the jaws of defeat—and crosses firmly to his desk and takes out his gun] You see, Inspector, I was working in the morning room when I heard a noise. I seized my gun and came in here. I saw the figure of a man, apparently carrying my wife's fur coat. I shouted for him to put his hands up, but instead he ran toward the front door, trying to escape. Though I aimed low, I'm afraid I shot him dead. [INSPECTOR's voice] Mustn't blame yourself, sir, could have happened to anybody!

> [MILO *returns, carrying fur coat. He comes down the stairs, but does not see the gun hidden behind* ANDREW's *back*]

ANDREW: I'm not going to let you go, you know.

MILO: No? What *are* you going to do, Andrew? Shoot me down? Play that old burglar game again?

ANDREW: Yes, that's precisely what I could do.

MILO: It wouldn't work, you know, even if you had the guts to go through with it.

ANDREW: Why not?

MILO: [*Fetches a suitcase from the hall and packs the fur coat*] Because of what happened when I left here on Friday night. I lurched home in the moonlight, numb and dazed, and soiled. I sat up all night in a chair—damaged—contaminated by you and this house. I remembered something my father said to me: "In this country, Milo," he said, "there's justice, but sometimes for a foreigner it is difficult." In the morning I went to the police station and told them what had happened. One of them, Sergeant Tarrant—yes, he's real—took me into a room and we had quite a long chat. But I don't think he really believed me, even though I showed him the powder burn on my head. He seemed more interested in my relationship with Marguerite, which by the way they all appeared to know about. I felt this terrible anger coming over me. I thought "they're not going to believe me because I'm a stranger from London who's screwing the wife of the local nob and has got what he deserved." So I thought of my father, and what I might have done in Italy, and I took my *own* revenge. But remember, Andrew, the police might still come.

ANDREW: [*Slowly*] Then why haven't they, then?

MILO: I don't know, perhaps they won't. But even if they don't, you can't play your burglar game now, they'd never swallow it. So you see, you've lost.

ANDREW: I don't believe one word you're saying.

MILO: [*Deliberately*] It's the truth.

ANDREW: You're lying!

MILO: Why don't you phone Sergeant Tarrant if you don't believe me.

ANDREW: And say what? Please, Sergeant, has Milo Tindle been in saying that I framed him as a burglar and then shot him? I'm not *that* half-witted.

MILO: Suit yourself.

ANDREW: I *shall* shoot you, Milo. You come here and ask my permission to steal away my wife, you pry into my manhood, you lecture me on dead worlds and ignoble minds, and you mock Merridew. Well, they're all *real* bullets this time.

MILO: I'm going home now.

> [MILO *starts to leave,* ANDREW *fires.* MILO *drops in pain, fatally shot.* ANDREW *kneels and holds his head up*]

ANDREW: You're a bad liar, Milo, and in the final analysis, an uninventive games-player. Can you hear me? Then listen to this, NEVER play the same game three times running!

> [*There is the sound of a car approaching and pulling to a halt. A flashing blue police car light shines through the window. The doorbell rings. There is a loud knocking on door. Painfully,* MILO *lifts his head from the floor; he laughs*]

MILO: Game, set and match!

> [*His laugh becomes a cough. Blood trickles from his mouth. He grimaces in surprise at the pain and dies. The knocking on the door is repeated more loudly.* ANDREW *staggers to his desk and accidentally presses the button on it. This sets off the sailor who laughs ironically. The knocking becomes more insistent.* ANDREW *leans weakly against pillar. He shouts in anguish as:*]

THE CURTAIN FALLS

The Letter

W. SOMERSET MAUGHAM

W. Somerset Maugham

Ever since 1927 when Gladys Cooper, the original Leslie Crosbie, with smoking pistol in hand pursued her inamorato onto the veranda of her bungalow in the Malay Peninsula, W. Somerset Maugham's heroine has had a compelling fascination for leading actresses. And it does not require a windy pundit to detail reasons for this: few roles in modern drama offer to an actress such a wide and varied range of emotional pyrotechnics. On the surface, Leslie represents the devoted, serene, remarkably self-controlled young wife of a suitably proper British overseer of a rubber plantation. Beneath the surface it is quite another matter, as we become well aware as Maugham scrupulously strips the veils from his character during the play's action. As in much of the author's work, illusions, stability, and especially fidelity not only can be threatened but more likely torn to revealing shreds in the exotic ambiance of the tropics. And so it was with Leslie Crosbie . . .

The Letter was founded on a Maugham short story of similar title that appeared in his 1926 collection, *The Casuarina Tree*. Toward the end of his life, Maugham was asked which of his own stories he could reread with pleasure and he admitted that there were two for which he had a lingering affection, one of these being *The Letter*. Although an established dramatist as well as a master creator of fiction, Maugham apparently was not the first to see its possibilities as a play. (For that matter, neither did he perceive the dramatic potentials in his story *Rain*, later dramatized by John Colton and Clemence Randolph.) The suggestion to make a play of *The Letter* came from Anthony Prinsep, who in 1923 had successfully produced the author's satiric comedy *Our Betters*. Prinsep wanted the play for his actress-wife Margaret Bannerman, but when

Maugham completed the dramatization he felt that the woman's
part would be more suited to Gladys Cooper, London's foremost star
actress of that period. Prinsep wouldn't agree, but as it turned out,
during the early rehearsals Miss Bannerman personally became convinced that the part was not right for her and she relinquished it.
Miss Cooper, at Maugham's behest, agreed to do the role for Prinsep.
The latter was away at the time and when his manager wired him:
"Can get Gladys Cooper for *The Letter*," he promptly wired back:
"I won't have her."

In the end, however, *The Letter* was turned over to Miss Cooper
and it became her first venture as actress-manager. As she herself
recalled: "All I had at the time was four hundred pounds for the
production. I had eight hundred pounds in the world, but I put half
of it away for myself and the children in case the play turned out a
failure. When we opened about two hundred pounds was left in my
theatre account, but luck was with us. *The Letter* was a success: it
played to more than two thousand pounds in its first full week at the
Playhouse, ran for sixty weeks—including the tour—and I made
forty thousand pounds out of it. Forty thousand pounds out of four
hundred! It was my biggest 'romance of the theatre.'" *The Letter*
also became one of Maugham's three most popular successes in the
English theatre.

Toward the conclusion of the play, Maugham originally had Leslie
narrate her quarrel with Hammond which led to the shooting, but
according to Miss Cooper's autobiography: "After we'd been re-
hearsing *The Letter* for some days, both Gerald du Maurier (the
director) and I felt uncertain about the dramatic values of a 'blackout' in it. I rang up Maugham and told him this, and his reply was
characteristic of him. 'All right, if you don't feel it's right, change it,'
he said with the greatest amiability. I wonder how many—if any—
playwrights would say a thing like that."

Despite good intentions, Miss Cooper obviously put the case the
wrong way round, as it was the *flash-back* sequence that was substituted at rehearsals. This was proven by Maugham's own note in the
published play (1927): "Since a play is published not only to gratify
an author's vanity, but also for the convenience of amateurs, I have
thought it well to print here the version acted at the Playhouse.

After two or three rehearsals, I replaced Leslie Crosbie's final confession with a 'throw-back,' because I thought it would bore the audience to listen to two long narratives in one play. I have a notion that an author may prudently take a risk to avoid tediousness." (Both versions are included in this collection.)

While Miss Cooper still was enjoying her London triumph, and profits, another actress of stellar rank, Katharine Cornell, opened in the play at the Morosco Theatre, New York, on September 26, 1927. The engagement lasted for thirteen weeks, then, in accordance with Miss Cornell's custom, toured for the balance of the season.

In 1929, the legendary Jeanne Eagels, who scored in the play *Rain*, portrayed Leslie Crosbie in the film version of *The Letter*. Since it was a chaotic period of transition from silents to talkies, Paramount Pictures decided to work both sides of the street and consequently made two versions, silent and sound.

Though Miss Eagels was lauded for her portrayal of Maugham's complex heroine, it was Bette Davis who truly immortalized the role on screen in the 1940 Warner Brothers production directed by William Wyler. Miss Davis's fire-and-ice performance and Wyler's superb craftsmanship combined to make *The Letter* a tense, enthralling drama that frequently is revived today. As a matter of record, Warner Brothers turned out another, lesser, version of *The Letter*, retitled *The Unfaithful*, with Ann Sheridan in 1947.

One of the giants of modern literature, W. Somerset Maugham (1874–1965) reached the height of his popularity as a dramatist in 1908 when he created a theatrical record by having four plays performed in London concurrently. During his long and extraordinary career, Maugham wrote more than thirty plays, but in the early 1930's, while still at the height of his creative powers, he declared that the sardonic comedy *Sheppey* would be his last play, and he kept to his vow in spite of general disbelief.

It has been said of Maugham (who was created a Companion of Honour in 1954): "There is a finish, a neatness, an air of accomplishment about every work of Maugham's, whatever its subject-matter, which ensures for playgoers and readers alike a certain quality of pleasure. He could always revive the oldest of themes, relacquer it, and make it look as good as new. He achieved popularity without being good-natured, expansive, optimistic, romantic, or soothing. His humor was sardonic, tending to hard epigram: his attitude toward the virtues mistrustful; but he took care to give the public what he himself liked, a good story."

The Letter was first produced by Gladys Cooper at the Playhouse, London, on February 24, 1927. The cast was as follows:

HOWARD JOYCE	*Leslie Faber*
ROBERT CROSBIE	*Nigel Bruce*
ONG CHI SENG	*George Carr*
GEOFFREY HAMMOND	*S. J. Warmington*
JOHN WITHERS	*James Raglan*
CHUNG HI	*A. G. Poulton*
MRS. JOYCE	*Clare Harris*
MRS. PARKER	*Marion Lind*
CHINESE WOMAN	*Marie Chen Sing*
A SIKH SERGEANT OF POLICE	*Tom Mills*
LESLIE CROSBIE	*Gladys Cooper*
CHINESE BOYS, MALAY SERVANTS	*Chong, Low Ping, Lun Kun Tar, Chung Kin, See Young Sing, Chung Ah Ker*

Directed by	Gerald du Maurier
Settings by	J. A. Fraser

The Letter was first presented in the United States at the Morosco Theatre, New York, on September 26, 1927, by Messmore Kendall. The cast was as follows:

LESLIE CROSBIE	*Katharine Cornell*
GEOFFREY HAMMOND	*Burton McEvily*
HEAD BOY	*M. Wada*
JOHN WITHERS	*John Buckler*
ROBERT CROSBIE	*J. W. Austin*
HOWARD JOYCE	*Allan Jeayes*
ONG CHI SENG	*James Vincent*
A SIKH SERGEANT OF POLICE	*B. Landon*
MRS. PARKER	*Mary Scott Seton*
CHINESE WOMAN	*Lady Chong Goe*
MRS. JOYCE	*Eva Leonard-Boyne*
CHINESE BOYS, MALAY SERVANTS	*K. Tanaka, Yong Mung, Ho Poi Kee, Lo Sing, Lum Hee, Tong See*

Directed by	Guthrie McClintic
Settings by	Raymond Sovey

The action of the play takes place on a plantation in the Malay Peninsula, and at Singapore.

ACT ONE

The sitting room of the Crosbies' bungalow. Midnight.

ACT TWO

The visitors' room in the gaol at Singapore. Six weeks later.

ACT THREE

SCENE 1: *A room in the Chinese quarter of Singapore. The same night.*

SCENE 2: *The sitting room of the Crosbies' bungalow. Afternoon; the next day.*

ACT ONE

The sitting room of the Crosbies' bungalow on a planta-
tion in the Malay Peninsula. Midnight.

The room is comfortably but quite simply furnished.
There are three rattan armchairs, with cushions, one above
the door right and one each side of a circular table. The
chair on the right of the table has an extending leg-rest.
A writing desk stands below the door with a small rattan
chair pushed into it. There is an occasional table with a
bowl of flowers. A cottage piano with a small rattan chair
in front of it is in the corner up left and a piece of music
is open on the stand. Below the piano there is a bookcase.
A long stool completes the furniture. A door in the right
wall leads to the bedroom. On the walls are water-color
pictures with here and there an arrangement of krises and
parangs and some hunting trophies. There are rattan mats
on the floor. The room is lit by two lamps, one on the
piano and the other on the round table, on which also is
LESLIE's lace pillow. Across the back of the room runs a
veranda, approached by steps from the garden. Rattan
blinds, at present rolled up, can be lowered to separate the
room from the veranda. A lamp hangs over the center of
the veranda.

When the curtain rises, the lamps are lit. The sound of a
shot is heard and a cry from HAMMOND, *who is seen stag-*
gering toward the veranda. LESLIE, *with a revolver in her*
right hand, is standing near the table. She fires again.

HAMMOND: Oh, my God!

[*He falls face down on the veranda.* LESLIE *follows, and*
stands over him. She fires several more shots in rapid suc-

cession into the prostrate body. There is a little click as she mechanically pulls the trigger and the six chambers are empty. She looks at the revolver and lets it drop from her hand; then her eyes fall on the body, they grow enormous as though they would start out of her head, and a look of horror comes into her face. She gives a shudder as she looks at the dead man, and then, her gaze still fixed on the dreadful sight, backs into the room. There is an excited jabbering from the garden and LESLIE *gives a start as she hears it. It is immediately followed by the appearance of the* HEAD BOY *and another servant. The* HEAD BOY *is a small, fat Chinese man of about forty. While he is speaking, two or three more Chinese servants wearing white trousers and singlets, and some Malays in sarongs, appear*]

HEAD BOY: [*As he ascends the steps; calling*] Missy! Missy! Whatchee matter? I hear gunfire. [*He catches sight of the body*] Oh!

[*The* BOY *with him speaks to him excitedly in Chinese*]

LESLIE: Is he dead?

HEAD BOY: Missy! Missy! Who kill him? [*He bends over and looks at the corpse*] That Mr. Hammond.

LESLIE: Is he dead?

[*The* HEAD BOY *kneels down and feels the man's face. The others stand round and chatter among themselves*]

HEAD BOY: Yes, I think him dead.

LESLIE: Oh, my God!

HEAD BOY: [*Rising*] Missy, what for you do that?

LESLIE: Do you know where the Assistant District Officer lives?

HEAD BOY: Mr. Withers, Missy? Yes, I savvy. He live jolly long way from here.

LESLIE: Fetch him.

HEAD BOY: More better we wait till daylight, Missy.

LESLIE: There's nothing to be frightened of. Hassan will drive you over in the car. Is Hassan there?

HEAD BOY: [*Pointing to one of the Malays*] Yes, Missy.

LESLIE: Wake Mr. Withers and tell him to come here at once. Say there's been an accident and Mr. Hammond's dead.

HEAD BOY: Yes, Missy.

LESLIE: Go at once.

[*The* HEAD BOY *turns to* HASSAN *the chauffeur and gives him instructions in Malay to get out the car.* HASSAN *exits down the veranda steps*]

HEAD BOY: I think more better we bring body in, Missy, and put him on bed in spare room.

LESLIE: [*With a broken cry of anguish*] No!

HEAD BOY: No can leave him here, Missy.

LESLIE: Don't touch it. When Mr. Withers comes he'll say what's to be done.

HEAD BOY: [*Moving into the room*] All right, Missy. I tell Ah Sing to wait here maybe.

LESLIE: If you like. [*She pauses*] I want Mr. Crosbie sent for.

HEAD BOY: Post office all closed up, Missy, no can telephone till tomollow morning.

LESLIE: What's the time?

HEAD BOY: I think, maybe, twelve o'clock.

LESLIE: You must wake the man up at the post office as you go through the village, and he must get on to Singapore somehow or other. Or try at the police station. Perhaps they can get on.

HEAD BOY: All light, Missy. I try.

LESLIE: Give the man two or three dollars. Whatever happens they must get on to him at once.

HEAD BOY: If I catchee speak master, what thing I say, Missy?

LESLIE: I'll write the message down for you.

[*She sits at the desk, takes a sheet of paper and pencil*]

HEAD BOY: All light, Missy. You write.

LESLIE: [*Trying to write*] Oh, my hand! [*She puts the pencil down*] I can't hold the pencil. [*She beats with her fist on the desk in anger with herself, and takes the pencil again. She writes a few words and then rises, paper in hand*] Here's the message. That's the telephone number. Master is spending the night at Mr. Joyce's house.

HEAD BOY: I savvy. The lawyer.

LESLIE: They must ring and ring till they get an answer. They can give the message in Malay if they like. Read it and see if you understand.

[*She holds the paper out toward him*]

HEAD BOY: [*Peering over the paper*] Yes, Missy. I understand.

LESLIE: [*Reading*] "Come at once. There's been a terrible accident. Hammond is dead."

[*She gives him the paper*]

HEAD BOY: All light, Missy.

[*There is the sound of a car being started*]

LESLIE: There's the car. Be quick now.

HEAD BOY: Yes, Missy.

[*He exits by the veranda steps.* LESLIE *stands for a moment looking down at the floor. One or two* MALAY WOMEN *come softly up the veranda steps. They look at the corpse and talk excitedly to each other in whispers.* LESLIE *becomes conscious of their presence*]

LESLIE: What do you want? Go away, all of you.

[*All leave silently down the veranda steps except* AH SING, *a Chinese boy.* LESLIE *gives the body a long look, then turns and goes into her bedroom and locks the door.* AH SING *comes into the room, moves to the circular table, helps himself to a cigarette and lights it. He then sits in the armchair, crosses one leg over the other, and blows the smoke into the air. The lights dim out.*

When the lights come up again it is three hours later. The scene is the same, but the body has been removed. JOHN WITHERS, *a young man, neatly dressed in a white duck suit, is walking up and down the room. His topee is on a table. The* HEAD BOY *comes in*]

HEAD BOY: My believe I hear motorcar on road.

WITHERS: [*Moving on to the veranda and listening*] I don't. [*He turns irritably*] I can't imagine why he's so long. [*There is the faint sound of a motor horn. He turns to peer out again into the darkness*] Yes, by George! That's a car. Thank the Lord for that. [*The* HEAD BOY *exits down the veranda steps as he crosses to the bedroom door, knocks and calls*] Mrs. Crosbie . . . [*There is no answer and he knocks again*] Mrs. Crosbie.

LESLIE: [*Off; calling*] Yes?

WITHERS: There's a car on the road. That must be your husband. [*There is no reply to this. He listens for a moment and then with a gesture of impatience crosses to the veranda. The sound is heard of a car arriving. It stops*] Is that you, Crosbie?

CROSBIE: [*Off; calling*] Yes.

WITHERS: I thought you were never coming.

> [CROSBIE *enters by the veranda steps. He is a man of powerful build, forty years old, with a large sunburned face; he is dressed in khaki shorts, a shirt without a tie, a khaki coat and a broad-brimmed hat*]

CROSBIE: Where's Leslie?

WITHERS: She's in her room. She's locked herself in. She wouldn't see me till you came.

CROSBIE: What's happened? [*He knocks urgently on the bedroom door and calls*] Leslie! Leslie!

> [*There is a moment's pause.* JOYCE *enters by the veranda steps. He is a thin, spare, clean-shaven man of about forty-five. He wears ducks and a topee*]

JOYCE: [*Holding out his hand to* WITHERS] My name is Joyce. Are you the A.D.O.?

WITHERS: [*Shaking hands with* JOYCE] Yes. Withers.

JOYCE: Crosbie was spending the night with us. I thought I'd better come along with him.

CROSBIE: Leslie! It's me! Open the door!

WITHERS: [*To* JOYCE] Oh, are you the lawyer?

JOYCE: Yes. Joyce and Simpson.

WITHERS: I know.

[*The bedroom door is unlocked and slowly opened.* LESLIE *enters. She closes the door behind her and stands against it*]

CROSBIE: [*Stretching out his hands as though to take her in his arms*] Leslie.

LESLIE: [*Warding him off with a gesture*] Oh, don't touch me.

CROSBIE: What's happened? What's happened?

LESLIE: Didn't they tell you over the telephone?

CROSBIE: They said Hammond was killed.

LESLIE: [*Looking toward the veranda*] Is he there still?

WITHERS: No. I had the body taken away.

[LESLIE *looks at the three men with haggard eyes and then throws back her head*]

LESLIE: He tried to rape me and I shot him.

CROSBIE: Leslie!

WITHERS: My God!

LESLIE: Oh, Robert, I'm so glad you've come.

CROSBIE: Darling! Darling!

[LESLIE *throws herself in his arms and he embraces her tightly. Now at last she breaks down and sobs convulsively*]

LESLIE: Hold me tight. Don't let me go. I'm so frightened. Oh, Robert, Robert.

CROSBIE: It'll be all right. There's nothing to be frightened about. Don't let yourself go to pieces.

LESLIE: I've got you, haven't I? Oh, Robert, what shall I do? I'm so unhappy.

CROSBIE: Sweetheart!

LESLIE: Hold me close to you.

WITHERS: Do you think you could tell us exactly what happened?

LESLIE: Now?

CROSBIE: Come and sit down, dear heart. You're all in.

[*He leads her to the long chair and she sinks into it with exhaustion*]

WITHERS: I'm afraid it sounds awfully brutal, but my duty is . . .

LESLIE: Oh, I know, of course. I'll tell you everything I can. I'll try to pull myself together. [*She looks up at* CROSBIE, *who is standing beside her*] Give me your hankie.

> [*She takes a handkerchief out of his pocket and dries her eyes*]

CROSBIE: Don't hurry yourself, darling. Take your time.

LESLIE: [*Forcing a smile to her lips*] It's so good to have you here.

CROSBIE: It's lucky Howard came along.

LESLIE: Oh, Mr. Joyce, how nice of you! [*She stretches out her hand*] Fancy your coming all this way at this time of night!

JOYCE: [*Crossing to her and shaking hands*] Oh, that's all right.

LESLIE: How's Dorothy?

JOYCE: Oh, she's very well, thank you.

LESLIE: I feel so dreadfully faint.

CROSBIE: Would you like a drop of whisky?

LESLIE: [*Closing her eyes*] It's on the table.

> [CROSBIE *crosses to the drinks table while* LESLIE *leans back in the chair, with her eyes closed, her face pale and wan.* JOYCE *eases softly toward* WITHERS]

JOYCE: [*In an undertone to* WITHERS] How long have you been here?

WITHERS: Oh, an hour or more. I was fast asleep. My boy woke me up and said the Crosbies' head boy was there and wanted to see me at once.

> [CROSBIE *pours out a whisky and soda*]

JOYCE: Did he tell you she'd shot him?

WITHERS: Yes. When I got here Mrs. Crosbie had locked herself in her room and refused to come out till her husband came.

JOYCE: Was Hammond dead?

WITHERS: Oh, yes, he was just riddled with bullets.

JOYCE: [*In a tone of faint surprise*] Oh!

WITHERS: [*Taking the revolver from his pocket*] Here's the revolver. All six chambers are empty.

[LESLIE *slowly opens her eyes and looks at the two men talking.* JOYCE *takes the revolver in his hand and looks at it*]

JOYCE: [*To* CROSBIE *as he crosses back with the drink*] Is this yours, Bob?

CROSBIE: Yes.

[*He goes to* LESLIE *and supports her while she sips*]

JOYCE: [*To* WITHERS] Have you questioned the boys?

WITHERS: Yes, they know nothing. They were asleep in their own quarters. They were awakened by the firing, and when they came here they found Hammond lying on the floor.

JOYCE: Where exactly?

WITHERS: [*Pointing*] There. On the veranda under the lamp.

LESLIE: Thank you. I shall feel better in a minute. I'm sorry to be so tiresome.

JOYCE: Do you feel well enough to talk now?

LESLIE: I think so.

CROSBIE: You needn't be in such a devil of a hurry. She's in no condition to make a long statement now.

JOYCE: It'll have to be made sooner or later.

LESLIE: It's all right, Robert, really. I feel perfectly well now.

JOYCE: I think we ought to be put in possession of the facts as soon as possible.

WITHERS: Take your time, Mrs. Crosbie. After all, we're all friends here.

LESLIE: What do you want me to do? If you've got any questions to ask, I'll do my best to answer them.

JOYCE: [*Sitting*] Perhaps it would be better if you told us the whole story in your own way. Do you think you can manage that?

LESLIE: [*Rising*] I'll try.

CROSBIE: What do you want to do?

LESLIE: I want to sit upright. [*She sits again, upright on the chair extension, and hesitates a moment. The eyes of all of them are on her face. Finally, she addresses* WITHERS] Robert was spending the night in Singapore, you know.

WITHERS: Yes, your boy told me that.

LESLIE: I was going in with him, but I wasn't feeling very well and I thought I'd stay here. I never mind being alone. [*With a half-smile at* CROSBIE] A planter's wife gets used to that, you know.

CROSBIE: That's true.

LESLIE: I had dinner rather late, and then I started working on my lace. [*She points to the pillow on which a piece of lace half made is pinned with little pins*]

CROSBIE: My wife is rather a dab at lacemaking.

WITHERS: Yes, I know. I've heard that.

LESLIE: I don't know how long I'd been working. It fascinates me, you know, and I lose all sense of time. Suddenly I heard a footstep outside and someone came up the steps of the veranda and said: "Good evening. Can I come in?" I was startled, because I hadn't heard a car drive up.

WITHERS: Hammond left his car about a quarter of a mile down the road. It's parked under the trees. Your chauffeur noticed it as we were driving back.

JOYCE: I wonder why Hammond left his car there?

WITHERS: Presumably, he did not want anyone to hear him drive up.

JOYCE: Go on, Mrs. Crosbie.

LESLIE: At first I couldn't see who it was. I work in spectacles, you know, and in the half-darkness of the veranda it was impossible for me to recognize anybody. "Who is it?" I said. "Geoff Hammond." "Oh, of course, come in and have a drink," I said. And I took off my spectacles. I got up and shook hands with him.

JOYCE: Were you surprised to see him?

LESLIE: I was, rather. He hadn't been up to the house for ages, had he, Robert?

CROSBIE: Three months at least, I should think.

LESLIE: I told him Robert was away. He'd had to go to Singapore on business.

WITHERS: What did he say to that?

LESLIE: He said: "Oh, I'm sorry. I felt rather lonely tonight, so I thought I'd just come along and see how you were getting on." I asked him how he'd come, as I hadn't heard a car, and he said he'd left it on the road because he thought we might be in bed and asleep and he didn't want to wake us up.

JOYCE: I see.

LESLIE: As Robert was away there wasn't any whisky in the room, but I thought the boys would be asleep, so I didn't call them; I just went and fetched it myself. Hammond mixed himself a drink and lit his pipe.

JOYCE: Was he quite sober?

LESLIE: [*After a slight pause*] I never thought about it. I suppose he had been drinking, but just then it didn't occur to me.

JOYCE: What happened?

LESLIE: Well, nothing very much; I put on my spectacles again and went on with my work. We chatted about one thing and another. He asked me if Robert had heard that a tiger had been seen on the road two or three days ago. It had killed a couple of goats and the villagers were in a state about it. He said he thought he'd try to get it over the weekend.

CROSBIE: Oh, yes, I know about that. Don't you remember, I spoke to you about it at tiffin yesterday.

LESLIE: Did you? I believe you did.

WITHERS: Fire away, Mrs. Crosbie.

LESLIE: Well, we were just chatting. Then suddenly he said something rather silly.

JOYCE: What?

LESLIE: It's hardly worth repeating. He paid me a little compliment.

JOYCE: I think perhaps you'd better tell us exactly what he said.

LESLIE: He said: "I don't know how you can bear to disfigure yourself with those horrible spectacles. You've got very pretty eyes indeed, you know, and it's too bad of you to hide them."

JOYCE: Had he ever said anything of the sort to you before?

LESLIE: No, never. I was a little taken aback, but I thought it best to take it quite lightly. "I make no pretensions to being a raving beauty, you know," I said. "But you are," he said. It sounds awfully silly to repeat things like this.

JOYCE: Never mind. Please let us have his exact words.

LESLIE: Well, he said: "It's too bad of you to try to make yourself look plain, but thank God you don't succeed." [*She gives the two strangers a faintly deprecating look*] I shrugged my shoulders. I thought it rather impertinent of him to talk to me like that.

CROSBIE: I don't wonder.

JOYCE: Did you say anything?

LESLIE: Yes, I said: "If you ask me point blank I'm bound to tell you that I don't care a row of pins what you think about me." I was trying to snub him, but he only laughed. "I'm going to tell you all the same," he said. "I think you're the prettiest thing I've seen for many a long year." "Sweet of you," I said, "but in that case I can only think you half-witted." He laughed again. He'd been sitting over there, and he got up and drew up a chair near the table I was working at. "You're not going to have the face to deny that you have the prettiest hands in the world," he said. That rather put my back up. In point of fact, my hands are not very good, and I'd just as soon people didn't talk about them. It's only an awful fool of a woman who wants to be flattered on her worst points.

CROSBIE: Leslie, darling.

[He takes one of her hands and kisses it]

LESLIE: Oh, Robert, you silly old thing.

JOYCE: Well, when Hammond was talking in that strain, did he just sit still with his arms crossed?

LESLIE: Oh, no. He tried to take one of my hands. But I gave him a little tap. I wasn't particularly annoyed, I merely thought he was rather silly. I said to him: "Don't be an idiot. Sit down where you were before and talk sensibly, or else I shall send you home."

WITHERS: But, Mrs. Crosbie, I wonder you didn't kick him out there and then.

LESLIE: I didn't want to make a fuss. You know, there are men who think it's their duty to flirt with a woman when they get the chance. I believe they think women expect it of them, and for all I know a good many do. But I'm not one of them, am I, Robert?

CROSBIE: Far from it.

LESLIE: A woman only makes a perfect fool of herself if she makes a scene every time a man pays her one or two compliments. She doesn't need much experience of the world to discover that it means rather less than nothing. I didn't suspect for an instant that Hammond was serious.

JOYCE: When did you suspect?

LESLIE: Then. What he said next. You see, he didn't move. He just looked at me straight in the face, and said: "Don't you know that I'm awfully in love with you?"

CROSBIE: The cad.

LESLIE: "I don't," I answered. You see, it meant so little to me that I hadn't the smallest difficulty in keeping perfectly cool. "I don't believe it for a minute," I said, "and even if it were true I don't want you to say it."

JOYCE: Were you surprised?

LESLIE: Of course I was surprised. Why, we've known him for seven years, Robert.

CROSBIE: Yes, he came here after the war.

LESLIE: And he's never paid me the smallest attention. I didn't suppose he even knew what color my eyes were. If you'd asked me, I should have said I didn't begin to exist for him.

CROSBIE: [To JOYCE] You must remember that we never saw very much of him.

LESLIE: When he first came here he was ill and I got Robert to go over and fetch him; he was all alone in his bungalow.

JOYCE: Where was his bungalow?

CROSBIE: About six or seven miles from here.

LESLIE: I couldn't bear the idea of his lying there without anyone to look after him, so we brought him here and took care of him till he was fit again. We saw a certain amount of him after that, but we had nothing very much in common, and we never became very intimate.

CROSBIE: For the last two or three years we've hardly seen him at all. To tell you the truth, after all that Leslie had done for him when he was ill I thought he was almost too casual.

LESLIE: He used to come over now and then to play tennis, and we used to meet him at other people's houses now and again. But I don't think I'd set eyes on him for a month.

JOYCE: I see.

LESLIE: He helped himself to another whisky and soda. I began to wonder if he'd been drinking. Anyhow, I thought he'd had enough. "I wouldn't drink any more if I were you," I said. I was quite friendly about it. I wasn't the least frightened or anything like that. It never occurred to me that I couldn't manage him. He didn't pay any attention to what I said. He emptied his glass and put it down. "Do you think I'm talking to you like this because I'm drunk?" he asked in a funny abrupt way. "That's the most obvious explanation, isn't it?" I said. It's awful having to tell you all this. I'm so ashamed. It's so disgraceful.

JOYCE: I know it's hard. But for your own sake I beg you to tell us the whole story now.

WITHERS: If Mrs. Crosbie would like to wait a little, I don't see any great harm in that.

LESLIE: No, if I've got to tell it I'll tell it now. What's the good of waiting? My head's simply throbbing.

CROSBIE: Don't be too hard on her, Howard.

LESLIE: He's being as kind as he can be.

JOYCE: I hope so. "That's the most obvious explanation," you said.

LESLIE: "Well, it's a lie," he said. "I've loved you ever since I first knew you. I've held my tongue as long as I could, and now it's got to come out. I love you. I love you. I love you." He repeated it just like that.

CROSBIE: The swine.

LESLIE: [Rising from her seat and standing] I got up and I put away the pillow with my lace. I held out my hand. "Good night," I said. He didn't take it. He just stood and looked at me and his eyes were all funny. "I'm not going now," he said. Then I began to lose my temper. I think I'd kept it too long. I think I'm a very even-tempered woman, but when I'm roused I don't care very much what I say. "But, you poor fool," I cried at him, "don't you know that I've never loved anyone but Robert, and even if I don't love Robert you're the last man I should care for." "What do I care?" he said. "Robert's away."

CROSBIE: The cur! The filthy cur! Oh, by God . . .

JOYCE: Be quiet, Bob.

LESLIE: That was the last straw. I was beside myself. Even then I wasn't frightened. It never occurred to me he'd dare—he'd dare . . . I was just angry. I thought he was just a filthy swine to talk to me like that because he knew Robert was safely out of the way. "If you don't go away this minute," I said, "I shall call the boys and have you thrown out." He gave a filthy look. "They're out of earshot," he said. I walked past him quickly. I wanted to get out onto the veranda, so that I could give the boys a call. I knew they'd hear me from there. But he took hold of my arm and swung me back. "Let me go," I screamed. I was furious. "Not much," he said. "Not much. I've got you now." I opened my mouth and shouted as loud as I could: "Boy! Boy!" But he put his hand over it . . . Oh, it's horrible. I can't go on. It's asking too much of me. It's so shameful, shameful.

CROSBIE: Oh, Leslie, my darling. I wish to God I'd never left you.

LESLIE: Oh, it was awful.

[*She sobs brokenheartedly*]

JOYCE: I beseech you to control yourself. You've been wonderful up till now. I know it's very hard, but you must tell us everything.

LESLIE: I didn't know what he was doing. He flung his arms round me. He began to kiss me. I struggled. His lips were burning, and I turned my mouth away. "No, no, no!" I screamed. "Leave me alone. I won't!" I began to cry. I tried to tear myself away from him. He seemed like a madman.

CROSBIE: I can't bear much more of this.

JOYCE: Be quiet, Bob.

LESLIE: I don't know what happened. I was all confused. I was so frightened. He seemed to be talking, talking. He kept on saying that he loved me and wanted me. Oh, the misery! He held me so tight that I couldn't move. I never knew how strong he was. I felt as weak as a rat. It was awful to feel so helpless. I'm trying to tell you everything, but it's all in a blur. I felt myself growing weaker and weaker, and I thought I'd faint. His breath was hot on my face, and it made me feel desperately sick.

WITHERS: The brute.

LESLIE: He kissed me. He kissed my neck. Oh, the horror! And he held me so tight that I felt I couldn't breathe. Then he lifted me right off my feet. I tried to kick him. He only held me tighter. Then I felt he was carrying me. He didn't say anything. I didn't look at him, but somehow I saw his face, and it was as white as a sheet and his eyes were burning. He wasn't a man any more, he was a savage; I felt my heart pounding against my ribs . . . Don't look at me. I

don't want any of you to look at me. It flashed across me that he
was carrying me to the bedroom. Oh!

CROSBIE: If he weren't dead I'd strangle him with my own hands.

LESLIE: It all happened in a moment. He stumbled and fell. I don't
know why. I don't know if he caught his foot in something or if it
was just an accident. I fell with him. It gave me a chance. Somehow
his hold on me loosened and I snatched myself away from him.
It was all instinctive; it was the affair of a moment; I didn't know
what I was doing. I jumped up and I ran round the table. He was
a little slow at getting up.

WITHERS: He had a game leg.

CROSBIE: Yes. He had his kneecap smashed in the war.

LESLIE: Then he made a dash at me. There was a revolver on the
table and I snatched it. I didn't even know I'd fired. I heard a report. I saw him stagger. He cried out. He said something. I don't
know what it was. I was beside myself. I was in a frenzy. He
lurched out of the room onto the veranda and I followed him. I
don't remember anything. I heard the reports one after the other.
I don't ask you to believe me, but I didn't even know I was pulling
the trigger. I saw Hammond fall down. Suddenly I heard a funny
little click and it flashed through my mind that I'd fired all the
cartridges and the revolver was empty. It was only then that I knew
what I'd done. It was as if scales dropped from my eyes, and all at
once I caught sight of Hammond, and he was lying there in a heap.

CROSBIE: [*Taking her in his arms*] My poor child.

LESLIE: Oh, Robert, what have I done?

CROSBIE: You've done what any woman would have done in your
place, only nine-tenths of them wouldn't have had the nerve.

JOYCE: [*Rising*] How did the revolver happen to be there?

CROSBIE: I don't very often leave Leslie alone for the night, but when
I do I feel safer if she's got a weapon handy. I saw that all the bar-
rels were loaded before I left, and thank God I did.

LESLIE: That's all, Mr. Withers. You must forgive me if I wouldn't
see you when you came. But I wanted my husband.

WITHERS: Of course. May I say that I think you behaved magnifi-
cently. I'm fearfully sorry we had to put you to the ordeal of telling

us all this. But I think Mr. Joyce was right. It was much better that we should be in possession of all the facts immediately.

LESLIE: Oh, I know.

WITHERS: It's quite obvious the man was drunk, and he only got what he deserved.

LESLIE: And yet I'd give almost anything if I could bring him back to life. It's so awful to think that I killed him.

CROSBIE: It was an easy death for him. By God, if ever I've wanted to torture anyone . . .

LESLIE: No, don't, Robert, don't. The man's dead.

JOYCE: Could I see the body for a minute?

WITHERS: Yes. I'll take you to where it is.

LESLIE: [*With a little shudder*] You don't want me to come?

JOYCE: No, of course not. You stay here with Bob. We shall only be a minute.

[JOYCE *and* WITHERS *go out*]

LESLIE: I'm so tired. I'm so desperately tired.

CROSBIE: I know you are, darling. I'd do anything to help you, and yet there doesn't seem to be a thing I can do.

LESLIE: You can love me.

CROSBIE: I've always loved you with all my heart.

LESLIE: Yes, but now.

CROSBIE: If I could love you any more I would now.

LESLIE: You don't blame me?

CROSBIE: Blame you? I think you've been splendid. By God, you're a plucky little woman.

LESLIE: [*Tenderly*] This is going to give you an awful lot of anxiety, my dear.

CROSBIE: Don't think about me. I don't matter. Only think about yourself.

LESLIE: What will they do to me?

CROSBIE: Do? I'd like to see anyone talk of doing anything to you. Why, there isn't a man or a woman in the colony who won't be proud to know you.

LESLIE: I so hate the idea of everyone talking about me.

CROSBIE: I know, darling.

LESLIE: Whatever people say you'll never believe anything against me, will you?

CROSBIE: Of course not. What should they say?

LESLIE: How can I tell? People are so unkind. They might easily say that he would never have made advances to me if I hadn't led him on.

CROSBIE: I think that's the last thing anyone who's ever seen you would dream of saying.

LESLIE: Do you love me very much, Robert?

CROSBIE: I can never tell you how much.

LESLIE: We have been happy together all these years, haven't we?

CROSBIE: By George, yes! We've been married for ten years and it hardly seems a day. Do you know that we've never even had a quarrel?

LESLIE: [With a smile] Who could quarrel with anyone as kind and good-natured as you are?

CROSBIE: You know, Leslie, it makes me feel stupid and awkward to say some things. I'm not one of those fellows with the gift of the gab. But I do want you to know how awfully grateful I am to you for all you've done for me.

LESLIE: Oh, my dear, what are you talking about?

CROSBIE: You see, I'm not in the least clever. And I'm a great ugly hulking devil. I'm not fit to clean your boots really. I never knew at the beginning why you ever thought of me. You've been the best wife a man ever had.

LESLIE: Oh, what nonsense!

CROSBIE: Oh, no, it isn't. Because I don't say much you mustn't fancy I don't think a lot. I don't know how I've deserved all the luck I've had.

LESLIE: Darling! It's so good to hear you say that.

[He takes her in his arms and lingeringly kisses her mouth. JOYCE and WITHERS return. Without self-consciousness, LESLIE releases herself from her husband's embrace and turns to the two men]

LESLIE: Wouldn't you like something to eat? You must be perfectly ravenous.

WITHERS: Oh, no, don't bother, Mrs. Crosbie.

LESLIE: It's no bother at all. I expect the boys are about still, and if they're not I can easily make you a little something myself.

JOYCE: Personally, I'm not at all hungry.

LESLIE: Robert?

CROSBIE: No, dear.

JOYCE: In point of fact, I think it's about time we started for Singapore.

LESLIE: [A *trifle startled*] Now?

JOYCE: It'll be dawn when we get there. By the time you've had a bath and some breakfast it'll be eight o'clock. We'll ring up the Attorney General and find out when we can see him. Don't you think that's the best thing we can do, Withers?

WITHERS: Yes. I suppose so.

JOYCE: You'll come with us, of course?

WITHERS: I think I'd better, don't you?

LESLIE: Shall I be arrested?

JOYCE: [*With a glance at* WITHERS] I think you're by way of being under arrest now.

WITHERS: It's purely a matter of form, Mrs. Crosbie. Mr. Joyce's idea is that you should go to the Attorney General and give yourself up. . . . Of course, all this is entirely out of my line. I don't know exactly what I ought to do.

LESLIE: Poor Mr. Withers, I'm so sorry to give you all this trouble.

WITHERS: Oh, don't bother about me. The worst that can happen to me is that I shall get hauled over the coals for doing the wrong thing.

LESLIE: [*With a faint smile*] And you've lost a good night's rest, too.

JOYCE: Well, we'll start when you're ready, my dear.

LESLIE: Shall I be imprisoned?

JOYCE: That is for the Attorney General to decide. I hope that after you've told him your story we shall be able to get him to accept bail. It depends on what the charge is.

CROSBIE: He's a very good fellow. I'm sure he'll do everything he can.

JOYCE: He must do his duty.

CROSBIE: What do you mean by that?

JOYCE: I think it not unlikely that he'll say only one charge is possible, and in that case I'm afraid that an application for bail would be useless.

LESLIE: What charge?

JOYCE: Murder.

[*There is a moment's pause. The only sign that* LESLIE *gives that the word startles her is the clenching of one of her hands. But it requires quite an effort for her to keep her voice level and calm*]

LESLIE: I'll just go and change into a jumper. I won't be a minute. And I'll get a hat.

JOYCE: Oh, very well. You'd better go and give her a hand, Bob. She'll want someone to do her up.

LESLIE: Oh, no, don't bother. I can manage quite well by myself. A jumper doesn't have to be done up, my poor friend.

JOYCE: Doesn't it? I forgot. I think you'd better go along all the same, old man.

LESLIE: I'm not thinking of committing suicide, you know.

JOYCE: I should hope not. The idea never occurred to me. I thought I'd like to have a word or two with Withers.

LESLIE: Come along, Robert.

[*She goes off into bedroom, followed by Crosbie*]

WITHERS: By George! That woman's a marvel.

JOYCE: [*Good-humoredly*] In what way?

WITHERS: I never saw anyone so calm in my life. Her self-control is absolutely amazing. She must have nerves of iron.

JOYCE: She has a great deal more character than I ever suspected.

WITHERS: You've known her a good many years, haven't you?

JOYCE: Ever since she married Crosbie. He's my oldest pal in the colony. But I've never known her very well. She hardly ever came into Singapore. I always found her very reserved, and I supposed she was shy. But my wife has been down here a good deal and she raves about her. She says that when you really get to know her she's a very nice woman.

WITHERS: Of course she's a very nice woman.

JOYCE: [*With the faintest irony*] She's certainly a very pretty one.

WITHERS: I was very much impressed by the way in which she told that terrible story.

JOYCE: I wish she could have been a little more explicit here and there. It was rather confused toward the end.

WITHERS: My dear fellow, what do you expect? You could see that she was just holding on to herself like grim death. It seemed to me a marvel that she was so coherent. I say, what a swine that man was!

JOYCE: By the way, did you know Hammond?

WITHERS: Yes, I knew him a little. I've only been here three months, you know.

JOYCE: Is this your first job as A.D.O.?

WITHERS: Yes.

JOYCE: Was Hammond a heavy drinker?

WITHERS: I don't know that he was. He could take his whack, but I never saw him actually drunk.

JOYCE: Of course I've heard of him, but I never met him myself. He was by way of being rather a favorite with the ladies, wasn't he?

WITHERS: He was a very good-looking chap. You know the sort, very breezy and devil-may-care and generous with his money.

JOYCE: Yes, that is the sort they fall for.

WITHERS: I've always understood he was one of the most popular men in the colony. Before he hurt his leg in the war he held the tennis championship, and I believe he had the reputation of being the best dancer between Penang and Singapore.

JOYCE: Did you like him?

WITHERS: He was the sort of chap you couldn't help liking. I should have said he was a man who hadn't an enemy in the world.

JOYCE: Was he the sort of chap you'd expect to do a thing like this?

WITHERS: How should I know? How can you tell what a man will do when he's drunk?

JOYCE: My own opinion is that if a man's a blackguard when he's drunk he's a blackguard when he's sober.

WITHERS: What are you going to do, then?

JOYCE: Well, it's quite evident that we must find out about him.

[LESLIE *returns. She has changed her clothes and is carrying her hat. She is followed by* CROSBIE]

LESLIE: Well, I haven't been long, have I?

JOYCE: I shall hold you up as an example to my Dorothy.

LESLIE: She's probably not half as slow as you are. I can always dress in a quarter of the time that Robert can.

CROSBIE: [*Crossing to the veranda*] I'll just go and start her up.

WITHERS: Is there room for me, or shall I come along in the other car?

LESLIE: Oh, there'll be plenty of room.

[CROSBIE *and* WITHERS *exit.* LESLIE *is about to follow*]

JOYCE: [*To* LESLIE] There's just one question I'd like to ask you.

LESLIE: [*Stopping and turning*] Yes, what is it?

JOYCE: Just now, when I was looking at Hammond's body, it seemed to me that some of the shots must have been fired when he was actually lying on the ground. It gives me the impression that you must have stood over him and fired and fired.

LESLIE: [*Putting her hand wearily on her forehead*] I was trying to forget for a minute.

JOYCE: Why did you do that?

LESLIE: I didn't know I did.

JOYCE: It's a question you must expect to be asked.

LESLIE: I'm afraid you think I'm more cold-blooded than I am. I lost my head. After a certain time everything is all blurred and confused. I'm awfully sorry.

JOYCE: Don't let it worry you, then. I daresay it's very natural. I'm sorry to make a nuisance of myself.

LESLIE: Shall we go?

JOYCE: Come on.

[*They exit. The* HEAD BOY *comes in and draws down the blinds that lead onto the veranda. He puts out the lights and goes, leaving the room in darkness*]

CURTAIN

ACT TWO

The visitors' room in the gaol at Singapore. Six weeks later.

It is a bare room of which we see only one corner. In the wall right there is a barred window through which can be seen the prison yard and wall. There are doors, down right and left. The only furniture is a large table of polished pitch pine and four plain chairs.

CROSBIE is standing at the window. He wears an air of profound dejection. He has on the clothes in which he is accustomed to walk over the estate—shorts and a khaki shirt; he holds his shabby old hat in his hand. He sighs deeply. The door left opens and JOYCE enters. He is followed by ONG CHI SENG, carrying a brief case. He is a Cantonese, small but trimly built; he is very neatly dressed in white ducks, patent-leather shoes and gay silk socks. He wears a gold wrist watch and invisible pince-nez. From his breast pocket protrudes a rolled-gold fountain pen. He expresses himself with elaborate accuracy; he has learned English as a foreign language, and speaks it perfectly; but he has trouble with his rs, he always turns them into ls, and this gives his careful speech every now and then a faintly absurd air.

CROSBIE: [*Turning*] Howard.

JOYCE: I heard you were here.

CROSBIE: I'm waiting to see Leslie.

JOYCE: I've come to see her too.

CROSBIE: Do you want me to clear out?

JOYCE: No, of course not. You go along and see her when they send for you, and then she can come here.

CROSBIE: I wish they'd let me see her here. It's awful having to see her in a cell with that damned matron always there.

JOYCE: I thought you'd probably look in at the office this morning.

CROSBIE: I couldn't get away. After all, the work on the estate has got to go on, and if I'm not there to look after it everything goes to blazes. I came into Singapore the moment I could. Oh, how I hate that damned estate!

JOYCE: In point of fact, I don't think it's been a bad thing for you during these last few weeks to have some work that you were obliged to do.

CROSBIE: I daresay not. Sometimes I've thought I should go mad.

JOYCE: You know you must pull yourself together, old man. You mustn't let yourself go to pieces.

CROSBIE: Oh, I'm all right.

JOYCE: You look as if you hadn't had a bath for a week.

CROSBIE: Oh, I've had a bath all right. I know my kit's rather grubby, but it's all right for tramping over the estate. I came just as I was. I hadn't the heart to change.

JOYCE: It's funny that you should have taken it all so much harder than your missus. She hasn't turned a hair.

CROSBIE: She's worth ten of me. I know that. I don't mind confessing it, I'm all in. I'm like a lost sheep without Leslie. It's the first time we've been separated for more than a day since we were married. I'm so lonely without her. [*He indicates* ONG CHI SENG] Who's that?

JOYCE: Oh, that's my confidential clerk, Ong Chi Seng.

[ONG CHI SENG *gives a little bow and smiles with a flash of white teeth*]

CROSBIE: What's he come here for?

JOYCE: I brought him with me in case I wanted him. Ong Chi Seng is as good a lawyer as I am. He took his degree in the University of Hong Kong, and as soon as he's learned the ins and outs of my business he's going to set up in opposition.

ONG CHI SENG: Hi, hi.

JOYCE: Perhaps you'd better wait outside, Ong. I'll call you if I want you.

ONG CHI SENG: Very good, sir. I shall be within earshot.

JOYCE: It'll do if you're within call.

[ONG CHI SENG *exits*]

CROSBIE: Oh, Howard, I wouldn't wish my worst enemy the agony that I've gone through during these horrible weeks.

JOYCE: You look as if you hadn't had much sleep lately, old man.

CROSBIE: I haven't. I don't think I've closed my eyes the last three nights.

JOYCE: Well, thank God it'll be over tomorrow. By the way, you'll clean yourself up a bit for the trial, won't you?

CROSBIE: Oh, yes, rather. I'm staying with you tonight.

JOYCE: Oh, are you? I'm glad. And you'll both come back to my house after the trial. Dorothy's determined to celebrate.

CROSBIE: I think it's monstrous that they should have kept Leslie in this filthy prison.

JOYCE: I think they had to do that.

CROSBIE: Why couldn't they let her out on bail?

JOYCE: It's a very serious charge, I'm afraid.

CROSBIE: Oh, this red tape. She did what any decent woman would do in her place. Leslie's the best girl in the world. She wouldn't hurt a fly. Why, hang it all, man, I've been married to her for ten years; do you think I don't know her? God, if I'd got hold of that man I'd have wrung his neck, I'd have killed him without a moment's hesitation. So would you.

JOYCE: My dear fellow, everybody's on your side.

CROSBIE: Thank God nobody's got a good word to say for Hammond.

JOYCE: I don't suppose a single member of the jury will go into the box without having already made up his mind to bring in a verdict of "Not guilty."

CROSBIE: Then the whole thing's a farce. She ought never to have been arrested in the first place; and then it's cruel, after all the poor girl's gone through, to subject her to the ordeal of a trial. There's not a soul I've met in Singapore, man or woman, who hasn't told me that Leslie was absolutely justified.

JOYCE: The Law is the Law. She admits that she killed the man. It is terrible, and I'm dreadfully sorry both for you and for her.

CROSBIE: I don't matter two straws.

JOYCE: But the fact remains that murder has been committed, and in a civilized community a trial is inevitable.

CROSBIE: Is it murder to exterminate noxious vermin? She shot him as she would have shot a mad dog.

JOYCE: I should be wanting in my duty as your legal adviser if I didn't tell you that there is one point which causes me a little anxiety. If your wife had only shot Hammond once the whole thing would have been absolutely plain sailing. Unfortunately she fired six times.

CROSBIE: Her explanation is perfectly simple. Under the circumstances anyone would have done the same.

JOYCE: I daresay, and, of course, I think the explanation is very reasonable.

CROSBIE: Then what are you making a fuss about?

JOYCE: It's no good closing our eyes to the facts. It's always a good plan to put yourself in another man's place, and I can't deny that if I were prosecuting for the Crown that is the point on which I would center my inquiry.

CROSBIE: Why?

JOYCE: It suggests not so much panic as uncontrollable fury. Under the circumstances which your wife has described one would expect a woman to be frightened out of her wits, but hardly beside herself with rage.

CROSBIE: Oh, isn't that rather farfetched?

JOYCE: I daresay. I just thought it was a point worth mentioning.

CROSBIE: I should have thought the really important thing was Hammond's character, and, by heaven! we've found out enough about him.

JOYCE: We've found out that he was living with a Chinese woman, if that's what you mean.

CROSBIE: Well, isn't that enough?

JOYCE: I daresay it is. It was certainly an awful shock to his friends.

CROSBIE: She'd been actually living in his bungalow for the last eight months.

JOYCE: It's strange how angry that's made people. It's turned public opinion against him more than anything.

CROSBIE: I can tell you this, if I'd known it I'd never have dreamed of letting him come to my place.

JOYCE: I wonder how he managed to keep it so dark.

CROSBIE: Will she be one of the witnesses?

JOYCE: I shan't call her. I shall produce evidence that he was living with her, and, public feeling being what it is, I think the jury will accept that as proof that Hammond was a man of notorious character.

> [A SIKH SERGEANT OF POLICE *enters. He is tall, bearded, dark, and dressed in blue*]

SIKH: [*To* CROSBIE] You come now, Sahib.

CROSBIE: At last.

JOYCE: You haven't got very long to wait now. In another twenty-four hours she'll be a free woman. Why don't you take her somewhere for a trip? Even though we're almost dead certain to get an acquittal, a trial of this sort is anxious work, and you'll both of you want a rest.

CROSBIE: I think I shall want it more than Leslie. She's been a brick. Why, d'you know, when I've been to see her it wasn't I who cheered her up, it was she who cheered me up. By God, there's a plucky little woman for you, Howard!

JOYCE: I agree. Her self-control is amazing.

CROSBIE: I won't keep her long. I know you're busy.

JOYCE: Thanks.

> [CROSBIE *exits right*]

JOYCE: [*To the* SIKH] Is my clerk outside, Sergeant? [*He has hardly spoken the words before* ONG CHI SENG *sidles in. The* SIKH *exits*] Give me those papers you've got there, will you?

ONG CHI SENG: Yes, sir.

> [*He opens his brief case, extracts a bundle of papers and hands them to* JOYCE]

JOYCE: [*Taking the papers and seating himself at the table*] That's all, Ong. If I want you, I'll call.

ONG CHI SENG: May I trouble you for a few words private conversation, sir?

[*He places his brief case on the table*]

JOYCE: [*Smiling slightly*] It's no trouble, Ong.

ONG CHI SENG: The matter upon which I desire to speak to you, sir, is delicate and confidential.

JOYCE: Mrs. Crosbie will be here in five minutes. Don't you think we might find a more suitable occasion for a heart-to-heart talk?

ONG CHI SENG: The matter on which I desire to speak with you, sir, has to do with the case of R. v. Crosbie.

JOYCE: Oh?

ONG CHI SENG: Yes, sir.

JOYCE: I have a great regard for your intelligence, Ong. I am sure I can trust you not to tell me anything that, as Mrs. Crosbie's counsel, it is improper that I should be advised of.

ONG CHI SENG: I think, sir, that you may rest assured of my discretion. I am a graduate of the University of Hong Kong, and I won the Chancellor's Prize for English composition.

JOYCE: Fire away, then.

ONG CHI SENG: A circumstance has come to my knowledge, sir, which seems to me to put a different complexion on this case.

JOYCE: What circumstance?

ONG CHI SENG: It has come to my knowledge, sir, that there is a letter in existence from the defendant to the unfortunate victim of the tragedy.

JOYCE: I should not be at all surprised. In the course of the last seven years I have no doubt that Mrs. Crosbie often had occasion to write to Mr. Hammond.

ONG CHI SENG: That is very probable, sir. Mrs. Crosbie must have communicated with the deceased frequently, to invite him to dine with her, for example, or to propose a tennis game. That was my first idea when the matter was brought to my notice. This letter, however, was written on the day of the late Mr. Hammond's death.

[*There is an instant's pause.* JOYCE, *a faint smile of amusement in his eyes, continues to look intently at* ONG CHI SENG]

JOYCE: Who told you this?

ONG CHI SENG: The circumstances were brought to my notice, sir, by a friend of mine.

JOYCE: I have always known that your discretion was beyond praise, Ong Chi Seng.

ONG CHI SENG: You will no doubt recall, sir, that Mrs. Crosbie has stated that until the fatal night she had had no communication with the deceased for several weeks.

JOYCE: Yes, I do.

ONG CHI SENG: This letter indicates in my opinion that her statement was not in every respect accurate.

JOYCE: [Stretching out his hand for the letter] Have you got the letter?

ONG CHI SENG: No, sir.

JOYCE: Oh! I suppose you know its contents?

ONG CHI SENG: My friend very kindly gave me a copy. Would you like to peruse it, sir?

JOYCE: I should. [ONG CHI SENG takes from an inside pocket a bulky wallet. It is filled with papers, Singapore dollar bills, and cigarette cards. He searches among the papers] Ah, I see you collect cigarette cards.

ONG CHI SENG: Yes, sir. I am happy to say that I have a collection which is almost unique and very comprehensive.

[From the confusion of papers he extracts a half-sheet of notepaper and places it on the table in front of JOYCE]

JOYCE: [Reading slowly, as though he could hardly believe his eyes] "Robert will be away for the night. I absolutely must see you. I shall expect you at eleven. I am desperate, and if you don't come I won't answer for the consequences. Don't drive up. Leslie." What the devil does it mean?

ONG CHI SENG: That is for you to say, sir.

JOYCE: What makes you think that this letter was written by Mrs. Crosbie?

ONG CHI SENG: I have every confidence in the veracity of my informant, sir.

JOYCE: That's more than I have.

ONG CHI SENG: The matter can very easily be put to the proof. Mrs. Crosbie will no doubt be able to tell you at once whether she wrote such a letter or not.

[JOYCE *rises and walks once or twice up and down the room. Then he stops and faces* ONG CHI SENG]

JOYCE: It is inconceivable that Mrs. Crosbie should have written such a letter!

ONG CHI SENG: If that is your opinion, sir, the matter is, of course, ended. My friend spoke to me on the subject only because he thought, as I was in your office, you might like to know of the existence of this letter before a communication was made to the Public Prosecutor.

JOYCE: Who has the original?

ONG CHI SENG: You will remember, sir, no doubt, that after the death of Mr. Hammond it was discovered that he had had relations with a Chinese woman. The letter is at present in her possession.

[*They face each other for a moment silently*]

JOYCE: I am obliged to you, Ong. I will give the matter my consideration.

ONG CHI SENG: Very good, sir. Do you wish me to make a communication to that effect to my friend?

[*He picks up his brief case*]

JOYCE: I daresay it would be as well if you kept in touch with him.

ONG CHI SENG: Yes, sir.

[*He leaves.* JOYCE *reads through the letter once more with knitted brows. Footsteps are heard off right, and he realizes that* LESLIE *is coming. He places the copy of the letter among the papers on the table.* LESLIE *enters, followed by the Matron,* MRS. PARKER, *a stout middle-aged Englishwoman in a white dress.* LESLIE *is very simply and neatly dressed; her hair is done with her habitual care; she is cool and self-possessed*]

JOYCE: Good morning, Mrs. Crosbie.

[LESLIE *comes forward graciously. She holds out her hand as calmly as though she were receiving him in her drawing room*]

LESLIE: [*Shaking hands with* JOYCE] How do you do? I wasn't expecting you so early.

JOYCE: How are you today?

LESLIE: I'm in the best of health, thank you. This is a wonderful place for a rest cure. And Mrs. Parker looks after me like a mother.

JOYCE: How do you do, Mrs. Parker?

MRS. PARKER: Very well, thank you, sir. This I can't help saying, Mrs. Crosbie, no one could be less trouble than what you are. I shall be sorry to lose you, and that's a fact.

LESLIE: [*With a gracious smile*] You've been very kind to me, Mrs. Parker.

MRS. PARKER: Well, I've been company for you. When you're not used to it, it's lonely-like in a place like this. It's a shame they ever put you here, if you want to know what I think about it.

JOYCE: Well, Mrs. Parker, I daresay you won't mind leaving us. Mrs. Crosbie and I have got business to talk about.

MRS. PARKER: Very good, sir.

[*She exits*]

LESLIE: Sometimes she drives me nearly mad, she's so chatty, poor dear. Isn't it strange how few people there are who can ever realize that you may be perfectly satisfied with your own company?

JOYCE: You must have had plenty of that lately.

LESLIE: I've read a great deal, you know, and I've worked at my lace.

JOYCE: I need hardly ask if you've slept well.

LESLIE: I've slept like a top. The time has really passed very quickly.

JOYCE: It's evidently agreed with you. You're looking very much better and stronger than a few weeks ago.

LESLIE: That's more than poor Robert is. He's a wreck, poor darling. I'm thankful for his sake that it'll all be over tomorrow. I think he's just about at the end of his tether.

JOYCE: He's very much more anxious about you than you appear to be about yourself.

LESLIE: Won't you sit down?

JOYCE: Thank you.

[*He sits at the table*]

LESLIE: [*Sitting*] I'm not exactly looking forward to the trial, you know.

JOYCE: One of the things that has impressed me is that each time you've told your story you've told it in exactly the same words. You've never varied a hair's breadth.

LESLIE: [*Gently chaffing him*] What does that suggest to your legal mind?

JOYCE: Well, it suggests either that you have an extraordinary memory or that you're telling the plain, unvarnished truth.

LESLIE: I'm afraid I have a very poor memory.

JOYCE: I suppose I'm right in thinking that you had no communication with Hammond for several weeks before the catastrophe?

LESLIE: [*With a friendly little smile*] Oh, quite. I'm positive of that. The last time we met was at a tennis party at the McFarrens'. I don't think I said more than two words to him. They have two courts, you know, and we didn't happen to be in the same sets.

JOYCE: And you hadn't written to him?

LESLIE: Oh, no.

JOYCE: Are you perfectly certain of that?

LESLIE: Oh, perfectly. There was nothing I should write to him for except to ask him to dine or play tennis, and I hadn't done either for months.

JOYCE: At one time you'd been on fairly intimate terms with him. How did it happen that you had stopped asking him to anything?

LESLIE: [*With a little shrug of the shoulders*] One gets tired of people. We hadn't anything very much in common. Of course, when he was ill, Robert and I did everything we could for him, but the last year or two he's been quite well. And he was very popular. He had a good many calls on his time, and there didn't seem to be any need to shower invitations upon him.

JOYCE: Are you quite certain that was all?

[LESLIE *hesitates for a moment and reflectively looks down*]

LESLIE: Well, of course, I knew about the Chinese woman. I'd actually seen her.

JOYCE: Oh! You never mentioned that.

LESLIE: It wasn't a very pleasant thing to talk about. And I knew you'd find out for yourselves soon enough. Under the circumstances I didn't think it would be very nice of me to be the first to tell you about his private life.

JOYCE: What was she like?

[LESLIE *gives a slight start and a hard look suddenly crosses her face*]

LESLIE: Oh, horrible. Stout and painted and powdered. Covered with gold chains and bangles and pins. Not even young. She's older than I am.

JOYCE: And it was after you knew about her that you ceased having anything to do with Hammond?

LESLIE: Yes.

JOYCE: But you said nothing about it to your husband.

LESLIE: It wasn't the sort of thing I cared to talk to Robert about.

[JOYCE *watches her for a moment. Any suggestion of emotion that showed itself on her face when she spoke of the Chinese woman has left it and she is now once more cool and self-possessed*]

JOYCE: I think I should tell you that there is in existence a letter in your handwriting from you to Geoff Hammond.

LESLIE: In the past I've often sent him little notes to ask him to something or other or to get me something when I knew he was going into Singapore.

JOYCE: This letter asks him to come and see you because Robert was going to Singapore.

LESLIE: [*Smiling*] That's impossible. I never did anything of the kind.

JOYCE: [*Taking the letter from among his papers*] You'd better read it for yourself.

[*He hands her the letter*]

LESLIE: [*Taking it and glancing quickly at it*] That's not my handwriting.

[*She gives it back*]

JOYCE: I know. It's said to be an exact copy of the original.

[LESLIE *takes the letter again and now reads the words. And as she reads a horrible change comes over her. Her colorless face grows dreadful to look at. The flesh seems on a sudden to fall away and her skin is tightly stretched over the bones. She stares at* JOYCE *with eyes that start from their sockets*]

LESLIE: [*In a whisper*] What does it mean?

JOYCE: That is for you to say.

LESLIE: I didn't write it. I swear I didn't write it.

JOYCE: Be very careful what you say. If the original is in your handwriting, it would be useless to deny it.

LESLIE: It would be forgery.

JOYCE: It would be difficult to prove that. It would be easy to prove that it was genuine.

[*A shiver passes through* LESLIE's *body. She takes out a handkerchief and wipes the palms of her hands. She looks at the letter again*]

LESLIE: [*Returning the letter*] It's not dated. If I had written it and forgotten all about it, it might have been written years ago. If you'll give me time I'll try to remember the circumstances.

JOYCE: I noticed there was no date. If this letter were in the hands of the prosecution they would cross-examine your houseboys. They would soon find out whether someone took a letter to Hammond on the day of his death.

[LESLIE *clasps her hands violently and sways on her chair so that you might think she would faint*]

LESLIE: I swear to you that I did not write that letter.

JOYCE: In that case we need not go into the matter further. If the person who possesses this letter sees fit to place it in the hands of the prosecution you will be prepared . . . [*There is a long pause.* JOYCE *waits for* LESLIE *to speak, but she stares straight in front of her*] If you have nothing more to say to me, I think I'll be getting back to my office.

LESLIE: [*Still not looking at him*] What would anyone who read the letter be inclined to think that it meant?

JOYCE: He'd know that you had told a deliberate lie.

LESLIE: When?

JOYCE: When you stated definitely that you had had no communication with Hammond for at least six weeks.

LESLIE: The whole thing has been a terrible shock to me. The events of that horrible night have been a nightmare. It's not very strange if one detail has escaped my memory.

JOYCE: Your memory has reproduced very exactly every particular of your interview with Hammond. It is very strange that you should have forgotten so important a point as that he came to the bungalow on the night of his death at your express desire.

LESLIE: I hadn't forgotten.

JOYCE: Then why didn't you mention it?

LESLIE: I was afraid to. I thought you'd none of you believe my story if I admitted that he'd come at my invitation. I daresay it was very stupid of me. I lost my head, and after I'd once said that I'd had no communication with Hammond I was obliged to stick to it.

JOYCE: You will be required to explain then why you asked Hammond to come to you when Robert was away for the night.

LESLIE: [*With a break in her voice*] It was a surprise I was preparing for Robert's birthday. I knew he wanted a new gun, and, you know, I'm dreadfully stupid about sporting things. I wanted to talk to Geoff about it. I thought I'd get him to order it for me.

JOYCE: Perhaps the terms of the letter are not very clear to your recollection. Will you have another look at it?

LESLIE: [*Quickly drawing back*] No, I don't want to.

JOYCE: Then I must read it to you. "Robert will be away for the night. I absolutely must see you. I shall expect you at eleven. I am desperate, and if you don't come I won't answer for the consequences. Don't drive up. Leslie." Does it seem to you the sort of letter a woman would write to a rather distant acquaintance because she wanted to consult him about buying a gun?

LESLIE: I daresay it's rather extravagant and emotional. I do express myself like that, you know. I'm quite prepared to admit it's rather silly.

JOYCE: I must have been very much mistaken. I always thought you a very reserved and self-possessed woman.

LESLIE: And after all, Geoff Hammond wasn't quite a distant acquaintance. When he was ill I nursed him like a mother.

JOYCE: By the way, did you call him Geoff?

LESLIE: Everybody did. He wasn't the kind of man anyone would think of calling Mr. Hammond.

JOYCE: Why did you ask him to come at so late an hour?

LESLIE: [*Recovering her self-possession*] Is eleven very late? He was always dining somewhere or other. I thought he'd look in on his way home.

JOYCE: And why did you ask him not to drive up?

LESLIE: [*With a shrug of the shoulder*] You know how Chinese boys gossip. If they'd heard him come, the last thing they'd have ever thought was that he was there for a perfectly innocent purpose.

[JOYCE *rises and walks once or twice up and down the room. Then, leaning over the back of his chair, he speaks in a tone of deep gravity*]

JOYCE: Mrs. Crosbie, I want to talk to you very, very seriously. This case was comparatively plain sailing. There was only one point that seemed to me to require explanation. So far as I could judge, you had fired no less than four shots into Hammond when he was lying on the ground. It was hard to accept the possibility that a delicate, frightened woman, of gentle nurture and refined instincts, should have surrendered to an absolutely uncontrollable frenzy. But, of course, it was admissible. Although Geoffrey Hammond was much liked, and on the whole thought highly of, I was prepared to prove that he was the sort of man who might be guilty of the crime which in justification of your act you accused him of. The fact, which was discovered after his death, that he had been living with a Chinese woman gave us something very definite to go upon. That robbed him of any sympathy that might have been felt for him. We made up our minds to make every use of the odium that such a connection cast upon him in the minds of respectable people. I told your husband just now that I was certain of an acquittal, and I wasn't just telling him that to cheer him up. I do not believe the jury would have left the box. [*They look into each other's eyes.* LESLIE *is strangely still. She is like a bird paralyzed by the fascination of a snake*] But this letter has thrown an entirely different complexion on the case. I am your legal adviser. I shall represent you in court. I take your story as you tell it to me, and I shall conduct your defense according to its terms. It may be that I believe your statements, or it may be that I doubt them. The duty of counsel is to persuade the jury that the evidence placed before them is not such as to justify them in bringing in a verdict of guilty, and any private opinion he may have of the innocence or guilt of his client is entirely beside the point.

LESLIE: I don't know what you're driving at.

JOYCE: You're not going to deny that Hammond came to your house at your urgent and, I may even say, hysterical invitation?

> [LESLIE *does not answer for a moment. She seems to consider*]

LESLIE: They can prove that the letter was taken to his bungalow by one of the houseboys. He rode over on his bicycle.

JOYCE: You mustn't expect other people to be stupider than you. The letter will put them on the track of suspicions that have entered nobody's head. I will not tell you what I personally thought when I read it. I do not wish you to tell me anything but what is needed to save your neck.

> [LESLIE *crumples up suddenly and slips from her chair to the floor in a dead faint before* JOYCE *can catch her. He glances round the room for water, but there is none to be seen. He looks toward the door, but will not call for help. He does not wish to be disturbed. He moves and*

*kneels down on one knee beside her, waiting for her to
recover, and in a few moments she opens her eyes]*

JOYCE: Keep quite still. You'll be better in a minute.

LESLIE: [*Raising herself with his help to a sitting position*] Don't
let anyone come.

JOYCE: [*Supporting her*] No, no.

LESLIE: [*Clasping her hands and looking up at him appealingly*]
Mr. Joyce, you won't let them hang me!

     [*She begins to cry hysterically*]

JOYCE: [*Trying to calm her; in undertones*] Sh! Sh! Don't make a
noise. Sh! Sh! It's all right. Don't, don't, don't! For goodness'
sake, pull yourself together.

LESLIE: Give me a minute.

     [*She makes an effort to regain her self-control, and soon
she is once more calm*]

JOYCE: [*With almost unwilling admiration*] You've got pluck. I
think no one could deny that.

LESLIE: Let me get up now. It was silly of me to faint.

     [JOYCE *helps her to her feet and leads her to a chair and
she sinks down wearily*]

JOYCE: Do you feel a little better?

LESLIE: [*With her eyes closed*] Don't talk to me for a moment or
two.

JOYCE: Very well.

     [*He moves up to the window and stands gazing out of it.
There is a pause*]

LESLIE: [*With a little sigh*] I'm afraid I've made rather a mess of
things.

JOYCE: [*Turning*] I'm sorry.

LESLIE: For Robert, not for me. You distrusted me from the beginning.

JOYCE: That's neither here nor there.

[LESLIE *gives him a glance and then looks down*]

LESLIE: Isn't it possible to get hold of the letter?

JOYCE: [*With a frown to conceal his embarrassment*] I don't think anything would have been said to me about it if the person in whose possession it is, was not prepared to sell it.

LESLIE: Who's got it?

JOYCE: The Chinese woman who was living in Hammond's house.

[LESLIE *instinctively clenches her hands; but again controls herself*]

LESLIE: Does she want an awful lot for it?

JOYCE: I imagine that she has a pretty shrewd idea of its value. I doubt if it would be possible to get hold of it except for a very large sum.

LESLIE: [*Hoarsely*] Are you going to let me be hanged?

JOYCE: [*With some irritation*] Do you think it's so simple as all that to secure possession of an unwelcome piece of evidence?

LESLIE: You say the woman is prepared to sell it.

JOYCE: But I don't know that I'm prepared to buy it.

LESLIE: Why not?

JOYCE: I don't think you know what you're asking me. Heaven knows, I don't want to make phrases, but I've always thought I was by way of being an honest man. You're asking me to do something that is no different from suborning a witness.

LESLIE: [*Her voice rising*] Do you mean to say you can save me and you won't? What harm have I ever done you? You can't be so cruel.

JOYCE: I'm sorry it sounds cruel. I want to do my best for you, Mrs. Crosbie. A lawyer has a duty not only to his client, but to his profession.

LESLIE: [*With dismay*] Then what is going to happen to me?

JOYCE: [*Very gravely*] Justice must take its course.

[LESLIE *grows very pale. A little shudder passes through her body. When she answers her voice is low and quiet*]

LESLIE: I put myself in your hands. Of course, I have no right to ask you to do anything that isn't proper. I was asking more for

Robert's sake than for mine. But if you knew everything, I believe you'd think I was deserving of your pity.

JOYCE: Poor old Bob, it'll nearly kill him. He's utterly unprepared.

LESLIE: If I'm hanged it certainly won't bring Geoff Hammond back to life again.

[*There is a moment's silence while* JOYCE *reflects upon the situation*]

JOYCE: [*Almost to himself*] Sometimes I think that when we say our honor prevents us from doing this or that we deceive ourselves, and our real motive is vanity. I ask myself, what really is the explanation of that letter? I daren't ask you. It's not fair to you to conclude from it that you killed Hammond without provocation. [*With emotion*] It's absurd how fond I am of Bob. You see, I've known him for so long. His life may very well be ruined too.

LESLIE: I know I have no right to ask you to do anything for me, but Robert is so kind and simple and good. I think he's never done anyone any harm in his life. Can't you save him from this bitter pain and this disgrace?

JOYCE: You mean everything in the world to him, don't you?

LESLIE: I suppose so. I'm very grateful for the love he's given me.

JOYCE: [*Making his resolution*] I'm going to do what I can for you. [LESLIE *gives a little gasp of relief*] But don't think I don't know I'm doing wrong. I am. I'm doing it with my eyes open.

LESLIE: [*Rising*] It can't be wrong to save a suffering woman. You're doing no harm to anybody else.

JOYCE: You don't understand. It's only natural. Let's not discuss that. Do you know anything about Bob's circumstances?

LESLIE: He has a good many tin shares and a part interest in two or three rubber estates. I suppose he could raise money.

JOYCE: He would have to be told what it was for.

LESLIE: Will it be necessary to show him the letter?

JOYCE: Don't you want him to see it?

LESLIE: No.

JOYCE: I shall do everything possible to prevent him from seeing it till after the trial. He will be an important witness. I think it

very necessary that he should be as firmly convinced of your innocence as he is now.

LESLIE: And afterwards?

JOYCE: I'll still do my best for you.

LESLIE: Not for my sake—for his. If he loses his trust in me he loses
everything.

JOYCE: [*Moving to the door*] It's strange that a man can live with
a woman for ten years and not know the first thing about her.
It's rather frightening.

LESLIE: He knows that he loves me. Nothing else matters.

JOYCE: [*Opening the door and calling*] Mrs. Parker, I'm just going.

[MRS. PARKER *enters*]

MRS. PARKER: Gracious, how white you look, Mrs. Crosbie. Mr. Joyce
hasn't been upsetting you, has he? You look like a ghost.

LESLIE: [*Smiling graciously, with an instinctive resumption of her
social manner*] No, he's been kindness itself. I daresay the strain
is beginning to tell on me a little. [*She holds out her hand to*
JOYCE] Good-bye. It's good of you to take all this trouble for me.
I can't begin to tell you how grateful I am.

JOYCE: [*Shaking hands with her*] I shan't see you again till just before the trial tomorrow.

LESLIE: I've got a lot to do before then. I've been making Mrs.
Parker a lace collar, and I want to get it done before I leave here.

MRS. PARKER: It's so grand. I shall never be able to bring myself to
wear it. She makes beautiful lace, you'd be surprised.

JOYCE: I know she does.

LESLIE: I'm afraid it's my only accomplishment.

[*She goes out*]

JOYCE: Good morning, Mrs. Parker.

MRS. PARKER: Good morning, sir.

[*She exits.* JOYCE *moves to the table and begins to collect
his papers together. There is a knock at the door*]

JOYCE: Come in.

[*The door is opened, and* ONG CHI SENG *enters*]

ONG CHI SENG: I desire to remind you, sir, that you have an appointment with Mr. Reed, of Reed and Pollock, at twelve thirty.

JOYCE: [*Glancing at his watch*] He'll have to wait.

ONG CHI SENG: Very good, sir. [*He crosses to the door and is about to go out, then stops and turns, as though on an afterthought*] Is there anything further you wish me to say to my friend, sir?

JOYCE: What friend?

ONG CHI SENG: About the letter which Mrs. Crosbie wrote to Hammond, deceased, sir.

JOYCE: [*Very casually*] Oh, I'd forgotten about that. I mentioned it to Mrs. Crosbie and she denies having written anything of the sort. It's evidently a forgery.

[*He takes out the copy of the letter from the papers in front of him and offers it to* ONG CHI SENG]

ONG CHI SENG: [*Ignoring the gesture*] In that case, sir, I suppose there would be no objection if my friend delivered the letter to the Public Prosecutor.

JOYCE: None. But I don't quite see what good that would do your friend.

ONG CHI SENG: My friend thought it was his duty, sir, in the interests of justice.

JOYCE: [*Grimly*] I'm the last man in the world to interfere with anyone who wishes to do his duty, Ong.

ONG CHI SENG: I quite understand, sir, but from my study of the case, R. v. Crosbie, I am of the opinion that the production of such a letter would be damaging to our client.

JOYCE: I have always had a high opinion of your legal acumen, Ong Chi Seng.

ONG CHI SENG: It has occurred to me, sir, that if I could persuade my friend to induce the Chinese woman who has the letter to deliver it into our hands it would save a great deal of trouble.

JOYCE: I suppose your friend is a businessman. Under the circumstances do you think he would be induced to part with the letter?

ONG CHI SENG: He has not got the letter.

JOYCE: Oh, has he got a friend, too?

ONG CHI SENG: The Chinese woman has got the letter. He is only a relation of the Chinese woman. She is an ignorant woman; she did not know the value of the letter till my friend told her.

JOYCE: What value did he put on it?

ONG CHI SENG: Ten thousand dollars, sir.

JOYCE: Good God! Where on earth do you suppose Mrs. Crosbie can get ten thousand dollars? I tell you the letter's a forgery.

ONG CHI SENG: Mr. Crosbie owns an eighth share of the Bekong Rubber Estate, and a sixth share of the Kelanton River Rubber Estate. I have a friend who will lend him the money on the security of his properties.

JOYCE: You have a large circle of acquaintances, Ong.

ONG CHI SENG: Yes, sir.

JOYCE: Well, you can tell them all to go to hell. I would never advise Mr. Crosbie to give a penny more than five thousand for a letter that can be very easily explained.

ONG CHI SENG: The Chinese woman does not want to sell the letter, sir. My friend took a long time to persuade her. It is useless to offer her less than the sum mentioned.

JOYCE: Ten thousand dollars is an awful lot.

ONG CHI SENG: Mr. Crosbie will certainly pay it rather than see his wife hanged by the neck, sir.

JOYCE: Why did your friend fix upon that particular amount?

ONG CHI SENG: I will not attempt to conceal anything from you, sir. Upon making inquiry, sir, my friend came to the conclusion that ten thousand dollars was the largest sum Mr. Crosbie could possibly get.

JOYCE: Ah, that is precisely what occurred to me. Well, I will speak to Mr. Crosbie.

ONG CHI SENG: Mr. Crosbie is still here, sir.

JOYCE: Oh! What's he doing?

ONG CHI SENG: We have only a very short time, sir, and the matter, in my opinion, brooks of no delay.

JOYCE: In that case be brief, Ong.

ONG CHI SENG: It occurred to me that you would wish to speak to Mr. Crosbie and, therefore, I took the liberty of asking him to wait. If it would be convenient for you to speak to him now, sir, I could impart your decision to my friend when I have my tiffin.

JOYCE: Where is the Chinese woman now?

ONG CHI SENG: She is staying in the house of my friend, sir.

JOYCE: Will she come to my office?

ONG CHI SENG: I think it more better you go to her, sir. I can take you to the house tonight, and she will give you the letter. She is a very ignorant woman and she does not understand checks.

JOYCE: I wasn't thinking of giving her a check. I should bring banknotes with me.

ONG CHI SENG: It would only be waste of time to bring less than ten thousand dollars, sir.

JOYCE: I quite understand.

ONG CHI SENG: [*Moving to the door*] Shall I tell Mr. Crosbie that you wish to see him, sir?

JOYCE: Ong Chi Seng.

ONG CHI SENG: [*Turning*] Yes, sir.

JOYCE: Is there anything else you know?

ONG CHI SENG: No, sir. I am of the opinion that a confidential clerk should have no secrets from his employer. May I ask why you make this inquiry, sir?

JOYCE: Call Mr. Crosbie.

ONG CHI SENG: Very good, sir.

[*He goes off right. After a few moments* CROSBIE *enters*]

JOYCE: It's good of you to have waited, old man.

CROSBIE: Your clerk said that you particularly wanted me to.

JOYCE: [*As casually as he can*] A rather unpleasant thing has happened, Bob. It appears that your wife sent a letter to Hammond asking him to come to the bungalow on the night he was killed.

CROSBIE: But that's impossible. She's always stated that she had had no communication with Hammond. I know from my own knowledge that she hadn't set eyes upon him for a couple of months.

JOYCE: The fact remains that the letter exists. It's in the possession of the Chinese woman Hammond was living with.

CROSBIE: What did she write to him for?

JOYCE: Your wife meant to give you a present on your birthday, and she wanted Hammond to help her to get it. Your birthday was just about then, wasn't it?

CROSBIE: Yes. In point of fact it was a fortnight ago today.

JOYCE: In the emotional excitement that she suffered from after the tragedy she forgot that she'd written a letter to him, and having once denied having any communication with Hammond she was afraid to say she'd made a mistake.

CROSBIE: Why?

JOYCE: My dear fellow. It was, of course, very unfortunate, but I daresay it was not unnatural.

CROSBIE: That's unlike Leslie. I've never known her afraid of anything.

JOYCE: The circumstances were exceptional.

CROSBIE: Does it very much matter? If she's asked about it she can explain.

JOYCE: It would be very awkward if this letter found its way into the hands of the prosecution. Your wife has lied, and she would be asked some difficult questions.

CROSBIE: Leslie would never tell a lie intentionally.

JOYCE: [*With a shadow of impatience*] My dear Bob, you must try to understand. Don't you see that it alters things a good deal if Hammond did not intrude, an unwanted guest, but came to your house by invitation? It would be easy to arouse in the jury a certain indecision of mind.

CROSBIE: I may be very stupid, but I don't understand. You lawyers, you seem to take a delight in making mountains out of molehills. After all, Howard, you're not only my lawyer, you're the oldest friend I have in the world.

JOYCE: I know. That is why I'm taking a step the gravity of which I can never expect you to realize. I think we must get hold of that letter. I want you to authorize me to buy it.

CROSBIE: I'll do whatever you think is right.

JOYCE: I don't think it's right, but I think it's expedient. Juries are very stupid. I think it's just as well not to worry them with more evidence than they can conveniently deal with.

CROSBIE: Well, I don't pretend to understand, but I'm perfectly prepared to leave myself in your hands. Go ahead and do as you think fit. I'll pay.

JOYCE: [*Collecting his papers*] All right. And now put the matter out of your mind.

CROSBIE: That's easy. I could never bring myself to believe that Leslie had ever done anything that wasn't absolutely square and above board.

JOYCE: [*Moving to the door*] Let's go to the club. I badly want a whisky and soda.

[*They start to go as:*]

CURTAIN

ACT THREE

A room in the Chinese quarter of Singapore. The same night.

The room is small, with dirty and bedraggled whitewashed walls. There is a small window over which a dirty piece of lace curtain is roughly hung and a door right. The only furniture consists of a low Chinese pallet bed, with a lacquered neck-rest, a stool, and a low circular coffee table. On the floor there is a rattan sleeping mat, also with a neck-rest. On the back wall are pinned a cheap Chinese oleograph, stained and discolored, and a picture of a nude from one of the illustrated papers. The room is lit by one electric light, a globe without a shade.

CHUNG HI is lying on the pallet bed with his opium pipe. On the table is a tray with a lighted spirit lamp, tin of opium and a couple of long needles. He is a fat Chinese man, in white trousers, singlet and slippers. He is reading a Chinese newspaper. A Chinese BOY, dressed in the same way, is sitting on the floor idly playing a Chinese flute. He plays a strange Chinese tune. CHUNG HI dips a needle in the tin of opium, extracts a small pellet and heating it over the spirit flame, puts it in his pipe. He inhales and presently blows out a thick cloud of smoke. There is a scratching at the door. CHUNG HI speaks a few words in Chinese and the BOY rises, moves to the door and opens it a little. He speaks to someone outside, then turns and says something in Chinese to CHUNG HI, who makes answer, rises and puts his opium pipe and paper down. The BOY opens the door wider and ONG CHI SENG enters.

ONG CHI SENG: This way, sir, please. Come in.

[JOYCE *enters, wearing his topee. The* BOY *closes the door and sits on the stool*]

JOYCE: I nearly broke my neck on those stairs.

ONG CHI SENG: This is my friend, sir.

JOYCE: Does he speak English?

CHUNG HI: Yes, my speakee velly good English. How do you do, sir. I hope you are quite well. Please to come in.

JOYCE: Good evening. I say, the air in here is awful. Couldn't we have the window open?

CHUNG HI: Night air velly bad, sir. Him bring fever.

JOYCE: We'll risk it.

ONG CHI SENG: [*Crossing to the window*] Very good, sir. I will open the window.

[*He does so*]

JOYCE: I see you've been smoking.

CHUNG HI: Yes, my suffer velly bad from my belly. Smokee two, thlee pipes make it more better.

JOYCE: We'd better get to our business.

ONG CHI SENG: Yes, sir. Business is business, as we say.

JOYCE: What is your friend's name, Ong?

CHUNG HI: My callee all same Chung Hi. You no see him written on shop? Chung Hi. General Dealer?

JOYCE: I suppose you know what I've come for?

CHUNG HI: Yes, sir. My velly glad to see you in my house. Me give you my business card. Yes?

JOYCE: I don't think I need it.

CHUNG HI: My sell you velly good China tea. All same Suchong. Number one quality. My can sell more cheap than you buy at stores.

JOYCE: I don't want any tea.

CHUNG HI: My sell you Swatow silk. Velly best quality. No can get more better in China. Make velly good suits. My sell you cheap.

JOYCE: I don't want any silk.

CHUNG HI: Velly well. You take my business card. Chung Hi, General

Dealer, two-six-four, Victoria Street. Maybe you want some to-mollow or next day.

JOYCE: Have you got this letter?

CHUNG HI: Chinese woman have got.

JOYCE: Where is she?

CHUNG HI: She come presently.

JOYCE: Why the devil isn't she here?

CHUNG HI: She here all light. She come presently. She wait till you come. See?

ONG CHI SENG: Much better you tell her to come, I think.

CHUNG HI: Yes, I tell her come this minute. [*He turns to the* BOY *and speaks to him in Chinese. The* BOY *gives a guttural, monosyllabic reply, rises and exits. To* JOYCE] You sit down. Yes?

JOYCE: I prefer to stand.

CHUNG HI: [*Offering him a tin of cigarettes from the table*] You smokee cigarette. Velly good cigarette. All same Thlee Castles.

JOYCE: I don't want to smoke.

CHUNG HI: You wantchee buy China tea velly cheap. Number one quality.

JOYCE: Go to hell.

CHUNG HI: All light. My no savee. Maybe you likee Swatow silk. No! You wantchee see jade? Have got string number one quality. My sell you one thousand dollars. Velly nice plesent your missus.

JOYCE: Go to hell.

CHUNG HI: All light. I smokee cigarette.

> [*He takes a cigarette from the tin and lights it with the spirit lamp. The* BOY *returns, carrying a tray on which are three bowls of tea. He offers one to* JOYCE, *who shakes his head and turns away.* ONG CHI SENG *and* CHUNG HI *each take one. The* BOY *then sits on the stool*]

JOYCE: Why the devil doesn't this woman come?

ONG CHI SENG: I think she come now, sir.

> [*There is a scratching at the door*]

JOYCE: I'm curious to see her.

[*The* BOY *rises and opens the door*]

ONG CHI SENG: My friend say that poor Mr. Hammond, deceased, was completely under her thumb, sir.

CHUNG HI: She no speakee English. She speakee Malay and Chinese.

[*The* CHINESE WOMAN *enters. She wears a silk sarong and a long muslin coat over a blouse. On her arms are heavy gold bangles; she wears a gold chain round her neck and gold pins in her shining, black hair. Her cheeks and mouth are painted, and she is heavily powdered; arched eyebrows make a thin dark line over her eyes. She walks slowly to the pallet bed and sits on the edge of it with her legs dangling.* ONG CHI SENG *makes an observation to her in Chinese and she answers briefly. She takes no notice of* JOYCE]

JOYCE: Has she got the letter?

ONG CHI SENG: Yes, sir.

JOYCE: Where is it?

ONG CHI SENG: She's a very ignorant woman, sir. I think she wants to see the money before she gives the letter.

JOYCE: Very well.

[*He takes a bundle of bills from his pocket, counts them, and hands them to* ONG CHI SENG. *The* CHINESE WOMAN *takes a cigarette from the tin and lights it. She appears to take no notice of what is proceeding.* ONG CHI SENG *counts the bills for himself, watched by* CHUNG HI. *All are grave and businesslike, the* CHINESE WOMAN *oddly unconcerned*]

ONG CHI SENG: The sum is quite correct, sir.

[*The* CHINESE WOMAN *takes the letter from her tunic and hands it to* ONG CHI SENG]

ONG CHI SENG: [*Glancing at the letter*] This is the right document, sir.

[*He hands it to* JOYCE]

JOYCE: [*Taking the letter and reading it*] There's not very much for the money.

[*He places it in his pocket*]

ONG CHI SENG: I am sure you will not regret it, sir. Considering all the circumstances, it is what you call dirt cheap.

JOYCE: [*Ironically*] I know that you have too great a regard for me to allow me to pay more for an article than the market price.

ONG CHI SENG: Shall you want me for anything else tonight, please, sir?

JOYCE: I don't think so.

ONG CHI SENG: In that case, sir, if it is convenient, I will stay here and talk to my friend.

JOYCE: [*Sardonically*] I suppose you want to divide the swag.

ONG CHI SENG: I am sorry, sir, that that is a word I have not come across in my studies.

JOYCE: You'd better look it up in the dictionary.

ONG CHI SENG: Yes, sir. I will do it without delay.

JOYCE: I have been wondering how much you were going to get out of this, Ong Chi Seng.

ONG CHI SENG: The laborer is worthy of his hire, as Our Lord said, sir.

JOYCE: I didn't know you were a Christian, Ong.

ONG CHI SENG: I am not, sir, to the best of my belief.

JOYCE: In that case he certainly isn't your Lord.

ONG CHI SENG: I was only making use of the common English idiom, sir. In point of fact, I am a disciple of the late Herbert Spencer. I have also been much influenced by Nietzsche, Shaw, and Herbert G. Wells.

JOYCE: [*Crossing to the door*] It is no wonder that I am no match for you.

[*He leaves quickly*]

CURTAIN

SCENE 2

The sitting room at the Crosbies' bungalow. Next day.
About five o'clock in the afternoon.

The piano is closed and there are no flower bowls. The
light is soft and mellow. When the curtain rises the stage
is empty, but immediately the sound is heard of a car ar-
riving and stopping. MRS. JOYCE *and* WITHERS *enter by the*
veranda steps followed by the HEAD BOY *carrying a large*
basket, and another Chinese SERVANT *carrying a suitcase.*
MRS. JOYCE *is a buxom, florid, handsome woman of about*
forty.

MRS. JOYCE: [*Looking around*] Good gracious, how desolate the place
looks. You can see in the twinkling of an eye that there hasn't
been a woman here to look after things.

WITHERS: I must say it does look a bit dreary.

MRS. JOYCE: I knew it. I felt it in my bones. That's why I wanted
to get here before Leslie. I thought we might have a chance to do
a little something before she came.

[*She opens the piano and puts a piece of music from the*
top onto the stand]

WITHERS: A few flowers would help.

MRS. JOYCE: I wonder if these wretched boys will have had the sense
to pick some. [*She turns to the* HEAD BOY] Is the ice all right, boy?

HEAD BOY: Yes, Missy.

MRS. JOYCE: Well, put it in some place where it won't melt. Are there
any flowers?

HEAD BOY: My lookee see.

MRS. JOYCE: [*To the Chinese* SERVANT] Oh, that's my bag. Put it
in the spare room.

[*The* HEAD BOY *and the Chinese* SERVANT *exit*]

WITHERS: You know, I can't help wondering how Mrs. Crosbie can
bring herself to come back here.

[*He takes out his pipe and lights it*]

MRS. JOYCE: [*Seating herself on the stool*] My poor friend, the Crosbies haven't got half a dozen houses to choose from. When you've only one house I suppose you've got to live in it no matter what's happened.

WITHERS: At all events I should have liked to wait a bit.

MRS. JOYCE: I wanted her to. I'd made all my plans for them both to come back to my house after the trial. I wanted them to stay with me till they were able to get away for a holiday.

WITHERS: I should have thought that much the most sensible thing to do.

MRS. JOYCE: But they wouldn't. Bob said he couldn't leave the estate, and Leslie said she couldn't leave Bob. So then I said Howard and I would come down here. I thought it would be easier for them if they had someone with them for a day or two.

WITHERS: [*With a smile*] And I think you were determined not to be robbed of your celebration.

MRS. JOYCE: [*Gaily*] You don't know my million-dollar cocktails, do you? They're celebrated all through the F.M.S. When Leslie was arrested I made a solemn vow that I wouldn't make another until she was acquitted. I've been waiting for this day and no one is going to deprive me of my treat.

WITHERS: Hence the ice, I suppose?

MRS. JOYCE: Hence the ice, wise young man. As soon as the others come I'll start making them.

WITHERS: With your own hands?

MRS. JOYCE: With my own hands. I don't mind telling you I never knew anyone who could make a better cocktail than I can.

WITHERS: [*With a grin*] We all think the cocktails we make ourselves better than anybody else's, you know.

MRS. JOYCE: [*Merrily*] Yes, but you're all lamentably mistaken, and I happen to be right.

WITHERS: The ways of Providence are dark.

> [*The* HEAD BOY *and the Chinese* SERVANT *return, carrying bowls of flowers, which are placed, one on the table, one on the writing-desk, and one on the piano*]

MRS. JOYCE: Oh, good. That makes the room look much more habitable.

WITHERS: They ought to be here in a minute.

MRS. JOYCE: We went very fast, you know. And I daresay a good many people wanted to say a word or two to Leslie. I don't suppose they were able to get away as quickly as they expected.

[*The* HEAD BOY *and the Chinese* SERVANT *exit*]

WITHERS: I'll wait till they come, shall I?

MRS. JOYCE: Of course you must wait.

WITHERS: I thought the Attorney General was very decent.

MRS. JOYCE: I knew he would be. I know his wife, you know. She said she thought Leslie should never be tried at all. But, of course, men are so funny.

WITHERS: I shall never forget the shout that went up when the jury came in and said, "Not guilty."

MRS. JOYCE: It was thrilling, wasn't it? And Leslie absolutely impassive, sitting there as though it had nothing to do with her.

WITHERS: I can't get over the way she gave her evidence. By George, she's a marvel.

MRS. JOYCE: It was beautiful. I couldn't help crying. It was so modest and so restrained. Howard, who thinks me very hysterical and impulsive, told me the other day he'd never known a woman who had so much self-control as Leslie. And that's real praise, because I don't think he very much likes her.

WITHERS: Why not?

MRS. JOYCE: Oh, you know what men are. They never care very much for the women their particular friends marry.

[*The* HEAD BOY *comes in, carrying the lace pillow, covered by a cloth*]

WITHERS: Hulloa, what's this?

HEAD BOY: Missy pillow lace.

MRS. JOYCE: [*Rising*] Oh, did you bring that?

[*She moves to him, and takes the cloth off*]

HEAD BOY: I thought maybe Missy wantchee.

[*He puts the pillow down on the circular table as it was in Act One*]

MRS. JOYCE: I'm sure she will. That was very thoughtful of you, boy. [*To* WITHERS, *as the* HEAD BOY *exits, taking the cloth with him*] You know, sometimes you could kill these Chinese boys, and then all of a sudden they'll do things that are so kind and so considerate that you forgive them everything.

WITHERS: [*Moving to the table to look at the lace*] By George, it is beautiful, isn't it? You know, it's just the sort of thing you'd expect her to do.

MRS. JOYCE: Mr. Withers, I want to ask you something rather horrible. When you came that night, where exactly was Geoff Hammond's body lying?

WITHERS: Out on the veranda, just under that lamp. By God, it gave me a turn when I ran up the steps and nearly fell over him.

MRS. JOYCE: Has it occurred to you that every time Leslie comes into the house she'll have to step over the place where the body lay? It's rather grim.

WITHERS: Perhaps it won't strike her.

MRS. JOYCE: Fortunately she's not the sort of hysterical fool that I am. But I . . . Oh, dear, I could never sleep again.

[*There is the sound of a car approaching and stopping*]

WITHERS: There they are. They haven't been so long, after all.

MRS. JOYCE: [*Going to the veranda*] No, they must have started within ten minutes of us. [*She calls*] Leslie! Leslie!

[LESLIE *enters, followed by* CROSBIE *and* JOYCE. CROSBIE *is wearing a neat suit of ducks.* LESLIE *wears a silk wrap and a hat*]

LESLIE: [*To* MRS. JOYCE] You haven't been here long, have you?

MRS. JOYCE: [*Taking* LESLIE *in her arms*] Welcome. Welcome back to your home.

LESLIE: [*Releasing herself*] Darling. [*She looks around*] How nice and cozy it looks. I can hardly realize that I've ever been away.

MRS. JOYCE: Are you tired? Would you like to go and lie down?

LESLIE: Tired? Why, I've been doing nothing but rest for the last six weeks.

MRS. JOYCE: Oh, Bob, aren't you happy to have her back again?

JOYCE: Now, Dorothy, don't gush, and if you must gush, gush over me.

MRS. JOYCE: I'm not going to gush over you, you old brute. What have you done?

LESLIE: [*Holding out her hand to* JOYCE, *with a charming smile*] He's done everything. I can never thank him enough. You don't know what he's been to me through all this dreary time of waiting.

MRS. JOYCE: I don't mind confessing that I thought you made rather a good speech, Howard.

JOYCE: Thank you for those kind words.

MRS. JOYCE: I think perhaps you might have been a little more impassioned without hurting yourself.

WITHERS: I don't agree with you, Mrs. Joyce. It's just because it was so cold and measured and businesslike that it was so effective.

JOYCE: Let's have this drink you've been talking about, Dorothy.

MRS. JOYCE: Come and help me, Mr. Withers. When I make a cocktail, I want a great many assistants.

LESLIE: [*Taking off her hat*] I know what an elaborate business your million-dollar cocktail is, Dorothy.

MRS. JOYCE: Don't be impatient. I can't hurry it. I must take my time.

[MRS. JOYCE *and* WITHERS *exit*]

LESLIE: I'll go and tidy myself up.

CROSBIE: You don't need it. You look as if you'd just come out of a bandbox.

LESLIE: I shan't be a minute.

CROSBIE: There's something I particularly want to say to you.

JOYCE: I'll make myself scarce.

CROSBIE: No, I want you, old man. I want your legal opinion.

JOYCE: Oh, do you? Fire away.

[LESLIE *puts her hat on the table and then sits on the stool*]

CROSBIE: Well, look here, I want to get Leslie away from here as quickly as possible.

JOYCE: I think a bit of a holiday would do you both good.

LESLIE: Could you get away, Robert? Even if it's only for two or three weeks I'd be thankful.

CROSBIE: What's the use of two or three weeks? We must get away for good.

LESLIE: But how can we?

JOYCE: You can't very well throw up a job like this. You'd never get such a good one again, you know.

CROSBIE: That's where you're wrong. I've something in view that's much better. We can neither of us live here. It would be impossible. We've gone through too much in this bungalow. How can we ever forget . . . ?

LESLIE: [With a shudder] No, don't, Bob, don't.

CROSBIE: [To JOYCE] You see. Heaven knows, Leslie has nerves of iron, but there is a limit to human endurance. You know how lonely the life is. I should never have a moment's peace when I was out and thought of her sitting in this room by herself. It's out of the question.

LESLIE: Oh, don't think of me, Bob. You've made this estate, it was nothing when you came here. Why, it's like your child. It's the apple of your eye.

CROSBIE: I hate it now. I hate every tree on it. I must get away, and so must you. You don't want to stay?

LESLIE: It's all been so miserable. I don't want to make any more difficulties.

CROSBIE: I know our only chance of peace is to get to some place where we can forget.

JOYCE: But could you get another job?

CROSBIE: Yes, that's just it. Something has suddenly cropped up. That's why I wanted to talk to you about it at once. It's in Sumatra. We'd be right away from everybody, and the only people round us would be Dutch. We'd start a new life, with new friends. The only thing is that you'd be awfully lonely, darling.

LESLIE: Oh, I wouldn't mind that. I'm used to loneliness. [With *sudden vehemence*] I'd be glad to go, Robert. I don't want to stay here.

CROSBIE: That settles it then. I'll go straight ahead and we can fix things up at once.

JOYCE: Is the money as good as here?

CROSBIE: I hope it'll be better. At all events I shall be working for myself and not for a rotten company in London.

JOYCE: [*Startled*] What do you mean by that? You're not buying an estate?

CROSBIE: Yes, I am. Why should I go on sweating my life out for other people? It's a chance in a thousand. It belongs to a Malacca Chinese who's in financial difficulties, and he's willing to let it go for thirty thousand dollars if he can have the money the day after tomorrow.

JOYCE: But how are you going to raise thirty thousand dollars?

CROSBIE: Well, I've saved about ten thousand since I've been in the East, and Charlie Meadows is willing to let me have the balance on mortgage.

[LESLIE *and* JOYCE *exchange a glance of consternation*]

JOYCE: It seems rather rash to put all your eggs in one basket.

LESLIE: I shouldn't like you to take such a risk on my account, Robert. You needn't worry about me, really. I shall settle down here quite comfortably.

CROSBIE: Don't talk nonsense, darling. It's only a moment ago that you said you'd give anything to clear out.

LESLIE: I spoke without thinking. I believe it would be a mistake to run away. The sensible thing to do is to sit tight. Everybody's been so kind, there's no reason to suppose they're not going to continue. I'm sure all our friends will do all they can to make things easy for us.

CROSBIE: You know, dear, you mustn't be frightened at a little risk. It's only if one takes risks that one can make big money.

JOYCE: These Chinese estates are never any good. You know how haphazard and careless the Chinese are.

CROSBIE: This is not that sort of thing at all. It belongs to a very progressive Chinese, and he's had a European manager. It's not a leap in the dark. It's a thoroughly sound proposition, and I reckon that in ten years I can make enough money to allow us to retire. Then we'll settle down in England and live like lords.

LESLIE: Honestly, Robert, I'd prefer to stay here. I'm attached to the place, and when I've had time to forget all that has happened . . .

CROSBIE: How can you forget?

JOYCE: Anyhow, it's not a thing that you must enter into without due consideration. You'd naturally want to go over to Sumatra and look for yourself.

CROSBIE: That's just it. I've got to make up my mind at once. The offer only holds for thirty-six hours.

JOYCE: But my dear fellow, you can't pay thirty thousand dollars for an estate without proper investigation. None of you planters are any too businesslike, but really there are limits.

CROSBIE: Don't try to make me out a bigger fool than I am. I've had it examined and it's worth fifty thousand if it's worth a dollar. I've got all the papers in my office. I'll go and get them and you can see for yourself. And I have a couple of photographs of the bungalow to show Leslie.

LESLIE: I don't want to see them.

CROSBIE: Oh, come, darling. That's just nerves. That shows how necessary it is for you to get away. Darling, in this case you must let me have my own way. I want to go, too. I can't stay here any more.

LESLIE: [*With anguish*] Oh, why are you so obstinate?

CROSBIE: Come, come, dear, don't be unreasonable. Let me go and get the papers. I shan't be a minute.

[*He exits. There is a moment's silence.* LESLIE *looks at* JOYCE *with terrified appeal; he makes a despairing gesture*]

JOYCE: I had to pay ten thousand dollars for the letter.

LESLIE: [*Rising*] What are you going to do?

JOYCE: [*Miserably*] What can I do?

LESLIE: Oh, don't tell him now. Give me a little time. I'm at the end of my strength. I can't bear anything more.

JOYCE: You heard what he said. He wants the money at once to buy this estate. He can't. He hasn't got it.

LESLIE: Give me a little time.

JOYCE: I can't afford to give you a sum like that.

LESLIE: No, I don't expect you to. Perhaps I can get it somehow.

JOYCE: [*Turning*] How? You know it's impossible. It's money I put by for the education of my boys. I was glad to advance it, and I wouldn't have minded waiting a few weeks . . .

LESLIE: [*Interrupting*] If you'd only give me a month I'd have time to think of something. I could prepare Robert and explain to him by degrees. I'd watch for my opportunity.

JOYCE: If he buys this estate the money will be gone. No, no, no. I can't let him do that. I don't want to be unkind to you, but I can't lose my money.

LESLIE: Where is the letter?

JOYCE: I have it in my pocket.

LESLIE: [*Sitting*] Oh, what shall I do?

JOYCE: I'm dreadfully sorry for you.

LESLIE: Oh, don't be sorry for me. I don't matter. It's Robert. It'll break his heart.

JOYCE: If there were only some other way. I don't know what to do.

[*He sits despondently on the stool*]

LESLIE: I suppose you're right. There's only one thing to do. Tell him. Tell him and have done with it. I'm broken.

[CROSBIE *returns, carrying a bundle of papers*]

CROSBIE: Of course, if it hadn't been for Leslie I should have run over to Sumatra last week. I'd just like you to have a look first at the report I've had.

JOYCE: Look here, Bob, has it struck you that your costs over this affair will be pretty heavy?

CROSBIE: I know all you lawyers are robbers. I daresay this will leave me a little short of money, but I don't suppose you'll mind if I keep you waiting till I've had time to settle down. You know I can be trusted, and if you like I'll pay you interest.

JOYCE: I don't think you have any idea how large the sum is. Of course, we don't want to press you, but we can't be out of our money indefinitely. I think I should warn you that when you've settled with us, you won't have much money left over to embark in rather hazardous speculations.

CROSBIE: You're putting the fear of God into me. How much will the costs come to?

JOYCE: I'm not going to charge you anything for my personal services. Whatever I've done has been done out of pure friendship, but there are certain out-of-pocket expenses that I'm afraid you must pay.

CROSBIE: Of course. It's awfully good of you not to wish to charge me for anything else. I hardly like to accept. What do the out-of-pocket expenses amount to?

JOYCE: You remember that I told you yesterday that there was a letter of Leslie's that I thought we ought to get hold of.

CROSBIE: Yes, I really didn't think it mattered very much, but, of course, I put myself in your hands. I thought you were making a great deal out of something that wasn't very important.

JOYCE: You told me to do what I thought fit, and I bought the letter from the person in whose possession it was. I had to pay a great deal of money for it.

CROSBIE: What a bore. Still, if you thought it necessary, I'm not going to grouse. How much was it?

JOYCE: I'm afraid I had to pay ten thousand dollars for it.

CROSBIE: [Aghast] Ten thousand dollars! Why, that's a fortune. I thought you were going to say a couple of hundred. You must have been mad.

JOYCE: You may be sure that I wouldn't have given it if I could have got it for less.

CROSBIE: But that's everything I have in the world. It reduces me to beggary.

JOYCE: Not that exactly, but you must understand that you haven't got money to buy an estate with.

CROSBIE: But why didn't you let them bring the letter in and tell them to do what they damned well liked?

JOYCE: I didn't dare.

CROSBIE: Do you mean to say it was absolutely necessary to suppress the letter?

JOYCE: If you wanted your wife acquitted.

CROSBIE: But—but . . . I don't understand. You're not going to tell me that they could have brought in a verdict of guilty. They couldn't have hanged her for putting a noxious vermin out of the way.

JOYCE: Of course, they wouldn't have hanged her. But they might have found her guilty of manslaughter. I daresay she'd have got off with two or three years.

CROSBIE: Three years. My Leslie. My little Leslie. It would have killed her. But what was there in the letter?

JOYCE: I told you yesterday.

LESLIE: It was very stupid of me. I . . .

CROSBIE: [Interrupting] I remember now. You wrote to Hammond to ask him to come to the bungalow.

LESLIE: Yes.

CROSBIE: You wanted him to get something for you, didn't you?

LESLIE: Yes, I wanted to get a present for your birthday.

CROSBIE: Why should you have asked him?

LESLIE: I wanted to get you a gun. He knew all about that sort of thing, and you know how ignorant I am.

CROSBIE: Bertie Cameron had a brand new gun he wanted to sell. I went into Singapore on the night of Hammond's death to buy it. Why should you want to make me a present of another?

LESLIE: How should I know that you were going to buy a gun?

CROSBIE: [Abruptly] Because I told you.

LESLIE: I'd forgotten. I can't remember everything.

CROSBIE: You hadn't forgotten that.

LESLIE: What do you mean, Robert? Why are you talking to me like this?

CROSBIE: [To JOYCE] Wasn't it a criminal offense that you committed in buying that letter?

JOYCE: [Trying not to take it seriously] It's not the sort of thing that a respectable lawyer does in the ordinary way of business.

CROSBIE: [Pressing him] It was a criminal offense?

JOYCE: I've been trying to keep the fact out of my mind. But if you must insist on a straight answer I'm afraid I must admit it was.

CROSBIE: Then why did you do it? You, you of all people. What were you trying to save me from?

JOYCE: Well, I've told you. I felt that . . .

CROSBIE: [*Hard and stern*] No, you haven't.

JOYCE: Come, come, Bob, don't be a fool. I don't know what you mean. Juries are very stupid, and you don't want them to get any silly ideas in their heads.

CROSBIE: Who has the letter now? Have you got it?

JOYCE: Yes.

CROSBIE: Where is it?

JOYCE: Why do you want to know?

CROSBIE: [*Violently*] God damn it, I want to see it!

JOYCE: [*Rising*] I've no right to show it to you.

CROSBIE: [*Violently*] Is it your money you bought it with, or mine? I've got to pay ten thousand dollars for that letter, and by God I'm going to see it! At least I'd like to know that I've had my money's worth.

LESLIE: Let him see it.

[*Without a word* JOYCE *takes his notecase from his pocket and extracts the letter which he hands to* CROSBIE, *who reads it*]*

CROSBIE: [*Hoarsely*] What does it mean?

LESLIE: It means that Geoff Hammond was my lover.

CROSBIE: [*Covering his face with his hands*] No, no.

JOYCE: Why did you kill him?

LESLIE: [*Rising and moving away*] He'd been my lover for years.

CROSBIE: [*In agony*] It's not true!

LESLIE: [*Turning*] For years. And then he changed. I didn't know what was the matter. I couldn't believe that he didn't care for me any more. I loved him; I didn't want to love him. I couldn't help myself. I hated myself for loving him, and yet he was everything in the world to me. He was all my life. And then I heard that he was living with a Chinese woman. I couldn't believe it. At last I saw her, I saw her with my own eyes, walking in the village, with her gold bracelets and her necklaces—a Chinese woman. Horrible! They all knew in the kampong that she was his mistress. And when I passed her, she looked at me, and I saw that she knew I was his mistress, too. I sent for him.

[*The lights fade to blackout. When the lights come up again,* LESLIE *is seated by the table working at her lace. She is dressed as in Act One. It is night, and the lamps are lit.* GEOFFREY HAMMOND *enters up the veranda steps. He is a good-looking fellow in the late thirties, with a breezy manner and abundant self-confidence*]

LESLIE: [*Rising and placing the lace pillow on the table*] Geoff! I thought you were never coming.

HAMMOND: What's that bold bad husband of yours gone to Singapore for?

LESLIE: He's gone to buy a gun that Bertie Cameron wants to sell.

HAMMOND: I suppose he wants to bag that tiger the natives are talking about. I bet I get him first. What about a little drink?

LESLIE: Help yourself.

[HAMMOND *goes to the drinks table*]

HAMMOND: [*Pouring out a whisky and soda*] I say, is anything the matter? That note of yours was rather hectic.

LESLIE: What have you done with it?

HAMMOND: I tore it up at once. What do you take me for?

LESLIE: [*Suddenly*] Geoff, I can't go on like this any more. I'm at the end of my tether.

HAMMOND: Why, what's up?

LESLIE: Oh, don't pretend. What's the good of that? Why have you left me all this time without a sign?

HAMMOND: I've had an awful lot to do.

[*He drinks and then returns his glass to the table*]

LESLIE: You haven't had so much to do that you couldn't spare a few minutes to write to me.

HAMMOND: There didn't seem to be any object in taking useless risks. If we don't want a bust-up, we must take elementary precautions. We've been very lucky so far. It would be silly to make a mess of things now.

LESLIE: Don't treat me like a perfect fool!

HAMMOND: I say, Leslie, darling, if you sent for me just to make a scene, I'm going to take myself off. I'm sick of these eternal rows.

LESLIE: A scene? Don't you know how I love you?

HAMMOND: Well, darling, you've got a damned funny way of showing it.

LESLIE: You drive me to desperation.

[HAMMOND *looks at her for a moment reflectively, then, with his hands in his pockets, goes up to her with deliberation*]

HAMMOND: Leslie, I wonder if you've noticed that we hardly ever meet now without having a row.

LESLIE: Is that my fault?

HAMMOND: I don't say that. I daresay it's mine. But when that happens with two people who are on the sort of terms that we are, it looks very much as though things were wearing a bit thin.

LESLIE: What do you mean by that?

HAMMOND: Well, when that happens, I'm not sure if the common-sense thing is not to say: "We've had a ripping time, but all good things must come to an end, and the best thing we can do is to make a break while we've still got the chance of keeping friends."

LESLIE: [*Frightened*] Geoff!

HAMMOND: I'm all for facing facts.

LESLIE: [*Suddenly flaming up*] Facts! What is that Chinese woman doing in your house?

HAMMOND: My dear, what are you talking about?

LESLIE: Do you think I don't know that you've been living with a Chinese woman for months?

HAMMOND: Nonsense.

LESLIE: What sort of a fool do you take me for? Why, it's the gossip of the kampong.

HAMMOND: [*With a shrug of the shoulders*] My dear, if you're going to listen to the gossip of the natives . . .

LESLIE: [*Interrupting him*] Then what is she doing in your bungalow?

HAMMOND: I didn't know there was a Chinese woman about. I don't bother much about what goes on in my servants' quarters as long as they do their work properly.

LESLIE: What does that mean?

HAMMOND: Well, I shouldn't be surprised if one of the boys had got a girl there. What do I care as long as she keeps out of my way.

LESLIE: I've seen her!

HAMMOND: What is she like?

LESLIE: Old and fat.

HAMMOND: You're not paying me a very pretty compliment. My head boy's old and fat, too.

LESLIE: Your head boy isn't going to dress a woman in silk at five dollars a yard. She had a couple of hundred pounds' worth of jewelry on her.

HAMMOND: It sounds as though she were of a thrifty disposition. Perhaps she thinks that the best way to invest her savings.

LESLIE: Will you swear she's not your mistress?

HAMMOND: Certainly.

LESLIE: On your honor?

HAMMOND: On my honor.

LESLIE: [Violently] It's a lie!

HAMMOND: All right, then, it's a lie. But in that case, why won't you let me go?

LESLIE: Because, in spite of everything, I love you with all my heart. I can't let you go now. You're all I have in the world. If you have no love for me, have pity on me. Without you I'm lost. Oh, Geoff, I love you! No one will ever love you as I've loved you. I know that often I've been beastly to you and horrible, but I've been so unhappy.

HAMMOND: My dear, I don't want to make you unhappy, but it's no good beating about the bush. The thing's over and done with. You must let me go now. You really must.

LESLIE: Oh, no, Geoff, you don't mean that, you can't mean that!

HAMMOND: Leslie, dear, I'm terribly sorry, but the facts are there and you've got to face them. This is the end and you've got to make the best of it. I've made up my mind, and there it is.

LESLIE: How cruel. How monstrously cruel! You wouldn't treat a dog as you're treating me.

HAMMOND: [Turning] Is it my fault if I don't love you? Damn it all, one either loves or one doesn't.

LESLIE: Oh, you're of stone. I'd do anything in the world for you, and you won't give me a chance.

HAMMOND: Oh, my God, why can't you be reasonable? I tell you I'm sick and tired of the whole thing. Do you want me to tell you in so many words that you mean nothing to me? Don't you know that? Haven't you felt it? You must be blind.

LESLIE: [*Desperately*] Yes, I've known it only too well. And I've felt it. I didn't care. It's not love any more that seethes in my heart; it's madness; it's torture to see you, but it's torture ten times worse not to see you. If you leave me now, I'll kill myself. [*She picks up the revolver that is lying on the table*] I swear to God I'll kill myself.

HAMMOND: [*Impatiently*] Oh, don't talk such damned rot!

LESLIE: Don't you think I mean it? Don't you think I have the courage?

HAMMOND: [*Beside himself with irritation*] I have no patience with you. You're enough to drive anyone out of his senses. If you'd got sick of me, would you have hesitated to send me about my business? Not for a minute. D'you think I don't know women?

LESLIE: [*Replacing the revolver on the table*] You've ruined my life, and now you're tired of me you want to cast me aside like a worn-out coat. No, no, no!

HAMMOND: You can do what you like, and say what you like, but I tell you it's finished.

LESLIE: [*Flinging her arms round his neck*] I'll never let you go. Never! Never!

> [HAMMOND *releases himself roughly. The touch of her exasperates him*]

HAMMOND: I'm fed up. Fed up. I'm sick of the sight of you!

LESLIE: [*Collapsing into a chair*] No, no, no. . . .

HAMMOND: [*Violently*] If you want the truth you must have it. [*He stands over her*] Yes, the Chinese woman *is* my mistress, and I don't care who knows it. If you ask me to choose between you and her, I choose her. Every time. And now for God's sake leave me alone!

LESLIE: [*Rising*] You cur!

[*She seizes the revolver and fires at him.* HAMMOND *staggers toward the veranda and falls. The lights quickly fade to blackout*]

LESLIE: . . . I ran after him and fired again. He fell, and then I stood over him and I fired till there were no more cartridges.

[*The lights come up again.* CROSBIE *and* JOYCE *are listening to* LESLIE's *story. She is dressed as at the beginning of the scene*]

CROSBIE: Have I deserved this of you, Leslie?

[*He moves to the stool and sits*]

LESLIE: No, I have no excuses to offer for myself. I betrayed you.
CROSBIE: What do you want to do now?
LESLIE: It is for you to say.
CROSBIE: How could you, Leslie? The awful part is that, notwithstanding everything—I love you still. Oh, God, how you must despise me. I despise myself.

[LESLIE *shakes her head slowly*]

LESLIE: I don't know what I've done to deserve your love. Oh, if only I could blame anybody but myself. I can't. I deserve everything I have to suffer. Oh, Robert, my dear.

[CROSBIE *buries his head in his hands*]

CROSBIE: Oh, what shall I do? It's all gone. All gone.

[*He begins to sob with the great, painful, difficult sobs of a man unused to tears*]

LESLIE: [*Sinking on her knees beside him*] Oh, don't cry. My dear —my dear.

[CROSBIE *springs up and pushes her to one side*]

CROSBIE: I'm a fool! There's no need for me to make an exhibition of myself. I'm sorry.

[*He goes hastily out of the room.* LESLIE *rises to her feet*]

JOYCE: No. Don't go to him. Give him a moment to get hold of himself.

LESLIE: I'm so dreadfully sorry for him.

JOYCE: He's going to forgive you. He can't do without you.

LESLIE: If only he'd give me another chance.

JOYCE: Don't you love him at all?

LESLIE: No. I wish to God I did.

JOYCE: Then, what's to be done?

LESLIE: I swear to you that I'll do everything in the world to make him happy. I'll make amends. I'll oblige him to forget. He shall never know that I don't love him as he wants to be loved.

JOYCE: It's not easy to live with a man you don't love. But you've had the courage and the strength to do evil; perhaps you will have the courage and the strength to do good. That will be your retribution.

LESLIE: No, that won't be my retribution. I can do that and do it gladly. He's so kind and good. My retribution is greater! With all my heart I still love the man I killed.

CURTAIN

* THE FOLLOWING IS W. SOMERSET MAUGHAM'S ORIGINAL ENDING TO THE PLAY.

[*Without a word* JOYCE *takes his notecase from his pocket and extracts the letter which he hands to* CROSBIE, *who reads it*]

CROSBIE: [*Hoarsely*] What does it mean?

LESLIE: It means that Geoff Hammond was my lover.

CROSBIE: [*Covering his face with his hands*] No, no, no.

JOYCE: Why did you kill him?

LESLIE: He'd been my lover for years. He became my lover almost immediately after he came back from the war.

CROSBIE: [*In agony*] It's not true!

LESLIE: I used to drive out to a place we knew and he met me, two or three times a week, and when Robert went to Singapore he used to come to the bungalow late, when the boys had gone for the night. We saw one another, constantly, all the time.

CROSBIE: I trusted you. I loved you.

LESLIE: And then lately, a year ago, he began to change. I didn't know what was the matter. I couldn't believe that he didn't care for me any more. I was frantic. Oh, if you knew what agonies I endured. I passed through hell. I knew he didn't want me any more, and I wouldn't let him go. Sometimes I thought he hated me. . . . I loved him. I didn't want to love him. I couldn't help myself. I hated myself for loving him, and yet he was everything in the world to me. He was all my life.

CROSBIE: Oh, God! Oh, God!

LESLIE: And then I heard he was living with a Chinese woman. I couldn't believe it. I wouldn't believe it. At last I saw her, I saw her with my own eyes, walking in the village, with her gold bracelets and her necklaces—a Chinese woman. Horrible! They all knew in the kampong that she was his mistress. And when I passed her, she looked at me, and I saw that she knew I was his mistress, too.

CROSBIE: Oh, the shame . . .

LESLIE: I sent for him. I told him I must see him. You've read the letter. I was mad to write it. I didn't know what I was doing. I didn't care. I hadn't seen him for ten days. It was a lifetime. And when last we'd parted he held me in his arms and kissed me, and told me not to worry. And he went straight from my arms to hers.

JOYCE: He was a rotter. He always was.

LESLIE: That letter. We'd always been so careful. He always tore up any word I wrote to him the moment he'd read it. How was I to know he'd leave that one?

JOYCE: That doesn't matter now.

LESLIE: He came, and I told him I knew about the Chinese woman. He denied it. He said it was only scandal. I was beside myself. I don't know what I said to him. Oh, I hated him then. I hated him because he'd made me despise myself. I tore him limb from limb. I said everything I could to wound him. I insulted him. I could have spat in his face. And at last he turned on me. He told me he was sick and tired of me and never wanted to see me again. He said I bored him to death. And then he acknowledged that it *was* true about the Chinese woman. He said he'd known her for years, and she was the only woman who really meant anything to him, and the rest was just pastime. And he said he was glad I knew, and now, at last, I'd leave him alone. He said things to me that I thought it impossible a man could ever say to a woman. He couldn't have been more vile if I'd been a harlot on the streets. And then I don't know what happened; I was beside myself; I seized the revolver and fired. He gave a cry and I saw I'd hit him. He staggered and rushed for the veranda. I ran after him and fired again. He fell, and then I stood over him, and I fired and fired till there were no more cartridges.

[*There is a pause and then* CROSBIE *goes up to her*]

CROSBIE: Have I deserved this of you, Leslie?

LESLIE: No. I've been vile. I have no excuses to offer for myself. I betrayed you.

CROSBIE: What do you want to do now?

LESLIE: It is for you to say.

CROSBIE: It was for your sake I wanted to go away. I only saved that money for you. I shall have to stay here now, but I could manage to give you enough to live on in England.

LESLIE: Where am I to go? I have no family left and no friends. I'm quite alone in the world.

CROSBIE: How could you, Leslie? What did I do wrong that I couldn't win your love?

LESLIE: What can I say? It wasn't me that deceived you. It wasn't me that loved that other. It was a madness that seized me, and I was as little my own mistress as though I were delirious with fever. It brought me no happiness, that love—it only brought me shame and remorse.

CROSBIE: The awful part is that, notwithstanding everything—I love you still. Oh, God, how you must despise me. I despise myself.

[LESLIE *shakes her head slowly*]

LESLIE: I don't know what I've done to deserve your love. I'm worthless. Oh, if only I could blame anybody but myself. I can't. I deserve everything I have to suffer. Oh, Robert, my dear.

[*He sits, and buries his head in his hands*]

CROSBIE: Oh, what shall I do? It's all gone. All gone.

[*He begins to sob with the great, painful, difficult sobs of a man unused to tears. She sinks on her knees beside him*]

LESLIE: Oh, don't cry. Darling. Darling . . .

[CROSBIE *springs up and pushes her to one side*]

CROSBIE: I'm a fool! There's no need for me to make an exhibition of myself. I'm sorry.

[*He goes hastily out of the room.* LESLIE *rises to her feet*]

JOYCE: No. Don't go to him. Give him a moment to get hold of himself.

LESLIE: I'm so dreadfully sorry for him.

JOYCE: He's going to forgive you. He can't do without you.

LESLIE: If he'd only give me another chance.

JOYCE: Don't you love him at all?

LESLIE: No. I wish to God I did.

JOYCE: Then, what's to be done?

LESLIE: I'll give my life such as it is to him, to him only. I swear to you that I'll do everything in the world to make him happy. I'll make amends. I'll oblige him to forget. He shall never know that I don't love him as he wants to be loved.

JOYCE: It's not easy to live with a man you don't love. But you've had the courage and the strength to do evil; perhaps you will have the courage and the strength to do good. That will be your retribution.

LESLIE: No, that won't be my retribution. I can do that and do it gladly. He's so kind, he's so tender. My retribution is greater! With all my heart I still love the man I killed.

CURTAIN

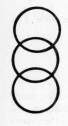

Child's Play

ROBERT MARASCO

Robert Marasco

Just as the 1969–1970 Broadway season seemed to be at its lowest ebb, *Child's Play*, an unheralded suspense drama by an unknown author, Robert Marasco, was brought to the stage of the Royale Theatre by producer David Merrick (customarily associated with gilt-edged theatrical packages and planetary marquee names) and it turned out to be the "sleeper" of the year.

Mr. Marasco's evocation of the sinister in a Roman Catholic prep school promptly was extolled as a melodramatic triumph, a play of dark and deepening mystery and Gothic horror. Clive Barnes, kindled by the unexpected event, proclaimed in *The New York Times*: "Robert Marasco has written a wonderfully powerful melodrama that will thrill audiences for a long time to come. . . . Nor is Mr. Marasco's play simply a melodrama, for his theme of the encroachment of evil is a serious one. Never for a moment does he lose his grip on the attention, and as the mystery is chillingly unraveled, he produces one stroke after another of genuine Grand Guignol horror. This is one of the most satisfyingly scary shows in years."

Not only was *Child's Play* lauded by a majority of the reviewers as "a fascinating new American play by a talented new playwright" and as "a highly original, spellbinding drama of suspense," it also was greeted as a harbinger of a possible resurgence of "straight" drama on Broadway which, for too many seasons, had languorously drifted into the more commercially secure lagoons of comedies and musicals.

The latter contemplation proved, to a degree, to be prophetic, for in spite of the fact that there wasn't a single female in the cast— extraordinary in itself, for in melodrama, more often than not, it is the tangled fate of a beleaguered heroine that induces maximum audience involvement and compassion—*Child's Play* had demonstrated its power at the box office as well as on stage. And at season's end, the play garnered five Antoinette Perry (Tony) Awards (the theatre's highest honor), an unprecedented amount for a nonmusical presentation; and *Variety's* poll of New York's drama critics cited the author as the year's "most promising playwright." (*Child's Play* will be filmed by Paramount Pictures in 1971 under the supervision of David Merrick, in his official debut as a motion picture producer.)

Robert Marasco, a native New Yorker, was born on September 22, 1936. He attended a Catholic prep school (which, he hastens to emphasize, bears no relation to St. Charles's in the play) and is an alumnus of Fordham University where, as an undergraduate, he wrote "humor" for two campus magazines, and a comedy, *Life of the Party*, their 1958 varsity show.

After leaving Fordham, he put in a year at *The New Yorker*. "At first I thought I wanted to write short stories. That's why I went to the magazine. But I soon found that I couldn't write short stories, so I left." The next move brought him full circle: he returned to the prep school of his youth to teach English, Latin, and Greek. Although his plan was to remain on faculty for a single year, his tenure lasted for nine years, and conversely to the events in his play, his experience was "pleasant."

Mr. Marasco's determination eventually to become a playwright had its genesis in "the mists of a not-specifically-remembered boyhood dream," deliberately postponed. "I decided that no one really is ready to write a play until he's thirty, so I waited." Characteristically, he wrote *Child's Play*, which he describes as "a metaphysical kind of melodrama," soon after he had passed thirty, during summer vacations in 1967 and 1968. Though he found the act of creation "very painful," the work crystalized rather swiftly and from the beginning manifested his predilection for melodrama, "the Elizabethan thing with lots of exits and entrances."

After his jubilant Broadway première, Mr. Marasco promptly returned to the solitude of his bachelor apartment and completed an original screenplay, *Burnt Offerings*. It started life as a comedy but then, somehow, "the sinister aspect took over." His next project for the stage, tentatively titled *The Christmas Assembly*, similarly was conceived as a comedy but again, according to the author, "the same appalling sense of menace began seeping in, mysteriously and uninvited."

Perhaps like his characters in *Child's Play*, who are caught in a seemingly inexplicable vortex of evil, Robert Marasco, though wary of being stereotyped as a playwright, may have been inexplicably appropriated by fate to channel his creative gifts toward the perpetuation of engrossing and chilling suspense drama.

Phoebus, our lord, plainly orders us
to drive out a defiling thing which, he says,
has been harbored in this land.

—*Oedipus Rex*

Child's Play was first produced at the Royale Theatre, New York, on February 17, 1970, by David Merrick. The cast was as follows:

FACULTY

PAUL REESE	*Ken Howard*
FATHER GEORGE PENNY	*David Rounds*
FATHER WILLIAM GRIFFIN	*Peter MacLean*
JEROME MALLEY	*Fritz Weaver*
JOSEPH DOBBS	*Pat Hingle*
FATHER FRANK MOZIAN	*Michael McGuire*

STUDENTS

CARRE	*Bryant Fraser*
MEDLEY	*Christopher Deane*
BANKS	*Robbie Reed*
JENNINGS	*Mark Hall*
O'DONNELL	*Frank Fiore*
SHEA	*Patrick Shea*
WILSON	*Ron Martin*
MC ARDLE	*Lloyd Kramer*
TRAVIS	*John Handy*

Directed by	Joseph Hardy
Associate Producer:	Samuel Liff
Scenery and Lighting by	Jo Mielziner
Costumes by	Sara Brook
Sound created by	Gary Harris

SCENE: *The play takes place at St. Charles' School. The time is the present, a week in midwinter.*

SCENE ONE

The scene is the lay Faculty Room and the adjacent stair-case and corridor in St. Charles', a Catholic boarding school for boys. Both areas are vast, Gothic, with huge arches disappearing into the shadows above. Windows in the Faculty Room, framed by dusty red drapes, reach up two stories, cut in half by a balcony which has now become a cluttered office area containing files, a ditto machine, typewriter, etc. Doors lead to this balcony from an upper landing in the hall area, and from the offstage stairway leading down to the Faculty Room.

Directly under the balcony is JEROME MALLEY's *private area, a small alcove with a wing chair, a lamp, and a library table piled with books. Across the room is* JOSEPH DOBBS' *worn leather chair, a small table with a lamp, a phone and a few textbooks. A common work table, with three chairs, is set in front of a massive Renaissance fireplace. Near the table are a cupboard, a bookcase with a few cups, a hotplate, a coffeepot, a small refrigerator—* JOSEPH DOBBS' *touches of comfort in the room.*

A door at the left leads to a locker room and lavatory, and to the balcony stairs offstage. Another door at the right leads to the hall area.

In the hall, the staircase descends to the floor below. The balustrades are huge, with a statue of a saint atop the center newel. The staircase continues up to the next floor. There is an open area in front of the stairs, and a corridor leading back past the Faculty Room door and off to the right, under the stairs.

It is three o'clock on an afternoon in midwinter. The Faculty Room is dimly lit as the curtain rises. PAUL REESE,

*a teacher in his early twenties, genial, athletic-looking, is
seated at the work table, reading. The hall lights come up
as a class bell rings.* REESE *gets up slowly and goes into the
lavatory.*

*With the bell, the boys begin to appear from the gym
area down the corridor, and at the top of the staircase.*
FATHER PENNY, *a rather aristocratic-looking young priest,
is coming down the stairs, brushing past the boys. He
wears a cassock with a sash, as do all the priests of this
order. He is carrying a schoolbag and a freshly typed
stencil. As he reaches the landing and starts for the Faculty
Room, a boy,* JENNINGS, *steps in front of him and blocks
his passage. The other boys stop all movement.* FATHER
PENNY *makes an attempt to get past* JENNINGS *but can't.
There is silence in the corridor.*

FATHER PENNY: Get out of my way.

[FATHER GRIFFIN, *the prefect of discipline, appears at the
top of the staircase. The boys continue to stare at* FATHER
PENNY *and* JENNINGS]

FATHER GRIFFIN: You heard what he said. Get out of his way.

[*There is a pause.* JENNINGS *steps aside slowly, allowing*
FATHER PENNY *to move toward the Faculty Room.* FATHER
GRIFFIN *comes down the stairs, clipboard in hand*]

FATHER PENNY: [*Going into the Faculty Room*] Bastards!
FATHER GRIFFIN: [*Coming down the stairs*] All right, Martin, Callino
—move! And you, Jennings, go down and wait outside my office.
[*He crosses in front of* JENNINGS *and stops when he sees that none
of the boys have moved*] You heard what I said. Go downstairs and
wait outside my office. [JENNINGS *pauses before taking a step toward* FATHER GRIFFIN, *challenging him. There is a pause, and then*
FATHER GRIFFIN *slaps him hard across the face. No one moves.*
JENNINGS *stands defiantly, inviting another blow.* FATHER GRIFFIN'S
*eyes shift quickly to the other boys, who remain motionless, watch-
ing him tensely*] Keep moving!

[*No one does.* JEROME MALLEY *begins to descend the stairs, carrying texts and his red markbook. He is in his mid-forties, tall, somewhat forbidding. He wears a dark three-piece suit. He does not look at the boys, who remain quiet but make way for him to pass.* MALLEY *acknowledges* FATHER GRIFFIN *as he passes him on his way to the Faculty Room.* JENNINGS *turns slowly now and starts downstairs. Gradually the other boys begin to move*]

FATHER GRIFFIN: [*Lamely; more rattled than angry*] All right, lift those feet!

[*He looks after them a moment, then down at his hand. He goes back up the stairs and out, to the right. During all this,* FATHER PENNY *has gone up to the dittoing machine on the balcony. He is running off a biology test.* MALLEY, *seemingly distracted and angry, has put his books down on the common table, and sits down in his study area.* DOBBS *and a boy,* MCARDLE, *can be heard coming up the stairs.* DOBBS *is in his late fifties, the oldest teacher on the faculty. He wears an old corduroy jacket—rumpled and comfortable, like* DOBBS *himself. They reach the corridor outside the Faculty Room*]

DOBBS: All right, McArdle, I'll see the headmaster for you. But you knew that call would upset Mr. Malley. So why'd you do it?

MCARDLE: It was just a joke, Mr. Dobbs.

DOBBS: The joke is that he recognized your voice. If you fellows called me in the middle of the night, I'd have you on the carpet, too.

MCARDLE: Yeah, but you wouldn't have me thrown out of here.

DOBBS: You haven't been thrown out yet.

MCARDLE: Well, give him time. He's mean enough to do it. Lash would really get a charge out of that.

DOBBS: McArdle, don't call him Lash. [MEDLEY, *a boy in a gym suit, appears behind* DOBBS. *He is carrying a basketball*] He's Mr. Malley to you.

MCARDLE: Well, it's the truth, sir. He enjoys watching us sweat it out. I mean, there's gotta be something wrong with a man like that. All the guys say so.

DOBBS: I don't care what all the guys say. [MEDLEY *bounces the basketball—loudly, deliberately—to* MC ARDLE. DOBBS *turns to face him*] What do you want, Medley?

[MEDLEY *keeps his eyes on* MC ARDLE. *There is an obvious silent communication between the two boys*]

MC ARDLE: Time for basketball practice.

DOBBS: [*Looking from one to the other*] I'll tell Mr. Reese; you go on.

MEDLEY: [*Without moving*] I need the ball, sir.

[DOBBS *nods at* MC ARDLE, *whose hands have tightened around the ball. There is a long pause; the boys continue to stare at each other*]

DOBBS: [*Puzzled*] Give him the ball. [MC ARDLE *waits, then bounces the ball to* MEDLEY: *the same loud signal. The boy catches the ball but does not move*] Medley, I thought I told you to go on. [*There is a pause. Then the boy leaves.* DOBBS *turns back to* MC ARDLE] What is it with you fellows lately?

MC ARDLE: [*Quickly*] I have to go, sir.

DOBBS: [*Put off by the change in him*] What? Yes, all right. I'll see if I can find Mr. Malley . . . [MC ARDLE *is moving away*] But remember, no promises.

MC ARDLE: Yes, sir. Thank you.

[*The boy leaves;* DOBBS *is watching him*]

DOBBS: [*Calling, at the door*] McArdle . . . ?

[*There is no reply.* MALLEY *hears the boy's name and rises.* DOBBS *stands there a moment, his hand on the door-knob. He gives a puzzled shake of his head as he enters the Faculty Room.* MALLEY *turns away and picks up a book*]

FATHER PENNY: [*Greeting*] Mr. Dobbs.

DOBBS: [*Looks up to the balcony*] Father Penny. Working after the final bell. Admirable.

[*He places his books on the table and turns on the electric percolator*]

FATHER PENNY: I have a biology test to run off . . . fodder for filthy little minds. I'll be through with the machine in a moment.

DOBBS: I won't be using it, Father. [*Calling* REESE, *who's in the lavatory*] Youngsters want to know if Mr. Reese can come out to play.

REESE: Be right out!

> [MALLEY *and* DOBBS *do not look at each other.* REESE *comes out of the lavatory. He has changed into a sweat suit. He bustles around the room*]

REESE: Where's my whistle?

> [*He goes to a cabinet*]

DOBBS: [*Takes a whistle out of* REESE's *canvas bag, and hands it to* REESE] How about that?

REESE: How'd it get there? [*Puts the whistle around his neck*] Don't suppose I can interest you in a game of kick-the-can?

DOBBS: With the wee ones? Father Penny's your man.

FATHER PENNY: [*Acknowledging the reference as he turns the mimeo machine*] . . . fifty-three . . .

REESE: How 'bout showing the fellows what a regular guy you are, hunh, Father? [*He heads for the lavatory, looking for his keys*]

FATHER PENNY: Thanks, but my truss is being laundered.

REESE: [*Laughs*] You're a flabby bunch.

DOBBS: [*Busy at the work table; refers to* REESE] I taught this one when he was a freshman here, Father; wonderful, how some people never seem to change . . . What are you looking for now?

REESE: Keys, keys.

> [DOBBS *reaches for a ring of keys under* REESE's *books on the table and throws them to* REESE]

DOBBS: How about that? I suppose that's why he gets on so well with the boys; emotionally he's just about a year behind them.

> [*He sits, looking through his schoolbag*]

REESE: Mr. Chips, what did you teach me, anyway?

DOBBS: Obviously nothing.

REESE: That cuts both ways, doesn't it?

[MALLEY *goes into the locker-room area, offstage*]

DOBBS: I was the first layman they hired, the old Fathers. [*Pointing to* REESE] Look what it's led to.

REESE: Charm, vitality.

FATHER PENNY: [*Sarcastically*] . . . sixty-seven . . .

[FATHER GRIFFIN *reappears at the head of the stairs and starts down*]

REESE: I gotta go.

DOBBS: Please do. [*To* FATHER PENNY *as he goes toward the kitchenette*] Cup of coffee, Father?

FATHER PENNY: No, devil's brew.

REESE: [*At the door*] Be here later?

DOBBS: I've been here thirty years. I'll be here later.

[REESE *starts to go toward the gym.* FATHER GRIFFIN *sees* REESE *and calls to him*]

FATHER GRIFFIN: Paul!

REESE: [*Turning to him*] Hello, Father.

FATHER GRIFFIN: Going to the gym?

REESE: Yeah. How 'bout a game of handball?

FATHER GRIFFIN: I'll take a rain check on that.

[MALLEY *comes out of the locker room*]

REESE: [*Starts for the gym*] Whenever you say.

FATHER GRIFFIN: Listen, Paul, do me a favor— [REESE *moves over to* FATHER GRIFFIN] Keep an eye on the kids.

REESE: Sure, what's wrong?

FATHER GRIFFIN: Just watch them. If they get out of hand, clear the gym.

REESE: Anybody in particular?

FATHER GRIFFIN: Yes, all of them. I'll be in here or down in my office if you want me.

[*He starts to go downstairs*]

REESE: Okay. That it?

FATHER GRIFFIN: That's it.

REESE: Tomorrow on that handball game, hunh?

FATHER GRIFFIN: Let you know tomorrow. [REESE *goes out toward the gym.* FATHER GRIFFIN *calls after him*] Paul! Watch them.

REESE: [*Offstage*] Sure, sure.

> [FATHER GRIFFIN *looks down the corridor, and moves toward the rear, out of view briefly.* FATHER PENNY *is still at the machine*]

FATHER PENNY: [*Triumphant*] One hundred!

DOBBS: A shaft for the boys, is it?

> [*He pours a cup of coffee*]

FATHER PENNY: Something to drive them back into the woodwork.

DOBBS: Ah, yes, it's that time of year—the long push toward Easter.

FATHER PENNY: [*Arranging test papers*] It's always that time of year.

DOBBS: These are the dark months; or the hornbusters . . . depending on which side of the desk you sit.

FATHER PENNY: We'll see whose horns go first—theirs or mine.

FATHER GRIFFIN: [*Comes back to the door and enters the room. Looking up at* FATHER PENNY] Bellyachin' as usual, George?

> [DOBBS *pours another cup of coffee*]

FATHER PENNY: The goon squad . . . The pain, alas, is not in the belly, but rather *ad podicem.* In the ass to you.

FATHER GRIFFIN: [*Closing the door*] George, you are very erudite. [MALLEY *has once more absorbed himself in a book*] How are you, Joe?

> [*He puts his clipboard on the table; sits in a chair and lights a cigarette*]

DOBBS: My, my—more clergy in the secular compound. Does this mean an Inquisition? Cup of coffee, Father?

FATHER GRIFFIN: Yes, thanks, Joe. [*He takes the coffee*] George, you didn't mean to send fifteen kids to detention today, did you?

FATHER PENNY: [*Putting papers into his bag*] Have they all been proscribed?

FATHER GRIFFIN: They're all here.

FATHER PENNY: Then fifteen it was. Every one of them a killer at heart.

FATHER GRIFFIN: Sending a kid to detention is serious, George.

FATHER PENNY: Thanks for the advice. Read through the list. I think you'll find the evidence warrants it.

> [FATHER GRIFFIN *gets up and walks to the fireplace.* MALLEY *moves down to the table to pick up his red markbook, then heads for the door.* DOBBS *calls after him*]

DOBBS: Jerome . . . [MALLEY *stops at the door as* DOBBS *starts to move toward him*] Can I speak to you for a minute?

MALLEY: The headmaster is waiting.

> [*He moves out into the corridor*]

DOBBS: Yes, I know . . . [*Following* MALLEY] Excuse me, Father . . . [*Catching* MALLEY *just before he starts downstairs*] . . . it's about McArdle.

MALLEY: Yes?

DOBBS: Jerome, it's . . . not my place, I know, but if you could manage to go a little easy on the boy . . .

MALLEY: You're right, Dobbs, it's *not* your place. You were speaking to him just now. Why?

DOBBS: The boy is frightened. Jerome, it was an innocent phone call, an adolescent prank. Why crucify him for that?

MALLEY: You'd let it pass, wouldn't you?

DOBBS: I've let worse than that pass. McArdle's a good boy; a little imprudent maybe, but certainly there was no malice intended.

MALLEY: Your solicitude is very touching, Dobbs; it always is. This does *not* concern you.

DOBBS: But it does; the boy will be graduating in June.

MALLEY: [*Starts down the stairs*] I'm late.

DOBBS: Don't ask the headmaster to expel him, not for an innocent prank.

MALLEY: And if I didn't . . . wouldn't that disappoint you?

DOBBS: Jerome! As a favor . . .

MALLEY: To you?

DOBBS: To the boy.

MALLEY: Don't be ridiculous.

> [He goes down the stairs. DOBBS looks after him, then returns to the room. FATHER PENNY has come down from the balcony. He pulls a paper from his bag and begins to speak as DOBBS comes back in]

FATHER PENNY: Would you like to see exhibit A? The Travis boy. [Reads paper] "The male reproductive cells are formed in the organs known as the balls." [DOBBS is amused] Condoning it, Mr. Dobbs? Blasphemy, considering my office, my charisma. What has happened to the Judeo-Christian tradition?

FATHER GRIFFIN: George generally sleeps in the reliquary, just behind the main altar.

FATHER PENNY: [Snapping shut his bag] Father Griffin, you can see, has been a great comfort to me during my trial in this wilderness. Seven priests and three laymen on the faculty; why am I always the victim?

FATHER GRIFFIN: Has it been all that bad, George?

FATHER PENNY: Every day I mount the pillory of that podium, exposing myself to those monsters who sit there dissecting me as if I were some large anointed frog. Do you know what they call me? Do you have any idea?

DOBBS: It's never flattering if it's any good.

FATHER PENNY: King Kong. King Kong.

FATHER GRIFFIN: Could've been a helluva lot worse, eh, Joe?

FATHER PENNY: Quiet, you! One day I happened to ask them, "But who is this Kong individual you keep referring to? A new boy come from the East? A pious devotion?" Jeers and catcalls, of course. I gave them a test immediately.

> [He moves to the door]

DOBBS: You have my sympathy, Father. There's nothing more deflating than fifteen minutes on a platform in front of those keen young eyes.

FATHER PENNY: Ah, they're gifted with a higher vision, then? Those unwashed hordes whooping up and down the stairwells? Horse shit!

[*He opens the door*]

FATHER GRIFFIN: Where're you going, George?
FATHER PENNY: Into shock.

[*He slams the door as he goes downstairs*]

FATHER GRIFFIN: [*Calls*] Watch the dark stretches, George!
DOBBS: I never know quite how to take him.
FATHER GRIFFIN: George is all right. [*Trying to order his thoughts, he pauses, then looks at* DOBBS] What's wrong with them, Joe?
DOBBS: [*Trying to follow*] Wrong?
FATHER GRIFFIN: The kids . . . what *is* it with them?
DOBBS: They're always jumpy after midterms. It's their way of unwinding.
FATHER GRIFFIN: That's what it's called, hunh? [*Picks up his clipboard and goes over to* DOBBS] You ever see eighty kids on a detention list before? You managed to nail a few yourself.
DOBBS: I'm getting old and crochety.
FATHER GRIFFIN: Joe . . . something is wrong with them. Have you been watching them? Between classes, on the stairs, in the gym after school?
DOBBS: The gym I leave to young Mr. Reese.
FATHER GRIFFIN: Well, watch them sometime. We've never had so many kids getting hurt around here. Hell, if it were just good old vandalism, protest; but they're going *at* one another. Deliberately, whenever they can, they try to hurt one another . . . physical hurt.
DOBBS: Father, I don't believe that.
FATHER GRIFFIN: Believe it! And then try to get something out of them. [*Moves around the table to* DOBBS' *chair*] You ask how'd it happen and the kid'll just look up at you and shrug. Yesterday a brawl in the dormitory and a kid breaks an arm; the day before, that accident in the chem lab. We need your help, Joe . . .
DOBBS: If it's as you say, of course. In thirty years here, though, I've never known a situation that collar couldn't control.
FATHER GRIFFIN: Well, we're getting less starch in them nowadays.

[*Puts down his coffee cup*] You know, it used to scare the hell out of them being sent to detention. They'd be more scared of coming into my office than the headmaster's. Now they seem to go out of their way to get sent down. Some of them—I think they're waiting for me to lay into them.

DOBBS: What do you want me to do, Father?

FATHER GRIFFIN: Speak to Paul and Jerome when you get a chance; and keep your eyes open to see what's going on with the boys.

DOBBS: I'll speak to young Reese, but Jerome isn't going to pay much attention to anything I have to say.

FATHER GRIFFIN: Think it would be better coming from me?

DOBBS: You or the headmaster. What another teacher does in a classroom is none of my business, I know, but sometimes . . . we can push them too hard.

FATHER GRIFFIN: Jerome's always been rough on the boys, but he's a damn good teacher.

DOBBS: That may be so, but from what the boys are telling me, he's even rougher on them now. They can take so much pressure and who can say how they'll let it out? There was a boy a few years ago, Walter Paxton . . .

FATHER GRIFFIN: Yes, I know about Paxton, but from what I hear it wasn't all Jerome's fault.

DOBBS: Well, maybe not, Father, but I do know the boy couldn't measure up to Jerome's standards. The pressure was too much for him. So one afternoon he went downstairs and tried to hang himself from the pipes in the furnace room. Just like that. Fortunately your predecessor was patrolling the halls at the time.

FATHER GRIFFIN: [*A pause*] All right, Joe, I'll speak to Jerome.

DOBBS: [*Rising and going to the percolator*] Thank you, Father. Now how about another cup of coffee?

FATHER GRIFFIN: No thanks. Time for *me* to start patrolling the halls. [*He starts for the door as* REESE *comes into the room from the gym*] What's wrong?

REESE: Nothing. Thirsty . . . need some fuel.

FATHER GRIFFIN: Who's with the kids?

REESE: One of the seniors. Weyland.

FATHER GRIFFIN: One of the seniors is a kid! Paul, you hurry back there.

REESE: Okay if I treat the kids?

[*He goes to the refrigerator for a Coke*]

FATHER GRIFFIN: Yes, yes. Just don't let them leave the empties around. [*To* DOBBS] Any other ideas, Joe . . . please pass them on.

DOBBS: I'll think about it. And let's see more of you here.

[*He goes into the lavatory to rinse the cups*]

FATHER GRIFFIN: Shake a leg, Paul.

[*He leaves and goes downstairs*]

REESE: What're you going to think about?

DOBBS: [*Returns from the lavatory; dries and hangs up the cups*] Problems. He's worried about the boys.

REESE: What's wrong?

DOBBS: I don't know. Neither does he. You haven't been having any trouble with them?

REESE: [*Taking Cokes from the refrigerator*] I never have trouble with anybody.

DOBBS: [*Indicating* REESE's *Coke*] Real drinks are on me tonight; a feed too, if I remain *ambulatory*.

REESE: Thanks, but I can't tonight.

DOBBS: Oh? Something on?

REESE: Date.

DOBBS: New girl?

REESE: No, my age.

[*He chuckles*]

DOBBS: She's sharpened your wit, I see. Payday's two days off. What's a witty boy like you using for money?

[REESE *gets up, putting his Coke on the table, then reaches into his canvas bag and pulls out a bag of change. He moves toward* DOBBS]

REESE: It's all right this time. You don't have to bail me out. I finally busted up my piggy bank.

DOBBS: [*Peering in*] By George, must be a dollar in there.

REESE: [*Replaces change. He notices* MALLEY's *schoolbag*] What's Lash doing in here this late? Flogging a kid?

DOBBS: [*Pointedly*] I expect Mr. Malley has a very good reason for being here. Let me remind you, you're one of *us* now.

REESE: [*Gathering Cokes*] I'm sorry. I forget.

DOBBS: Well, don't forget.

REESE: Hey, Joe, you want to hear something funny? He still scares me, Lash. He scares the hell out of me. I keep expecting him to send me to detention. You know, whenever we have a free period together, I go sit in the john for forty minutes.

DOBBS: You're not serious?

REESE: So help me! Pretty stupid, hunh?

DOBBS: It sure is.

REESE: Poor kids, I really feel for them. That lousy red markbook of his could stop a heart. What's he doing working with kids, anyway?

DOBBS: I imagine you learned some Latin with Mr. Malley.

REESE: Oh, I learned Latin. But I learned English, too, and it wasn't nearly so painful.

DOBBS: Well, that's because I'm the grand old man of the faculty, beloved of all the boys.

REESE: You're what made me become a teacher. I figured . . . nice, cushy job; don't have to know much. In fact, don't really have to know anything. Hell, nobody teaches English I for thirty years.

DOBBS: [*Silence; then a look*] It's my vocation, boy. And it's your vocation, too, let me remind you. Now, don't you think you'd better get back to the gym, where you're supposed to be?

[MALLEY *comes into the room, his red markbook in hand.* REESE *becomes suddenly uneasy*]

REESE: [*Quick smile*] Mr. Malley.

MALLEY: Reese.

[*He goes to sit in his chair at the table and starts arranging papers.* REESE *watches self-consciously as* DOBBS *returns to correcting papers*]

REESE: [*Fumbling*] You're . . . around late today.

MALLEY: [*Looking up*] Pardon?

REESE: You're usually . . . this is late for you.

MALLEY: Yes, I suppose it is.

[*He gets up to pick up some test papers*]

REESE: [*Looking at* DOBBS, *who smiles slightly, then back to* MALLEY. *Struggling as he moves toward* MALLEY] I can never get out of here before five. I . . . get involved with the kids and . . . basketball.

MALLEY: [*Turning to him; polite, no warmth*] You're enjoying the year?

REESE: Oh, yeah. Yes. The kids are great.

MALLEY: You're not too much older than them yourself, are you?

REESE: [*Lamely*] I guess not.

[*There is a silence.* DOBBS *is obviously listening to* REESE's *discomfort. There is noise from the gym: a distant cheer*]

DOBBS: [*Rescuing* REESE] Isn't that the sound of the rafters being pulled down?

REESE: Hunh?

DOBBS: Your charges are kicking up their heels some.

REESE: Oh, jeez, the kids! [*Grabbing the remaining Cokes; to* MALLEY] Nice talking to you. Excuse me.

[*He exits to the gym.* MALLEY *goes to the cabinet where he sharpens his pencil, then returns to sit at the table. Pause*]

DOBBS: All right, Jerome, what about McArdle?

MALLEY: [*Busy with papers*] He's been suspended.

DOBBS: How long will he be out?

MALLEY: Indefinitely.

DOBBS: That's a bit harsh, isn't it?

MALLEY: For an innocent prank?

DOBBS: For a senior to miss all that work?

MALLEY: I'm sorry you weren't consulted first. One of your boys, isn't he, Dobbs?

DOBBS: So are they all, Jerome, so are they all. I take it the suspension was the headmaster's idea. You would have preferred expulsion, I'm sure.

MALLEY: Why not ask him yourself? As I understand it, you'll be going down to see him as soon as I've left the building.

DOBBS: The headmaster? Why should I see him?

MALLEY: The boy's given him to understand you'll be going down to plead for him.

DOBBS: I made no promises.

MALLEY: No, you never do. You were misinterpreted as usual.

DOBBS: [Clearing the table of the creamer and sugar bowl] You've made it quite clear this doesn't concern me.

MALLEY: When has that ever stopped you?

DOBBS: That's not fair.

MALLEY: I'm never fair, Dobbs; your boys must have told you that.

[More noise is heard from the gym]

DOBBS: Jerome, we spend so much time in this room . . .

[He slams the refrigerator door and returns to the table]

MALLEY: I'm trying to work, Dobbs!

DOBBS: I'm sorry I spoke to the boy. It was a mistake.

MALLEY: You deliberately set them against me, the boys. You always have.

DOBBS: That's all in your mind. [He gets a dust rag from the cupboard and comes back to dust off the table]

MALLEY: It's not in my mind! [Looking directly at DOBBS] You have got to stop undermining my position here.

[Another distant cheer is heard from the gym]

DOBBS: You still don't see it, after all these years. It's not me setting them against you; it's yourself . . . Jerome, the boys are afraid of you. You terrify them. It's as simple as that.

MALLEY: Simpler, Dobbs. You encourage it. Whatever their absurd fears are, you magnify them.

DOBBS: Do I? And what about the counselors and the headmaster, do they encourage it as well? [Going to the cupboard to return *the dust rag*] Young Reese is uncomfortable being in the same room with you.

MALLEY: Ah yes, you've got yourself an ally there.

DOBBS: [*Checks the time of the clock on the mantel; then moves minute hand*] No one is allied with me against you.

MALLEY: Another in your long line of McArdles.

DOBBS: I'd rather the McArdles than the Paxtons, Jerome. It's a hell of a lot easier on the conscience. [MALLEY *stops; looks up*] It's the truth isn't it? The boy tried to kill himself. He couldn't take the pressure.

MALLEY: The boy should not have been in this school in the first place. The *work* was too much for him.

DOBBS: Maybe so, but as long as he was here he was our responsibility. [*A long shout from the gym*] He managed to survive his other classes all right.

MALLEY: Your class.

DOBBS: My class, yes.

MALLEY: What sort of criterion is that?

DOBBS: None, I suppose. Your command of Greek and Latin may be awesome, Jerome, but you know absolutely nothing about boys. Look, all I'm asking is that you ease up on McArdle. Forget methods, forget personalities. For God's sake, what malice can there be in a child?

MALLEY: Listen to me, Dobbs. I'll suffer, since I must, the humiliation of this room with you, and the daily spectacle of a pathetic old man—

DOBBS: All right, Jerome, that's enough.

MALLEY: —living on the affection of adolescent boys—

DOBBS: That's enough, I said!

MALLEY: . . . that *too*, Dobbs, as degrading as it is. But I won't be lectured by you on my responsibility. You are not to see the headmaster! You are not to interfere!

> [*Now a cry is heard from the gym, rising to a shriek.* MALLEY *listens without moving.* DOBBS *rushes out into the corridor.* REESE *is coming from the gym area, dragging a boy whose face and gym shirt are covered with blood*]

REESE: [*Yelling into the stairwell*] Father Griffin! Father Griffin! [DOBBS *joins in the cry.* REESE *has gotten the boy to the Faculty Room. He pulls him across the room. The boy,* BANKS, *is screaming, fighting him.* DOBBS *follows*] Oh, God, oh, God, Joe—help me! HELP ME!

[*The boy screams louder as* DOBBS *and* REESE *bring him into the lavatory.* MALLEY *still does not move. After a pause he turns slightly toward the lavatory as:*]

THE LIGHTS FADE

SCENE TWO

FATHER MOZIAN, *the headmaster, a rather commanding figure, is coming up the stairs as the lights build.* MALLEY *has moved into his study area.* FATHER MOZIAN *enters.*

MALLEY: How is the boy, Father?

FATHER MOZIAN: I haven't heard anything yet. Paul's still here, isn't he? [*The phone rings before* MALLEY *can reply.* FATHER MOZIAN *places the leather folder he has been carrying down on* DOBBS' *chair and answers the phone*] Yes, yes, put her through . . . Yes, Mrs. Banks . . . I don't know. Mr. Dobbs is at the hospital with him now. All I know is that there was an accident . . . No, I'm not excusing it, Mrs. Banks. I'm as upset as you are. [DOBBS, *wearing an overcoat, and* FATHER GRIFFIN *come up the stairs and enter the Faculty Room.* FATHER MOZIAN *nods and indicates his impatience with the phone conversation. There is a first-aid kit on the common table.* DOBBS *moves toward it now, and places it back on the shelf*] There's always a teacher in the gym with them.

[REESE *enters from the lavatory, dressed now, but without his jacket*]

REESE: [*To* DOBBS] Christ, this is all my fault!

DOBBS: Relax, now relax, will you?

FATHER MOZIAN: That has to be your decision, of course, but I don't think it's wise at all . . .

[FATHER GRIFFIN *moves down to* FATHER MOZIAN *with his clipboard*]

FATHER GRIFFIN: Eleven boys, Frank.

FATHER MOZIAN: [*Anxious to get off the phone*] . . . Look, Mrs. Banks, I'm with the teacher now. [*Looking quickly at* FATHER GRIFFIN's *clipboard*] Can I call you back as soon as I've found out what's happened?

FATHER GRIFFIN: [*Moving to* REESE *and showing him the list*] Paul, are these all the boys?

[REESE *looks over the list and nods*]

FATHER MOZIAN: Mrs. Banks, he's getting the best of care. That's all I can tell you right now . . . Of course, of course, whenever you say. [*Hangs up. Picks up his folder*] She wants to take him out of the school. How is Freddy?

DOBBS: He's a brave boy but I'm afraid he's going to lose an eye.

[REESE *is putting on his jacket at the cabinet. He stops*]

FATHER MOZIAN: Dear God!

REESE: [*In disbelief*] Lose his eye . . . ?

FATHER MOZIAN: [*Moves to the table and sits down, trying to control himself*] You know what she said to me? "What are you doing to those boys?" Not just *my* boy, *those* boys. [*Angrily*] What happened down there, Paul?

REESE: I don't know! I was there, I saw it all happen and I swear I don't understand it.

FATHER GRIFFIN: They just went for him, is that it?

REESE: No, they were tossing the ball around, playing . . .

DOBBS: Dodge-ball, I've seen them playing it.

FATHER MOZIAN: That can get pretty rough, can't it?

REESE: Not the way they were playing—just killing time till they got enough men together for a game. They were lined up, three or four on either side of the gym.

FATHER GRIFFIN: Then you really weren't paying much attention to the game.

REESE: I was. I remembered what you said. I was sitting on the benches, waiting to ref the game, talking to some of the seniors.

FATHER GRIFFIN: Well, you were in here getting Cokes. How long did you stay?

DOBBS: [*To* FATHER GRIFFIN] Not long, Father, no more than five minutes.

> [MALLEY *remains in the alcove, listening almost guiltily. He has gotten his coat from the closet; he places it on the back of his chair, careful not to distract anyone in the center of the room. During the next exchange, he gathers the rest of his books quickly, becoming more absorbed in* REESE's *narration. Gradually he stops and listens*]

FATHER MOZIAN: [*Sitting in* MALLEY's *chair at the table*] Go on, Paul.

REESE: [*Moving nervously*] Well, Holleran got the ball and flipped it to McCarthy and McCarthy flipped it to the kid next to him. Then they sort of . . . formed a circle, very slowly. [*He illustrates with his hands*]

FATHER MOZIAN: As if it were something planned?

DOBBS: [*Explaining it away*] Of course it's planned. What game doesn't have rules?

REESE: Let me finish. The fellows kept flipping the ball to one another. They didn't stop flipping it while they were changing position . . . just flipping the ball. So I said, "What's up, guys?" But they didn't seem to hear me . . . just flipping the ball to one another—real serious, their faces, and silence—flipping the ball and forming this circle.

FATHER GRIFFIN: And you were still up on the benches.

> [MALLEY *is changing his shoes, putting on rubbers*]

REESE: No! I was down on the court with them.

FATHER GRIFFIN: Then why didn't you break it up?

REESE: Why should I? All they were doing was flipping the ball back and forth.

FATHER MOZIAN: It's possible that you missed some kind of signal, isn't it?

REESE: No, I don't think so. Freddy had the ball and held it for maybe a couple of seconds longer than the other guys . . . and they were all looking at him, not saying anything, just looking.

DOBBS: Of course they were looking at him, the boy had the ball.

REESE: [*Crossing to* DOBBS] No, no. Joe, this was different. They were staring at him. And so I said, "Okay, Freddy, let's go!" But they didn't seem to hear me, they were all staring at Freddy . . . blank, no expression.

FATHER MOZIAN: Isn't that when you should have stopped them?

REESE: [*His voice rising*] All right, I should have. I didn't! [*Stops himself*] . . . Freddy waited, maybe for a few seconds, then he flipped the ball and walked into the middle of the circle . . . and they all waited until he was in the center. I could see him take a deep breath and I said, [*Looks to* FATHER GRIFFIN] "Okay, let's break it up, you guys!" And just as I said it, I saw the guy with the ball step back a few feet . . . [*Looks to* DOBBS] and Freddy was watching him . . . [*Looks back to* FATHER MOZIAN] and this guy lifted the ball over his shoulder. And then, then he let go and smashed it into Freddy's stomach. I could see Freddy's arms come in—like this—and then . . . God! They—stopped—just before the ball hit him.

[*He illustrates the reflex*]

FATHER MOZIAN: He didn't try to protect himself?

DOBBS: Of course he did.

REESE: I swear he didn't!

DOBBS: Someone throws something at you, you—

REESE: [*Very worked up now*] His arms stopped—here! I heard the ball hit him, and he doubled over . . . And when it hit him, the kids—the kids . . . let out a cry—not a cry, a kind of . . . cheer! A cheer! I heard it.

FATHER GRIFFIN: You couldn't stop them, you couldn't get to Freddy?

REESE: I tried, I ran for him, but they were on him. I couldn't reach him, the eight, nine of them were on him—beating him, clawing him, tearing at his face.

FATHER GRIFFIN: Paul, you knew where I was. Why didn't you call me?

REESE: There wasn't time! Even the kids on the other side of the gym, they were running over and I yelled, "Help me!"

DOBBS: You mean Freddy yelled.

REESE: No, *I yelled*, not Freddy. I yelled and these kids who had run over grabbed me! Held me while the others were on Freddy. And I heard somebody yell, "Hold that bastard!" and . . . and then I hit one of them . . . [*His voice catches*] . . . a couple of them— I don't know—and started to pull them off Freddy, who was crouching against the wall under them . . . pulled them off him. And Freddy, when I got to him, Freddy was covered with blood, coughing, spitting up blood. I raised his head, and when he saw me—God, I don't understand this, Freddy pushed himself against the wall, away from me, pushed himself away and screamed "NO!" *At me!* He was trying to get away from *me!* Trying to fight me off . . . until I grabbed him, lifted him up and . . . They didn't move, the other kids; just drew back . . . And I brought him . . . I didn't know where I was bringing him . . . God, God . . .

[*He stops, almost dazed. There is a pause.* FATHER MOZIAN *watches him, still unable to believe what he's heard.* REESE *gestures helplessly with both hands as he sits in* DOBBS' *chair at the table.* FATHER MOZIAN *gets up and paces*]

DOBBS: You brought him up here. You did the right thing.

REESE: He pulled away, he was fighting me! I swear it, Joe—he didn't want me to stop them!

DOBBS: Oh, come on Paul. That doesn't make sense. I know those boys.

REESE: Joe, I saw it!

DOBBS: What you saw was a schoolboy brawl, some kind of feud that just got out of hand.

FATHER MOZIAN: No, the boy obviously *wanted* to be hurt. There've been other incidents here the past few weeks; more and more violent, and senseless.

DOBBS: [*Still puzzled*] Come on, Paul, I'll buy you a drink.

REESE: [*Annoyed*] No, Joe, I don't want a drink.

DOBBS: C'mon, it'll do you good.

[FATHER MOZIAN *pulls a slip of paper from his folder and hands it to* REESE]

FATHER MOZIAN: Paul, is this all of them? Are those all the names?

REESE: Yes, Father.

DOBBS: What will you do to those boys?

FATHER MOZIAN: [*To* FATHER GRIFFIN] I don't know. How can I expel eleven boys?

DOBBS: Eleven? That's half a class.

FATHER MOZIAN: [*To* FATHER GRIFFIN] Are they still in your office?

FATHER GRIFFIN: Father Gerard's with them.

FATHER MOZIAN: Send them back to their rooms for now. Wait for me in my office. [*Hands the list to* FATHER GRIFFIN] We'll decide what to do with them when I'm through here.

FATHER GRIFFIN: [*To* DOBBS] Coming down, Joe?

DOBBS: Paul, I'll wait for you downstairs. [*Turns out the lamp*] Father, I know those boys. I've taught every one of them. And if you want, I'll go down and talk to them and get this story straight. The boys always level with me.

FATHER MOZIAN: Well, they'll have to level with me as well, Joe. Thanks anyway.

[DOBBS *leaves with* FATHER GRIFFIN. MALLEY *has put his coat on silently.* REESE *looks up as the door closes*]

FATHER MOZIAN: Jerome, I'd like to talk to you before you go.

MALLEY: [*Checking his watch*] The nurse leaves my mother at five. She shouldn't be alone.

FATHER MOZIAN: It won't take long. Paul?

REESE: I'm sorry, Father. The kids *liked* me.

FATHER MOZIAN: Paul, it's not your fault. There's nothing more you could have done. Go take Joe up on that drink and let me worry about this.

REESE: I've got to close the gym.

FATHER MOZIAN: Leave it for now.

REESE: [*Getting his coat and bag*] No, I want to go in there. There's got to be something I missed. Those kids wanted me to hit them. "Hold that bastard!" Crazy, but that hits me more than anything. Why'd they want to say that about me?

[*He leaves and exits into the gym*]

FATHER MOZIAN: [*A pause*] Jerome, about McArdle. What say we let him back in Thursday? I think two days is long enough.

MALLEY: The suspension was to be indefinite.

FATHER MOZIAN: That was before this incident. Besides, he's not a bad fellow from what I hear, and he's never been in serious trouble before this.

MALLEY: He's had his champions, I'd imagine. Forgive me, Father, but this sort of leniency has a way of getting back to the boys.

FATHER MOZIAN: Let it then. Maybe this sort of leniency is what we need right now. Sleep on it, all right?

MALLEY: I don't foresee any changes overnight.

FATHER MOZIAN: Sleep on it anyway. [Pause] How have they been for you in class lately, the boys?

MALLEY: My students, I'm afraid, don't lend themselves to lengthy analysis.

FATHER MOZIAN: Then you underestimate your students.

MALLEY: If anything, I'm being excessively charitable. They might spend more time on their Latin and less on their coiffures. That's hardly to the point, is it?

FATHER MOZIAN: No, hardly. Jerome, are you aware of what's been going on in the classrooms? Some of the teachers seem to be losing any kind of control, especially the priests, and I'm not just talking about Father Penny.

MALLEY: It's the teacher's role to enforce discipline, to insist on it. [Pointedly] And with the cooperation of the administration.

FATHER MOZIAN: Under ordinary circumstances, yes. But the classroom pranks have become more than pranks, more than adolescent defiance. What they're doing is deliberate and violent. Why?

MALLEY: I'm sure I don't know, Father.

FATHER MOZIAN: Jerome, it frightens me the way they've started going after one another. We've all got to try to understand what it is driving these boys. Maybe even revise our methods for a while.

[He is watching MALLEY, trying to determine whether he's implied enough. MALLEY has been tense, distracted during the exchange; more so now]

MALLEY: I'm too rough on them, is that it?

FATHER MOZIAN: If you put it that way, yes.

MALLEY: Why? Because I expect them to do a little work? For forty minutes a day, possibly even think?

FATHER MOZIAN: That's not what I'm talking about.

MALLEY: Then I don't know what you're talking about.

FATHER MOZIAN: Jerome, you've been here longer than I have, and that puts me in an awkward position.

MALLEY: Why should it? You're the headmaster.

[*They are standing at opposite ends of the room:* MALLEY *beside the door,* FATHER MOZIAN *next to the common table*]

FATHER MOZIAN: So I am. All right, everything right on the line. Jerome, I want you to ease up on those boys.

MALLEY: I see.

FATHER MOZIAN: Do you?

MALLEY: Perfectly. And perhaps you can suggest an appropriate pose as well. A friend, a chum . . .

FATHER MOZIAN: Please, don't make this any harder for me.

MALLEY: . . . a Mr. Dobbs—of course that's it—kindly, paternal!

FATHER MOZIAN: I'm not asking you to assume any kind of pose. All I'm saying is that we must all adjust to these peculiar circumstances.

MALLEY: [*A pause*] No.

FATHER MOZIAN: Jerome?

MALLEY: No.

FATHER MOZIAN: And that's final?

MALLEY: That's final.

FATHER MOZIAN: No, Jerome, I'm afraid it can't be final.

MALLEY: [*Less controlled*] What is it you think I've been doing to these boys? I've been teaching here for ten years. My students have always been important to me. I wouldn't be here if that weren't true.

FATHER MOZIAN: Jerome, I have great respect for you as a teacher, but I know your methods.

MALLEY: You know what you've *heard* of my methods.

FATHER MOZIAN: It's not what I've heard, it's what I've seen happening here that concerns me.

MALLEY: What has that to do with me? My methods are not Dobbs' methods. Why must you judge me by him?

FATHER MOZIAN: I am not judging you by Joe Dobbs.

MALLEY: I am paid to teach Latin and Greek. That's the extent of my responsibility to the school.

FATHER MOZIAN: And the human element?

MALLEY: I am not their chum! I will not tolerate laziness or stupidity, but I am not an ogre, not what Dobbs would have me!

FATHER MOZIAN: It's not what Dobbs would have you that concerns me. It's what the boys would have you. What they scrawl on the walls and pass to each other under the desks.

MALLEY: I'm not interested in what's written on the walls of a lavatory.

FATHER MOZIAN: Well, maybe you should be aware of it . . . the obscenity, the malevolence directed against you in this school.

MALLEY: Oh, I'm aware of it, the malevolence. I've been made aware of it . . .

FATHER MOZIAN: [Moving toward him] Are you? [He takes a sheet of paper from his folder and holds it out to MALLEY] Fully aware of it?

MALLEY: What is that?

FATHER MOZIAN: A note some of the boys were passing.

MALLEY: I'm not interested in notes.

FATHER MOZIAN: Read it, please.

[MALLEY takes the note, reads it slowly, and then crumples it]

MALLEY: Where did you get this?

FATHER MOZIAN: That doesn't matter.

MALLEY: [Giving the note back to FATHER MOZIAN] I have a right to know where this filth came from!

FATHER MOZIAN: That does not matter! What does matter is there've been other notes, uglier than that.

MALLEY: From whom? From what boys? I WANT THEIR NAMES!

FATHER MOZIAN: All of them directed against you. None of the other teachers, Jerome.

MALLEY: They wouldn't write such things about me . . . the boys.

FATHER MOZIAN: I'm sorry for all of this, Jerome. But whether you like it or not, you must cooperate. There are two hundred boys in this school, and more than any of you, they're my responsibility.

MALLEY: So he's reached you all, has he? As easily as he's reached those two hundred boys. [*Looking directly* at FATHER MOZIAN] *He's* the malevolence. *He's* the obscenity. [*Emphatically*] Dobbs wrote that note!

FATHER MOZIAN: You actually believe that?

MALLEY: I know it! I know what he's capable of.

FATHER MOZIAN: What you're saying is *insane*. Jerome, I know what the boys think of you, I've seen the way they react to you.

MALLEY: They react the way he's taught them to react. They're all his boys. This room is his . . . the school is his . . . everything here is *his* and it's all being used against me. [*Pointing to the note*] Dobbs wrote that note! There are no names, it was just handed to you. You know what I'm saying is true.

FATHER MOZIAN: No, Jerome. I took the note from those boys.

MALLEY: [*Shocked; shaking his head*] No, that's not possible. [*He lifts his schoolbag and pulls open the door with a quick gesture. A slight catch in his voice:*] That is not possible!

[*He leaves the room quickly, slamming the door behind him*]

THE LIGHTS FADE

SCENE THREE

Liturgical music is briefly heard as the lights come up on the chapel. The light is dim, reddish. On the wall is one of the Stations of the Cross in white marble: Christ falling beneath the weight of the cross. DOBBS is standing in the rear of the chapel, behind a pew. He holds a string of rosary beads in one hand. MALLEY enters the chapel through the rear door, genuflects and moves into the pew. He kneels and buries his face in his hands. DOBBS watches him silently, the sound of the rosary beads hitting against the wooden pew. MALLEY becomes aware of his presence.

MALLEY: [*Whispers*] What are you doing here?

DOBBS: I saw those boys, Jerome. I came in here to pray for them.

MALLEY: Yes, Dobbs, you're a great comfort to all your boys.

DOBBS: Well, who else have they got here but me? [*Putting the beads into his pocket, he pauses, looking straight ahead*] I remember, in grade school years ago, I remember the nuns telling us that God Himself was present on the altar whenever that small red light was burning. And how easy it was, in my child's mind, for the light itself to become God. I used to think . . . what if a wind were to blow into the church and find that light? Poof! . . . no more God? [*He gives a soft smile as he looks at the back of* MALLEY's *head*] Jerome, can we talk . . . calmly for once?

MALLEY: [*Wearily*] I don't want to talk to you, Dobbs. Just leave me alone. You've all made your point, haven't you?

DOBBS: I don't think so, no. Because you'll come in again tomorrow and it'll be the same pressure, the same going at the boys, all in the name of learning. They're children, Jerome.

MALLEY: And I'm a teacher, nothing more than that. This school is my life.

DOBBS: And mine as well.

MALLEY: All I have is here. I'm a good teacher. I belong here.

DOBBS: We all know that. If we're concerned—the headmaster, Father Griffin, all of us . . .

MALLEY: It's for your boys, I know. The headmaster has made that very clear. As clear as you've made it to him.

DOBBS: I've never said anything to him against you.

MALLEY: I wouldn't expect the truth from you, Dobbs. Not even in here. [*Staring straight ahead*] The hate—the hate between us . . . How terrible, isn't it . . . that the two of us should find ourselves together here? Two such . . . second-rate human beings . . . two such empty lives . . . shackled together here.

DOBBS: My life empty? With all I have here? [*Pauses; softly*] I don't hate you, Jerome.

MALLEY: More, I think, than I hate you. All right, Dobbs, if it's finally to destroy one of us, then let it be just that—*one of us.* [*Half turns*] Listen to me. My mother is very ill.

DOBBS: I know, Jerome, I know the strain you're under. Take it out on me if you have to, but leave the boys alone.

MALLEY: [*More emphatic*] She's dying. I have no defense against that. If . . . I go along with you, if I try . . . will you at least have a little pity on her?

DOBBS: Of course I pity her.

MALLEY: You know what I'm talking about, don't you?

DOBBS: I don't think I do.

MALLEY: There have been other calls besides McArdle's. Someone has been calling her. Terrible calls . . . terrible lies about me . . . Please, Dobbs, no more.

DOBBS: Do you know what you're saying to me?

MALLEY: I know exactly what I'm saying. For her sake, Dobbs—*no more!* I'll do whatever you want; whatever it does to me, I'll at least attempt it. But please leave her alone. Because you must know by now . . . there are kinder ways to destroy me.

> [*He leans forward in the pew, covering his face with his hands.* DOBBS *makes a helpless gesture, then crosses himself and leaves the chapel slowly. There is a long pause.* MALLEY *is motionless. The light in the chapel has been growing redder. There is a movement then, very quiet, at the chapel's side door. A boy comes in and slips into the pew, staring straight ahead.* MALLEY *becomes aware of his presence. More movement: the rear door opens. Two more boys enter, supporting a third who is semiconscious. They stand directly behind* MALLEY *and wait.* MALLEY's *hands fall from his face; he tries to see behind him. A pause; he gets up, lifts his schoolbag and leaves the pew without looking at the boys around him. He leaves the chapel. As soon as he does, the semiconscious boy collapses over the back of the pew. The boys press close to him now and tear off his jacket, exposing his whiplashed back. He moans as they raise him up and hang him by his wrists from the cross hanging on the wall. They leave the chapel quickly. The boy does not make a sound now. The chapel bells begin to ring. After a few moments,* FATHER MOZIAN *enters from the rear door, crosses himself and kneels in the pew. The bells continue to ring.* FATHER GRIFFIN *follows him in;*

as he genuflects, the boy moans loudly. They turn toward the sound]

FATHER GRIFFIN: [*Rushing toward the boy*] Dear God! Frank! Frank, help me! What are they doing, what are they—?

[*They lift the boy from the cross and cradle him with his head resting on the back of the pew*]

FATHER MOZIAN: [*Voice rising*] I want this chapel closed!

[*The bells are growing louder*]

FATHER GRIFFIN: It's the chapel, Frank, you can't close the chapel!
FATHER MOZIAN: I said lock it! *Lock it, lock it!*

[*His voice is covered by the sound of the bells. The red light goes out*]

SCENE FOUR

The lights come up in the Faculty Room. DOBBS *is handing* SHEA, *a senior, composition books.*

DOBBS: I appreciate the help, Shea.
SHEA: It's nothing, sir.
DOBBS: [*A little breathless*] Try not to grow old, boy. The body's not built to take it. [*Handing him the last of the books*] There you go. Put those on the table and count them. Should be thirty of 'em. [SHEA *puts the books on the table.* DOBBS *is looking for an opening*] Shea? [SHEA *stops counting*] I want you to give it to me straight now: What happened in the chapel yesterday?

[SHEA *goes back to counting*]

SHEA: [*Tonelessly*] I don't know anything about it, sir.
DOBBS: That may be a good enough answer for the headmaster and Father Griffin; this is Mr. Dobbs asking. You do know a boy was beaten up and left in the chapel. I want you to tell me how something so terrible could happen here.
SHEA: I don't know, sir. I wasn't there.

DOBBS: I'm not saying you were. I don't want any names. I just want to know why any boys in this school would desecrate their own chapel.

[FATHER GRIFFIN *enters the room and sees* SHEA]

FATHER GRIFFIN: Shea, what are you doing in here?
DOBBS: He's helping me, Father.
FATHER GRIFFIN: Where's your next class?
SHEA: Library.
FATHER GRIFFIN: Are you finished with him, Mr. Dobbs?
DOBBS: I don't know. Am I, Shea?
SHEA: [*Very clearly*] Yes, sir.

[*He starts to pick up his books*]

DOBBS: [*Stopping* SHEA] Are you sure? [SHEA *nods*] Okay. Put them on the desk in One C.

[*The class bell rings.* SHEA *starts for the door*]

FATHER GRIFFIN: Shea, three minutes. You've got three minutes to deliver those books and get to class.

[SHEA *leaves and goes down the stairs as* REESE *enters from the gym*]

DOBBS: Morning, Paul.
REESE: Morning.
DOBBS: Father, I hope you're bringing us some good news this morning.
FATHER GRIFFIN: I'm afraid not, Joe. We're canceling all masses and services in the school till further notice.
DOBBS: You can't be serious. Father, the boys need to feel the presence of God more than ever now. I don't have to tell you that.
FATHER GRIFFIN: I'm very serious, Joe. [*Checks his clipboard*] All students will report to their home rooms for study during the chapel period. You hear that, Paul?
REESE: I'm afraid I did.
FATHER GRIFFIN: Well, I've got a little more for you. [*Reads*] The school building is closed immediately after the last period.

DOBBS: You're locking the kids out of the building, locking . . . God out of the building.

FATHER GRIFFIN: Any boy found in the building after three-fifteen is on suspension.

DOBBS: Father, there was no faculty meeting on this. I wasn't consulted.

FATHER GRIFFIN: That's straight from the headmaster's office, Joe.

DOBBS: What about my conferences with the boys?

FATHER GRIFFIN: You're going to have to take that up with him.

DOBBS: I will, Father. I will.

REESE: I suppose that knocks out intramurals?

FATHER GRIFFIN: It knocks out all extracurriculars. And, Paul, the gym is out of bounds except for gym classes.

DOBBS: Father, wait a minute . . .

FATHER GRIFFIN: Joe, Frank is headmaster. This is the way he wants to handle the situation. [DOBBS *shrugs and moves away*] I'm sorry.

DOBBS: So am I, so am I.

[FATHER GRIFFIN *leaves and goes downstairs*]

REESE: Fifteen minutes to get out of the building. If he's running that scared, why open it at all?

DOBBS: Don't worry about it, young man. I've been in this school thirty years. No boy has ever held anything back from me in all that time, and I don't intend for it to start now.

> [*The class bell rings.* DOBBS *leaves the room angrily and goes down the stairs.* REESE *is setting his books up on the table. Two boys come up the stairs stealthily. One moves ahead to check that the way is clear. He signals to the other. They continue up and stop in the middle of the staircase. One of the boys is carrying a red markbook. He takes careful aim and throws it against the Faculty Room door. Both run up the stairs and disappear.* REESE *rushes to the door, opens it, and picks up the book and the scattered papers. As he puts them together, he notices something scrawled in the markbook. A look of distaste crosses his face as he rips the page from the book and crumples it.*

MALLEY *is coming down the stairs now, slowly, uncertainly.* REESE *moves back to the table, deciding what to do with the torn-out page. He slips it into his pocket as* MALLEY *enters the room. A bit rattled,* REESE *holds the book out to him*]

REESE: Here's your markbook, Mr. Malley.

MALLEY: [*Going to him*] My markbook? Where did you get that?

REESE: Found it . . . outside. You must've dropped it.

[MALLEY *takes the book and checks it, trying to remember*]

MALLEY: How could I have done that? I had it in my last class; I'm sure I did.

REESE: Me, I'm always forgetting things.

[*He looks quickly at* MALLEY, *who hasn't heard him*]

MALLEY: I never go to class without my markbook.

[*He goes to the alcove*]

REESE: I gave back a history test once and forgot all about recording the marks.

MALLEY: [*Still trying to figure it out*] I've never done that before.

REESE: Joe told me to bluff it—tell them I wanted to look over one of the essay questions again. Boy, did they see through that! [*Sees that* MALLEY *isn't listening; his voice trails off*] Guess Joe can . . . hand them a better line.

[MALLEY *looks up, not exactly at* REESE]

MALLEY: Just now . . . I found myself walking through the halls . . . I don't think I knew where I was going.

REESE: Sir?

MALLEY: [*With difficulty, trying to explain it more to himself. Sitting*] After my last class . . . What could have come over me . . . to wander through the halls that way? I lost my way. [*Convincing himself*] I didn't know what I was doing!

REESE: [*Hand extended*] Can I . . . Is there anything I can do?

MALLEY: What happened to me?

REESE: [*Moves toward the door*] I'll get Joe.

MALLEY: No! Nobody. I'll be all right.

> [*He tries to compose himself.* REESE *watches him with great concern*]

REESE: Are you sure?

MALLEY: [*Hand on his markbook again*] I *know* I had this in class with me.

> [*Aware of* REESE's *stare, he starts flipping through some papers*]

REESE: Look, Mr. Malley, are you all right?

MALLEY: [*Speaks without looking up*] I'd be thankful if you could forget all about this . . . stupid episode. It was inexcusable of me.

REESE: [*Moving toward him*] You don't have to apologize.

MALLEY: I'm not apologizing! I . . . blacked out, that's all. I've been under a great strain lately.

REESE: I know. Your mother.

MALLEY: Yes. My mother. [*With difficulty*] Her condition is much worse the last few days.

REESE: I'm sorry to hear that. That's rough on top of everything else. Look, if there's anything I can do . . .

> [FATHER GRIFFIN *is coming down the stairs quickly. He opens the Faculty Room door; looks in*]

FATHER GRIFFIN: Is George Penny in here?

REESE: No, he's not, Father.

> [FATHER PENNY *runs up the staircase*]

FATHER GRIFFIN: Well, if he comes in, will you tell him . . . [*He hears* FATHER PENNY, *turns and calls loudly*] . . . 2C is waiting for him to teach biology.

FATHER PENNY: [*Breathless*] Sorry. I was in levitation and I couldn't get down.

> [FATHER PENNY *continues up the stairs*]

FATHER GRIFFIN: What does it take to make that guy sober up?

[*He leaves, down the stairs*]

REESE: [*After a pause; peering at* MALLEY's *papers*] Test, hunh?

MALLEY: [*Uncomfortable, aware of* REESE] No. Composition. Caesar.

REESE: Caesar . . . [*Thinks hard; starts to recite*] *Gallia est omni divida . . . in tres . . . partes . . .*

MALLEY: . . . *omnis divisa in partes tres.*

REESE: [*Abashed; smiles*] You probably remember what a brain I was in Latin 2. The old 2B. I was the clod in the last seat near the window. That seems like such a helluva long time ago—nine years. [*With great effort*] A lot can happen in nine years. I have been trying, you know? To fit in here.

MALLEY: And now you're apologizing to me? [*Looks up*] Why?

REESE: Because I'm afraid you don't have much respect for me as a teacher.

MALLEY: Does what I think of you really matter?

REESE: Well, yes. I mean . . . we're sort of . . . colleagues.

[*The word comes out with difficulty*]

MALLEY: Yes, I suppose, we are . . . colleagues. And it's time we came to grips with that.

REESE: Yeah, because . . . I'm afraid of you. Isn't that something? So it's important to me just to work up enough courage to talk to you like this. I hate like hell to have to hide in the john every time we have a free period together.

MALLEY: I'm sorry I make you so uncomfortable.

REESE: It's not you, Lash, it's me.

[*He grimaces; waits for an explosion*]

MALLEY: [*A quick look*] Afraid of me.

REESE: *Still.*

MALLEY: Well, why not? I'm frightening, a menacing figure. I'm sure you've heard that over and over. Coupled with your own memories of my classroom . . . tyranny. I'm sure that's all been refreshed for you.

REESE: [*Defeated*] I'm sorry. [*Gathers his books*] I'll get out of your way now. I'll work in the gym.

[*He gets up and heads for the door.* MALLEY *raises one hand*]

MALLEY: No, *wait!* [*Just to say something*] You . . . stay around late, do you?

REESE: [*Stops*] Yes, I do. Often. Stay late.

MALLEY: [*Nods; can't pursue it*] A singularly stupid class, wasn't it, your old 2B?

REESE: The worst.

MALLEY: The worst. I have a newspaper clipping somewhere. That was your 2B, wasn't it?

REESE: [*Moving back into the room*] Yeah.

MALLEY: Yes. You boys had left it on the desk for me.

REESE: You weren't too happy about it.

MALLEY: Someday I must look for that clipping; something about . . .

REESE: [*Very cautiously*] A student stabbing his teacher.

MALLEY: Ah, yes, I remember feeling vaguely threatened at the time.

[REESE *puts down his books, and moves toward the refrigerator*]

REESE: [*Tentative*] Would you like a Coke?

MALLEY: [*A few seconds to absorb the offer*] Thank you, I have some tea. [*He gets up and goes to his schoolbag. Takes out a Thermos and pours himself a cup of tea*] That became a famous incident among you boys, didn't it? Something to add to the Lash catalogue of infamy.

REESE: [*Sitting at the table*] You had us all kneeling in the aisle.

MALLEY: Did I?

REESE: Forty minutes.

MALLEY: [*Drinking his tea and moving out of the alcove toward* REESE] I imagine . . . that's the sort of reminiscing you do when you boys get together.

REESE: Oh, yeah.

MALLEY: Do you keep in touch?

REESE: Sometimes.

MALLEY: Dwyer . . . do you ever see him?

REESE: Not since graduation, no.

MALLEY: Dirty fingernails, but a first-rate mind, one of the best I've ever taught. And Peter Jackmin?

REESE: He's still in the seminary.

MALLEY: He may actually pick up a bit of Latin. It was Jackmin who put the clipping on my desk.

REESE: [Surprised] You knew that?

MALLEY: Not then. I had a Christmas card from him once, with a note. Sometimes I hear from you boys . . . after a while. More than you'd think. [Moves over to the alcove table with his Thermos] A singularly stupid class; a trying year—like all of them, I suppose. You boys are afraid of me, I know. Maybe I am too hard on you. Maybe I shouldn't be teaching, at least not in a high school. It's not that I dislike you. It's just that . . . you're children, and some of you are so slow. I don't have much patience with the slow ones. [Pause] You'll find that . . . the pattern of one's life can be formed so suddenly, without realizing it. So suddenly and, for some of us, so irrevocably. And if it's wrong? Well, one comes in and goes through the motions, thinking at first that next year will be different . . . and realizing gradually that, no, next year will be the same and the year after that and, well, if that's the way it's to be . . . that's the way it's to be. And so . . . I save newspaper clippings and Christmas cards. Why do I save them? I don't know. But wouldn't it be comforting some day to take out all those bits of the past and lay them out on the floor like paths through a maze, and see what the course of my life has been . . . perhaps see what's been there all along, tucked away in a drawer? [Pause] If I've hurt you, any of you boys, I'm sorry . . . but that's what I am . . . [Pause. The phone rings] . . . that's the only way I know . . . [Pause. The phone rings again. MALLEY stops and looks at it. REESE has been standing, absorbed in MALLEY's sudden opening up to him. The ringing breaks his concentration. REESE sees that MALLEY, who is closer to the phone, will not answer it. MALLEY stares at the phone, his expression darkening. REESE moves toward the phone quietly] No! . . . Don't answer it! I won't speak to him!

[REESE *looks at him as the phone rings. No movement;
the phone keeps ringing*]

REESE: Maybe I better . . . ? [REESE's *hand is on the receiver, and
his eyes on* MALLEY. *He lifts the receiver*] Mr. Reese . . . [*To*
MALLEY] It's for you . . . Mrs. Carter . . . Your mother's nurse?

[MALLEY *takes the receiver and holds it for a moment
without speaking.* REESE *is watching him*]

MALLEY: Yes . . . I see . . . All right . . . Yes . . . [*Pause; then the
barest whisper*] All right . . . Thank you . . .

[*Slowly he lowers the receiver to the table. No movement
for several moments. He seems unaware of* REESE's *stare
as he goes to the closet for his coat, and then slowly walks
toward the door*]

REESE: Jerome? [MALLEY *looks at him and begins to weep.* REESE
*takes a step toward him; his hand moves in a helpless quieting
motion. He seems near tears himself now*]

MALLEY: [*At the door, holding it open*] It's just that . . . I should
have been with her . . . for that . . .

[*He goes out into the corridor and down the stairs.* REESE
remains motionless as:]

THE LIGHTS FADE

SCENE FIVE

It is evening, three days later. The lighting is dim. REESE
*is at the ditto machine on the balcony. A boy is moving
up the stairs from the lower floor. He stops at the landing,
listening for sounds from the Faculty Room. He is about
to go up to the next floor when distant laughter is heard
from the dining hall downstairs. He goes down the corridor quickly, toward the gym area.*

Now there is silence. FATHER PENNY, *glass in hand, is*

climbing the stairs. He starts for the Faculty Room, and
stops as he sees the statue atop the newel post.

FATHER PENNY: [*Addressing the statue*] What's a nice saint like
you . . . ? [*He leaves it incomplete, and moves—just a bit un-*
steadily—into the Faculty Room. He sees REESE] Ah! There you
are. Ten o'clock and nothing's well. You're missing the high point
of the faculty meeting—the booze.

[*He holds up the glass*]

REESE: [*With little interest*] Everybody still down there?
FATHER PENNY: Oh, yes. The faculty, having met in extraordinary
session, has dragged its collective ass to the dining hall, where
they are raising their glasses like a wall against the plague. The
feeling seems to be: we survived the Colosseum, we'll survive this
blood bath. We are dancing on the ruins.

[*He does a quick soft-shoe*]

REESE: [*Looking down*] George, George—I don't think I'm ready for
that tonight.
FATHER PENNY: Don't you go sour on me too. I came up here to get
away from all those craggy faces farting around down there. [*Sits*
in DOBBS' *chair*] Isn't that why you sneaked away?
REESE: I had a history test to run off.
FATHER PENNY: Anybody left to take it?

[*He laughs rowdily, then beats his breast in expiation*]

REESE: Nice to know there are some twisted minds left.

[*He starts to come down to the lower level. Noise is heard*
from below: voices raised, some laughter]

FATHER PENNY: Ah! Father Headmaster has pinned the tail on the
donkey.

[*He rises and dances quickly, professionally, across the*
room]

REESE: [*At the table now*] Very smooth. [FATHER PENNY *falls over*
the arm of DOBBS' *chair*]

FATHER PENNY: Thank you. One never knows where liturgical reform will lead.

REESE: George? You ever think of going over the wall?

FATHER PENNY: All the time.

REESE: I was only kidding.

FATHER PENNY: I wasn't.

REESE: You're a bad influence on me, George.

FATHER PENNY: [*Touching his cassock*] Don't be put off by the cassock. Its sanctity is becoming one of the great mysteries of faith. In view of what's happening around here, it dwarfs the Immaculate Conception. [*Getting up*] Come on downstairs with me; we'll shake them up.

REESE: [*Packing his schoolbag*] I'm going home.

FATHER PENNY: Father Headmaster will be displeased.

REESE: Tough shit.

FATHER PENNY: Ah, spunk! You may make it out of here yet.

REESE: Sorry, George, this place is beginning to get to me.

FATHER PENNY: [*Sitting in* MALLEY's *chair at the table*] Don't know why you say that. Chapel sealed, boys flagellating themselves— happens in the best of cloisters. But we're not to think of that tonight. Orders from On High. None of us may make it out of here alive, but tonight we're . . . *having fun.* Someone dropped a glass a few minutes ago and we all reached for our rosaries. [*He makes a quick "rosary" motion, and begins to sing dissonantly*] You're telling your beads more than you're telling me . . .

[*He chuckles again*]

REESE: [*More seriously now*] You wouldn't really go over the wall, would you?

FATHER PENNY: [*Pause*] I have taken vows. [*Getting up*] May I use the lay toilets? The urinals downstairs have suspicious wires running from the flushers. [*Moves toward the lavatory*] I shall be blown up decorously or not at all.

REESE: Don't write on the walls.

FATHER PENNY: I'll leave that to the already moving finger.

[*He goes into the lavatory.* REESE *takes his canvas bag to the table, and begins to pack up. A soft, wordless moan comes from the stairwell, then a distinct "no," followed by whispering. A boy comes up the stairs, his back against the rail. A second boy pursues slowly in the middle of the stairs, his arms extended to prevent the first boy's escape. A third boy comes from the gym and stops at the top of the stairs as the first boy reaches the landing and starts to back down to the right. Another boy has appeared at the head of the stairs. He comes down quickly and grabs the first boy, putting his hand over his mouth. One of the other boys punches him in the stomach; the victim doubles over. The boys drag him up the stairs.* REESE *moves slowly toward the door as the sounds build in the hallway. He opens the Faculty Room door, and moves slowly out into the corridor. There is silence; the boys have disappeared.* REESE *goes back into the Faculty Room and closes the door as* FATHER PENNY *comes out of the lavatory*]

FATHER PENNY: What's wrong?

REESE: I think there are kids in the building.

FATHER PENNY: It's after ten. They've all been flushed back to their rooms.

REESE: I know I heard them a minute ago.

FATHER PENNY: [*Tries to pass it off*] Well, *I've* had a revelation in the terlet! The boys are clearly possessed. Which means we need an exorcist and a herd of swine, fast.

REESE: Something's wrong with those kids. I'm sure they're in the building.

FATHER PENNY: Well, I'm sure about that possession idea. [*Touching his cassock, serious now*] This might have been the wrong way for me to go . . . but I believe in God, and I believe in Satan. [*Pauses; looks at his glass*] And now I believe I'll go have another drink.

REESE: Be careful, George.

FATHER PENNY: On second thought, I'll go back to the reliquary. [*Handing his glass to* REESE] A little free advice? You haven't taken vows. Why don't you get out of here?

REESE: I don't want to get out of here. I want to be a teacher.

FATHER PENNY: Be one somewhere else. You don't want to turn into one of those dried-up old celibates down there, clacking their beads and their teeth. That's my role.

[FATHER PENNY *leaves the room, and goes back down the stairs quickly.* REESE *closes the door after him. He looks at the glass* FATHER PENNY *has handed him, thinks a moment; he seems to dismiss a thought. He throws the glass into the wastebasket. The glass shatters. Two more boys have come quietly into the corridor, from the gym area. They stop at the sound of the glass breaking. One of them turns front, the light on his face. He waits for something, his companion watching him.* REESE *is looking at the broken glass in the wastebasket. He bends slowly and retrieves a piece of it. The boy in the corridor tenses, leaning against the newel post.* REESE *rises, and opens his palm; he looks from his hand to the glass. He brings the glass to his hand slowly. The boy in the hall moans softly and closes his eyes. A pause, and then* REESE *presses the jagged edge into his palm.* REESE *and the boy cry out in pain at the same time.* REESE *bends forward, covering his bleeding hand with the uninjured one. The second boy has grabbed the first; he leads him up the stairs.* REESE *grabs a towel from the rack beside the refrigerator, and wraps it around his hand. His back is to the Faculty Room door as he bites his lip, waiting for the pain to pass. There is a long pause.* DOBBS *comes up the stairs and enters the Faculty Room*]

REESE: [*Turns quickly at the sound*] Jesus, Joe! Don't creep up on me like that.

DOBBS: [*His mind back downstairs*] Those black robes think they know it all. They'll handle it their way. Well, their way is making it impossible for me to talk to my boys. They're frightening the boys. That's why those boys are avoiding me. [*Notices* REESE's *hand*] What's wrong with your hand?

REESE: I cut myself.

DOBBS: Well, the doctor just happens to be in. Sit down there.

REESE: It's all right.

DOBBS: Sit down, sit down. [REESE *sits in* MALLEY's *chair while* DOBBS *takes the first-aid kit from a shelf*] I've patched torn hands, knees, elbows, trousers. Been doing it for years. Everything needed to repair an adolescent boy is somewhere in this room.

REESE: [*Impatient*] I'm not an adolescent boy.

DOBBS: You're still a freshman to me, young man. You just got your growth a little faster than the other boys. You're all freshmen to me, whatever you go on to when you leave the old man. Doctors, bishops, councilmen—what do I care? I knew them when their faces were changing. Hold still.

[DOBBS *touches* REESE's *hand.* REESE *pulls away*]

REESE: Leave it alone, hunh?

DOBBS: Come on, boy. [*Takes* REESE's *hand again and begins to bandage the cut*] How'd you manage this?

REESE: I cut myself.

DOBBS: I'm asking how you did it.

REESE: Joe . . . I did it deliberately.

DOBBS: What do you mean, deliberately?

REESE: Just what I said. I broke a glass and cut myself deliberately!

DOBBS: You don't cut yourself deliberately. When we cut ourselves we call that an accident. Now you can all put that in your notebooks.

REESE: Joe, I don't understand. Why would I want to hurt myself? Why? What's in this building that made me want to hurt myself?

DOBBS: All right, Paul, you cut yourself. Now let's leave it at that.

REESE: That's not enough.

DOBBS: Well, it'll just have to be enough for now. You're too excitable, boy. I meant to tell you that downstairs.

REESE: Why, because I got pissed off at that meeting? Let me tell you something, Joe. Your friends downstairs are panicking. They're just looking for a scapegoat. Something's gone wrong in this school and you're all looking for something to pin it on and it looks like you've all elected Jerome.

DOBBS: Nobody says it's just Jerome.

REESE: Well, you were all sure hinting at it.

WITNESS FOR THE PROSECUTION
(New York production)
Courtroom scene

DIAL "M" FOR MURDER
Gusti Huber, Maurice Evans,
Richard Derr

SLEUTH
Keith Baxter, Anthony Quayle

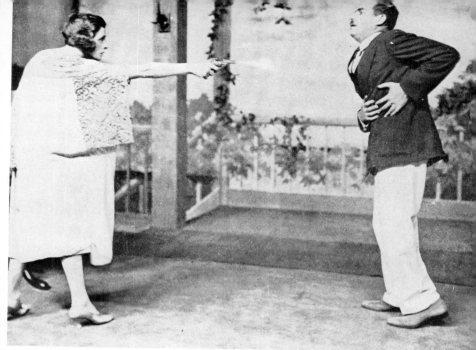

THE LETTER
(*London production*)
Gladys Cooper,
S. J. Warmington

THE LETTER
(*New York production*)
Katharine Cornell,
J. W. Austin

CHILD'S PLAY
Foreground: Robbie Reed, Ken Howard, Middle Row: Fritz Weaver, Pat
Hingle, Peter MacLean, David Rounds

ARSENIC AND OLD LACE
Edgar Stehli, Boris Karloff, Josephine Hull, Jean Adair

ANGEL STREET
Vincent Price,
Judith Evelyn

BAD SEED
Patty McCormack,
Nancy Kelly

DANGEROUS CORNER
Colin Keith-Johnston, Jean Dixon, Mary Servoss

DRACULA
Bela Lugosi as Count Dracula (Screen version)

DOBBS: If I remember correctly, there was a time when you were afraid to be in the same room with—*Jerome*.

REESE: Well, maybe that was my fault more than his. We talked for the first time . . . just before he got the call about his mother. Did I tell you that?

DOBBS: [*More slowly*] No. And what was it you talked about—Jerome and you?

REESE: I don't know—just talked. Joe, he's different, changed. You didn't see him at the funeral this morning.

DOBBS: I had a class.

REESE: Well, you should have seen him. He's not the same person. If it means anything, he's not here now; he hasn't been anywhere near the place for three days. And I'm still afraid. Whatever there is in this building is in here *now*. And Joe . . . the kids are in here.

DOBBS: The boys? In here?

REESE: I know they're in here. I heard them. Why, Joe? What do they want in here? What are they looking for?

DOBBS: You're sure full of questions tonight, young man.

REESE: Well, nobody around here's been coming up with any answers. What about you, old man? You've always had them. All right, why are the kids in the building now?

DOBBS: They're not in the building!

REESE: They are, for Chrissake!

DOBBS: They're not! I'd know it if they were. I'll show you. [*He gets up, crosses out into the corridor and goes halfway up the stairs. When he speaks, it is almost a litany*] Bassman? Blake? Curran? DeLeo? Enright? Hartnett? Keaney? Kearney? Landis? Martin? Sheppard? Tapken? [*Starts back down the stairs*] Uzzo? Weeks? [*Stops, meditative*] And Bennie Zeller . . . English 1D. Nineteen fifty-two. Nobody there . . . [*He stands beside the statue.* REESE *has come out into the corridor.* DOBBS *looks at him, his eyes suddenly glazed, distant*] I've taught over two thousand boys, do you know that? Other men's sons, two thousand of them. I've always valued it, the affection of all those boys, their friendship . . . years of it. You know me, you boys. It's you, you I trust. Not myself, but you, all those boys. And what you see, what all those boys have seen in me, that must be what I am . . . truly, isn't that so? This is my school. I've spent thirty years in this building . . . And what you see is all there is. There's nothing to frighten you.

REESE: I *am* scared, Joe. This place scares the hell out of me.

DOBBS: It's just a school, for God's sake.

REESE: I know it's just a school. I went here. [DOBBS *moves in front of* REESE *and goes back into the Faculty Room.* REESE *follows, closing the door*] I know every room and every corridor. I can take you downstairs and show you my old desk, my locker; but it's changed. It's not the same. Something's come into this place.

DOBBS: Your imagination, that's what.

REESE: No, Joe, it's not my imagination. It's something real. It's real enough to touch. [*He holds up his hand, and looks at it, as if realizing something for the first time*] And I touched it. *I touched it!* [*There is a shrill scream from the offstage corridor upstairs. The victim the boys had selected is pushed out into the corridor. He stumbles down the top steps, and flails about for the bannister to break his fall. The boy's glasses have been shattered; his eyes are bloody. He feels his way down the remaining steps as* DOBBS *and* REESE *rush out into the hall.* DOBBS *grabs the boy as* REESE *stops suddenly, too shocked to move. The boy pulls away from* DOBBS *and falls against* REESE, *whose arms go around him*]

REESE: [*Almost inaudibly*] God . . . his eyes . . . his . . .

[*He lifts the boy and begins to carry him down the stairs.* DOBBS' *hands reach out helplessly. Faculty voices are heard again from downstairs—louder, more jovial now*]

THE LIGHTS FADE

SCENE SIX

The lights come up. A boy is coming from the gym, another from the floor below. Both look, almost instinctively, toward the Faculty Room, for just a moment, then continue. They meet beside the statue on the newel post, exchange a look without speaking, and then continue. The first boy descends the stairs, the second boy continues up.

FATHER GRIFFIN *has appeared at the head of the stairs. He stops and watches the boys. The second boy passes him without seeing him.* FATHER GRIFFIN *has stepped aside to let the boy pass. After a pause,* FATHER GRIFFIN *continues down.*

When he reaches the landing he stops; someone else is coming up. He waits. It is MALLEY, *climbing slowly, his eyes downcast. His expression, when he looks up at* FATHER GRIFFIN, *is one of profound weariness.*

FATHER GRIFFIN: [*Seeing the change in him*] Jerome. Why have you come back so soon? We told you to stay out the whole week.

MALLEY: Three days were enough. You were a great help to me yesterday at the funeral, Father. Thank you. I had hoped more of the priests would have come.

FATHER GRIFFIN: [*Very gently*] Go home now, Jerome.

MALLEY: No, Father. I have a class.

FATHER GRIFFIN: I don't think that's wise.

MALLEY: I'm all right now. Thank you.

[*He enters the Faculty Room.* FATHER GRIFFIN *looks after him as* FATHER MOZIAN *comes up the stairs. During the following,* MALLEY *takes off his coat and goes through his routine activity, almost numbly, preparing for the class*]

FATHER GRIFFIN: Frank . . .

FATHER MOZIAN: [*His voice low and troubled, before* FATHER GRIFFIN *can say more*] I know, Bill, I saw him.

FATHER GRIFFIN: Then go easy on him, hunh?

FATHER MOZIAN: I only wish I could. Make sure his classes are being covered. And there's to be a general assembly second period. Please see that it's announced. [FATHER GRIFFIN *goes up the stairs, and* FATHER MOZIAN *enters the Faculty Room quietly*] Jerome . . .

MALLEY: Good morning, Father.

FATHER MOZIAN: [*Watching him*] I hardly expected to see you here today, Jerome.

MALLEY: [*Busy with books*] I know, but it's better for me this way.

FATHER MOZIAN: Your classes are being covered.

MALLEY: There's no need for that.

FATHER MOZIAN: Father Brooke's been reassigned to second-year Latin. I'll handle your Greek class myself.

MALLEY: I've never had another teacher take my classes. A week without me and they'll forget everything.

FATHER MOZIAN: That's not our major concern right now.

MALLEY: If this is still a school, then it should be. The boys are lazy, you've got to keep at them.

[*He crosses up to the alcove for a pencil*]

FATHER MOZIAN: [*Pauses; as gently as possible*] The new assignments are permanent, Jerome.

MALLEY: Permanent?

FATHER MOZIAN: As of first period today. Jerome, this is very painful for me.

MALLEY: Then please, don't. There's no need, there's . . . I've thought it over . . . and of course you're right. I'll change my methods . . .

FATHER MOZIAN: Jerome, I'm afraid that doesn't matter now.

MALLEY: If you'll just give me a little time to get my thoughts in order . . . I'll explain . . . I can revise the course . . . we can discuss that . . .

FATHER MOZIAN: There's nothing to discuss. I know what you've been through the past few days . . .

MALLEY: You don't. You wouldn't be saying this to me now if that were true. I . . . won't be dismissed. I'll do whatever you say, I'll go against what I believe, but I won't be dismissed. Not for something I'm not responsible for. Not from this school. And please, not now. I'll change my methods . . .

FATHER MOZIAN: [*Taking an envelope from his leather folder*] This is addressed to you. You know what it is?

[MALLEY *takes a long look at the envelope*]

MALLEY: [*Almost inaudibly*] Yes.

FATHER MOZIAN: Have you received them before?

MALLEY: [*Same*] Yes.

FATHER MOZIAN: Pictures like this? . . . You're teaching young boys, Jerome.

MALLEY: [*Very slowly, painfully*] Whatever there is in my life, I have never brought it into this school.

FATHER MOZIAN: Well, I'm afraid it *has* come into the school now. How long have you been getting this kind of thing here?

MALLEY: Here? Never.

FATHER MOZIAN: Jerome, there's no point in lying to me.

MALLEY: No, never here. At my home, yes, but not here. But I should have expected that, shouldn't I? That's why Father Griffin was so concerned about me. I imagine it's all over the faculty by now. Mr. Malley is, after all, just another dirty joke. Has it been passed down to the students yet?

FATHER MOZIAN: I'm sorry, Jerome. You do understand my position?

[*He places the envelope back in his folder*]

MALLEY: [*Thinking; his hands moving nervously*] Yes, yes, of course I do. [FATHER MOZIAN *starts to leave*] Wait! Father . . . ? [*Trying to control himself as he moves toward* FATHER MOZIAN] Try to understand mine. Those pictures are being sent to me. Deliberately sent to me.

FATHER MOZIAN: [*Has stopped*] Sent to you?

MALLEY: Yes. I have nothing to do with them.

FATHER MOZIAN: They're addressed to you. You've involved the school—all of us—in this.

MALLEY: I've tried to stop them. I have always destroyed them. You must believe that.

FATHER MOZIAN: Jerome, I have no other choice. You admit you've received them before.

MALLEY: [*More desperate*] But they're being *sent* to me! Don't you understand?

FATHER MOZIAN: [*Challenging; he knows*] Sent to you by whom, Jerome?

MALLEY: You'd believe me? You'd believe that such deliberate . . . malevolence could be directed at me by . . . Dobbs? Dobbs?

FATHER MOZIAN: [*Pause. Directly at him*] No, Jerome.

MALLEY: And if it's the truth?

FATHER MOZIAN: Then it's a truth I can't afford to face. Not now, Jerome, not with everything else I've got to face here. And we both know that something like that cannot be true. Don't we?

MALLEY: Of course you're right. How could it be so easy to select a victim . . . and turn everything against him?

FATHER MOZIAN: I cannot afford something like this now, Jerome. Please, let's end it!

MALLEY: End it. And how easily it solves the problem of Mr. Malley. Anything would have worked, wouldn't it?

FATHER MOZIAN: [*Harder*] I think it would be best if you left this school as soon as possible.

MALLEY: Best for whom?

FATHER MOZIAN: For all of us.

MALLEY: No! How can I make you understand it's true? *He is destroying me!* My mother first, and now me. There must be some way I can make you understand that what is happening to me is true. He can't win this easily, can he?

FATHER MOZIAN: [*A step away*] I'm sorry, Jerome.

MALLEY: Wait! You're a priest, before everything you're a priest. If I got down on my knees to you . . . would you believe me?

[*He is beside him*]

FATHER MOZIAN: [*Moving away further*] That's enough, please!

MALLEY: If I were to humiliate myself before you . . . make my confession to you . . . then you'd have to believe me . . . [*Falls to his knees before* FATHER MOZIAN] Bless me, Father, bless me for I have sinned . . .

FATHER MOZIAN: [*Pulling away*] I said that's enough!

MALLEY: [*Overwhelmed*] But you're a priest! You can't deny me confession, not if you're a priest—

FATHER MOZIAN: [*His back to him*] Your contract with this school is terminated. [*Turns to him. Voice quavering*] And I forbid you, I absolutely forbid you to go up to those boys!

[*He leaves the room quickly*]

MALLEY: [*Still on his knees*] Then . . . what are you . . . all of you?

[*He pulls himself up, very slowly. Looks around the room*

*and then moves, almost blindly, toward the table. He
picks up his books and walks out into the corridor, leaving
the Faculty Room door open. He stops beside the staircase, suddenly unsure of his direction. The class bell rings,
like a blow against his brain. He is motionless now.* REESE
is coming up the stairs. He sees MALLEY *immediately*]

REESE: Jerome? [*Reaching out for him*] Come into the Faculty Room.

MALLEY: I have a class.

REESE: No, you can't go up like this. Come and sit down for a while.

[*He leads* MALLEY *toward the Faculty Room*]

MALLEY: I told you I have a class!

REESE: All right, later.

[*Seating* MALLEY. MALLEY *grabs* REESE'S *arm*]

MALLEY: Now. Second period. There's no way he can stop me. I'm
not responsible, not for any of it. He's a priest before everything;
and if I tell him that again, if I explain everything to him when
my mind is clearer, when I can think more clearly . . . then he's
got to believe me. Because it's the truth, all of it is true.

REESE: [*Bending before him*] Jerome, I can't follow you, I don't
understand what you're saying. Let me get somebody—

MALLEY: *There is nobody!* Paul . . . there was no need . . . no reason to torment her like that . . . an old woman who was dying
. . . my mother. He was sending those pictures to my home. He
was calling her, telling her lies about me, destroying her with those
terrible lies . . . All of it deliberate. And I don't understand, I
don't understand why he's doing this to me!

REESE: What calls? Who was calling?

MALLEY: *Dobbs. Dobbs.*

REESE: Joe? . . . Jerome, I don't know what you're saying.

MALLEY: How could I protect myself against someone like that?
Someone who could know me so completely? What defense do
I have against so much hate?

[DOBBS *comes down the corridor and opens the Faculty
Room door*]

DOBBS: [*A long look. Slowly*] What are you doing here, Jerome?

REESE: He was going upstairs and I brought him in here . . .

DOBBS: You don't belong in this school, Jerome.

MALLEY: It's all yours now, Dobbs, isn't it?

REESE: [*Standing up beside* MALLEY's *chair*] What do you mean, he doesn't belong in this school?

DOBBS: Just what I said.

MALLEY: It's taken you ten years, but you've won.

DOBBS: [*To* REESE] What's he been telling you?

REESE: [*Challenging*] I don't know.

DOBBS: All the old lies, the old accusations? Everything wrong in his life is Joe Dobbs? Well, look at him, for God's sake.

MALLEY: How can you hate me so much . . . How can so much hate exist?

REESE: What calls is he talking about, what pictures?

DOBBS: I don't know!

MALLEY: *You're lying!*

REESE: Joe, what were you doing to him?

DOBBS: Nothing!

MALLEY: Destroying me! With all, *all* the malevolence in him! [*He springs up and rushes at* DOBBS, *hands raised*] Devil! [DOBBS *moves back quickly.* REESE *is too stunned to move immediately*] Devil! [*Now* REESE *comes behind him and grabs him just as he is about to strike* DOBBS] DEVIL!

REESE: Jerome, no!

MALLEY: [*Trying to break away*] Wasn't it enough—me? Me? [*He frees himself and turns to face* REESE] And he's got you all, hasn't he? Every last one of you. [*He begins to move out of the room*] Well, I'll show you, I'll find a way to show you the evil he's brought down on every last one of you. [*He is mounting the stairs. Stops*] But I'll bring you down with me . . . *Mr. Dobbs!*

[*He disappears up the stairs.* REESE *moves toward the door suddenly.* DOBBS *steps into the doorway*]

REESE: [*Calls*] Jerome!

DOBBS: Let him go!

REESE: Get out of my way, Joe!

DOBBS: I said let him go!

REESE: [*Pushing* DOBBS *aside*] I've got to help him!

[REESE *is rushing up the stairs*]

DOBBS: [*Steps into the hall*] Did you hear me?

REESE: He can't go up like that! Jerome!

[REESE *disappears upstairs*]

DOBBS: [*Enormous power*] LET HIM GO! [*There is a sudden great sound—a shriek of boys' voices. The shriek fills the room, the school. Another sound—a rush, the toppling of furniture.* DOBBS *stands rooted by the terrible sounds.* FATHER GRIFFIN *rushes down the stairs*] What is it? What's happened?

FATHER GRIFFIN: My God! Jerome! He's—jumped, he—! Keep those kids up here, we've got to keep them out of the courtyard!

[*He runs down the stairs. The boys appear at the top of the staircase, screaming. They come down to the landing and stop when they see* DOBBS. *Silence*]

DOBBS: [*As the boys rush down*] All right, you boys, listen to me . . . stay here . . .

[*One of the boys moves slowly toward* DOBBS, *his face lighting up with some kind of terrible recognition.* DOBBS *puts out his hands to stop the boy. The boy pulls back violently. His hands rise suddenly and come down with a cry against* DOBBS' *face.* DOBBS *staggers under the blow, and falls to his knees as* REESE *comes down the stairs. The boys surround* DOBBS *now, striking him; he is trying to protect himself.* REESE *fights his way to him, pulling the boys off. The boys continue down the stairs.* REESE *is standing over* DOBBS *now, looking down at him.* DOBBS *looks up, a plea for help.* REESE *turns away and goes downstairs.* DOBBS *is alone, a single spot on him now. He pulls himself up slowly and moves toward the Faculty Room. The sounds in the building diminish gradually.* DOBBS *falls into a chair, staring at nothing. Long wait. Silence. The light builds slowly.* DOBBS *has not moved. Three boys appear, on the upper landing, from the gym area, and on the staircase*]

*from the lower floor. They are moving toward the statue.
A door slams downstairs. The boys stand still and wait.*
REESE *comes up the stairs. He stops when he sees the boys.
They exchange a long look of recognition.* REESE *moves
past them, to the Faculty Room. The boys assume set
positions in the corridor, their eyes on the Faculty Room
as* REESE *opens the door and enters*]

REESE: [*Pause; at door*] Maybe you haven't heard, old man: this
building is closed. They want us out of here. What are you waiting for? There's nothing left.

DOBBS: [*Without looking up*] I've been sitting here, thinking . . .
Those boys . . . couldn't have known what they were doing. To
hit me? I mean, what reason would any of my boys have to do
something like that to the old man?

REESE: What old man are you talking about? The one I saw beaten
to his knees an hour ago?

DOBBS: You need a longer memory than that, boy.

REESE: [*A step into the room*] I've got one, Joe. I remember all the
beers and the handouts. Well, a quick beer isn't going to help me
forget what happened here today. Jerome is dead.

DOBBS: [*Looks up*] Well, then God rest his soul.

REESE: And that's all you've got to say?

DOBBS: What do you want, boy—tears? [*Another boy comes up the
stairs and stops on the second step from the top*] Well, I have
no tears for Jerome.

REESE: Then maybe I have enough for both of us. I could have
stopped him. But you wouldn't let me go up there. Why?

DOBBS: Why should you stop him? What did Jerome ever do for you
boys? That door was always open to you boys whenever you needed
me. Any of you felt free to come in and talk to me until he moved
in here . . . [*A boy appears on the balcony in the Faculty Room.*
DOBBS *does not see him*] All right, it's back the way it should be,
so what does it matter that Jerome is dead?

REESE: My God! What are you?

DOBBS: What I've always been to all you boys. And you know it.
That's why I say those boys didn't know what they were doing.

REESE: And did they know what they were doing to themselves downstairs after they sent you crawling back into this room? You want to know what your boys were doing to each other?

DOBBS: No . . .

REESE: Kids fighting for bits of broken glass . . . to tear themselves . . . [*Another boy appears at the opposite end of the balcony*] your boys, all of them your boys . . .

DOBBS: Is that why you've come back? To blame me for what's happened to my school, my boys?

REESE: You don't need me for that, Joe. Your boys showed you that out in the hall.

DOBBS: I told you . . . they didn't know what they were doing.

REESE: They knew what they were doing. And everything he said was true. What were you doing to him? [*No reply.* DOBBS *is still deep within himself.* REESE *has come to the table; he sits beside* DOBBS] You wanted him dead, didn't you, Joe?

DOBBS: No. I wanted him out of my school.

REESE: Your school! What makes it *your* school?

DOBBS: Thirty years.

REESE: Thirty years of what?

DOBBS: Thirty years of my life. My life is this school. That makes it mine.

REESE: Well, it's all yours now. [*Another boy appears on the stairs*] My God, you did want him dead.

DOBBS: No! I never wanted that.

REESE: [*Building*] You wanted him dead.

DOBBS: [*Same*] I wanted him out of my life!

REESE: You wanted him dead!

DOBBS: [*Bursting out*] All right, I wanted him dead! If that's what you want me to say, then I wanted him dead! If that was the only way to get him out of my school, out of my life, then I wanted him dead!

REESE: Well, he's dead. It took you ten years, didn't it, but you finally found a way to break him. Well, what are you going to do with all the hate that's in you now?

DOBBS: There's no more hate left in me.

REESE: Of course not. [*A boy moves down a step*] You've managed

to infect this whole place with it . . . this room is *filled* with it
. . . And, Joe, you've infected your boys, every last one of them.
[*Looks at his hand*] Is that what I tried to tear out of myself. The
hate?

DOBBS: My boys? I've never done anything to hurt my boys.

[*A boy enters the corridor from the gym. He moves down
opposite the Faculty Room door and leans against the rail*]

REESE: You still think you're the grand old man of the faculty. Well,
you're not, Joe. You're a killer. [*The boys are moving toward the
door: one step*] And Jerome was only one victim. [REESE *opens
the Faculty Room door, and a boy throws open the locker-room
door. He is in the room*] The others are here. They're still your
boys. They've come back for the old man. Maybe they'll forgive
you for what you've done.

DOBBS: My boys . . . ?

REESE: Are you afraid, Joe?

DOBBS: I've never been afraid of any of my boys.

[DOBBS *starts to get up*]

REESE: Well then, I'll leave you with them. After all, what's the old
man without his boys?

[REESE *leaves the room. He stops in the corridor, and looks
at the boys waiting. Then he moves past them and down
the stairs. The boys enter the room slowly.* DOBBS *moves to
the center of the room*]

DOBBS: [*Calling as he moves back*] Paul? Paul, wait? [*The boys are
circling him. He does not move as he looks at each of them*] Mc-
Ardle? Jennings? Carre? Medley? Shea? Wilson? Banks? Travis?
[*A pause. They are very close to him. He raises his hands, just
slightly*] Please. [*Quietly*] Please?

[*They close in on him*]

CURTAIN

Arsenic and Old Lace

JOSEPH KESSELRING

Joseph Kesselring

The theatre, which is several thousand years old, has never produced anything quite like *Arsenic and Old Lace*. Nor have there ever been two more disarmingly homicidal characters on stage than the Brewster sisters of Joseph Kesselring's murder charade. Beaming with benevolence and as devout as any of Norman Rockwell's parishioners, they go about their charitable duties of proffering lethal elderberry wine to lonely old men with all the grace and innocent pleasure of hostessing a church tea. And not only has their erratic behavior brought permanent solace to the hapless victims, it also has established *Arsenic and Old Lace* as a modern classic and one of the theatre's all-time highest-grossing plays.

The macabre comedy made its debut at the Fulton Theatre, New York, on January 10, 1941, and ran for 1,444 performances. During that period, the original Broadway production and four touring companies grossed more than four million dollars. In London, where it opened on December 23, 1942, the Kesselring murder romp established a new mark for an American importation—1,337 performances. During the harrowing period of the London blitz, when other West End offerings were forced to seek shelter in the provinces, *Arsenic and Old Lace* nonchalantly stayed right on at the Strand Theatre until 1946. The Brewster sisters, as usual, persevered.

Nor did these uncommonly genteel poison-cup artists confine their feral activities to the English-language stage: through numerous foreign translations, they roamed the globe, providing chills and laughter in equal and profitable doses. And to add to the account: a motion picture version was made by Frank Capra in 1944, with Cary Grant abetted by Josephine Hull and Jean Adair in a re-creation of their famed stage roles.

Arsenic and Old Lace nimbly combines the humor of farce with the mystery and suspense of melodrama. As Brooks Atkinson reported in *The New York Times:* "Mr. Kesselring has written a murder play as legitimate as farce-comedy. It is full of chuckles even when the scene is gruesome by nature. Swift, dry, satirical and exciting, it kept the first-night audience roaring with laughter."

Joseph Kesselring (1902–1967) was born in New York City. At the age of twenty he joined the faculty of Bethel College, Kansas, as a professor of music and remained on campus until 1924. During the next eight years, he wrote, produced, and acted in vaudeville sketches and also turned out a number of published short stories and poems.

Aggie Appleby, Maker of Men (1933) was Kesselring's first play to reach Broadway. It was not a success, nor were his two succeeding attempts: *There's Wisdom in Women* (1935), and *Cross-Town* (1937).

Indeed, there was little in Kesselring's professional dossier to prepare Broadway for the riotous comedy and fresh invention of *Arsenic and Old Lace.* Consequently, rumors were rife that Howard Lindsay and Russel Crouse, producers of the play, had transformed the show from straight melodrama to farce by adding humorous embellishments. Though they consistently denied this, it was logical that the suspicion persisted, for Lindsay and Crouse had an almost unbeatable track record in the comedy department and were old and experienced hands at doctoring as well as at creating.

Subsequent to 1941, when the Brewster menage took firm hold, Joseph Kesselring produced at least a half dozen other plays, but all are more or less forgotten. What matters most, however, is that he gave us *Arsenic and Old Lace,* a wildly satiric thriller, "one so funny that none of us will ever forget it."

Arsenic and Old Lace was first produced at the Fulton Theatre, New York, on January 10, 1941, by Howard Lindsay and Russel Crouse. The cast was as follows:

ABBY BREWSTER	*Josephine Hull*
THE REV. DR. HARPER	*Wyrley Birch*
TEDDY BREWSTER	*John Alexander*
OFFICER BROPHY	*John Quigg*
OFFICER KLEIN	*Bruce Gordon*
MARTHA BREWSTER	*Jean Adair*
ELAINE HARPER	*Helen Brooks*
MORTIMER BREWSTER	*Allyn Joslyn*
MR. GIBBS	*Henry Herbert*
JONATHAN BREWSTER	*Boris Karloff*
DR. EINSTEIN	*Edgar Stehli*
OFFICER O'HARA	*Anthony Ross*
LIEUTENANT ROONEY	*Victor Sutherland*
MR. WITHERSPOON	*William Parke*

Directed by	Bretaigne Windust
Setting and Costumes by	Raymond Sovey

Arsenic and Old Lace was first presented in London by Firth Shephard (by arrangement with Howard Lindsay and Russel Crouse) on December 23, 1942, at the Strand Theatre. The cast was as follows:

ABBY BREWSTER	*Lilian Braithwaite*
THE REV. DR. HARPER	*Clarence Bigge*
TEDDY BREWSTER	*Frank Pettingell*
OFFICER BROPHY	*George Dillon*
OFFICER KLEIN	*E. J. Kennedy*
MARTHA BREWSTER	*Mary Jerrold*
ELAINE HARPER	*Eileen Bennett*
MORTIMER BREWSTER	*Naunton Wayne*
MR. GIBBS	*Fred Beck*
JONATHAN BREWSTER	*Edmund Willard*
DR. EINSTEIN	*Martin Miller*
OFFICER O'HARA	*Cyril Smith*
LIEUTENANT ROONEY	*Frank Tilton*
MR. WITHERSPOON	*Wilfred Caithness*

Directed by	Marcel Varnel
Setting by	Roger Furse

SCENE: *The living room of the Brewster home in Brooklyn.*
TIME: *1941.*

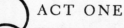

ACT ONE
An afternoon in September.

ACT TWO
That same night.

ACT THREE
SCENE 1: *Later that night.*
SCENE 2: *Early the next morning.*

ACT ONE

The living room of the old Brewster home in Brooklyn. It is just as Victorian as the two sisters, ABBY *and* MARTHA BREWSTER, *who occupy the house with their nephew,* TEDDY.

Downstage, right, is the front door of the house, a large door with frosted glass panels in the upper half, beyond which, when it is open, can be seen the front porch and the lawn and shrubbery of the front garden of the Brewster house. On either side of the door are narrow windows of small panes of glass, curtained. Over the door is a small arch of colored glass. The remainder of the right wall is taken up by the first flight of stairs leading to the upper floors. In the upstage corner is a landing where the stairs turn to continue along the back wall of the room. In the right wall of the landing is an old-fashioned window, also looking out on to the porch. At the top of the stairs, along the back wall, is another landing, from which a door leads into the second-floor bedrooms, and an arch at the left end of this landing suggests the stairs leading to the third floor.

On stage level under this landing is a door which leads to the cellar. To the left of this door is a recess which contains a sideboard, on the top of which at either end are two small cabinets, where the sisters keep, among other things, bottles of elderberry wine. On the sideboard, among the usual impedimenta, are colored wine glasses. To the left of the recess is the door leading to the kitchen.

In the left wall of the room, there is a large window looking out over the cemetery of the neighboring Episcopal Church. This window has the usual lace curtains and thick

*drapes, which open and close by the use of a heavy curtain
cord. Below the window is a large window seat, the lid of
which has a thin pad of the same material as the drapes.
When this lid is raised, the hinges creak audibly.*

*At the left of the foot of the stairs is a small desk, on
which stands a dial telephone, and by this desk is a stool.
Along the back wall, to the right of the cellar door, is an
old-fashioned sofa. Left center in the room is a round table. There is a small chair right of this table and behind
it, to the left of the table, a larger, comfortable armchair.
On the walls are the usual pictures, including several portraits of the rather eccentric Brewster ancestors.*

*The time is 1941. Late afternoon in September. As the
curtain rises,* ABBY BREWSTER, *a plump little darling in her
late sixties, is presiding at tea. She is sitting behind the
table in front of a high silver tea service. At her left, in
the comfortable armchair, is the* REV. DR. HARPER, *the
elderly rector of the nearby church. Standing, at her right,
thoughtfully sipping a cup of tea, is her nephew,* TEDDY,
*in a frock coat, and wearing pince-nez attached to a black
ribbon.* TEDDY *is in his forties and has a large mustache.*

ABBY: My sister Martha and I have been talking all week about your
sermon last Sunday. It's really wonderful, Dr. Harper—in only two
short years you've taken on the spirit of Brooklyn.

DR. HARPER: That's very gratifying, Miss Brewster.

ABBY: You see, living here next to the church all our lives, we've seen
so many ministers come and go. The spirit of Brooklyn, we always
say, is friendliness—and your sermons are not so much sermons as
friendly talks.

TEDDY: Personally, I've always enjoyed my talks with Cardinal Gib-
bons—or have I met him yet?

ABBY: No, dear, not yet. [*Changing the subject*] Are the biscuits
good?

TEDDY: Bully! [TEDDY *retires to the sofa, with his teacup and his
thoughts*]

ABBY: Won't you have another biscuit, Dr. Harper?

DR. HARPER: Oh, no, I'm afraid I'll have no appetite for dinner now. I always eat too many of your biscuits just to taste that lovely jam.

ABBY: But you haven't tried the quince. We always put a little apple in with it to take the tartness out.

DR. HARPER: No, thank you.

ABBY: We'll send you over a jar.

DR. HARPER: No, no! You keep it here so I can be sure of having your biscuits with it.

ABBY: I do hope they don't make us use that imitation flour again. I mean with this war trouble threatening us. It may not be charitable of me, but I've almost come to the conclusion that this Mr. Hitler isn't a Christian.

DR. HARPER: [*With a sigh*] If only Europe were on another planet!

TEDDY: [*Sharply*] Europe, sir?

DR. HARPER: Yes, Teddy.

TEDDY: Point your gun the other way!

DR. HARPER: Gun?

ABBY: [*Trying to calm him*] Teddy!

TEDDY: To the West! There's your danger! There's your enemy! Japan!

DR. HARPER: Why, yes—yes, of course.

ABBY: Teddy!

TEDDY: No, Aunt Abby! Not so much talk about Europe and more about the Canal!

ABBY: Let's not talk about war. Have another cup of tea, dear?

TEDDY: No, thank you, Aunt Abby.

ABBY: Dr. Harper?

DR. HARPER: No, thank you. I must admit, Miss Abby, that war and violence seem far removed from these surroundings.

ABBY: It is peaceful here, isn't it?

DR. HARPER: Yes—peaceful. The virtues of another day—they're all here in this house. The gentle virtues that went out with candle-light and good manners and low taxes.

ABBY: [*Glancing about her contentedly*] It's one of the oldest houses in Brooklyn. It's just as it was when Grandfather Brewster built and furnished it—except for the electricity. We use it as little as possible—it was Mortimer who persuaded us to put it in.

DR. HARPER: [*Dryly*] Yes, I can understand that. Your nephew Mortimer seems to live only by electric light.

ABBY: The poor boy has to work so late. I understand he's taking Elaine to the theater again tonight. Teddy, your brother Mortimer will be here a little later.

TEDDY: [*Bearing his teeth in a broad grin*] Dee-lighted!

ABBY: We're so happy it's Elaine Mortimer takes to the theater with him.

DR. HARPER: Well, it's a new experience for me to wait up until three o'clock in the morning for my daughter to be brought home.

ABBY: Oh, Dr. Harper, I hope you don't disapprove of Mortimer.

DR. HARPER: Well . . .

ABBY: We'd feel so guilty if you did—sister Martha and I. I mean since it was here in our home that your daughter met Mortimer.

DR. HARPER: Of course, Miss Abby. And so I'll say immediately that I believe Mortimer himself to be quite a worthy gentleman. But I must also admit that I have watched the growing intimacy between him and my daughter with some trepidation. For one reason, Miss Abby.

ABBY: You mean his stomach, Dr. Harper?

DR. HARPER: Stomach?

ABBY: His dyspepsia—he's bothered with it so, poor boy.

DR. HARPER: No, Miss Abby, I'll be frank with you. I'm speaking of your nephew's unfortunate connection with the theater.

ABBY: The theater! Oh, no, Dr. Harper! Mortimer writes for a New York newspaper.

DR. HARPER: I know, Miss Abby, I know. But a dramatic critic is constantly exposed to the theater, and I don't doubt but that some of them do develop an interest in it.

ABBY: Well, not Mortimer! You need have no fear at all. Why, Mortimer hates the theater.

DR. HARPER: Really?

ABBY: Oh, yes! He writes awful things about the theater. But you can't blame him, poor boy. He was so happy writing about real estate, which he really knew something about, and then they just made him take this terrible night position.

DR. HARPER: My! My!

ABBY: But as he says, the theater can't last much longer and in the meantime, it's a living. [*Complacently*] I think if we give the theater another year or two . . . [*There is a knock at the door. They all rise.* TEDDY *starts toward door*] Now who do you suppose that is? [*To* TEDDY] Never mind, Teddy, I'll go. [*She goes to door and opens it*] Come right in, Mr. Brophy. [*Two uniformed policemen enter. They are* BROPHY *and* KLEIN]

BROPHY: Hello, Miss Brewster.

ABBY: How are you, Mr. Klein?

KLEIN: Very well, Miss Brewster.

TEDDY: [*To the policemen*] Gentlemen, what news have you brought me?

BROPHY: [*As he and* KLEIN *salute him*] Colonel, we have nothing to report.

TEDDY: [*Returning the salute*] Splendid! Thank you, gentlemen! At ease!

ABBY: [*To the policemen*] You know Dr. Harper.

KLEIN: Sure! Hello, Dr. Harper.

BROPHY: [*To* ABBY] We've come for the toys for the Christmas Fund.

ABBY: Oh, yes!

DR. HARPER: That's a splendid work you men do—fixing up discarded toys to give poor children a happier Christmas.

KLEIN: It gives us something to do when we have to sit around the station. You get tired playing cards and then you start cleaning your gun and the first thing you know you've shot yourself in the foot.

ABBY: Teddy, go upstairs and get that box in your Aunt Martha's room. [TEDDY *starts for the stairs*] How is Mrs. Brophy today? Mrs. Brophy has been quite ill, Dr. Harper.

BROPHY: [*To* DR. HARPER] Pneumonia.

DR. HARPER: I'm sorry to hear that.

[TEDDY *has reached the landing, where he stops and draws an imaginary sword*]

TEDDY: [*Shouting*] CHARGE! [*He charges up the stairs and exits through the door to the bedrooms. The others pay no attention to this*]

BROPHY: Oh, she's better now. A little weak still . . .

ABBY: I'm going to get you some beef broth to take to her.

BROPHY: Don't bother, Miss Abby! You've done so much for her already.

ABBY: We made it this morning. Sister Martha is taking some to poor Mr. Benitzky right now. I won't be a minute. Sit down and be comfortable, all of you. [*She goes into the kitchen.* DR. HARPER *sits again*]

BROPHY: She shouldn't go to all that trouble.

KLEIN: Listen, try to stop her or her sister from doing something nice —and for nothing! They don't even care how you vote. [*He sits on the window seat*]

DR. HARPER: When I received my call to Brooklyn and moved next door, my wife wasn't well. When she died—and for months before —well, if I know what pure kindness and absolute generosity are, it's because I've known the Brewster sisters.

[*At this moment* TEDDY *steps out on the balcony with a large brass bugle and blows a bugle call*]

BROPHY: [*To* TEDDY] Colonel, you promised not to do that!

TEDDY: But I have to call a Cabinet meeting to get the release of those supplies. [*He wheels and exits*]

BROPHY: He used to do that in the middle of the night. The neighbors raised Cain with us. They're a little afraid of him, anyway.

DR. HARPER: Oh, he's quite harmless.

KLEIN: Suppose he does think he's Teddy Roosevelt. There's a lot worse people he could think he was.

BROPHY: Damn shame—a nice family like this hatching a cuckoo.

KLEIN: Well, his father—the old girls' brother—was some sort of a genius, wasn't he? And their father—Teddy's grandfather—seems to me I've heard he was a little crazy, too.

BROPHY: Yeah—he was crazy like a fox. He made a million dollars.

DR. HARPER: Really? Here in Brooklyn?

BROPHY: Yeah—patent medicine. He was kind of a quack of some sort. Old Sergeant Edwards remembers him. He used the house here as sort of a clinic—tried 'em out on people.

KLEIN: Yeah, I hear he used to make mistakes occasionally, too.

BROPHY: The department never bothered him much because he was pretty useful on autopsies sometimes, especially poison cases.

KLEIN: Well, whatever he did, he left his daughters fixed for life. Thank God for that.

BROPHY: Not that they ever spend any of it on themselves.

DR. HARPER: Yes, I'm well acquainted with their charities.

KLEIN: You don't know a tenth of it. When I was with the Missing Persons Bureau I was trying to trace an old man that we never did find . . . [Rising] Do you know there's a renting agency that's got this house down on its list for furnished rooms? They don't rent rooms, but you can bet that anybody who comes here looking for a room goes away with a good meal and probably a few dollars in their kick.

BROPHY: It's just their way of digging up people to do some good to.

[The doorknob rattles, the door opens and MARTHA BREWSTER enters. MARTHA is also a plump, sweet, elderly woman with Victorian charm. She is dressed in the old-fashioned manner of ABBY, but with a high lace collar that covers her neck]

MARTHA: [Closing the door] Well, isn't this nice?

BROPHY: Good afternoon, Miss Brewster.

MARTHA: How do you do, Mr. Brophy?

DR. HARPER: Good afternoon, Miss Brewster.

MARTHA: How do you do, Dr. Harper, Mr. Klein?

KLEIN: How do you do, Miss Brewster? We dropped in to get the Christmas toys.

MARTHA: Oh, yes! Teddy's Army and Navy. They wear out. They're all packed.

BROPHY: The Colonel's upstairs after them—it seems the Cabinet has to O.K. it.

MARTHA: Yes, of course. I hope Mrs. Brophy's better?

BROPHY: She's doing fine, ma'am. Your sister's getting some soup for me to take to her.

MARTHA: Oh, yes, we made it this morning. I just took some to a poor man who broke ever so many bones.

[ABBY *enters from the kitchen, carrying a small covered pail*]

ABBY: Oh, you're back, Martha. How was Mr. Benitzky?

MARTHA: It's pretty serious, I'm afraid. The doctor was there. He's going to amputate in the morning.

ABBY: [*Hopefully*] Can we be present?

MARTHA: No. I asked him, but he says it's against the rules of the hospital.

DR. HARPER: You couldn't be of any service—and you must spare yourselves something.

[TEDDY *enters on balcony with a box of toys and comes downstairs and puts the box down on the stool by the desk*]

ABBY: Here's the broth, Mr. Brophy. [*She hands the pail to* BROPHY]

BROPHY: Thank you, Miss Brewster.

ABBY: Be sure it's good and hot.

KLEIN: [*Looking into the box of toys*] This is fine—it'll make a lot of kids happy. [*Holding up a toy soldier*] That O'Malley boy is nuts about soldiers.

TEDDY: That's General Miles. I've retired him. [KLEIN *holds up a toy ship*] What's this! The *Oregon*! [*He takes the ship from* KLEIN]

MARTHA: Put it back, dear.

TEDDY: But the *Oregon* goes to Australia.

ABBY: Now, Teddy . . .

TEDDY: No, I've given my word to Fighting Bob Evans.

MARTHA: But, Teddy . . .

KLEIN: What's the difference what kid gets it—Bobby Evans, Izzy Cohen? We'll run along, ma'am, and thank you very much.

[*He picks up the box and he and* BROPHY *salute* TEDDY *and exit*]

ABBY: [*Closing door*] Not at all. Good-bye.

MARTHA: Good-bye.

DR. HARPER: I must be getting home.

ABBY: Before you go, Doctor—

[TEDDY *has reached the stair landing*]

TEDDY: CHARGE! [*He dashes up the stairs. At top, he stops and with a sweeping gesture over the balcony rail:*] Charge the blockhouse! [*He dashes through the door*]

DR. HARPER: The blockhouse?

MARTHA: The stairs are always San Juan Hill.

DR. HARPER: Have you ever tried to persuade him that he wasn't Teddy Roosevelt?

ABBY: Oh, no!

MARTHA: He's so happy being Teddy Roosevelt.

ABBY: Once, a long time ago, we thought if he would be George Washington it would be a change and we suggested it to him.

MARTHA: But he stayed under his bed for days and wouldn't be anybody.

ABBY: And we'd so much rather he'd be Mr. Roosevelt than nobody.

DR. HARPER: Well, if he's happy—and what's more important, *you're* happy. You will see that he signs these. [*He takes some legal documents from his pocket and hands them to* ABBY]

MARTHA: What are they?

ABBY: Dr. Harper has made all the arrangements for Teddy to go to Happy Dale Sanitarium after we pass on.

MARTHA: But why should Teddy sign any papers now?

DR. HARPER: It's better to have it all settled. If the Lord should take you away suddenly, perhaps we couldn't persuade Teddy to commit himself and that would mean an unpleasant legal procedure. Mr. Witherspoon understands they're to be filed away until the time comes to use them.

MARTHA: Mr. Witherspoon? Who's he?

DR. HARPER: He's the Superintendent of Happy Dale.

ABBY: [*To* MARTHA] Dr. Harper has arranged for him to drop in tomorrow or the next day to meet Teddy.

DR. HARPER: I'd better be running along or Elaine will be over here looking for me. [*He leaves*]

ABBY: [*At door; calling after him*] Give Elaine our love . . . And please don't think harshly of Mortimer because he's a dramatic critic. *Somebody* has to do those things.

MARTHA: [*Noticing the tea things*] Did you just have tea?

ABBY: [*As one who has a secret*] Yes—and dinner's going to be late, too.

[TEDDY *enters on the balcony*]

MARTHA: So? Why?

[TEDDY *starts downstairs*]

ABBY: Teddy! [*He stops halfway downstairs*] Good news for you! You're going to Panama and dig another lock for the Canal.

TEDDY: Dee-lighted! Bully! Bully, bully! I shall prepare at once for the journey. [*He turns to go back upstairs, stops as if puzzled, then hurries to the landing and cries:*] CHARGE! [*He rushes up and disappears*]

MARTHA: [*Elated*] Abby! While I was out?

ABBY: Yes, dear! I just couldn't wait for you. I didn't know when you'd be back and Dr. Harper was coming.

MARTHA: But all by yourself?

ABBY: Oh, I got along fine!

MARTHA: I'll run right downstairs and see! [*She starts happily for the cellar door*]

ABBY: Oh, no, there wasn't time. I was all alone.

[MARTHA *looks around the room and toward the kitchen*]

MARTHA: Well?

ABBY: Martha . . . [*Coyly*] You just look in the window seat. [MARTHA *almost skips to the window seat, but just as she gets there, a knock is heard on the door. She stops. They both look toward the door.* ABBY *hurries to the door and opens it.* ELAINE HARPER *enters.* ELAINE *is an attractive girl in her twenties; she looks surprisingly smart for a minister's daughter*] Oh, it's Elaine! Come in, dear.

ELAINE: Good afternoon, Miss Abby. Good afternoon, Miss Martha. I thought Father was here.

MARTHA: He just this minute left. Didn't you meet him?

ELAINE: [*Pointing to the window*] No, I took the short cut through the cemetery. Mortimer hasn't come yet?

ABBY: No, dear.

ELAINE: Oh? He asked me to meet him here. Do you mind if I wait?

MARTHA: [*Cordially*] Not at all.

ABBY: Why don't you sit down?

MARTHA: But we really must speak to Mortimer about doing this to you.

ELAINE: Doing what?

MARTHA: He was brought up to know better. When a gentleman is taking a young lady out he should call for her at her house.

ELAINE: Oh, there's something about calling for a girl at a parsonage that discourages any man who doesn't embroider.

ABBY: He's done this too often—we're going to speak to him!

ELAINE: Don't bother! After young men whose idea of night life was to take me to prayer meeting, it's wonderful to go to the theater almost every night of my life.

MARTHA: It's comforting for us too, because if Mortimer has to see some of those plays he has to see, at least he's sitting next to a minister's daughter.

ABBY: My goodness, Elaine, what must you think of us—not having tea cleared away by this time. [*She picks up the tea tray and starts toward the kitchen*]

MARTHA: [*To* ABBY] Now don't bother with anything in the kitchen until Mortimer comes. Then I'll help you. [ABBY *exits into the kitchen. To* ELAINE] He should be here any minute now.

ELAINE: Yes. Father must have been surprised not to find me at home—I'd better run over and say good night to him.

MARTHA: It's a shame you missed him.

ELAINE: If Mortimer comes you tell him I'll be right back. [*She has opened the door, but sees* MORTIMER *just outside*] Hello, Mort!

[MORTIMER BREWSTER *walks in. He is a dramatic critic*]

MORTIMER: Hello, Elaine. [*As he passes her going toward* MARTHA, *thus placing himself between* ELAINE *and* MARTHA, *he reaches back and pats* ELAINE *on the fanny*] Hello, Aunt Martha. [*He kisses her*]

MARTHA: [*Calling off*] Abby, Mortimer's here!

MORTIMER: [*To* ELAINE] Were you going somewhere?

ELAINE: I was just going over to tell Father not to wait up for me.

MORTIMER: I didn't know that was still being done, even in Brooklyn.

[ELAINE *closes the door, staying inside, as* ABBY *comes in from the kitchen*]

ABBY: Hello, Mortimer.

MORTIMER: Hello, Aunt Abby. [*He kisses her*]

ABBY: How are you, dear?

MORTIMER: All right. And you look well. You haven't changed much since yesterday.

ABBY: It was yesterday, wasn't it? We're seeing a great deal of you lately. [*She laughs and looks at* ELAINE] Sit down! Sit down! [*It looks as though she's going to settle down, too*]

MARTHA: [*Knowingly*] Abby—haven't we something to do in the kitchen? You know—the tea things.

ABBY: [*Getting it*] Oh, yes! Yes! [*Backing toward kitchen, joining* MARTHA] Well—you two just make yourselves at home. Just . . .

MARTHA: Just make yourselves at home!

[ABBY *and* MARTHA *exit happily into the kitchen.* ELAINE *moves over to* MORTIMER *ready to be kissed*]

ELAINE: Well, can't you take a hint?

MORTIMER: No. That was pretty obvious. A lack of inventiveness, I should say.

ELAINE: Yes—that's exactly what you'd say! [*She walks away, ruffled*]

MORTIMER: [*Not noticing the ruffle*] Where do you want to go for dinner?

ELAINE: I don't care. I'm not very hungry.

MORTIMER: Well, I just had breakfast. Suppose we wait until after the show?

ELAINE: But that'll make it pretty late, won't it?

MORTIMER: Not with the little stinker we're seeing tonight. From what I've heard about it, we'll be at Bleeck's by ten o'clock.

ELAINE: You ought to be fair to these plays.

MORTIMER: Are these plays fair to me?

ELAINE: I've never seen you walk out on a musical.

MORTIMER: That musical isn't opening tonight.

ELAINE: [*Disappointed*] No?

MORTIMER: Darling, you'll have to learn the rules. With a musical there are always four changes of title and three postponements. They liked it in New Haven but it needs a lot of work.

ELAINE: Oh, I was hoping it was a musical.

MORTIMER: You have such a light mind.

ELAINE: Not a bit! Musicals somehow have a humanizing effect on you. [*He gives her a look*] After a serious play we join the proletariat in the subway and I listen to a lecture on the drama. After a musical you bring me home in a taxi and you make a few passes.

MORTIMER: Now wait a minute, darling, that's a very inaccurate piece of reporting.

ELAINE: Oh, I will admit that after the Behrman play you told me I had authentic beauty—and that's a hell of a thing to say to any girl. It wasn't until after our first musical you told me I had nice legs. And I have, too. [MORTIMER *stares at her legs for a moment, then walks over and kisses her*]

MORTIMER: For a minister's daughter you know a lot about life. Where did you learn it?

ELAINE: [*Casually*] In the choir loft.

MORTIMER: I'll explain that to you sometime, darling—the close connection between eroticism and religion.

ELAINE: Religion never gets as high as the choir loft. Which reminds me, I'd better tell Father please not to wait up for me tonight.

MORTIMER: [*Almost to himself*] I've never been able to rationalize it.

ELAINE: What?

MORTIMER: My falling in love with a girl who lives in Brooklyn.

ELAINE: Falling in love? You're not stooping to the articulate, are you?

MORTIMER: [*Ignoring this*] The only way I can regain my self-respect is to keep you in New York.

ELAINE: Did you say *keep*?

MORTIMER: No, I've come to the conclusion you're holding out for the legalities.

ELAINE: I can afford to be a good girl for quite a few years yet.

MORTIMER: And *I* can't wait that long. Where could we be married in a hurry—say tonight?

ELAINE: I'm afraid Father will insist on officiating.

MORTIMER: Oh, God! I'll bet your father could make even the marriage service sound pedestrian.

ELAINE: Are you, by any chance, writing a review of it?

MORTIMER: Forgive me, darling. It's an occupational disease. [*She smiles at him lovingly and walks toward him. He meets her halfway and they forget themselves for a moment in a sentimental embrace and kiss. When they come out of it, he turns away from her quickly*] I may give that show tonight a good notice!

ELAINE: Now, darling, don't pretend you love me *that* much.

[MORTIMER *looks at her with polite lechery*]

MORTIMER: Be sure to tell your father not to wait up tonight.

ELAINE: [*Aware that she can't trust either of them*] I think tonight I'd better tell him *to* wait up.

MORTIMER: [*Reassuringly*] Darling, I'll telephone Winchell to publish the banns.

ELAINE: Nevertheless . . .

MORTIMER: All right, everything formal and legal. But not later than next month.

ELAINE: Darling. [*She kisses him*] I'll talk it over with Father and set the date.

MORTIMER: Oh, no! We'll have to consult the Zolotow list. There'll be a lot of other first nights in October.

[TEDDY *enters from above and comes down the stairs carrying his bugle and dressed in tropical clothes and a solar topee. He sees* MORTIMER]

TEDDY: Hello, Mortimer! [*He goes to* MORTIMER *and they shake hands*]

MORTIMER: [*Gravely*] How are you, Mr. President?

TEDDY: Bully, thank you. Just bully. What news have you brought me?

MORTIMER: Just this, Mr. President—the country is squarely behind you.

TEDDY: [*Beaming*] Yes, I know. Isn't it wonderful? [*He shakes* MORTI-MER's *hand again*] Well, good-bye. [*He shakes hands with* ELAINE] Good-bye.

ELAINE: Where are you off to, Teddy?

TEDDY: *Panama.* [*He exits through the cellar door.* ELAINE *looks at* MORTIMER *inquiringly*]

MORTIMER: Panama's the cellar. He digs locks for the Canal down there.

ELAINE: You're so sweet with him—and he's very fond of you.

MORTIMER: Well, Teddy was always my favorite brother.

ELAINE: Favorite? Were there more of you?

MORTIMER: There's another brother—Jonathan.

ELAINE: I never heard of him. Your aunts never mention him.

MORTIMER: No, we don't like to talk about Jonathan. He left Brooklyn very early—by request. Jonathan was the kind of boy who liked to cut worms in two—with his teeth.

ELAINE: [*Shuddering*] What became of him?

MORTIMER: I don't know. He wanted to be a surgeon like Grandfather, but he wouldn't go to medical school—and his practice got him into trouble.

[ABBY *enters from the kitchen*]

ABBY: Aren't you going to be late for the theater?

MORTIMER: We're skipping dinner. [*Consulting his wristwatch, then to* ELAINE] We won't have to start for half an hour.

ABBY: Then I'll leave you two alone again.

ELAINE: Don't bother, darling. I'm going to run over to speak to Father. [*To* MORTIMER] Before I go out with you, he likes to pray over me a little. I'll be right back—I'll cut through the cemetery.

MORTIMER: Well, if the prayer isn't too long, I'd have time to lead you beside distilled waters.

[ELAINE *laughs and exits*]

ABBY: [*Happily*] That's the first time I ever heard you quote the Bible! We knew Elaine would be a good influence on you.

MORTIMER: Oh, by the way—I'm going to marry her.

ABBY: Oh, Mortimer! [*She runs to him and embraces him. Then she dashes to the kitchen door, as* MORTIMER *crosses toward the window*] Martha, Martha! Come right in here! I've got wonderful news for you! [MARTHA *hurries in from the kitchen*] Mortimer and Elaine are going to be married!

MARTHA: Married! Oh, Mortimer. [*She runs over to* MORTIMER, *who is looking out the window, embraces and kisses him*]

ABBY: We hoped it would happen just like this!

MARTHA: Elaine must be the happiest girl in the world!

MORTIMER: [*Looking out the window*] Happy! Just look at her leaping over those gravestones! [*He and* ABBY *wave to* ELAINE, *outside. He starts to turn away from the window but his attention is drawn to something*] Say! What's that?

MARTHA: [*Looking out*] What's what, dear?

MORTIMER: See that statue there? That's a horundinida carnina.

MARTHA: Oh, no—that's Emma B. Stout ascending to heaven.

MORTIMER: No—standing on Mrs. Stout's left ear. That bird—that's a red-crested swallow. I've only seen one of those before in my life.

ABBY: I don't know how you can think of birds now—with Elaine and the engagement and everything.

MORTIMER: It's a vanishing species. Thoreau was very fond of them. By the way, I left a large envelope around here last week. It's one of the chapters of my book on Thoreau. Have you seen it?

MARTHA: Well, if you left it here, it must be here somewhere.

[MORTIMER *starts searching the room, looking in drawers, cupboards, desks, etc.*]

ABBY: When are you going to be married? What are your plans? There must be something more you can tell us about Elaine.

MORTIMER: Elaine? Oh, yes, Elaine thought it was brilliant.

MARTHA: What, Mortimer?

MORTIMER: My chapter on Thoreau!

ABBY: Well, when Elaine comes back I think we ought to have a little celebration. We must drink to your happiness. Martha, isn't there some of that Lady Baltimore cake left?

MARTHA: Oh, yes!

ABBY: And we'll open a bottle of wine.

MARTHA: And to think that it happened in this room! [*She exits into the kitchen*]

MORTIMER: Now, where could I have put that . . . ?

ABBY: Well, with your fiancée sitting beside you tonight, I do hope the play will be something you can enjoy for once. It may be something romantic. What's the name of it?

> [MORTIMER *is still searching for the envelope with the chapter in it*]

MORTIMER: *Murder Will Out!*

ABBY: Oh, dear!

> [*She disappears into the kitchen.* MORTIMER *doesn't notice her absence and goes on talking. He is beside the window seat*]

MORTIMER: When the curtain goes up the first thing you see will be a dead body . . . [*He lifts the window seat and sees one. Not believing it, he drops the window seat again and turns away. He looks back quickly toward the window seat, opens it again, stares in. He goes slightly mad for a moment. He drops the window seat again and sits on it, as if to hold it down.* ABBY *comes into the room, carrying the silencer and tablecloth, which she puts on a chair and turns to the table, clearing it of its impedimenta. When* MORTIMER *speaks to her it is in a somewhat strained voice*] Aunt Abby!

ABBY: Yes, dear?

MORTIMER: You were going to make plans for Teddy to go to that sanitarium—Happy Dale.

ABBY: Yes, dear, it's all arranged. Dr. Harper was here today and brought the things for Teddy to sign. Here they are.

> [*She takes the papers from the sideboard and hands them to him*]

MORTIMER: He's got to sign them right away!

ABBY: That's what Dr. Harper thinks . . . [MARTHA *enters from the kitchen, carrying a tray with the table silver. Throughout the scene*

the two sisters go ahead setting the table—three places] Then
there won't be any legal difficulties after we pass on.

MORTIMER: [*Glancing through the papers*] He's got to sign them
this minute! He's down in the cellar—get him up here right away.

MARTHA: There's no such hurry as that.

ABBY: When he starts working on the Canal you can't get his mind
on anything else.

MORTIMER: Teddy's got to go to Happy Dale *now—tonight!*

MARTHA: Oh, no, Mortimer! That's not until after we're gone!

MORTIMER: Right away, I tell you!—right away!

ABBY: Mortimer, how can you say such a thing? Why, as long as we
live we won't be separated from Teddy.

MORTIMER: [*Trying to be calm*] Listen, darlings, I'm frightfully sorry,
but I've got some shocking news for you. [*The sisters stop work
and look at him with some interest*] Now, we've all got to try to
keep our heads. You know, we've sort of humored Teddy because
we thought he was harmless.

MARTHA: Why, he *is* harmless!

MORTIMER: He *was* harmless. That's why he has to go to Happy Dale
—why he has to be confined.

ABBY: Mortimer, why have you suddenly turned against Teddy?—
your own brother!

MORTIMER: You've got to know sometime. It might as well be now.
Teddy's killed a man!

MARTHA: Nonsense, dear.

[MORTIMER *rises and points to the window seat*]

MORTIMER: There's a body in the window seat!

ABBY: [*Not at all surprised*] Yes, dear, we know.

MORTIMER: You *know?*

MARTHA: Of course, dear, but it has nothing to do with Teddy.

[*Relieved, they resume setting the table*]

ABBY: Now, Mortimer, just forget about it—forget you ever saw the
gentleman.

MORTIMER: *Forget?*

ABBY: We never dreamed you'd peek.

MORTIMER: But who is he?

ABBY: His name's Hoskins—Adam Hoskins. That's really all I know about him—except that he's a Methodist.

MORTIMER: That's all you know about him? Well, what's he doing here? What happened to him?

MARTHA: He died.

MORTIMER: Aunt Martha, men don't just get into window seats and die.

ABBY: No, he died first.

MORTIMER: But how?

ABBY: Mortimer, don't be so inquisitive! The gentleman died because he drank some wine with poison in it.

MORTIMER: How did the poison get in the wine?

MARTHA: We put it in wine because it's less noticeable. When it's in tea it has a distinct odor.

MORTIMER: *You* put it in the wine?

ABBY: Yes. And I put Mr. Hoskins in the window seat because Dr. Harper was coming.

MORTIMER: So you knew what you'd done! You didn't want Dr. Harper to see the body!

ABBY: Not at tea! That wouldn't have been very nice! Now you know the whole thing and you can forget all about it. I do think Martha and I have the right to our own little secrets.

MARTHA: And don't you tell Elaine! [MORTIMER *stands looking at his aunts, stunned.* MARTHA *turns to* ABBY] Oh, Abby, while I was out I dropped in on Mrs. Schultz. She's much better, but she would like to have us take Junior to the movies again.

ABBY: We must do that tomorrow or the next day. [*They start toward the kitchen*]

MARTHA: This time we'll go where *we* want to go. Junior's not going to drag me into another one of those scary pictures.

ABBY: They shouldn't be allowed to make pictures just to frighten people.

> [*They exit into the kitchen.* MORTIMER, *dazed, looks around the room, goes to the telephone and dials a number*]

MORTIMER: [*Into telephone*] City desk. . . . Hello, Al. Do you know who this is? [*Pause*] That's right. Say, Al, when I left the office, I told you where I was going, remember? [*Pause*] Well, where did I say? [*Pause*] Uh-huh. Well, it would take me about half an hour to get to Brooklyn. What time have you got? [*He looks at his watch*] That's right. I must be here. [*He hangs up, sits for a moment, then suddenly leaps out of the chair toward the kitchen*] Aunt Martha! Aunt Abby! Come in here! [*The two sisters bustle in.* MORTIMER *turns to them in great excitement*] What are we going to do? What are we going to do?

MARTHA: What are we going to do about what, dear?

MORTIMER: There's a body in there!

ABBY: Yes, Mr. Hoskins'.

MORTIMER: Good God, I can't turn you over to the police. But what am I going to do?

MARTHA: Well, for one thing, stop being so excited.

ABBY: And for pity's sake stop worrying. We told you to forget the whole thing.

MORTIMER: *Forget it?* My dear Aunt Abby, can't I make you realize that something has to be done!

ABBY: [*A little sharply*] Mortimer, you behave yourself! You're too old to be flying off the handle like this!

MORTIMER: But Mr. Hotchkiss . . .

ABBY: Hoskins, dear.

MORTIMER: Well, whatever his name is, you can't leave him there!

MARTHA: We don't intend to, dear.

ABBY: Teddy's down in the cellar now digging a lock.

MORTIMER: You mean you're going to bury Mr. Hotchkiss in the cellar?

MARTHA: Why, of course, dear. That's what we did with the others.

MORTIMER: Aunt Martha, you can't bury Mr. . . . . *Others?*

ABBY: The other gentlemen.

MORTIMER: When you say others—do you mean—others? More than one others?

MARTHA: Oh, yes, dear. Let me see, this is eleven, isn't it, Abby?

ABBY: No, dear, this makes twelve.

[MORTIMER *backs up and sinks stunned on the stool be-side the desk*]

MARTHA: Oh, I think you're wrong, Abby. This is only eleven.

ABBY: No. When Mr. Hoskins first came in, it occurred to me that he would make a round dozen.

MARTHA: Well, you really shouldn't count the first one.

ABBY: Oh, I was counting the first one. So that makes it twelve.

[*The telephone rings.* MORTIMER, *in a daze, turns toward it and without picking up the receiver speaks*]

MORTIMER: Hello! [*It rings the second time and he realizes it's the telephone and picks up the receiver*] Hello. Oh, hello, Al. My, it's good to hear your voice!

ABBY: [*To* MARTHA] But he *is* in the cellar, dear.

MORTIMER: [*To aunts*] Ssh! [*Into telephone*] Oh, no, Al, I'm as sober as a lark. No, I just called you because I was feeling a little Pirandello. Pirandel . . . You wouldn't know, Al. Look, I'm glad you called. Get hold of George right away. He's got to review the play tonight. I can't make it. No, you're wrong, Al. I'll tell you about it tomorrow . . . No— Well, George has got to cover the play tonight! This is my department and I'm running it! You get hold of George! [*He hangs up and sits for a moment, trying to collect himself*] Now, let's see, where were we? [*He suddenly leaps from his chair*] Twelve!

MARTHA: Yes, Abby thinks we ought to count the first one and that makes twelve.

MORTIMER: Now, let me get this. . . . [*Grabs* MARTHA *and sits her in a chair*] Who was the first one?

ABBY: Mr. Midgely. He was a Baptist.

MARTHA: Of course, I still think we can't take full credit for him because he just died.

ABBY: Martha means without any help from us. You see, Mr. Midgely came here looking for a room.

MARTHA: It was right after you moved to New York.

ABBY: And it didn't seem right that your nice room should go to waste when there were so many people who needed it.

MARTHA: He was such a lonely old man.

ABBY: All his kith and kin were dead and it left him so forlorn and unhappy.

MARTHA: We felt so sorry for him.

ABBY: And then when his heart attack came, and he sat dead in that chair, so peaceful—remember, Martha?—well, we decided then and there that if we could help other lonely old men to find that peace, we would.

[MORTIMER *is immersed in their story for a moment*]

MORTIMER: He dropped dead, right in that chair. How awful for you!

MARTHA: Not at all! It was rather like old times. Your grandfather always used to have a cadaver or two around the house. You see, Teddy had been digging in Panama and he thought Mr. Midgely was a yellow fever victim.

ABBY: That meant he had to be buried immediately.

MARTHA: So we all took him down to Panama and put him in the lock. [*Rising*] You see, that's why we told you not to bother about it. We know exactly what's to be done.

MORTIMER: And that's how all this started? That man walking in here and dropping dead?

ABBY: Well, we realized we couldn't depend on that happening again.

MARTHA: Remember those jars of poison that have been up on the shelves in Grandfather's laboratory all these years?

ABBY: You know the knack your Aunt Martha has for mixing things. You've eaten enough of her piccalilli!

MARTHA: Well, Mortimer, for a gallon of elderberry wine I take a teaspoonful of arsenic, and add a half-teaspoonful of strychnine, and then just a pinch of cyanide.

MORTIMER: [*Appraisingly*] Should have quite a kick.

ABBY: As a matter of fact, one of our gentlemen found time to say, "How delicious!"

MARTHA: Well, I'll have to get things started in the kitchen.

[*She starts out*]

ABBY: [*To* MORTIMER] I wish you could stay to dinner, dear.

MARTHA: I'm trying out a new recipe.

MORTIMER: I couldn't eat a thing.

[MARTHA *exits into the kitchen*]

ABBY: [*Calling after* MARTHA] I'll come and help you. [*She turns to* MORTIMER, *relieved*] Well, I feel better now that you understand. You have to wait for Elaine, don't you? [*She smiles*] How happy you must be! I'll leave you alone with your thoughts.

[ABBY *exits, smiling.* MORTIMER *stands dazed and then summons his courage and goes to the window seat, opens it and peeks in, then closes it and backs away. He backs around the table and is still looking at the window seat when there is a knock at the door, immediately followed by* ELAINE's *entrance. This, however, does not arouse him from his thought. She smiles at him softly*]

ELAINE: I'm sorry I took so long, dear. [*She starts slowly toward him. As she approaches he looks in her direction and as her presence dawns on him he speaks*]

MORTIMER: Oh, it's you!

ELAINE: Don't be cross, darling! Father saw I was excited—so I told him about us and that made it hard for me to get away. [*She goes to him and puts her arm around him*] But, listen, darling—he's not going to wait up for me tonight.

MORTIMER: Elaine—you run on back home and I'll call you up to-morrow.

ELAINE: Tomorrow!

MORTIMER: [*Irritated*] You know I always call you up every day or two.

ELAINE: But we're going to the theater tonight.

MORTIMER: No—no, we're not.

ELAINE: Well, why not?

MORTIMER: Elaine, something's come up.

ELAINE: What, darling? Mortimer—you've lost your job!

MORTIMER: No—no! I haven't lost my job! I'm just not covering the play tonight. Now, you run along home, Elaine.

ELAINE: But I've got to know what's happened. Certainly, you can tell me.

MORTIMER: No, I can't, dear.

ELAINE: But if we're going to be married . . .

MORTIMER: Married?

ELAINE: Have you forgotten that not fifteen minutes ago you proposed to me?

MORTIMER: I did? Oh—yes! Well, as far as I know, that's still on. But you go home now. I've got to do something.

ELAINE: Listen, you can't propose to me one minute and throw me out of the house the next.

MORTIMER: I'm not throwing you out of the house, darling. Will you get out of here?

ELAINE: No, I won't get out of here. Not until I've had some kind of explanation!

> [*She stalks across the room and almost sits on the window seat. He intercepts her*]

MORTIMER: Elaine! [*The telephone rings. He goes to it and answers*] Hello! Oh, hello, Al. Hold on just a minute, will you, Al? I'll be right with you. All right, it's important! But it can wait a minute, can't it? Hold on! [*He puts the receiver down on the table and goes back to* ELAINE] Elaine, you're a sweet girl and I love you. But I have something on my mind now and I want you to go home and wait until I call you.

ELAINE: Don't try to be masterful!

MORTIMER: [*Annoyed to the point of being literate*] When we're married and I have problems to face I hope you're less tedious and uninspired!

ELAINE: And when we're married, *if* we're married, I hope I find you adequate! [*She exits*]

MORTIMER: Elaine! [*He runs out on the porch after her, calling*] Elaine! [*He rushes back in, slams the door, and runs across to call to her out of the window. When he kneels on the window seat, he suddenly remembers Mr. Hoskins, and leaps off it. He dashes toward the kitchen, then he remembers Al is waiting on the telephone. He hurries across the room and picks up the receiver*]

Al . . . ? Al . . . ? [*He hangs up and starts to dial again, when the doorbell rings. He lifts the receiver and speaks into it*] Hello . . . Hello . . . ?

[ABBY *enters from the kitchen, followed by* MARTHA]

ABBY: It's the doorbell ringing. [*She goes to door and opens it, as* MORTIMER *hangs up and starts to dial*] How do you do? Come in.

[MR. GIBBS *enters. A very disgruntled old man*]

GIBBS: I understand you have a room to rent.

ABBY: Yes. Won't you step in?

GIBBS: Are you the lady of the house?

ABBY: Yes, I'm Miss Brewster. This is my sister, another Miss Brewster.

GIBBS: My name is Gibbs.

ABBY: Oh, won't you sit down? I'm sorry we're just setting the table for dinner.

MORTIMER: [*Into the telephone*] Hello . . . Let me talk to Al again. City desk! *Al! City desk!* What . . . I'm sorry . . . wrong number.

[*He hangs up and dials again*]

GIBBS: May I see the room?

MARTHA: Why don't you sit down and let's get acquainted?

GIBBS: That won't do much good if I don't like the room.

ABBY: Is Brooklyn your home?

GIBBS: Haven't got a home. Live in a hotel. Don't like it.

MORTIMER: [*Into the telephone*] Hello. City desk.

MARTHA: Are your family Brooklyn people?

GIBBS: Haven't got any family.

ABBY: All alone in the world? Why, Martha . . . [MARTHA *crosses to the sideboard for the wine*] Well, you've come to just the right place. Do sit down.

[*She eases* GIBBS *into a chair by the table*]

MORTIMER: [*Into the telephone*] Hello, Al? Mort. We got cut off. . . . Al, I can't cover the play tonight. That's all there is to it. I can't!

MARTHA: What church do you go to? There's an Episcopal church practically next door.

GIBBS: I'm Presbyterian. Used to be.

MORTIMER: [*Into the telephone*] What's George doing in Bermuda? Certainly, I told him he could go to Bermuda. . . . It's my department, isn't it? Well, Al, you've got to get somebody. Who else is there around the office?

GIBBS: [*Rising*] Is there always this much noise?

MARTHA: Oh, he doesn't live with us.

MORTIMER: [*Into the telephone*] There must be *somebody* around the place. How about the office boy? You know, the bright one. The one we don't like. Well, look around the office . . . I'll hold on.

GIBBS: I'd really like to see the room.

ABBY: It's upstairs. Won't you try a glass of our wine before we start up?

GIBBS: Never touch it.

MARTHA: We make this ourselves. It's elderberry wine.

GIBBS: [*To* MARTHA] Elderberry. [*Looking at the wine*] Haven't tasted elderberry wine since I was a boy. Thank you.

[*He sits.* ABBY *pours a glass of wine for* MR. GIBBS]

MORTIMER: [*Into the telephone*] Well, there must be some printers around. Look, Al, the fellow who sets my copy. He ought to know about what I'd write. His name is Joe. He's the third machine from the left. . . . But, Al, he might turn out to be another Burns Mantle!

GIBBS: Do you have your own elderberry bushes?

MARTHA: No, but the cemetery's full of them.

MORTIMER: [*Into the telephone*] No, I'm not drinking, but I'm going to start now!

[*He hangs up and starts for the sideboard. When he sees the wine bottle on the table, he rushes and gets a glass from the sideboard and starts pouring himself a glass of wine*]

MARTHA: [*Seeing* MORTIMER *pouring the wine*] Mortimer, eh . . . eh . . . eh!

MORTIMER: [*Engrossed in pouring the wine*] Huh?

MARTHA: [*To* MORTIMER] Eh . . . eh . . . eh! . . .

ABBY: [*Seeing what* MORTIMER *is doing*] Mortimer! Not that!

> [*She drags his arm down as he is about to drink.* MORTIMER *puts his glass down, then realizes that it must be the poisoned wine. Suddenly, he sees* MR. GIBBS *is about to drink.* MORTIMER *utters a blood-curdling cry and points his finger at* MR. GIBBS, *who puts his glass down on the table and stares at* MORTIMER, *terrified*]

MORTIMER: Get out of here! Do you want to be killed? Do you want to be poisoned? Do you want to be murdered?

> [*In the middle of the above speech,* MR. GIBBS *starts to run and dashes out of the house, with* MORTIMER *chasing him.* MORTIMER *slams the door behind* MR. GIBBS *and leans against it weakly*]

ABBY: [*To* MORTIMER] Now, you've spoiled everything.

MORTIMER: You can't do things like that! I don't know how I can explain this to you. But it's not only against the law, it's wrong! It's not a nice thing to do! People wouldn't understand. *He* wouldn't understand.

MARTHA: Abby, we shouldn't have told Mortimer.

MORTIMER: What I mean is . . . Well—this has developed into a very bad habit.

ABBY: Now, Mortimer, we don't try to stop you from doing the things you like to do. I don't see why you should interfere with us.

> [*The telephone rings.* MORTIMER *answers it*]

MORTIMER: [*Into the telephone*] Hello? Yes, Al. . . . All right, Al, I'll see the first act and I'll pan the hell out of it. But, Al, you've got to do this for me. Get hold of O'Brien. Our lawyer . . . the head of our legal department! Have him meet me at the theater. Now, don't let me down. O.K. I'm starting now. [*He hangs up, then speaks to his aunts*] I've got to go to the theater. I can't get out of it. But before I go will you promise me something?

MARTHA: We'd have to know what it was first.

MORTIMER: I love you very much and I know you love me. You know I'd do anything in the world for you and I want you to do this little thing for me.

ABBY: What do you want us to do?

MORTIMER: Don't *do* anything. I mean—don't do *anything!* Don't let anyone in this house—and leave Mr. Hoskins right where he is.

MARTHA: Why?

MORTIMER: I want time to think—and I've quite a little to think about. You know I wouldn't want anything to happen to you.

ABBY: Well, what on earth could happen to us?

MORTIMER: Anyway—you'll do that for me, won't you?

MARTHA: Well, we were planning to hold services before dinner.

MORTIMER: Services?

MARTHA: [*A little indignant*] You don't think we'd bury Mr. Hoskins without a full Methodist service? He *was* a Methodist.

MORTIMER: Can't that wait until I get back?

ABBY: Oh, then you could join us!

MORTIMER: Yes! Yes!

ABBY: You'll enjoy the services, Mortimer—especially the hymns. [*To* MARTHA] Remember how beautifully Mortimer sang in the choir before his voice changed?

MORTIMER: And you're not going to let anybody in this house until I get back? It's a promise.

MARTHA: Well . . .

ABBY: Oh, Martha—we can do that now that Mortimer's cooperating with us. All right, Mortimer.

MORTIMER: Have you got any paper? [ABBY *goes to the desk and gets a sheet of stationery*] I'll be back as soon as I can. [MORTIMER *takes out the commitment papers, looks at them*] There's a man I've got to see.

ABBY: Here's some stationery. Will this do?

MORTIMER: [*Taking it*] That's fine. I can save some time if I write my review on the way to the theater.

[*He hurries out.* MARTHA *closes the door behind him.* ABBY *returns to setting the table*]

MARTHA: Mortimer didn't seem quite himself today.

ABBY: [*Lighting the candelabra*] Well, that's only natural—I think I know why.

MARTHA: [*Going up to landing to close the drapes on the window of the landing*] Why?

ABBY: He's just become engaged to be married. I suppose that always makes a man nervous.

MARTHA: I'm so happy for Elaine. And their honeymoon ought to give Mortimer a real vacation. I don't think he got much rest this summer.

[*She comes down into the room again, turns off the electric lights, straightens the telephone on the desk, lights the standing lamp beside the desk*]

ABBY: Well, at least he didn't go kiting off to China or Spain.

MARTHA: I could never understand why he wanted to go to those places.

ABBY: Well, I think to Mortimer the theater has always seemed pretty small potatoes. He needs something really big to criticize—something like the human race.

MARTHA: Abby, if Mortimer's coming back for the services for Mr. Hoskins, we'll need another hymnal. There's one in my room.

[*She starts upstairs*]

ABBY: It's really my turn to read the services, but since you weren't here when Mr. Hoskins came I want you to do it.

[MARTHA *stops on the stairs*]

MARTHA: [*Pleased*] That's very nice of you, dear. Are you sure you want me to?

ABBY: It's only fair.

MARTHA: I think I'll wear my black bombazine—and Mother's old brooch.

[*She starts up again and* ABBY *starts toward the kitchen. The doorbell rings*]

ABBY: I'll go, dear.

MARTHA: [*Hushed*] We promised Mortimer we wouldn't let anyone in.

ABBY: Who do you suppose it is?

MARTHA: Wait a minute—I'll look. [*She is at the landing and turns to the landing window and peeks out the curtains*] It's two men—and I've never seen them before.

ABBY: Are you sure?

MARTHA: [*Peeking out again*] There's a car at the curb—they must have come in that.

ABBY: Let me look!

[*She hurries up the stairs. There is a knock at the door.* ABBY *peeks out the window*]

MARTHA: Do you recognize them?

ABBY: They're strangers to me.

MARTHA: We'll just have to pretend we're not home.

[*There is another knock, then the door is slowly opened and a tall man walks into the center of the room. He walks in with assurance and ease as though the room were familiar to him. He stands and looks about him—in every direction but that of the stairs. There is something sinister about the man—something that brings a slight chill in his presence. It is in his walk, his bearing and his strange resemblance to Boris Karloff. From the stair landing,* ABBY *and* MARTHA *watch him, almost afraid to speak. Having completed his survey of the room, the man turns and addresses someone outside the front door*]

JONATHAN: Come in, Doctor. [DR. EINSTEIN *enters. He is somewhat ratty in his appearance. His face wears the benevolent smirk of a man who lives in a haze of alcohol. There is something about him that suggests the unfrocked priest. He stands just inside the door, timid but expectant*] This is the home of my youth. [DR. EINSTEIN *looks about him timidly*] As a boy, I couldn't wait to escape from this house. And now I'm glad to escape back into it.

EINSTEIN: Yah, Chonny, it's a good hideout.

JONATHAN: The family must still live here. There's something so unmistakably Brewster about the Brewsters. I hope there's a fatted calf awaiting the return of the prodigal.

EINSTEIN: Yah, I'm hungry. [*He sees the fatted calf in the form of the two glasses of wine*] Look, Chonny! Drinks!

JONATHAN: As if we were expected! A good omen.

[EINSTEIN *almost scampers to the table, passing* JONATHAN, *also on his way to the table. As they are about to reach for the glasses,* ABBY *speaks*]

ABBY: Who are you? What are you doing here?

[EINSTEIN *and* JONATHAN *turn and see the two sisters*]

JONATHAN: Aunt Abby! Aunt Martha! It's Jonathan.

MARTHA: You get out of here!

JONATHAN: I'm Jonathan! Your nephew, Jonathan!

ABBY: Oh, no, you're not! You're nothing like Jonathan, so don't pretend you are! You just get out of here!

[*A little belligerent, she comes two or three steps down the stairs*]

JONATHAN: Yes, Aunt Abby. I *am* Jonathan. And this is Dr. Einstein.

ABBY: And he's not Dr. Einstein either.

JONATHAN: Not Dr. Albert Einstein—Dr. Herman Einstein.

ABBY: Who are you? You're not our nephew, Jonathan!

JONATHAN: I see you're still wearing the lovely garnet ring that Grandma Brewster bought in England. [ABBY *gasps, looks at the ring and then looks toward* MARTHA] And you, Aunt Martha, still the high collar—to hide the scar where Grandfather's acid burned you.

[MARTHA'S *hand goes to her throat. The two sisters stare at each other, then back at* JONATHAN]

MARTHA: His voice is like Jonathan's.

ABBY: Have you been in an accident?

JONATHAN: No . . . [*His hand goes up to his neck*] My face . . . [*He clouds*] Dr. Einstein is responsible for that. [*The two sisters look at* EINSTEIN] He's a plastic surgeon. [*Flatly*] He changes people's faces.

MARTHA: But I've seen that face before. [*To* ABBY] Remember when we took the little Schultz boy to the movies—and I was so frightened. It was that face!

[JONATHAN *grows tense and looks toward* EINSTEIN]

EINSTEIN: Easy, Chonny—easy! [*He goes quickly between* JONATHAN *and his aunts*] Don't worry! The last five years I give Chonny three faces. I give him another one right away. The last face—I saw that picture, too—just before I operate. And I was intoxicated.

JONATHAN: [*With a growing and dangerous intensity*] You see, Doctor—what you've done to me. Even my own family . . .

EINSTEIN: [*To calm him*] Chonny—you're home!—in this lovely house! [*To the aunts*] How many times he tells me about Brooklyn—about this house—about his aunts that he loves so much! [*To* JONATHAN] They know you, Chonny. [*To the aunts*] You know it's Jonathan. Speak to him! Tell him so!

[ABBY *starts slowly downstairs*]

ABBY: Well—Jonathan—it's been a long time—what have you been doing all these years?

[MARTHA *starts to follow her cautiously*]

MARTHA: Yes, Jonathan, where have you been?

JONATHAN: [*Recovering his composure*] England, South Africa, Australia—the last five years, Chicago. Dr. Einstein and I have been in business together there.

ABBY: Oh! We were in Chicago for the World's Fair.

MARTHA: [*For want of something to say*] We found Chicago awfully warm.

EINSTEIN: Yah—it got hot for us, too.

JONATHAN: [*Turning on the charm*] It's wonderful to be in Brooklyn again. And you—Abby—Martha—you don't look a day older. Just as I remembered you—sweet, charming, hospitable. [*They ex-*

change a quick look] And dear Teddy? [*He indicates with his hand a lad of eight or ten*] Did he go into politics? [*Turns to* EINSTEIN] My little brother, Doctor, was determined to become President.

ABBY: Oh, Teddy's fine! Just fine. Mortimer's well, too.

JONATHAN: [*Grimly*] I know about Mortimer. I've seen his picture at the head of his column. He's evidently fulfilled all the promise of his early nasty nature.

ABBY: [*Defensively*] We're very fond of Mortimer.

[*There is a pause*]

MARTHA: [*Uneasily*] Well, Jonathan, it's very nice to have seen you again.

JONATHAN: [*Expanding*] Bless you, Aunt Martha! It's good to be home again.

[*He sits down. The two women look at each other with dismay*]

ABBY: Martha, we mustn't let what's on the stove boil over.

[*She tugs at* MARTHA]

MARTHA: Yes. If you'll excuse us for just a minute, Jonathan—unless you're in a hurry to go somewhere.

[JONATHAN *looks at her balefully.* ABBY *exits to the kitchen taking the glasses of wine with her.* MARTHA *takes the bottle of wine from the table, puts it in the compartment of the sideboard, then hurries out after* ABBY]

EINSTEIN: Well, Chonny, where do we go from here? We got to think fast. The *police!* They got pictures of that face. I got to operate on you right away. We got to find some place—and we got to find some place for Mr. Spenalzo, too.

JONATHAN: Don't waste any worry on that rat.

EINSTEIN: But, Chonny, we got a hot stiff on our hands.

JONATHAN: Forget Mr. Spenalzo!

EINSTEIN: But we can't leave a dead body in the rumble seat! You shouldn't have killed him, Chonny. He's a nice fellow—he gives us a lift—and what happens . . . ?

[*He gestures strangulation*]

JONATHAN: He said I looked like Boris Karloff! That's your work, Doctor. You did that to me!

EINSTEIN: Now, Chonny—we find a place somewhere—I fix you up quick!

JONATHAN: *Tonight!*

EINSTEIN: Chonny, I got to eat first. I'm hungry. I'm weak.

[ABBY *enters and comes spunkily up to* JONATHAN. MARTHA *hovers in the doorway*]

ABBY: Jonathan, we're glad that you remembered us and took the trouble to come and say "Hello." But you were never happy in this house and we were never happy while you were here. So we've just come in to say good-bye.

JONATHAN: [*Smoothly*] Aunt Abby, I can't say your feeling toward me comes as a surprise. I've spent a great many hours regretting the heartaches I must have given you as a boy.

ABBY: You were quite a trial to us, Jonathan.

JONATHAN: But my great disappointment is for Dr. Einstein. [*The aunts look at* EINSTEIN] I promised him that no matter how rushed we were in passing through Brooklyn, I would take the time to bring him here for one of Aunt Martha's homecooked dinners.

[MARTHA *rises to this a bit*]

MARTHA: Oh?

ABBY: I'm sorry. I'm afraid there wouldn't be enough.

MARTHA: Abby, it's a good-sized pot roast.

JONATHAN: Pot roast!

MARTHA: I think the least we can do is . . .

JONATHAN: Thank you, Aunt Martha! We'll stay to dinner!

ABBY: Well, we'll hurry it along.

MARTHA: Yes!

[*She exits into the kitchen*]

ABBY: If you want to freshen up, Jonathan—why don't you use the washroom in Grandfather's laboratory?

JONATHAN: Is that still there?

ABBY: Oh, yes! Just as he left it. Well, I'll help Martha get things started—since we're all in a hurry.

[*She exits into kitchen*]

EINSTEIN: Well, we get a meal, anyway.

JONATHAN: Grandfather's laboratory! [*He looks upstairs*] And just as it was! Doctor, a perfect operating room!

EINSTEIN: Too bad we can't use it.

JONATHAN: After you finished with me . . . Doctor, we could make a fortune here! The laboratory—that large ward in the attic—ten beds, Doctor—and Brooklyn is crying for your talents.

EINSTEIN: Why work yourself up, Chonny? Anyway, for Brooklyn we're a year too late.

JONATHAN: You don't know this town, Doctor. Practically everybody in Brooklyn needs a new face.

EINSTEIN: But so many of the old faces are locked up.

JONATHAN: A very small percentage—and the boys in Brooklyn are famous for paying generously to stay out of jail.

EINSTEIN: Take it easy, Chonny. Your aunts—they don't want us here.

JONATHAN: We're here for dinner, aren't we?

EINSTEIN: Yah—but after dinner?

JONATHAN: Leave that to me, Doctor, I'll handle it. This house will be our headquarters for years.

EINSTEIN: Oh, that would be beautiful, Chonny! This nice quiet house! Those aunts of yours—what sweet ladies! I love them already. [*Starts to the door*] I get the bags, yah?

JONATHAN: [*Stopping him*] Doctor! We must wait until we're invited.

EINSTEIN: But you just said . . .

JONATHAN: We'll be invited.

EINSTEIN: And if they say no?

JONATHAN: [*Grimly*] Doctor—two helpless old women . . . ?

[*He sits on the sofa*]

EINSTEIN: [*Taking out flask, and relaxing on the window seat*] It's like comes true a beautiful dream. Only I hope you're not dreaming. [*Takes a swig from the flask*] It's so peaceful.

JONATHAN: [*Stretching out on the sofa*] Yes, Doctor, that's what makes this house so perfect for us. It's so peaceful.

[TEDDY *enters from the cellar, blows a blast on his bugle, then marches to the stairs and on up to the landing as the two men look at his tropical garb with some astonishment*]

TEDDY: [*On the landing*] CHARGE! [*He rushes up the stairs and off through the balcony door.* JONATHAN *has risen, watching him.* EINSTEIN *stares and takes another hasty swig from his flask*]

CURTAIN

ACT TWO

JONATHAN, *smoking an after-dinner cigar, is occupying the most comfortable chair, completely at his ease.* ABBY *and* MARTHA, *sitting together on the window seat, are giving him a nervous attention in the attitude of people who wish their guests would go home.* EINSTEIN *is relaxed and happy. The dinner dishes have been cleared and the room has been restored to order.*

JONATHAN: Yes, those five years in Chicago were the busiest and happiest of my life.

EINSTEIN: And from Chicago, we go to South Bend, Indiana.

> [*He shakes his head as though he wishes they hadn't.* JON-ATHAN *gives him a look*]

JONATHAN: They wouldn't be interested in our experience in Indiana.

ABBY: Well, Jonathan, you've led a very interesting life, I'm sure. But we shouldn't have allowed you to talk so late. [*She starts to rise*]

JONATHAN: My meeting Dr. Einstein in London, I might say, changed my whole life. Remember, I had been in South Africa in the diamond business—then Amsterdam, the diamond market. I wanted to go back to South Africa—and Dr. Einstein made it possible for me.

EINSTEIN: A good job, Chonny. [*To the aunts*] When we take off the bandages, he look so different the nurse had to introduce me.

JONATHAN: I loved that face. I still carry the picture with me.

> [*He produces a picture from his pocket, looks at it a moment and then hands it to* MARTHA, *who takes it.* ABBY *looks over her shoulder*]

ABBY: That looks more the way you used to look, but still I wouldn't know you.

[MARTHA *returns the picture to* JONATHAN]

JONATHAN: I think we'll go back to that face, Doctor.

EINSTEIN: Yah! It's safe now.

ABBY: [*Rising*] I know that you both want to get to—where you're going.

MARTHA: Yes.

[*She rises, too, hintingly*]

JONATHAN: My dear aunts—I am so full of that delicious dinner that I just can't move a muscle.

[*He takes a puff of his cigar*]

EINSTEIN: Yes, it's nice here.

[*He relaxes a little more*]

MARTHA: After all, it's very late and . . .

[TEDDY *appears at the head of the stairs, wearing his solar topee, carrying an open book and another solar topee*]

TEDDY: I found it! I found it!

JONATHAN: What did you find, Teddy?

TEDDY: [*Descending*] The story of my life—my biography. [*He goes to* EINSTEIN] Here's the picture I was telling you about, General. Here we are, both of us. [*He shows the open book to* EINSTEIN] "President Roosevelt and General Goethals at Culebra Cut." That's me, General, and that's you.

[EINSTEIN *looks at the picture*]

EINSTEIN: My, how I've changed!

[TEDDY *looks at* EINSTEIN, *a little puzzled, but makes the adjustment*]

TEDDY: Well, you see that picture hasn't been taken yet. We haven't even started work on Culebra Cut. We're still digging locks. And now, General, we will go to Panama and inspect the new lock.

[*He puts the book down and hands* EINSTEIN *the solar topee*]

ABBY: No, Teddy—not to Panama!

EINSTEIN: We go some other time. Panama's a long way off.

TEDDY: Nonsense, it's just down in the cellar.

JONATHAN: The cellar?

MARTHA: We let him dig the Panama Canal in the cellar.

TEDDY: General Goethals, as President of the United States, Commander-in-Chief of the Army and Navy, and the man who gave you this job, I demand that you accompany me on the inspection of the new lock.

JONATHAN: Teddy! I think it's time for you to go to bed.

[TEDDY *turns and looks at* JONATHAN]

TEDDY: I beg your pardon. Who are you?

JONATHAN: I'm Woodrow Wilson. Go to bed.

TEDDY: No—you're not Wilson. But your face is familiar. [JONATHAN *stiffens*] Let me see. You're not anyone I know now. Perhaps later —on my hunting trip to Africa—yes, you look like someone I might meet in the jungle.

[JONATHAN *begins to burn*]

ABBY: It's your brother, Jonathan, dear . . .

MARTHA: He's had his face changed.

TEDDY: So that's it—a nature faker!

ABBY: Perhaps you had better go to bed—he and his friend have to get back to their hotel.

[JONATHAN *looks at* ABBY *and then, rising, turns to* EINSTEIN]

JONATHAN: General Goethals—inspect the Canal.

EINSTEIN: All right, Mr. President. We go to Panama.

TEDDY: [*On his way to the cellar door*] Bully! Bully! [EINSTEIN *follows him.* TEDDY *opens the cellar door*] Follow me, General. It's down south, you know.

[EINSTEIN *puts on the solar topee*]

EINSTEIN: Well—bon voyage.

> [TEDDY *exits,* EINSTEIN *follows him off. When the cellar door closes* JONATHAN *turns to* ABBY]

JONATHAN: Aunt Abby, I must correct your misapprehension. You spoke of our hotel. We have no hotel. We came directly here . . .

MARTHA: Well, there's a very nice little hotel just three blocks down the street . . .

JONATHAN: Aunt Martha, this is my home!

ABBY: But, Jonathan, you can't stay here. [JONATHAN *gives her a look*] We need our rooms.

JONATHAN: You need them?

ABBY: Yes, for our lodgers.

JONATHAN: [*Alarmed for a moment*] Are there lodgers in this house?

MARTHA: Well, not just now, but we plan to have some.

JONATHAN: Then my old room is still free.

ABBY: But, Jonathan, there's no place for Dr. Einstein.

JONATHAN: He'll share the room with me.

ABBY: No, Jonathan, I'm afraid you can't stay here.

JONATHAN: [*Coldly*] Dr. Einstein and I need a place to sleep. This afternoon, you remembered that as a boy I could be disagreeable. It wouldn't be pleasant for any of us if . . .

MARTHA: [*To* ABBY, *frightened*] Perhaps we'd better let them stay here tonight.

ABBY: Well, just overnight, Jonathan.

JONATHAN: That's settled. Now, if you'll get my room ready . . .

MARTHA: [*Starting upstairs*] It only needs airing out . . .

ABBY: [*Following*] We keep it ready to show to our lodgers. I think you and Dr. Einstein will find it comfortable.

JONATHAN: You have a most distinguished guest in Dr. Einstein. I'm afraid you don't appreciate his skill. But you shall. In a few weeks you'll see me looking like a very different Jonathan.

MARTHA: [*Stopping on the balcony*] But he can't operate here!

JONATHAN: When Dr. Einstein and I get organized . . . when we resume practice . . . I forgot to tell you—we're turning Grandfather's laboratory into an operating room. We expect to be very busy.

ABBY: [*On the balcony*] Jonathan, we're not going to let you turn this house into a hospital.

JONATHAN: A hospital! Heavens, no! It will be a beauty parlor!

[EINSTEIN *enters excitedly from the cellar*]

EINSTEIN: Hey, Chonny! Down in the cellar . . .

[*He sees the aunts and stops*]

JONATHAN: Dr. Einstein. My dear aunts have invited us to live with them.

EINSTEIN: Oh, you fixed it?

ABBY: Well, you're sleeping here tonight.

JONATHAN: Please get our room ready immediately.

MARTHA: Well . . .

ABBY: For tonight.

[*They exit to the third floor*]

EINSTEIN: Chonny, when I was in the cellar, what do you think I find?

JONATHAN: What?

EINSTEIN: The Panama Canal.

JONATHAN: The Panama Canal!

EINSTEIN: Chonny, it just fits Mr. Spenalzo! A hole Teddy dug, four feet wide and six feet long.

JONATHAN: [*Pointing*] Down there?

EINSTEIN: You'd think they knew we were bringing Mr. Spenalzo along. Chonny, that's hospitality.

JONATHAN: Rather a good joke on my aunts, Doctor, their living in a house with a body buried in the cellar.

EINSTEIN: How do we get him in, Chonny?

JONATHAN: Yes, we can't just walk him through the door. [*Looks from door to window*] We'll drive the car up between the house and the cemetery and, after they've gone to bed, we'll bring Mr. Spenalzo in through the window.

EINSTEIN: Bed! Just think! We got a bed tonight.

[*He takes out his bottle and starts to take a swig*]

JONATHAN: Easy, Doctor. Remember you're operating tomorrow. And this time you'd better be sober.

EINSTEIN: I fix you up beautiful.

JONATHAN: And if you don't . . .

[ABBY *and* MARTHA *enter on the balcony*]

ABBY: Your room's all ready, Jonathan.

JONATHAN: [*Crossing to the outside door*] Then you can go to bed. We're moving the car up behind the house.

MARTHA: It will be all right where it is—until morning.

[EINSTEIN *has opened the door*]

JONATHAN: I don't want to leave it in the street—that might be against the law.

[*He and* EINSTEIN *exit*]

MARTHA: Abby, what are we going to do?

ABBY: [*Coming downstairs*] Well, we're not going to let them stay more than one night in this house, for one thing. What would the neighbors think? People coming into this place with one face and going out with another.

MARTHA: What are we going to do about Mr. Hoskins?

ABBY: Oh, yes, Mr. Hoskins. It can't be very comfortable for him in there. He's been so patient, the poor dear. I think Teddy ought to get Mr. Hoskins downstairs right away.

MARTHA: Abby, I will not invite Jonathan to the services.

ABBY: Oh, no, dear—we'll wait until they've gone to bed and then come down and hold the services.

[TEDDY *enters from the cellar*]

TEDDY: General Goethals was very pleased. He said the Canal was just the right size.

ABBY: Teddy, there's been another yellow fever victim.

TEDDY: Dear me—that will be a shock to the General.

MARTHA: Then we mustn't tell him about it.

TEDDY: But it's his department.

ABBY: No, we mustn't tell him about it. It would just spoil his visit, Teddy.

TEDDY: I'm sorry, Aunt Abby. It's out of my hands—he'll have to be told. Army regulations, you know.

ABBY: No, Teddy, we'll have to keep it a secret.

MARTHA: Yes!

TEDDY: A state secret?

ABBY: Yes, a state secret.

MARTHA: Promise?

TEDDY: You have the word of the President of the United States. Cross my heart and hope to die. [*Following the childish formula, he crosses his heart and spits*] Now let's see—how are we going to keep it a secret?

ABBY: Well, Teddy, you go back down in the cellar and when I turn out the lights—when it's dark—you come up and take the poor man down to the Canal. Go along, Teddy.

MARTHA: We'll come down later and hold services.

TEDDY: You may announce the President will say a few words. [*He starts to the cellar door, then stops*] Where is the poor devil?

MARTHA: In the window seat.

TEDDY: It seems to be spreading. We've never had yellow fever *there* before.

[*He exits into the cellar*]

ABBY: When Jonathan and Dr. Einstein come back, let's see whether we can't get them to go to bed right away.

MARTHA: Yes, then they'd be asleep by the time we got dressed for the funeral. Abby, I haven't even seen Mr. Hoskins yet.

ABBY: Oh, my goodness, that's right—you were out. Well, you just come right over and see him now. [*They go to the window seat*] He's really very nice-looking—considering he's a Methodist.

[MARTHA *is about to lift the window seat when* JONATHAN *thrusts his head through the window curtains. They jump back in fright*]

JONATHAN: We're bringing our luggage through here. [*He climbs into the room*]

ABBY: Your room's waiting for you. You can go right up.

[*Two bags and a large instrument case are passed through the window.* JONATHAN *puts them down*]

JONATHAN: I'm afraid we don't keep Brooklyn hours. You two run along to bed.

ABBY: You must be very tired—both of you—and we don't go to bed this early.

JONATHAN: Well, you should. It's time I came home to take care of you.

MARTHA: Oh, we weren't planning to go until . . .

JONATHAN: [Sternly] Did you hear me say go to bed, Aunt Martha? [MARTHA retreats upstairs. EINSTEIN comes through the window] Take the bags upstairs. [Putting the instrument case beside the window seat] The instruments can go to the laboratory in the morning. [He closes the window] Now we're all going to bed.

[EINSTEIN starts upstairs, reaching the upper landing, where he stops]

ABBY: I'll wait till you're up, then turn out the lights. [She retreats toward the light switch]

JONATHAN: Another flight, Doctor. Run along, Aunt Martha. [MARTHA goes to the upstairs door and opens it. EINSTEIN goes through the arch with the bags and JONATHAN stops on the landing, looks down at ABBY] All right, Aunt Abby.

ABBY: [Looking toward cellar door] I'll be right up.

JONATHAN: Now, Aunt Abby! Turn out the lights.

[ABBY snaps out the lights. JONATHAN waits until ABBY has come upstairs and she and MARTHA have gone through their door and closed it, then turns and goes up through the arch. The stage is entirely dark. TEDDY opens the cellar door, looks out and sees everything is safe, then switches the cellar light on and moves toward the window seat. In the darkness we hear the familiar creak of the window seat as it is opened. A few seconds later we see the faint shadow of TEDDY carrying a burden, passing through the cellar door, then this door is closed behind him shutting off the light. After a second or two JONATHAN and EINSTEIN come out on the upper landing. JONATHAN lights a match and in its light he comes down the stairs]

EINSTEIN: [*On the balcony, listening at the aunts' door*] It's all right, Chonny.

[*He comes downstairs*]

JONATHAN: I'll open the window. You go around and hand him through.

EINSTEIN: Chonny, he's too heavy for me. You go outside and push. I stay here and pull. Then together we get him down to Panama.

JONATHAN: All right. But be quick. I'll take a look around outside the house. When I tap on the glass you open the window.

[*JONATHAN goes out front door, closing it behind him. EINSTEIN moves toward the window, holding lighted match. He bumps into the table, burns his finger, and we hear him suck the burnt place. He continues to window in darkness. Then we hear a crash*]

EINSTEIN: Ach! Himmel! [*He lights a match and in its wavering light we see that he has fallen into the window seat*] Who left this open, the dummkopf? [*We hear tapping on the glass, as he closes the window seat and then we hear him open the window*] Chonny? O.K. Allez oop! Wait a minute, Chonny. You lost a leg somewhere. Ach! Now I got him. [*There is a crash of a body and then the sound of a "Sh-h!" from outside*] That was me, Chonny. I schlipped.

JONATHAN'S VOICE: [*Off*] Quiet!

EINSTEIN: Well, his shoe came off. [*Pause*] All right, Chonny. I got him. Whew! [*In the silence there is a knock at the door*] Chonny! Somebody at the door! Go quick. No, I manage here. Go quick!

[*There is a second knock at the door. There is a moment's silence and we hear the creak of the window seat, the noise of EINSTEIN struggling with Mr. Spenalzo's body, then another creak of the window seat. There is a third knock at the door, then it is opened and by the dim glow of a remote street light we see ELAINE peering into the room*]

ELAINE: [*Calling softly*] Miss Abby! Miss Martha! [*In the dim path*

*of light she comes in and moves toward the center of the room,
calling toward the staircase*] Miss Abby! Miss Martha! [JONATHAN
enters hurriedly and we hear the closing of the door. ELAINE
whirls and gasps] Who is it? Is that you, Teddy? [JONATHAN *advances on her*] Who *are* you?

JONATHAN: Who are *you?*

ELAINE: I'm Elaine Harper—I live next door!

JONATHAN: What are you doing here?

[EINSTEIN *circles around* ELAINE *toward front door*]

ELAINE: I came over to see Miss Abby and Miss Martha.

JONATHAN: Turn on the lights, Doctor. [EINSTEIN *switches on the
lights*] I'm afraid you've chosen an untimely moment for a social
call.

[*He moves past her toward the window expecting to see
Mr. Spenalzo there. He doesn't, and this bewilders him*]

ELAINE: [*Trying to summon courage*] I think you'd better explain
what you're doing here.

JONATHAN: We happen to live here. [JONATHAN *looks out the window
in his search for the missing Mr. Spenalzo*]

ELAINE: You don't live here. I'm in this house every day and I've
never seen you before. Where are Miss Abby and Miss Martha?
What have you done to them?

JONATHAN: Perhaps we had better introduce ourselves. May I present
Dr. Einstein . . .

ELAINE: Dr. Einstein!

[JONATHAN *moves toward the table and looks under the
table cloth for Mr. Spenalzo*]

JONATHAN: A surgeon of great distinction—and—[*Not finding Mr.
Spenalzo*] something of a magician.

ELAINE: And I suppose you're going to tell me you're Boris . . .

[JONATHAN *stiffens and speaks sharply*]

JONATHAN: I'm Jonathan Brewster!

ELAINE: [*Almost with fright*] Oh—you're Jonathan!

JONATHAN: I see you've heard of me.

ELAINE: Yes—just this afternoon—for the first time . . .

JONATHAN: And what did they say about me?

ELAINE: Only that there was another brother named Jonathan—that's all that was said. Well, that explains everything. Now that I know who you are I'll run along back home [*She runs to the door and finds it locked*]—if you'll kindly unlock the door.

> [JONATHAN *goes to the door and unlocks it.* ELAINE *starts toward the door, but* JONATHAN *turns and stops her with a gesture*]

JONATHAN: "That explains everything?" Just what did you mean by that? Why did you come here at this time of night?

ELAINE: I thought I saw someone prowling around the house. I suppose it was you.

> [JONATHAN *reaches back and locks the door again, leaving the key in the lock.* EINSTEIN *and* JONATHAN *both move slowly toward* ELAINE]

JONATHAN: You thought you saw someone prowling about the house?

ELAINE: Yes—weren't you outside? Is that your car?

JONATHAN: Oh, you saw someone at the car!

ELAINE: Yes.

JONATHAN: What else did you see?

ELAINE: Just that—that's all. That's why I came over here. I wanted to tell Miss Abby to call the police. But if it was you, and that's your car, I don't need to bother Miss Abby. I'll be running along.

> [*She takes a step toward the door.* JONATHAN *blocks her way*]

JONATHAN: What was the man doing at the car?

ELAINE: I don't know. You see I was on my way over here.

JONATHAN: I think you're lying.

EINSTEIN: Chonny, I think she tells the truth. We let her go now, huh?

JONATHAN: I think she's lying. Breaking into a house at this time of night. I think she's dangerous. She shouldn't be allowed around loose.

[*He seizes* ELAINE'S *arm. She pulls back*]

ELAINE: [*In a hoarse frightened tone*] Take your hands off me . . .
JONATHAN: And now, young lady . . .

[*The cellar door suddenly opens and* TEDDY *comes through and closes it with a bang. They all jump.* TEDDY *looks them over*]

TEDDY: [*Blandly*] It's going to be a private funeral.

[*He starts for the steps*]

ELAINE: [*Struggling*] Teddy! Teddy! Tell these men who I am!
TEDDY: That's my daughter, Alice.

[*She struggles to get away from* JONATHAN]

ELAINE: No! No! Teddy! Teddy!

[*Still struggling*]

TEDDY: Now, Alice, don't be a tomboy. Don't play rough with the gentlemen. [*He has reached the landing on the stairs, draws his imaginary sword*] CHARGE!

[*He charges up the stairs and off*]

ELAINE: Teddy! Teddy!

[JONATHAN *pulls her arm behind her back and claps a hand over her mouth*]

JONATHAN: Doctor, your handkerchief! [JONATHAN *takes* EINSTEIN'S *handkerchief in his free hand and starts to stuff it in her mouth. As he releases his hand for this,* ELAINE *lets out a scream.* JONATHAN *claps his hand over her mouth again*] Doctor, the cellar!

[EINSTEIN *opens the cellar door, then dashes for the light switch and turns off the lights.* JONATHAN *forces* ELAINE *into the cellar and waits until* EINSTEIN *takes hold of her. In the dark, we hear:*]

ABBY: What's the matter?
MARTHA: What's happening down there?

[JONATHAN *closes the cellar door on* EINSTEIN *and* ELAINE *as* ABBY *turns on the lights from the balcony switch and we see* ABBY *and* MARTHA *on the balcony. They are dressed for Mr. Hoskins' funeral. Mr. Hoskins is being paid the respect of deep and elaborate mourning*]

ABBY: What's the matter? What are you doing?

[JONATHAN *is holding the cellar door*]

JONATHAN: We caught a burglar—a sneak thief. Go back to your room.

ABBY: I'll call the police!

[*She starts downstairs*]

JONATHAN: We've called the police. We'll handle this. You go back to your room. [*They hesitate*] Did you hear me? [ABBY *turns as if to start upstairs when the knob of the outside door is rattled followed by a knock. They all turn and look toward the door.* ABBY *starts down again*] Don't answer that!

[ELAINE *rushes out of the cellar.* EINSTEIN *follows, grabbing for her*]

ELAINE: Miss Abby! Miss Martha!
MARTHA: Why, it's Elaine!

[*There is a peremptory knock at the door.* ABBY *hurries over, unlocks it and opens it.* MORTIMER *enters carrying a suitcase. At the sight of him* ELAINE *rushes into his arms. He drops the suitcase and puts his arms around her.* EINSTEIN *and* JONATHAN *have withdrawn toward the kitchen door, ready to make a run for it*]

ELAINE: Oh, Mortimer, where have you been?
MORTIMER: To the Nora Bayes Theatre—and I should have known better. [*He sees* JONATHAN] My God, I'm still there!
ABBY: This is your brother Jonathan—and this is Dr. Einstein.

[MORTIMER *surveys the roomful*]

MORTIMER: I know this isn't a nightmare, but what is it?

JONATHAN: I've come back home, Mortimer.

MORTIMER: [*Looking at him and then at* ABBY] Who did you say that was?

ABBY: It's your brother Jonathan. He's had his face changed. Dr. Einstein performed the operation on him.

MORTIMER: Jonathan, you always were a horror, but do you have to look like one?

> [JONATHAN *takes a step toward him.* EINSTEIN *pulls his sleeve*]

EINSTEIN: Easy, Chonny! Easy!

JONATHAN: Mortimer, have you forgotten the things I used to do to you? Remember the time you were tied to the bedpost—the needles—under your fingernails. I suggest you don't ask for trouble now.

MORTIMER: Yes, I remember. I remember you as the most detestable, vicious, venomous form of animal life I ever knew.

> [JONATHAN *gets tense and takes a step toward* MORTIMER. ABBY *steps between them*]

ABBY: Now, don't you boys start quarreling again the minute you've seen each other.

MORTIMER: There won't be any fight, Aunt Abby. Jonathan, you're not wanted here, so get out!

JONATHAN: Dr. Einstein and I have been invited to stay.

MORTIMER: Oh, no—not in this house!

ABBY: Just for tonight.

MORTIMER: I don't want him anywhere near me.

ABBY: But we did invite them for tonight, Mortimer, and it wouldn't be very nice to go back on our word.

MORTIMER: [*Reluctantly giving in*] All right, tonight—but the first thing in the morning—out. Where are they sleeping?

ABBY: We put them in Jonathan's old room.

MORTIMER: [*Picking up his suitcase and starting up the stairs*] That's my old room. I'm moving into that room. I'm here to stay.

MARTHA: Oh, Mortimer, I'm so glad!

EINSTEIN: [*To* JONATHAN] Chonny, we sleep down here.

MORTIMER: You bet your life you'll sleep down here.

EINSTEIN: [*To* JONATHAN] You sleep on the sofa—I sleep on the window seat.

MORTIMER: [*Stopping suddenly, as he remembers Mr. Hoskins*] The window seat! Oh, well, let's not argue about it. That window seat's good enough for me tonight. [*Descending as he talks*] I'll sleep on the window seat.

EINSTEIN: Chonny—all this argument—it makes me think of Mr. Spenalzo.

JONATHAN: Spenalzo! Well, Mortimer, there's no real need to inconvenience you. We'll sleep down here.

MORTIMER: Jonathan, this sudden consideration for me is very unconvincing.

EINSTEIN: Come, Chonny, we get our things out of the room, yes?

MORTIMER: Don't bother, Doctor.

JONATHAN: You know, Doctor, I've completely lost track of Mr. Spenalzo.

MORTIMER: Who's this Mr. Spenalzo?

EINSTEIN: [*On the stairs*] Just a friend of ours Chonny's been looking for.

MORTIMER: Don't you bring anybody else in here!

EINSTEIN: [*Reassuringly*] It's all right, Chonny. While we pack I tell you about him.

[JONATHAN *starts upstairs*]

ABBY: Mortimer, you don't have to stay down here. I could sleep with Martha and you could have my room.

JONATHAN: [*On the balcony*] No trouble at all, Aunt Abby. We'll be packed in a few minutes, and then you can have the room, Mortimer.

MORTIMER: You're just wasting time. I told you I'm sleeping down here! [JONATHAN *exits through the arch.* MORTIMER *starts for stairs and almost bumps into* ELAINE] Oh, hello, Elaine!

ELAINE: Mortimer!

MORTIMER: [*Taking her in his arms*] What's the matter with you, dear?

ELAINE: I've almost been killed!

MORTIMER: You've almost been . . . Abby! Martha!

[*He looks quickly at the aunts*]

MARTHA: It was Jonathan.

ABBY: He mistook her for a sneak thief.

ELAINE: No, it was more than that. He's some kind of a maniac. [*She draws close to* MORTIMER *again*] Mortimer, I'm afraid of him.

MORTIMER: Why, darling, you're trembling. [*Sitting* ELAINE *on sofa. To the aunts*] Have you got any smelling salts?

MARTHA: No, but do you think some hot tea or coffee . . . ?

MORTIMER: Coffee. Make some for me too—and some sandwiches. I haven't had any dinner.

MARTHA: We'll get something for both of you.

[ABBY *takes off her hat and gloves and puts them on sideboard*]

ABBY: Martha, we can leave our hats downstairs here.

MORTIMER: You weren't going out anywhere, were you? Do you know what time it is? It's after twelve. Twelve! [*He glances hurriedly at the cellar door, remembering*] Elaine, you go along home.

ELAINE: What?

ABBY: Why, Mortimer, you wanted some sandwiches for you and Elaine. It won't take us a minute.

MARTHA: Remember, we wanted to celebrate your engagement . . . That's what we'll do. We'll have a nice supper for you—and we'll open a bottle of wine.

MORTIMER: [*Reluctantly*] All right. [*The aunts exit to the kitchen. He calls after them*] No wine!

ELAINE: [*Rising*] Mortimer, what's going on in this house?

MORTIMER: What do you mean—what's going on in this house?

ELAINE: You were supposed to take me to dinner and the theater tonight . . . You called it off. You asked me to marry you . . . I said I would . . . five minutes later you threw me out of the house. Tonight, just after your brother tries to strangle me, you want to chase me home. Now, listen, Mr. Brewster . . . before I go home, I want to know where I stand. Do you love me?

MORTIMER: [Going to her] I love you very much, Elaine. In fact, I love you so much I can't marry you.

ELAINE: [Drawing away] Have you suddenly gone crazy?

MORTIMER: I don't think so—but it's just a matter of time. [He seats her on sofa] You see, insanity runs in my family. [He looks toward the kitchen] It practically gallops! That's why I can't marry you, dear.

ELAINE: [Unconvinced] Now wait a minute. You've got to do better than that.

MORTIMER: No, dear—there's a strange taint in the Brewster blood. If you really knew my family—well—it's what you would expect if Strindberg had written Hellzapoppin!

ELAINE: Now, just because Teddy . . .

MORTIMER: No, it goes way back. The first Brewster—the one who came over on the Mayflower. You know, in those days the Indians used to scalp the settlers—he used to scalp the Indians.

ELAINE: Mortimer, that's ancient history.

MORTIMER: No, the whole family! Take my grandfather—he tried his patent medicines out on dead people to be sure he wouldn't kill them!

ELAINE: He wasn't so crazy. He made a million dollars.

MORTIMER: And then there's Jonathan. You just said he was a maniac. He tried to kill you.

ELAINE: But he's your brother, not you. I'm in love with you.

MORTIMER: And Teddy! You know Teddy. He thinks he's Roosevelt.

ELAINE: Even Roosevelt thinks he's Roosevelt.

MORTIMER: No, dear, no Brewster should marry. I realize now that if I'd met my father in time I would have stopped him.

ELAINE: Now, darling, all of this doesn't prove you're crazy. Just look at your aunts—they're Brewsters, aren't they?—and the sanest, sweetest people I've ever known.

MORTIMER: [Glancing at the window seat and moving toward it] Well, even they have their peculiarities!

[ELAINE walks away from him]

ELAINE: Yes, but what lovely peculiarities!—kindness, generosity, human sympathy!

[MORTIMER *lifts the window seat to take a peek at* MR. HOSKINS *and sees* MR. SPENALZO]

MORTIMER: [*To himself*] There's another one!

ELAINE: [*Turning to* MORTIMER] There are plenty of others! You can't tell me anything about your aunts.

MORTIMER: I'm not going to! [*Crossing to* ELAINE] Elaine, you've got to go home. Something very important has just come up.

ELAINE: Come up from where? We're here alone together.

MORTIMER: Elaine, I know I'm acting irrationally, but just put it down to the fact that I'm a mad Brewster.

ELAINE: If you think you're going to get out of this by pretending you're insane, you're crazy. Maybe you're not going to marry me, but I'm going to marry you. I love you, you dope!

MORTIMER: [*Pushing her toward the door*] Well, if you love me, will you get the hell out of here?

ELAINE: Well, at least take me home. I'm afraid!

MORTIMER: Afraid! A little walk through the cemetery?

ELAINE: [*Changing tactics*] Mortimer, will you kiss me good night?

[MORTIMER *goes over to her*]

MORTIMER: Of course. [*What* MORTIMER *plans to be a desultory peck,* ELAINE *turns into a production number.* MORTIMER *comes out of it with no loss of poise*] Good night, dear. I'll call you up in a day or two.

[*She walks to the door in a cold fury, opens it and starts out, then wheels on* MORTIMER]

ELAINE: You—you critic!

[*She exits, slamming the door.* MORTIMER *turns and rushes determinedly to the kitchen door*]

MORTIMER: Aunt Abby, Aunt Martha! Come in here!

ABBY'S VOICE: We'll be in in just a minute, dear.

MORTIMER: Come in here now!

[ABBY *enters from the kitchen*]

ABBY: What do you want, Mortimer? Where's Elaine?

MORTIMER: I thought you promised me not to let anyone in this house while I was gone!

ABBY: Well, Jonathan just walked in.

MORTIMER: I don't mean Jonathan!

ABBY: And Dr. Einstein was with him.

MORTIMER: I don't mean Dr. Einstein! Who is that in the window seat?

ABBY: We told you—it's Mr. Hoskins.

MORTIMER: It is *not* Mr. Hoskins.

> [*He opens the window seat.* ABBY *goes over and looks down at* MR. SPENALZO]

ABBY: [*Puzzled at the sight of a stranger*] Who can that be?

MORTIMER: Are you trying to tell me you've never seen this man before?

ABBY: I certainly am! Why, this is a fine how-do-you-do! It's getting so anyone thinks he can walk into our house.

MORTIMER: Now, Aunt Abby, don't try to get out of this. That's another one of your gentlemen!

ABBY: Mortimer, that man's an impostor! Well, if he came here to be buried in our cellar, he's mistaken.

MORTIMER: Aunt Abby, you admitted to me that you put Mr. Hoskins in the window seat.

ABBY: Yes, I did.

MORTIMER: Well, this man couldn't have just got the idea from Mr. Hoskins. By the way, where *is* Mr. Hoskins?

ABBY: He must have gone to Panama.

MORTIMER: You buried him?

ABBY: Not yet, he's just down there waiting for the services, poor dear! We haven't had a minute what with Jonathan in the house.

MORTIMER: Jonathan . . .

> [*At the mention of* JONATHAN's *name, he closes the window seat*]

ABBY: We've always wanted to hold a double funeral, but we're not going to read services over a perfect stranger.

MORTIMER: A stranger! Aunt Abby, how can I believe you? There are twelve men in the cellar and you admit you poisoned them.

ABBY: [*Drawing herself up*] I did. But you don't think I'd stoop to telling a fib? [*She bustles indignantly into the kitchen, calling:*] Martha!

[MORTIMER *starts to pace.* JONATHAN, *having learned where* MR. SPENALZO *is, enters from above and comes down the stairs hurriedly, making for the window seat. He sees* MORTIMER *and stops*]

JONATHAN: Mortimer, I'd like to have a word with you.

MORTIMER: A word's about all you'll have time for, Jonathan, because I've decided you and your doctor friend are going to have to get out of this house as quickly as possible.

JONATHAN: I'm glad you recognize the fact that you and I can't live under the same roof. But you have arrived at the wrong solution. Take your suitcase and get out!

[*He starts toward the window seat*]

MORTIMER: Jonathan, you're beginning to bore me! [*He circles around the table, heading* JONATHAN *off*] You've played your one-night stand in Brooklyn. Move on!

JONATHAN: My dear Mortimer, just because you've graduated from the back fence to the typewriter, don't think you're grown up. [*He slips past* MORTIMER, *and sits on window seat*] I'm staying—you're leaving—and I mean now!

MORTIMER: If you think I can be frightened, Jonathan, if you think there's anything I fear . . .

JONATHAN: [*Rising and facing* MORTIMER] I've led a strange life, Mortimer. But it's taught me one thing—to be afraid of nothing!

[*For a second they glare at each other with equal courage.* ABBY *marches in from kitchen, followed by* MARTHA]

ABBY: Martha, you just look and see what's in that window seat.

[*Both men throw themselves on the window seat and speak and gesture simultaneously*]

MORTIMER AND JONATHAN: Now, Aunt Abby . . . [*Light dawns on* MORTIMER'*s face. He rises with smiling assurance*]

MORTIMER: Jonathan, let Aunt Martha see what's in the window seat. [JONATHAN *freezes dangerously*] Aunt Abby, I owe you an apology. I have very good news for you. Jonathan is leaving. He's taking Dr. Einstein and their cold companion with him. [*He walks to* JONATHAN] You're my brother, Jonathan. You're a Brewster. I'm giving you a chance to get away and take the evidence with you. You can't ask for more than that. [JONATHAN *doesn't move*] All right. In that case, I'll have to call the police.

[MORTIMER *starts for the telephone*]

JONATHAN: Don't reach for that telephone! [*He crosses quickly toward* MORTIMER] Are you still giving me orders after seeing what's happened to Mr. Spenalzo?

MARTHA: Spenalzo?

ABBY: I knew he was a foreigner.

JONATHAN: [*To* MORTIMER] Remember, what happened to Mr. Spenalzo can happen to you, too.

[*There is a knock at the door; it opens and* OFFICER O'HARA *sticks his head in*]

O'HARA: Oh, hello . . .

ABBY: Hello, Officer O'Hara. Is there anything we can do for you?

O'HARA: Saw your lights on—thought there might be sickness in the house. Oh, you got company. Sorry I disturbed you.

[MORTIMER *hurries to* O'HARA *and pulls him through the door into the room*]

MORTIMER: No! Come in!

ABBY: Yes, come in!

MARTHA: Come right in, Officer O'Hara. This is our nephew, Mortimer.

O'HARA: Pleased to meet you.

ABBY: And this is another nephew, Jonathan.

O'HARA: Pleased to make your acquaintance. Well, it must be nice having your nephews visiting you. Are they going to stay with you for a bit?

MORTIMER: I'm staying. My brother Jonathan is just leaving.

[JONATHAN *starts for stairs.* O'HARA *stops him*]

O'HARA: I've met you here before, haven't I?

ABBY: I'm afraid not. Jonathan hasn't been home for years.

O'HARA: [*To* JONATHAN] Your face looks familiar to me. Perhaps I've seen a picture of you somewhere.

JONATHAN: I don't think so.

[*He hurries up the stairs*]

MORTIMER: I'd hurry if I were you, Jonathan. You're all packed anyway, aren't you?

[JONATHAN *exits upstairs*]

O'HARA: Well, you'll be wanting to say your good-byes. I'll be running along.

[*He starts for the door*]

MORTIMER: [*Stopping him*] What's the rush? I'd like to have you stick around until my brother goes.

O'HARA: I just dropped in to make sure everything was all right.

MORTIMER: We're going to have some coffee in a minute. Won't you join us?

ABBY: Oh, I forgot the coffee.

[*She hurries out*]

MARTHA: I'd better make some more sandwiches. I ought to know your appetite by this time, Mr. O'Hara.

[*She exits into the kitchen*]

O'HARA: [*Calling after her*] Don't bother. I'm due to ring in in a few minutes.

MORTIMER: You can have a cup of coffee with us. My brother will be going soon.

O'HARA: Haven't I seen a photograph of your brother around here some place?

MORTIMER: I don't think so.

O'HARA: He certainly reminds me of somebody.

MORTIMER: He looks like somebody you've probably seen in the movies.

O'HARA: I never go to the movies. I hate 'em. My mother says the movies is a bastard art.

MORTIMER: Yes. It's full of them. Your mother said that?

O'HARA: Yeah. My mother was an actress—a stage actress. Perhaps you've heard of her—Peaches Latour.

MORTIMER: Sounds like a name I've seen on a program. What did she play?

O'HARA: Her big hit was *Mutt and Jeff*. Played it for three years. I was born on tour—the third season.

MORTIMER: You were?

O'HARA: Yeah. Sioux City, Iowa. I was born in the dressing-room at the end of the second act and mother made the finale.

MORTIMER: What a trouper! There must be a good story in your mother. You know, I write about the theater.

O'HARA: You do? Say, you're not Mortimer Brewster, the dramatic critic? [MORTIMER *nods*] Say, I'm glad to meet you. We're in the same line of business.

MORTIMER: We are?

O'HARA: Yes, I'm a playwright. This being on the police force is just temporary.

MORTIMER: How long have you been on the force?

O'HARA: Twelve years. I'm collecting material for a play.

MORTIMER: I'll bet it's a honey.

O'HARA: Well, it ought to be. With all the drama I see being a cop. Mr. Brewster, you got no idea what goes on in Brooklyn.

MORTIMER: I think I have!

O'HARA: What time you got?

MORTIMER: Ten after one.

O'HARA: Gee, I got to ring in.

[*He starts to go*]

MORTIMER: [*Stopping him*] Wait a minute! On that play of yours—you know, I might be able to help you.

O'HARA: You would? Say, it was fate my walking in here tonight. Look, I'll tell you the plot.

[JONATHAN *and* EINSTEIN *enter on the balcony carrying suitcases*]

MORTIMER: Oh, Jonathan, you're on your way, eh? Good! You haven't got much time, you know.

ABBY: [*Entering from kitchen*] Everything's about ready. [*She sees* JONATHAN *and* EINSTEIN] Oh, you leaving now, Jonathan? Well, good-bye. Good-bye, Dr. Einstein. [*She notices the instrument case by the window*] Oh, doesn't this case belong to you?

MORTIMER: Yes, Jonathan. You can't go without *all* of your things! [*To* O'HARA] Well, O'Hara, it was nice meeting you. I'll see you again—we'll talk about your play.

O'HARA: Oh, I'm not leaving now, Mr. Brewster.

MORTIMER: Why not?

O'HARA: Well, you just offered to help me with my play, didn't you? You and me are going to write my play together.

MORTIMER: No, O'Hara, I can't do that. You see, I'm not a creative writer.

O'HARA: I'll do the creating. You just put the words to it.

MORTIMER: But, O'Hara . . .

O'HARA: No, sir, Mr. Brewster, I ain't going to leave this house till I tell you the plot.

[O'HARA *sits on the window seat*]

JONATHAN: In that case, Mortimer, we'll be running along.

[*He starts toward the outside door*]

MORTIMER: No, Jonathan! Don't try that! You can't go yet. You're taking *everything* with you. . . . [*To* O'HARA] Look, O'Hara, you run along now. My brother's just going and . . .

O'HARA: I can wait. I've been waiting twelve years.

[MARTHA *enters with sandwiches and coffee on a tray*]

MARTHA: I'm sorry I was so long.

MORTIMER: Don't bring that in here! O'Hara, would you join us for a bite in the kitchen?

MARTHA: The kitchen?

ABBY: Jonathan's leaving.

MARTHA: Oh, that's nice! Come along, Mr. O'Hara.

[*She takes the tray back into the kitchen*]

ABBY: Mr. O'Hara, you don't mind eating in the kitchen?

O'HARA: Where else would you eat?

[*He exits to the kitchen*]

ABBY: Good-bye, Jonathan, it's nice to have seen you again.

[*She hurries into kitchen*]

MORTIMER: [*Closing the kitchen door after* ABBY] Jonathan, I'm glad you came back to Brooklyn because it gives me a chance to throw you out! [*He opens window seat*] And the first one out is your boy friend, Mr. Spenalzo.

O'HARA: [*Appearing in doorway*] Look, Mr. Brewster! [MORTIMER *hurriedly closes the window seat*] We can talk in here.

MORTIMER: No. I'll be right out, O'Hara.

[*He pushes* O'HARA *back into the kitchen*]

JONATHAN: [*Scornfully*] I might have known you'd grow up to write a play with a policeman.

MORTIMER: Get going, now—all *three* of you!

[*He exits; closing the door*]

JONATHAN: [*Putting the bags down*] Doctor, this affair between my brother and me has got to be settled.

EINSTEIN: Now, Chonny, we got trouble enough. Your brother gives us a chance to get away—what more could you ask?

JONATHAN: You don't understand, Doctor. [*Opening window seat*] This goes back many years.

EINSTEIN: Now, Chonny, let's get going.

JONATHAN: We're not going—we're going to sleep right here tonight.

EINSTEIN: With a cop in the kitchen and Mr. Spenalzo in the window seat?

JONATHAN: That's all he's got on us, Doctor. [*He closes the window seat*] We'll take Mr. Spenalzo down and dump him in the bay. That done, we're coming back here. And then if he tries to interfere . . .

EINSTEIN: Now, Chonny!

JONATHAN: Doctor, you know when I make up my mind . . .

EINSTEIN: Yeah—when you make up your mind, you lose your head! Brooklyn ain't a good place for you, Chonny.

JONATHAN: [*Peremptorily*] Doctor!

EINSTEIN: O.K. We got to stick together. Some day we get stuck together. [*He points to the bags*] If we're coming back do we got to take them with us?

JONATHAN: No. Leave them here. [*He looks toward upstairs, then toward the cellar door*] Hide them in the cellar. [EINSTEIN *moves toward the cellar with the instrument case*] Move fast! Spenalzo can go out the same way he came in.

> [EINSTEIN *exits into the cellar.* JONATHAN *goes to the foot of the staircase, takes the other bags to the cellar door, goes to the window and opens it.* EINSTEIN *comes up from the cellar, excited*]

EINSTEIN: Hey, Chonny! Come quick!

JONATHAN: What's the matter?

EINSTEIN: You know that hole in the cellar?

JONATHAN: Yes.

EINSTEIN: Well—we got an ace in the hole.

> [*They both disappear down the cellar steps.* MORTIMER *enters from kitchen, finishing a sandwich and looks around the room. He sees their two bags and notices the open window. He goes to the window seat, looks in and sees* MR. SPENALZO *is still there, closes the window seat and, kneeling on it, leans out the window and calls softly*]

MORTIMER: Jonathan! Jonathan! [JONATHAN *and* EINSTEIN *come in through the cellar door unnoticed by* MORTIMER *and walk into the room*] Jonathan!

JONATHAN: Yes, Mortimer!

MORTIMER: [*Turning around and seeing* JONATHAN, *he speaks angrily*] Where have you two been? I thought I told you . . .

JONATHAN: We're not going.

MORTIMER: Oh, you're not? You think I'm not serious about this, eh? Do you want the police to know what's in that window seat?

JONATHAN: [*Firmly*] We're staying here.

MORTIMER: All right! You asked for it! This gets me rid of you and O'Hara both at the same time. [*He goes to the kitchen door*] Officer O'Hara!

JONATHAN: If you tell O'Hara what's in the window seat, I'll tell him what's in the cellar.

MORTIMER: [*Closing the door swiftly*] The cellar?

JONATHAN: There's an elderly gentleman down there who seems to be very dead.

MORTIMER: What were you doing in the cellar?

EINSTEIN: What's *he* doing in the cellar?

[OFFICER O'HARA's *voice is heard off-stage*]

O'HARA: [*Off-stage*] No, thank you, ma'am. I've had plenty! They were fine!

JONATHAN: Now, what are you going to say to Officer O'Hara?

[O'HARA *walks in*]

O'HARA: Say, your aunts want to hear it, too. Shall I get them in here?

MORTIMER: [*Pulling him toward the outside door*] No, O'Hara! You can't do that now! You've got to ring in!

O'HARA: The hell with ringing in! I'll get your aunts in and tell you the plot.

MORTIMER: No, O'Hara, not in front of all these people! We'll get together alone someplace, later.

O'HARA: Say, how about the back room at Kelly's?

MORTIMER: [*Hurrying him toward door*] Fine! You go ring in and I'll meet you at Kelly's.

JONATHAN: Why don't you two go down in the cellar?

o'HARA: That's all right with me. [*He starts for the cellar door*] Is this the cellar?

MORTIMER: [*Grabbing him*] No! We'll go to Kelly's. But you're going to ring in on the way, aren't you?

o'HARA: All right, that will only take a couple of minutes.

> [MORTIMER *pushes him through the outside door, then turns to get his hat*]

MORTIMER: [*To* JONATHAN] I'll ditch this guy and be back in five minutes. I expect to find you gone. No! Wait for me.

> [*He exits, closing the door*]

JONATHAN: We'll wait for him, Doctor. I've waited a great many years for a chance like this.

EINSTEIN: We got him where we want him. Did he look guilty!

JONATHAN: Take the bags back to our room, Doctor.

> [*He goes to the window and closes it.* ABBY, *who is wiping her hands on her apron, enters, followed by* MARTHA, *who has a saucer and dish towel in her hand*]

ABBY: Have they gone? [*She sees* JONATHAN *and* EINSTEIN] Oh— we thought we heard somebody leave.

JONATHAN: Just Mortimer—he'll be back in a few minutes. Is there any food left in the kitchen? I think Dr. Einstein and I would enjoy a bite.

MARTHA: You won't have time . . .

ABBY: Yes, if you're still here when Mortimer gets back, he won't like it.

EINSTEIN: He'll like it! He's gotta like it!

JONATHAN: Get something for us to eat, while we bury Mr. Spenalzo in the cellar.

MARTHA: Oh, no!

ABBY: [*Spiritedly*] He can't stay in our cellar, Jonathan. You've got to take him with you.

JONATHAN: There's a friend of Mortimer's downstairs waiting for him.

ABBY: A friend of Mortimer's?

JONATHAN: He and Mr. Spenalzo will get along fine together. They're both dead.

MARTHA: They must mean Mr. Hoskins.

EINSTEIN: Mr. Hoskins?

JONATHAN: So you know about what's downstairs?

ABBY: Of course we do, and he's no friend of Mortimer's. He's one of our gentlemen.

EINSTEIN: Your gentlemen?

MARTHA: [Firmly] And we won't have any strangers buried in our cellar.

JONATHAN: But Mr. Hoskins . . .

MARTHA: Mr. Hoskins isn't a stranger.

ABBY: Besides, there's no room for Mr. Spenalzo. The cellar's crowded already.

JONATHAN: Crowded? With what?

ABBY: There are twelve graves down there now.

JONATHAN: Twelve graves!

ABBY: That leaves very little room and we're going to need it.

JONATHAN: You mean you and Aunt Martha have murdered . . .

ABBY: Murdered! Certainly not! It's one of our charities.

MARTHA: What we've been doing is a mercy.

ABBY: [With a gesture of dismissal] So you take your Mr. Spenalzo out of here.

JONATHAN: [Amazed and impressed] You've done that—right in this house—and buried them down there?

EINSTEIN: Chonny, we been chased all over the world . . . They stay right here in Brooklyn and do just as good as you do.

JONATHAN: What?

EINSTEIN: You got twelve, Chonny. They got twelve.

JONATHAN: [His pride wounded] I've got thirteen.

EINSTEIN: No, twelve, Chonny.

JONATHAN: Thirteen! There's Mr. Spenalzo! Then the first one in London. Two in Johannesburg—one in Sydney—one in Melbourne—two in San Francisco—one in Phoenix, Arizona . . .

EINSTEIN: Phoenix?

JONATHAN: The filling station—the three in Chicago, and the one in South Bend. That makes thirteen!

EINSTEIN: But, Chonny, you can't count the one in South Bend. He died of pneumonia.

JONATHAN: [*His record at stake*] He wouldn't have got pneumonia if I hadn't shot him.

EINSTEIN: No, Chonny, he died of pneumonia. He don't count.

JONATHAN: He counts with me! I say *thirteen!*

EINSTEIN: No, Chonny. You got twelve. They got twelve. The old ladies are just as good as you are.

JONATHAN: [*Wheeling on them*] Oh, they are, are they? That's easily taken care of! All I need is one more!—that's all—just one more!

> [MORTIMER *enters hastily, closing the door behind him and turns to them with a nervous smile*]

MORTIMER: Well—here I am!

> [JONATHAN *looks at* MORTIMER *with the widening eyes of someone who has just solved a problem*]

CURTAIN

ACT THREE

SCENE 1

The curtain rises on an empty stage. We hear voices, voices in disagreement, from the cellar, through the open cellar door.

MARTHA: *[Off-stage]* You stop doing that!

ABBY: *[Off-stage]* This is our house and this is our cellar and you can't do that!

EINSTEIN: *[Off-stage]* Ladies! Please go back upstairs where you belong.

JONATHAN: *[Off-stage]* Abby! Martha! Go upstairs!

MARTHA: *[Off-stage]* There's no use of your doing what you're doing because it will just have to be undone!

ABBY: *[Off-stage]* I tell you we won't have it!

[MARTHA *enters from the cellar*]

MARTHA: You'll find out! You'll find out whose house this is!

[*She goes to the street door, opens it and looks out.* ABBY *enters from the cellar. Both women are wearing their hats*]

ABBY: I'm warning you! You'd better stop! [*To* MARTHA] Hasn't Mortimer come back yet?

MARTHA: [*She closes the door*] No.

ABBY: It's a terrible thing—burying a good Methodist with a foreigner!

MARTHA: I won't have our cellar desecrated!

ABBY: And we promised Mr. Hoskins a full Christian funeral. . . . Where do you suppose Mortimer went?

MARTHA: I don't know. But he must be doing something. He said to Jonathan, "You just wait, I'll settle this!"

ABBY: Well, he can't settle it while he's out of the house. [*Turning to the cellar door*] That's all we want settled—what's going on down there.

[MORTIMER *enters from the street carrying* TEDDY's *commitment papers in his hand*]

MORTIMER: [*Grimly*] All right. Now, where's Teddy?

ABBY: Mortimer, where have you been?

MORTIMER: I've been over to Dr. Gilchrist's. I've got his signature on Teddy's commitment papers.

MARTHA: Mortimer, what's the matter with you?

ABBY: Running around getting papers signed at a time like this!

MARTHA: Do you know what Jonathan is doing?

ABBY: He's putting Mr. Hoskins and Mr. Spenalzo in together.

MORTIMER: Oh, he is, is he? Well, let him. Is Teddy in his room?

MARTHA: Teddy won't be any help.

MORTIMER: When he signs these commitment papers, I can tackle Jonathan.

ABBY: What have they got to do with it?

MORTIMER: You had to tell Jonathan about those twelve graves! If I can make Teddy responsible for those, I can protect you, don't you see?

ABBY: No, I don't see. And we pay taxes to have the police protect us.

MORTIMER: [*Starting upstairs*] I'll be back down in a minute.

ABBY: Come, Martha. [*To* MORTIMER] We're going for the police.

[*The sisters get their gloves*]

MORTIMER: All right. [*He suddenly realizes what has been said*] The police! You can't go for the police!

[*He rushes downstairs to the street door*]

MARTHA: Why can't we?

MORTIMER: Because, if you told them about Mr. Spenalzo, they'd find Mr. Hoskins too; and that might make them curious, and they'd find out about the other gentlemen.

ABBY: Mortimer, we know the police better than you do. I don't think they'd pry into our private affairs if we asked them not to.

MORTIMER: But if they found your twelve gentlemen they'd have to report to headquarters.

MARTHA: [*Pulling on her gloves*] I'm not so sure they'd bother. They'd have to make out a very long report. And if there's one thing a policeman hates to do, it's to write.

MORTIMER: You can't depend on that! It might leak out! And you couldn't expect a judge and jury to understand.

MARTHA: Judge Cullman would.

ABBY: [*Drawing on her gloves*] We know him very well.

MARTHA: He always comes to church to pray just before election.

ABBY: And he's coming here to tea some day. He promised.

MARTHA: We'll have to speak to him again about that, Abby. [*To* MORTIMER] His wife died a few years ago and it's left him very lonely.

ABBY: Come along, Martha.

> [*She starts toward the door.* MORTIMER, *however, gets there first*]

MORTIMER: You can't do this! I won't let you. You can't leave this house and you can't have Judge Cullman to tea!

ABBY: Well, if you're not going to do something about Mr. Spenalzo, we are.

MORTIMER: But I am going to do something. We may have to call the police in later, but if we do, I want to be ready for them.

MARTHA: You've got to get Jonathan out of this house!

ABBY: And Mr. Spenalzo, too!

MORTIMER: Will you please let me do it my own way? I've got to see Teddy.

> [*He starts upstairs*]

ABBY: If they're not out of here by morning, Mortimer, we're going to call the police.

> [MORTIMER *turns at the top of the stairs*]

MORTIMER: They'll be out. I promise you that! Go to bed, will you? And for God's sake get out of those clothes. You look like Judith Anderson.

[*He exits upstairs*]

MARTHA: Well, that's a relief, Abby.

ABBY: If Mortimer is doing something at last then Jonathan's just going to a lot of unnecessary trouble. We'd better tell him. [JONATHAN *comes up the cellar steps and into the room*] Jonathan, you might as well stop what you're doing.

JONATHAN: It's all done. Did I hear Mortimer?

ABBY: Well, it will just have to be undone. You're all going to be out of this house by morning.

JONATHAN: Oh, we are? In that case, you and Aunt Martha can go to bed and have a peaceful night's sleep.

MARTHA: [*Always a little frightened by* JONATHAN] Yes. Come, Abby.

[*They start up the stairs*]

JONATHAN: Good night, aunties.

[*The sisters turn at the top of the stairs*]

ABBY: Not good night, Jonathan. Good-bye! By the time we get up you'll be out of this house. Mortimer's promised.

MARTHA: And he has a way of doing it, too!

JONATHAN: Then Mortimer is back?

ABBY: Yes, he's up here talking to Teddy.

MARTHA: Good-bye, Jonathan.

ABBY: Good-bye, Jonathan.

JONATHAN: [*Quietly*] Perhaps you'd better say good-bye to Mortimer.

ABBY: Oh, you'll see Mortimer.

JONATHAN: [*Tense*] Yes, I'll see Mortimer.

> [ABBY *and* MARTHA *exit.* JONATHAN *stands without moving.*
> *There is murder on his mind. After an appreciable pause*
> EINSTEIN *comes up from the cellar dusting himself off. He*
> *is wearing Mr. Spenalzo's shoes*]

EINSTEIN: Whew! That's all fixed up. Smooth like a lake. Nobody'd ever know they're there. [JONATHAN *still stands without moving*] That bed feels good already. Forty-eight hours we didn't sleep. Whew! Come on, Chonny, let's go up, yes?

[JONATHAN's *eyes move to* EINSTEIN]

JONATHAN: You're forgetting, Doctor.

EINSTEIN: Vas?

JONATHAN: My brother Mortimer.

EINSTEIN: Chonny, tonight? I'm sleepy. We do that tomorrow—the next day.

JONATHAN: No, tonight. Now!

EINSTEIN: Chonny, please! I'm tired . . . Tomorrow I got to operate . . .

JONATHAN: You're going to operate tomorrow, Doctor. But tonight we take care of Mortimer.

EINSTEIN: Chonny, not tonight—we go to bed, eh?

JONATHAN: Doctor, look at me! [EINSTEIN *looks and straightens up*] You can see that it's going to be done, can't you?

EINSTEIN: Ach, Chonny! I can see! I know that look!

JONATHAN: It's a little late for us to dissolve our partnership.

EINSTEIN: OK, Chonny. We do it. But the quick way? The quick twist, like in London.

[*He gives that London neck another twist with his hands*]

JONATHAN: No, Doctor, I think this calls for something special. [JONA-THAN *begins to anticipate a rare pleasure*] I think, perhaps, the Melbourne method.

EINSTEIN: Chonny—No!—Not that! Two hours! And when it was all over—what? The fellow in London was just as dead as the fellow in Melbourne.

JONATHAN: We had to work too fast in London. There was no aesthetic satisfaction in it. Now, Melbourne—ah, there was something to remember.

EINSTEIN: Remember! [*He shivers*] I wish I didn't. No, Chonny—not Melbourne—not me . . .

JONATHAN: Yes, Doctor. Where are the instruments?

EINSTEIN: I won't do it, Chonny! I won't do it!

JONATHAN: Get your instruments!

EINSTEIN: No, Chonny!

JONATHAN: Where are they? Oh, yes. You hid them in the cellar. Where?

EINSTEIN: I won't tell you!

JONATHAN: I'll find them, Doctor.

> [*He exits to the cellar.* EINSTEIN *paces desperately for a moment.* TEDDY *steps out on the balcony with his bugle and lifts it as if to blow.* MORTIMER *dashes out after him and grabs his arm*]

MORTIMER: Don't do that, Mr. President!

TEDDY: I cannot sign any proclamation without consulting my cabinet.

MORTIMER: But this must be secret.

TEDDY: A secret proclamation? How unusual!

MORTIMER: Japan mustn't know until it's signed.

TEDDY: Japan? Those yellow devils! I'll sign it right away. You have my word for it. I can let the cabinet know later.

MORTIMER: Yes, let's go and sign it.

TEDDY: You wait here. If it's a secret proclamation it has to be signed in secret.

MORTIMER: At once, Mr. President.

TEDDY: I'll put on my signing clothes.

> [*He exits.* MORTIMER *comes downstairs.* EINSTEIN *takes* MORTIMER's *hat from the hall tree and meets him at the foot of the stairs*]

EINSTEIN: You go now, eh?

> [*He hands* MORTIMER *his hat*]

MORTIMER: No, Doctor, I'm waiting for something—something important.

> [MORTIMER *tosses his hat on the couch*]

EINSTEIN: [*Urging* MORTIMER *to the door*] Please, you go now!

MORTIMER: Dr. Einstein, I have nothing against you personally. You seem to be a nice fellow. If you'll take my advice, you'll get out of this house and get just as far away as possible . . . There's going to be trouble.

EINSTEIN: Trouble, yah! You get out!

MORTIMER: All right, don't say I didn't warn you.

EINSTEIN: I'm warning *you*—get away quick!

MORTIMER: Things are going to start popping around here any minute.

EINSTEIN: [*Glancing nervously toward the cellar*] Chonny is in a bad mood. When he is like this—he is a madman! Things happen— terrible things!

MORTIMER: Jonathan doesn't worry me now.

EINSTEIN: Ach! Himmel! Don't those plays you see teach you anything?

MORTIMER: About what?

EINSTEIN: At least people in plays act like they got sense.

MORTIMER: Oh, you think so, do you? You think people in plays act intelligently. I wish you had to sit through some of the ones I have to sit through. This little opus tonight—for instance. In this play, there's a man . . . [JONATHAN *enters from the cellar, carrying the instrument case. He pauses in the doorway, unseen by* MORTIMER] . . . he's supposed to be bright. He knows he's in a house with murderers—he ought to know he's in danger. He's even been warned to get out of the house. Does he go? No, he stays there. I ask you—is that what an intelligent person would do?

EINSTEIN: You're asking me!

MORTIMER: He didn't even have sense enough to be scared—to be on guard. For instance, the murderer invites him to sit down.

EINSTEIN: You mean "Won't you sit down"?

MORTIMER: Believe it or not, that one was in there, too.

EINSTEIN: And what did he do?

MORTIMER: He sat down! Mind you—this fellow is supposed to be bright. [MORTIMER *sits down*] There he is—all ready to be trussed up. And what do they use to tie him with?

EINSTEIN: What?

MORTIMER: The curtain cord.

[JONATHAN *finds an idea being thrust on him, draws his knife, and goes to the window*]

EINSTEIN: Well, why not? A good idea. Very convenient.

[JONATHAN *cuts the curtain cord*]

MORTIMER: A little too convenient. When are playwrights going to use some imagination? [JONATHAN *has coiled the curtain cord and is moving behind* MORTIMER] The curtain cord!

EINSTEIN: He didn't see him get it?

MORTIMER: See him? He sat there with his back to him. That's the kind of stuff we have to suffer through night after night. And they say the critics are killing the theater. It's the playwrights that are killing the theater. So there he sat—the big dope—this guy that's supposed to be bright—waiting to be tied up and gagged!

[JONATHAN *drops the looped curtain cord over* MORTIMER'S *shoulders, pulls it taut and ties it behind the back of the chair. Simultaneously* EINSTEIN *leaps to* MORTIMER, *pulls* MORTIMER'S *handkerchief out of his pocket and gags him with it.* JONATHAN *steps to* MORTIMER'S *side*]

EINSTEIN: [*Tying* MORTIMER'S *legs*] You're right about that fellow— he *wasn't* very bright.

JONATHAN: Now if you don't mind, Mortimer—we'll finish the story. [MORTIMER *is making muted, unintelligible sounds.* JONATHAN *goes to the sideboard and brings the candelabra down to the table and lights the candles*] Mortimer, I've been away for twenty years, but never, my dear brother, were you out of my mind. . . . In Melbourne one night—I dreamt of you. . . . When I landed in San Francisco—I felt a strange satisfaction— Once again I was in the same country with you. [JONATHAN *turns out the lights, throwing the room into an eerie candlelight. He picks up the instrument case and sets it down on the table between the candelabra*] Now, Doctor—we go to work.

EINSTEIN: Please, Chonny—for me—the quick way—eh?

JONATHAN: Doctor, this must be an artistic achievement! After all, we're performing before a very distinguished critic.

EINSTEIN: Chonny . . .

JONATHAN: [*Flaring*] Doctor . . .

EINSTEIN: All right. Let's get it over! [JONATHAN *takes several instruments out of the case, handling them as potential accessories to torture. The last of these is a long probe, which he measures to* MORTIMER'S *face. Finally he begins to put on rubber gloves.* EINSTEIN *takes a bottle from his pocket, finds it empty]* Chonny, I gotta have a drink, I can't do this without a drink.

JONATHAN: Pull yourself together, Doctor!

EINSTEIN: I gotta have a drink! Chonny, when we walked in this afternoon—there was wine there . . . [*He points to the table*] Remember? Where did she put it? [*He remembers*] Ah . . . [*He goes to sideboard and opens it, finding the wine*] Look, Chonny! [*He takes the wine bottle to the table with two wine glasses*] We got a drink [*He pours the wine into the two glasses, the second glass emptying the bottle.* MORTIMER, *who has been squirming, stops, eyeing the bottle, then* JONATHAN *and* EINSTEIN] That's all there is. I split it with you. We both need a drink!

> [EINSTEIN *hands one glass to* JONATHAN, *then raises the glass of poisoned wine and is about to drink*]

JONATHAN: One moment, Doctor! Please! Where are your manners? [*To* MORTIMER] Yes, Mortimer. I realize now that it was you who brought me back to Brooklyn. We drink to you! [*He raises his glass, sniffs the wine, hesitates, then proposes a grim toast*] Doctor—to my dear dead brother! [*They are raising their glasses to their lips, when* TEDDY, *fully and formally dressed, steps out of the upper door onto the balcony and blows a terrific blast on his bugle.* EINSTEIN *and* JONATHAN *drop their glasses, spilling the wine.* TEDDY *turns around and goes out again*]

EINSTEIN: Ach, Gott!

JONATHAN: Damn that idiot! He goes next! That's all. He goes next!

> [*He rushes to the staircase*]

EINSTEIN: No, Chonny, not Teddy! That's where I stop—not Teddy!

> [*He intercepts* JONATHAN *at the stairs*]

JONATHAN: We'll get to him later.

EINSTEIN: We don't get to him at all!

JONATHAN: Now we *have* to work fast!

EINSTEIN: Yah—the quick way—eh, Chonny?

JONATHAN: Yes—the quick way!

> [*He darts behind* MORTIMER, *pulling a large silk handkerchief from his pocket and drops it around* MORTIMER'S *neck. There is a knock at the door.* JONATHAN *and* EINSTEIN *are startled. The door opens and* OFFICER O'HARA *enters*]

O'HARA: Hey, the Colonel's gotta quit blowing that horn!

> [JONATHAN *and* EINSTEIN *quickly stand between* MORTIMER *and* O'HARA]

JONATHAN: It's all right, officer. We're taking the bugle away from him.

O'HARA: There's going to be hell to pay in the morning. We promised the neighbors he wouldn't do that any more.

JONATHAN: It won't happen again, officer. Good night.

O'HARA: I better speak to him myself. Where are the lights? [O'HARA *turns on the lights.* EINSTEIN *and* JONATHAN *break for the kitchen door but stop when the lights go on.* O'HARA *closes the door and starts up the stairs.* MORTIMER *mumbles through the gag.* O'HARA *turns and sees him*] Hey, you stood me up! I waited an hour at Kelly's for you [*He comes downstairs.* MORTIMER *is trying to talk.* O'HARA *turns to* EINSTEIN] What happened to him?

EINSTEIN: He was explaining the play he saw tonight. That's what happened to a fellow in the play.

O'HARA: Did they have that in the play you saw tonight? [MORTIMER *nods his head*] Gee, they practically stole that from the second act of *my* play. In the second act just before . . . I'd better begin at the beginning. It opens in my mother's dressing room, where I was born—only I ain't born yet. [MORTIMER *mumbles and moves his head*] Huh? Oh, yes. [*He goes to* MORTIMER *and starts to remove the gag, then hesitates*] No! You've got to hear the plot! [O'HARA *goes enthusiastically into his plot as the curtain is coming down*] Well, she's sitting there making up, see—when out of a clear sky the door opens—and a man with a black mustache walks in . . .

CURTAIN

SCENE 2

When the curtain rises again, daylight is streaming through the windows. MORTIMER *is still tied in his chair and seems to be in a semi-conscious state.* JONATHAN *is asleep on the couch near the stairs.* EINSTEIN, *pleasantly intoxicated, is seated, listening. There is a bottle of whisky on the table and two glasses.* O'HARA, *with his coat off and his collar loosened, has progressed to the most exciting scene of his play.*

O'HARA: . . . there she is, lying unconscious across the table—in her longeray—the Chink is standing over her with a hatchet . . . [*He takes the pose*] . . . I'm tied up in a chair just like you are . . . The place is an inferno of flames—it's on fire—great effect we got there—when all of a sudden—through the window—in comes Mayor La Guardia! [MORTIMER *is startled into consciousness, then collapses again.* O'HARA *is pacing with self-satisfaction.* EINSTEIN *pours himself a drink*] Hey, remember who paid for that—go easy on it.

EINSTEIN: Well, I'm listening, ain't I?

O'HARA: How do you like it, so far?

EINSTEIN: It put Chonny to sleep. [EINSTEIN *goes over and shakes* JONATHAN] Hey, Chonny!—Chonny!—want a drink?

O'HARA: [*Pouring drink*] Let him alone—if he ain't got no more interest than that—he don't get a drink. [O'HARA *tosses a drink down and is ready to resume his story*] All right . . . it's three days later . . . I been transferred and I'm under charges—that's because somebody stole my badge—all right, I'm walking my beat on Staten Island—forty-sixth precinct—when a guy I'm following, it turns out is really following *me* . . . [*There is a knock at the door*] Don't let anybody in. [EINSTEIN *hurries to the landing window and looks out*] So I figure I'll outsmart him. There's a vacant house on the corner. I goes in.

EINSTEIN: [*Looking out*] It's cops!

O'HARA: I stands there in the dark and I sees the door handle turn.

EINSTEIN: [*Shaking* JONATHAN's *shoulder*] Chonny! It's cops! It's cops!

[EINSTEIN *hurries up the stairs*]

O'HARA: I pulls my gun, I braces myself against the wall and I says "Come in!" [OFFICERS BROPHY *and* KLEIN *walk in, see* O'HARA *with his gun pointed toward them, and start to raise their hands.* EINSTEIN *exits upstairs*] Hello, boys!

BROPHY: [*Recognizing* O'HARA] What the hell's going on here?

O'HARA: Hey, Pat, what do you know? This is Mortimer Brewster! He's going to write my play with me! I'm just telling him the story.

KLEIN: Did you have to tie him up to make him listen?

[*He goes over and unties* MORTIMER]

BROPHY: Joe, you'd better report in at the station. The whole force is out looking for you.

O'HARA: Did they send you boys here for me?

KLEIN: We didn't know you was here.

BROPHY: We came to warn the old ladies that there's hell to pay. The Colonel blew that bugle again in the middle of the night.

KLEIN: From the way the neighbors have been calling in about it you'd think the Germans had dropped a bomb on Flatbush Avenue.

BROPHY: The Lieutenant's on the warpath. He says the Colonel's got to be put away some place.

[KLEIN *helps* MORTIMER *to his feet*]

MORTIMER: [*Weakly*] Yes!

[*He staggers toward the stairs.* O'HARA *follows him*]

O'HARA: Listen, Mr. Brewster. I got to go, so I'll just run through the third act quick.

MORTIMER: Get away from me!

[BROPHY *goes to the telephone and dials*]

KLEIN: Say, do you know what time it is? It's after eight o'clock in the morning.

O'HARA: It is? Gee, Mr. Brewster, them first two acts run a little long. But I don't see anything we can leave out.

MORTIMER: You can leave it *all* out.

[BROPHY *sees* JONATHAN *on the couch*]

BROPHY: Who the hell is this guy?

MORTIMER: It's my brother.

BROPHY: Oh, the one that ran away? So he came back.

MORTIMER: Yes, he came back!

[*He has reached the balcony*]

BROPHY: [*Into the telephone*] This is Brophy. Get me Mac. [*To* O'HARA] I'd better let them know I found you, Joe. [KLEIN *has wandered over to the other side of* JONATHAN *and looks down at him.* BROPHY *is looking at* O'HARA] Mac? Tell the Lieutenant he can call off the big man hunt. We got him. In the Brewster house. [JONATHAN *hears this and suddenly becomes very awake, looking up to see a policeman on each side of him*] Do you want us to bring him in? Oh, all right—we'll hold him right here. [*He hangs up*] The Lieutenant's on his way over.

[JONATHAN *is now on his feet between the two policemen, under the impression that he is cornered*]

JONATHAN: So, I've been turned in, eh? [BROPHY *and* KLEIN *look at him with interest*] All right, you've got me! I suppose you and my stool-pigeon brother will split the reward?

KLEIN: Reward?

[*Instinctively* KLEIN *and* BROPHY *both grab* JONATHAN *by an arm*]

JONATHAN: Now I'll do some turning in! You think my aunts are charming, sweet old ladies, don't you? Well, there are thirteen bodies buried in their cellar!

MORTIMER: [*Exits upstairs, calling:*] Teddy! Teddy!

KLEIN: What the hell are you talking about?

BROPHY: You'd better be careful what you say about your aunts— they happen to be friends of ours.

JONATHAN: I'll show you! I'll prove it to you! Come down in the cellar with me!

[*He starts to drag them toward the cellar door*]

KLEIN: Wait a minute!

JONATHAN: Thirteen bodies—I'll show you where they're buried!

KLEIN: [*Refusing to be kidded*] Oh, yeah?

JONATHAN: Oh, you don't want to see what's down in the cellar!

[BROPHY *releases* JONATHAN's *arm*]

BROPHY: Go on down in the cellar with him, Abe.

KLEIN: [*Stepping away from* JONATHAN] I'm not so sure I want to be down in the cellar with him. Look at that puss. He looks like Boris Karloff.

[JONATHAN, *at the mention of Boris Karloff, leaps at* KLEIN's *throat*]

BROPHY: What d'you think you're doing?

KLEIN: Get him off me. Pat! Grab him! [BROPHY *swings on* JONATHAN *with his nightstick.* JONATHAN *falls, unconscious*] Well, what do you know about that?

[*There is a knock at the door*]

O'HARA: Come in!

[LIEUTENANT ROONEY *bursts in. He is a very tough, driving, dominating police officer*]

ROONEY: What the hell are you men doing here? I told you *I* was going to handle this.

KLEIN: Well, sir, we was just . . .

[KLEIN's *eyes go to the prostrate* JONATHAN *and* ROONEY *sees him*]

ROONEY: What happened? Did he put up a fight?

BROPHY: This ain't the guy that blows the bugle. This is his brother. He tried to kill Klein.

KLEIN: [*Feeling his throat*] All I said was he looked like Boris Karloff.

[ROONEY *gives them a look*]

ROONEY: Turn him over!

BROPHY: We kinda think he's wanted somewhere.

[KLEIN *and* BROPHY *turn* JONATHAN *over and* ROONEY *takes a look at him*]

ROONEY: Oh, you kinda *think* he's wanted somewhere? If you guys don't look at the circulars we hang up in the station, at least you could read *True Detective*. Certainly he's wanted! In Indiana! Escaped from the Prison for the Criminal Insane—he's a lifer. For God's sake, that's how he was described—he looked like *Karloff!*

KLEIN: Was there a reward mentioned?

ROONEY: Yeah—and *I'm* claiming it.

BROPHY: He was trying to get us down in the cellar.

KLEIN: He said there was thirteen bodies buried down there.

ROONEY: Thirteen bodies buried in the cellar? And that didn't tip you off he came out of a nut house?

O'HARA: I thought all along he talked kinda crazy.

[ROONEY *sees* O'HARA *for the first time*]

ROONEY: Oh—it's Shakespeare! Where have you been all night—and you needn't bother to tell me!

O'HARA: I've been right here, sir, writing a play with Mortimer Brewster.

ROONEY: Yeah? Well, you're going to have plenty of time to write that play. You're suspended!

O'HARA: [*Getting his hat and coat*] Can I come over some time and use the station typewriter?

ROONEY: No! Get out! [O'HARA *gets out.* TEDDY *enters on the balcony and comes downstairs*] Take that guy somewhere else and bring him to. See what you can find out about his accomplice—the guy that helped him escape. He's wanted, too. [KLEIN *and* BROPHY *are bending over* JONATHAN] No wonder Brooklyn's in the shape it's in. With the police force full of flatheads like you. Falling for that kind of a story—thirteen bodies buried in the cellar!

[TEDDY *has reached* ROONEY'*s side*]

TEDDY: But there are thirteen bodies in the cellar.
ROONEY: [*Turning on him*] Who are you?
TEDDY: I'm President Roosevelt.

[ROONEY *goes slightly crazy*]

ROONEY: What the hell is this?
BROPHY: He's the fellow that blows the bugle.
KLEIN: Good morning, Colonel.

[BROPHY *and* KLEIN *salute* TEDDY. TEDDY *returns the salute.* ROONEY *almost salutes but stops halfway*]

ROONEY: Well, Colonel, you've blown your last bugle!

[TEDDY'*s attention has been attracted to the body on the floor*]

TEDDY: Dear me, another yellow fever victim!
ROONEY: What?
TEDDY: All the bodies in the cellar are yellow fever victims.

[ROONEY *takes a walk on this*]

BROPHY: No, Colonel, this is a spy we caught in the White House.
ROONEY: [*Pointing to* JONATHAN] Will you get that guy out of here?
[BROPHY *and* KLEIN *pick up* JONATHAN] Bring him to and question him.

[MORTIMER *enters on the balcony carrying* TEDDY'*s commitment papers, and starts downstairs*]

TEDDY: If there's any questioning of spies—that's my department!

[BROPHY *and* KLEIN *drag* JONATHAN *into the kitchen.* TEDDY *starts to follow*]

ROONEY: Hey, you—keep out of that!
TEDDY: You're forgetting! As President, I'm also head of the Secret Service.

[*He exits into the kitchen.* MORTIMER *has come down*]

MORTIMER: Captain—I'm Mortimer Brewster.

ROONEY: [*Dizzy by this time*] Are you sure?

MORTIMER: I'd like to talk to you about my brother Teddy—the one who blew the bugle.

ROONEY: Mr. Brewster, we ain't going to talk about that—he's got to be put away.

MORTIMER: I quite agree with you, Captain. In fact, it's all arranged for. I had these commitment papers signed by Dr. Gilchrist last night. Teddy has just signed them himself—you see. And I've signed them as next of kin.

[ROONEY *looks at the papers.* EINSTEIN *enters hurriedly through the arch, sees the policeman and sneaks back out of sight*]

ROONEY: Where's he going?

MORTIMER: Happy Dale . . .

ROONEY: All right. I don't care where he goes as long as he goes!

MORTIMER: Oh, he's going all right. But I want you to understand that everything that's happened around here Teddy's responsible for. Now, those thirteen bodies in the cellar . . .

ROONEY: Yeah—those thirteen bodies in the cellar! It ain't enough that the neighbors are afraid of him and his disturbing the peace with that bugle—but can you imagine what would happen if that cockeyed story about thirteen bodies in the cellar got around? And now he's starting a yellow fever scare. Cute, ain't it?

MORTIMER: [*Greatly relieved and with an embarrassed laugh*] Thirteen bodies! Do you think anybody would believe that story?

ROONEY: You can't tell. Some people are just dumb enough. You don't know what to believe sometimes. A year ago, a crazy guy started a murder rumor over in Greenpoint and I had to dig up a half-acre lot, just to prove . . .

[*There is a knock at the door*]

MORTIMER: Excuse me!

[*He goes to the door and admits* ELAINE *and* MR. WITHER-

SPOON, *an elderly, tight-lipped disciplinarian. He is carrying a briefcase*]

ELAINE: [*Briskly*] Good morning, Mortimer!

MORTIMER: Good morning, dear.

ELAINE: This is Mr. Witherspoon. He's come to meet Teddy.

MORTIMER: To meet Teddy?

ELAINE: Mr. Witherspoon's the Superintendent of Happy Dale.

MORTIMER: [*Eagerly*] Oh, come right in! This is Captain . . .

ROONEY: Lieutenant Rooney. I'm glad you're here, Super, because you're taking him back with you today!

WITHERSPOON: Today! I had no idea . . .

ELAINE: Not today!

MORTIMER: Elaine, I've got a lot of business to attend to, so you run along home and I'll call you up.

ELAINE: Nuts!

[*She walks over and plants herself on the window seat*]

WITHERSPOON: I didn't realize it was this immediate.

ROONEY: The papers are all signed. He goes today.

[TEDDY *enters from the kitchen*]

TEDDY: [*Looking back*] It's insubordination! You'll find out I'm no mollycoddle. [*He advances into the room angrily*] When the President of the United States is treated that way, what's this country coming to?

ROONEY: There's your man, Super.

MORTIMER: Just a minute! [*He goes to* TEDDY *and speaks with great dignity*] Mr. President! I have very good news for you. Your term of office is over.

TEDDY: Is this March fourth?

MORTIMER: Practically.

TEDDY: Let's see! [*He thinks it over*] Oh—now I go on my hunting trip to Africa! Well, I must get started immediately. [*He starts across, sees* WITHERSPOON, *steps back to* MORTIMER, *and speaks sotto voce*] Is he trying to move into the White House before I've moved out?

MORTIMER: Who, Teddy?

TEDDY: [*Indicating* WITHERSPOON] Taft!

MORTIMER: This isn't Mr. Taft, Teddy. This is Mr. Witherspoon. He's going to be your guide in Africa.

TEDDY: Bully! Bully! [*He shakes* MR. WITHERSPOON'S *hand*] Wait right here—I'll bring down my equipment. [MARTHA *and* ABBY *enter on the balcony and come downstairs*] When the safari comes tell them to wait. [*To his aunts as he passes them on the stairs*] Good-bye, Aunt Abby. Good-bye, Aunt Martha. I'm on my way to Africa. Isn't it wonderful? [*He has reached the landing*] CHARGE!

[*He charges up and out*]

MARTHA: Good morning, Mortimer.

MORTIMER: Good morning, darlings.

MARTHA: Good morning, Elaine. Well, we have visitors.

MORTIMER: This is Lieutenant Rooney.

ABBY: [*Going to him*] Well, Lieutenant, you don't look like the fuss-budget the policemen say you are.

MORTIMER: Why the Lieutenant is here—you know Teddy blew that bugle again last night.

MARTHA: Yes, we're going to speak to Teddy about that.

ROONEY: It's a little more serious than that, Miss Brewster.

MORTIMER: And you haven't met Mr. Witherspoon—he's the Superintendent of Happy Dale.

ABBY: How do you do?

MARTHA: Oh—you've come to meet Teddy.

ROONEY: He's come to *take* him.

MORTIMER: Aunties, the police want Teddy to go there *today*.

ABBY: Oh—no!

MARTHA: Not as long as we're alive!

ROONEY: I'm sorry, Miss Brewster, but it has to be done. The papers are all signed and he's going along with the Superintendent.

ABBY: We won't permit it! We'll promise to take the bugle away from him.

MARTHA: We won't be separated from Teddy!

ROONEY: I know how you feel, ladies, but the law's the law. He's committed himself and he's going.

ABBY: Well, if he goes, we're going too!

MARTHA: Yes, you'll have to take us with him!

MORTIMER: Well, why not?

WITHERSPOON: [*To* MORTIMER] It's sweet of them to want to, but it's impossible. You see, we can't take *sane* people at Happy Dale.

MARTHA: Mr. Witherspoon, if you'll let us live there with Teddy, we'll see that Happy Dale is in our will and for a very generous amount.

WITHERSPOON: The Lord knows we could use the money, but I'm afraid . . .

ROONEY: Now, let's be sensible about this, ladies. For instance, here I am wasting my morning when I've got serious work to do. You know there are still *murders* to be solved in Brooklyn.

MORTIMER: Yes! [*He remembers a few*] Oh, are there?

ROONEY: It ain't only his bugle-blowing and the neighbors all afraid of him, but things would just get worse. Sooner or later we'd be put to the trouble of digging up your cellar.

ABBY: Our cellar?

ROONEY: Yeah—your nephew is telling around that there are thirteen bodies buried in your cellar.

ABBY: But there are thirteen bodies in our cellar.

MARTHA: If that's why you think Teddy has to go away—you come down to the cellar with us and we'll prove it to you.

ABBY: There's one, Mr. Spenalzo—who doesn't belong there and is going to have to leave—and the other twelve are our gentlemen.

[MORTIMER *crosses and stands in front of the cellar door to head them off*]

MORTIMER: I don't think the Lieutenant wants to go down in the cellar. He was just telling me that last year he had to dig up a half-acre lot—weren't you, Lieutenant?

ABBY: Oh, he doesn't have to dig here. The graves are all marked. We put flowers on them every Sunday.

ROONEY: Flowers? [*He thinks that one over and looks at* WITHER-SPOON] Superintendent—don't you think you can find room for these ladies?

WITHERSPOON: Well, I . . .

ABBY: You come along with us—and see the graves.

ROONEY: I'll take your word for it, lady—I'm a busy man. How about it, Super?

WITHERSPOON: They'd have to be committed.

MORTIMER: Teddy committed himself. Can't they do that? Can't they sign the papers?

WITHERSPOON: Certainly.

MARTHA: Oh, if we can go with Teddy we'll sign the papers. Where are they?

ABBY: Yes, where are they?

> [*The sisters cross to the table and sit, ready to sign.* WITHERSPOON *produces the papers from his briefcase.* KLEIN *enters from kitchen*]

KLEIN: [*To* ROONEY] He's coming around, Lieutenant.

ABBY: Good morning, Mr. Klein.

MARTHA: Good morning, Mr. Klein. Are you here, too?

KLEIN: Yeah, me and Brophy have got your other nephew out in the kitchen.

ROONEY: Sign 'em up, Superintendent. I want to get this all cleaned up. Thirteen bodies!

> [*He and* KLEIN *exit into the kitchen.* WITHERSPOON *and* MORTIMER *produce fountain pens*]

WITHERSPOON: [*To* MARTHA] If you'll sign right here.

> [MARTHA *takes his pen*]

MORTIMER: [*Handing* ABBY *his pen*] And you here, Aunt Abby.

ABBY: I'm really looking forward to going. The neighborhood here has changed so.

MARTHA: Just think, a front lawn again!

> [*They both sign.* EINSTEIN *enters on the balcony and comes downstairs stealthily*]

WITHERSPOON: Oh—we're overlooking something.

MARTHA: What?

WITHERSPOON: Well, we're going to need the signature of a physician.

> [MORTIMER *straightens up, sees* EINSTEIN *slipping out the door*]

MORTIMER: Oh, Dr. Einstein! Will you come over here and sign some papers?

EINSTEIN: Please . . .

MORTIMER: Come right along, Doctor. At one time last night, I thought the doctor was going to operate on me. [EINSTEIN *crosses nervously to the table*] Just sign right here.

> [ROONEY *enters and goes to the telephone, unseen by* EINSTEIN, *and starts dialing.* KLEIN *has come in through the kitchen door*]

ABBY: Were you leaving, Doctor?

EINSTEIN: Yes, I think so.

MARTHA: Aren't you going to wait for Jonathan?

EINSTEIN: I don't think we're going to the same place.

> [EINSTEIN *signs the papers hurriedly.* MORTIMER *suddenly rediscovers* ELAINE *patiently sitting on the window seat*]

MORTIMER: Oh, hello, darling! Glad to see you. Stick around.

ELAINE: Don't worry. I'm going to.

ROONEY: [*Into the telephone*] Hello, Mac? Rooney. We've picked up that guy that's wanted in Indiana. There's a description of his accomplice on the circular—it's right on the desk there. Read it to me. [EINSTEIN *starts for the kitchen but sees* KLEIN. *He retreats toward the front door but is stopped by* ROONEY's *voice.* ROONEY's *eyes are somewhat blankly on* EINSTEIN *through the following description*] Yeah—about fifty-four—five-foot-six—a hundred and forty pounds—blue eyes—talks with a German accent—poses as a doctor— Thanks, Mac.

> [*He hangs up*]

WITHERSPOON: [*To* ROONEY] It's all right, Lieutenant. The doctor here has just completed the signatures.

ROONEY: [*Going to* EINSTEIN *and shaking his hand*] Thanks, Doc. You're really doing Brooklyn a service.

> [ROONEY *and* KLEIN *exit into kitchen*]

EINSTEIN: [*Bolts for the front door*] If you'll excuse me, I'd better hurry.

> [*He exits, waving a good-bye. The aunts wave gaily back*]

WITHERSPOON: [*To* MORTIMER] Mr. Brewster, you sign now as next of kin.

ABBY: [*A little upset by this*] Martha . . .

[*The sisters go into a huddle*]

MORTIMER: Oh, yes, of course. Right here?

[*He signs the papers*]

WITHERSPOON: Yes. . . . That's fine.

MORTIMER: That makes everything complete? Everything legal?

WITHERSPOON: Oh, yes.

MORTIMER: Well, Aunties, now you're safe!

WITHERSPOON: [*To the aunts*] When do you think you'll be ready to start?

ABBY: [*Nervously*] Well, Mr. Witherspoon, why don't you go up and tell Teddy what he can take along?

WITHERSPOON: Upstairs?

[*He starts across the room*]

MORTIMER: I'll show you.

[*He starts, but* ABBY *stops him*]

ABBY: No, Mortimer, you stay here. We want to talk to you. [*To* WITHERSPOON] Just up the stairs and turn left.

[WITHERSPOON *starts up, the sisters keeping an eye on him while talking to* MORTIMER]

MARTHA: Mortimer, now that we're moving—this house is really yours.

ABBY: Yes, Mortimer, we want you to live here.

MORTIMER: No, Aunt Abby, I couldn't do that. This house is too full of memories.

MARTHA: But you'll need a home when you and Elaine are married.

MORTIMER: Darlings, that's very indefinite.

ELAINE: [*Still in there fighting*] It's nothing of the kind. We're going to be married right away.

[*The sisters watch* WITHERSPOON *as he exits through the balcony door, then turn to* MORTIMER]

ABBY: Mortimer, we're really very worried about something.

MORTIMER: Now, Aunt Abby, you're going to love it at Happy Dale.

MARTHA: Oh, yes, we're very happy about the whole thing! That's just it! We don't want anything to go wrong.

ABBY: Will they investigate those signatures?

MORTIMER: Now, don't worry—they're not going to look up Dr. Einstein.

MARTHA: It's not his signature, dear, it's yours.

ABBY: You see, you signed as next of kin.

MORTIMER: Of course. Why not?

MARTHA: It's something we've never wanted to tell you, Mortimer. But now you're a man—and it's something Elaine should know, too. You see, you're not really a Brewster.

[MORTIMER *stares*]

ABBY: Your mother came to us as a cook—and you were born about three months afterward. But she was such a sweet woman—and such a good cook—and we didn't want to lose her—so brother married her.

MORTIMER: I'm—not—really—a—Brewster?

MARTHA: Now don't feel badly about it, Mortimer.

ABBY: And you won't let it make any difference, Elaine?

MORTIMER: Elaine! Did you hear—do you understand? I'm a bastard!

[ELAINE *leaps into his illegitimate arms*]

MARTHA: [*Relieved*] Well, I'll have to see about breakfast.

[*She starts for the kitchen*]

ELAINE: Mortimer's coming to my house. Father's gone to Philadelphia and Mortimer and I are going to have breakfast together.

MORTIMER: Yes, I need some coffee. I've had quite a night.

ABBY: Well, Mortimer, in that case, I should think you'd want to get to bed.

MORTIMER: [*With a glance at* ELAINE] I do.

[*He leads her out.* ABBY *closes the door.* WITHERSPOON *enters from balcony door, carrying an armful of canteens.* TEDDY *enters with an enormous, two-bladed canoe paddle*]

TEDDY: Just a minute, Mr. Witherspoon. Take this with you!

[*He hands the paddle to* WITHERSPOON *and goes back through the balcony door.* WITHERSPOON, *encumbered, comes downstairs.* ROONEY *enters from the kitchen, followed by* JONATHAN, *handcuffed to* KLEIN *and* BROPHY]

ROONEY: We won't need the wagon. My car's out front.

MARTHA: [*Pleasantly*] Oh, you leaving now, Jonathan?

ROONEY: Yes. He's going to Indiana. Some people out there want to take care of him the rest of his life. [*To* JONATHAN] Come on.

[*The handcuffed three start*]

ABBY: Well, Jonathan, it's nice to know you have some place to go.

[JONATHAN *stops*]

JONATHAN: Good-bye, Aunt Abby. Good-bye, Aunt Martha.

MARTHA: We're leaving, too.

ABBY: We're going to Happy Dale.

JONATHAN: Then this house is seeing the last of the Brewsters.

MARTHA: Unless Mortimer would like to live here.

JONATHAN: I have a suggestion. Why don't you turn this property over to the church?

[*The aunts look at each other*]

ABBY: Well, we never thought of that.

JONATHAN: [*Dryly*] After all, it *should* be a part of the cemetery. [*He starts, then turns back*] Well, I won't be able to better my record now, but neither will you. At least, I have that satisfaction. The score stands even—*twelve* to *twelve.*

[JONATHAN *and the policemen exit. The aunts bristle slightly, looking out after* JONATHAN]

MARTHA: Jonathan always was a mean boy. He never could stand to see anyone get ahead of him.

[*She closes the door*]

ABBY: I wish we could show him he isn't so smart! [*She turns and her eyes fall on* WITHERSPOON, *standing looking out the window. She studies him.* MARTHA *turns from the door and sees* ABBY's *contemplation*] Mr. Witherspoon, does your family live with you at Happy Dale?

WITHERSPOON: I have no family.

ABBY: Oh . . .

MARTHA: Well, I suppose you consider everyone at Happy Dale your family?

WITHERSPOON: I'm afraid you don't understand. As head of the institution, I have to keep quite aloof.

ABBY: That must make it very lonely for you.

WITHERSPOON: It does. But my duty is my duty.

ABBY: [*Benignly*] Well, Martha . . . [MARTHA *immediately starts for the sideboard*] If Mr. Witherspoon won't have breakfast with us, I think at least we should offer him a glass of elderberry wine.

WITHERSPOON: Elderberry wine?

[MARTHA *takes out a wine bottle but it is the one* EINSTEIN *has emptied. She reaches in for another*]

MARTHA: We make it ourselves.

[*She uncorks the fresh bottle*]

WITHERSPOON: Why, yes! Of course, at Happy Dale our relationship will be more formal, but here . . . [*He sits, as* MARTHA *brings the wine with a single wine glass to the table*] You don't see much elderberry wine nowadays. I thought I'd had my last glass of it.

ABBY: Oh, no . . .

MARTHA: [*Handing it to him*] Here it is!

[WITHERSPOON *bows to the ladies and lifts the glass to his lips, but* THE CURTAIN FALLS *before he does*]

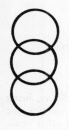

Angel Street

A VICTORIAN THRILLER

PATRICK HAMILTON

Patrick Hamilton

When Patrick Hamilton died in 1962, it was said editorially of him: "For more than thirty years Patrick Hamilton raised goose pimples on millions of theatregoers, and his plays are likely to continue to do so as long as thriller melodramas remain popular." There was more truth than poetry to this journalistic eulogy, for Hamilton's celebrated Victorian melodrama, *Angel Street*, remains to this day one of the most frequently revived of all suspense dramas.

Its perennial allurement may be attributed to a combination of factors. It is a work that never permits the attention to wander even for the briefest moment; characters, situation, and dialogue all minister to the desired thrill. It is compact in construction, economical in style, and as the British historian J. C. Trewin has said, "*Angel Street* has always kept a throat-constricting power, one bred of narrative and atmosphere and with an effect unfailing in performance, the *frisson* of the rising and falling light."

Undoubtedly Patrick Hamilton, who could drill upon the nerves as subtly as any writer, was familiar with the principles of the Grand Guignol. But unlike the French, who relied heavily on startling tricks and too little upon elemental passion, his period thriller is stripped down to the bare essentials to provide concentrated and deeply felt horror. As Ernest Short has observed in his survey, *Sixty Years of Theatre*: "In all plays of the Grand Guignol order, dramatist, players and director must concentrate upon the all-important unity of theme and presentation. All the dramatic elements must be interwoven, as the vital elements are associated in a living body. Psychological truth, love interests, charm of scenery must be sacrificed ruthlessly to the single end, the enchaining of the imagination to a compelling absorption in the terrible or the painful, for terror and pain (much as the individual may dislike them) are among the legitimate theatrical thrills."

When the play was presented in England in 1938, it was known as *Gaslight* (as was the subsequent film version that co-starred Ingrid Bergman and Charles Boyer). Following an engagement at the Richmond Theatre, it was brought to London where the Manninghams set up their rather demoniac housekeeping at the Apollo Theatre. Reports of its success gradually crossed the Atlantic and in due course contracts were arranged for an American presentation. Before its Broadway debut, however, the play encountered almost as many anxious moments as did the terrorized Mrs. Manningham. After a West Coast tryout that made little dent, Broadway regarded its chances for survival as practically nil. Production money was tight, and according to theatrical lore, when the play finally did manage to raise its curtain at the John Golden Theatre, tickets had been printed to cover only the opening night and the subsequent Saturday matinee and evening performances. In short, as the Broadway skeptics had prophesied, the Manninghams soon were destined to take up a more permanent residence at Cain's Warehouse. And as if that were not quite enough, the Victorian thriller opened on December 5, 1941, two days before Pearl Harbor.

Yet, the actualities of the theatre can be as astonishing as any piece of fiction, perhaps more so, and *Angel Street* reversed course and became an instant smash hit. It ran for over three years, achieving a record of 1,295 performances, making it one of the ten longest-running nonmusical plays in Broadway history.

New York's professional aisle-sitters were generous in their praise for both play and production. Brooks Atkinson, from his lofty perch at *The New York Times*, sounded the clarion call that led directly to the box office of the John Golden Theatre: "As a creep show, Patrick Hamilton's Victorian melodrama remains close to the top of the class—literate and harrowing simultaneously." His colleagues were in accordance: "One of the most satisfying theatre adventures of the last decade . . . it really can keep you anchored to your seat bolt upright . . . a masterpiece of suspense."

Two occasional, but highly influential, drama assessors, Eleanor

Roosevelt and Alexander Woollcott, presently joined in the chorus of commendation. Mrs. Roosevelt, as much at home with the arts as she was with politics, advised the devotees of her syndicated column, *My Day:* "In the evening we went to see *Angel Street* which I recommend to anyone who wants to be absorbed and taken out of his daily round of interests. You sit on the edge of your chair most of the time and it is really a grand mystery story." Woollcott, a man never to be outranked, chirped to his own faithful: "Not in ten years at least have I seen an audience, including myself, so spellbound by a melodrama."

The verdict was in. . . .

Patrick Hamilton was born in Sussex, England, on March 17, 1904. Educated at Westminster, he began his association with the theatre as an actor and made his first appearance on stage in 1921. He established himself as a playwright with *Rope,* a 1929 drama of two Oxford undergraduates who commit murder for thrills. Although Hamilton always stoutly denied that it was suggested by the notorious Leopold-Loeb murder case in Chicago, the parallel proved beneficial to the play's long career. Among the author's other works for the stage are: *John Brown's Body; The Duke in Darkness;* and *The Man Upstairs.* An accomplished novelist as well as dramatist, he published his first novel, *Monday Morning,* before he was twenty. Additional novels followed at brief intervals, but he is best known, perhaps, in the United States for *Hangover Square.*

In his foreword to *Rope,* Patrick Hamilton stated his credo as a dramatist: "I have gone all out to write a horror play and make your flesh creep. And there is no reason to believe that this reaction is medically or chemically any worse for you than making you laugh or cry. If I have succeeded, you will leave the theatre braced and recreated which is what you go to the theatre for."

Angel Street was first presented under the title, *Gaslight*, at the Richmond Theatre, Richmond, England, on December 5, 1938. The cast was as follows:

MRS. MANNINGHAM	*Gwen Ffrangcon-Davies*
MR. MANNINGHAM	*Dennis Arundell*
ROUGH	*Milton Rosmer*
ELIZABETH	*Beatrice Rowe*
NANCY	*Elizabeth Inglis*
Directed by	Gardner Davies

(*Gaslight* opened in London at the Apollo Theatre on January 31, 1939, under the auspices of O'Bryen, Linnit & Dunfee Ltd., in association with Alec L. Rea.)

Angel Street was first produced in the United States at the John Golden Theatre, New York, on December 5, 1941, by Shepard Traube (in association with Alexander H. Cohen). The cast was as follows:

MRS. MANNINGHAM	*Judith Evelyn*
MR. MANNINGHAM	*Vincent Price*
NANCY	*Elizabeth Eustis*
ELIZABETH	*Florence Edney*
ROUGH	*Leo G. Carroll*

Directed by	Shepard Traube
Setting and Costumes by	Lemuel Ayers
Lighting by	Feder

The entire action of the play occurs in a house on Angel Street, located in the Pimlico district of London. The time is 1880.

ACT ONE

Late afternoon.

ACT TWO

Immediately afterward.

ACT THREE

Later the same night.

ACT ONE

The scene is a living room on the first floor of a four-storied house in a gloomy and unfashionable quarter of London, in the latter part of the last century. The room is furnished in all the heavily draped and dingy profusion of the period, and yet, amidst this abundance of paraphernalia, an air is breathed of poverty, wretchedness and age.

Fireplace down right. Door at right above fireplace leading to little room. Settee below fireplace with stool in front of it. Table center with chairs right and left of it. Window at left. Desk in front of window with chairs back and above it. Secretary against wall up right. Lamp on table. Sliding double doors at back left center leading to hall, to left the front door, to right the servants' quarters. A circular stair leading to the upper floors is at back up right center. Chairs down right and left.

The curtain rises upon the rather terrifying darkness of the late afternoon—the zero hour, as it were, before the feeble dawn of gas light and tea. In front of the fire, on the settee, MANNINGHAM is stretched out and sleeping heavily. He is tall, good-looking, about forty-five. He is heavily moustached and bearded and perhaps a little too well dressed. His manner is suave and authoritative, with a touch of mystery and bitterness. MRS. MANNINGHAM is sitting sewing on the chair left of the table. She is about thirty-four. She has been good-looking, almost a beauty —but now she has a haggard, wan, frightened air, with rings under her eyes, which tell of sleepless nights and worse.

Big Ben strikes five. Pause. From the street below, in the distance, can be heard the intermittent jingling of a muffin-man ringing his bell.

MRS. MANNINGHAM *listens to this sound for a few moments, furtively and indecisively, almost as though she is frightened even of this. Then she rustles quickly over to the window and looks down into the street. Then to the bell cord by the door, which she pulls. Then back to her sewing, which she gathers up and puts into a box, at the same time taking a purse therefrom. There is a knock at the door, and* ELIZABETH, *the cook and housekeeper, enters. She is a stout, amiable, subservient woman of about fifty. Signaling that her husband is asleep,* MRS. MANNINGHAM *goes over and whispers to her at the door, giving her some money from the purse.* ELIZABETH *goes out closing the doors.*

MR. MANNINGHAM: [*Whose eyes have opened, but whose position has not changed a fraction of an inch*] What are you doing, Bella?

MRS. MANNINGHAM: Nothing, dear. [*She crosses quietly and quickly to the secretary with her sewing and starts back to the doors*] Don't wake yourself.

[*There is a pause. She starts to window*]

MR. MANNINGHAM: [*Whose eyes are closed again*] What are you doing, Bella? Come here . . .

MRS. MANNINGHAM: [*After hesitating, going to him*] Only for tea, my dear. Muffins—for tea— [*She takes his hand*]

MR. MANNINGHAM: Muffins—eh—?

MRS. MANNINGHAM: Yes, dear— He only comes so seldom—I thought I might surprise you.

MR. MANNINGHAM: Why are you so apprehensive, Bella? I was not about to reproach you.

MRS. MANNINGHAM: [*Nervously releasing her hand*] No, dear. I know you weren't.

MR. MANNINGHAM: That fire's in ashes. Ring the bell, will you, Bella dear, please?

MRS. MANNINGHAM: Yes . . . [*She is going over to bell, but stops*] Is it merely to put coal on, my dear? I can do that.

MR. MANNINGHAM: Now then, Bella. We've had this out before. Be so good as to ring the bell.

MRS. MANNINGHAM: But, dear—Lizzie's out in the street. Let me do it. I can do it so easily. [*She comes over to do it*]

MR. MANNINGHAM: [*Stopping her with outstretched hand*] No, no, no, no, no . . . Where's the girl? Let the girl come up if Lizzie's out.

MRS. MANNINGHAM: But, my dear . . .

MR. MANNINGHAM: Go and ring the bell, please, Bella—there's a good child. [MRS. MANNINGHAM *gives in, and goes back to ring the bell*] Now, come here. [*She does so*] What do you suppose the servants are for, Bella? [MRS. MANNINGHAM *does not answer. There is a pause; then gently*] Go on. Answer me. [*He rises*] What do you suppose servants are for?

MRS. MANNINGHAM: [*Shamefacedly, and scarcely audible, merely dutifully feeding him*] To serve us, I suppose, Jack—

MR. MANNINGHAM: Precisely. Then why—?

MRS. MANNINGHAM: But I think we should consider them a little, that's all.

MR. MANNINGHAM: Consider them? There's your extraordinary confusion of mind again. You speak as though they work for no consideration. I happen to consider Elizabeth to the tune of sixteen pounds per annum. And the girl ten. Twenty-six pounds a year all told. And if that is not consideration of the most acute and lively kind, I should like to know what is.

MRS. MANNINGHAM: Yes, Jack. I expect you are right.

MR. MANNINGHAM: I have no doubt of it, my dear. It's sheer weakmindedness to think otherwise. [*Pause*] What's the weather doing? Is it still as yellow?

MRS. MANNINGHAM: Yes, it seems to be denser than ever. Shall you be going out in this, Jack dear?

MR. MANNINGHAM: Oh—I expect so. Unless it gets very much worse after tea.

[*There is a knock at the door.* MRS. MANNINGHAM *hesitates. There is another knock*]

Come in.

[*Enter* NANCY, *the maid. She is a self-conscious, pretty, cheeky girl of nineteen*]

NANCY: [*Stands looking at both, as* MRS. MANNINGHAM *hesitates to tell her why she rang the bell*] Oh, I beg your pardon. I thought the bell rang—

MR. MANNINGHAM: Yes, we rang the bell, Nancy— [*Pause*] Go on, my dear, tell her why we rang the bell.

MRS. MANNINGHAM: Oh— Yes— We want some coal on the fire, Nancy, please.

[NANCY *looks at her impudently, and then, with a little smile and toss of the head, goes over to put coal on the fire*]

MR. MANNINGHAM: [*After pause*] And you might as well light the gas, Nancy. This darkness in the afternoon is getting beyond endurance.

NANCY: Yes, sir.

[*With another barely discernible little smile, she gets the matches, and goes to light the two incandescent mantles on each side of the fireplace. Manningham watches her as she lights the second mantle*]

MR. MANNINGHAM: You're looking very impudent and pretty this afternoon, Nancy. Do you know that?

NANCY: I don't know at all, sir, I'm sure.

MR. MANNINGHAM: What is it? Another broken heart added to your list?

NANCY: I wasn't aware of breaking any hearts, sir.

MR. MANNINGHAM: I'm sure that's not true. And that complexion of yours. That's not true, either. I wonder what mysterious lotions you've been employing to enhance your natural beauties.

NANCY: I'm quite natural, sir, I promise you. [*Crosses to light lamp on table*]

MR. MANNINGHAM: But you do it adroitly, I grant you that. What are your secrets? Won't you tell us the name of your chemist? Perhaps you could pass it on to Mrs. Manningham—and help banish her pallor. She would be most grateful, I have no doubt.

NANCY: I'd be most happy to, I'm sure, sir.

MR. MANNINGHAM: Or are women too jealous of their discoveries to pass them on to a rival?

NANCY: I don't know, sir— Will that be all you're wanting, sir?

MR. MANNINGHAM: Yes. That's all I want, Nancy— Except my tea.

NANCY: It'll be coming directly, sir.

[NANCY *goes out*]

MRS. MANNINGHAM: [*After a pause, reproachfully rather than angrily*] Oh, Jack, how *can* you treat me like that?

MR. MANNINGHAM: But, my dear, you're the mistress of the house. It was your business to tell her to put the coal on.

MRS. MANNINGHAM: It *isn't* that! It's humiliating me like that. As though I'd do anything to my face, and ask for *her* assistance if I did.

MR. MANNINGHAM: But you seem to look on servants as our natural equals. So I treated her as one. [*Sits down on settee and picks up newspaper*] Besides, I was only trifling with her.

MRS. MANNINGHAM: It's strange that you can't see how you hurt me. That girl laughs at me enough already.

MR. MANNINGHAM: Laughs at you? What an idea. What makes you think she laughs at you?

MRS. MANNINGHAM: Oh—I know that she does in secret. In fact, she does so openly—more openly every day.

MR. MANNINGHAM: But, my dear—if she does that, doesn't the fault lie with you?

MRS. MANNINGHAM: [*Pause*] You mean that I'm a laughable person?

MR. MANNINGHAM: I don't mean anything. It's you who read meanings into everything, Bella dear. I wish you weren't such a perfect little silly. Come here and stop it. I've just thought of something rather nice.

MRS. MANNINGHAM: Something nice? What have you thought of, Jack?

MR. MANNINGHAM: I shan't tell you unless you come here.

MRS. MANNINGHAM: [*Going over and sitting on stool beside him*] What is it, Jack? What have you thought of?

MR. MANNINGHAM: I read here that Mr. MacNaughton—the celebrated actor—is in London for another season.

MRS. MANNINGHAM: Yes. I read that. What of it, Jack?

MR. MANNINGHAM: What of it? What do you suppose?

MRS. MANNINGHAM: Oh, Jack dear. Do you mean it? Would you take me to see MacNaughton? You wouldn't take me to see MacNaughton, would you?

MR. MANNINGHAM: I not only would take you to see MacNaughton, my dear. I *am* going to take you to see MacNaughton. That is, if you want to go.

MRS. MANNINGHAM: Oh, Jack! What heaven—what heaven!

MR. MANNINGHAM: When would you like to go? You have only three weeks, according to his advertisement.

MRS. MANNINGHAM: Oh—what perfect heaven! Let me see. Do let me see!

MR. MANNINGHAM: There. You see? You can see him in comedy or tragedy—according to your choice. Which would you prefer, Bella —the comedy or the tragedy?

MRS. MANNINGHAM: Oh—it's so hard to say! Either would be equally wonderful. Which would you choose, if you were me?

MR. MANNINGHAM: Well—it depends—doesn't it—upon whether you want to laugh, or whether you want to cry.

MRS. MANNINGHAM: Oh—I want to laugh. But then, I should like to cry, too. In fact, I should like to do both. Oh, Jack, what made you decide to take me?

MR. MANNINGHAM: Well, my dear, you've been very good lately, and I thought it would be well to take you out of yourself.

MRS. MANNINGHAM: Oh, Jack dear. You have been so much kinder lately. Is it possible you're beginning to see my point of view?

MR. MANNINGHAM: I don't know that I ever differed from it, did I, Bella?

MRS. MANNINGHAM: Oh, Jack dear. It's true. It's true. All I need is to be taken out of myself—some little change—to have some attention from you. Oh, Jack, I'd be *better*—I could really try to be better

—you know in what way—if only I could get *out* of myself a little more.

MR. MANNINGHAM: How do you mean, my dear, exactly, *better?*

MRS. MANNINGHAM: You know . . . You know in what way, dear. About all that's happened lately. We said we wouldn't speak about it.

MR. MANNINGHAM: Oh, no—don't let's speak about that.

MRS. MANNINGHAM: No, dear, I don't want to—but what I say is so important. I *have* been better—even in the last week. Haven't you noticed it? And why is it? Because you have stayed in, and been kind to me. The other night when you stayed in and played cards with me, it was like old days, and I went to bed feeling a normal, happy, healthy, human being. And then, the day after, when you read your book to me, Jack, and we sat by the fire, I felt all my love for you coming back, then, Jack. And I slept that night like a child. All those ghastly dreads and terrible, terrible fears seemed to have vanished. And all just because you had given me your time, and taken me from brooding on myself in this house all day and night.

MR. MANNINGHAM: I wonder if it is that—or whether it's merely that your medicine is beginning to benefit you?

MRS. MANNINGHAM: No, Jack dear, it's not my medicine. I've taken my medicine religiously—haven't I taken it religiously? Much as I detest it! It's more than medicine that I want. It's the medicine of a sweet, sane mind, of interest in something. Don't you see what I mean?

MR. MANNINGHAM: Well—we *are* talking about gloomy subjects, aren't we?

MRS. MANNINGHAM: Yes. I don't want to be gloomy, dear—that's the last thing I want to be. I only want you to understand. Say you understand.

MR. MANNINGHAM: Well, dear. Don't I seem to? Haven't I just said I'm taking you to the theatre?

MRS. MANNINGHAM: Yes, dear— Yes, you have. Oh, and you've made me so happy—so happy, dear.

MR. MANNINGHAM: Well, then, which is it to be—the comedy or the tragedy. You must make up your mind.

MRS. MANNINGHAM: [*With exulting solemnity*] Oh, Jack, which *shall* it be? [*Rising and showing her pleasure with delighted gestures*] What *shall* it be? It matters so little! It matters so wonderfully little! I'm going to the play! Do you understand that, my husband! I'm going to the play! [*She throws her arms around him and kisses him. There is a knock on the door*] Come in. [*Enter* NANCY, *carrying tray. Pause, as she starts to desk*] No, Nancy, I think we'll have it on the table today.

NANCY: [*Still with impudence*] Oh—just as you wish, madam.

[*Pause, as she puts tray on table, arranges cups and puts books, etc., on one side*]

MRS. MANNINGHAM: [*At mantelpiece*] Tell me, Nancy—if you were being taken to the play, and had to choose between comedy and tragedy, which would *you* choose?

NANCY: Me, madam? Oh—I'd go for the comedy all the time.

MRS. MANNINGHAM: Would you? Why would you choose the comedy, Nancy?

NANCY: I like to laugh, madam, I suppose.

MRS. MANNINGHAM: Do you? Well—I daresay you're right. I must bear it in mind. Mr. Manningham's taking me next week, you see.

NANCY: Oh, yes? I hope you enjoy it. I'll bring the muffins directly.

[*As* NANCY *goes out,* MRS. MANNINGHAM *puts out her tongue at her.* MANNINGHAM *sees this*]

MR. MANNINGHAM: My dear—what are you doing?

MRS. MANNINGHAM: The little beast! Let her put that in her pipe and smoke it.

MR. MANNINGHAM: But what has she done?

MRS. MANNINGHAM: Ah—you don't know her. She tries to torment and score off me all day long. You don't see these things. A man wouldn't. [MR. MANNINGHAM *rises*] She thinks me a poor thing. And now she can suffer the news that you're taking me to the theatre.

MR. MANNINGHAM: I think you imagine things, my dear.

MRS. MANNINGHAM: Oh, no, I don't. We've been too familiar with her. [*Arranging chairs, in an emotionally happy state*] Come along, my dear. You sit one side, and I the other—like two children in the nursery.

MR. MANNINGHAM: [*Stands with back to fire*] You seem wonderfully pleased with yourself, Bella. I must take you to the theatre more often, if this is the result.

MRS. MANNINGHAM: [*Sitting at the table*] Oh, Jack—I wish you could.

MR. MANNINGHAM: I don't really know why we shouldn't. I used to like nothing so much when I was a boy. In fact, you may hardly believe it, but I even had an ambition to be an actor myself at one time.

MRS. MANNINGHAM: I can well believe it, dear. Come along to your tea now.

MR. MANNINGHAM: You know, Bella, that must be a very superb sensation. To take a part and lose yourself entirely in the character of someone else. I flatter myself I could have made an actor.

MRS. MANNINGHAM: [*Pouring tea*] Why, of course, my dear. You were cut out for it. Anyone can see that.

MR. MANNINGHAM: [*Crosses slowly*] No—do you think so—seriously? I always felt a faint tinge of regret. Of course, one would have required training, but I believe I should have made out—and might have reached the top of the tree for all I know.
"To be or not to be. That is the question.
Whether 'tis nobler in the mind to suffer
The slings and arrows of outrageous fortune,
Or to take arms against a sea of troubles,
And, by opposing, end them."

[NANCY *enters, sets the muffin dish down on table during the recitation and goes out*]

MRS. MANNINGHAM: You see how fine your voice is? Oh—you've made a great mistake.

MR. MANNINGHAM: [*Lightly*] I wonder.

MRS. MANNINGHAM: Then if you had been a famous actor, I should have had a free seat to come and watch you every night of my life. And then called for you at the stage door afterwards. Wouldn't that have been paradise?

MR. MANNINGHAM: [*As he sits at the table*] A paradise of which you would soon tire, my dear. I have no doubt that after a few nights you would be staying at home again, just as you do now.

MRS. MANNINGHAM: Oh, no, I wouldn't. I should have to keep my eye on you for all the hussies that would be after you.

MR. MANNINGHAM: There would be hussies after me, would there? That is an added inducement, then.

MRS. MANNINGHAM: Yes—I know it, you wretch. But you wouldn't escape me. [*Lifting cover of muffin dish*] They look delicious. Aren't you glad I thought of them? [*Passes the salt*] Here's some salt. You want heaps of it. Oh, Jack dear, you must forgive me chattering on like this, but I'm feeling so happy.

MR. MANNINGHAM: I can see that, my dear.

MRS. MANNINGHAM: I'm being taken to the play, you see. Here you are. I used to adore these as a child, didn't you? [*Offers muffin to* MR. MANNINGHAM] I wonder how long it is since we had them? We haven't had them since we've been married anyway. Or have we? Have we?

MR. MANNINGHAM: I don't know, I'm sure. [*Suddenly rising, looking at the wall upstage and speaking in a calm, yet menacing way*] I don't know—Bella—

MRS. MANNINGHAM: [*After pause, dropping her voice almost to a whisper*] What is it? What's the matter? What is it now?

MR. MANNINGHAM: [*Walking over to fireplace, and speaking with his back to her*] I have no desire to upset you, Bella, but I have just observed something very much amiss. Will you please rectify it at once, while I am not looking, and we will assume that it has not happened.

MRS. MANNINGHAM: Amiss? What's amiss? For God's sake don't turn your back on me: What has happened?

MR. MANNINGHAM: You know perfectly well what has happened, Bella, and if you will rectify it at once I will say no more about it.

MRS. MANNINGHAM: I don't know. I don't know. You have left your tea. Tell me what it is. Tell me.

MR. MANNINGHAM: Are you trying to make a fool of me, Bella? What I refer to is on the wall behind you. If you will put it back, I will say no more about it.

MRS. MANNINGHAM: The wall behind me? What? [*Turns*] Oh—yes— The picture has been taken down— Yes— The picture— Who has taken it down? Why has it been taken down?

MR. MANNINGHAM: Yes. Why has it been taken down? Why, indeed? You alone can answer that, Bella. Why was it taken down before? Will you please take it from wherever you have hidden it, and put it back on the wall again?

MRS. MANNINGHAM: But I haven't hidden it, Jack. [*Rises*] I didn't do it. Oh, for God's sake look at me. I didn't do it. I don't know where it is. Someone else must have done it.

MR. MANNINGHAM: Someone else? [*Turning to her*] Are you suggesting perhaps that I should play such a fantastic and wicked trick?

MRS. MANNINGHAM: No, dear, no! But someone else. [*Going to him*] Before God, I didn't do it! Someone else, dear, someone else.

MR. MANNINGHAM: [*Shaking her off*] Will you please leave go of me. [*Walking over to bell*] We will see about "someone else."

MRS. MANNINGHAM: Oh, Jack—don't ring the bell. Don't ring it. Don't call the servants to witness my shame. It's not my shame for I haven't done it—but *don't* call the servants! Tell them not to come. [*He has rung the bell. She goes to him*] Let's talk of this between ourselves! Don't call that girl in. Please!

MR. MANNINGHAM: [*Shaking her off violently*] Will you please leave go of me and sit down there! [*She sits in chair above the desk. He goes to fireplace*] Someone else, eh? Well—we shall see. [MRS. MANNINGHAM *sobs*] You had better pull yourself together, hadn't you?—[*There is a knock at the door*] Come in. [*Enter* ELIZABETH] Ah, Elizabeth. Come in please, Elizabeth— Shut the door—well, come in, come into the room. [*She does so*] Now, Elizabeth, do you notice anything amiss in this room?—Look carefully around the walls, and see if you notice anything amiss— [*Pause, as* ELIZABETH *looks around the room and when she sees the space of the missing picture she stands still*] Well, Elizabeth, what do you notice?

ELIZABETH: Nothing, sir— Except the picture's been taken down.

MR. MANNINGHAM: Exactly. The picture has been taken down. You noticed it at once. Now was that picture in its place when you dusted the room this morning?

ELIZABETH: Yes, sir. It was, sir. I don't understand, sir.

MR. MANNINGHAM: Neither do I, Elizabeth, neither do I. And now, before you go, just one question. Was it you who removed that picture, Elizabeth?

ELIZABETH: No, sir. Of course I ain't, sir.

MR. MANNINGHAM: You did not. And have you ever, at any time, removed that picture from its proper place?

ELIZABETH: No, sir. Never, sir. Why should I, sir?

MR. MANNINGHAM: Indeed, why should you?—And now please, Elizabeth, will you kiss that Bible, will you as a token of your truthfulness—fetch that Bible from my desk? [ELIZABETH *hesitates. Then she does so*] Very well, you may go. And please send Nancy in here at once.

ELIZABETH: Yes, sir.

[ELIZABETH *goes out looking at both*]

MRS. MANNINGHAM: [*Going to him*] Jack—spare me that girl. Don't call her in. I'll say anything. I'll say that I did it. I did it, Jack, I did it. Don't have that girl in. Don't!

MR. MANNINGHAM: Will you have the goodness to contain yourself?

[*There is a knock at the door.* MRS. MANNINGHAM *sits again*]

Come in.

NANCY: Yes, sir. Did you want me?

MR. MANNINGHAM: Yes, I do want you, Nancy.—If you will look at the wall behind you, you will see that the picture has gone.

NANCY: [*Going upstage*] Why. My word. So it has. [*Turns*] What a rum go!

MR. MANNINGHAM: I did not ask for any comment on your part, Nancy. Kindly be less insolent and answer what I ask you. Did *you* take that picture down, or did you not?

NANCY: Me? Of course I didn't. [*Comes to him slyly*] What should I want to move it for, sir?

MR. MANNINGHAM: Very good. Now will you kiss that Bible lying there, please, as a solemn oath that you did not—and you may go.

NANCY: Willingly, sir. [*She does so, and places Bible on table again with a little smile*] If I'd done it I'd've—

MR. MANNINGHAM: That is all, Nancy. You may go. [NANCY *goes out.*
Going to Bible as if to replace it on the desk] There! I think we
may now be said to have demonstrated conclusively—

MRS. MANNINGHAM: [*Rises*] Give me that Bible! Give it to me! Let
me kiss it, too! [*Snatches it from him*] There! [*Kisses it*] There!
Do you see? [*Kisses it*] There! Do you see that I kiss it?

MR. MANNINGHAM: For God's sake be careful what you do. Do you
desire to commit sacrilege above all else?

MRS. MANNINGHAM: It is no sacrilege, Jack. Someone else has committed sacrilege. Now see—I swear before God Almighty that I
never touched that picture. [*Kisses it*] There! [*She comes close to
him*]

MR. MANNINGHAM: [*He grabs Bible*] Then, by God, you are mad,
and you don't know what you do. You unhappy wretch—you're
stark gibbering mad—like your wretched mother before you.

MRS. MANNINGHAM: Jack—you promised you would never say that
again.

MR. MANNINGHAM: [*Crosses right. Pause*] The time has come to face
facts, Bella. If this progresses you will not be much longer under *my*
protection.

MRS. MANNINGHAM: Jack—I'm going to make a last appeal to you. I'm
going to make a last appeal. I'm desperate, Jack. Can't you see that
I'm desperate? If you can't, you must have a heart of stone.

MR. MANNINGHAM: [*Turns to her*] Go on. What do you wish to say?

MRS. MANNINGHAM: Jack, I may be going mad, like my poor mother—
but if I am mad, you have got to treat me gently. Jack—before God
—I never lie to you knowingly. If I have taken down that picture
from its place I have not known it. *I have not known it.* If I took
it down on those other occasions I did not know it, either. Jack, if
I steal your things—your rings—your keys—your pencils and your
handkerchiefs, and you find them later at the bottom of my box,
as indeed you do, then I do not know that I have done it— Jack, if
I commit these fantastic, meaningless mischiefs—so meaningless
—why should I take a picture down from its place? If I do all these
things, then I am certainly going off my head, and must be treated
kindly and gently so that I may get well. You must *bear* with me,
Jack, *bear* with me—not storm and rage. God knows I'm trying,

Jack, I'm trying! Oh, for God's sake believe me that I'm trying and be kind to me!

MR. MANNINGHAM: Bella, my dear—have you any idea where that picture is now?

MRS. MANNINGHAM: Yes, yes, I suppose it's behind the secretary.

MR. MANNINGHAM: Will you please go and see?

MRS. MANNINGHAM: [Vaguely] Yes—yes— [She goes to upper end of secretary and produces it] Yes, it's here.

MR. MANNINGHAM: [Reproachfully; as he crosses to the desk, places the Bible on it] Then you did know where it was, Bella. [Turns to her] You did know where it was.

MRS. MANNINGHAM: [As she starts toward him] No! No! I only supposed it was! I only supposed it was because it was found there before! It was found there twice before. Don't you see? I didn't know—I didn't!

MR. MANNINGHAM: There is no sense in walking about the room with a picture in your hand, Bella. Go and put it back in its proper place.

MRS. MANNINGHAM: [Pause, as she hangs the picture on wall, then comes to the back of the chair right of table] Oh, look at our tea. We were having our tea with muffins—

MR. MANNINGHAM: Now, Bella, I said a moment ago that we have got to face facts. And that is what we have got to do. I am not going to say anything at the moment, for my feelings are running too high. In fact, I am going out immediately, and I suggest that you go to your room and lie down for a little in the dark.

MRS. MANNINGHAM: No, no—not my room. For God's sake don't send me to my room!

MR. MANNINGHAM: There is no question of sending you to your room, Bella. You know perfectly well that you may do exactly as you please.

MRS. MANNINGHAM: I feel faint, Jack— [He goes quickly to her and supports her] I feel faint—

MR. MANNINGHAM: Very well— [Leading her to settee] Now, take things quietly and come and lie down, here. Where are your salts? [Crosses to secretary, gets salts and returns to her] Here they are— [Pause] Now, my dear, I am going to leave you in peace—

MRS. MANNINGHAM: [*Eyes closed, reclining*] Have you got to go? Must you go? Must you always leave me alone after these dreadful scenes?

MR. MANNINGHAM: Now, no argument, please. I had to go in any case after tea, and I'm merely leaving you a little earlier, that's all. [*Pause. Going into room up right and returning with undercoat on*] Now is there anything I can get for you?

MRS. MANNINGHAM: No, Jack dear, nothing. You go.

MR. MANNINGHAM: Very good— [*Goes toward his hat and overcoat which are on the chair above desk, and stops*] Oh, by the way, I shall be passing the grocer and I might as well pay that bill of his and get it done with. Where is it, my dear? I gave it to you, didn't I?

MRS. MANNINGHAM: Yes, dear. It's on the secretary. [*Half rising*] I'll—

MR. MANNINGHAM: No, dear—don't move—don't move. I can find it. [*At secretary and begins to rummage*] I shall be glad to get the thing off my chest. Where is it, dear? Is it in one of these drawers?

MRS. MANNINGHAM: No—it's on top. I put it there this afternoon.

MR. MANNINGHAM: All right. We'll find it— We'll find it— Are you sure it's here, dear? There's nothing here except some writing paper.

MRS. MANNINGHAM: [*Half rising and speaking suspiciously*] Jack, I'm quite sure it *is* there. Will you look carefully?

MR. MANNINGHAM: [*Soothingly*] All right, dear. Don't worry. I'll find it. Lie down. It's of no importance, I'll find it— No, it's not here— It must be in one of the drawers—

MRS. MANNINGHAM: [*She has rushed to the secretary*] It is not in one of the drawers! I put it out here on top! You're not going to tell me *this* has gone, are you?

MR. MANNINGHAM: My dear. Calm yourself. Calm yourself!

[*Together*]

MRS. MANNINGHAM: [*Searching frantically*] I laid it out here myself! Where is it? [*Opening and shutting drawers*] Where is it? Now you're going to say I've hidden this!

MR. MANNINGHAM: [*Moving away*] My God!—What new trick is this you're playing upon me?

MRS. MANNINGHAM: It was there this afternoon! I put it there! This is a plot! This is a filthy plot! You're all against me! It's a plot! [*She screams hysterically*]

MR. MANNINGHAM: [*Coming to her and shaking her violently*] Will you control yourself! Will you control yourself!— Listen to me, madam, if you utter another sound I'll knock you down and take you to your room and lock you in darkness for a week. I have been too lenient with you, and I mean to alter my tactics.

MRS. MANNINGHAM: [*Sinks to her knees*] Oh, God help me! God help me!

MR. MANNINGHAM: May God help you, indeed. Now listen to me. I am going to leave you until ten o'clock. In that time you will recover that paper, and admit to me that you have lyingly and purposely concealed it—if not, you will take the consequences. You are going to see a doctor, madam, more than one doctor—[*Puts his hat on and throws his coat over his arm*] and they shall decide what this means. Now do you understand me?

MRS. MANNINGHAM: Oh, God—be patient with me. If I am mad, be patient with me.

MR. MANNINGHAM: I have been patient with you and controlled myself long enough. It is now for you to control yourself, or take the consequences. Think upon that, Bella.

[*He starts to door*]

MRS. MANNINGHAM: Jack—Jack—don't go—Jack—you're still going to take me to the theatre, aren't you?

MR. MANNINGHAM: What a question to ask me at such a time. No, madam, emphatically, I am not. You play fair by me, and I'll play fair by you. But if we are going to be enemies, you and I, you will not prosper, believe me.

[MANNINGHAM *goes out. Whimperingly,* MRS. MANNINGHAM *rises, aiding herself by the mantel, and goes to the secretary searching through the drawers, then crosses to center, looks at the picture and shudders. Then turning to the table, she takes up the pitcher of water from the tea tray, crosses back to the secretary, opens the upper door, gets a glass, then opens a drawer and takes out a paper of medicine. She takes this medicine and follows it with a drink of water. This is obviously, incredibly nasty and almost chokes her. She staggers over to the table and replaces the pitcher of water and then turns down the table lamp. Then crossing to the settee, she sinks down on it with her head toward the fireplace and sobs. She mutters, "Peace—Peace —Peace." She breathes heavily as a clock in the house strikes six. Pause. There is a knock at the door. She does not hear it. There is another knock and* ELIZABETH *enters*]

ELIZABETH: Madam—madam—

MRS. MANNINGHAM: Yes!—Yes!—What is it, Elizabeth? Leave me alone.

ELIZABETH: [*Peering through the darkness*] Madam, there's somebody called.

MRS. MANNINGHAM: Who is it? I don't want to be disturbed.

ELIZABETH: It's a gentleman, madam—he wants to see you.

MRS. MANNINGHAM: Tell him to go, Elizabeth. He wants to see my husband. My husband's out.

ELIZABETH: No, madam—he wants to see you. You must see him, madam.

MRS. MANNINGHAM: Oh, leave me alone. Tell him to go away. I want to be left alone.

ELIZABETH: Madam, madam. I don't know what's going on between you and the Master, but you've got to hold up, madam. You've got to hold up.

MRS. MANNINGHAM: I am going out of my mind, Elizabeth. That's what's going on.

ELIZABETH: Don't talk like that, madam. You've got to be brave. You mustn't go on lying here in the dark, or your mind *will* go. You must see this gentleman. It's *you* he wants—not the Master. He's waiting to see you. Come, madam, it'll take you out of yourself.

MRS. MANNINGHAM: Oh, my God—what new torment is this? I'm not in a fit state, I tell you.

ELIZABETH: [*Crosses to table*] Come, madam, I'll turn up the light. [*She does so. Then, she picks up box of matches, crosses to the desk lamp, lights it*] There. Now you'll be all right.

MRS. MANNINGHAM: Elizabeth! What have you done? I can't have anyone in. I'm not fit to be seen.

ELIZABETH: You look all right, madam. You mustn't take on so. Now —I'll call him in.

> [ELIZABETH *goes to the door, and can be heard calling* "Will you come in, please, sir?" *The front door is heard to slam.* MRS. MANNINGHAM *rises, half paralyzed, then runs over to the mirror above the mantelpiece and adjusts her hair. She stands with her back to the fireplace, waiting.* ELIZABETH *returns, holding back the door.* DETECTIVE ROUGH *enters. He is middle-aged—graying, short, wiry, active, brusque, friendly, overbearing. He has a low warming chuckle and completely dominates the scene from the beginning*]

ROUGH: Thank you— Ah—good evening. [*As he crosses*] Mrs. Manningham, I believe— How are you, Mrs. Manningham?

MRS. MANNINGHAM: [*Shaking hands*] How do you do? I'm very much afraid—

ROUGH: You're very much afraid you don't know me from Adam? That's about the root of the matter, isn't it?

> [ELIZABETH *goes out, closing the doors*]

MRS. MANNINGHAM: Oh, no—it's not that—but no doubt you have come to see my husband?

ROUGH: [*Who is still holding her hand, and looking at her appraisingly*] Oh, no! You couldn't be further out. [*Chuckling*] On the contrary, I have chosen this precise moment to call when I knew your husband was out. May I take off my things and sit down?

MRS. MANNINGHAM: Why, yes, I suppose you may.

ROUGH: You're a good deal younger and more attractive than I thought, you know. But you're looking very pale. Have you been crying?

MRS. MANNINGHAM: Really—I'm afraid I don't understand at all.

ROUGH: You will do so, madam, very shortly. [*Goes left, and begins to remove scarf*] You're the lady who's going off her head, aren't you?

[*He puts his hat on the desk*]

MRS. MANNINGHAM: [*Terrified*] What made you say that? Who are you? What have you come to talk about?

ROUGH: Ah, you're running away with things, Mrs. Manningham, and asking me a good deal I can't answer at once. [*Taking off coat, and putting it on chair down left*] Instead of that, I am going to ask you a question or two— Now, please, will you come here, and give me your hands? [*Pause. She obeys*] Now, Mrs. Manningham, I want you to take a good look at me, and see if you are not looking at someone to whom you can give your trust. I am a perfect stranger to you, and you can read little in my face besides that. But I can read a great deal in yours.

MRS. MANNINGHAM: [*Pause*] What? What can you read in mine?

ROUGH: Why, madam, I can read the tokens of one who has traveled a very long way upon the path of sorrow and doubt—and will have, I fear, to travel a little further yet before she comes to the end. But I fancy she is coming toward the end, for all that. Come now, are you going to trust me, and listen to me?

MRS. MANNINGHAM: [*Pause*] Who are you? God knows I need help.

ROUGH: [*Still holding her hands*] I very much doubt whether God knows anything of the sort, Mrs. Manningham. If He did I believe He would have come to your aid before this. But I am here, and so you must give me your faith.

MRS. MANNINGHAM: [*Withdraws her hands*] Who are you? Are you a doctor?

ROUGH: Nothing so learned, ma'am. Just a plain police detective.

MRS. MANNINGHAM: Police detective?

ROUGH: Yes. Or was some years ago. At any rate, still detective enough to see that you've been interrupted in your tea. Couldn't you start again, and let me have a cup? [*He stands back of chair left of table and holds it for her*]

MRS. MANNINGHAM: Why, yes—yes. I will give you a cup. It only wants water. [*She begins to busy herself with hot water, cup, pot, etc., throughout the ensuing conversation*]

ROUGH: You never heard of the celebrated Sergeant Rough, madam? Sergeant Rough, who solved the Claudesley Diamond Case— Sergeant Rough, who hunted down the Camberwell dogs— Sergeant Rough, who brought Sandham himself to justice. [*He has his hand on back of chair, right of table, as he looks at her*] Or were all such sensations before your time?

MRS. MANNINGHAM: [*Looking up at* ROUGH] Sandham? Why, yes—I have heard of Sandham—the murderer—the Throttler.

ROUGH: Yes—madam—Sandham the Throttler. And you are now looking at the man who gave Sandham to the man who throttled *him*. And that was the common hangman. In fact, Mrs. Manningham—you have in front of you one who was quite a personage in his day—believe it or not.

MRS. MANNINGHAM: [*As she adds water to the tea*] I quite believe it. Won't you sit down? I'm afraid it won't be very hot.

ROUGH: Thank you— [*Sitting*] How long have you been married, Mrs. Manningham?

MRS. MANNINGHAM: [*Pouring tea*] Five years—and a little.

ROUGH: Where have you lived during all that time, Mrs. Manningham? Not here, have you?

MRS. MANNINGHAM: [*Putting milk in his cup and passing it to him*] No—first we went abroad—then we lived in Yorkshire, and then six months ago my husband bought this house.

ROUGH: You bought it?

MRS. MANNINGHAM: Yes. I had a bit of money. My husband thought this was an excellent investment.

ROUGH: You had a bit of money, eh? [*Taking cup*] That's very good. And does your husband always leave you alone like this in the evenings?

MRS. MANNINGHAM: Yes. He goes to his club, I believe, and does business.

ROUGH: Oh, yes— [*He is stirring his tea, thoughtfully*]

MRS. MANNINGHAM: Yes—

ROUGH: And does he give you a free run of the whole house while he's out?

MRS. MANNINGHAM: Yes— Well, no—not the top floor. Why do you ask?

ROUGH: Ah—not the top floor—

MRS. MANNINGHAM: No—no—will you have some sugar?

ROUGH: Thanks.

MRS. MANNINGHAM: [Bending over eagerly to answer his questions] What were you saying?

ROUGH: Before I go any further, Mrs. Manningham, I must tell you there's a leakage in this household. You have a maid called Nancy?

MRS. MANNINGHAM: Yes—yes—

ROUGH: And Nancy walks out of an evening with a young man named Booker in my employ. I only live a few streets away from you, you know.

MRS. MANNINGHAM: Oh, yes?

ROUGH: [With a chuckle] Well, there is hardly anything which goes on in this house, which is not described in detail to Booker, and from that quarter it reaches me.

MRS. MANNINGHAM: I knew it! I knew she talked. Now I know it, she shall be dismissed.

ROUGH: Oh, no—no such retribution is going to overtake her at the moment, Mrs. Manningham. In fact, I fancy you are going to be heavily in debt to your maid, Nancy. If it were not for her indiscretions I should not be here now, should I?

MRS. MANNINGHAM: What do you mean? What is this mystery? You must not keep me in the dark. What is it?

ROUGH: I'm afraid I shall have to keep you in the dark for a little, Mrs. Manningham, as I am still quite far down in the dark myself. Can I have another lump of sugar in this?

MRS. MANNINGHAM: Yes. [Passes bowl to him]

ROUGH: Thank you. [Pause] We were talking about the top floor. [Helping himself to several lumps] There is a bedroom above this, and above that again is the top floor? Is that right?

MRS. MANNINGHAM: Yes. But it's shut up. When we first took the house, my husband said we would not need the upstairs quarters —until there were children.

ROUGH: You've never been up to the top floor, Mrs. Manningham?

[*Pause*]

MRS. MANNINGHAM: No one goes up there.

ROUGH: Not even a servant to dust?

MRS. MANNINGHAM: No.

ROUGH: Rather funny?

MRS. MANNINGHAM: Funny? [*Pause*] I don't know— [*But she does think so*]

ROUGH: I think it is. Now, Mrs. Manningham, to ask a personal question. When did you first get the notion into your head that your reason was playing you tricks?

MRS. MANNINGHAM: [*About to drink her tea. Pause. Looks at* ROUGH *and then sets her cup down*] How did you know?

ROUGH: Never mind how I know. When did it begin?

MRS. MANNINGHAM: I always had that dread. My mother died insane, when she was quite young. When she was my age. But only in the last six months, in this house—things began to happen—

ROUGH: Which are driving you mad with fear?

MRS. MANNINGHAM: Yes. Which are driving me mad with fear.

ROUGH: Is it the house itself you fear, Mrs. Manningham?

MRS. MANNINGHAM: Yes. I suppose it is. I hate the house. I always did.

ROUGH: And has the top floor got anything to do with it?

MRS. MANNINGHAM: Yes, yes, it has. That's how all this dreadful horror began.

ROUGH: Ah—now you interest me beyond measure. Do tell me about the top floor.

MRS. MANNINGHAM: I don't know what to say. It all sounds so incredible— It's when I'm alone at night. I get the idea that—somebody's walking about up there— [*Looking up*] Up there— At night, when my husband's out— I hear noises, from my bedroom, but I'm too afraid to go up—

ROUGH: Have you told your husband about this?

MRS. MANNINGHAM: No. I'm afraid to. He gets angry. He says I imagine things which don't exist—

ROUGH: It never struck you, did it, that it might be your own husband walking about up there?

MRS. MANNINGHAM: Yes—that *is* what I thought—but I thought I must be mad. [*She turns to him*] Tell me how you knew.

ROUGH: Why not tell me first how *you* knew, Mrs. Manningham.

MRS. MANNINGHAM: [*Rises and goes toward fireplace*] It's true, then! It's true. I knew it. I knew it! When he leaves this house he comes back. He comes back and walks up there above—up and down—up and down. He comes back like a ghost. How does he get up there?

ROUGH: [*Rises, crosses to* MRS. MANNINGHAM] That's what we're going to find out, Mrs. Manningham. But there are such commonplace resources as roofs and fire escapes, you know. Now please don't look so frightened. Your husband is no ghost, believe me, and you are very far from mad. [*Pause*] Tell me now, what made you first think it was him?

MRS. MANNINGHAM: It was the light—the gas light— It went down and it went up— Oh, thank God I can tell this to someone at last. I don't know who you are, but I must tell you!

ROUGH: Now try to keep calm. You can tell me just as well sitting down, can't you? Won't you sit down?

MRS. MANNINGHAM: Yes—yes. [*She sits down on settee*]

ROUGH: [*Looks around*] The light, did you say? Did you see a light from a window?

MRS. MANNINGHAM: No. In this house, I can tell everything by the light of the gas. You see the mantle there. Now it's burning full. But if an extra light went on in the kitchen or someone lit it in the bedroom then this one would sink down. It's the same all over the house.

ROUGH: Yes—yes—that's just a question of insufficient pressure, and it's the same in mine. But go on, please.

MRS. MANNINGHAM: [*Pause*] Every night, after he goes out, I find myself waiting for something. Then all at once I look round the room and see that the light is slowly going down. Then I hear tapping sounds—persistent tapping sounds. At first I tried not to notice it, but after a time it began to get on my nerves. I would go all over the house to see if anyone had put on an extra light, but they never had. It's always at the same time—about ten minutes after he goes out. That's what gave me the idea that somehow *he* had come back and that it was *he* who was walking about up there. I go up to the bedroom but I daren't stay there because I hear noises overhead. I want to scream and run out of the house. I sit here for hours, terrified, waiting for him to come back, and I always know when he's coming, always. Suddenly the light goes up again and ten minutes afterwards I hear his key in the lock, and he's back again.

ROUGH: How very strange, indeed. You know, Mrs. Manningham, you should have been a policeman.

MRS. MANNINGHAM: Are you laughing at me? Do you think I imagine everything, too?

ROUGH: Oh, no! I was merely praising the keenness of your observation. I not only think you are right in your suppositions, I think you have made a very remarkable discovery, and one which may have very far-reaching consequences.

MRS. MANNINGHAM: Far-reaching? How?

ROUGH: Well, let's leave that for the moment. Tell me, that is not the only cause, is it, which has lately given you reason to doubt your sanity? Has anything else been happening? [*Pause*] Don't be afraid to tell me.

MRS. MANNINGHAM: Yes, there are other things. I hardly dare speak of them. It has been going on for so long. This business of the gas has only brought it to a head. It seems that my mind and memory are beginning to play me tricks.

ROUGH: Tricks? What sort of tricks? When?

MRS. MANNINGHAM: Incessantly—but more and more of late. He gives me things to look after, and when he asks for them they are gone, and can never be found. Then he misses his rings, or his studs, and I will hunt the place for them, and he will find them lying hidden at the bottom of my workbox. Twice the door of that room [*Looking at door up right*] was found locked with the key vanished. That was also found at the bottom of my box. Only today, before you came, that picture had been taken from the wall and hidden. [ROUGH *looks around at picture*] Who could have done it but myself? I try to remember. [*He turns to her*] I break my heart trying to remember. But I can't. Oh, and then there was that terrible business about the dog—

ROUGH: The dog?

MRS. MANNINGHAM: We have a little dog. A few weeks ago, it was found with its paw hurt.—He believes . . . Oh, God, how can I tell you what he believes—that *I* had hurt the dog. He does not let the dog near me now. He keeps it in the kitchen and I am not allowed to see it! I begin to doubt, don't you see? I begin to believe I imagine everything. Perhaps I do. Are *you* here? Is this a dream, too? Who are you? [*Rises*] I'm afraid they are going to lock me up.

ROUGH: Do you know, Mrs. Manningham, it has occurred to me that you'd be all the better for a little medicine.

MRS. MANNINGHAM: Medicine. Are you a doctor? You're not a doctor, are you?

ROUGH: [*Chuckling*] No, I'm not a doctor, but that doesn't mean that a little medicine would do you any harm.

MRS. MANNINGHAM: But I have medicine. He makes me take it. It does me no good, and I hate it. How can medicine help a mind that's ill?

ROUGH: Oh—but mine's an exceptional medicine. I have some with me now. You must try it.

MRS. MANNINGHAM: What medicine is it?

ROUGH: You shall sample it and see. [*He goes over to his coat*] You see, it has been employed by humanity, for several ages, for the purpose of the instantaneous removal of dark fears and doubts. That seems to fit you, doesn't it?

MRS. MANNINGHAM: The removal of doubt. How could a medicine effect that?

ROUGH: Ah—that we don't know. The fact remains that it does. Here we are. [*Produces what is obviously a bottle of whiskey*] You see, it comes from Scotland. Now, madam, have you such a thing handy as two glasses or a couple of cups?

MRS. MANNINGHAM: Why—are you having some, too?

ROUGH: Oh, yes. I am having some above all things. We could use these cups, if you like.

MRS. MANNINGHAM: No. I will get two—

[*She goes to secretary and brings out two glasses*]

ROUGH: Ah—thank you—the very thing. Now we shan't be long.

MRS. MANNINGHAM: What is it? I so dislike medicine. What does it taste like?

ROUGH: Delicious! Something between ambrosia and methylated spirits. Do you mean to say you've never tasted good Scotch whiskey, Mrs. Manningham?

MRS. MANNINGHAM: Whiskey? But I must not take whiskey. I can't do that!

ROUGH: [*Pouring it out*] You underestimate your powers, Mrs. Manningham. You see, I don't want you thinking you can't trust your reason. This will give you faith in your reason like nothing else— Now for some water— All right this will do. [*Takes water from pitcher and pours it into the glasses*] There! [*Hands glass to her*] Tell me— [*Is pouring water into his own*] Did you ever hear of the Cabman's Friend, Mrs. Manningham?

MRS. MANNINGHAM: The Cabman's Friend?

ROUGH: Yes. How nice to see you smile. Here's your very good health. [*Drinks*] Go on— [*She drinks*] There— Is it so nasty?

MRS. MANNINGHAM: No. I rather like it. My mother used to give us this as children when we had the fever.

ROUGH: Ah, then you're a hardened whiskey drinker. But you'll enjoy it better sitting down.

MRS. MANNINGHAM: Yes. [*Sitting down on chair below fireplace*] What were you saying? Who is the Cabman's Friend?

ROUGH: Ah. The Cabman's Friend. [*Crosses to her*] You should ask me who *was* the Cabman's Friend, Mrs. Manningham, for she was an old lady who died many years ago.

[*Pause, as he puts her whiskey on mantelpiece*]

MRS. MANNINGHAM: An old lady years ago? What has she to do with me?

ROUGH: A great deal, I fancy, if you will follow me patiently. Her name was Barlow—Alice Barlow, and she was an old lady of great wealth, and decided eccentricities. In fact, her principal mania in life was the protection of cabmen. You may think that an extraordinary hobby, but in her odd way she did a lot of good. She provided these men with shelters, clothing, pensions, and so forth, and that was her little contribution to the sum of the world's happiness; or rather her little stand against the sum of the world's pain. There is a great deal of pain in this world, Mrs. Manningham, you know. Well, it was not my privilege to know her, but it was my duty, on just one occasion, to see her. That was when her throat was cut open, and she lay dead on the floor of her own house.

MRS. MANNINGHAM: Oh, how horrible! Do you mean she was murdered?

ROUGH: Yes. She was murdered. I was only a comparatively young officer at the time. It made an extremely horrible, in fact I may say lasting, impression on me. You see the murderer was never discovered but the motive was obvious enough. Her husband had left her the Barlow rubies and it was well known that she kept them, without any proper precautions, in her bedroom on an upper floor. She lived alone except for a deaf servant in the basement. Well, for that she paid the penalty of her life.

MRS. MANNINGHAM: But I don't see—

ROUGH: There were some sensational features about the case. The man seemed to have got in at about ten at night, and stayed till dawn. Apart, presumably, from the famous rubies, there were only a few trinkets taken, but the whole house had been turned upside down, and in the upper room every single thing was flung about, or torn open. Even the cushions of the chairs were ripped up with his bloody knife, and the police decided that it must have been a revengeful maniac as well as a robber. I had other theories, but I was a nobody then, and not in charge of the case.

MRS. MANNINGHAM: What were your theories?

ROUGH: Well, it seemed to me, from all that I gathered here and there, that the old lady might have been an eccentric, but that she was by no means a fool. It seemed to me that she might have been one too clever for this man. We presume he killed her to silence her, but what then? What if she had *not* been so careless? What if she had got those jewels cunningly hidden away in some inconceivable place, in the walls, floored down, bricked in, maybe? What if the only person who could tell him where they were was lying dead on the floor? Would not that account, Mrs. Manningham, for all that strange confusion in which the place was found? Can't you picture him, Mrs. Manningham, searching through the night, ransacking the place, hour after hour, growing more and more desperate, until at last the dawn comes and he has to slink out into the pale street, the blood and wreckage of the night behind? And the deaf servant down in the basement sleeping like a log through it all.

MRS. MANNINGHAM: Oh, how horrible! How horrible indeed! And was the man never found?

ROUGH: No, Mrs. Manningham, the man was never found. Nor have the Barlow rubies ever come to light.

MRS. MANNINGHAM: Then perhaps he found them after all, and may be alive today.

ROUGH: I think he is almost certainly alive today, but I don't believe he found what he wanted. That is, if my theory is right.

MRS. MANNINGHAM: Then the jewels may still be where the old lady hid them?

ROUGH: Indeed, Mrs. Manningham, if my theory is right the jewels *must* still be where she hid them. The official conclusion was quite otherwise. The police, naturally and quite excusably, presumed that the murderer had got them, and there was no re-opening of matters in those days. Soon enough the public forgot about it. I almost forgot about it myself. But it would be funny, wouldn't it, Mrs. Manningham, if after all these years I should turn out to be right.

MRS. MANNINGHAM: Yes, yes, indeed. But what has this to do with me?

ROUGH: Ah, that is the whole question, Mrs. Manningham. What, indeed? What has the obscure murder of an old lady fifteen years ago to do with an attractive, though I am afraid at present, somewhat pale and wan young woman, who believes she is going out of her mind? Well, I believe there is a link, however remote, wild and strange it may be, and that is why I am here.

MRS. MANNINGHAM: It's all so confusing. Won't you—

ROUGH: Do you conceive it possible, Mrs. Manningham, that that man might never have given up hope of one day getting at the treasure which lay there?

MRS. MANNINGHAM: Yes. Yes. Possibly. But how—

ROUGH: Can you conceive that he may have waited years—gone abroad, got married even, until at last his chance came to resume the search begun on that terrible night? [*Crossing down to her*] You don't follow where I am leading at all, do you, Mrs. Manningham?

MRS. MANNINGHAM: Follow you? I think so.

ROUGH: You know, Mrs. Manningham, of the old theory that the criminal always returns to the scene of his crime.

MRS. MANNINGHAM: Yes?

ROUGH: Ah, yes, but in this case there is something more than morbid compulsion— There is real treasure there to be unearthed if only he can search again, search methodically, without fear of interruption, without causing suspicion. And how would he do that? [*All at once she rises*] Don't you think . . . What's the matter, Mrs. Manningham?

MRS. MANNINGHAM: [*As she looks at brackets and backs away*] Quiet! Be quiet! He has come back! Look at the light! It is going down! Wait!

[*Pause, as light sinks*]

There! He has come back, you see. He is upstairs now.

ROUGH: Dear me, now. How very odd that is. How very odd, indeed.

MRS. MANNINGHAM: [*Whispering*] He is in the house, I tell you. You must go. He will know you are here. You must go.

ROUGH: How dark it is. You could hardly see to read.

MRS. MANNINGHAM: You must go. He is in the house. Please go.

ROUGH: [*Quickly coming to her*] Quiet, Mrs. Manningham, quiet! You have got to keep your head. Don't you see my meaning, yet? Don't you understand that this was the house?

MRS. MANNINGHAM: House? What house?

ROUGH: The old woman's house, Mrs. Manningham— This house, here, these rooms, these walls. Fifteen years ago Alice Barlow lay dead on the floor in this room. Fifteen years ago the man who murdered her ransacked this house—below and above—but could not find what he sought. What if he is still searching, Mrs. Manningham? What if he is up there—*still searching?* Now do you see why you must keep your head?

MRS. MANNINGHAM: But my husband, my husband is up there!

ROUGH: Precisely that, Mrs. Manningham. Your husband. [*Going and fetching her drink from mantelpiece*] You see, I am afraid you are married to a tolerably dangerous gentleman. Now drink this quickly, as we have a great deal to do.

[*He stands there, holding out glass to her. She remains motionless*]

CURTAIN

ACT TWO

No time has passed. MRS. MANNINGHAM *takes the whiskey from* ROUGH *in a mechanical way, and stares at him.*

MRS. MANNINGHAM: This house— How do you know this was the house?

ROUGH: Why, ma'am, because I was on the case, and came here myself, that's all.

MRS. MANNINGHAM: The idea is mad. I have been married five years. How can you imagine my husband is—what you imagine he may be?

ROUGH: Mrs. Manningham—

MRS. MANNINGHAM: Yes?—

[*Pause*]

ROUGH: When the police came into this place fifteen years ago, as you can understand there was a great deal of routine work to be done—interviewing of relatives and friends and so forth. Most of that was left to me.

MRS. MANNINGHAM: Well?—

ROUGH: Well, amongst all the acquaintances and relatives, nephews and nieces, etc., that I interviewed, there happened to be a young man of the name of Sydney Power. I suppose you have never heard that name at all, have you?

MRS. MANNINGHAM: Power?—

ROUGH: Yes, Sydney Power. It conveys nothing to you?

MRS. MANNINGHAM: Sydney Power. No—

ROUGH: [*During the following speech, he pours himself out another drink*] Well, he was a kind of distant cousin, apparently much attached to the old lady, and even assisting her in her good works. The only thing was that I remembered his face. Well, I saw that face again just a few weeks ago. It took me a whole day to recollect where I had seen it before, but at last I remembered.

MRS. MANNINGHAM: Well—what of it? What if you did remember him?

ROUGH: It was not so much my remembering Mr. Sydney Power, Mrs. Manningham. What startled me was the lady on his arm, and the locality in which I saw him.

MRS. MANNINGHAM: Oh—who was the lady on his arm?

ROUGH: *You* were the lady on his arm, Mrs. Manningham, and you were walking down this street.

MRS. MANNINGHAM: What are you saying? Do you mean you think my husband—my husband is this Mr. Power?

ROUGH: Well, not exactly, for if my theories are correct— [*He drinks*]

MRS. MANNINGHAM: What are you saying? [*Sits*] You stand there talking riddles. You are so cold. You are as heartless and cold as he is.

ROUGH: No, Mrs. Manningham, I am not cold, and I am not talking riddles. [*Puts his drink on table*] I am just trying to preserve a cold and calculating tone, because you are up against the most awful moment in your life, and your whole future depends on what you are going to do in the next hour. Nothing less. You have got to *strike* for your freedom, and *strike* now, for the moment may not come again.

MRS. MANNINGHAM: Strike—

ROUGH: You are not going out of your mind, Mrs. Manningham. You are slowly, methodically, systematically being *driven* out of your mind. And why? Because you are married to a criminal maniac who is afraid you are beginning to know too much—a criminal maniac who steals back to his own house at night, still searching for something he could not find fifteen years ago. Those are the facts, wild and incredible as they may seem. His name is no more Manningham than mine is. He is Sydney Power and he murdered Alice Barlow in this house. Afterward he changed his name, and he has waited all these years, until he found it safe to acquire this house in a legal way. He then acquired the empty house next door. Every night, for the last few weeks, he has entered that house from the back, climbed up onto its roof and come into this house by the skylight. I know that because I have seen him do it. You have watched the gas light, and, without knowing it, been aware of the same thing. He is up there now. Why he should employ this mad, secretive, circuitous way of getting at what he wants, God Himself only knows. For the same reason perhaps, that he employs this mad, secretive, circuitous way of getting rid of you: that is, by slowly driving you mad and into a lunatic asylum.

MRS. MANNINGHAM: Why?

ROUGH: The fact that you had some money, enough to buy this house is part of it, I expect. For now that he's got that out of you he doesn't need you any longer. Thank God you are not married to him, and that I have come here to save you from the workings of his wicked mind.

MRS. MANNINGHAM: Not married?—Not married?—He married me.

ROUGH: I have no doubt he did, Mrs. Manningham. Unfortunately, or rather fortunately, he contracted the same sort of union with another lady many years before he met you. Moreover the lady is still alive, and the English law has a highly exacting taste in monogamy. You see, I have been finding things out about Mr. Sydney Power.

MRS. MANNINGHAM: Are you speaking the truth? [Rises] My God—are you speaking the truth? Where is this wife now?

ROUGH: I'm afraid, she is the length of the world away—on the continent of Australia to be precise, where I know for a fact he spent two years. Did you know that?

MRS. MANNINGHAM: No. [Pause. She crosses to front of settee and faces fireplace] I—did—not—know—that.

ROUGH: Ah, yes. If only I could find her, things would be easier, and that's the whole root of the matter, Mrs. Manningham. So far I am only dealing in guesses and half facts. I have got to have evidence, and that is why I came to see you. You have got to give me the evidence or help me find it.

MRS. MANNINGHAM: [Turning and facing ROUGH] This is my husband. Don't you understand—this is my husband. He married me. Do you ask me to betray the man who married me?

ROUGH: By which you mean, of course, the man who has betrayed you into thinking that you are married to him—don't you?

MRS. MANNINGHAM: But I'm married to him. You must go. I must

think this out. You must go. I must cling to the man I married.
Mustn't I?

ROUGH: Indeed, cling to him by all means, but do not imagine you are
the only piece of ivy on the garden wall. You can cling to him if
you desire, as his fancy women in the low resorts of the town cling
to him. That is the sort of wall you have to cling to, ma'am.

MRS. MANNINGHAM: [*Sits on settee*] Women? What are you
suggesting?

ROUGH: I'm not suggesting anything. I am only telling you what I
have seen. He comes to life at night, this gentleman upstairs, in
more ways than one. I have made it my business to follow him on
some of his less serious excursions, and I can promise you he has a
taste in *unemployed actresses* which he is at no pains to conceal.

MRS. MANNINGHAM: [*After pause*] God in heaven! . . . what *am* I
to believe?

ROUGH: Mrs. Manningham, it is hard to take everything from you,
but you are no more tied to this man, you are under no more ob-
ligation to him than those wretched women in those places. You
must learn to be thankful for that.

MRS. MANNINGHAM: [*Pause*] What do you want me to do? What do
you want?

ROUGH: I want his papers, Mrs. Manningham—his identity. There is
some clue somewhere in this house, and we have got to get at it.
Where does he keep his papers?

[ROUGH *has now completely changed his tone, and is
striding up and down in a businesslike way*]

MRS. MANNINGHAM: [*Rises*] Papers? I know of no papers. Unless his
bureau—

ROUGH: Yes. His bureau? His bureau?

MRS. MANNINGHAM: Yes. There. [*Points to desk*] But he keeps it always locked. I have never seen it open.

ROUGH: Ah—he keeps it locked, does he?

MRS. MANNINGHAM: It is just his desk—his bureau—

ROUGH: [*Crosses to desk*] Very well. We will have a look inside.

MRS. MANNINGHAM: But it is locked. How can you, if it is locked?

ROUGH: Oh—it doesn't look so very formidable. [*Going to overcoat,*

to fetch ring of keys and implements] You know, Mrs. Manningham, one of the greatest regrets of my life is that fate never made
me one of two things—one was a gardener, the other a burglar—
both quiet occupations, Mrs. Manningham. As for burgling I think,
if I'd started young, and worked my way up, I should have been a
genius. Now let's have a look at this.

MRS. MANNINGHAM: [*Crossing to him at desk*] But you must not
touch this. He will know what you have done.

ROUGH: Come now, ma'am. You're working with me, aren't you—not
against me? [*Looks at desk*] Yes— Yes— Now do you mind if I
take off my coat? I'm a man who never feels at work until his coat's
off. [*He is taking off his coat, and hanging it on chair down left,
revealing a pink fancy shirt*] Quite a saucy shirt, don't you think?
You didn't suspect I was such a dandy, did you? Now. [*Sits at
desk and gets out keys*] Let's have a real look at this.

MRS. MANNINGHAM: [*After a pause*] But you must not tamper with
that. He will know what you have done.

ROUGH: Not if we are clever enough. And this one here doesn't even
ask for cleverness— You see, Mrs. Manningham, there are all manner of . . .

MRS. MANNINGHAM: Stop—stop talking— Haven't you noticed?
Haven't you noticed something?

ROUGH: Noticed? I've only . . .

MRS. MANNINGHAM: Stop! Yes—I was right. Look. Can't you see?
The light! It's going up. He's coming back.

ROUGH: The light?—

MRS. MANNINGHAM: Quiet! [*Pause, after which the light slowly goes
up in a tense silence. Whispering:*] There. It's come back. You see.
You must go. Don't you see? He's coming back— He's coming
back and you must go!

ROUGH: [*Rises*] God bless my soul. This looks as if the unexpected
has entered in.

MRS. MANNINGHAM: Yes. He *always* does the unexpected. I never
know what he'll do. You must go.

ROUGH: [*Without moving, looking up ruminatively*] I wonder. Yes.
Well, well— [*Puts the keys in his pocket and begins to put on his
coat*] Now—will you go and ring that bell for Elizabeth?

MRS. MANNINGHAM: Elizabeth. Why do you want her?

ROUGH: Do as I say, and ring the bell. At once. Please. Or you can go and fetch her if you like. Now let me see.

MRS. MANNINGHAM: [*Ringing bell*] Go, please!—Go, please do! You must go at once. [*Crossing to above desk*] Why do you want Elizabeth?

ROUGH: [*Picks up overcoat, puts it on, then his scarf and crosses below desk to her*] All in good time. He's not going to jump through the window, you know. In fact he can't be round at our front door in less than five minutes—unless he's a magician. Now, can you see anything I've missed?

MRS. MANNINGHAM: No. No. [*Turns and sees whiskey bottle, quickly gets it and gives it to* ROUGH] Yes, the whiskey here.

ROUGH: Oh, yes. I told you you'd make a good policeman. Don't forget the glasses.

MRS. MANNINGHAM: Oh, do go, please, please go!

[ELIZABETH *enters*. MRS. MANNINGHAM *puts glasses away in secretary*]

ROUGH: Ah—Elizabeth—come here, will you?

ELIZABETH: [*Crosses to* ROUGH] Yes, sir?

ROUGH: Elizabeth, you and I have got to do a little quite calm, but rather quick thinking. You've told me you're anxious to help your mistress, Elizabeth?

ELIZABETH: Why, yes, sir, I told you I was, sir. But what's it all about?

ROUGH: Are you anxious to help your mistress, blindly, without asking any questions?

ELIZABETH: Yes, sir. But you see—

ROUGH: Come now, Elizabeth. Are you or are you not?

ELIZABETH: [*After pause, looking at* MRS. MANNINGHAM, *in quiet voice*] Yes, sir.

ROUGH: Good. Now, Elizabeth, Mrs. Manningham and I have reason to suppose that in about five minutes' time the master is returning to this house. He mustn't see me leaving. Would you be good enough to take me down to your kitchen and hide me away for a short space of time? You can put me in the oven if you like.

ELIZABETH: Yes, sir. But you see—

MRS. MANNINGHAM: [As ROUGH *crosses to window and looks out*] You must go! You must go! He won't see you if you go now.

ROUGH: What were you saying, Elizabeth?

ELIZABETH: Yes, sir. You could come to the kitchen. But—Nancy's down there, sir.

ROUGH: Nancy! What the devil's this now? I thought this was Nancy's afternoon off. Was it not arranged that I should come when Nancy was away?

ELIZABETH: [*Agitated*] Yes, sir. But for some reason she's stayed on. I think she's got a young man, and I couldn't make her go, could I, sir? If I'd done that, I'd've—

ROUGH: All right—all right. Then she was here when I came, and she knows I am here—is that it?

ELIZABETH: Oh, no— She was in the scullery when I answered the door, and I said it was a man who had come to the wrong house. She hasn't no idea, sir, and I'm—

ROUGH: All right. All right. That's better news. But it means you can't entertain me in the kitchen. Now where are you going to hide me, Elizabeth? Make up your mind quickly.

ELIZABETH: I don't know, sir. Unless you go to the bedroom. Mine and Nancy's, I mean.

ROUGH: That sounds altogether entrancing! Shall we go there now?

ELIZABETH: Yes, sir, but supposing Nancy went up there before she goes out?

ROUGH: You're a good soul and you think of everything, Elizabeth. [*Going to door up right*] Where does this lead to, and what's the matter with this?

ELIZABETH: [*Crossing to* ROUGH] It's where he dresses, where he keeps his clothes. Yes, sir. Go in there, sir. He won't see you there. There's a big wardrobe there, at the back.

ROUGH: Excuse me. [*He goes through door*]

MRS. MANNINGHAM: Oh, Elizabeth.

ELIZABETH: [*Crosses to* MRS. MANNINGHAM] It's all right, ma'am. Don't take on so. It'll be all right.

MRS. MANNINGHAM: I'm sure he ought to go.

ELIZABETH: No, ma'am. He knows best. He's bound to know best.

ROUGH: [*Coming back*] Perfect accommodation. [*As he trots across*

to window for another peep. Has seen something] Yes, there he is.
Now we really have got to hurry. Get off to bed, Mrs. Manningham,
quick. And you, Elizabeth, go to your room. You can't get downstairs in time. Hurry, please. Elizabeth, turn down that lamp.

[ELIZABETH *does so. He goes to turn down gas*]

MRS. MANNINGHAM: To bed? Am I to go to bed?
ROUGH: [*Really excited for the first time*] Yes, quick. He's coming.
Don't you understand? Go there and stay there. You have a bad
headache—[*He crosses to fireplace and starts to turn down upstage
gas bracket*]—a bad headache. [*Quite angry, turning from gas*]
Will you go, in heaven's name!

> [MRS. MANNINGHAM *goes upstairs and* ELIZABETH *exits,
> leaving the doors open, as* ROUGH *turns down the gas in
> the downstage bracket. There is a light from the hall
> through the open doors.* ROUGH *crosses to the left end of
> of the settee, pauses a moment watching the hall, then,
> nimbly on tiptoes, crosses up to the open doors and listens.
> After a short pause, there is the sound of the front door
> closing. He stiffens and starts to quietly trot to the door up
> right and as he just about reaches it, feels his head, dis-
> covers his hat missing, and, turning quickly, trots to the
> desk, gets his hat, puts it on as he quickly crosses back to
> door up right and exits. There is a short pause and* MR.
> MANNINGHAM *appears in the doorway, peers into the room
> and enters, closes the doors and looks up the stairway, then
> crosses to upstage bracket, turns it up, then to the down-
> stage bracket and turns it up. Then he goes back of the
> settee, puts his hat on the settee, crosses to the bell and
> rings it. Then leisurely, he starts to the fireplace. As he
> reaches the settee* ELIZABETH *opens the doors and enters*]

ELIZABETH: Did you ring, sir?
MR. MANNINGHAM: Yes, I did. [*Without yet saying why he has rung,
he removes his coat and places it over settee, and then comes and
stands with his back to the fireplace*] Where is Mrs. Manningham,
Elizabeth?

ELIZABETH: I think she's gone to bed, sir. I think she had a bad headache and went to bed.

MR. MANNINGHAM: Oh, indeed. And how long has she been in bed, do you know?

ELIZABETH: She went just a little while ago, sir—I think, sir—

MR. MANNINGHAM: Oh. I see. Then we must be quiet, mustn't we? Walk about like cats.—Can you walk about like a cat, Elizabeth?

ELIZABETH: [*Trying to smile*] Yes, sir. I think so, sir.

MR. MANNINGHAM: Very well, Elizabeth. Walk about like a cat. All right. That's all.

ELIZABETH: Yes, sir. Thank you, sir.

[*Just as* ELIZABETH *is about to exit, he calls her back*]

MR. MANNINGHAM: Er—Elizabeth.

ELIZABETH: [*Coming back*] Yes, sir? [MANNINGHAM *is again silent*] Did you call, sir?

MR. MANNINGHAM: Yes. Why haven't you cleared away the tea things?

ELIZABETH: [*Crossing to table*] Oh—I'm sorry, sir. I was really just about to, sir.

MR. MANNINGHAM: Yes. I think you had better clear away the tea things, Elizabeth.

ELIZABETH: Yes, sir. [*After pause, putting a dish on the tray*] Excuse me, sir, but were you going to have some supper, sir?

MR. MANNINGHAM: [*Crossing to desk*] Oh, yes. I am going to have supper. The question is, am I going to have supper here?

ELIZABETH: Oh, yes, sir. Are you having it out, sir?

MR. MANNINGHAM: Yes, I am having it out. [MANNINGHAM *takes off his undercoat and puts it carefully over a chair left of table. He is beginning to undo his tie*] I have come back to change my linen. [*He is undoing his collar. There is a pause*]

ELIZABETH: [*Looks up and realizes his coat is off*] Do you want a fresh collar, sir? Shall I get you a fresh collar?

MR. MANNINGHAM: Why, do you know where my collars are kept?

ELIZABETH: Why, yes, sir. In your room, there, sir. Shall I get you one, sir?

MR. MANNINGHAM: What a lot you know, Elizabeth. And do you know the sort of collar I want tonight?

ELIZABETH: Why, yes, sir— I think I know the sort of collar, sir.

MR. MANNINGHAM: [*As he crosses toward door up right*] Then all I can say is you know a great deal more than I do— No— I think you must let me choose my own collar— [*Stops, turns to* ELIZABETH] That is, if I have your permission, Elizabeth.

ELIZABETH: [*Gazing at him*] Yes, sir—yes, sir—

[MANNINGHAM *goes in.* ELIZABETH *puts on the table the plate she is holding and lowers her head, remaining motionless in suspense. Not a sound comes from the other room, and nearly a quarter of a minute goes by. At last,* MANNINGHAM *comes out in a perfectly leisurely way. He is putting his tie on and crosses down to mirror over fireplace, looking at himself in the mirror during the ensuing conversation*]

MR. MANNINGHAM: What did you think about Mrs. Manningham tonight, Elizabeth?

ELIZABETH: Mrs. Manningham, sir? In what way do you mean, sir?

MR. MANNINGHAM: Oh—just as regards her general health, Elizabeth.

ELIZABETH: I don't know, sir. She certainly seems very unwell.

MR. MANNINGHAM: Yes. I doubt if you can guess to what extent she is unwell. [*Turns to* ELIZABETH] Or are you beginning to guess?

ELIZABETH: I don't know, sir.

MR. MANNINGHAM: I'm afraid I was compelled to drag you and Nancy into our troubles tonight. Perhaps I should not have done that.

ELIZABETH: It all seems very sad, sir.

MR. MANNINGHAM: [*Smiling and somewhat appealingly, as he takes a step toward* ELIZABETH] I'm at my wits' end, Elizabeth. You know that, don't you?

ELIZABETH: I expect you are, sir.

MR. MANNINGHAM: I have tried everything. Kindness, patience, cunning—even harshness, to bring her to her senses. But nothing will stop these wild, wild hallucinations, nothing will stop these wicked pranks and tricks.

ELIZABETH: It seems very terrible, sir.

MR. MANNINGHAM: You don't know a quarter of it, Elizabeth. You only see what is forced upon your attention—as it was tonight.

You have no conception of what goes on all the time. [*He is looking at his tie*] No—not this one, I think—

ELIZABETH: Do you want another tie, sir?

MR. MANNINGHAM: Yes. [*He strolls again into the other room.* ELIZABETH *turns and watches the door intently. After a pause, he comes out with another tie. As he enters,* ELIZABETH *quickly turns to tea table. He crosses down to fireplace mirror. He is putting his tie on during the ensuing conversation*] I suppose you know about Mrs. Manningham's mother, Elizabeth?

ELIZABETH: No, sir. What of her, sir?

MR. MANNINGHAM: Not of the manner in which she died?

ELIZABETH: No, sir.

MR. MANNINGHAM: She died in the madhouse, Elizabeth, without any brain at all in the end.

ELIZABETH: Oh, sir!—How terrible, sir.

MR. MANNINGHAM: Yes, terrible indeed. The doctors could do nothing. [*Pause. Turns to* ELIZABETH] You know, don't you, that I shall have to bring a doctor to Mrs. Manningham before long, Elizabeth? [*As he crosses and gets his undercoat*] I have fought against it to the last, but it can't be kept a secret much longer.

ELIZABETH: No, sir— No, sir—

MR. MANNINGHAM: [*Putting on his undercoat*] I mean to say, you know what goes on. You can testify to what goes on, can't you?

ELIZABETH: Indeed, sir. Yes.

MR. MANNINGHAM: Indeed, you may *have* to testify in the end. Do you realize that? [*Pause. Sharp*] Eh?

ELIZABETH: [*Looking quickly up at him*] Yes, sir. I would only wish to help you both, sir.

MR. MANNINGHAM: [*Goes to settee, gets coat and puts it on, crosses to mirror and adjusts coat*] Yes, I believe you there, Elizabeth. You're a very good soul. I sometimes wonder how you put up with things in this household—this dark household. I wonder why you do not go. You're very loyal.

ELIZABETH: [*Looking at him in an extraordinary way. He cannot see her*] Always loyal to you, sir. Always loyal to you.

MR. MANNINGHAM: There now, how touching. I thank you, Elizabeth.

You will be repaid later for what you have said, and repaid in more ways than one. You understand that, don't you?

ELIZABETH: Thank you, sir. I only want to serve, sir.

MR. MANNINGHAM: [*Crosses back of settee, gets hat*] Yes, I know that. Well, Elizabeth, I am going out. In fact, I'm even going to try to be a little gay. Can you understand that, or do you think it is wrong?

ELIZABETH: Oh, no, sir. No. You should get all the pleasure you can, sir, while you can.

MR. MANNINGHAM: I wonder—yes—I wonder—it's a curious existence, isn't it— Well—good night, Elizabeth.

[MANNINGHAM *goes off*]

ELIZABETH: Good night, sir—good night.

[MANNINGHAM *has left the door open.* ELIZABETH *quickly crosses up to door and looks after him. After a pause,* ROUGH *comes forth and* ELIZABETH *turns to him. He and* ELIZABETH *stand there looking at each other. At last,* ROUGH *goes to the window and looks out. The front door is heard slamming*]

ROUGH: He was right when he said you would be repaid, Elizabeth. Though not in the way he thinks. [*Taking off hat, puts it on desk; then his overcoat and muffler and puts them on chair down left*] Will you go and get Mrs. Manningham?

ELIZABETH: Yes, sir. I'll get her, sir.

[*As she starts toward stairs,* MRS. MANNINGHAM *comes downstairs.* ROUGH *gets implements out of overcoat pocket*]

ROUGH: Ah—there you are.

MRS. MANNINGHAM: I saw him go.

[ELIZABETH *takes tray and exits*]

ROUGH: Now we must get back to work.

MRS. MANNINGHAM: What did he want? What did he come back for?

ROUGH: He only came to change his clothes. Turn up the lamp, will you? [MRS. MANNINGHAM *does so, and comes to him as he again reaches desk*] Now let's have another look at this.

MRS. MANNINGHAM: What if he comes back again? There is no light to warn us now.

ROUGH: Oh, you've realized that, have you? Well, Mrs. Manningham, we've just got to take that risk. [*Takes his keys from pocket*] This is going to be child's play, I fancy. Just a little patience—a little adroitness in the use . . . [*The front door slams*] What's that?— Go and have a look, will you? [MRS. MANNINGHAM *rushes over to the window*] We seem to be rather bothered this evening, don't we?

MRS. MANNINGHAM: It's all right. It's only Nancy. I forgot. She usually goes out at this time.

ROUGH: She uses the front door—does she?

MRS. MANNINGHAM: Oh, yes. Indeed she does. She behaves like the mistress in this house.

ROUGH: A saucy girl. [*The top of the bureau opens*] Ah—here we are. Next to a key there's nothing a lock appreciates like kindness.

MRS. MANNINGHAM: Will you be able to close it again?

ROUGH: Yes. No damage done. There we are. [*He pulls the upstage drawer out and puts it on top of desk*] Now. Let's see. Doesn't seem much here— And when she got there the cupboard was bare —and so the poor detective—[*He picks up a brooch*]

MRS. MANNINGHAM: What is that in your hand? What is that in your hand?

ROUGH: [*Holding up brooch*] Why, do you recognize this?

MRS. MANNINGHAM: Yes! My brooch! Yes! Is there anything else there? What else is there?—Look, my watch! Oh, God, it's my watch!

ROUGH: This also is your property then?

MRS. MANNINGHAM: Yes. Both of them. This watch I lost a week ago—my brooch has been missing three months. And he said he would give me no more gifts because I lost them. He said that in my wickedness I hid them away! Inspector, is there anything else—? [*She crosses anxiously to upper end of the desk and looks over his shoulder*] Is there a bill there? [*He looks up at her*] Is there a grocery bill?

ROUGH: [*Searching drawer*] A grocery bill?—No— There doesn't seem to be— [*He has pulled out a letter which he drops on the desk*]

MRS. MANNINGHAM: [*Picking up letter*] One moment— One moment— This letter!—this letter! [*She goes on reading it*] It's from my cousin—my cousin—

ROUGH: Is your husband's correspondence with your relations very much to the point at the moment, Mrs. Manningham?

MRS. MANNINGHAM: You don't understand. [*Speaking rapidly*] When I was married I was cast off by all my relations. I have not seen any of them since I was married. They did not approve my choice. I have longed to see them again more than anything in the world. When we came to London—to this house, I wrote to them, I wrote to them twice. There never was any answer. Now I see why there never was any answer. [*Dazed*] This letter is to me. It's from my cousin.

ROUGH: [*Cynically*] Yet you never got it. Now you're beginning to understand, Mrs. Manningham?

MRS. MANNINGHAM: [*As she crosses to chair and sits*] Listen. Let me read to you what he says. Let me read it to you. [*Feverishly*] "Dear Cousin— All of us were overjoyed to hear from you again." [*Looks up at* ROUGH] Overjoyed, do you hear that? [*Returns to reading the letter*] He goes on to say that his family are in Devonshire, and that they have gone to the country. He says we must meet and recapture old times. [*She is showing signs of great emotion*] He says that they all want to see me—that I must go and stay with them—that they will give me—that they will give me their Devonshire cream to fatten my cheeks, and their fresh air to bring the sparkle back to my eyes . . . they will give me . . . they'll give me . . . [*Breaking down*] Dear God, they wanted me back! They wanted me back all the time!

ROUGH: [*Coming to her as she cries softly*] Poor child. You shall have your Devonshire cream and you shall have the fresh air to bring the sparkle back into your eyes. [*She looks up at him*] Why, I can see a sparkle in them already. If you will be brave now and trust me, you will not have to wait long. Are you going to trust me?

MRS. MANNINGHAM: Thank you, Inspector, for bringing me this letter. [ROUGH *crosses back to desk*] What do you wish me to do?

ROUGH: For the moment, nothing. Tell me. This drawer here. It seems to me to have a special lock. Has it ever been open to your knowledge?

MRS. MANNINGHAM: [Hesitantly] No.

ROUGH: No?—I suspected as much. Yes, this is a tougher proposition, I'm afraid. [He goes to his overcoat and produces an iron instrument]

MRS. MANNINGHAM: [Rising and crossing to stop him] What are you going to do? Are you going to force it?

ROUGH: [Calmly] If I possibly can. I don't know that . . .

MRS. MANNINGHAM: But you must not do that. You must not. What shall I say when my husband comes back?

ROUGH: [Ironically. Getting his jimmy from coat] I have no idea what you will say when he comes back, Mrs. Manningham. But then I have no idea what you will do, Mrs. Manningham, if I have no evidence to remove you from his loving care for good.

MRS. MANNINGHAM: [Torn with doubts] Oh, God. I am afraid. What can I do?

ROUGH: [Sharply] There is only one thing we can do—go ahead. If we go back now, we are lost. I am going to force it and gamble on finding something. Are you with me?

MRS. MANNINGHAM: [Tormented as she studies him] But, don't you see— All right. Force it! Force it! But be quick.

ROUGH: There's no hurry, madam. He's quite happy where he is— Now, I don't like violent methods [He is straining at lock] of this sort—it makes me feel like a dentist— There— [There's a sound of splitting wood] All over now— Now, let's have a look.

MRS. MANNINGHAM: [After pause, in which she watches him. As he pulls out the drawer:] Is there anything there? Is there anything there?

ROUGH: [Looking at papers] No, I don't see anything yet—I don't see anything. Wait a minute— No— No— What's this? [As he picks up a bundle of papers] Mr. Manningham—Mr. Manningham —Mr. Manningham—

MRS. MANNINGHAM: Is there nothing?

ROUGH: No— Not a thing. We have lost our gamble, ma'am, I'm afraid.

MRS. MANNINGHAM: [*Frightened*] Oh, dear me, what are we to do? What are we to do?

ROUGH: Some rapid thinking at the moment. Don't have any fear, Mrs. Manningham, I've been in many a tighter corner than this. Let's get those things back to begin with, shall we? Give me the watch and the brooch. [*Takes watch and brooch*] We must put them back where they were.

MRS. MANNINGHAM: Yes—here they are.

ROUGH: Here on the right, was it not?

MRS. MANNINGHAM: Yes. There— That's right. There.

ROUGH: [*Holding up brooch*] A nice piece of jewelry. When did he give you this?

MRS. MANNINGHAM: Soon after we were married. But it was only secondhand.

ROUGH: Secondhand, eh? I'm afraid you got everything secondhand, from this gentleman, Mrs. Manningham. Well—that's all right. [*He puts brooch in drawer and drawer back in desk*] Now I must lock this up again, [*Closes the second drawer*] if I can— [*About to lock first drawer*] Secondhand did you say?— How did you know that brooch was secondhand, Mrs. Manningham?

MRS. MANNINGHAM: There's an affectionate inscription to someone else inside.

ROUGH: [*Vaguely*] Oh— Is there?—[*Opens first drawer*] Why didn't you tell me that—?

MRS. MANNINGHAM: Why—I only found it myself a little while ago.

ROUGH: [*As he takes out brooch*] Oh . . . really. Do you know, I have a feeling I have seen this somewhere before? Where is this inscription you speak of?

MRS. MANNINGHAM: It is a sort of trick. I only discovered it by accident. You pull the pin at the back. It goes to the right, and then to the left. It opens out like a star.

ROUGH: [*As he opens it*] Oh, yes— Yes— Ah—here we are. Yes. [*He sits at table and takes out his jeweler's glass*] How very odd. What are these spaces here?

MRS. MANNINGHAM: There were some beads in it, but they were all loose and falling out—so I took them out.

ROUGH: Oh—there were some beads in it, but they were all loose and falling out—so you took them out. [*Pause*] Have you got them by any chance?

MRS. MANNINGHAM: Yes. I think so. I put them in a vase.

ROUGH: May I see them, please?

MRS. MANNINGHAM: Yes. [*Going to vase on mantelpiece*] They should still be here.

ROUGH: There should be nine altogether, I think.

MRS. MANNINGHAM: Yes, that's right, I think there were. Yes. Here they are. Here are some of them at any rate.

ROUGH: Let me see, will you?—Ah— Thank you. Try and find them all, will you? [*She goes back to mantel*] Did you happen to read this inscription at any time, ma'am?

MRS. MANNINGHAM: Yes, I read it. Why?

ROUGH: [*Reading*] "Beloved A.B. from C.B. Eighteen fifty-one." [*Looking up at her*] Does nothing strike you about that?

MRS. MANNINGHAM: No. What of it? What should strike me?

ROUGH: Really, I should have thought that as simple as A.B.C. Have you got the others? There should be four more.

MRS. MANNINGHAM: Yes. Here they are.

ROUGH: Thank you. That's the lot. [*He is putting them in brooch on the table*] Now tell me this—have you ever been embraced by an elderly detective in his shirt sleeves?

MRS. MANNINGHAM: What do you mean?

ROUGH: For that is your immediate fate at the moment. [*Puts down brooch, rises and comes to her*] My dear Mrs. Manningham . . . [*Kisses her*] My dear, dear Mrs. Manningham! Don't you understand?

MRS. MANNINGHAM: No, what are you so excited about?

ROUGH: [*Picks up brooch*] There, there you are, Mrs. Manningham. The Barlow rubies—complete. Twelve thousand pounds' worth before your very eyes! [*Gives her brooch*] Take a good look at them before they go to the Queen.

MRS. MANNINGHAM: But it couldn't be—it couldn't. They were in the vase all the time.

ROUGH: Don't you see? Don't you see the whole thing? *This* is where the old lady hid her treasure—in a common trinket she wore all the day. I knew I had seen this somewhere before. And where was that? In portraits of the old lady—when I was on the case. She wore it on her breast. I remember it clearly though it was fifteen years ago. Fifteen years! Dear God in heaven, am I not a wonderful man!

MRS. MANNINGHAM: And I had it all the time. I had it all the time.

ROUGH: And all because he could not resist a little common theft along with the big game . . . Well, it is I who am after the big game now. [*He shows signs of going*]

MRS. MANNINGHAM: Are you going?

ROUGH: Oh, yes. I must certainly go. [*Begins to collect his coat and things*] And very quickly at that.

MRS. MANNINGHAM: Where are you going? Are you going to leave me? What are you going to do?

ROUGH: I am going to move heaven and earth—Mrs. Manningham —and if I have any luck I . . . [*Looking at his watch*] It's very early yet. What time do *you* think he'll be back?

MRS. MANNINGHAM: I don't know. He's not usually in till eleven.

ROUGH: Yes. So I thought. Let's hope so. That will give me time. Here, give me that. Have you closed it? [*Takes brooch*] We will put it back where we found it. [*He crosses to desk*]

MRS. MANNINGHAM: But what are you going to do?

ROUGH: It's not exactly what I am going to do. It's what the Government is going to do in the person of Sir George Raglan. Yes, ma'am. Sir George Raglan. No one less. The power above all the powers that be. [*Puts brooch in drawer; closes and locks drawer*] He knows I am here tonight, you see. But he didn't know I was going to find what I have found. [*Pause. Looks at broken drawer*] Yes—we've done for that, I'm afraid— Well, we must just risk it, that's all. [*Tries to force broken drawer into place*] Now, Mrs. Manningham, you will serve the ends of justice best by simply going to bed. Do you mind going to bed?

MRS. MANNINGHAM: No. I will go to bed. [*She starts upstairs*]

ROUGH: Good. Go there and stay there. Your headache is worse. Remember, be ill. Be anything. But stay there, you understand. I'll let myself out.

MRS. MANNINGHAM: [*Suddenly. Comes downstairs and crosses to*

ROUGH] Don't leave me. Please don't leave me. I have a feeling . . . Don't leave me.

ROUGH: Feeling? What feeling?

MRS. MANNINGHAM: A feeling that something will happen if you leave me. I'm afraid. I haven't the courage.

ROUGH: Have the goodness to stop making a fool of yourself, Mrs. Manningham. Here's your courage. [*He gives her whiskey, taking it from pocket*] Take some more of it, but don't get tipsy and don't leave it about. Good-bye. [*He is at doors, about to exit*]

MRS. MANNINGHAM: Inspector.

ROUGH: [*Turns to her*] Yes.

MRS. MANNINGHAM: [*Summoning courage*] All right. Good-bye. [*She starts up the stairs*]

ROUGH: Good-bye.

[*He goes, shutting the doors. Pause, as* MRS. MANNINGHAM *stops on the stairs and glances around the room.* ROUGH *suddenly opens the doors*]

ROUGH: Mrs. Manningham!

MRS. MANNINGHAM: Yes.

[ROUGH *motions to her to go upstairs. She does so and he watches her*]

ROUGH: Good-bye.

[*When she is out of sight around the curve on the stairs he exits and closes the doors*]

CURTAIN

ACT THREE

The time is eleven the same night. The room is in dark-ness, but the doors are open and a dim light in the passage outside can be seen. There is the sound of the front door shutting. Footsteps can be heard, and MANNINGHAM *appears outside. He stops to turn out the light in the passage. He enters the room and goes to the lamp on the center table and turns it up. Then he lights the two brackets and crosses to table up right and puts his hat on it. He goes in a slow and deliberate way over to the bell-cord and pulls it. He is humming to himself as he goes over to the fire-place.*

NANCY puts her head round the door. She has only just come in and is dressed for out-of-doors.

NANCY: Yes, sir. Did you ring, sir?

MR. MANNINGHAM: Yes, Nancy, I did ring. It seems that the entire household has gone to bed without leaving me my milk and with-out leaving me my biscuits.

NANCY: Oh, I'm sorry, sir. They're only just outside. I'll bring them in! [*Turns to door, then stops*] Mrs. Manningham usually gets them, doesn't she, sir? Cook's in bed and I've only just come in.

MR. MANNINGHAM: Quite, Nancy. Then perhaps you will deputize for Mrs. Manningham, and bring them into the room.

NANCY: Certainly, sir.

MR. MANNINGHAM: And after you do that, Nancy, will you go upstairs and tell Mrs. Manningham that I wish to see her down here.

NANCY: Yes, sir. Certainly, sir. [*She exits*]

[MR. MANNINGHAM *walks into room up right.* NANCY *returns. She has milk in a jug, a glass and biscuits on a tray, and puts them on the table. She goes upstairs. He comes back in and crosses slowly over to desk.* NANCY *comes downstairs and stops at the foot of the stairs*]

MR. MANNINGHAM: Well, Nancy?

NANCY: She says she has a headache, sir, and is trying to sleep.

MR. MANNINGHAM: Oh—she still has a headache, has she?

NANCY: Yes, sir. Is there anything else you want, sir?

MR. MANNINGHAM: Did you ever know a time when Mrs. Manningham did not have a headache, Nancy?

NANCY: No, sir. Hardly ever, sir.

MR. MANNINGHAM: Do you usually perform your domestic tasks in outdoor costume, Nancy?

NANCY: I told you, sir. I've only just come in, and I heard the bell by chance.

MR. MANNINGHAM: Yes, that's just the point.

NANCY: How do you mean, sir?

MR. MANNINGHAM: Will you be so good as to come closer, Nancy, where I can see you. [NANCY *comes closer. They look at each other in a rather strange way*] Have you any idea of the time of the day, or rather night, Nancy?

NANCY: Yes, sir. It's a little after eleven, sir.

MR. MANNINGHAM: Are you aware that you came in half a minute, or even less, before myself?

NANCY: Yes, sir. I thought I saw you, sir.

MR. MANNINGHAM: Oh—you thought you saw me. Well, I certainly saw you.

NANCY: [*Looking away*] Did you, sir?

MR. MANNINGHAM: Have you ever reflected, Nancy, that you are given a great deal of latitude in this house?

NANCY: I don't know, sir. I don't know what latitude means.

MR. MANNINGHAM: Latitude, Nancy, means considerable liberty—liberty to the extent of two nights off a week.

NANCY: [*Pause*] Yes, sir.

MR. MANNINGHAM: Well, that's all very well. It is not so well, however, when you return as late as the master of the house. We ought to keep up some pretenses, you know.

NANCY: Yes, sir. We must. [*She makes to go*]

MR. MANNINGHAM: Nancy.

NANCY: [*Stops*] Yes, sir?

MR. MANNINGHAM: [*In a more human tone*] Where the devil have you been tonight, anyway?

NANCY: [*Pause*] Only with some friends, sir.

MR. MANNINGHAM: You know, Nancy, when you say friends, I have an extraordinary idea that you mean gentlemen friends.

NANCY: [*Looking at him*] Well, sir, possibly I might.

MR. MANNINGHAM: You know, gentlemen friends have been known to take decided liberties with young ladies like yourself. Are you alive to such a possibility?

NANCY: Oh, no, sir. Not with me. I can look after myself.

MR. MANNINGHAM: Are you always so anxious to look after yourself?

NANCY: No, sir, not always, perhaps.

MR. MANNINGHAM: You know, Nancy, pretty as your bonnet is, it is not anything near so pretty as your hair beneath it. Won't you take it off and let me see it?

NANCY: [*As she removes hat*] Very good, sir. It comes off easy enough. There— Is there anything more you want, sir?

MR. MANNINGHAM: Yes. Possibly. Come here, will you, Nancy?

NANCY: [*Pause*] Yes, sir— [*She drops hat on chair. Coming to him*] Is there anything you want, sir?—[*Changing tone as he puts his arms on her shoulders*] What do you want?—eh— What do you want? [MANNINGHAM *kisses* NANCY *in a violent and prolonged manner. There is a pause in which she looks at him, and then she kisses him as violently*] There! Can she do that for you? Can she do that?

MR. MANNINGHAM: Who can you be talking about, Nancy?

NANCY: You know who I mean all right.

MR. MANNINGHAM: You know, Nancy, you are a very remarkable girl in many respects. I believe you are jealous of your mistress.

NANCY: She? She's a poor thing. There's no need to be jealous of her. You want to kiss me again, don't you? Don't you want to kiss me?

[MANNINGHAM *kisses* NANCY]

There! That's better than a sick headache—ain't it—a sick headache and a pale face all the day.

MR. MANNINGHAM: Why yes, Nancy, I believe it is. I think, however, don't you, that it would be better if you and I met one evening in different surroundings.

NANCY: Yes. Where? I'll meet you when you like. You're mine now —ain't you—'cos you want me. You want me—don't you?

MR. MANNINGHAM: And what of you, Nancy. Do you want me?

NANCY: Oh, yes! I always wanted you, ever since I first clapped eyes on you. I wanted you more than all of them.

MR. MANNINGHAM: Oh—there are plenty of others?

NANCY: Oh, yes—there's plenty of others.

MR. MANNINGHAM: So I rather imagined. And only nineteen.

NANCY: Where can we meet? Where do you want us to meet?

MR. MANNINGHAM: Really, Nancy, you have taken me a little by surprise. I'll let you know tomorrow.

NANCY: How'll you let me know, when she's about?

MR. MANNINGHAM: [Quietly] Oh, I'll find a way, Nancy, I don't believe Mrs. Manningham will be here tomorrow.

NANCY: Oh? Not that I care about her. I'd like to kiss you under her very nose. That's what I'd like to do.

MR. MANNINGHAM: All right, Nancy. Now you had better go. I have some work to do.

NANCY: Go? I don't want to go.

MR. MANNINGHAM: There, run along. I have some work to do.

NANCY: Work? What are you going to work at? What are you going to do?

MR. MANNINGHAM: Oh—I'm going to write some letters. Then I— Go along, Nancy, that's a good girl.

NANCY: Oh, very well, sir. You shall be master for a little more. [Her arms around his neck. Kisses him] Good night, your lordship [She starts to door and picks up her hat on the way]

MR. MANNINGHAM: Good night.

NANCY: [At door, stops and turns to him] When shall you let me know tomorrow?

MR. MANNINGHAM: When I find time, Nancy, when I find time. Good night.

NANCY: Good night! [She goes out]

[MANNINGHAM crosses to the desk and sits down. He rises

and crosses to the secretary, gets some papers, crosses back
to the desk and sits down again. He takes up the pen and
begins to write. He stops and takes out his key ring which
is on the other end of his watch chain and unlocks the
upstage drawer, then turns to unlock the downstage
drawer. He stops as he discovers it has been forced and
quickly rises. He turns to the upstage drawer, opens it and
rummages through it. He then looks toward the stairs,
crosses to the door, hesitates, then turns and goes to the
bell cord, pulls it, and goes back to desk and takes a quick
look at both drawers, then closes them]

NANCY: [Re-enters] Yes? What is it now?

MR. MANNINGHAM: Nancy, will you please go upstairs and take a message for me to Mrs. Manningham.

NANCY: Yes. What do you want me to say?

MR. MANNINGHAM: Will you please tell her that she is to come down
here this instant, whether she is suffering from a sick headache or
any other form of ailment.

NANCY: Just like that, sir?

MR. MANNINGHAM: Just like that, Nancy.

NANCY: With the greatest of pleasure, sir. [She goes upstairs]

[MANNINGHAM looks at the drawer again carefully. He
walks over to the fireplace and stands with his back to it,
waiting]

NANCY: [Returns] She won't come. She doesn't mean to come.

MR. MANNINGHAM: [Steps forward] What do you mean, Nancy—she
won't come?

NANCY: She said she can't come—she's not well enough. She's just
shamming, if you ask me.

MR. MANNINGHAM: Really? Then she forces me to be undignified.
[Walking over to the stairs] All right, Nancy, leave it to me.

NANCY: The door's locked. She's got it locked. I tried it.

MR. MANNINGHAM: Oh—really—the door is locked, is it? Very well . . .
[He starts up the stairs past her]

NANCY: She won't let you in. I can tell by her voice. She's got it locked and she won't open it. Are you going to batter it in?

MR. MANNINGHAM: [*Turns, comes down*] No—perhaps you are right, Nancy—let us try more delicate means of attaining our ends. [*He goes to desk, sits, and starts to write*] Perhaps you will take a note to this wretched imbecile and slip it under her door.

NANCY: Yes, I'll do that. [*Coming to desk*] What are you going to write?

MR. MANNINGHAM: Never mind what I am going to write. I'll tell you what you can do though, Nancy.

NANCY: Yes? What?

MR. MANNINGHAM: Just go down to the basement and bring the little dog here, will you?

NANCY: The dog?

MR. MANNINGHAM: The dog, yes.

NANCY: What's the game? What's the idea with the dog?

MR. MANNINGHAM: Never mind. Just go and get it, will you?

NANCY: [*Starts*] All right.

MR. MANNINGHAM: Or on second thought perhaps you need not get the dog. [*She stops. Turns to him*] We will just let it be supposed we have the dog. That will be even more delicate still. Here you are, Nancy. [*She crosses to desk*] Please go and put this under the door.

NANCY: [*Pause*] What's the idea? What have you written in this?

MR. MANNINGHAM: Nothing very much. Just a little smoke for getting rats out of holes. There. Run along.

NANCY: You're a rum beggar, ain't you? [*At stairs*] Can't I look?

MR. MANNINGHAM: Go on, Nancy!

> [NANCY *goes up. Left alone,* MANNINGHAM *shuts and locks the top of his desk. Then he comes down and carefully places an armchair facing the fireplace—as though he is staging some ceremony. He looks around the room. Then he takes up his place in front of the fire, and waits.* NANCY *comes downstairs*]

NANCY: She's coming. It's done the trick all right.

MR. MANNINGHAM: Ah—so I thought. Very well, Nancy. Now I shall be obliged if you will go to bed at once.

NANCY: Go on. What's the game? What's the row about?

MR. MANNINGHAM: Nancy, will you please go to bed?

NANCY: [Coming forward, to him] All right, I'm going. [Kisses him] Good night, old dear. Give her what-for, won't you.

MR. MANNINGHAM: Good night, Nancy.

NANCY: Ta-ta.

> [MRS. MANNINGHAM appears and stands on the stairs. MRS. MANNINGHAM says nothing. NANCY goes out. After a long pause, MANNINGHAM goes to the door, and looks to see that NANCY is not there, closes it. He comes back and standing again with his back to the fireplace, looks at her]

MR. MANNINGHAM: Come and sit down in this chair, please, Bella.

MRS. MANNINGHAM: [Unmoving] Where is the dog? Where have you got the dog?

MR. MANNINGHAM: Dog? What dog?

MRS. MANNINGHAM: You said you had the dog. Have you hurt it? Let me have it. Where is it? Have you hurt it again?

MR. MANNINGHAM: Again? This is strange talk, Bella—from you— after what you did to the dog a few weeks ago. Come and sit down here.

MRS. MANNINGHAM: I do not want to speak to you. I am not well. I thought you had the dog and were going—to hurt it. That is why I came down.

MR. MANNINGHAM: The dog, my dear Bella, was merely a ruse to compel you to pay me a visit quietly. Come and sit down where I told you.

MRS. MANNINGHAM: [Starts upstairs] No. I want to go.

MR. MANNINGHAM: [Shouting] Come and sit down where I told you!

MRS. MANNINGHAM: [Coming downstage to back of table] Yes—yes —what do you want?

MR. MANNINGHAM: Quite a good deal, Bella. Sit down and make yourself comfortable. We have plenty of time.

MRS. MANNINGHAM: [As she crosses back toward stairs] I want to go. You cannot keep me here. I want to go.

MR. MANNINGHAM: [*Calmly*] Sit down and make yourself comfortable, Bella. We have plenty of time.

MRS. MANNINGHAM: [*Going to chair which he did not indicate and which is nearer the door and sits*] Say what you have to say.

MR. MANNINGHAM: Now you are not sitting in the chair I indicated, Bella.

MRS. MANNINGHAM: What have you to say?

MR. MANNINGHAM: I have to say that you are not sitting in the chair I indicated. Are you afraid of me that you desire to get so near the door?

MRS. MANNINGHAM: No, I am not afraid of you.

MR. MANNINGHAM: No? Then you have a good deal of courage, my dear. However, will you now sit down where I told you?

MRS. MANNINGHAM: Yes. [*She rises and slowly crosses*]

MR. MANNINGHAM: Do you know what you remind me of, Bella, as you walk across the room?

MRS. MANNINGHAM: No. What do I remind you of?

MR. MANNINGHAM: A somnambulist, Bella. Have you ever seen such a person?

MRS. MANNINGHAM: No, I have never seen one.

MR. MANNINGHAM: Haven't you? Not that funny, glazed, dazed look of the wandering mind—the body that acts without the soul to guide it? I have often thought you had that look, but it's never been so strong as tonight.

MRS. MANNINGHAM: [*Sitting in armchair*] My mind is not wandering.

MR. MANNINGHAM: No?—When I came in, Bella, I was told that you had gone to bed.

MRS. MANNINGHAM: Yes. I had gone to bed.

MR. MANNINGHAM: Then may I ask why you are still fully dressed? [*She does not answer*] Did you hear what I said?

MRS. MANNINGHAM: Yes, I heard what you said.

MR. MANNINGHAM: Then will you tell me why, since you had gone to bed, you are still fully dressed?

MRS. MANNINGHAM: I don't know.

MR. MANNINGHAM: You don't know? Do you know anything about anything you do?

MRS. MANNINGHAM: I don't know. I forgot to undress.

MR. MANNINGHAM: You forgot to undress. A curious oversight, if I may say so, Bella. [*Leaning over her*] You know, you give me the appearance of having had a rather exciting time since I last saw you. Almost as though you have been up to something. Have you been up to anything?

MRS. MANNINGHAM: No. I don't know what you mean.

MR. MANNINGHAM: [*Straightens up*] Did you find that bill I told you to find?

MRS. MANNINGHAM: No.

MR. MANNINGHAM: [*Goes to milk on table*] Do you remember what I said would happen to you if you did not find that bill when I returned tonight?

MRS. MANNINGHAM: No.

MR. MANNINGHAM: No? [*Is pouring milk into glass*] No? [*She refuses to answer*] Am I married to a dumb woman, Bella, in addition to all else? The array of your physical and mental deficiencies is growing almost overwhelming. I advise you to answer me.

MRS. MANNINGHAM: What do you want me to say?

MR. MANNINGHAM: I asked you if you remembered something. [*Going back to fireplace with glass of milk*] Go on, Bella—what was it I asked you if you remembered?

MRS. MANNINGHAM: I don't understand your words. You talk round and round. My head is going round and round.

MR. MANNINGHAM: It is not necessary for you to tell me that, Bella. I am just wondering if it might interrupt its gyratory motion for a fraction of a second, and concentrate upon the present conversation. [*Sips milk*] Now please, what was it I a moment ago asked you if you remembered?

MRS. MANNINGHAM: [*Labored*] You asked me if I remembered what you said would happen to me if I did not find that bill.

MR. MANNINGHAM: Admirable, my dear Bella! Admirable! We shall make a great logician of you yet—a Socrates—a John Stuart Mill! You shall go down to history as the shining mind of your day. That is, if your present history does not altogether submerge you —take you away from your fellow creatures. And there is a danger

of that, you know, in more ways than one. [*Puts milk on mantel*]
Well—what did I say I would do if you did not find that bill?

MRS. MANNINGHAM: [*Choked*] You said you would lock me up.

MR. MANNINGHAM: Yes. And do you believe me to be a man of my
word? [*Pause in which she does not answer*] You see, Bella, in a
life of considerable and varied experience I have hammered out a
few principles of action. In fact, I actually fancy I know how to
deal with my fellowmen. I learned it quite early actually—at school
in fact. There, you know, there were two ways of getting at what
you wanted. One was along an intellectual plane, the other along
the physical. If one failed one used the other. I took that lesson
into life with me. Hitherto, with you, I have worked with what
forbearance and patience I leave you to judge, along the intellectual plane. The time has come now, I believe, to work along the
other as well— You will understand that I am a man of some
power . . . [*She suddenly looks at him*] Why do you look at me,
Bella? I said I am a man of some power and determination, and as
fully capable in one direction as in the other.—I will leave your
imagination to work on what I mean.—However, we are really
digressing . . . You did not find the bill I told you to find.

MRS. MANNINGHAM: No.

MR. MANNINGHAM: Did you look for it? [*He moves toward desk*]

MRS. MANNINGHAM: Yes.

MR. MANNINGHAM: Where did you look for it?

MRS. MANNINGHAM: Oh, around the room . . .

MR. MANNINGHAM: Around the room. Where around the room?
[*Pause. As he bangs on the desk with his right hand*] In my desk,
for instance?

MRS. MANNINGHAM: No—not in your desk.

MR. MANNINGHAM: Why not in my desk?

MRS. MANNINGHAM: Your desk is locked.

MR. MANNINGHAM: Do you imagine you can lie to me?

MRS. MANNINGHAM: I am not lying.

MR. MANNINGHAM: Come here, Bella.

MRS. MANNINGHAM: [*Coming to him*] What do you want?

MR. MANNINGHAM: [*Pause*] Now, listen to me. Your dark, confused, rambling mind has led you into playing some pretty tricks tonight —has it not?

MRS. MANNINGHAM: My mind is tired. [*She starts to stairs*] I want to go to bed.

MR. MANNINGHAM: Your mind indeed is tired! Your mind is so tired that it can no longer work at all. You do not think. You dream. Dream all day long. Dream everything. Dream maliciously and incessantly. Don't you know that by now? [*She starts to give way*] You sleepwalking imbecile, what have you been dreaming tonight —where has your mind wandered—that you have split [*Pounds on desk*] open my desk? What strange diseased dream have you had tonight—eh?

MRS. MANNINGHAM: Dream? Are you saying I have dreamed— Dreamed all that happened?—

MR. MANNINGHAM: All that happened when, Bella? Tonight? Of course you dreamed all that happened—or rather all that didn't happen.

MRS. MANNINGHAM: Dream— Tonight—are you saying I have dreamed? [*Pause*] Oh, God—have I dreamed? Have I dreamed again?—

MR. MANNINGHAM: Have I not told you—?

MRS. MANNINGHAM: [*Storming*] *I haven't dreamed. I haven't! Don't tell me I have dreamed. In the name of God don't tell me that!*

MR. MANNINGHAM: [*Speaking at the same time, and forcing her down into small chair left*] Sit down and be quiet. Sit down! [*More quietly and curiously*] What was this dream of yours, Bella? You interest me.

MRS. MANNINGHAM: I dreamt of a man— [*Hysterical*] I dreamt of a man—

MR. MANNINGHAM: [*Now very curious*] You dreamed of a man, Bella? What man did you dream of, pray?

MRS. MANNINGHAM: A man. A man that came to see me. Let me rest! Let me rest!

MR. MANNINGHAM: Pull yourself together, Bella! What man are you talking about?

MRS. MANNINGHAM: I dreamed a man came in here.

MR. MANNINGHAM: [*As he grasps her neck and slowly raises her*] I know you dreamed it, you gibbering wretch! I want to know more about this man of whom you dreamed. Do you hear! Do you hear me?

MRS. MANNINGHAM: I dreamed—I dreamed—

[*She looks off at door up right, transfixed.* MANNINGHAM *turns and looks as* ROUGH *enters door up right.* MANNINGHAM *releases her and she sinks back into the chair*]

ROUGH: Was I any part of this curious dream of yours, Mrs. Manningham?—Perhaps my presence here will help you to recall it.

MR. MANNINGHAM: [*After pause*] May I ask who the devil you are, and how you got in?

ROUGH: Well, who I am seems a little doubtful. Apparently I am a mere figment of Mrs. Manningham's imagination. As for how I got in, I came in, or rather I came back—or better still, I effected an entrance a few minutes before you, and I have been hidden away ever since.

MR. MANNINGHAM: And would you be kind enough to tell me what you are doing here?

ROUGH: Waiting for some friends, Mr. Manningham, waiting for some friends. Don't you think you had better go up to bed, Mrs. Manningham? You look very tired.

MR. MANNINGHAM: Don't you think you had better explain your business, sir?

ROUGH: Well, as a mere figment, as a mere ghost existing only in your wife's mind, I can hardly be said to have any business. Tell me, Mr. Manningham, can you see me? No doubt your wife can, but it must be difficult for you. Perhaps if she goes to her room I will vanish, and you won't be bothered by me any more.

MR. MANNINGHAM: Bella. Go to your room. [*She rises, staring at both in turn in apprehension and wonderment, goes to the stairs*] I shall find out the meaning of this, and deal with you in due course.

MRS. MANNINGHAM: I—

MR. MANNINGHAM: Go to your room. I will call you down later. I have not finished with you yet, madam.

[MRS. MANNINGHAM *looks at both again, and goes upstairs*]

ROUGH: You know, I believe you're wrong there, Manningham. I believe that is just what you have done.

MR. MANNINGHAM: Done what?

ROUGH: Finished with your wife, my friend. [*He sits down easily in armchair*]

MR. MANNINGHAM: Now, sir—will you have the goodness to tell me your name and your business if any?

ROUGH: I have no name, Manningham, in my present capacity. I am, as I have pointed out, a mere spirit. Perhaps a spirit of something that you have evaded all your life—but in any case, only a spirit. Will you have a cigar with a spirit? We may have to wait some time.

MR. MANNINGHAM: Are you going to tell me your business, sir, or am I going to fetch a policeman and have you turned out?

ROUGH: [*Puts cigar back in pocket*] Ah—an admirable idea. I could have thought of nothing better myself. Yes, fetch a policeman, Manningham, and have me turned out— [*Pause*] Why do you wait?

MR. MANNINGHAM: Alternatively, sir, I can turn you out myself.

ROUGH: [*Standing and facing him*] Yes. But why not fetch a policeman?

MR. MANNINGHAM: [*After pause*] You give me the impression, sir, that you have something up your sleeve. Will you go on with what you were saying?

ROUGH: Yes, certainly. Where was I? Yes. [*Pause*] Excuse me, Manningham, but do you get the same impression as myself?

MR. MANNINGHAM: What impression?

ROUGH: An impression that the light is going down in this room?

MR. MANNINGHAM: I have not noticed it.

ROUGH: Yes—surely— There—[*The light goes slowly down. As* ROUGH *moves,* MANNINGHAM *keeps his eyes on him*]—Eerie, isn't it? Now we are almost in the dark— Why do you think that has happened? You don't suppose a light has been put on somewhere else— You don't suppose there are other spirits—fellow spirits of mine— spirits surrounding this house now—spirits of justice, even, which have caught up with you at last, Mr. Manningham?

MR. MANNINGHAM: [*His hand on the back of chair right of table*] Are you off your head, sir?

ROUGH: No, sir. Just an old man seeing ghosts. It must be the atmosphere of this house. [*As he looks about*] I can see them everywhere. It's the oddest thing. Do you know one ghost I can see, Mr. Manningham? You could hardly believe it.

MR. MANNINGHAM: What ghost do you see, pray?

ROUGH: Why, it's the ghost of an old woman, sir—an old woman who once lived in this house, who once lived in this very room. Yes—in this very room. What things I imagine!

MR. MANNINGHAM: What are you saying?

ROUGH: Remarkably clear, sir, I see it— An old woman getting ready to go to bed—here in this very room—an old woman getting ready to go up to bed at the end of the day. Why! There she is. She sits just there. [*Points to chair right of table.* MANNINGHAM *removes his hand from the chair*] And now it seems I see another ghost as well. [*Pause. He is looking at* MANNINGHAM] I see the ghost of a young man, Mr. Manningham—a handsome, tall, well-groomed young man. But this young man has murder in his eyes. Why, God bless my soul, he might be you, Mr. Manningham—he might be you! [*Pause*] The old woman sees him. Don't you see it all? She screams—screams for help—screams before her throat is cut—cut open with a knife. She lies dead on the floor—the floor of this room—of this house. There! [*Pointing to floor in front of table. Pause*] Now I don't see that ghost any more.

MR. MANNINGHAM: What's the game, eh? What's your game?

ROUGH: [*Confronting* MANNINGHAM] But I still see the ghost of the man. I see him, all through the night, as he ransacks the house, hour after hour, room after room, ripping everything up, turning everything out, madly seeking the thing he cannot find. Then years pass and where is he?— Why, sir, is he not back in the same house, the house he ransacked, the house he searched—and does he not now stand before the ghost of the woman he killed—in the room in which he killed her? A methodical man, a patient man, but perhaps he has waited too long. For justice has waited too, and here she is, in my person, to exact her due. And justice found, my friend, in one hour what you sought for fifteen years, and still could not find. See here. Look what she found. [*Goes to desk*] A letter which never reached your wife. Then a brooch which you gave your wife but which she did not appreciate. How wicked of her! But then she didn't know its value. How was she to know that it held the Barlow rubies! There! [*Opening it out*] See. Twelve thousand pounds' worth before your eyes! There you are, sir. You killed one woman for those and tried to drive another out of her mind. And all the time they lay in your own desk, and all they have brought you is a rope around your neck, Mr. Sydney Power!

MR. MANNINGHAM: [*Pause*] You seem, sir, to have some very remarkable information. Do you imagine you are going to leave this room with such information in your possession?

[*Going up to doors as though to lock them*]

ROUGH: Do you imagine, sir, that you are going to leave this room without suitable escort?

MR. MANNINGHAM: May I ask what you mean by that?

ROUGH: Only that I have men in the house already. Didn't you realize that they had signaled their arrival from above, your own way in, Mr. Manningham, when the lights went down?

MR. MANNINGHAM: [*Pause. He looks at* ROUGH] Here you— What the devil's this? [*He rushes to the door, where two* POLICEMEN *are standing*] Ah, Gentlemen— Come in. Come in. Make yourselves at home. Here. [*He makes a plunge. They grab him*] Leave go of me, will you? Here. Leave go of me! Here's a fine way of going on. Here's a fine way!

[*A struggle ensues.* ROUGH, *seeing help is needed, jerks down the bell cord. With this, they secure* MANNINGHAM. ROUGH *kicks him in the shins. He falls*]

ROUGH: [*Taking paper from his pocket*] Sydney Charles Power, I have a warrant for your arrest for the murder of Alice Barlow. I should warn you that anything you may say now may be taken down in writing and used as evidence at a later date. Will you accompany us to the station in a peaceful manner? You will oblige us all, and serve your own interests best, Power, by coming with

us quietly. [MANNINGHAM *renews struggle*] Very well—take him
away—

> [*They are about to take him away when* MRS. MANNING-
> HAM *comes down the stairs. There is a silence*]

MRS. MANNINGHAM: Inspector Rough . . .

> [*The two* POLICEMEN *turn so that* MANNINGHAM *faces*
> MRS. MANNINGHAM]

ROUGH: [*Going to her*] Yes, my dear, now don't you think you'd
better—

MRS. MANNINGHAM: [*In a weak voice*] Inspector . . .

ROUGH: Yes?

MRS. MANNINGHAM: I want to speak to my husband.

ROUGH: Now, surely, there's nothing to be—

MRS. MANNINGHAM: I want to speak to my husband.

ROUGH: Very well, my dear, what do you want to say?

MRS. MANNINGHAM: I want to speak to him alone.

ROUGH: Alone?

MRS. MANNINGHAM: Yes, alone. Won't you please let me speak to
him alone? I beg of you to allow me. I will not keep him long.

ROUGH: [*Pause*] I don't quite understand. Alone?— [*Pause*] Very
well. You may speak to him alone. [*To* POLICEMEN] Very well.
Make him fast in this chair. [*He signifies that they are to tie him
to chair. They do so and exit*] This is anything but in order—but
we will wait outside. [MRS. MANNINGHAM *crosses to desk.* ROUGH
examines fastenings on MANNINGHAM *and crosses up to door*] I'm
afraid you must not be long, Mrs. Manningham.

MRS. MANNINGHAM: I do not want you to listen.

ROUGH: No, I will not listen. [ROUGH *hesitates, then exits*]

> [MRS. MANNINGHAM *stands looking at her husband. At last
> she goes over to door, locks it and then comes to him*]

MRS. MANNINGHAM: Jack! Jack! What have they done to you? What
have they done?

MR. MANNINGHAM: [*Struggling at his bonds, half whispering*] It's all
right, Bella. You're clever, my darling. Terribly clever. Now get

something to cut this. I can get out through the dressing room window and make a jump for it. Can you fetch something?

MRS. MANNINGHAM: [*Hesitating*] Yes—yes. I can get something. What can I get?

MR. MANNINGHAM: I've just remembered— There's a razor in my dressing room. Quick! Can you get it, Bella?

MRS. MANNINGHAM: [*Feverishly*] Razor—yes—I'll get it for you.

MR. MANNINGHAM: Hurry—yes— In my dresser— Hurry—quick and get it.

[*She goes into room up right, talking and mumbling, and comes back with the razor and crosses to desk. As she takes the razor from case, a scrap of paper falls to the floor. She stoops to pick it up, almost unconsciously tidy. She glances at it and a happy smile illuminates her face*]

MRS. MANNINGHAM: [*Joyously*] Jack! Here's the grocery bill! [*She comes to him, the grocery bill in one hand, the razor in the other. She is half-weeping, half-laughing*] You see, dear, I didn't lose it. I told you I didn't!

MR. MANNINGHAM: [*Uncomfortably*] Cut me loose, Bella.

MRS. MANNINGHAM: [*She stares at him for a moment, then at the grocery bill, then back at him*] Jack—how did this get in here? You said that I . . . [*Her voice trails off, a wild look comes into her eyes*]

MR. MANNINGHAM: [*Trying to placate her with charm*] I must have been mistaken about the bill. Now—quickly, dear, use the razor! Quick!

[*She stares at him for a moment, then moves a step closer. His look falls upon the razor. He glances up at her and a momentary hint of terror comes into his face. He draws back in the chair*]

MRS. MANNINGHAM: Razor? What razor? [*She holds it up, under his face*] You are not suggesting that this is a razor I hold in my hand? Have you gone mad, my husband?

MR. MANNINGHAM: Bella, what are you up to?

MRS. MANNINGHAM: [*With deadly rage that is close to insanity*] Or

is it I who am mad? [*She hurls the razor across the room*] Yes.
That's it. It's *I*. Of course, it *was* a razor. Dear God—I have lost it,
haven't I? I am always losing things. And I can never find them.
I don't know *where* I put them.

MR. MANNINGHAM: [*Desperately*] Bella!

MRS. MANNINGHAM: I must look for it, mustn't I? Yes—if I don't find
it you will lock me in my room—you will lock me in the madhouse for my mischief. [*Her voice is compressed with bitterness
and hatred*] Where could it be now? [*Turns and looks around*]
Could it be behind the picture? Yes, it must be there! [*She goes
to the picture swiftly and takes it down*] No, it's not there—how
strange! I must put the picture back. I have taken it down, and I
must put it back. There. [*She puts it back askew*] Where now
shall I look? [*She is raging like a hunted animal. Turns and sees
the desk*] Where shall I look? The desk. Perhaps I put it in the
desk. [*Goes to the desk*] No—it is not there—how strange! But
here is a letter. Here is a watch. And a bill— See, I've found them
at last. [*Going to him*] You see! But they don't help you, do they?
And I am trying to help you, aren't I?—to help you escape— But
how can a mad woman help her husband to escape? What a
pity . . . [*Getting louder and louder*] If I were not mad I could
have helped you—if I were not mad, whatever you had done, I
could have pitied and protected you! But because I am mad I
have hated you, and because I am mad I am rejoicing in my heart
—without a shred of pity—without a shred of regret—watching you
go with glory in my heart!

MR. MANNINGHAM: [*Desperately*] Bella!!

MRS. MANNINGHAM: Inspector! Inspector! [*Up to door; pounds on
door then flings it open*] Come and take this man away! Come and
take this man away! [ROUGH *and the others come in swiftly.* MRS.
MANNINGHAM *is completely hysterical*] Come and take this man
away!

[ROUGH *gestures to the men. They remove* MANNINGHAM.
MRS. MANNINGHAM *stands apart, trembling with homicidal
rage.* ROUGH *takes her by the shoulders sternly. She struggles to get away. He slaps her across the face. She is mo-*

mentarily stunned. ELIZABETH *enters, quickly takes in the situation, gets a glass of water from table up right and brings it down to* MRS. MANNINGHAM *and gives her a drink.* ROUGH *stands watching them for a second*]

ROUGH: [*His eyes on* MRS. MANNINGHAM *whose wild fury has resolved in weeping. He leads her to chair*] Now, my dear, come and sit down. You've had a bad time. I came in from nowhere and gave you the most horrible evening of your life. Didn't I? The most horrible evening of anybody's life, I should imagine.

MRS. MANNINGHAM: The most horrible? Oh, no,—the most wonderful.—Far and away the most wonderful.

CURTAIN

Bad Seed

MAXWELL ANDERSON

The Dramatization of William March's
Novel, "The Bad Seed"

Maxwell Anderson

Maxwell Anderson (1888–1959) was one of America's foremost dramatists. Never content to follow any one dramatic or artistic formula, he varied his themes and styles to conform with his aims as thinker and practical playwright intent upon providing entertainment for the public. During his long career he touched upon almost every conceivable dramatic genre, ranging from contemporary realistic comedy to historical verse tragedy. Undeniably, there were the high peaks and the low, yet, in retrospect, his important achievements far outweigh the occasional creative lapses.

Anderson was born in Atlantic, Pennsylvania, the son of a Baptist minister. After being educated at the University of North Dakota and Stanford University, he taught for a while, then drifted into journalism. From there it was a logical step to try his hand at drama, and his first play, *White Desert*, was produced in 1923. Undeterred by its failure, he embarked on a second theatrical project, this time in collaboration with Laurence Stallings. The result was *What Price Glory?* (1924), an enormous hit and the first play written by an American "to question the sacredness of our mission in the First World War."

A long stream of plays followed. To list some in nonchronological order: *Saturday's Children; Elizabeth the Queen; Mary of Scotland; Both Your Houses* (which won the Pulitzer Prize in 1933); *Valley Forge; Winterset* (winner of the New York Drama Critics' Circle Award, 1936); *High Tor* (recipient of the same award, 1937); *The Eve of St. Mark; Key Largo; Candle in the Wind; The Wingless Victory; The Masque of Kings; Joan of Lorraine; Night Over Taos; Anne of the Thousand Days;* and *Bad Seed.*

As librettist and lyricist, he participated in two notable musicals, both with scores by Kurt Weill: *Knickerbocker Holiday* and *Lost In the Stars*, the latter based on Alan Paton's novel, *Cry the Beloved Country*.

A point that seems to have been overlooked in most studies and treatises dealing with his work is the salient fact that Anderson often wrote in the grand manner, with strong stress upon star roles. While this may be denied by some, it is nonetheless verifiable if one takes a moment to scrutinize the list of stars who appeared in his plays: Alfred Lunt, Lynn Fontanne, Katharine Cornell, Helen Hayes, Walter Huston, Paul Muni, Ingrid Bergman, Ruth Gordon, Rex Harrison, Lillian Gish, Richard Bennett, Joyce Redman, Uta Hagen, José Ferrer, Burgess Meredith, Nancy Kelly, and dozens more. A star does not glisten without a strong role, and Anderson, a consummate man of the theatre, surely was aware of their contributions and significance to a property when planning a new play.

He also was an outspoken man. Although twice accoladed by the New York drama critics, he was not averse to heaping his scorn upon them when the occasion arose. Indeed, it was on just such an occasion in 1946 when one of his minor efforts, *Truckline Café*, received an unmerciful trouncing from the press that he publicly labeled the Broadway critics "the Jukes family of journalism," a descriptive phrase that since has become part of theatrical folklore.

In 1938, Anderson openly expressed his dissatisfaction with the vagaries and tastes of the average commercial producer and joined forces with Robert E. Sherwood, Elmer Rice, Sidney Howard, S. N. Behrman, and attorney John F. Wharton to found The Playwrights' Company, an organization that mainly was to produce the plays of its noted officer-members. As Anderson stated at the time, its aims were "to make a center for ourselves within the theatre, and possibly rally the theatre as a whole to new levels by setting a high standard of writing and production." The organization flourished for more than two decades and during its period of activity frequently fulfilled its initial objectives.

When Maxwell Anderson's adaptation of William March's novel *The Bad Seed* opened on Broadway in 1954, it came to some as a shocker, both on stage and off stage, for as far as could be determined, the author had not attempted a pure "thriller" before. To those more familiar with the Anderson prolificacy, however, it was still further proof of his varied range as a dramatist. Brooks Atkinson of *The New York Times* characterized it as: "An extraordinarily literate horror story and a superior bit of theatre. But the plot is not the only virtue of the play. For *Bad Seed* is a perceptive drama that is equally interested in the frightful tragedy of a mother who takes the responsibility for her daughter's guilt, continues to love her daughter and tries desperately and selflessly to administer justice to everyone. It is a shattering story, largely because it involves such decent people."

Walter Kerr, as drama arbiter for the now-vanished *New York Herald Tribune* (and like Marlene Dietrich's celebrated flowers, one often wonders where have all the city's newspapers gone?) also expressed his admiration: "A genuine fourteen-carat, fifteen-below chiller . . . thrilling entertainment. As a work of purely theatrical excitement, it is beautifully carpentered, suspensefully acted, craftily sustained. *Bad Seed* is an ingenious piece of straight showmanship."

The play ran for 332 performances in New York and later was made into a film with Nancy Kelly and Patty McCormack repeating their stage roles.

Bad Seed was Anderson's last successful play on the Broadway stage.

In spite of a growing concern over the complexities and problems of contemporary civilization and his lifelong preoccupation with poetic form, to the end Maxwell Anderson remained a man of the theatre, a conscientious and dedicated craftsman who knew that the theatre, basically, always has been and always will be a medium of inspiration and entertainment.

Bad Seed was first produced at the Forty-sixth Street Theatre, New York, on December 8, 1954, by The Playwrights' Company. The cast was as follows:

RHODA PENMARK	*Patty McCormack*
COL. KENNETH PENMARK	*John O'Hare*
CHRISTINE PENMARK	*Nancy Kelly*
MONICA BREEDLOVE	*Evelyn Varden*
EMORY WAGES	*Joseph Holland*
LEROY	*Henry Jones*
MISS FERN	*Joan Croydon*
REGINALD TASKER	*Lloyd Gough*
MRS. DAIGLE	*Eileen Heckart*
MR. DAIGLE	*Wells Richardson*
MESSENGER	*George Gino*
RICHARD BRAVO	*Thomas Chalmers*

Directed by	Reginald Denham
Setting and Lighting by	George Jenkins

Bad Seed was first presented in London by H. M. Tennent, Ltd., on April 14, 1955 at the Aldwych Theatre. The cast was as follows:

RHODA PENMARK	*Carol Wolveridge*
COL. KENNETH PENMARK	*Robert Ayres*
CHRISTINE PENMARK	*Diana Wynyard*
MONICA BREEDLOVE	*Margalo Gillmore*
EMORY WAGES	*Jon Farrell*
LEROY	*Bernard Bresslaw*
MISS FERN	*Joan Sanderson*
REGINALD TASKER	*Andrew Crawford*
MRS. DAIGLE	*Miriam Karlin*
MR. DAIGLE	*Mark Baker*
MESSENGER	*David Geary*
RICHARD BRAVO	*Malcolm Keen*

Directed by	Frith Banbury
Décor by	Stewart Chaney

SCENE: *The apartment of Colonel and Mrs. Penmark, in the suburb of a southern city.*

ACT ONE

ACT TWO

ACT ONE

SCENE 1

The one set is the apartment of COLONEL *and* MRS. PEN-
MARK, *in a suburb of a southern city. We see a tastefully
furnished living room, with colonial pieces and reproduc-
tions, expensive but not too gaudy. The pictures on the
walls are views of New York City in the early nineteenth
century. The door to the front hall is at stage left, the door
to an inner hallway at stage right, a door to the kitchen—
which is partially visible—is at right rear, a door to a den
containing a piano is at left rear. Large windows with heavy
drapes flood the room with early morning light. There is a
dining table at the bay window with chairs about it, a
couch at the left with a coffee table nearby. There are two
or three easy chairs in a semi-circle facing the coffee table.
A rug on the floor is varicolored rag colonial.*

RHODA PENMARK, *a neat, quaint and pretty little girl of
eight, sits, seriously reading a book, on the chair right. She
turns a page carefully, absorbed in the story.* COLONEL KEN-
NETH PENMARK, *a good-looking officer of thirty-five or so,
comes in from the right, carrying two fairly new suitcases.
He sets them down near the outer door and turns, seeing*
RHODA.

KENNETH: Why, 'morning, Rhoda! Up, and dressed and ready for the
day! Wearing your best perfume?

RHODA: [*Marking her place*] Yes, I am, daddy.

KENNETH: That's right, this is the day of the picnic. I hope there's a
breeze off the water.

RHODA: Miss Fern says there always is.

KENNETH: She says it never rains on the first of June, too. Don't count on it.

RHODA: Are you leaving today, daddy?

KENNETH: My plane goes in an hour. Back to Washington and the Pentagon and a climate that coddles eggs.

RHODA: I like coddled eggs.

KENNETH: You like everything. You're just too good to be true.

[*He pulls her braids, and she smiles up at him*]

RHODA: How long will you be gone?

KENNETH: Sealed orders, darling. All I know is I'll be home as soon as I can. What will you give me if I give you a basket of kisses?

RHODA: I'll give you a basket of hugs.

[*He leans down to hug and kiss her*]

KENNETH: I like your hugs.

RHODA: I like your kisses, daddikins! You're so big and strong!

KENNETH: I'll miss you. The General doesn't have one pretty girl on his whole staff!

RHODA: I wish he didn't have my daddy! I'll miss you every day!

KENNETH: Will you write to me?

RHODA: Do you want me to?

KENNETH: Of course I want you to.

RHODA: Then I'll write to you every day.

KENNETH: Every time I write to mother I'll put in a note for you!

RHODA: Will you really?

KENNETH: Really and truly. And every time the General tells a good joke I'll send you an official report!

RHODA: Oh, daddy, that won't be very often! You'd better send me the bad ones too!

KENNETH: Sweetheart, I will! [MRS. PENMARK *comes in from the den in a becoming morning gown. She is somewhat under thirty, a very pretty, gentle and gracious woman, quite obviously dedicated to her husband and child. The kind of woman whose life is given meaning by the affection she gives and receives*] I shall write daily to both my sweethearts unless somebody makes a mistake and starts a shooting war and we all have to go underground. [*He kisses*

CHRISTINE, *his wife, who has brought his briefcase and goes into his arms without a word.* *They have said goodbye previously, but she can't let him go without another embrace*]

RHODA: Would you go underground if there was a war?

KENNETH: Yes, I would, and, by gum, I'd go fast!

RHODA: You said "by gum" because I was here.

KENNETH: That's right, I did.

CHRISTINE: Take care.

KENNETH: I will. I'll wire you the minute we're on the ground. Take care of each other, you two.

CHRISTINE: We will. [*The doorbell rings a delicate little chime*] That's Monica and Emory. They wanted to say a last goodbye to you.

KENNETH: Oh.

> [*He goes to the door. Meanwhile* CHRISTINE *looks at* RHODA's *hair*]

RHODA: Is it all right?

CHRISTINE: It's perfect, darling, braids and all.

KENNETH: [*At the door*] Come in, Monica. Come in, Emory.

> [MRS. MONICA BREEDLOVE *is a widow of fifty-five or so, plump, intelligent, voluble and perhaps over-friendly. Her brother,* EMORY WAGES, *is a few years younger than she, also plump and friendly, but in contrast almost taciturn*]

MONICA: Just the effusive neighbors from upstairs, darlings! Have to be in on everything. No lives of their own, so they live other people's. I speak for my brother as well as myself, because he never gets a chance to speak when I'm around. There, I've talked enough. Say something, Colonel.

KENNETH: I guess it will have to be goodbye, because the taxi's here and I don't want to rush through traffic.

EMORY: Don't worry about your two pretty girls, Ken. We'll keep an eye on them, and if one of them begins to look peaked, we'll send up smoke signals.

KENNETH: I'm counting on you, Emory. [*He gives* MONICA *his hand*] And on Monica.

MONICA: Goodbye.

KENNETH: Well, sweetheart, this is it. [*He waves across the room to* RHODA] Goodbye, big eyes!

RHODA: Goodbye, daddy.

CHRISTINE: I promised myself I wouldn't come down, but—

KENNETH: Don't, sweet. It's just another empty month or two. We'll get through them somehow.

EMORY: I'm taking these.

[*He precedes* KENNETH *out with both bags.* KENNETH *and* CHRISTINE *embrace*]

KENNETH: Goodbye.

[KENNETH *takes his briefcase and goes out*]

MONICA: Poor boy. He hates to go. And you hate to let him go.

CHRISTINE: I'm—not very self-sufficient.

MONICA: You're in love, both of you, you lucky characters. I wish I were. Oh, by the way, nobody has to take Rhoda to the bus, because I made some cupcakes for Miss Fern, and she's coming by to pick them up.

CHRISTINE: Oh, good.

MONICA: [*To* RHODA] But before she comes I have two little presents for you, my darling.

RHODA: Presents?

MONICA: The first is from Emory. It's a pair of dark glasses with rhinestone decorations, and he said to tell you they're intended to keep the sun out of those pretty blue eyes. [*She produces the glasses, and* RHODA *goes toward her with an eager expression which her mother knows as* RHODA's *"acquisitive look"*] I'll try them on you. [RHODA *stands obediently while* MONICA *adjusts the glasses*] Now who is this glamorous Hollywood actress? Can it really be little Rhoda Penmark who lives with her delightful parents on the first floor of my apartment house?

RHODA: [*Looking at her reflection in the glass of a picture*] I like them. Where's the case?

MONICA: Here it is. And now for the second prize, which is from me. [*She takes from her purse a little gold heart with a chain attached*] This was given to me when I was eight years old, and it's a little young for me now, but it's still just right for an eight-year-old. However, it has a garnet set in it, and we'll have to change that for a turquoise, since turquoise is your birthstone. So I'll have it changed and cleaned, and then it's yours.

RHODA: Could I have both stones? The garnet, too?

CHRISTINE: Rhoda! Rhoda! What a—

MONICA: [*Laughing*] But of course you may! How wonderful to meet such a natural little girl! She knows what she wants and asks for it—not like these overcivilized little pets that have to go through analysis before they can choose an ice cream soda!

[RHODA *goes to her, puts her arms around her waist and hugs her with an intensity which gives* MONICA *great delight*]

RHODA: [*Purring*] Aunt Monica! Dear, sweet Aunt Monica!

[MONICA *is completely captivated, but* CHRISTINE *looks on with a slightly skeptical and concerned attitude. She knows that* RHODA *is not really affectionate, that she is acting*]

MONICA: I know I'm behind the times, but I thought children wore coveralls and play-suits to picnics. Now you, my love, look like a princess in that red and white dotted Swiss. Tell me, aren't you afraid you'll get it dirty? Or fall and scuff those new shoes?

CHRISTINE: She won't soil the dress and she won't scuff the shoes. Rhoda never gets anything dirty, though how she manages it, I don't know.

RHODA: I don't like coveralls. They're not—

[*She hesitates*]

MONICA: You mean coveralls aren't quite ladylike, don't you, my darling? [*She embraces the tolerant* RHODA *again*] Oh, you old-fashioned little dear!

RHODA: [*Looking at the locket*] Am I to keep this now?

MONICA: You're to keep it till I find out where I can get the stone changed.

RHODA: Then I'll put it in my box.

[*She goes to her table, opens a drawer and takes out a box which once held Swiss chocolates. She opens it and places the locket carefully inside. A voice says "Leroy" as the door swings open. The houseman, or* JANITOR, *stands in the doorway*]

LEROY: Guess I'm pretty early, Mrs. Penmark, but it's my day for doing the windows on this side.

CHRISTINE: Oh, yes, you can begin in the bedrooms, Leroy.

LEROY: [*To* MONICA] Excuse me, ma'am. [*To* RHODA] Mornin'.

[*He crosses through to the inner hall with pail and paraphernalia.* RHODA *skips across the room*]

RHODA: I like garnets, but I like turquoise better.

MONICA: You sound like Fred Astaire, tap-tapping across the room. What have you got on your shoes?

RHODA: I run over my heels, and mother had these iron pieces put on so they'd last longer.

CHRISTINE: I'm afraid I can't take any credit. It was Rhoda's idea entirely.

RHODA: I think they're very nice. They save money.

MONICA: Oh, you penurious little sweetheart! But I'll tell you one thing, Rhoda, I think you worry too much when you're not the very best at everything. That's one reason Emory and I thought you should have some presents today. You wanted that penmanship medal very much, didn't you?

RHODA: It's the only gold medal Miss Fern gives. And it was really mine. Everybody knew I wrote the best hand and I should have had it.

[LEROY *comes through toward the kitchen with his pail*]

LEROY: 'Scuse me, just gettin' some water.

[*He goes to the kitchen*]

RHODA: I just don't see why Claude Daigle got the medal.

CHRISTINE: These things happen to us all the time, Rhoda, and when they do we simply accept them. I've told you to forget the whole thing. [*She puts an arm around* RHODA, *trying to soften her.* RHODA *pulls away impatiently*] I'm sorry. I know you don't like people pawing over you.

RHODA: It was mine! The medal was mine!

CHRISTINE: Try to forget it, Rhoda. Put it out of your mind.

RHODA: [*Stamping in anger*] I won't! I won't! I won't!

[LEROY *comes out of the kitchen with his pail, passes near* RHODA, *and manages to spill a splash of water on her shoes*]

MONICA: Leroy! Have you completely lost your senses? You spilled water on Rhoda's shoes!

LEROY: I'm sorry, ma'am. I guess I was just trying to hurry.

[*In turning he spills more water on the floor near* CHRISTINE]

MONICA: Leroy!

LEROY: I'm sorry, Mis' Breedlove.

[*Kneels*]

MONICA: [*Under her breath*] One, two, three, four, five, six, seven, eight, nine, ten! Leroy, I own this apartment house! I employ you! I've tried to give you the benefit of every doubt! I've thought of you as emotionally immature, torn by irrational rages, a bit on the psychopathic side! But after this demonstration I think my diagnosis was entirely too mild! You're definitely a schizophrenic with paranoid overtones! I've had quite enough of your discourtesy and surliness—and so have the tenants in the building! My brother Emory has wanted to discharge you! I've been on your side, though with misgivings! I shall protect you no longer!

CHRISTINE: He didn't mean it, Monica. It was an accident, I'm sure it was.

RHODA: He meant to do it! I know Leroy well.

MONICA: It was no accident, Christine! It was deliberate—the spiteful act of a neurotic child!

RHODA: He meant to do it. [*To* LEROY] You made up your mind to do it when you went through the room.

CHRISTINE: Rhoda!

RHODA: I was looking at you when you made up your mind to wet us.

LEROY: Oh, I never, I never, I'm just clumsy!

[*He takes out his handkerchief and cleans* RHODA'S *shoes*]

CHRISTINE: [*Not wishing the man to humble himself*] Oh, Leroy, please, please!

[RHODA *draws away*]

MONICA: My patience is at an end, and you may as well know it. Go about your work!

LEROY: Yes, ma'am.

[*He goes out*]

MONICA: He has the mind of an eight-year-old, but he's managed to produce a family so I keep him on. [*The doorbell rings*] It's probably Miss Fern.

CHRISTINE: [*Going to door*] Yes. Come in, Miss Fern. We're nearly ready, I think.

MISS FERN: I'm a bit ahead of time, as usual.

[*She comes in primly. As the head of the most aristocratic school in the state she has achieved a certain savoir faire, though she is in herself a timid and undistinguished little old maid, making the most of the remains of once quite remarkable beauty*]

MONICA: Oh, Miss Fern, the old scatterbrain left her two dozen cupcakes upstairs. Rhoda, will you help me carry them down?

RHODA: Yes, of course I will.

MONICA: They're all packed.

RHODA: [*She curtsies to* MISS FERN] Morning, Miss Fern.

MISS FERN: That's a perfect curtsy, Rhoda.

RHODA: Thank you, Miss Fern.

[*She goes out the front door with* MONICA]

CHRISTINE: She does such things well?

MISS FERN: She does everything well. As you must know better than I.

CHRISTINE: And, as a person, does she fit in well—at the school?

MISS FERN: Let me think—in what way, Mrs. Penmark?

CHRISTINE: Well, Rhoda has been—I don't quite know how to say it. There's a mature quality about her that's disturbing in a child. My husband and I thought that a school like yours, where you believe in discipline and the old-fashioned virtues, might perhaps teach her to be a bit more of a child.

MISS FERN: Yes—yes, I know what you mean. In some ways, in many ways, Rhoda is the most satisfactory pupil the school has ever had. She's never been absent. She's never been tardy. She's the only child in the history of the school who has made a hundred in deportment each month in every class, and a hundred in self-reliance and conservation on the playground each month for a full school year. If you had dealt with as many children as I have, you'd realize what a remarkable record that is. And she's the neatest little girl I've ever encountered.

CHRISTINE: Kenneth says he doesn't know where she gets her tidiness. Certainly not from him or me.

MISS FERN: She has many good qualities. She's certainly no tattletale.

CHRISTINE: Oh?

MISS FERN: One of our children broke a window across the street and we knew that Rhoda knew who it was. When we questioned her about it, and told her it was her duty as an honorable citizen to report the offender, she just went on eating her apple, shaking her head, denying that she knew anything about it—and looking us over with that pitying, calculating look she has at certain times.

CHRISTINE: Oh, I know that look so well!

MISS FERN: But that was admirable too, for she was merely being loyal to a playmate.

CHRISTINE: Then—do the other children like her? Is she popular?

MISS FERN: The other children? Well, I . . .

[MISS FERN *hesitates, trying to think of something to say, and is saved from having to answer by the re-entry of* MONICA *and* RHODA, *carrying two small packed baskets*]

MONICA: Here we are!

MISS FERN: Then I suppose we should go, for my sisters and the others will be waiting. Goodbye, Mrs. Penmark.

CHRISTINE: Goodbye! May it be everything a picnic should be!

MISS FERN: Thank you! Come, Rhoda!

[*She takes one of the baskets and goes to the door*]

RHODA: Yes, Miss Fern.

[*She goes to be kissed by her mother*]

MONICA: Calm sea and prosperous voyage!

MISS FERN: Thank you! We'll take care of her! [RHODA *runs to* MONICA *for a last quick hug*] No time! We're off!

MONICA: We stole time, didn't we, Rhoda?

MISS FERN: Bless you both!

[*She goes out with* RHODA]

MONICA: So now the older set's left behind with nothing to do.

CHRISTINE: I could go through the dreary business of trying to make my face presentable. It happens every morning.

MONICA: Your face! Think of mine!

CHRISTINE: It always makes me gloomy when Kenneth goes away. Anything could happen—before I see him again. There's an old saying—we die a little at parting.

MONICA: Oh, my dear. We die a little every day if you want to brood about it! Why don't we make some kind of party of this? You're having Emory and Reginald Tasker to lunch—can't I help with that?

CHRISTINE: What does one feed a criminologist?

MONICA: Oh, prussic acid, blue vitriol, ground glass—

CHRISTINE: Hot weather things!

MONICA: Nothing would hurt Reggie. He thrives on buckets of blood and sudden death.

CHRISTINE: How many mysteries has he written?

MONICA: A complete set of his works would encircle the Empire State building—or me. Come on—I'm a garrulous old hag, but I can grind glass. We're not going to let you be lonely.

[*They go into the kitchen together.* LEROY *comes in with pail and brush, and opens one of the windows, muttering to himself*]

LEROY: That know-it-all, that Monica Breedlove, she don't think nobody knows anything but her. I'll show that bitch plenty. And that young trough-fed Mrs. Penmark. She don't get enough of what she needs, and I could give it to her. Now Rhoda's smart. That's a smart little girl. She's almost as smart as I am. She sees through me and I see through her. By damn she's smart!

CURTAIN

SCENE 2

It is 2:30 p.m. the same day. CHRISTINE *has served lunch in her apartment to* EMORY WAGES *and his sister* MONICA, *also to* REGINALD TASKER, *a friend of theirs who writes detective stories and has made himself a minor expert in the history of crime. The luncheon dishes have mostly been removed, and the guests still linger over their iced drinks. The men have taken off their coats.* TASKER *and* EMORY *are laughing as the curtain goes up.*

MONICA: But I did meet him! Nobody ever believes that I met Sigmund Freud—

EMORY: Now, come—they believe you—

MONICA: You mean it's automatic flattery. They know I'm old enough, but they voice doubts to make me feel better— Well, perhaps. Anyway, it wasn't Dr. Freud who analyzed me; it was Dr. Kettlebaum in London.

EMORY: Now we're off.

MONICA: And this was my choice, too. Not that I minimize Freud's professional standing, for I still consider him the great genius of our time—but Dr. Kettlebaum was more—more *simpatico*, if you know what I mean, Reggie.

EMORY: It means *simpatico*, if you know what that means.

MONICA: Freud loathed American women—

CHRISTINE: Oh?

MONICA: Especially those that talked back to him, and I loathed his Germanic prejudice against feminine independence, which he couldn't conceal.

CHRISTINE: Was Freud prejudiced?

MONICA: Indeed he was. Not consciously, you know. He just bristled when I suggested that women had more sense than men. Now Dr. Kettlebaum believed in the power of the individual soul, and considered sex of only trivial interest. His mind was less literal, more mystic, like my own.

CHRISTINE: Oh, Monica! Did the analysis do you any good, really?

MONICA: Well, it broke up my marriage. I looked into the very bottom of my soul. What a spectacle! When I came back I asked Mr. Breedlove for a divorce and he didn't oppose it. Then I decided that what I'd always really wanted was to make a home for my brother—and so I did. I don't think dear Emory appreciates it, but what woman—

EMORY: I can stand anything except talk about your analysis—and analyzing of your friends—and me. I don't want to look at the bottom of my soul.

MONICA: I can understand that perfectly. We're all so sensitive about these things. The truth absolutely disgusts us. Now I've come to the conclusion that Emory is a "larvated homosexual"—

CHRISTINE: What?

EMORY: Thank you! What does larvated mean?

MONICA: It means covered as with a masque—concealed.

TASKER: It means something that hasn't come to the surface—as yet.

EMORY: You can say that again. If I'm a homosexual, they'll have to change the whole concept of what goes on among 'em.

TASKER: Where do you get that idea, Monica?

MONICA: Pure association, the best evidence of all. Emory's fifty-two years old, and he's never married. I doubt if he's ever had a serious love affair.

EMORY: How would you know if they're serious?

MONICA: Please, let's look at things objectively. What are Emory's deepest interests in life? They are— [*She counts them on her fingers*]—fishing, murder mysteries in which housewives are dismembered, canasta, baseball games, and singing in male quartets. How does Emory spend Sundays? He spends them on a boat with Reggie and other men—fishing. And are there ladies present on these occasions? There are not.

EMORY: You're damned right there are not!

MONICA: I guess you are all shocked, aren't you? But you shouldn't be. Actually, homosexuality is triter than incest. Dr. Kettlebaum considered it was all a matter of personal preference. I'm perfectly frank about myself. Subconsciously I have an incestuous fixation on Emory. It's not normal, but that's the way it is.

EMORY: Thanks a million, little sister. Can't we talk about something normal, like murder? Anybody mind if I smoke a cigar?

MONICA: What are you trying to prove, Emory?

CHRISTINE: Let's relax away from the table and have our tea over here.

MONICA: Yes, we've run through sex, let's try homicide. Reggie, you're the expert.

EMORY: Any change is for the better.

TASKER: All right, I'll oblige. I've been collecting data on Mrs. Allison lately. *News Budget* wants an article on her, but I can't say she's a very flaming subject. Just an unimaginative nurse who decided she was in a position to kill folks off for their insurance—and ran through quite a list before anybody suspected her.

EMORY: Was this recent?

TASKER: Well, last year and the year before. She'd be going still only she was too stupid to vary her poisons, with the result that all her victims had similar symptoms—nausea, burning throat, intestinal pain and convulsions—to say nothing of the conventional life insurance policies made out to the old girl with the arsenic.

CHRISTINE: Please, I don't like to hear about such things.

MONICA: You don't?

CHRISTINE: No.

MONICA: Now that's an interesting psychic block. Why would Christine dislike hearing about murders?

CHRISTINE: I don't know—I have an aversion to violence of any kind. I even hate the revolver Kenneth keeps in the house.

MONICA: Oh, do you dislike the revolver more than the poisons?

CHRISTINE: I hate them both.

MONICA: Hmm, perhaps if you'll try saying the first thing that comes into your mind we can get at the root anxiety. Say it, no matter how silly it seems to you! Tell your story, Reggie, and Christine will associate.

EMORY: Oh, nonsense, Monica.

CHRISTINE: What do you mean by "associate?"

MONICA: Just speak up—because any idea that comes into your mind will be an associated idea.

CHRISTINE: Oh.

TASKER: Well, the end of the story was like this. Toward the middle of May, last year, Mrs. Allison visited her sister-in-law's family. She got there in time for lunch, and her niece Shirley reminded her that she had promised to bring a present for her birthday. Mrs. Allison was so upset about forgetting the present that she went to the neighborhood store and bought candy and soft drinks for the family.

MONICA: [Nudging CHRISTINE] Do you think of anything?

CHRISTINE: Oh, absolutely nothing.

TASKER: Actually Mrs. Allison had brought her niece a present. It was ten cents' worth of arsenic.

MONICA: But there must be something in your mind—something!

CHRISTINE: Well, I was thinking at the moment of how devoted the Fern sisters were to my father, when he was a radio commentator.

MONICA: Hmm—I don't think I understand that—so far. How did you know of this?

CHRISTINE: Oh, they spoke of it when I entered Rhoda in their school.

EMORY: Isn't your father Richard Bravo?

CHRISTINE: Yes.

EMORY: Yes, I thought so. Well, the whole nation was devoted to him during the last war.

TASKER: Yes, listened to Bravo every evening.

MONICA: Is there any more of the story?

TASKER: Yes. When Mrs. Allison returned from the store she opened a bottle of sarsaparilla for her niece, and then watched the little girl's convulsions for an hour—

MONICA: Now—without thinking at all—what's your second association? [CHRISTINE hesitates] No editing—no skipping—

CHRISTINE: Well, what I was thinking was even sillier. I've always had a feeling that I was an adopted child, and that the Bravos weren't my real parents.

MONICA: Oh, you poor innocent darling! Don't you know that the changeling fantasy is one of the commonest of childhood? I once believed I was a foundling with royal blood—Plantagenet, I think it was. Emory was a Tudor. But have you really always had this—suspicion—that you were adopted?

CHRISTINE: Yes, always.

MONICA: But no evidence?

CHRISTINE: Only that I dream about it.

MONICA: What kind of dream?

CHRISTINE: Oh, Monica, must I tell my dreams too? I'd rather hear the murder story.

MONICA: Well, let's hear more story, then hear more from Christine.

EMORY: Why do you always want to dig at people's insides? Monica, you're a ghoul.

MONICA: Of course, who isn't? Furnish the final details, Reggie.

TASKER: Well, Mrs. Allison hurried back to town on an urgent errand. She hadn't paid the current premium on the policy on Shirley's life, and this was the last day of grace.

EMORY: Stupid!

TASKER: Allison was certainly crude. But there have been artists in her line, really gifted operators like Bessie Denker. Bessie never made a mistake, never left a trace, never committed an imperfect crime—

CHRISTINE: [Suddenly interested] Who was this?

TASKER: The most amazing woman in all the annals of homicide, Bessie Denker. She was beautiful, she was brainy, and she was ruthless. She never used the same poison twice. Her own father, for example, died of rabies, contracted supposedly from a mad dog. It just happened that all his money went to Bessie—

CHRISTINE: Did you say Bessie Denker?

TASKER: Yes.

CHRISTINE: Excuse me. I, I think—I—

EMORY: I guess Christine has had enough of this, Reggie. Couldn't we talk about something else?

TASKER: We certainly could.

MONICA: And we will—though I'm still puzzled—

CHRISTINE: No, no—tell us more about Dr. Kettlebaum—

EMORY: If you leave it to Monica, she has three subjects: sex, psychiatry, and pills. Sex and psychiatry are synonymous. Better try pills.

MONICA: By pills Emory means the modern pharmaceutical discoveries which have revolutionized medicine since 1935. If you took them, Emory, you'd be a better man.

TASKER: [*Looking at his watch*] I should have looked at this before. I've got a lecture date at three-thirty, and I won't be much ahead of time if I start now. Will you forgive me for filling the air with horror stories, Mrs. Penmark?

CHRISTINE: Oh, you must forgive me, Mr. Tasker! I have some kind of phobia or mania so that I'm quite unreasonable when I hear such things.

TASKER: I'm sick of the bloody stuff myself and only keep on with it to make a living—so let's be friends.

[*He puts out a hand.* CHRISTINE *shakes with him*]

CHRISTINE: Yes, of course.

TASKER: I do have to go. Goodbye, Monica.

MONICA: Goodbye, Bluebeard.

EMORY: Goodbye, Reggie. See you Sunday. I hear the red-fish are running.

[TASKER *goes out*]

TASKER: [*From outside*] Good.

EMORY: I wonder if it wouldn't be about time for the news. [*He goes to the radio*] Do you mind, Christine?

CHRISTINE: Of course not. I'll just clear these off.

MONICA: I'll lend a hand.

[*The women carry plates into the kitchen.* EMORY *finds the local news broadcast*]

THE RADIO: "Nothing more important has happened for many years in the field of foreign affairs." [*There is a brief pause, then the voice proceeds on a somewhat different note]* "I interrupt this broadcast to—I have been asked to announce that one of the children on the annual outing of the Fern Grammar School was accidentally drowned in the bay this afternoon. The name of the victim is being withheld until the parents are first notified. More news of the tragic affair is expected momentarily. This is Station WWB—in Tallahassee, bringing you the 3:15 news, brought to you by Pickets Hardware, Best For Your Home Needs."

> [MONICA *and* CHRISTINE *hurry into the room, listening.* MONICA *puts her arm around* CHRISTINE. EMORY *turns the voice down]*

MONICA: It was not Rhoda. Rhoda is too self-reliant a child. It was some timid, confused youngster, afraid of its own shadow. It certainly wasn't Rhoda.

> [EMORY *turns the radio up]*

THE RADIO: "To return to local affairs, I am now authorized to give the name of the victim of the drowning at the Fern School picnic. It was Claude Daigle, the only child of Mr. and Mrs. Dwight Daigle of 126 Willow Street. He appears to have fallen into the water from an abandoned wharf on the Fern property. It is a mystery how the little boy got on the wharf, for all the children had been forbidden to play near or on it, but his body was found off the end of the landing, wedged among the pilings. The guards who brought up the body applied artificial respiration without result. There were bruises on the forehead and hands, but it is assumed these were caused by the body washing against the pilings. And now back to the national news."

> [EMORY *turns the radio off]*

CHRISTINE: Poor child—poor little boy!

MONICA: They'll send the children home immediately. They must be on their way now.

EMORY: This will be the end of the picnic.

CHRISTINE: I don't know what to say to her. Rhoda is eight. I remember I didn't know about death—or it didn't touch me closely—till

I was much older. A teacher I adored died. My whole world changed and darkened.

MONICA: We'd better go. This is no time for well-meaning friends to look on from the sidelines.

CHRISTINE: I don't know what to say to her!

EMORY: You'll meet it better alone. Honestly you will.

MONICA: Yes, you will, dear. We'll go. It's between you and Rhoda, dear. Nobody else can help.

CHRISTINE: Yes, I suppose so.

EMORY: Children get these shocks all the time. Life's a grim business.

CHRISTINE: I'm glad you were here. She'll have missed lunch, so I'll make her a sandwich.

MONICA: We'll be upstairs in case you need us.

CHRISTINE: Thank you, Monica. Thank you both.

> [MONICA *and* EMORY *go out. The clock strikes once—three-thirty.* CHRISTINE *carries some dishes from the table to the kitchen, leaving the table practically clear. The door opens while she is in the kitchen and* RHODA *comes in, quiet and unruffled. She sits and removes her shoes.* CHRISTINE *re-enters from the kitchen*]

CHRISTINE: Darling!

RHODA: Mother, you know we didn't really have our lunch because Claude Daigle was drowned.

CHRISTINE: I know. It was on the radio.

RHODA: He was drowned, so then they were all rushing and calling and hurrying to see if they could make him alive again, but they couldn't, so then they said the picnic was over and we had to go home.

CHRISTINE: I'm glad you're home!

RHODA: So could I have a peanut-butter sandwich and milk?

> [CHRISTINE *puts her arm around her*]

CHRISTINE: Did you see him, dear?

RHODA: Yes, of course. Then they put a blanket over him.

CHRISTINE: Did you see him taken from the water?

RHODA: Yes, they laid him out on the lawn and worked and worked. But it didn't help.

CHRISTINE: You must try to get these pictures out of your mind. I don't want you to be frightened or bothered at all. These things happen and we must accept them.

RHODA: I thought it was exciting. Could I have the peanut-butter sandwich?

CHRISTINE: [*Taking away her arm, rising*] Yes, I'm getting it ready for you. [*She goes into the kitchen.* RHODA *puts her shoes in the cupboard and takes out skates.* CHRISTINE *enters with a glass of milk and a sandwich as* RHODA *sits*] Here, dear. Darling, you're controlling yourself very well, but just the same it was an unfortunate thing to see and remember. I understand how you feel, my darling.

RHODA: I don't know what you're talking about. I don't feel any way at all.

[*She tastes the milk.* CHRISTINE *is puzzled.* RHODA, *feeling that she has displeased her mother somehow, grabs* CHRISTINE's *hand and rubs it against her cheek*]

CHRISTINE: Have you been naughty?

RHODA: Why, no, mother. What will you give me if I give you a basket of kisses?

CHRISTINE: [*Feeling a great rush of affection*] I'll give you a basket of hugs!

RHODA: I want to go out and skate on the asphalt.

CHRISTINE: Then you should, dear.

[CHRISTINE *goes to the kitchen to do the dishes.* RHODA *puts the skates on.* LEROY *opens the door and comes in to empty waste baskets*]

LEROY: [*Under his breath*] How come you go skating and enjoying yourself when your poor little schoolmate is still damp from drowning in the bay? Looks to me like you'd be in the house crying your eyes out; either that or be in church burning a candle in a blue cup.

[RHODA *stares at* LEROY *but gives no answer. Then with*

*her sandwich in her hand, she gets up and walks on her
skates to the door]*

RHODA: 'Bye, mother!

CHRISTINE: [*From the kitchen*] Goodbye, Rhoda.

LEROY: Ask me, and I'll say you don't even feel sorry for what happened to that little boy.

RHODA: Why should I feel sorry? It was Claude Daigle got drowned, not me.

[*She goes out.* LEROY *shakes his head*]

CURTAIN

SCENE 3

It is evening of the same day and RHODA, *ready for bed, is
lying on the couch while her mother reads to her. A pillow
from her bedroom is under her head, and a half-empty
glass sits on the coffee-table beside her.*

CHRISTINE: [*Reading*] "Then the knight alit from his steed and sought what way he could find out of this labyrinth, and a path appearing he began to make his way along it and it began at that time to grow dark. The knight had not gone more than a dozen paces before he saw beside the path a beautiful lady who laid out a fair damask cloth under an oak and set thereon cates and dainties and a flagon with two silver cups."

[*She pauses*]

RHODA: Mother?

CHRISTINE: Yes.

RHODA: Why aren't you reading?

CHRISTINE: I was just thinking.

RHODA: What about? The accident?

CHRISTINE: Partly—and about my phone call. The circuits were busy.

RHODA: What are cates and dainties?

CHRISTINE: Little cakes, I think.

RHODA: Oh.

CHRISTINE: [*Reading*] . . . "and set thereon cates and dainties and a flagon with two silver cups. 'Knight,' she called, 'knight, come eat and drink with me, for you are hungry and thirsty and I am alone.'" Did you take your vitamins, dear?

RHODA: [*Sitting up, taking a capsule, sipping from the glass*] I took one before. This is the second. I was saving them because I like the juice. [*She lies back*] This is wonderful, to have you read to me out here.

CHRISTINE: You'd better take the third one now.—You'll be too sleepy.

RHODA: All right. [*She sits up and takes another capsule and the last of the drink, then lies back*] I'll close my eyes, but I won't be asleep.

CHRISTINE: I know. [*She reads*] "Then the knight answered her, 'I thank you, fair lady, for I am not only hungry and thirsty but I am lost within the forest.' Then he let his palfrey graze nearby and he feasted with the lady, who gave him loving looks, sweeter than the wine from the flagon, though the wine was sweet and strong, and in this fashion the time passed till the light was gone out of the wood and it was dark." [*She pauses*] "The knight heard the music of hautbois softly playing and he perceived that a fair pavilion stood nearby under the oak trees, lighted by a torch at the entrance where there were servants going to and fro. And he was aware that the pavilion had not been there in the daylight, but had been created out of darkness—by magic—" Rhoda? Rhoda? [*There's no answer.* CHRISTINE *rises, takes the empty glass to the kitchen, returns and bends over* RHODA *to pick her up. The phone rings.* CHRISTINE *goes quickly to answer it, so that it won't wake the child. She picks up the receiver*] Yes, I was calling Washington, D.C. Yes, Bethesda 7-1293. Mr. Richard Bravo. That's right. Daddy? I'm so glad I found you at home! I've been trying to get you all evening. You said in your letter you might be coming to Tallahassee? Are you well enough to be doing such things? Well that's not really far from here—Couldn't you come to see me? Daddy, couldn't you make it sooner? Could you . . . Well as soon as you can?—No, we're well. It's not that. You met Kenneth at the airport? Tell him I'm writing my first letter to him tonight. I'll send it Air Mail Special in the morning.—Tell him I love him and miss him. And remember I love you and miss you.—No, nothing like that. Daddy, do you remember that recurrent dream I used to have when I was a child?—Now, I'm beginning to have it again and again.—I know what the Freudians say—but even *they* tell you dreams can't come out of any past but your own!— Tell me, daddy, is there some terrible thing in my past that I don't know? No—nobody. It's something I dream. Yes, I'll be good. And I will see you? You always help! You always have! I do feel better. Already. Good night, daddy.

[*She hangs up.* RHODA *still sleeps.* CHRISTINE *goes to the couch, watches her a moment, then picks her up and carries her to her room*]

CURTAIN

SCENE 4

Midmorning, a few days later, in the same apartment. The living room is empty; RHODA *can be heard practicing "Au Clair de la Lune" on the piano in the den.* CHRISTINE *is in the kitchen. The doorbell chimes and she answers it.* MISS FERN *is at the door.*

MISS FERN: May I come in, Mrs. Penmark?

CHRISTINE: Yes, of course, Miss Fern. I meant to come and see you. I got your note.

MISS FERN: [*Entering*] We're in such distress, all of us at the school, and we've suffered such a blow, losing one of the children that way, I'm sure you'll excuse us for going over and over things!

CHRISTINE: I think everybody has been puzzled and worried and saddened.

MISS FERN: I don't think I've ever known any happening to puzzle so many people in so many ways. And I can help so few of them. I've just come from seeing Mrs. Daigle. Of course, our first thought was of her. The rest of us are touched only lightly by this tragedy. She will have to live with it the rest of her days.

CHRISTINE: I know.

MISS FERN: I have seen her several times, and each time she has asked me to find out from you if you had any possible clue to where the penmanship medal might be.

CHRISTINE: It was lost?

MISS FERN: Yes, it wasn't found with the body and has completely disappeared.

CHRISTINE: I didn't know of this.

> [At this moment RHODA comes out with a book in her hand, dressed immaculately as usual]

RHODA: [Curtsying] Good morning, Miss Fern.

MISS FERN: Good morning, Rhoda.

RHODA: Mother, could I sit under the scuppernong arbor for a while and read my book?

CHRISTINE: Of course, Rhoda.

RHODA: It's shady there, and I can see your window, and you can watch me from the window, and I like to be where you can see me.

CHRISTINE: Is it a new book?

RHODA: Yes. It's *Elsie Dinsmore*. The one I got for a prize at Sunday school.

CHRISTINE: I'll be here.

RHODA: I'll be right there all the time. Goodbye, Miss Fern.

> [Curtsy. She runs out]

MISS FERN: It did occur to me that—that Rhoda might have told you a detail or two which she hadn't remembered when she talked with me. You see, she was the last to see the little Daigle boy alive—

CHRISTINE: Are you sure of that?

MISS FERN: Yes.

CHRISTINE: I hadn't realized—

MISS FERN: About an hour after we arrived at the estate one of our older pupils came on Rhoda and the Daigle boy at the far end of the grounds. The boy was upset and crying, and Rhoda was stand-ing in front of him, blocking his path. The older girl was among the trees, and neither child saw her. She was just about to intervene when Rhoda shoved the boy and snatched at his medal, but he broke away and ran down the beach in the direction of the old wharf where he was later found. Rhoda followed him, not running, just walking along, taking her time, the older girl said.

CHRISTINE: Has it occurred to you that the older girl might not be telling the truth?

MISS FERN: That isn't at all likely. She was one of the monitors we'd appointed to keep an eye on the younger children. She's fifteen and has been with us since kindergarten days. No, Mrs. Penmark, she was telling precisely what she saw. We know her well.

CHRISTINE: And that was the last time Claude was seen?

MISS FERN: Yes. A little later—it might have been about noon—one of the guards saw Rhoda coming off the wharf. He shouted a warning, but by then she was on the beach again and he decided to forget the matter. The guard didn't identify the girl by name, but she was wearing a red dress, he said, and Rhoda was the only girl who wore a dress that day. At one o'clock the lunch bell rang and Claude was missing when the roll was called. You know the rest, I think.

CHRISTINE: Yes. But this is very serious—that Rhoda was on the wharf—

MISS FERN: Not serious, really, when you've seen as much of how children behave as I have. Children conceal things from adults. Suppose Rhoda did follow the Daigle child onto the wharf—so many things could have happened quite innocently. He may have hidden himself in the old boathouse, and then, when discovered, may have backed away from Rhoda and fallen in the water.

CHRISTINE: Yes, that could have happened.

MISS FERN: Now Claude, although he looked frail, was an excellent swimmer—and, of course, Rhoda knew that. Once he was in the water she would have expected him to swim ashore. How could she know that the treacherous pilings were at the exact spot where he fell?

CHRISTINE: No.

MISS FERN: Perhaps the thought in Rhoda's mind when he fell in the water was that he'd ruin his new suit and she'd get a scolding for causing it. When he didn't swim ashore at once she may have thought, with the logic of childhood, that he'd hidden under the wharf to frighten her—or to escape her. Later on, when it was too late to do anything, she was afraid to admit what had happened.

CHRISTINE: Then you think she does know something she hasn't told?

MISS FERN: Yes. I think that, like many a frightened soldier, she deserted under fire. This is not a serious charge. Few of us are courageous when tested.

CHRISTINE: She has lied, though.

MISS FERN: Is there any adult who hasn't lied? Smooth the lines from your brow, my dear. You're so much prettier when smiling.

CHRISTINE: I shall question Rhoda.

MISS FERN: I wish you would, though I doubt that you'll learn more than you know.

CHRISTINE: And there's something I want to ask you. There was a floral tribute at Claude's funeral sent by the children of the Fern School. I suppose the children shared the expense—but I haven't been asked to pay my part of it.

MISS FERN: The tribute wasn't nearly so expensive as the papers seemed to think. The money has been collected, and the flowers paid for.

CHRISTINE: Perhaps you telephoned me, and I was out.

MISS FERN: No, my dear. We thought perhaps you'd want to send flowers individually.

CHRISTINE: But why should we have sent flowers individually? Rhoda wasn't friendly with the boy, and my husband and I had never met the Daigles.

MISS FERN: I don't know, my dear. I really—there are three of us, you know, and in the hurry of making decisions—

[She pauses]

CHRISTINE: You make excuses for Rhoda—and then you admit that you didn't ask me to help pay for the flowers—and the reasons you give for not asking me are obviously specious. Does this mean that in your mind, and the minds of your sisters, there is some connection between the drowning and Rhoda's presence on the wharf?

MISS FERN: I refuse to believe there is any connection.

CHRISTINE: And yet you have acted as if there were.

MISS FERN: Yes, perhaps we have.

CHRISTINE: This is a terrible tragedy for Mrs. Daigle, as you say. She has lost her only son. But if there were any shadow over Rhoda—from what has happened—I shall have to live under it, too—and my husband. As for Rhoda—she would not be happy in your school next year.

MISS FERN: No, she would not. And since she would not, it would be as well to make up our minds now that she will not be there.

CHRISTINE: Then there *is* a shadow over her—and you have decided that she will not be invited to return to the Fern School?

MISS FERN: Yes. We have made that decision.

CHRISTINE: But you can't tell me why?

MISS FERN: I think her behavior in the matter of the medal would be sufficient explanation. She has no sense of fair play. She's a poor loser. She doesn't play the game.

CHRISTINE: But you're not saying that Rhoda had anything to do with Claude's death?

MISS FERN: Of course not! Such a possibility never entered our minds!

[*At this moment the doorbell chimes*]

CHRISTINE: I'd better answer.

MISS FERN: Of course, my dear.

[CHRISTINE *goes to the door, hesitates a moment, and then opens it.* MR. *and* MRS. DAIGLE *come in, he tentatively, she boldly. She has been drinking*]

CHRISTINE: Yes?

MRS. DAIGLE: Thanks. We're Mrs. Daigle and Mr. Daigle. You didn't have to let us in, you know. [*To* MISS FERN] You realize we followed you. We shouldn't have done it. I'm a little drunk. [*To* CHRISTINE] I guess you never get a little drunk.

CHRISTINE: You're quite welcome, both of you.

MRS. DAIGLE: Oh, pay no attention to him. He's all for good breeding. He was trying to stop me. Now, you, Mrs. Penmark. You've always had plenty. You're a superior person.

CHRISTINE: No, I'm not.

MRS. DAIGLE: Oh, yes. Father was rich. Rich Richard Bravo. I know. Now I worked in a beauty parlor. Miss Fern used to come there. She looks down on me.

MISS FERN: Please, Mrs. Daigle!

MRS. DAIGLE: I was that frumpy blonde. Now I've lost my boy and I'm a lush. Everybody knows it.

MR. DAIGLE: We're worried about Mrs. Daigle. She's under a doctor's care. She's not herself.

MRS. DAIGLE: But I know what I'm about just the same. Just the same. May I call you Christine? I'm quite aware that you come from a higher level of society. You prolly made a debut and all that. I always considered Christine such a gentle name. Hortense sounds fat—that's me, Hortense. "My girl Hortense," that's what they used to sing at me, "Hasn't got much sense. Let's write her name on the privy fence." Children can be nasty, don't you think?

MR. DAIGLE: Please, Hortense.

MRS. DAIGLE: You're so attractive, Christine. You have such exquisite taste in clothes, but of course you have amples of money to buy 'em with. What I came to see you about, I asked Miss Fern how did Claude happen to lose the medal, and she wouldn't tell me a thing.

MISS FERN: I don't know, Mrs. Daigle. Truly.

MRS. DAIGLE: You know more than you're telling. You're a sly one —because of the school. You don't want the school to get a bad name. But you know more than you're telling, Miss Butter-Wouldn't-Melt Fern. There's something funny about the whole thing. I've said so over and over to Mr. Daigle. He married quite late, you know. In his forties. But I wasn't exactly what the fellow calls a "spring chicken" either. We won't have any more children. No more.

MR. DAIGLE: Please, Hortense. Let me take you home where you can rest.

MRS. DAIGLE: Rest. Sleep. When you can't sleep at night, you can't sleep in the daylight. I lie and look at the water where he went down. There's something funny about the whole thing, Christine. I heard that your little girl was the last who saw him alive. Will you ask her about the last few minutes and tell me what she says?

Maybe she remembers some little thing. I don't care how *small* it is! No matter *how* small! You know something, Miss Fern dyes her hair! She knows something and she won't tell me. Oh, my poor little Claude! What did they do to you?

[CHRISTINE *goes to* MRS. DAIGLE *and puts her arm around her*]

CHRISTINE: I will ask Rhoda, Hortense. Oh, if I only knew!

MRS. DAIGLE: Somebody took the medal off his shirt, Christine. It couldn't come off by accident. I pinned it on myself, and it has a clasp that locks in place. It was no accident. You can wear such simple things, can't you? I never could wear simple things. I couldn't even buy 'em. When I got 'em home they didn't look simple.—He was such a lovely, dear little boy. He said I was his sweetheart. He said he was going to marry me when he grew up. I used to laugh and say, "You'll forget me long before then. You'll find a prettier girl, and you'll marry her." And you know what he said then? He said, "No, I won't, because there's not a prettier girl in the whole world than you are." If you don't believe me, ask the girl who comes in and cleans. She was present at the time.

MR. DAIGLE: Hortense—Hortense!

MRS. DAIGLE: Why do you put your arms around me? You don't give a damn about me. You're a superior person and all that, and I'm— oh, God forgive me! There were those bruises on his hands, and that peculiar crescent-shaped mark on his forehead that the undertaker covered up. He must have bled before he died. That's what the doctor said. And where's the medal? *Who took the medal?* I have a right to know what became of the penmanship medal! If I knew, I'd have a good idea what happened to him.—I don't know why you took it on yourself to put your arms around me? I'm as good as you are. And Claude was better than your girl. He won the medal, and she didn't.—I'm drunk. It's a pleasure to stay drunk when your little boy's been killed. Maybe I'd better lay down.

MR. DAIGLE: We'll go home, and you can lie down there.

MRS. DAIGLE: Why not? Why not go home, and lay down?

MR. DAIGLE: I'm sorry.

MRS. DAIGLE: Oh, who cares what they think? I drank a half bottle of bonded corn in little sips. I'm drunk as holy hell.

[*The* DAIGLES *go out*]

CHRISTINE: Oh, the poor woman!

MISS FERN: I've tried to think of any little thing I could to tell her. But nothing helps.

CHRISTINE: Nothing will ever help.

MISS FERN: No.—I'll be getting back. Thank you for bearing with her, and with me.

CHRISTINE: I'll try again with Rhoda. There's no help for that poor creature, [*She indicates the door*] but I'll try.

MISS FERN: We both have to do what we can. Goodbye, Mrs. Penmark.

CHRISTINE: Goodbye, Miss Fern. [*She suddenly goes to* MISS FERN *as she is about to turn in the doorway, and kisses her, her eyes filling with tears*] She will have to live with it till she dies.

MISS FERN: Yes. Till she dies. Thank you.

> [*She goes, closing the door.* CHRISTINE *turns and looks at the apartment, then goes to the window from which she can see* RHODA. *After a moment she waves, and we know that* RHODA *has looked up from her book. The telephone rings, and* CHRISTINE *answers*]

CHRISTINE: Yes, yes, speaking.—Oh, Kenneth, I'm so glad you called! She's well and I'm well. The little boy who was drowned? Oh, no, Rhoda's her usual self. She's across the street where I can look out and see her reading a book. Do you really, darling?—I hope it won't be too much longer. Four weeks is a long, long time. Call me as often as you can, darling! I love you. Then don't be late. Goodbye, dear.

[*She hangs up and* MONICA *opens the door*]

CHRISTINE: Oh, Monica.

MONICA: Yes, Christine, the fluttery one with the typically inane conversation, but I do have an errand this time, not just gab—

CHRISTINE: Come in, please.

MONICA: [*Entering*] It's Rhoda's locket I'm using for an excuse. I've actually found a place where they'll engrave and clean it in one day. They didn't agree to this unusual effort without a little pressure—in fact, I had to threaten—

CHRISTINE: Not really?

MONICA: Oh, you don't know the old busybody. She uses pressure, influence, bribery, blackmail—and I had to pull them *all* on old Mr. Pageson. He said this little job would take at least two weeks—

CHRISTINE: I'll get the locket. I know where she keeps it.

MONICA: Good. I told him straight that I'm handling the Community Chest again this year, and if he were as busy as all that, I'd be happy to revise my estimate of his contribution upward by a considerable amount. [CHRISTINE *has opened* RHODA'*s table drawer and found the locket in the chocolate box. Her fingers feel something under the oilcloth lining of the drawer and she extracts it also, concealing it from* MONICA, *but turning toward her with the locket*] Ah, you found it! The darling! She keeps her treasures so carefully it's a kind of miserly delight.

CHRISTINE: Shall I wrap it?

MONICA: No, no! I'll just drop it in my purse. [*She does so*] And now I'll take to the air, dear Christine—only do forgive me bursting in and rushing out!

CHRISTINE: No ceremony, please.

MONICA: No ceremony, no; just plain pragmatism! Goodbye, darling.

CHRISTINE: Goodbye, Monica.

> [MONICA *goes out.* CHRISTINE *regards the medal in her hand with a kind of horror mixed with incredulity. After a moment she goes to the window from which* RHODA *was seen. Evidently* RHODA *is not there. She turns from the window and sits on the couch, staring at the medal. The door opens and* RHODA *comes in quietly*]

RHODA: Did you want me to come in, mother? When you waved?

CHRISTINE: So you had the medal, after all. Claude Daigle's medal.

> [*She puts it on coffee table*]

RHODA: [*Warily*] Where did you find it?

CHRISTINE: How did the penmanship medal happen to be hidden under the lining of the drawer of your table? Tell me the truth, Rhoda.

[RHODA *takes off one of her shoes and examines it. Then, smiling a little in a fashion she has always found charming, she asks:*]

RHODA: When we move into our new house can we have a scuppernong arbor, mother? Can we, mother? It's so shady, and pretty, and I love sitting in it!

CHRISTINE: Answer my question. And remember I'm not as innocent about what went on at the picnic as you think. Miss Fern has told me a great deal. So please don't bother to make up a story for my benefit. [RHODA *is silent, her mind working*] How did Claude Daigle's medal get in your drawer? It certainly didn't get there by itself. [RHODA *is silent*] I'm waiting for your answer.

RHODA: I don't know how the medal got there, mother. How could I?

CHRISTINE: [*Controlling herself*] You know. You know quite well how it got there. Did you go on the wharf at any time during the picnic? At *any* time?

RHODA: [*After a pause*] Yes, mother. I—I went there once.

CHRISTINE: Was it before or after you were bothering Claude?

RHODA: I didn't bother Claude, mother. What makes you think that?

CHRISTINE: Why *did* you go on the wharf?

RHODA: It was real early. When we first got there.

CHRISTINE: You knew it was forbidden. Why did you do it?

RHODA: One of the big boys said there were little oysters that grew on the pilings. I wanted to see if they did.

CHRISTINE: One of the guards saw you coming off the wharf. But he says it was just before lunch time.

RHODA: I don't know why he says that. He's wrong, and I told Miss Fern he was wrong. He hollered at me to come off the wharf and I did. I went back to the lawn and that's where I saw Claude. But I wasn't bothering him.

CHRISTINE: What did you say to Claude?

RHODA: I said if I didn't win the medal, I was glad he did.

CHRISTINE: [*Wearily*] Please, please, Rhoda. I know you're an adroit liar. But I must have the *truth*.

RHODA: But it's all true, mother. Every word.

CHRISTINE: One of the monitors saw you try to snatch the medal off Claude's shirt. Is that true? Every word?

RHODA: Oh, that big girl was Mary Beth Musgrove. She told everybody she saw me. Even Leroy knows she saw me. [*She opens her eyes wide, and smiles as though resolving on complete candor*] You see, Claude and I were playing a game we made up. He said if I could catch him in ten minutes and touch the medal with my hand—it was like prisoner's base—he'd let me wear the medal for an hour. How can Mary Beth say I took the medal? I didn't.

CHRISTINE: She didn't say you took the medal. She said you grabbed at it. And that Claude ran away down the beach. Did you have the medal even then?

RHODA: No, mommy. Not then.

[*She runs to her mother and kisses her ardently. This time* CHRISTINE *is the passive one*]

CHRISTINE: How did you get the medal?

RHODA: Oh, I got it later on.

CHRISTINE: How?

RHODA: Claude went back on his promise and I followed him up the beach. Then he stopped and said I could wear the medal all day if I gave him fifty cents.

CHRISTINE: Is that the truth?

RHODA: [*With slight contempt*] Yes, mother. I gave him fifty cents and he let me wear the medal.

CHRISTINE: Then why didn't you tell this to Miss Fern when she questioned you?

RHODA: Oh, mommy, mommy! [*She whimpers a little*] Miss Fern doesn't like me at all! I was afraid she'd think bad things about me if I told her I had the medal!

CHRISTINE: You knew how much Mrs. Daigle wanted the medal, didn't you?

RHODA: Yes, mother, I guess I did.

CHRISTINE: Why didn't you give it to her? [RHODA *says nothing*] Mrs.

Daigle is heartbroken over Claude's death. It's destroyed her. I don't think she'll ever recover from it. [*She disengages herself*] Do you know what I mean?

RHODA: Yes, mother, I guess so, mother.

CHRISTINE: No! You don't know what I mean.

RHODA: It was silly to want to bury the medal pinned on Claude's coat. Claude was dead. He wouldn't know whether he had the medal pinned on him or not. [*She senses her mother's sudden feeling of revulsion, and kisses her cheek with hungry kisses*] I've got the sweetest mother. I tell everybody I've got the sweetest mother in the world!—If she wants a little boy that bad, why doesn't she take one out of the Orphans' Home?

CHRISTINE: Don't touch me! Don't talk to me! We have nothing to say to each other!

RHODA: Well, okay. Okay, mother.

[*She turns away and starts to the den*]

CHRISTINE: Rhoda! When we lived in Baltimore, there was an old lady, Mrs. Clara Post, who liked you very much.

RHODA: Yes.

CHRISTINE: You used to go up to see her every afternoon. She was very old, and liked to show you all her treasures. The one you admired most was a crystal ball, in which opals floated. The old lady promised this treasure to you when she died. One afternoon when the daughter was shopping at the supermarket, and you were alone with Mrs. Post, the old lady somehow managed to fall down the spiral backstairs and break her neck. You said she heard a kitten mewing outside and went to see about it and somehow missed her footing and fell five flights to the courtyard below.

RHODA: Yes, it's true.

CHRISTINE: Then you asked the daughter for the crystal ball. She gave it to you, and it's still hanging at the head of your bed.

RHODA: Yes, mother.

CHRISTINE: Did you have anything to do, anything at all, no matter how little it was, with Claude getting drowned?

RHODA: What makes you ask that, mother?

CHRISTINE: Come here, Rhoda. Look me in the eyes and tell me. I must know!

RHODA: No, mother. I didn't.

CHRISTINE: You're not going back to the Fern School next year. They don't want you any more.

RHODA: Okay. Okay.

CHRISTINE: [*Crosses to telephone*] I'll call Miss Fern and ask her to come over.

RHODA: She'll think I lied to her.

CHRISTINE: You did lie to her!

RHODA: But not to you, mother! Not to you!

[CHRISTINE *rises and goes to the telephone.* RHODA *watches her with apprehension.* CHRISTINE *dials a number*]

CHRISTINE: The Fern School? Is Miss Claudia Fern there?—No. No message. [*She hangs up*] She's not home yet.

RHODA: What would you tell her, mother?

CHRISTINE: No! It can't be true! It can't be true!

[*She turns and looks at* RHODA, *then embraces her*]

CURTAIN

ACT TWO

SCENE 1

The same apartment, late afternoon, the next day. RHODA *is seated at her little table putting a jig-saw puzzle together. She works with intense concentration, trying, rejecting, considering sizes and angles.* CHRISTINE *comes out of the inner hall after* RHODA *calls.*

MONICA: Anybody here?

RHODA: Hello, Aunt Monica!

MONICA: Hi, honey.

RHODA: Mother!

MONICA: Oh, Christine! You said I might have Rhoda for a while. And there's a package for you.

CHRISTINE: Thank you, Monica. You're always the bringer of gifts.

[*She takes a rather bulky carton from* MONICA]

MONICA: This is from somebody else. It was in the package room.

CHRISTINE: Oh—for Rhoda, from daddy—

RHODA: [*Up at once*] For me?

CHRISTINE: Oh, not yet. "In anticipation of her ninth birthday."

RHODA: What does anticipation mean?

MONICA: Looking forward to it.

CHRISTINE: "Not to be opened till—"

RHODA: Oh. It's a long time to wait. But I will.

MONICA: Isn't she the perfect old-fashioned girl? She'll wait!

CHRISTINE: No—there's more in daddy's writing—"Open when you get it—there'll be a real one later."

RHODA: But then he wants me to open it now!

CHRISTINE: Yes. All it needs is to be slit down this side with the scissors.

RHODA: There's excelsior—I can see it.

CHRISTINE: It should be opened in the kitchen, Rhoda.

RHODA: Okay.

[*She takes the package to the kitchen*]

MONICA: [*Watching* RHODA, *waiting till she's out of earshot*] I wish she were mine! Every time I look at her I wish I had just such a little girl.

CHRISTINE: She's not wanted in the Fern School next year.

MONICA: Why?

CHRISTINE: She doesn't fit in, doesn't play the game, she's a poor sport.

MONICA: Honestly, the longer I live, the more I see, the less I'm able to understand the tight little minds of people like the Fern girls! The truth of the matter is, Rhoda is much too charming, too clever, too unusual for them! She makes those others look stupid and stodgy by comparison! [*She lights a cigarette*] Have one?

CHRISTINE: I seem to have quit.

MONICA: Seem to have! Good God, if I were to quit you'd hear the repercussions in New Orleans! I string along with St. Paul—it's better to smoke than to burn.—Could Rhoda stay up and have dinner with me tonight?

CHRISTINE: Yes, she could. I've asked Reginald Tasker over for cocktails and to talk to me about some writing I want to try.

MONICA: Fine; there's no reason why Rhoda should hear about his strychnines and belladonnas. [RHODA *comes to the kitchen door with a large pasteboard box in her hands*] Rhoda, you're to have dinner with me tonight.

RHODA: I am? May I bring my new puzzle?

MONICA: You surely may.

CHRISTINE: Is that what it was?

RHODA: I think it must be the best jig-saw puzzle in the whole world.

[*There is a tap at the door and as* LEROY *speaks it swings open*]

LEROY: [*Outside*] Leroy.

[LEROY *enters with a garbage pail*]

RHODA: Oh, Leroy, there was a lot of excelsior.

MONICA: He'll take care of it.

LEROY: Yes, surely, ma'am.

CHRISTINE: Don't bother to sweep the kitchen. I'll do it.

[LEROY *carries the garbage pail into the kitchen*]

RHODA: It's a map of Asia with all the animals.

MONICA: I have an aversion to cobras, but it's Freudian.

LEROY: [*Emerging from the kitchen*] There's a lot of this stuff scattered around, Mis' Penmark.

MONICA: Let him sweep it, dear. I shall run up and look at the simmering meat sauce.

RHODA: Oh, is it spaghetti?

MONICA: It is. Approve?

RHODA: My favorite!

MONICA: Come up any time. It must be nearly ready.

[*She goes out.* LEROY *begins to sweep in the kitchen.*
RHODA *puts her new puzzle on the table and examines it*]

MESSENGER: [*In the hall outside*] Mrs. Penmark?

MONICA: Yes. This is her door. [MONICA *looks in*] Western Union for you, dear.

CHRISTINE: Thank you. [MONICA *disappears, leaving a* MESSENGER *in her place in the doorway. He hands* CHRISTINE *a yellow envelope. She takes the envelope and the* MESSENGER *goes, closing the door.* CHRISTINE *opens the envelope, and reads the message with pleasure*] Ah!

RHODA: Is it daddy?

CHRISTINE: Not your daddy this time; mine. He's coming here.

RHODA: Grandfather?

CHRISTINE: Yes. He'll be here tonight.—He can sleep—I think Monica has an extra room—I must run up and ask her! Be right back.

[*She goes out.* LEROY *comes from the kitchen again with the box of excelsior*]

LEROY: [*Quietly*] There she sits at her little table, doing her puzzle and looking cute and innocent. Looking like she wouldn't melt

butter, she's that cool. She can fool some people with that innocent look she can put on and put off when she wants to, but not
me. Not even part way, she can't fool me. [RHODA *looks at* LEROY
as though he bored her, then turns back to the puzzle] She don't
want to talk to nobody smart. She likes to talk to people she can
fool, like her mama and Mrs. Breedlove and Mr. Emory.

RHODA: Go empty the excelsior. You talk silly all the time. I know
what you do with the excelsior. You made a bed of excelsior in the
garage behind that old couch, and you sleep there where nobody
can see you.

LEROY: I been way behind the times here-to-fore, but now I got your
number, miss. I been hearing things about you that ain't nice. I
been hearing you beat up that poor little Claude in the woods,
and it took all three the Fern sisters to pull you off him. I heard
you run him off the wharf, he was so scared.

RHODA: [*Picking up a piece*] If you tell lies like that you won't go to
heaven when you die.

LEROY: I heard plenty. I listen to people talk. Not like you who's
gabbling all the time and won't let anybody get a word in edgewise.
That's why I know what people are saying and you don't.

RHODA: People tell lies all the time. I think you tell them more than
anybody else.

LEROY: I know what you done to that boy when you got him out on
the wharf. You better listen to me if you want to keep out of bad
trouble.

RHODA: What did I do, if you know so much?

LEROY: You picked up a stick and hit him with it. You hit him because he wouldn't give you that medal like you told him to. I
thought I'd seen some mean little girls in my time, but you're the
meanest. You want to know how I know how mean you are? Because I'm mean. I'm smart and I'm mean. And you're smart and
you're mean, and I never get caught and you never get caught.

RHODA: I know what you think. I know everything you think. Nobody
believes anything you say.

LEROY: You want to know what you did after you hit that boy? You
jerked the medal off his shirt. Then you rolled that sweet little
boy off the wharf, among them pilings.

RHODA: You don't know anything. None of what you said is true.

LEROY: You know I'm telling the God's truth. You know I got it figured out.

RHODA: You figured out something that never happened. And so it's all lies. Take your excelsior down to the garage and put it where you can sleep on it when you're supposed to be working.

LEROY: You ain't no dope—that I must say—and that's why you didn't leave that stick where nobody could find it. Oh, no, you got better sense than that. You took that bloody stick and washed it off good, and then you threw it in the woods where nobody could see it.

RHODA: I think you're a very silly man.

LEROY: It was you was silly, because you thought you could wash off blood—and you can't.

RHODA: [After a pause, putting down a piece] Why can't you wash off blood?

LEROY: Because you can't, and the police know it. You can wash and wash, but there's always some left. Everybody knows that. I'm going to call the police and tell them to start looking for that stick in the woods. They got what they call "stick bloodhounds" to help them look—and them stick bloodhounds can find any stick there is that's got blood on it. And when they bring in that stick you washed so clean the police'll sprinkle that special blood powder on it, and that little boy's blood will show up on the stick. It'll show up a pretty blue color like a robin's egg.

RHODA: You're scared about the police yourself!

LEROY: Shhh!

RHODA: What you say about me, it's all about you! They'll get you with that powder!

[LEROY hears MRS. PENMARK coming]

LEROY: As far as I'm concerned I wish there was more excelsior. I could use it.

CHRISTINE: [Coming in] What were you saying to Rhoda?

LEROY: Why, Mrs. Penmark, we was just talking. She said it was a big box of excelsior.

CHRISTINE: [Seeing the anger on RHODA's face, the smirk of triumph

on LEROY'*s*] Just the same you're not to speak to her again. If
you do I'll report you! Is that entirely clear?

RHODA: I started it, mama. I told him it was a puzzle all about Asia,
and I hardly know where anything is in Asia.

CHRISTINE: Very well—but don't speak to her!

LEROY: Yes, ma'am.

[*He goes*]

CHRISTINE: [*Turning on the lights*] You're really working in the dark
here. I think you strain your eyes over these things.

[CHRISTINE *wheels a small bar out of the kitchen, set up
to serve drinks*]

RHODA: Mother, is it true that when blood has been washed off anything a policeman can still find it was there if he puts powder on
the place? Will the place really turn blue?

CHRISTINE: Who's been talking to you about such things? Leroy?

RHODA: No, mommy, it wasn't he. It was some men went by the gate
in the park.

CHRISTINE: I don't know how they test for blood. But I could ask
Reginald Tasker. Or Miss Fern; she might know.

RHODA: No—don't ask her! Mommy, mommy, mommy! [*She breaks
down and cries, deliberately*] Nobody helps me! Nobody believes
me! I'm your little girl, and I'm all alone!

CHRISTINE: It's not a very good act, Rhoda. You may improve it
enough to convince someone who doesn't know you, but at present it's easy to see through.

RHODA: [*Wiping away tears with the back of her hand*] Maybe I'd
better go up to Monica's and have dinner.

CHRISTINE: Yes. She said any time. [*The doorbell rings*] And my
company is here. [*She opens the door*] Good evening, Mr. Tasker.

TASKER: [*Entering*] Good evening.

CHRISTINE: This is my daughter, Rhoda.

TASKER: Hello, Rhoda. [*He puts out his hand. She takes it and gives
him her best smile*] Well, isn't she a little sweetheart!

RHODA: [*Making her curtsy*] Thank you.

TASKER: That's the kind of thing makes an old bachelor wish he were married.

RHODA: You like little girls to curtsy?

TASKER: It's the best thing left out of the Middle Ages!

RHODA: I'm having dinner upstairs.

TASKER: The loss is ours, all ours.

CHRISTINE: You may go now, Rhoda.

RHODA: Yes, mommy.

[*She throws* CHRISTINE *a kiss and runs out*]

TASKER: That's a little ray of sunshine, that one. Isn't she?

CHRISTINE: I've seen her stormy.

TASKER: No doubt. But she's going to make some man very happy. Just that smile.

CHRISTINE: Since I called you I've had a wire from my father, and he'll be here tonight. It's a year since I've seen him.

TASKER: Bravo's coming?

CHRISTINE: Yes.

TASKER: Now there's a man I always wanted to meet.

CHRISTINE: He may be here before long. He said perhaps for dinner.

TASKER: Good. By the way, if you're thinking of writing mystery stories Bravo was quite an authority on crime and criminals early in his career.

CHRISTINE: Yes, I know he was.

TASKER: He could probably help you more than I could. Before he began covering wars he covered practically all the horror cases, from Leopold and Loeb on.

CHRISTINE: What will it be?

TASKER: Gin and tonic?

CHRISTINE: Good. I'll have it too.—You see, what I wanted to ask was a psychological question and I doubt that it was asked or answered—if it has been—till recently.

[*She pauses, pouring into the jigger, getting out the ice*]

TASKER: I may not know all the answers.

CHRISTINE: Well, perhaps nobody does. But the story I was thinking of writing made me wonder—tell me, do children ever commit murders? Or is crime something that's learned gradually, and grows as the criminal grows up, so that only adults do really dreadful things?

TASKER: Well, I have thought about that, and so have several authorities I've consulted lately. Yes, children have often committed murders, and quite clever ones too. Some murderers, particularly the distinguished ones who are going to make great names for themselves, start amazingly early.

CHRISTINE: In childhood?

TASKER: Oh, yes. Just like mathematicians and musicians. Poets develop later. There's never been anything worth while in poetry written before eighteen or twenty. But Mozart showed his genius at six, Pascal was a master mathematician at twelve, and some of the great criminals were top-flight operators before they got out of short pants and pinafores.

CHRISTINE: They grew up in the slums, or among criminals, and learned from their environment? [*The doorbell chimes*] Oh—I wonder if that could be father!

TASKER: If it is I would like to stay and see him a moment—

CHRISTINE: Oh, that's understood! [*She opens the door*] Daddy!

[BRAVO *comes into the doorway, a man of fifty-five or sixty, handsome once, but somewhat stern and weary*]

BRAVO: Hello, darling. I'm early.

[CHRISTINE *goes into his arms and they kiss, then stand looking at each other. He sets down a small bag*]

CHRISTINE: You're here! You're actually here!

BRAVO: I guess I'm something of a truant, sweetheart, but you said you wanted to see me, and I wanted to see you, so—

CHRISTINE: I'm so glad! This is Reginald Tasker, father.

BRAVO: [*Giving his hand to* TASKER] Ah, one of my favorites!

TASKER: Puts you to sleep regularly?

BRAVO: Sometimes keeps me awake. You've done some impressive research for the Classic Crime Club.

TASKER: Now I've always thought the best papers they ever printed were by Richard Bravo.

BRAVO: That old dodo! No, no, he's written himself out, and talked himself out and now he's drifting round the country, working for a second-rate news service.

TASKER: You're really looking into this off-side oil?

BRAVO: That's what they've got me doing. But I took off and left them, for the moment anyway. I wanted to see my long-lost daughter.

[*He puts his arm around* CHRISTINE]

TASKER: I've sometimes wanted to ask you if you've ever considered coming back into the criminology racket. There's been nobody like you since you left.

BRAVO: Well, all compliments aside, my later books didn't sell as well as the early ones—and the war came along. Now I write filler.

TASKER: You've written some things that won't be forgotten.

BRAVO: Let's hope.

TASKER: And now your daughter is going to try her hand.

BRAVO: At writing? She can't even spell.

CHRISTINE: I do get lonely here with Kenneth away, and I thought I'd try to work out a murder mystery, in the evenings.

BRAVO: [*To* TASKER] And you're encouraging this competition?

TASKER: Well, I was rather stumped by her last question. She was asking whether criminal children are always the product of environment.

BRAVO: Nothing difficult about that, little one. They are.

TASKER: Now, I'd have said the same, a few years ago—

BRAVO: Look, can't I have some of this wicked mixture you're lapping up?

CHRISTINE: Of course, daddy—I'm sorry. Do you really think they're always the product of environment?

BRAVO: Always.

TASKER: I couldn't prove you're wrong, of course. But some doctor friends of mine assure me that we've all been putting too much emphasis on environment and too little on heredity lately. They say there's a type of criminal born with no capacity for remorse or guilt—born with the kind of brain that may have been normal among humans fifty thousand years ago—

BRAVO: Do you believe this?

TASKER: Well, yes, I guess I do.

BRAVO: Well, I don't.

TASKER: I've been convinced that there are people—only a few, and certainly very unfortunate—who are incapable from the beginning of acquiring a conscience, or a moral character. Not even able to love, except physically. No feeling for right or wrong.

BRAVO: I've heard such assertions, but never found any evidence behind them. If you encounter a human without compassion or pity or morals, he grew up where these things weren't encouraged. That's final and absolute. This stuff you're talking is tommyrot.

[He sips his drink]

CHRISTINE: Do your doctor friends have any evidence?

TASKER: They can't prove it, but they think there are such people. They say there are children born into the best families, with every advantage of education and discipline—that never acquire any moral scruples. It's as if they were born blind—you couldn't expect to teach them to see.

CHRISTINE: And do they look—like brutes?

BRAVO: Are you sold on this?

CHRISTINE: I want to find out.

TASKER: Sometimes they do. But often they present a more convincing picture of virtue than normal folks. A wax rosebud or a plastic peach can look more perfect than the real thing. They imitate humanity beautifully.

CHRISTINE: But that's—horrible.

TASKER: Some of them seem to have done some pretty horrible things and kept on looking innocent and sweet.

BRAVO: I'd like to examine the evidence. Not much sense discussing it till we do.

TASKER: Well, this clinic I frequent came long ago to the conclusion that there are bad seeds—just plain bad from the beginning, and nothing can change them.

CHRISTINE: And this favorite murderess of yours—the one you were speaking of the other day—is she an instance?

TASKER: Bessie Denker—was she a bad seed? Well, she may have been, because the deaths started so early in her vicinity. Bessie earned her sobriquet of "The Destroying Angel" in early childhood.

CHRISTINE: Then she began young?

TASKER: Yes. The name wasn't applied to her till much later, when the whole story of her career came out, but Bessie was lethal and accurate from the beginning. One of her most famous murders involved the use of the deadly amanita, a mushroom known as "the destroying angel," and some clever reporter transferred the term to her.—In fact, it was a colleague of Mr. Bravo's, unless I've misread something—

BRAVO: It may have been—I don't know.

CHRISTINE: How did she end?

TASKER: Well, Mr. Bravo knows more about it than I do—

BRAVO: I've forgotten the whole thing. Put it out of my mind. I'm in oil now.

CHRISTINE: Tell me—how did she end?

BRAVO: You don't want to probe into this mess, sweetheart—

CHRISTINE: Yes, I do.

BRAVO: Can't we change the subject?

CHRISTINE: No, darling, I want to know. What was the rest of the story, Mr. Tasker?

TASKER: There's the mystery. By the time the authorities got really roused about her she disappeared from the Middle West—just seemed to vanish. She had quite a fortune by that time. The fellow that seems to know most about her maintains that she went to Australia. A similar beauty emerged in Melbourne; her name was Beulah Demerest, so if it was the same person she didn't have to change the initials on her linen or silver.

CHRISTINE: How could she—kill so many—and leave no trace?

TASKER: [To BRAVO] You wrote a famous essay listing all her methods —you must know it better than I do—

BRAVO: Not at all. I've dropped all that—haven't read the recent literature.

CHRISTINE: Did she ever use violence?

TASKER: Forgive me, sir, I'll make it short. She made a specialty of poisons—studied not only drugs and toxins but the lives of those she wished to kill. It's practically impossible to prove murder when the victim dies of rattlesnake venom in Western Colorado. Too many diamondbacks about. And tetanus can be picked up in any barnyard. She made use of such things.—It all came to a sudden end—she was indicted again and took off for parts unknown—leaving no—but wasn't there a child, a little girl?

BRAVO: Never heard of one. That must be a recent addition to the myth.

CHRISTINE: I wanted to ask one more question. Was she ever found out here?

TASKER: Not in this country. Three juries looked at that lovely dewy face and heard that melting cultured voice and said, "She couldn't have done it."

CHRISTINE: She wasn't convicted?

TASKER: "Not guilty." Three times.

CHRISTINE: You think she was one of these poor deformed children, born without pity?

TASKER: Personally, I guess I do.

CHRISTINE: Did she have an enchanting smile?

TASKER: Dazzling, by all accounts.

CHRISTINE: She was doomed?

TASKER: Absolutely. Doomed to commit murder after murder till somehow or other she was found out.

CHRISTINE: She'd have been better off if she'd died young.

TASKER: And society would. And yet sometimes I wonder whether these malignant brutes may not be the mutation that survives on this planet in this age. This age of technology and murder-for-empire. Maybe the softies will have to go, and the snake-hearted will inherit the earth.

BRAVO: I'm betting on the democracies.

TASKER: And so am I. But we're living in an age of murder. In all history there have never been so many people murdered as in our century. Add up all the murders from the beginning of history to 1900, and then add the murders after 1900, and our century wins. All alone.—And on that merry note I think I should take my leave, for I meant not to bother you and I've been lecturing.

BRAVO: You've got a highly questionable theory there—about heredity.

TASKER: I'd like to go into that with you when there's more time.

BRAVO: Let's do that next time I'm in town.

TASKER: Right. And now I'll say good evening, Mrs. Penmark—I'm afraid the pleasure's been all mine.

CHRISTINE: Not at all. I'll call you early in the week.

TASKER: I'm always about. [*To* BRAVO] Good-night, sir.

BRAVO: Good-night, Mr. Tasker.

CHRISTINE: Good-night.

[TASKER *goes out*]

BRAVO: Are you really planning to write something?

CHRISTINE: I was just asking questions. You saw Kenneth in Washington?

BRAVO: Yes. He's looking well. As well as possible when a fellow's hot, sticky, tired, and, most of all, lonesome.

CHRISTINE: We'd counted on going somewhere this summer. Then there was a sudden change of orders.

BRAVO: Am I looking too close, or is there something heavy on your mind?

CHRISTINE: Does something show in my face?

BRAVO: Everything shows in your face. It always did.

CHRISTINE: I'm not sure I'm worried about anything—now that you're here. I always felt so safe and comfortable when you were in the room. And you have the same effect now.

BRAVO: To tell you the truth you did a magic for me. I'd always wanted a little girl and you were everything lovely a little girl could be for her old dad. But, Christine, what did you want to ask me— that night you phoned?

CHRISTINE: Let me think a minute.—Would you have another drink?

BRAVO: Yes, I guess I will. [*He looks at the bar*] Let me fix something. Will you have more gin and tonic?

[*He goes to the bar*]

CHRISTINE: No, thank you.

BRAVO: Speak up, darling. It's between us, whatever it is.

CHRISTINE: My landlady here is—is a sort of amateur psychiatrist— a devotee of Freud, constantly analyzing.

BRAVO: I know the sort.

CHRISTINE: Her name is Breedlove. You'll meet her, because she's offered a wonderful room for you to stay in while you're here. Rhoda's having dinner with her tonight.

BRAVO: You were going to come out with something.

CHRISTINE: Yes. Well, what I was going to ask reminded me of her. I confessed to her the other day that I had always worried about being an adopted child—had always been afraid that mommy wasn't really my mother and the daddy I love so much wasn't really my daddy.

BRAVO: What did she say?

CHRISTINE: She said it was one of the commonest fantasies of childhood. Everybody has it. She had it herself.

BRAVO: It certainly is common.

CHRISTINE: But that doesn't help me. I still feel, just as strongly as ever, that old fear that you're not really mine.

BRAVO: Has something made you think of this lately?

CHRISTINE: Yes.

BRAVO: What is it?

CHRISTINE: My little girl, Rhoda.

BRAVO: What about her?

CHRISTINE: She terrifies me. I'm afraid for her. I'm afraid of what she may have inherited from me.

BRAVO: What could she have inherited?

CHRISTINE: Father—daddy—whose child am I?

BRAVO: Mine.

CHRISTINE: Daddy, dear, don't lie to me. It's gone beyond where that will help. I've told you about a dream I have—and I'm not sure it's all a dream. Whose child am I? Are you my father? [BRAVO is silent] This is a strange question to greet you with after being so long away from you—but I—I have to ask it. And for Rhoda's sake —and mine—you must tell me.

BRAVO: What has Rhoda done?

CHRISTINE: I don't know. But I'm afraid.

BRAVO: It cannot be inherited. It cannot.

[*He draws a deep breath, then takes a step and staggers slightly, putting out a hand for support*]

CHRISTINE: Father, you're not well!

[*She goes to him. He sinks into a chair*]

BRAVO: I'm all right, just get me a glass of water. [*She gets a glass from the kitchen*] Perfectly well. A trace of fibrillation once in a while, quite normal at my age. Thank you. And with fibrillation there's a slight dizziness, also normal. I'm all right now.

CHRISTINE: I won't ask any more questions. I'm sorry.

BRAVO: I think that's better. Let's just close the book.

CHRISTINE: [*After a pause*] Only I have the answer now.

BRAVO: The answer?

CHRISTINE: Yes.

BRAVO: I've been a very fortunate man, Christine. I could tell you a long history of jobs that came in the nick of time, of lost money found, of friends who showed up to pay old debts just when I had to have the money. At every main turning-point in my life some good fairy has seemed to intervene to flip things my way. And the biggest piece of luck I ever had—the luck that saved my reason and kept me going—was a little girl named Christine. You were the only child I ever had. My life was futile and barren before you came, but you were magic for me, as I said, and you made life bearable. I kept on—because of you.

CHRISTINE: You don't have to say any more.

BRAVO: I don't, do I?

CHRISTINE: You found me somewhere.

BRAVO: Yes. In a very strange place—in a strange way.

CHRISTINE: I know the place.

BRAVO: I don't think you could. You were less than two years old.

CHRISTINE: I either remember it or I dreamed it.

BRAVO: What kind of dream?

CHRISTINE: I dream of a bedroom in a farmhouse in a countryside where there are orchards. I sleep in the room with my brother, who is older than I—and my—is it my mother?—comes to take care of him. She is a graceful, lovely woman, like an angel. I suppose my brother must have died, for afterward I'm alone in the room. One night I awake feeling terrified and for some reason I can't stay in that house. It's moonlight and I somehow get out the window, drop to the grass below and hide myself in the tall weeds beyond the first orchard. I don't recall much more except that toward morning I'm thirsty and keep eating the yellow pippins that fall from the tree—and when the first light comes up on the clouds I can hear my mother calling my name. I hide in the weeds and don't answer. Is this a dream? Is it only a dream?

BRAVO: What name did she call?

CHRISTINE: It isn't Christine. It—is it—could it be Ingold?

BRAVO: You remember that name?

CHRISTINE: Yes, it comes back to me. "Ingold! Ingold Denker," she was calling. *Denker?* You've concealed something from me all these years, haven't you, daddy? I came out of that terrible household! You found me there!

BRAVO: The neighbors found you after your mother vanished. Where she went I never knew, nor did they, but she had quite a fortune by that time, and something had panicked her—so she quickly got away, leaving one child, an astonishingly sweet and beautiful little thing with the most enchanting smile I've ever seen. I was covering the case for a Chicago paper, and I wired my wife to join me. We couldn't resist you.

CHRISTINE: Oh, daddy, daddy! Oh, God help me! Why didn't you leave me there? Why didn't I die in the orchard and end the agony then?

BRAVO: It was the neighbors found you and saved you. Would you rather have stayed with them?

CHRISTINE: Oh, no, you know I wouldn't. You've been a wonderful father! But—that place—and that evil woman—my mother—!

BRAVO: There are places and events in every man's life he'd rather not remember. Don't let it hurt you now. It's past and doesn't touch you.

CHRISTINE: I wish I had died then! I wish it! I wish it!

BRAVO: It hasn't mattered where you came from! You've been sound and sweet and loving! You've given me more than I ever gave or could ever repay! If you'd been my own I couldn't have hoped for more! You knew nothing but love and kindness and you've given love and kindness and sweetness all your life! Kenneth loves you, and you've made him happy. And Rhoda's a perfect, sweet, sound little girl!

CHRISTINE: Is she, father? Is she?

BRAVO: What has she done?

CHRISTINE: She's—it's as if she were born blind!

BRAVO: It cannot happen! It does not happen!

[*The doorbell chimes and* MONICA *comes in*]

MONICA: Excuse me, please, but Rhoda has eaten her dinner, tired of her puzzle and now she wants a book.

CHRISTINE: We haven't even started yet.

MONICA: And I haven't met Mr. Bravo. [*She puts out her hand*] I'm Mrs. Breedlove. The oversized analyst who's going to put you up, and promises not to annoy you.

BRAVO: You know what newspaper men are like—crusty, bitter, irascible. If you can put up with me you're a saint.

[RHODA *enters*]

RHODA: Granddaddy!

BRAVO: Rhoda!

[*He picks her up and puts her down*]

MONICA: Isn't she perfection?

RHODA: Next to daddy, you lift me up best! Why do you look at me?

BRAVO: I want to see your face.

MONICA: You know, Mr. Bravo, these Penmarks are the most enchanting neighbors I've ever had. Now I'll want Rhoda for dinner every night. Tell me, didn't you write the Fingerprint Series?

BRAVO: I'm afraid I was very guilty of that about twenty years ago.

MONICA: I read the first volume to pieces, and wept over it till the parts I loved most were illegible—and then bought another!

BRAVO: I've finally met my public.

MONICA: I don't disappoint you? Anyway I'm large.

BRAVO: I like the way you read books to pieces. It's good for royalties.

CHRISTINE: It's time to get dinner for us.

BRAVO: Maybe I should find my room and get ready for the evening.

MONICA: I'll take you up if you'd like to go now.

BRAVO: If you'll be so kind.

MONICA: It's the floor above. Be back, Christine.

[BRAVO *picks up his small bag and goes out with* MONICA. CHRISTINE *goes into the kitchen to get dinner.* RHODA *goes to the inner hall, and then comes out furtively, carrying a newspaper package.* CHRISTINE *emerges from the kitchen*]

CHRISTINE: What are you doing?

RHODA: Nothing.

CHRISTINE: Is that for the incinerator?

RHODA: Yes.

CHRISTINE: What is it?

RHODA: Some things you told me to throw away.

CHRISTINE: Let me see what's in the package.

RHODA: No.

CHRISTINE: Let me see it! [*She tries to take the bundle from a sullen* RHODA. RHODA *suddenly snatches it back and tries to run.* CHRISTINE *holds on determinedly, and* RHODA *begins to bite and kick like a little animal. The package tears, revealing* RHODA's *shoes.* CHRISTINE *wrests the bundle away, and pushes* RHODA *violently from her, so that she falls into a chair, staring at her mother with cold, fixed hatred*] You hit him with one of the shoes, didn't you? Tell me! Tell me the truth! You hit him with those shoes! That's how those half-moon marks got on his forehead and hands! Answer me! Answer me!

RHODA: I hit him with the shoes! I had to hit him with the shoes, mother! What else could I do?

CHRISTINE: Do you know that you murdered him?

RHODA: It was his fault! If he'd given me the medal like I told him to I wouldn't have hit him!

[*She begins to cry, pressing her forehead against table*]

CHRISTINE: Tell me what happened. I want the truth this time. Start from the beginning and tell me how it happened. I know you killed him, so there's no sense in lying again.

RHODA: [*Throwing herself into her mother's arms*] I can't, mother! I can't tell you!

CHRISTINE: [*Shaking* RHODA] I'm waiting for your answer! Tell me. I must know now!

RHODA: He wouldn't give me the medal like I told him to, that's all. So then he ran away from me and hid on the wharf, but I found him there and told him I'd hit him with my shoe if he didn't give me the medal. He shook his head and said, "No," so I hit him the first time and then he took off the medal and gave it to me.

CHRISTINE: What happened then?

RHODA: Well, he tried to run away, so I hit him with the shoe again. He kept crying and making a noise, and I was afraid somebody would hear him. So I kept on hitting him, mother. I hit him harder this time, and he fell in the water.

CHRISTINE: Oh, my God, my God! What are we going to do, what are we going to do?

RHODA: [*Coquettishly*] Oh, I've got the prettiest mother! I've got the nicest mother! That's what I tell everybody! I say, "I've got the sweetest—"

CHRISTINE: How did the bruises get on the back of his hands?

RHODA: He tried to pull himself back on the wharf after he fell in the water. I wouldn't have hit him any more only he kept saying he was going to tell on me. Mother, mother, please say you won't let them hurt me! Please!

CHRISTINE: [*Putting her arms around* RHODA] Nobody will hurt you. I don't know what must be done now, but I promise you nobody will hurt you.

RHODA: I want to play the way we used to, mommy. Will you play with me? If I give you a basket of kisses what will you give me?

CHRISTINE: Please, please.

RHODA: Can't you give me the answer, mother? If I give you a basket of kisses—

CHRISTINE: Rhoda, go into your room and read. I must think what to do.—You must promise you won't tell anyone else what you've told me. Do you understand?

RHODA: [*With contempt*] Why would I tell and get killed?

CHRISTINE: What happened to old Mrs. Post in Baltimore? I know so much, another won't matter now.

RHODA: There was ice on the steps—and I slipped and fell against her, and—and that was all.

CHRISTINE: That was all?

RHODA: No. I slipped on purpose.

CHRISTINE: Take the shoes and put them in the incinerator! Hurry! Hurry, Rhoda! Put them in the incinerator! Burn them quickly!

[RHODA *takes the bundle*]

RHODA: What will you do with the medal, mother?

CHRISTINE: I must think of something to do.

RHODA: You won't give it to Miss Fern?

CHRISTINE: No, I won't give it to Miss Fern.

[RHODA *smiles and goes toward the door*]

CURTAIN

SCENE 2

After breakfast in the apartment, the next morning. At rise the stage is empty and the phone ringing. LEROY enters the front door.

LEROY: Leroy. [*He looks at phone, starts toward kitchen and decides to answer phone. Goes back and takes it off the hook and hangs up. He starts back toward the kitchen and the phone rings again. RHODA enters from the kitchen*] You better answer that phone.

RHODA: [*At the phone*] Hello—no, Mr. Bravo isn't here. Yes, I could write down a number.—Yes, sir.—I'll tell him. Goodbye. [*To LEROY*] I found out about one lie that you told. There's no such thing as a "stick bloodhound."

LEROY: I'm not supposed to talk to little Miss Goody-goody.

RHODA: Then don't.

LEROY: Where's your mother?

RHODA: Upstairs.

LEROY: For your own sake, though, I'll tell you this much. There may not be any stick bloodhounds, but there's a stick. And you better find that stick before they do, because it'll turn blue and then they'll fry you in the electric chair.

RHODA: There wasn't any stick any more than there were stick bloodhounds.

LEROY: You know the noise the electric chair makes? It goes z—z—z, and then you swivel all up the way bacon does when your mother's frying it.

RHODA: Go empty the garbage. They don't put little girls in the electric chair.

LEROY: They don't? They got a little blue chair for boys and a little pink one for girls. I just remembered something. Just the morning of the picnic I wiped off your shoes with the cleats on 'em. You used to go tap-tap-tap on the walk. How come you don't wear 'em any more?

RHODA: You're silly. I never had a pair of shoes like that.

LEROY: They used to go tap-tap when you walked and I didn't like it. I spilled water on 'em and I wiped 'em off.

RHODA: They hurt my feet and I gave them away.

LEROY: You know one thing? You didn't hit that boy with no stick. You hit him with them shoes. Ain't I right this time?

RHODA: You're silly.

LEROY: You think I'm silly because I said about the stick. All I was trying was to make you say "No, it wasn't no stick. It was my shoes." Because I knew what it was.

RHODA: You lie all the time. All the time.

LEROY: How come I've got those shoes then?

RHODA: Where did you get them?

LEROY: I came in and got them right out of your apartment.

RHODA: [Looking at book] It's just more lies. I burned those shoes. I put them down the incinerator and burned them. Nobody's got them.

LEROY: [After a pause] I don't say that wasn't smart. That was.— Only suppose I heard something coming rattling down the incinerator and I says to myself, "It sounds to me like a pair of shoes with cleats." Oh, I'm not saying you didn't burn 'em a little, but you didn't burn 'em all up like you wanted to.

RHODA: [*Waits with a new frightening stillness and intensity*] Yes?—

LEROY: Now listen to this and figure out which of us is the silly one. I'm in the basement working, and I hear them shoes come rattling down the pipe. I open the door quick and there they is on top of the coals only smoking the least little bit. I grab them out. Oh, they're scorched some, but there's plenty left to turn blue and show where the blood was. There's plenty left to put you in the electric chair!

[*He laughs a foolish little laugh of triumph*]

RHODA: [*Calmly*] Give me those shoes back.

LEROY: Oh, no. I got them shoes hid where nobody but me can find them.

RHODA: You'd better give me those shoes. They're mine. Give them back to me.

LEROY: I'm not giving them shoes back to nobody, see?

RHODA: [*With cold fury*] You'd better give them back to me, Leroy.

LEROY: [*Laughing*] I'm keeping them shoes until—[*His laughter dies under her fixed, cold stare. He begins to be afraid of her. He no longer wants to play this game*] Who said I had any shoes except mine?

RHODA: You did. You get them and give them back.

LEROY: Now, listen, Rhoda, I was just fooling and teasing you. I haven't got any shoes. I've got work to do.

[*He starts toward front door.* RHODA *quickly moves up to door and blocks his way*]

RHODA: Give me back my shoes.

LEROY: I haven't got nobody's shoes. Don't you know when anybody's teasing you?

RHODA: Give them back!

LEROY: Go and practice your piano lesson! I haven't got 'em, I keep telling you.

RHODA: Will you bring them back!

LEROY: I was just fooling at first, but now I really believe you killed that little boy. I really believe you did kill him with your shoes.

RHODA: You've got them hid, but you'd better get them and bring them back here! Right here to me!

LEROY: Quit talking loud. There's someone in the hall!

[CHRISTINE *enters*]

CHRISTINE: What was Leroy saying to you?

RHODA: Nothing.

CHRISTINE: I heard you say, "Bring them back here!"

RHODA: He said he had my shoes.

LEROY: I got nobody's shoes but my own. There's a number for Mr. Bravo to call.

CHRISTINE: You may go, Leroy.

LEROY: Yes, ma'am.

[*He exits*]

CHRISTINE: Daddy, there is a message for you.

BRAVO: [*Entering*] Thank you, sweetheart.

[*He takes the phone and dials*]

MONICA: [*Entering*] Look what I have for you, Rhoda! Turquoise! And the garnet, too!

RHODA: Thank you, Aunt Monica.

BRAVO: Hello. Listen, Murry, I know I ran out on you but this was imperative. Just wouldn't wait.—When does it leave?—Yes, I've had breakfast. If I get a taxi now I could just make it.—Yes, I've never been on the rig. I'd like to see it. And remember I've never missed a deadline. Think nothing of it. [*He hangs up*] I'll be gone a couple of days, but I plan to make this my headquarters the next few weeks if I may—

MONICA: As long as you can stand us—

BRAVO: Rhoda.

RHODA: Yes, granddaddy.

BRAVO: You ought to patent your smile. It does unfair things to your elders. . . . I really have to go, dear. I'll pick up the taxi at the corner. [*He puts his arms around* CHRISTINE] You are the bright thing in my life, Christine. It was you I lived for. You I loved. No

matter what happens I want you to remember that. Don't worry.
It will come out well.

CHRISTINE: Come back soon.

BRAVO: I will, sweetheart. [*He kisses* CHRISTINE *briefly*] My bag's upstairs. Don't come along. It'll be quicker.

[*He goes out*]

MONICA: What a trouper! [*There is a sound of ice cream bells*] Ah,
the ice cream man!

RHODA: Mother, could I have a popsicle?

CHRISTINE: Yes. Take the money from my purse. [RHODA *runs into
the kitchen, then, coming out, stops to pick up matches as she
passes the stove*] It is hot today.

MONICA: Yes, the streets seem deserted.

CHRISTINE: Rhoda, what have you got those for?

RHODA: I guess I just wasn't thinking.

CHRISTINE: I'll take them, please.

[*She takes the matches and goes into the kitchen.* RHODA
picks up another box and runs out. CHRISTINE *re-enters*]

MONICA: You won't mind too much if I'm nosey and ridiculous,
Christine. You haven't been yourself lately. It's as if something's
dragging you down.

CHRISTINE: Oh, dear. Do I seem that way to others?

MONICA: You mean you feel it?

CHRISTINE: Yes.

MONICA: Do you take vitamins regularly?

CHRISTINE: No.

MONICA: You should. That's one of the things we know. I have an
awfully good combination, and I'll bring some down if I may.—
And now you must really forgive me. Have you and Kenneth come
to a parting of the ways? Is his secretary more to him than an expert on politics? Does she make a nest for him among the office
buildings?

CHRISTINE: It's nothing like that, Monica. I wish I were as sure of
other things as I am of Kenneth.

MONICA: Then do you suspect some disease—something like cancer, for example? If you do, we must face it and do everything that can be done. And a lot can be.

CHRISTINE: I'm perfectly healthy as far as I know.

MONICA: Do you sleep enough?

CHRISTINE: Well, no. Not always.

MONICA: You must have some sleeping pills. That much we can do. And now I won't bully you any more, Christine. I'm only going to say that I love you truly and deeply, my dear, as though you were my own; in fact Emory feels the same way about you, but I needn't tell you that, for you know it already. [CHRISTINE *puts her head down on the table and sobs*] Tell me what it is, dear. You can trust me. [CHRISTINE *gets up blindly, puts her arms around* MONICA, *and weeps without restraint*] Dear, dear Christine. You'll feel better now. Perhaps you can get some sleep.

[*The doorbell rings, and* CHRISTINE *stirs herself slowly to answer it*]

MONICA: Damn, I'll get rid of whatever—

[*She goes to the door and opens it.* MRS. DAIGLE *stands in the doorway*]

MRS. DAIGLE: Well, Mrs. Breedlove. Hi. You don't want me here, and I don't want to be here, but I can't stay away, so I got a little drunk and came over. Excuse it, please.

MONICA: You're very welcome.

[*But the words come hard*]

MRS. DAIGLE: Like a skunk, I know. Mrs. Breedlove knows everybody. Knows even me.

CHRISTINE: How are you, Mrs. Daigle?

MRS. DAIGLE: I'm half seas over, as the fellow—I just want to talk to your little girl. She was one of the last to see my Claude alive.

CHRISTINE: Yes, I know.

MRS. DAIGLE: Where do you keep the perfect little lady that was the last to see Claude? I thought I'd just hold her in my arms and we'd have a nice talk and maybe she'd remember something. Any little thing.

CHRISTINE: She's out playing.

MRS. DAIGLE: I'm just unfortunate, that's all. Drunk and unfortunate. Only she was right outside when I came by, ladies and gentlemen.

CHRISTINE: [*Going to the window*] She isn't there now. I don't see her.

[*But she couldn't, for her life, call* RHODA]

MRS. DAIGLE: She's a perfect little lady, never gives any trouble, that's what I heard. Have you got anything to drink in the house? Anything at all. I'm not the fussy type. I prefer bourbon and water but anything will do. [CHRISTINE *goes to kitchen and wheels out the bar*] Oh, ain't we swank? Really Plaza and Astor! [MRS. DAIGLE *pours herself a straight drink and downs it at a gulp, then takes a taste of water*] What I came here for was to have a little talk with Rhoda, because she knows something. I've called Miss Fern on the telephone a dozen times, but she just gives me the brush-off. [*She sits rather clumsily*] She knows something, all right.

CHRISTINE: Are you comfortable there?

MRS. DAIGLE: I'm not intoxicated in the slightest degree. Kindly don't talk down to me, Mrs. Penmark. I've been through enough, without that.

[*The door opens and* RHODA *enters, delicately eating her popsicle*]

RHODA: I brought back change, mother.

CHRISTINE: Very well. Mrs. Daigle wants to see you.

MRS. DAIGLE: So this is your little girl? Claude spoke of you so often, and in such high terms. You were one of his dearest friends, I'm sure. He said you were so bright in school. So you're Rhoda.

RHODA: Yes.

MRS. DAIGLE: Come let me look at you, Rhoda. Now how about giving your Aunt Hortense a big kiss? [RHODA *gives her popsicle to* MONICA *and goes dutifully to be kissed*] You were with Claude when he had his accident, weren't you dear? You're the little girl who was so sure she was going to win the penmanship medal, and worked so hard. But you didn't win it after all, did you, darling? Claude won the medal, didn't he? Now tell me this: would you say he won it fair and square or he cheated? These things are so important to me now he's dead. Would you say it was fair Claude had the medal? Because if it was fair why did you go after him for it?

RHODA: I want my popsicle.

MONICA: Rhoda, if you're going shopping with me, you'll have to come now. Mr. Pageson is going to show us his collection.

MRS. DAIGLE: Right now?

MONICA: We're a little late as it is. Bring your popsicle, Rhoda. You can wash upstairs.

[MONICA *disengages* RHODA *from* MRS. DAIGLE *and ushers her out of the room*]

MRS. DAIGLE: Well, I must say!

CHRISTINE: They do have an appointment.

MRS. DAIGLE: I'm sure they do, practically sure. Of course, I didn't know Rhoda had all these social obligations. I thought she was like any little girl that stayed home and minded her mother, and didn't go traipsing all over town with important appointments. I'm sorry I interfered with Rhoda's social life. I'm sorry, Christine, and I offer my deepest apologies. I'll apologize to Rhoda too when I can have an interview with her.

CHRISTINE: You haven't interfered at all.

[*The telephone rings.* CHRISTINE *answers it*]

MRS. DAIGLE: I wasn't going to contaminate Rhoda in the slightest degree, I assure you.

CHRISTINE: [*On the phone*] Hello. Yes, Mr. Daigle. Yes, she's here. Not at all.

[*She hangs up*]

MRS. DAIGLE: Did you tell him I was drinking and making a spectacle of myself? Did you tell him to call the patrol wagon?

CHRISTINE: You heard what I said. I said only that you were here. Your husband said he was in the drugstore on the corner.

MRS. DAIGLE: I was just going to hold her in my arms and ask her a few simple questions.

CHRISTINE: Perhaps another time would be better.

MRS. DAIGLE: You think because I'm lit, but I'm not lit in the slightest degree, I assure you. But Rhoda knows more than she's told anybody, if you'll pardon me for being presumptuous. I talked to that guard, remember. It was a long interesting conversation, and he said he saw Rhoda on the wharf just before Claude was found among the pilings. She knows something she hasn't told, all right. I know what you're thinking. You're thinking, "How can I get rid of this pest?" You may fool some with that mealy mouth, but you look like "Ned in the primer" to me.

CHRISTINE: Then perhaps you'd better not come here again.

MRS. DAIGLE: I wouldn't come here again for a million dollars laid out in a line! I wouldn't have come this time if I'd known about Rhoda's social obligations. [*She pours herself another drink*] I won't wait for Mr. Daigle. I'll go home by myself. I know where I'm not wanted, and I'm not wanted in a place where people have all these social obligations, if you get what I mean. You're looking sort of sick and sloppy. Come over to my house and I'll give you a free beauty treatment if you're pressed for ready cash. It won't cost you a nickel.

[*The doorbell rings and* CHRISTINE *opens the door.* MR. DAIGLE *is there*]

MR. DAIGLE: Thank you, Mrs. Penmark. Come, Hortense, it's time to go home.

MRS. DAIGLE: Oh, my God, oh, my God, it's time to go home! [*She embraces* CHRISTINE *at the door, resting her head on* CHRISTINE's *shoulder*] Christine, you know something! You know something, and you won't tell me!

[*The* DAIGLES *go out.* CHRISTINE *stands for a moment, thinking, then goes to the phone and dials the operator*]

CHRISTINE: [*Into the phone*] Operator, I want to call Washington, D.C. [*She covers the speaker*] Kenneth, darling, Kenneth, my dear love, what can I say to you? That our daughter is a—— [*She speaks into the phone*] Never mind, then. No, cancel it.

[*She hangs up. The door opens and* MONICA *comes in, looks quickly around*]

MONICA: Good, she's gone. Sweet, I know I shouldn't take things into my all too capable hands, but I couldn't let her paw Rhoda any longer.

CHRISTINE: Mr. Daigle came for her.

MONICA: And I fear I've loosened discipline just a little. I let Rhoda go down for another popsicle.

CHRISTINE: Did she want a second? That's most unusual.

MONICA: She seemed quite eager. And since she's not one of these fat and self-indulgent little blobs I doubt that it can do any harm. —By the way, here are the vitamins and the sleep-capsules, both plainly marked.

CHRISTINE: Thank you, Monica. I'll keep them separate.

MONICA: Emory called while I was upstairs. He's coming by with Reggie Tasker to store some fishing equipment they bought this morning, so I'll get lunch for them. Wouldn't you like to run up and eat with us—you and Rhoda both?

CHRISTINE: Monica—I'd—I'd rather not, really.

MONICA: You poor girl, I do bully you, and I promised not to!

A VOICE: [*Off-stage*] Fire! Fire!

CHRISTINE: What was that?

MONICA: It sounded a little like somebody shouting, "Fire! Fire!" It sounded nearby.

[*Other voices are now heard shouting, this time much nearer, and they are definitely crying "fire"*]

EMORY: [*Off-stage*] Fire! Fire!

TASKER: [*Off-stage*] Fire! Emory! This way!

[RHODA *comes in. She has finished her second popsicle, and goes calmly to the den*]

CHRISTINE: Rhoda, who was shouting?

RHODA: I don't know, mother.

CHRISTINE: It sounds as if there were a fire!

RHODA: I don't think so, mother.

[*She goes to den, closes door, and begins to play "Au Clair de la Lune"*]

TASKER: [*Outside*] Fire! Fire!

EMORY: [*Outside*] Fire! Fire! The garage door!

[*There is a rush of feet off-stage, and other voices add to the calling*]

VOICES: [*Outside*] Break the door down! Is anybody in there? Fire! Fire! That's Leroy's door! Break it down! Fire! I can hear him! Break it down! Break it down!

[*There is a sudden ragged crash below, as if a door were split from top to bottom, and a man's screaming, as if he were in extreme pain*]

THE MAN: [*Screaming unintelligibly*] I haven't got 'em! I wasn't gonna do nothing! I was just saying it to tease you! I haven't got 'em, I never had 'em, I was just— Oh God, oh God!

MONICA: [*At the window*] There's a man on fire!

CHRISTINE: His clothes are burning! His hair is burning!

[*The piano continues to tinkle*]

MONICA: Emory's there—and Reggie!

[*There is a man's scream, then silence*]

CHRISTINE: It's too late! He fell just before he got to the pond! He's lying still!

[*She slips to her knees, half-fainting*]

MONICA: [*Trying to draw* CHRISTINE *from the window*] Whatever can be done will be done.

CHRISTINE: I should have known it was coming! I should have known! Why am I so blind?

MONICA: Thank God Rhoda was in the den playing the piano!

CHRISTINE: The fire was in the garage! Where Leroy was!

MONICA: There's nothing we can do.

CHRISTINE: This time I saw it! I saw it with my own eyes. Tell them to stop screaming! It won't help to scream!

MONICA: Christine, Christine! You aren't making sense!

CHRISTINE: Tell her to stop the piano—and stop the screaming—I can hear it still, the man is still screaming, Monica, still screaming, and the piano going on and on while he's dying in fire, screaming, screaming a man's scream! [*The doorbell rings*] I don't want to see anybody now.

MONICA: It's probably Emory and Reggie, dear.

[CHRISTINE *remains sobbing on the chair,* MONICA *goes to open the door*]

EMORY: [*At the door*] Everything all right?

MONICA: Come in.

[EMORY *and* TASKER *come in, coats off and somewhat disarranged from a sudden encounter with fire-fighting*]

EMORY: We thought you'd be here. It was just a little flare-up in the garage; it's out now, but I guess Leroy—

MONICA: Never mind—

CHRISTINE: You can say it. I know about Leroy—I saw him burning, I saw him run down the walk and die! Could there be any worse than that?

TASKER: I guess you did see the worst of it, Mrs. Penmark. What seems to have happened is that he fell asleep on a bed he'd made out of excelsior, out in the garage, and his cigarette set fire to the stuff.

EMORY: And excelsior burns like gasoline when it's dry.

[*A siren is heard approaching*]

MONICA: You'd better leave me alone with Christine for a minute.

TASKER: That will be the ambulance.

EMORY: We can take care of that.

[EMORY *and* TASKER *go out. The tune continues in the den*]

CHRISTINE: I can't bear it! I can't bear it! She's driving me mad! [*She leaps up and runs toward the den*] How can she play that tinkle now? Rhoda! Rhoda!

MONICA: What is it, Christine? What is it?

[*She catches* CHRISTINE'S *shoulders and holds her*]

CHRISTINE: It's heartless; I can't bear it! I can't, I tell you! Rhoda! Rhoda! Will you stop that music!

[*But it continues*]

MONICA: Try to make sense, dear!

CHRISTINE: Rhoda! Rhoda! Stop that music!

[RHODA *comes out of the den, wide-eyed and innocent*]

RHODA: Is mommy sick, Monica?

CHRISTINE: Don't let me get my hands on her.

MONICA: Christine, she's only a child.

CHRISTINE: You didn't see it! You could look away and play the piano, but it happened!

MONICA: Christine. Please be sensible. What has she done?

CHRISTINE: It's not what *she's* done—it's what *I've* done!

RHODA: What does she mean, Monica?

MONICA: I don't know, Rhoda. She'd better have lunch upstairs with me, Christine. She'll stay till you're calmer.

CHRISTINE: Yes, take her.

[*She sinks into a chair, shivering*]

MONICA: Will you be all right?

CHRISTINE: Yes, I'm all right. Only the screaming goes on and on.

[*She covers her eyes*]

MONICA: We'll come down for you. Come, Rhoda.

[RHODA *takes* MONICA's *hand and they go out.* CHRISTINE *still sits, shivering, and her voice drops to a moan*]

CHRISTINE: She killed him. And I love her.—Oh, my baby, my baby!
[*She puts her head in her arms and weeps silently*]

CURTAIN

SCENE 3

After dinner in the apartment, the same day. RHODA *is on the couch, in pajamas, ready for bed.* CHRISTINE *is reading to her.*

CHRISTINE: "Polly put one toe out from under the covers to find out how cold it was, and it was nipping cold. She remembered why she had wanted to wake up, and got out of bed very softly, shivering and pulling on her dress and her stockings. She had never seen a Christmas tree decorated and lighted the way they are at Christmas in houses where children have fathers and it isn't hard times. She had promised herself that she would see one." [CHRISTINE *pauses and looks at* RHODA] You have some new vitamins to take tonight.

RHODA: New ones?

CHRISTINE: Yes.

RHODA: Are those the vitamins?

CHRISTINE: Yes.

RHODA: May I see them please?

[CHRISTINE *gives* RHODA *the bottle*]

CHRISTINE: Yes, of course. They're some that Monica sent down for us.

RHODA: Okay, mommy. I think Monica likes me.

CHRISTINE: I'm sure she does.

RHODA: Swallowing pills is just a trick.

CHRISTINE: You're very good at it.

RHODA: Do you love me, mommy?

CHRISTINE: Yes.

RHODA: Mommy, do you know about Leroy?

CHRISTINE: Yes.

RHODA: You told me to put my shoes in the incinerator, didn't you?

CHRISTINE: Yes.

RHODA: Did you do something with the medal?

CHRISTINE: I drove out to Benedict today to see Miss Fern. And then I made an excuse to go on the pier alone—and dropped the medal in the deep water there.

RHODA: Mommy, Leroy had my shoes, and he said he was going to give them to the police and then tell them about me—and they'd put me in the electric chair. So—I had to—

CHRISTINE: You don't need to say any more.

RHODA: Will you read more now?

CHRISTINE: Take these first.

[*Giving her a number of pills*]

RHODA: So many?

CHRISTINE: They're a new kind. I'm to take them, too.

RHODA: [*Taking the pills*] I like apricot juice. It doesn't even need ice. Mommy, I took another box of matches, and I lit the excelsior and I locked the door. But it wasn't my fault, mommy. It was Leroy's fault. He shouldn't have said he'd tell the police about me and give them my shoes.

CHRISTINE: I know.

RHODA: There. That's all. Don't let them hurt me, mommy.

CHRISTINE: No, dear, I won't let them hurt you. [*She leans over and kisses* RHODA] Good night.

RHODA: Good night, mommy. Now will you read to me?

CHRISTINE: [*Reading*] "When Polly was all dressed she found her shawl and crept very quietly out of the room and out the front door. The door creaked, and she waited and listened, but nobody woke up. She closed the door carefully and looked at the bright moon and the shining, cold snow. The Carters must have a tree. They lived two blocks away, and if they left the curtains open you could look in and see it. If only there weren't any dogs. Polly walked carefully on the hard snow on the walk, keeping the warm shawl close around her. It was further than she remembered to the Carters' house, but she could see that there were lights in the windows. She came near it, only making a little creaking noise on the snow, and stood for a while in front of the house before she dared go near. Then she gathered all her courage and walked across the yard, her shoes sinking through the crust. The Christmas tree was right in the front window, and the lights were on in the house, so she could see the fruits and bells and strings of popcorn and candy—and the silver star at the top." [CHRISTINE *pauses and looks at* RHODA. *She makes no sign, and her breathing is deep and regular.* CHRISTINE *lays down the book*] Rhoda, dear. Rhoda, dear—you are mine, and I carried you, and I can't let them hurt you. I can't let them take you away and shut you up. They'd put you in some kind of institution. Nobody can save you from that unless I save you.

So sleep well, and dream well, my only child, and the one I love. I shall sleep, too.

> [*She gathers* RHODA *up in her arms gently, and carries her into the bedroom. After a moment she returns and opens a drawer in a spice cabinet high on the wall, takes out a bunch of keys and goes to the den. There is a shot and the lights go out*]

CURTAIN

SCENE 4

Morning, a few days later. The sun is shining in at the window and MONICA *enters from the kitchen with a coffee tray. She sets it down and turns toward the kitchen.* EMORY, TASKER, *and* KENNETH *come in from the outer hall.*

MONICA: I've made coffee if anybody wants it.

EMORY: That's a thought.

TASKER: I'm in favor.

MONICA: [*Coming from the kitchen with a plate of sandwiches*] Kenneth? Coffee?

KENNETH: No, thanks, Monica. [*He goes to the window, looks out*] Now I must face living without her. Somehow I could almost believe she was still with me till they lowered that coffin into the earth—and I knew I'd never see her face again. Now the earth is empty, and I'm empty.

EMORY: She's left all of us feeling pretty much the same way.

KENNETH: And why did she do it? Why, in God's name, did she do such a thing? She wasn't unhappy when I left! Monica, she was closer to you than anyone else lately; did she say anything—that was any kind of a reason?

MONICA: I've gone over and over everything she said, till I'm almost distracted—and it just doesn't fit any pattern! And I've talked to everybody who knew her—and they're just incredulous and shocked. There seems to be no reason at all!

KENNETH: There was a reason. Christine didn't do things without a reason.—Her father died suddenly, you said?

TASKER: He'd had a series of attacks, and the news of Christine's death seems to have been too much for his heart.

EMORY: She had some worry or other and I think it was connected with her father.

TASKER: I think she brooded over the Daigle boy's death and about the death of Leroy.

MONICA: She was hysterical at the time of the fire, but that was understandable.

KENNETH: [To MONICA] When it happened how did you find her? Did you hear the shot?

MONICA: Yes—we heard it—and ran down. She'd shot herself and given Rhoda a deadly dose of sleeping pills. She had obviously planned that they should die together.

KENNETH: Could she—could Christine have been insane?

TASKER: No. We can rule that out. I talked with her not long ago. She shuddered somewhat—at my murder cases—but her comments were completely level-headed.

EMORY: No, Christine wasn't crazy.

KENNETH: I don't know how I'll live. I don't know that I will.

EMORY: I guess nothing helps.

KENNETH: Nothing.—I don't think it's much good without Christine. The army—and promotion—and—a career—it was Christine that kept me afloat—not any of that.

EMORY: She was a wonderful girl.

KENNETH: And she left me—crept away into the earth—and I don't know why! [His voice breaks, and he chokes down an uncontrollable sob, then another and another] I'm sorry.

MONICA: You cry if you feel like it. She was worth it.

KENNETH: She didn't want to live.

[The piano in the den is heard playing "Au Clair de la Lune"]

MONICA: Kenneth, you have a lot to be grateful for. If we hadn't heard the shot you'd have lost Rhoda too. [She goes to den, opens door and calls] Rhoda.

[RHODA *enters*]

RHODA: Did you like it, daddy? I played it for you.

KENNETH: Oh, Rhoda, my Rhoda, there's a little of Christine left! It's in your smile!

RHODA: I love you, daddy! What will you give me for a basket of kisses?

KENNETH: For a basket of kisses? [*He looks at* RHODA] Oh, my darling —I'll give you a basket of hugs!

[*His arms go round her*]

CURTAIN

Dangerous Corner

J. B. PRIESTLEY

J. B. Priestley

John Boynton Priestley, who prefers to be known simply as J. B. Priestley, was born at Bradford, England, on September 13, 1894. He was educated there and at Trinity Hall, Cambridge, where he began his illustrious career as a writer, though it actually wasn't until 1929 that he hit his apogee with his picaresque novel, *The Good Companions*. In 1931 he collaborated with Edward Knoblock on a dramatization; it opened at His Majesty's Theatre, London, with John Gielgud, who had just left the Old Vic after performing *King Lear* at the age of twenty-six, which led James Agate to remark in his coverage of *The Good Companions*: "The young man rattling away at the piano was Mr. John Gielgud, and perhaps this time some of the applause might be taken as a tribute to all those kings over the water whose sceptres our young tragedian had just laid down."

The Good Companions ran for 331 performances and thereafter Priestley, as dramatist, tended to overshadow the other Priestleys: novelist, journalist, and essayist. Encouraged by its reception, he decided to persevere as a playwright and in 1932 turned out *Dangerous Corner*, written in a week, "chiefly to prove that a man might produce long novels and yet be able to write effectively, using the strictest economy, for the stage."

Paradoxically, according to Priestley: "It was received in Shaftesbury Avenue so tepidly that only my own insistence carried it past the initial five performances. It then became the most popular play I have ever written. I doubt if there is any country in the world possessing a playhouse that has not seen *Dangerous Corner*, or if any other play written during the last thirty years has had more performances."

In the years that followed its West End première, *Dangerous Corner*, one of the most ingenious suspense plays of the modern theatre, accumulated much praise from leading critics, who in reconsideration termed it "a masterfully constructed play on a split-time theory" and "a suspenseful display of virtuosity." It is held in high regard today and indeed most consider it to be Priestley's finest work for the stage.

In the play a casual conversation takes a chance turn and compels the characters to unmask themselves and also to reconstruct a past event, a presumed suicide that turns out to have been murder. Each character makes new and surprising revelations about his or her connection with the deceased, which leads to tragic results. In the brief epilogue, Mr. Priestley makes his underlying theme—at certain moments a chance remark may seriously alter the course of lives—visibly plain when the characters return to where they started from, tracing what would have happened if a single sentence remained unspoken (by Olwen), thus enabling the Chatfield family to round that "dangerous corner."

This last twist foreshadows a later development in Priestley's career: his "time" plays that started in 1937 with *Time and the Conways*, bringing to the theatre his dramatic demonstration of J. W. Dunne's theory of Serialism, "the curious feeling which almost everyone has now and then experienced—that sudden, fleeting, disturbing conviction that something which is happening at the moment happened before."

Since 1931, Mr. Priestley has contributed over thirty plays to the theatre. In addition to the aforementioned, they include: *An Inspector Calls*; *Eden End*; *I Have Been Here Before*; *Johnson Over Jordan*; *The Linden Tree*; *Laburnum Grove*; *When We Are Married*; *They Came to a City*; *Mr. Kettle and Mrs. Moon*; *Music at Night*; *Bees on the Boat Deck*; and *A Severed Head*, adapted with Iris Murdoch from her novel of the same name. He also has collaborated on two plays, *Dragon's Mouth* and *The White Countess*, with his present wife, Jacquetta Hawkes, a well-known archaeologist and writer.

His novels, stories, essays, criticisms, histories, and autobiographical writings fill more than forty published volumes, indisputably making him one of the century's most prolific authors.

Although an acknowledged leader in English letters, Priestley nonetheless has come under critical fire on any number of occasions. Ironically, and possibly in keeping with his known predilection for expounding the theory of eternal recurrence in human experience, identical charges have been leveled at him at different intervals: he wrote too much, too rapidly, and his plays lacked the poetry of drama.

On the other hand, he has been championed by some of the world's foremost drama assessors. Alan Dent said of Priestley: "We urgently need his fine, uncommon, questing mind in the theatre. He is a true dramatist—always an interesting one, and sometimes a first-rate one." To J. C. Trewin he is "one of the first of our dramatists: an exasperating, obstinate fellow, no doubt, but a dramatist with a love of life, a love of the theatre, a great capacity for work, and a gift for exploration and inquiry."

There is little doubt, when one considers his voluminous portfolio of works for the stage, that J. B. Priestley has a masterly technique and an exceptional flair for the theatre and is a writer to whom good humor comes naturally.

Priestley's passion for the theatre has not been confined to playwriting: for two eventful years he was associated in the management of the Duchess Theatre (London) and he devoted considerable energy and effort to his duties as the first president of the worldwide International Theatre Institute.

Priestley himself has described the compulsion, the force that hurled him toward the mettlesome milieu of the theatre when he very well could have conducted a successful writer's career in the tranquillity of his study: "It was the ancient witchery of the work itself, the eternal fascination of the theatre. As a youth I was a passionate playgoer, and for some time was determined to go on the stage myself. (A good comic actor was lost in me, or almost lost.) Then other ambitions came, sweeping me away from the theatre, through poetry and journalism, the barren interlude of the war, then afterwards through criticism, essays, and fixation; but the movement was circular, and after twenty years or so I found myself thinking hard about the theatre again; but this time, being a professional writer, as a dramatist. And I did not hesitate to turn manager for myself too, learning a good deal in the rather grim process. The witchery still remained . . ."

Dangerous Corner was first presented by Gilbert Miller at the Lyric Theatre, London, on May 17, 1932. The cast was as follows:

ROBERT CAPLAN	*Richard Bird*
FREDA CAPLAN	*Marie Ney*
GORDON WHITEHOUSE	*William Fox*
BETTY WHITEHOUSE	*Isla Bevan*
OLWEN PEEL	*Flora Robson*
CHARLES TREVOR STANTON	*Frank Allenby*
MAUD MOCKRIDGE	*Esmé Church*

Directed by	Tyrone Guthrie
Scenery and Decorations designed by	Sibyl Colefax and P. Beaumont Hambrow
Costumes by	Eva Lutyens

Dangerous Corner was first produced in the United States at the Empire Theatre, New York, on October 27, 1932, by Harry Moses. The cast was as follows:

MAUD MOCKRIDGE, a novelist	*Jane Wheatley*
OLWEN PEEL, secretary to the publishers	*Mary Servoss*
FREDA CHATFIELD, Robert's wife	*Jean Dixon*
BETTY WHITEHOUSE, Gordon's wife	*Barbara Robbins*
CHARLES STANTON, one of the publishers	*Stanley Ridges*
GORDON WHITEHOUSE, Freda's brother	*John Cecil Holm*
ROBERT CHATFIELD, head of the publishing firm	*Colin Keith-Johnston*

Directed by	Elsa Lazareff
Setting by	Woodman Thompson

ACT ONE

SCENE: *The living room of the Chatfield country home, after dinner.*

FOUR WOMEN *discovered sitting and talking.*

MISS MOCKRIDGE: [*Lighting cigarette*] And what do you say this novel is called?

OLWEN: *The Sleeping Dog.*

MISS MOCKRIDGE: *The Sleeping Dog.* I must remember that. When will you publish it?

OLWEN: Next spring, I suppose.

MISS MOCKRIDGE: I must look out for it.

OLWEN: We'll send you a copy. If you're here when it comes out, I'll give you a ring about it.

MISS MOCKRIDGE: Oh, of course you're in the city office now.

OLWEN: Yes, I am. Though I still come up here as often as I can.

MISS MOCKRIDGE: You know you people make such an intimate little group that you confuse me. I can't make out who's here and who's in the city office.

FREDA: It's very simple. It's so arranged now that the married ones —my brother Gordon and Betty and Robert and I are here—and the single ones, Olwen and Stanton, are in the city office.

OLWEN: And come back here every time there's the smallest excuse. Only I haven't the luck to have as many excuses as Charles Stanton has. But I do my best.

MISS MOCKRIDGE: I'm sure you do. So would I. [*To* OLWEN] Miss Peel, I think you ought to marry Mr. Stanton. [OLWEN *laughs. To the other two*] Don't you think she ought to marry Mr. Stanton?

OLWEN: Oh? Why should I?

BETTY: I didn't know you were a matchmaker, Miss Mockridge.

MISS MOCKRIDGE: I'm not. In the ordinary way, I consider it a disgusting business. But I like things symmetrical. I like a neat pattern. And you see, if you married Mr. Stanton, that would complete the pattern here. Then you'd have your three directors, and also three pairs of adoring husbands and wives.

FREDA: I must say the adoring husbands don't seem in a hurry to join their wives tonight.

BETTY: [*Turning head*] Aren't they pigs! What's keeping them?

FREDA: Well, I think I know one thing that's keeping them. Robert has just acquired some old brandy that he's terribly proud of [*Sudden burst of laughter from* MEN *off*], and I suppose they're sampling that.

MISS MOCKRIDGE: They're probably laughing at something very improper.

BETTY: No. I know them. It's just gossip. Men like gossip.

FREDA: Of course they do.

OLWEN: Well, why shouldn't they?

MISS MOCKRIDGE: Exactly. Why shouldn't they? People who don't like gossip aren't interested in their fellow creatures. So I insist upon my three publishers gossiping.

BETTY: Yes, but they always say it's business. I don't mind Gordon drinking Robert's old brandy—and I don't mind him gossiping. But I do object to him coming in—as he will, you'll see—looking very important and pretending he knows all the secrets of the publishing business.

FREDA: Well, Betty, you may know Gordon better than I do, but even if he is your husband, he's my brother and I've known him long enough to realize he has to look important now and again about *something* rather absurd.

MISS MOCKRIDGE: I hope you don't mean by that, Mrs. Chatfield, that you think the publishing business absurd. As a woman who gets her living through it, I protest.

OLWEN: And as another woman who also gets her living by it—though in a humbler capacity—I also protest.

MISS MOCKRIDGE: Meanwhile, I'm almost prepared to marry Mr. Stanton myself to be one of your charmed circle here. What a snug little group you are!

FREDA: Are we?

MISS MOCKRIDGE: Well, aren't you?

FREDA: Snug little group! How awful.

MISS MOCKRIDGE: Not awful at all. I think it's charming.

FREDA: It sounds disgusting.

BETTY: Yes, like Dickens or a Christmas card.

MISS MOCKRIDGE: And very nice things to be like, too, let me tell you. In these days almost too good to be true.

BETTY: Oh, why should it be?

OLWEN: I didn't know you were such a pessimist, Miss Mockridge.

MISS MOCKRIDGE: Didn't you? Then you don't read the reviews of my books—and you ought to, you know, being an employee of my publishers. I shall complain of that to my three directors when they come in. Certainly I'm a pessimist. I'm an intelligent woman. [*Snuffling*] But I didn't mean in that way, of course. I think it's wonderful here.

FREDA: It is rather nice here. We've been lucky.

OLWEN: It's enchanting. I hate to leave it.

MISS MOCKRIDGE: I'm sure you do. It must be comforting to be all so settled.

FREDA: Quite the cosy little nest!

BETTY: Oh, talking about nests! What about that white bird that comes into your garden nearly every night? [*Rising*] Do you suppose we might see it now?

FREDA: [*Rising*] We might try. It usually comes about this time. Perhaps we might get a glimpse of it. [*Crosses up to window*] That is, if it's condescending to visit us tonight.

MISS MOCKRIDGE: [*Rising*] That sounds interesting. [*Going to window*] What does it look like?

FREDA: [*Pulling curtains open*] I suppose it's a white owl. But it looks like the ghost of a bird.

[OLWEN *rises and joins them at window*]

MISS MOCKRIDGE: How exciting!

BETTY: I can't see anything at all.

FREDA: Just a second, I'll turn out the lights. [FREDA *switches off the lights and the stage is in complete darkness, except for the moonlight which silhouettes the four women against the window, and*

*a light from the hall coming through the half-open door up right.
After a moment's pause there is the sound of a revolver shot offstage right.* BETTY *gives a sharp little scream. Startled exclamations
from the other three women.* FREDA *advances toward the door*]
Robert, Robert, what was that! [*Pause*] ROBERT!!!

ROBERT'S VOICE: [*Off*] It's all right. I was showing them my gun and
took a crack at a flower pot.

[FREDA *switches on the lights*]

GORDON'S VOICE: [*Off*] Pretty good shot. . . .

ROBERT'S VOICE: And what's more, I hit it!

STANTON'S VOICE: [*Off*] Pretty lucky, I'll say. . . .

ROBERT'S VOICE: We'll be in in a minute!

FREDA: I should hope so. Those idiots, firing Robert's revolver out
the window!

BETTY: You ought to take it away from him. They nearly frightened
the life out of me.

[MISS MOCKRIDGE *moves down and sits as* BETTY *speaks*]

FREDA: There's no chance of seeing our bird *now*. If it was there,
it must have cleared out pretty quickly.

BETTY: [*Sitting on sofa*] I should think so—after all that racket.

OLWEN: Perhaps it will come back later.

[*She sits*]

FREDA: No, no, I hardly think so. I've never caught sight of it much
after ten.

MISS MOCKRIDGE: I suppose you all miss your brother-in-law. He used
to be up here with you too, didn't he?

FREDA: [*Turning*] You mean Robert's brother, Martin?

MISS MOCKRIDGE: Yes.

FREDA: What made you think of Martin just then?

MISS MOCKRIDGE: Well, I don't quite know. He just came into my
head, I suppose.

FREDA: [*Sits*] It must have been the shot.

MISS MOCKRIDGE: Oh, surely not. I was away at the time and never quite understood what happened. Something rather dreadful, wasn't it? I'm sorry if I—

FREDA: No. It's all right. It was very distressing for us at the time, but it's done with now. Martin shot himself. It happened a year ago—last October, in fact—at his own cottage about twenty miles from here.

MISS MOCKRIDGE: Oh, yes. Dreadful business, of course. I only met him twice, I think. I remember I thought him very amusing and charming. He was very handsome, wasn't he?

[STANTON *and* GORDON *enter*]

OLWEN: Yes, very handsome.

STANTON: Who's very handsome?

FREDA: Not you, Charles.

STANTON: Well, who is it? Or is it a secret?

GORDON: They must have been talking about me. Betty, why do you let them rave about your husband like that?

BETTY: Darling, I'm sure you've had too much manly gossip and old brandy. You're beginning to look purple in the face and bloated— a typical financier.

[ROBERT *enters: closes door*]

ROBERT: Why so dim? [*Switching on extra light*] Sorry about that gun, Freda. It was stupid. I hope it didn't frighten anybody.

FREDA: As a matter of fact, it did. All of us.

MISS MOCKRIDGE: Yes, and I'd just been saying what a charming little group you've made here, all of you.

ROBERT: I'm glad you think so.

MISS MOCKRIDGE: I think you've all been lucky.

ROBERT: [*Sits on sofa, next to* BETTY] I agree, we have.

STANTON: It's not all luck, Miss Mockridge. You see, we all happen to be nice easy-going people.

ROBERT: Except Betty—she's terribly wild.

STANTON: That's only because Gordon doesn't beat her often enough —yet.

MISS MOCKRIDGE: You see, Miss Peel, Mr. Stanton is *still* the cynical bachelor. I'm afraid he rather spoils the picture.

STANTON: Oh. You must have a dark relief—

[*He crosses to chair and sits*]

GORDON: [*Picks up radio section of* Times *from piano*] I wonder if there's any dance music on the radio tonight?

ROBERT: I hope not. Let's be quiet. [GORDON *goes to radio*] What have you people been talking about?

FREDA: Olwen has been telling us about *The Sleeping Dog.*

ROBERT: *The Sleeping Dog?* Oh yes—that novel we're going to publish, the one she's so keen on.

STANTON: Why does he call it that?

OLWEN: Don't you know the proverb—Let Sleeping Dogs Lie?

STANTON: Where does that come into it?

FREDA: From what Olwen says, the sleeping dog represents *truth.*

OLWEN: Yes, and the chief character—the husband—insisted upon disturbing it.

ROBERT: Well, he was quite right to disturb it.

STANTON: Was he? I think it a very sound idea—the truth as a sleeping dog.

MISS MOCKRIDGE: But of course we do spend too much of our time telling lies and acting them.

BETTY: Oh, but one has to. I'm always fibbing. I do it all day long.

GORDON: [*Still at radio*] You do, darling. You do.

BETTY: It's the secret of my charm.

MISS MOCKRIDGE: Very likely. But we meant something more serious.

ROBERT: Serious or not, I'm all for it coming out. It's healthy.

STANTON: [*Picks up puzzle from table*] I think telling the truth is about as healthy as skidding round a corner at sixty.

FREDA: And life's got a lot of dangerous corners—hasn't it, Charles?

STANTON: It can have—if you don't choose your route well. To lie or not to lie—what do you think, Olwen? You're looking terribly wise.

OLWEN: I agree with you. I think telling everything is dangerous. The point is, I think—there's truth *and* truth.

GORDON: I always agree to that. Something *and* something.

STANTON: Keep quiet, Gordon. Go on, Olwen.

MISS MOCKRIDGE: Yes—go on.

OLWEN: Well—the real truth—that is, every single little thing, with nothing missing at all, wouldn't be dangerous. I suppose that's God's truth. But what most people mean by truth is only *half* the real truth. It doesn't tell you all that went on inside everybody. It simply gives you a lot of facts that happened to have been hidden away and were perhaps a lot better hidden away. It's rather treacherous stuff.

GORDON: Yes, like the muck they drag out of everybody in the law courts. Where were you on the night of the 27th of November? Answer yes or no.

MISS MOCKRIDGE: [*Looking at* GORDON] Yes! [*Turns to* OLWEN] I'm not convinced, Miss Peel. I'm ready to welcome what you call half the truth—the facts.

ROBERT: So am I. I'm all for it.

FREDA: You would be, Robert.

ROBERT: What do you mean by that, Freda?

FREDA: Anything, nothing. [*Rises*] Let's talk about something more amusing. Who wants a drink? Drinks, Robert. And cigarettes. [ROBERT *rises, crosses to drinks.* FREDA *takes up musical cigarette box from table, being careful to keep it closed. Turns toward* MISS MOCKRIDGE, *offering the box*] A cigarette, Miss Mockridge?

MISS MOCKRIDGE: [*Rises*] No, thanks, I'm a slave to my own brand.

[*She crosses to table and picks up her bag*]

FREDA: Cigarette, Olwen?

OLWEN: [*Taking the box*] Oh, I remember that box! It plays a tune, doesn't it? I remember the tune. [*Opens the box*] Yes, it's the Wedding March, isn't it?

[*She takes a cigarette, as the box plays*]

ROBERT: Good, isn't it?

FREDA: [*Taking the box from* OLWEN *and snapping it shut*] It *can't* have been this box you remember. This is the first time I've had it out.

[MISS MOCKRIDGE *sits in nearby chair*]

OLWEN: It belonged to Martin, didn't it? He showed it to me.

FREDA: He couldn't have shown it to you, Olwen. He hadn't got it when you saw him last.

STANTON: How do you know, Freda?

FREDA: That doesn't matter. I know. Martin couldn't have shown you this box, Olwen.

[*She puts box down on piano*]

OLWEN: Couldn't he? . . . [*Turns to* ROBERT] No, perhaps he couldn't. I suppose I got mixed up. I must have seen a box like this somewhere else and then pushed it on to poor Martin because he was always so fond of things like this.

ROBERT: Olwen, I'm going to be rather rude, but I know you won't mind. You know you suddenly stopped telling the truth then, didn't you? [*Strikes match and lights cigarette for* OLWEN] You're absolutely positive that this is the box Martin showed you, just as Freda is equally positive it isn't.

OLWEN: Well, does that matter?

GORDON: [*Fiddling with radio*] Not a hoot. I'm trying to find some dance music, but this thing has suddenly decided not to function.

ROBERT: Then don't fiddle about with it.

BETTY: Don't bully Gordon.

ROBERT: Well, you stop him.

BETTY: Stop it, Gordon! [GORDON *turns off radio*]

ROBERT: No. I don't suppose it does matter, Olwen, but after what we'd been saying, I couldn't help thinking that it was rather an odd, provoking situation.

MISS MOCKRIDGE: Just what I was thinking—it's all terribly provoking—. More about the cigarette box, please!

FREDA: It's all perfectly simple. . . .

OLWEN: Wait a minute, please, Freda. I don't think it *is* all perfectly simple, but I can't see that it matters now.

FREDA: I don't understand you.

ROBERT: Neither do I. First you say it can't have been the same box and now you say it's not all perfectly simple and begin to hint at grand mysteries. I believe you're hiding something, Olwen, and that isn't like you. Either that box you saw was Martin's or it wasn't—

STANTON: Oh, damn that box!

[FREDA *turns, moves up to piano*]

MISS MOCKRIDGE: Oh, but Mr. Stanton, we'd like to hear—

STANTON: Sorry—but I hate a box that plays tunes. Let's forget it.

GORDON: [*Moves away from radio*] Yes, and Martin *too!* He isn't here —and we are.

ROBERT: Gordon, please—

GORDON: Don't let's mention Martin or think about him. He's dead.

FREDA: Well, there's no need to be tragic about it, Gordon. One would think you owned Martin, to hear you talk.

[GORDON *turns away*]

BETTY: Instead of which, *nobody* owned Martin. He belonged to himself. He had some sense.

ROBERT: What does all that mean, Betty?

BETTY: It means that I'm being rather stupid and that you're all talking a lot of rot and that I think I'm going to have a headache any minute.

ROBERT: Is that all?

BETTY: Isn't that quite enough?

ROBERT: More about the box, Freda.

[GORDON *sits on arm of sofa*]

FREDA: I wish you wouldn't be so absurdly persistent, Robert. It came to us with some other of Martin's things from the cottage. I put it away and this is the first time it's been out here. Now the last time Olwen was at Martin's cottage was that Saturday when we all went over—you remember, at the very beginning of October.

[*She sits on settee*]

GORDON: Gosh—yes. What a day that was! And a marvelous night, wasn't it? That was the time we all sat in the garden for hours and Martin told us all about those ridiculous people he'd stayed with in Cornwall—the handwoven people.

BETTY: Yes—and the long long thin woman who always said, "Do you belong?"

GORDON: I don't think I ever had a better day. We'll never have another like that.

ROBERT: [*Crosses to drinks*] Yes, it was a good day. Though I'd no idea you felt so deeply about it, Gordon.

[*Pours drink*]

FREDA: Neither had anybody else. Gordon seems to have decided that he ought to be sentimental every time Martin is mentioned.

BETTY: I suspect it's Robert's old brandy. And those enormous glasses. They go to his head.

GORDON: Well, where do you want them to go to?

ROBERT: The point is then, that that first Saturday in October was the last time Olwen was at Martin's cottage—

FREDA: Yes, and I know that he hadn't got this cigarette box then.

ROBERT: No, he'd have shown it to us if he'd had it then. As a matter of fact, I never remember seeing the thing at the cottage. So there you are, Olwen.

OLWEN: There I am.

ROBERT: Yes, but—hang it all—where are you?

OLWEN: You *are* a baby, Robert. I don't know where I am. Out of the dock or the witness box, I hope.

MISS MOCKRIDGE: Oh, no, that would be too disappointing.

BETTY: You know, that *wasn't* the last time you were at the cottage, Olwen. Don't you remember, you and I ran over the next Sunday afternoon, to see Martin about those little etchings?

OLWEN: Yes.

ROBERT: Yes, that's true.

BETTY: But I don't remember his showing us this cigarette box. In fact, I've never seen it before.

STANTON: Neither have I, and I don't think I ever want to see it again. I never heard such a lot of fuss about nothing.

FREDA: [*To* STANTON] I agree with you, Charles. [*To* OLWEN] But I may as well tell you—if only to have done with it—that Martin *couldn't* have shown it to you that Sunday anyhow, because he hadn't got it then.

STANTON: You seem to know a *lot* about that box, Freda.

GORDON: That's just what I was going to say. Why are you so grand and knowing about it?

BETTY: I know why. *You* gave it to him.

ROBERT: Did you, Freda?

FREDA: Yes, I gave it to him.

ROBERT: That's queer. I don't mean it's queer your giving it to him —why shouldn't you? But your never mentioning it. When did you give it to him? Where did you pick it up?

FREDA: That's easily explained. You remember the day before that awful Saturday? You were staying in town, and I came up for the day. Well, I happened to see the cigarette box in a shop. It was amusing and rather cheap, so I bought it and had it sent parcel post to Martin.

ROBERT: Oh! so that he never got it until that last Saturday.

FREDA: Yes.

ROBERT: [*Crosses to platform, puts down glass*] Well, that's that.

GORDON: I'm sorry, Freda, but it's not quite so simple as all that. You mustn't forget that I was with Martin at the cottage that very Saturday morning.

ROBERT: Well, what about it?

GORDON: Well, I was there when the parcel post came, with the letters in the morning. I remember Martin had a parcel of books— I don't forget anything about that morning, and neither would you if you'd been dragged into that hellish inquest, as I was. But he *didn't* have that cigarette box!

FREDA: I suppose it must have arrived by the afternoon post then. What does it matter?

GORDON: [*Rises*] It doesn't matter at all, Freda darling, except that parcels are never delivered there by the afternoon post.

FREDA: Yes, they are.

GORDON: No.

FREDA: How do you know?

GORDON: Because Martin used to grumble about it and say that he always got books and manuscripts a day late. That cigarette box didn't arrive in the morning, because I saw the post opened, and it couldn't have been delivered in the afternoon. Freda, I don't believe you ever *sent* the box. You took it to Martin yourself. You did, didn't you?

FREDA: You are a fool, Gordon!

GORDON: Possibly. But, you *did* take it to Martin, didn't you?

ROBERT: Did you?

FREDA: Well, if you must know— I did.

ROBERT: Freda!

GORDON: I thought so.

ROBERT: But, Freda, if you went to the cottage to give Martin the box after Gordon had left, you must have seen Martin later than anybody, only a few hours before he—before he shot himself.

FREDA: I did. I saw him shortly before dinner.

ROBERT: But why have you never said anything about it? Why didn't you come forward at the inquest? You could have given evidence.

FREDA: I could, but why should I? What good would it have done? It was bad enough Gordon having to do it—

GORDON: It was hell.

FREDA: If it could have helped Martin, I'd have gone. But it couldn't have helped *anybody*.

[GORDON *crosses to radio*]

STANTON: That's true. You were quite right.

ROBERT: Yes, I can understand that. But why didn't you tell me? Why did you keep it to yourself, why have you kept it to yourself all this time? You were the very last person to talk to Martin.

FREDA: Was I the last person?

ROBERT: You must have been.

FREDA: Then what about Olwen?

ROBERT: Olwen? Oh—the cigarette box.

FREDA: Yes, of course—the cigarette box. [STANTON *rises, moves to the piano bench*] Martin didn't get that box until late Saturday afternoon, and Olwen admitted that he showed it to her.

BETTY: No, she didn't. She said it was some other box, and I vote we believe her and have done with it.

MISS MOCKRIDGE: No, no—Mrs. Whitehouse—

BETTY: Yes, I do. It's all wrong going on and on like this.

STANTON: And I second that.

ROBERT: And I don't.

BETTY: Oh! But Robert.

ROBERT: I'm sorry, Betty. After all you don't come into this. Martin was my brother and I don't like all these mysteries and I've a right to know.

OLWEN: All right, Robert. But must you know now?

FREDA: I don't see the necessity. [*Rises*] But then I didn't see why I should have been cross-examined, with the entire approval of the company, apparently. But now that it's your turn, Olwen, I've no doubt that Robert will relent.

ROBERT: I don't see why you should say that, Freda.

FREDA: You might as well admit it, Olwen. Martin showed you that box, didn't he? So you must have seen him, you must have been at the cottage that Saturday night.

OLWEN: Yes, he did show me the box. That was after dinner—about nine o'clock—on that Saturday night.

ROBERT: You were there? But this is crazy. First Freda—then you. And neither of you has said a word about it.

OLWEN: I'm sorry, Robert. I couldn't.

ROBERT: But why were you there?

OLWEN: I'd been worried about—something—something that I'd heard—it had been worrying me for days. I felt I had to see Martin to ask him about it. So I motored up to see him. I had some dinner on the way, and got to the cottage just before nine. Nobody saw me go and nobody saw me leave—you know how quiet it was there. Like Freda, I thought it wouldn't serve any good purpose to come forward at the inquest—[FREDA *crosses to chair and sits*] so I didn't. That's all.

ROBERT: But you can't dismiss it like that. You must have been the very last person to talk to Martin. You must know something about it.

OLWEN: [*Rises*] Please Robert! It's all over and done with! Let's leave it alone! We don't mean to discuss it, do we, Freda? There's nothing to discuss. It's all over.

ROBERT: But look here, Olwen, you must tell me this. Had your visit to Martin that night anything to do with the firm? You said you'd been worried about something.

FREDA: Oh, Robert, please.

ROBERT: I'm sorry, but I must know this. Was that *something* to do with that missing money?

GORDON: [*Comes forward*] Oh—for God's sake—don't drag that money into it! We don't want that all over again. Martin's gone. Leave him alone, can't you, and shut up about the rotten money.

FREDA: Gordon, be quiet. You're behaving like an hysterical child tonight. I'm sure we must be boring Miss Mockridge with all this!

MISS MOCKRIDGE: No, no, I'm enjoying it very much!

GORDON: I'm sorry! I beg your pardon, Miss Mockridge.

FREDA: I think we'd better change the subject, Robert.

MISS MOCKRIDGE: [*Rising*] Not at all. Well, I think—I'd better be going! It must be getting late.

FREDA: [*Rises*] Oh, no.

ROBERT: Oh, don't go yet.

MISS MOCKRIDGE: The Pattersons said they'd send their car over for me to take me back. It hasn't arrived yet, do you know?

ROBERT: Yes, I heard it when we left the dining room and I told the man to wait in the kitchen. I'll get hold of him for you.

[*He exits*]

FREDA: Oh, must you really go?

MISS MOCKRIDGE: Yes, I really think I ought. It's at least half an hour's run to the Pattersons', and I don't suppose they like their car and chauffeur to be kept out too late. [*To* FREDA] Thank you so much. [*To* OLWEN] It's been so delightful seeing you all again.

STANTON: Good-night, Miss Mockridge.

MISS MOCKRIDGE: [*To* BETTY] Good-bye, Mrs. Whitehouse. Good-bye.

BETTY: Good-night.

FREDA: I think you left your wrap in my room. I'll get it for you.

[MISS MOCKRIDGE *leaves.* FREDA *follows and shuts door.* STANTON *crosses to drinks*]

GORDON: I'm glad she's gone.

[OLWEN *sits*]

BETTY: I am too! I can't bear that woman. She reminds me too much of a geometry teacher I used to have.

STANTON: I've always suspected your geometry, Betty. [*Picks up glass*] Drink, Gordon?

GORDON: [*Lighting cigarette*] No, thanks.

STANTON: [*Fixing drink*] That was mean—. Because after all, she's not at all a bad novelist. I don't mean she's just a good seller, but she's a good novelist too. Why is it there seems to be always something rather unpleasant about good novelists?

GORDON: [*Sits*] I give up. But I don't call Maud Mockridge a good novelist, Charles!

BETTY: I'll bet she's a good *gossiper*.

STANTON: She is. She's notorious for it. She'll embroider that cigarette box story and have it all around town within a week. The Pattersons will have it tonight, to begin with. It must have been agony for her to go away and not hear any more.

GORDON: She wouldn't have gone if she'd thought she'd have heard any more. But she's got enough to go on with. She'll probably start a new novel in the morning and we'll all be in it.

BETTY: Well, she'll have to use her imagination a bit about me.

STANTON: And me. Perhaps she'll invent the most frightful vices for us, Betty.

BETTY: She can't really do much with what she's just heard, you know. After all, why shouldn't Freda have taken Martin a cigarette box, and why shouldn't Olwen have gone to see him?

OLWEN: [*Reading magazine*] Yes, why not?

BETTY: I'd forgotten you were there, Olwen. May I ask something? After all, I don't think I've asked anybody anything, so far, have I?

OLWEN: You may ask. I don't promise to answer.

BETTY: I'll risk it then. Were you in love with Martin, Olwen?

OLWEN: Not in the least.

BETTY: I thought you weren't.

OLWEN: As a matter of fact, to be absolutely candid, I rather disliked him.

BETTY: Yes, I thought so.

GORDON: [*Rises*] Oh—rot! I'll never believe that, Olwen. You couldn't dislike him. Nobody could. I don't mean he hadn't any faults or anything, but with him they just didn't matter. He was one of those people. You *had* to like him. He was Martin.

BETTY: In other words—your god! [GORDON *turns sharply*] You know, Gordon literally adored him. Didn't you, darling?

STANTON: [*Puts down glass*] Well, he could be fascinating. And he was very clever. I must admit the firm's never been the same without him.

GORDON: I should think not!

BETTY: How could it be?

[ROBERT *returns, followed by* FREDA, *who closes door*]

ROBERT: Now we can thrash this out.

OLWEN: Oh, no, please, Robert.

[GORDON *crosses to piano and puts out cigarette*]

ROBERT: I'm sorry, Olwen. But I want to know the truth now. There's something very queer about all this. First Freda going to see Martin, and never saying a word about it. Then you going to see him, too, Olwen, and never saying a word about it either. It's not good enough. You've both been hiding this all along. You may be hiding other things too. It's about time some of us began telling the truth—for a change.

FREDA: Do *you* always tell the truth, Robert?

ROBERT: I try to.

STANTON: Noble fellow. But don't expect too much of us ordinary mortals. Spare our weaknesses. Please!

FREDA: What weaknesses?

STANTON: Anything you like, my dear Freda. Buying musical cigarette boxes, for instance. I'm sure that's a weakness.

FREDA: Or making rather too much use of one's little country cottage. I think that too under circumstances might be described as a weakness.

STANTON: Do you mean Martin's cottage? I hardly ever went there.

FREDA: No, I wasn't thinking of Martin's.

STANTON: I'm afraid I don't understand.

ROBERT: Look here, what's all this about? Are you starting now, Stanton?

STANTON: Certainly not.

ROBERT: Well, I want to get to the bottom of this Martin business. And I want to do it now.

GORDON: Oh, Lord, is this going to be another inquest?

ROBERT: Well, it wouldn't be necessary if we'd heard more of the truth perhaps when there *was* an inquest. And it's up to you, Olwen. You were the last to see Martin. Why did you go to see him like that? Was it about the missing money?

OLWEN: Yes, it was.

ROBERT: Did you know then that Martin had taken it?

OLWEN: No.

ROBERT: But you thought he had?

OLWEN: I thought there was a possibility he had.

GORDON: You were *all* damned ready to think that!

BETTY: Gordon, I want to go home now.

ROBERT: So soon, Betty?

BETTY: I'm going to have an awful headache if I stay any longer. I'm going home—

[*She rises*]

GORDON: All right. Just a minute.

STANTON: I'll take you along, Betty, if Gordon wants to stay on.

BETTY: No, I want Gordon to come along too.

GORDON: All right. But hang on a minute.

BETTY: I tell you I want to go now. Take me home.

ROBERT: [*Taking her hand*] Why, what's the matter, Betty?

BETTY: I don't know. I'm stupid, I suppose.

GORDON: All right. We'll go.

ROBERT: But, Betty, I'm awfully sorry if all this stuff has upset you.

BETTY: Oh, don't go on and on about it! Why can't you leave things alone?

[*She rushes out*]

GORDON: Well—good-night, everybody.

[*He exits*]

STANTON: I'll see these infants home and then turn in myself.

OLWEN: Very good of you.

STANTON: Yes, isn't it? Good-night.

FREDA: Good-night.

[STANTON *exits*]

ROBERT: Now, Olwen, you can tell me exactly why you rushed to see Martin like that about the missing money.

OLWEN: We're all being truthful now, aren't we?

ROBERT: I want to be.

OLWEN: What about you, Freda?

FREDA: Yes, yes, yes. I don't care. What does it matter?

ROBERT: Queer way of putting it.

FREDA: Is it? Well sometimes, Robert, I'm rather a queer woman. You'd hardly know me.

OLWEN: You started all this, you know, Robert. Now it's your turn. Will you be truthful, with me?

ROBERT: Good God. Yes—of course I will. I loathe all these silly mysteries. [FREDA *sits*] But it's not my turn. I asked you a question that you haven't answered yet.

OLWEN: I know you have. But I'm going to ask you one before I answer yours. I've been waiting to do it for some time but I've never had the chance or never dared. Now I don't care. It might as well come out. Robert—did you take that money?

ROBERT: Did *I* take the money?

OLWEN: Yes.

ROBERT: Of course not! You must be crazy, Olwen. Do you think even if I had taken it, I'd let Martin shoulder the blame like that? But Martin took it, of course. We all know that.

OLWEN: Oh, what a fool I've been.

ROBERT: I don't understand. Surely you must have known that Martin took it. You can't have been thinking all this time that I did!

OLWEN: Yes, I have. And I've not been thinking it— I've been torturing myself with it!

[FREDA *rises, moves to piano*]

ROBERT: Damn it all—it doesn't make sense! I might have taken the money—I suppose we're all capable of that, under certain circumstances—but never on earth could I let somebody else—and especially Martin, take the blame for it. How could you think me capable of such a thing? I thought you were a friend of mine, Olwen —one of my best and oldest friends.

FREDA: You might as well know, Robert—

OLWEN: Oh, no, Freda. Please! Please!

FREDA: Why not? What does it matter! [*To* ROBERT] You might as well know, Robert—and how you can be so dense baffles me!— that Olwen is not a *friend* of yours.

ROBERT: Of course she is!

FREDA: She's not! She's a woman who's in *love* with you. A very different thing! She's been in love with you for ages!

OLWEN: Freda, that's damnably unfair! That's cruel!

FREDA: It's not going to hurt you, and he *wanted* the truth. Let him have it!

ROBERT: I'm terribly sorry, Olwen. We've always been very good friends and I've always been very fond of you.

OLWEN: Stop! Freda, that's unforgivable! You'd no right to say that!

FREDA: But it's true, isn't it? You wanted the truth, Robert, and here it is—some of it. Olwen's been in love with you for ages. I don't know exactly how long, but I've been aware of it for the last eighteen months. Wives always are aware of these things. And, I'll tell you now what I've longed to tell you for some time. I think you're a fool for not being aware of it yourself, for not having responded to it, for not having done something drastic about it long before this. If somebody loves you like that, for God's sake enjoy it, make the most of it, hold on to it, before it's too late!

OLWEN: Freda, I understand now.

FREDA: Understand what?

OLWEN: About you. I ought to have understood before.

ROBERT: If you mean by that, that you understand now Freda doesn't care for me very much—you're right. We've not been very happy together—somehow our marriage hasn't worked. Nobody knows.

FREDA: Of course they know!

ROBERT: Do you mean you've told them?

FREDA: Of course I haven't. If you mean by *them* the people we know intimately—our own group here—they didn't need to be told!

ROBERT: But Olwen has just said she understood about it for the first time.

OLWEN: No, I knew about that before, Robert. It was something else I've just—

ROBERT: Well, what is it?

OLWEN: I'd rather not explain.

FREDA: Being noble, now, Olwen? You needn't, you know. We're past that.

OLWEN: No, it's not that. It's—it's because I can't talk about it! There's something horrible to me about it. And I can't tell you why.

FREDA: Something horrible?

OLWEN: Yes, something really horrible. Don't let's talk about that side of it!

FREDA: But Olwen . . .

OLWEN: I'm sorry I said I understood. It just slipped out! Please!

FREDA: Very well. But you've got to talk about that money now. You said you believed all along Robert had taken it.

OLWEN: It looked to me as if he must have.

ROBERT: [To OLWEN] But if you believed that, why didn't you say something?

FREDA: Oh, Robert—can't you see why she couldn't?

ROBERT: You mean—she was shielding me?

FREDA: Yes, of course!

ROBERT: Olwen—I'm terribly sorry. I'd no idea. Though it's fantastic, I must say, that you could think I was that kind of man and yet you go on caring enough not to say anything.

OLWEN: But it's not fantastic at all.

FREDA: If you're in love with somebody, you're in love with them, and they can do all sorts of things, be mean as hell, and you'll forgive them or just not bother about it. At least, some women will.

ROBERT: I don't see that in you, Freda.

FREDA: Don't you? But there are a lot of things about me you don't see. [To OLWEN] But this is what I wanted to say, Olwen. If you thought that Robert had taken that money, then you knew that Martin hadn't.

OLWEN: Yes, I was sure—after I had talked with him that last night—that Martin *hadn't* taken it.

FREDA: But you let us all think he had.

OLWEN: I know. But it didn't seem to matter then. It couldn't hurt Martin any more. He wasn't there to be hurt. And I felt I had to keep quiet.

ROBERT: Because of me?

OLWEN: Yes, because of you, Robert.

ROBERT: But Martin *must* have taken it.

OLWEN: No.

ROBERT: That's why he shot himself. He thought he'd be found out. He was terribly nervous—always was. And he simply couldn't face it.

OLWEN: [*Rises*] No, it wasn't that at all. You *must* believe me. I'm positive Martin never touched that money.

FREDA: I've always thought it queer that he should. It wasn't his style at all—doing some sneaky work with a check. I knew he could be wild—and rather cruel sometimes. But he couldn't be a cautious cunning little sneak-thief. It wasn't like him and he didn't care at all about money.

ROBERT: He spent enough of it. He was badly in debt.

FREDA: Yes, but that's just the point. He didn't mind being in debt. He could have cheerfully gone on being in debt. Money simply didn't matter. Now, *you* loathe it. You're entirely different.

OLWEN: Yes, that was one of the reasons I thought that you—

ROBERT: Yes, I see that. Though I think those fellows who don't care about money, who don't mind being in debt, are just the sort who might help themselves to other people's.

FREDA: Yes, but not in a cautious sneaky way. That wasn't like Martin at all.

ROBERT: . . . Olwen, where did you get the idea that *I'd* taken it?

OLWEN: Because Martin himself was sure that you had taken it. He told me so.

ROBERT: Martin told you so?

OLWEN: Yes. That was the first thing we talked about.

ROBERT: Martin thought I had taken it?

OLWEN: Yes.

ROBERT: But he knew me better than that. Why should he have thought that?

FREDA: You thought *he'd* been the thief. You didn't know him any better, it seems!

ROBERT: There were special circumstances, I'd been told something. Besides, I wasn't at all sure. It wasn't until after he shot himself that I felt certain.

OLWEN: You say you'd been told something? But then Martin had been told something too! He'd practically been told that you'd taken that check.

ROBERT: What!

OLWEN: And do you know who told him?

ROBERT: I can guess now.

FREDA: Who?

ROBERT: Stanton, wasn't it?

OLWEN: Yes, Stanton.

ROBERT: But he told *me* that Martin had taken that check.

FREDA: Oh, but he— }
OLWEN: Oh! }

ROBERT: He practically proved it to me. He said he didn't want Martin given away—said we'd all stand in together, all that sort of thing.

OLWEN: But don't you see—he told Martin all that too. And Martin would never have told me if he hadn't known—well, that I would never give you away.

ROBERT: Stanton.

FREDA: Then it was Stanton himself who got that money?

OLWEN: It looks like it.

FREDA: I'm sure it was! He played Martin and Robert against each other. Could anything be more vile?

ROBERT: You know, it doesn't follow that Stanton himself was the thief.

FREDA: Of course he was!

ROBERT: Wait. Let's get this clear. That check made payable to bearer was on your father's desk, Freda, in his private office. Remember, only three of us had access to his office. Martin, Stanton, and I. The check disappeared. Cashed at one of the branch banks where none of us were known. The teller was rather vague about it all except that the person who cashed it was about the age and build of Martin or myself, so it couldn't have been Stanton.

FREDA: How could you believe Martin had taken the check?

ROBERT: The evidence pointed to him or to me, and I knew *I* hadn't taken it.

FREDA: And Stanton told you—?

ROBERT: That he'd seen Martin coming out of your father's office.

OLWEN: Stanton told Martin he'd seen *you* coming out of that office.

FREDA: Stanton took that money himself.

ROBERT: [*Fiercely*] Whether he took the money or not, Stanton's got to explain this! [*He goes up steps to phone and dials*] No wonder he didn't approve of this business and was glad to get out of it! He's got too much to hide.

OLWEN: We *all* have too much to hide.

ROBERT: Then we'll let some daylight into it for once, if it kills us! Stanton's got to explain this.

FREDA: Not tonight!

ROBERT: Tonight!!

OLWEN: They've probably all gone to bed.

FREDA: Are you going to get them all back, Robert?

ROBERT: Yes. Hello, is that you, Gordon? . . . He is, is he? Well, I want you *both* to come back here. . . . Yes, more and more of it. . . . It's damned important! . . . Oh, no, we can keep Betty out of it. All right, then. Be as quick as you can! [*Puts back receiver*] They're coming back.

QUICK CURTAIN

ACT TWO

ROBERT, FREDA *and* OLWEN *are discovered in exactly the same positions as they were at the end of Act One.*

FREDA: Are they all coming back?

ROBERT: [*On platform*] No, not Betty. She's going to bed.

> [FREDA *crosses to drinks, throws* OLWEN *a look—then takes cigarette*]

OLWEN: [*On* FREDA's *look*] Wise little Betty.

ROBERT: [*Comes down steps*] What do you mean, Olwen? You know very well she's not mixed up in this business.

OLWEN: Do I?

ROBERT: Well, don't you?

FREDA: Poor Robert, look at him now. [*Sitting*] This is really serious, he's saying to himself. How we give ourselves away. It's a mystery we have any secrets at all.

ROBERT: No, but—hang it all, Olwen—you've no right to sneer at Betty like that. You know very well it's better to keep her out of all this.

OLWEN: No, we mustn't soil her pure young mind.

ROBERT: Well, after all, she's younger than we are—and she's terribly sensitive. You saw what happened to her just before they went. She can't stand the atmosphere of all this.

OLWEN: [*Sitting*] I suppose not.

ROBERT: Obviously you dislike her, Olwen. I can't imagine why. She's always had a great admiration for you.

OLWEN: Well, I'm sorry, Robert, but I can't return her admiration— except for her looks. I don't dislike her. But—well, I can't be as sorry for her as I'd like to be or ought to be.

> [*She lights a cigarette*]

ROBERT: Is it necessary for you or anybody else to be sorry for her? You're talking wildly now, Olwen.

FREDA: I suspect not. And anyhow it seems to be our evening for talking wildly. Also, I'm now facing a most urgent problem, the sort of problem that only women have to face. If a man has been dragged back to your house to be told he's a liar, a cad, and a possible thief, oughtn't you to make a few sandwiches for him?

ROBERT: He'll get no sandwiches from me!

FREDA: No sincerity, no sandwiches—that's your motto, is it? No? Oh, dear—how heavy we are without Martin. And how he would have adored all this. He'd have invented the most extravagant and incredible sins to confess to. Oh, don't look so dreadfully solemn, you two. You might be a bit brighter—just for a minute.

ROBERT: I'm afraid we haven't your light touch, my dear Freda.

FREDA: I suppose I feel like this because, in spite of everything I *am* a hostess expecting company, and I can't help thinking about bright remarks and sandwiches. [A *bell rings out in the hall*] And there they are! [*Rises*] You'll have to let them in yourself, Robert.

[OLWEN *puts out cigarette.* ROBERT *goes out*]

OLWEN: Freda.

FREDA: Yes?

OLWEN: [*Rising*] Have you really known a long time?

FREDA: Yes. More than a year. I've often wanted to say something to you about it.

OLWEN: What would you have said?

FREDA: I don't quite know. Something idiotic. But friendly, very friendly.

OLWEN: And I only guessed about you tonight, Freda. And now it all seems so obvious. I can't think why I never guessed before.

FREDA: Neither can I.

OLWEN: This is quite mad, isn't it?

FREDA: And rapidly getting madder. I don't care, do you? It's rather a relief.

OLWEN: Yes, it is—in a way. But it's rather frightening too. Like being in a car when the brakes are gone.

[*Noise of* MEN *outside.* STANTON *enters first,* GORDON *follows.* ROBERT *follows, closing door*]

STANTON: [*As he enters*] I can't see why? [OLWEN *sits*] I'm sorry about this, Freda. But it's Robert's doing. He insisted on our coming back.

FREDA: I think Robert was right.

GORDON: That's a change, anyhow. Well, what's it all about?

ROBERT: Chiefly about that money.

GORDON: Oh—hell—I thought as much. Why can't you leave poor Martin alone?

ROBERT: Wait a minute, Gordon. Martin didn't take that check.

GORDON: What? Is that true? Are you sure?

FREDA: Yes.

GORDON: You know, I never could understand that. It wasn't like him.

STANTON: [*To* FREDA *and* ROBERT] Do you really believe that Martin didn't get that money? If he didn't, who did? And if he didn't, why did he shoot himself?

ROBERT: We don't know, Stanton. But we're hoping that you'll tell us.

STANTON: Being funny, Robert?

ROBERT: Not a bit. I wouldn't have dragged you back here to be funny. You told me—didn't you—that you were practically certain that Martin took that check?

STANTON: Certainly I did. And I told you why I thought so. All the evidence pointed that way. And what happened afterwards proved I was right.

ROBERT: Did it?

STANTON: Well, didn't it?

FREDA: [*By piano*] If it did, then why did you tell Martin you thought Robert had done it?

STANTON: Don't be ridiculous, Freda! Why should I tell Martin I thought Robert had done it?

FREDA: Yes, why should you? That's *exactly* what we want to know.

STANTON: But of course I didn't.

OLWEN: Yes, you did!

STANTON: Olwen. Are you in this too?

OLWEN: Yes, I'm in it too! [*Rises*] Because you lied like that to Martin, telling him you were sure Robert took the check. You've given me hours of misery.

STANTON: But I never meant to, Olwen. How could I know that you would go and see Martin and he would tell you?

OLWEN: It doesn't matter whether you knew or not. It was a mean vile lie! After this I feel that I never want to speak to you again.

STANTON: I'm sorry, Olwen. I'd rather anything had happened than that. You do believe that, don't you?

FREDA: Apparently the rest of us don't matter very much. But you owe us a few explanations.

ROBERT: You'd better stop lying now, Stanton. [OLWEN *sits on sofa*] You've done enough. Why did you play Martin and me against each other like that?

FREDA: There can only be one explanation. Because he took that check himself.

GORDON: My God—you didn't, did you, Stanton?

STANTON: [*Turning*] Yes, I did.

GORDON: Then you're a rotten swine, Stanton! I don't care about the money. But you let Martin take the blame. You let everybody think he was a thief.

[*He closes in on* STANTON]

STANTON: Don't be such a hysterical young fool.

ROBERT: [*Seizes* GORDON's *right hand, pins it on back of chair*] Keep quiet, Gordon!

GORDON: I won't keep quiet!

STANTON: Sit down and behave yourself. We don't want this to develop into a free fight.

GORDON: But you let—

STANTON: I didn't let Martin take the blame, as you call it. He wasn't the sort to take the blame, and you ought to know that. It happened that in the middle of all the fuss about this money, he shot himself. You all jumped to the conclusion that it was because he had taken the money and was afraid of being found out. I let you go on thinking it, that's all. You might as well think he shot himself for that as for anything else. And anyhow he was done with it, out of it. Besides—where he's gone, it doesn't matter a damn whether people here think you've stolen money or not.

ROBERT: But you deliberately tried to fasten the blame on to Martin or me.

FREDA: Of course he did! That's what makes it so foul.

[*She goes to chair, sits*]

STANTON: Not really. I'd not the least intention of letting anybody else be punished for what I'd done. I took that check because I needed some money quickly and I didn't know where to turn. I knew I could square it up in a week. But when it all came out, I had to play for time, and that seemed to me the easiest way of doing it.

ROBERT: But you couldn't have cashed the check at the bank yourself.

STANTON: No, I got somebody else to do that—a fellow who could keep his mouth shut. It was pure coincidence that he was about the same age and build as you and Martin. Don't go thinking there was any deep-laid plot. There wasn't. It was all improvised and haphazard and damned stupid.

ROBERT: Why didn't you confess to this before?

STANTON: Why the devil should I?

FREDA: If you can't understand why, it's hopeless for us to try and show you. But there is such a thing as common honesty and decency.

STANTON: [*Crosses to* FREDA] Is there? Don't forget—before you become too self-righteous—that you happen to be taking the lid off me. It might be somebody else's turn before we've finished.

ROBERT: Possibly. But that doesn't explain why you've kept so quiet about all this.

STANTON: [*To* ROBERT] I should have thought it did. Martin's suicide put "paid" to the whole thing. Nobody wanted to talk about it after that. Dear Martin must have done it, so we won't mention it. That was the line. It wasn't the money. I'd have been glad to replace that. But I knew damned well that if I confessed, the old man would have had me out of the firm in two minutes. I wasn't one of his pets like you and Martin. I had to work myself up from nothing in the firm. I hadn't been brought in because I had the right university and social backgrounds. If the old man had thought for a minute that I'd done it, there'd have been none of this hush-hush business. He'd have felt like calling in the police. Don't forget, I'd been a clerk in the office. You fellows hadn't. It makes a difference, I can tell you.

FREDA: But my father retired from the firm six months ago.

STANTON: Well, what if he did? The whole thing was over and done with. Why open it up again? It might never have been mentioned if this damn fool inquisition hadn't been started tonight. Robert, Gordon and I were all working well together in the firm. What would have happened if I'd confessed? Where are we now? Who's better off because of this?

FREDA: You're not, it's true. But Martin is. And the people who cared about him.

STANTON: Are they?

FREDA: Of course they are.

STANTON: Don't be too sure.

FREDA: At least we know now that he wasn't a mean thief.

STANTON: And that's all you do know. But for all that he shot himself. And you don't suppose he did it for fun, do you?

FREDA: [Rises] Oh—you—you—!

GORDON: You are a rotter, Stanton!

ROBERT: Drop that sort of talk, Stanton.

STANTON: [To ROBERT] Why should I? You wanted the truth, and now you're getting it. I didn't want to come back here and be put in the witness box. It's your own doing. I'll say what I damn well like! Martin shot himself, and he did it knowing that he'd never touched the money. So it must have been something else. Well, what was it? You see what you've started now.

FREDA: What have we started? You're talking now as if you knew a lot more about Martin than we did.

STANTON: What I do know is that he must have had some reason for doing what he did, and that if it wasn't the money, it must have been something else. You're probably a lot better off for not knowing what that something is, just as you'd have been a lot better off if you'd never started poking about and prying into all this business.

ROBERT: Perhaps he did it because he thought I'd taken the money.

STANTON: And then again—perhaps not. If you think that Martin would have shot himself because he thought you'd taken some money—then you didn't know your own brother. Why, he laughed when I told him. It amused him. A lot of things amused that young man.

OLWEN: That's true, I know. He didn't care. He didn't care at all.

ROBERT: Look here—do you know why Martin *did* shoot himself?

STANTON: [*Back to fireplace*] No. How should I?

FREDA: You talk as if you do.

STANTON: I can imagine reasons.

FREDA: What do you mean by that?

STANTON: I mean he was that sort. He'd got his life into a mess, and I don't blame him.

FREDA: You don't blame him! Who are you to blame him or not to blame him? You're not fit to mention his name. You hung your mean little piece of thieving round his neck, tried to poison our memory of him, and now when you're found out and Martin's name is clear of it, you want to begin all over again and start hinting that he was a criminal or a lunatic or something.

ROBERT: The less you say now, the better.

STANTON: The less we *all* say, the better! You should have thought of that before. I told you as much before you began dragging all this stuff out. Like a fool, you wouldn't leave well enough alone.

ROBERT: Anyway, I've cleared Martin's name.

STANTON: You've cleared nothing yet, and if you'd a glimmer of sense you'd see it. But now I don't give a damn. You're going to get all you ask for.

FREDA: One of the things we shall ask for is to be rid of you.

GORDON: Do you think you'll stay on with this firm after this?

STANTON: I don't know and I don't care.

FREDA: You did a year ago.

STANTON: Yes, but now I don't. I can get along better now without the firm than they can without me.

GORDON: Well, after this, at least it will be a pleasure to try. You always hated Martin, and I knew it.

STANTON: I had my reasons! Unlike the Whitehouse family—father, daughter and son—who all fell in love with him.

ROBERT: Does that mean anything, Stanton? If it doesn't just take it back—now. If it does, you'll kindly explain yourself.

STANTON: I'll take nothing back.

OLWEN: [*Rises*] Stanton—please! Don't let's have any more of this. We've all said too much already.

STANTON: I'm sorry, Olwen. But you can't blame me.

[OLWEN *moves up to window*]

ROBERT: [*To* STANTON] I'm waiting for your explanation.

FREDA: Don't you see, he's getting at me.

ROBERT: Is that true, Stanton?

STANTON: I'm certainly not leaving *her* out.

ROBERT: Be careful.

STANTON: It's too late to be careful. [FREDA *sits in chair*] Why do you think Freda's been so angry with me? There's only one reason, and I've known that reason for a long time. She was in love with Martin.

ROBERT: Is that true, Freda? I must know, because if it isn't I'm going to kick Stanton out of this house.

STANTON: Don't talk like a man in a melodrama. I wouldn't have said it if I hadn't known it was true. Whether she admits it or not is another matter. But even if she doesn't admit it, you're not going to kick me out of the house. I'll go in the ordinary way, thank you.

[GORDON *moves to platform, sits on step*]

ROBERT: [*Facing* FREDA] Freda, is it true?

[OLWEN *sits*]

FREDA: Yes.

ROBERT: Has that been the trouble all along?

FREDA: Yes. All along.

ROBERT: When did it begin?

FREDA: A long time ago. Or it seems a long time ago, ages.

ROBERT: Before we were married?

FREDA: Yes. I thought I could—break it—then. I did for a little time. But it came back, worse than ever.

ROBERT: I wish you'd told me. Why didn't you tell me?

FREDA: I wanted to. Hundreds of times I tried to. . . . I said the opening words to myself so often— Sometimes I've hardly known whether I didn't actually say them out loud to you.

ROBERT: I wish you had. But why didn't I see it for myself? It seems plain enough now. I know now when it began. It was when we were all up at the lake that summer.

FREDA: Yes, it began then. Oh, that lovely lovely summer! Nothing's ever been quite real since then.

ROBERT: Martin went away, and you said you'd stay a few days with the Hutchinsons. Was that—?

FREDA: Yes, Martin and I spent that little time together. It was the only time we really did spend together. It didn't mean much to him—a sort of experiment, that's all.

ROBERT: Didn't he care?

FREDA: No, not really. If he had, it would have been all so simple. That's why I never told you. And I thought when we were married, it would be—different. It wasn't fair to you, I know, but I thought it would be all right. But it wasn't. You know that too. It was hopeless. But you don't know how hopeless it was—for me.

ROBERT: But why didn't Martin tell me? He knew how unhappy I was.

FREDA: He couldn't. He was rather afraid of you.

ROBERT: Martin afraid of me?

GORDON: Yes, he was.

ROBERT: Nonsense! He wasn't afraid of anybody—and certainly not of me.

FREDA: Yes, he was, in some strange way.

GORDON: I know that! He told me that when you're really angry, you'll stop at nothing.

ROBERT: Queer. I never knew he felt like that. [*To* FREDA] It couldn't have been—this—

FREDA: [*Rises, crosses to fireplace*] No, no. He didn't care. Oh, Martin, Martin—

OLWEN: [*Rises*] Freda—don't.

STANTON: That's how it goes on, you see. A good evening's work.

ROBERT: I'm not regretting it. I'm glad all this has come out. I wish to God I'd known earlier, that's all.

STANTON: What difference would it have made? You couldn't have done anything.

ROBERT: To begin with, I'd have known the *truth*. And then something might have been done about it. I wouldn't have stood in their way.

STANTON: You didn't stand in their way.

GORDON: [*Rises*] No, it was Martin himself. As Freda says he didn't care. He told me about it.

FREDA: Gordon, I don't believe you!

GORDON: Why should I lie about it? Martin told me. He used to tell me everything.

FREDA: Rubbish! He thought you were a little nuisance—always hanging about him.

GORDON: That's not true!

FREDA: It is! He told me so that—that very last Saturday, when I took him the cigarette box. He told me then he'd had to do everything he could to get rid of you.

GORDON: Freda—you're making this up, every word of it. I know you are! Martin would never have said that about me. He knew how fond I was of him, and he was fond of me too in his own way.

FREDA: He wasn't.

GORDON: You're just saying this because you're jealous.

FREDA: I'm not.

GORDON: You've *always* been jealous of Martin's interest in me.

FREDA: Gordon, that's a disgusting lie!

GORDON: It isn't.

FREDA: It is. He told me himself how tired he was of having you around him and suddenly becoming hysterical. I see what he meant now. Every time he's been mentioned tonight, you've been hysterical. What are you trying to make me believe you are?

ROBERT: Freda, you're mad.

GORDON: It's all jealousy, jealousy! If he'd thought I was a nuisance, he wouldn't have kept asking me down to the cottage. [*Turning to* FREDA] But he was tired of you, pestering him and worrying him all the time. He didn't care for women. He was sick of them. He wanted me to tell you so that you'd leave him alone.

FREDA: [*Sits*] You're making me feel sick.

GORDON: Well, you just leave me—

OLWEN: Stop it. Stop it, both of you!

GORDON: And I *was* going to tell you too! Only then—he killed himself.

FREDA: [*Rises*] I don't believe it! I don't believe it! Martin couldn't have been so cruel.

[OLWEN *sits on piano bench*]

GORDON: Couldn't he? What did he say to you that afternoon when you took him the cigarette box?

FREDA: What does it matter what he said? You're just making up those abominable lies.

ROBERT: [*Comes between* FREDA *and* GORDON] Look here, I'm not having any more of this. I understand about you, Freda, and I'm sorry—but for God's sake keep quiet about it now. I can't stand any more. As for you, Gordon—you must be tight or something—

GORDON: I'm not. I'm as sober as you are.

ROBERT: Well, behave as if you were. You're not a child. I know Martin was a friend of yours—

GORDON: [*Turning on* ROBERT, *hotly and scornfully*] Of course he was! Martin was the only person on earth I *really* cared about. I couldn't help it. There it was. I'd have done *anything* for him. Money, my God, I'd have stolen ten times the amount from the firm if Martin had asked me to. He was the most marvelous person I'd ever known. Sometimes I tried to hate him. Sometimes he gave me a hell of a time. But it didn't really matter. He was Martin, and I'd rather be with him, even if he was jeering at me all the time, than be with anybody else I've ever known. I'm like Freda—since he died, I haven't really cared a damn. He didn't really care for women. He tried to amuse himself with them, but he distrusted them, disliked them. He told me so, many times. Martin told me everything. And that was the finest thing that ever happened to me. [*Sits on sofa*] And now you can call me any name you like, I don't care.

ROBERT: But what about Betty?

GORDON: You can leave her out of this.

ROBERT: I want to. But I can't help thinking about her.

GORDON: Well, you needn't. She can look after herself.

ROBERT: That's just what she can't do and she shouldn't have to. You ought to see that.

GORDON: Well, I don't see it. And I know Betty better than you do.

FREDA: You know everybody better than anybody else does, don't you?

GORDON: You would say that, wouldn't you? I can't help it if Martin liked me better than he liked you.

FREDA: How do you know that he—

OLWEN: [*Rises*] Stop it, both of you! Can't you see that Martin was making mischief, just to amuse himself?

GORDON: No, I can't! He wasn't like that.

STANTON: [*Crosses to drinks*] Oh, no. Not at all like that. You couldn't ask for a quieter, simpler, more sincere fellow.

FREDA: Nobody's going to pretend he was that. But at least he didn't steal money and then try to put the blame on other people!

STANTON: We could all start talking like that, Freda. Just throwing things at each other's heads. But I suggest we don't.

OLWEN: I agree. But I do want Freda and Gordon to understand that it's simply madness quarreling over anything Martin ever said to them. He was a born mischief-maker, cruel as a cat. That's one of the reasons why I disliked him so much.

ROBERT: Olwen!

OLWEN: Yes, I'm sorry, Robert, but I didn't like Martin. I *detested* him. You ought to have seen that.

STANTON: And you were quite right, Olwen. I'm afraid you always are.

OLWEN: No, I'm not.

STANTON: I'd trust your judgment. And you're the only one of us who will come out of this as sound as you went in.

OLWEN: No, that's not true.

GORDON: No—it was Olwen and that damned cigarette box that began the whole business.

STANTON: Oh, that was nothing. I knew about that all along.

OLWEN: You knew about what?

STANTON: [*Facing* OLWEN] I knew you'd been to see Martin that Saturday night.

OLWEN: You knew?

STANTON: Yes.

OLWEN: But how could you? I don't understand.

STANTON: I was spending that weekend at my own cottage. You remember that garage, where the road forks? You stopped there that night for some gas.

OLWEN: Yes, I believe I did.

STANTON: They told me, and said you'd taken the old road, and so I knew you must have been going to see Martin. You couldn't have been going anywhere else, could you? Quite simple.

OLWEN: And you've known all this time?

STANTON: Yes, all this time.

[OLWEN *turns and crosses to window platform*]

ROBERT: I suppose, Stanton, it's no use asking you why you've never said a word about it?

STANTON: I'm afraid not. I think I've done my share in the confession box tonight.

[OLWEN *sits at window*]

GORDON: Well, I wish I'd known a bit more, that's all. There was I, dragged into that foul inquest. Did I know *this*? Did I know *that*? My God—and all the time, I wasn't the *last* person he'd talked to at all! [*Rises*] Freda had been there some time in the afternoon. And Olwen was there that very night, at the very moment—for all we know.

STANTON: Don't talk rubbish!

GORDON: Well, is it rubbish? After all, what *do* we know? What was Olwen doing there?

ROBERT: She's told us that. She was there to talk to Martin about the money.

GORDON: And how far does that take us?

STANTON: What do you mean by that?

FREDA: He means—I imagine—that Olwen hasn't told us very much so far. We know she went to Martin to talk to him about the missing money. And that he thought Robert had taken it and that she thought so too. And that's all we do know.

GORDON: Yes, we don't know how long she was there or what Martin said to her, or anything. It's a good thing she wasn't pushed in front of that coroner or they'd have had it out of her in no time! I think it's up to her to tell us a little more.

STANTON: Well, there's no need to sound so damned vindictive about it.

[OLWEN, *looking out through the window, suddenly gives a little start and rises*]

OLWEN: Somebody's out there!

ROBERT: [*Hastens to window, opens it and looks out*] There's no one there now.

OLWEN: No, they darted away. But I'll swear there was somebody! They'd been listening.

STANTON: Well, they couldn't have chosen a better night for it.

ROBERT: [*Closing window*] It's impossible, Olwen. And there isn't a sign of anybody.

GORDON: Thank the Lord for that.

[*There are several short rings of a doorbell heard from the hall*]

ROBERT: Who on earth can this be?

FREDA: Don't ask me. I haven't the slightest idea. Go and see.

ROBERT: Yes, I know. But we don't want anybody interrupting us now.

FREDA: Well, don't let them interrupt us, whoever they are. But you'll have to see who it is.

[*The bell rings again and* ROBERT *goes out*]

ROBERT: [*Off*] But we haven't, I tell you. You've never been mentioned.

BETTY: [*Off*] I know you have. I can feel it. That's why I *had* to come back.

ROBERT: [*Off*] I tell you we haven't.

[ROBERT *opens the door and* BETTY *is seen in front of him*]

GORDON: [*As* BETTY *enters*] I thought you'd gone to bed, Betty. What's the matter?

[ROBERT *enters and shuts door*]

BETTY: You're talking about me, all of you. [*Looking round at them all*] I know you are! I wanted to go to bed. I started to go. And then I couldn't. I knew you were all talking about me. I couldn't stand it. I had to come.

FREDA: Well, you were wrong. As a matter of fact, you're the one person we *haven't* been talking about.

BETTY: Is that true?

ROBERT: Yes, of course.

OLWEN: [*To* BETTY] You were outside just now, weren't you? Outside the window, listening.

BETTY: No, I wasn't listening. I was trying to look in, to see exactly who was here and what you all looked like. You see, I was sure you were all saying things about me. I meant to go to bed and I was tired, but I felt too excited to sleep and now I'm so damn nervous. God knows what I shall be saying in a minute. You mustn't mind me.

[*She sits*]

ROBERT: I'm so sorry, Betty. [OLWEN *crosses up to window and sits*] Not a word's been said about you. In fact, we all wanted to keep you out of this. It's all rather unpleasant.

FREDA: Seeing that Betty has married into one of the families concerned, I think she ought not to be too carefully protected from the sordid truth.

ROBERT: Keep quiet, Freda.

FREDA: I thought we should see a different Robert now.

ROBERT: After what you've said tonight, I can't see that it matters much to you how different I may be.

FREDA: Perhaps not, but I still like reasonably decent manners.

ROBERT: Then set us an example.

GORDON: Oh, be still, both of you.

BETTY: But what have you been talking about then?

GORDON: It began with the money.

BETTY: You mean that Martin took—?

GORDON: [*Back of* BETTY's *chair*] Martin *didn't* take it. We know that now. Stanton took that money. He's admitted it.

BETTY: Admitted it! Stan—Stanton. Oh, surely—it's impossible.

STANTON: It sounds impossible, doesn't it, Betty, but it isn't. I'm sorry to go down with such a bump in your estimation, my dear Betty, but this is our night for telling the truth, and I've had to admit that I took that money. Terrible, isn't it?

ROBERT: What did you mean by that, Stanton?

STANTON: I meant what I said. I nearly always do.

ROBERT: Why did you use that tone of voice to Betty?

STANTON: Perhaps because I think that Betty has not a very high opinion of me—and so she need not have sounded so surprised and shocked.

ROBERT: I don't quite understand that.

FREDA: I'm sure you don't, Robert.

ROBERT: Do you?

FREDA: Yes, I think so.

BETTY: But if Martin didn't take the money—then why—why did he shoot himself?

GORDON: That's what we want to know. Olwen saw him last of all, that very evening, and she knew he hadn't taken the money, but that's *all* she's told us.

OLWEN: I've told you that he thought Robert had taken the money.

ROBERT: And that was enough—in the state he was in then—to throw him clean off his balance. All that stuff about his merely being amused is nonsense. That was just his bluff. Martin hated anybody to think he was really moved or alarmed by anything.

GORDON: That's true.

ROBERT: And he depended on me. He used to laugh at me a lot, but that was nothing. He depended on me. You've told me yourselves—that he was secretly rather frightened of me. It was because Martin had a respect for me. He thought I was the solid steady one. I tell you, it must have been a hell of a shock to poor Martin.

OLWEN: I don't think it was, Robert.

STANTON: Neither do I.

ROBERT: But neither of you knew him as I did. What's the good of talking. He was in a wretched state, all run down and neurotic, and when he heard that I'd taken the check he must have felt that there was nobody left he could depend on, that I'd let him down. He'd probably been brooding over it day and night—he was that sort. He wouldn't let you see it, Olwen. He wouldn't let *anybody* see it. But it would be there all the time, giving him hell. Oh! what a fool I was. I ought to have gone straight to him and told him what Stanton had told me.

GORDON: If this is true, then the person *really* responsible is Stanton.

FREDA: Yes.

STANTON: Rubbish!

FREDA: It isn't. Don't you see what you did?

STANTON: No, because I don't believe it.

GORDON: No, because you don't choose to, that's all.

STANTON: Oh, talk sense. Can't you see Martin had his own reasons?

ROBERT: No. What drove him to suicide was my stupidity and your damned lying, Stanton! That settles it once and for all!

STANTON: You're not in a state to settle anything.

ROBERT: Listen to me, Stanton—

STANTON: Oh, drop it, man.

GORDON: You've got to answer.

ROBERT: I'll never forgive you for telling Martin what you did—by God! I won't!

STANTON: You've got it all wrong.

GORDON: [*Crosses furiously to* STANTON] They haven't, you rotten liar! You made Martin shoot himself.

OLWEN: Wait a minute, Gordon. Martin *didn't* shoot himself.

MEDIUM CURTAIN

ACT THREE

ALL are discovered in exactly the same positions as they were in at the end of Act Two.

FREDA: Martin didn't shoot himself?

OLWEN: [*On window platform*] No. I shot him.

[*She comes away from window.* BETTY *rises*]

FREDA: *Olwen!*

ROBERT: That's impossible, Olwen! You couldn't have done it.

GORDON: Are you joking?

OLWEN: I wish I were.

GORDON: Olwen!

ROBERT: She must be hysterical.

STANTON: Olwen's not hysterical. She means it.

BETTY: Oh, Lord!— She can't mean—she murdered him? Can she?

STANTON: You might as well tell us exactly what happened now, Olwen. And I might as well tell you—before you begin—that I'm not at all surprised. I suspected this from the first.

OLWEN: You suspected I had done it? But why?

STANTON: For three reasons. The first was, that I couldn't understand why Martin should shoot himself. You see, I knew he hadn't taken the money, and though he was in every kind of mess, he didn't seem to me the sort who'd get out of it that way. Then I knew you'd been with him quite late, because—as I said before— I'd been told you'd gone that way. And the third reason—well, that'll keep. You'd better tell us what happened now. [OLWEN *sits on sofa*] It was an accident, wasn't it?

[BETTY *sits on piano bench*]

OLWEN: Yes, it was really an accident. I'll tell you what happened but I can't go into details. It's all too muddled and horrible. But

I'll tell you the complete truth. I won't hide anything more, I promise you. I think we'd all better tell everything we know now, really speak our minds.

STANTON: Yes, of course.

OLWEN: I went to see Martin that Saturday night, as you know, to talk to him about the missing money. Mr. Whitehouse had told me about it. He thought that either Martin or Robert must have taken it. I gathered it was more likely Robert. So I went to see Martin. I didn't like Martin and he knew it but he knew too what I felt about Robert, and after all, he was Robert's brother. He believed that Robert had taken the money and he wasn't a bit worried about it. I'm sorry, Robert, but he wasn't. I hated him for that too. He was rather maliciously amused. The good brother fallen at last—that sort of thing.

FREDA: I can believe that. I hate to, but I know he could be like that!

OLWEN: I've never seen him as bad as he was that night. He wasn't really sane.

ROBERT: Olwen!

OLWEN: I'm sorry, Robert. I didn't want you to know all this, but there's no help for it now. You see, Martin had been taking some sort of drug!

ROBERT: Drug!

OLWEN: Yes. He'd had a lot of it.

ROBERT: Are you sure? I can't believe it.

GORDON: It's true. You remember when he went to Berlin and how nervous he was just then? Well, a fellow he met there put him on to it—some new drug that a lot of the so-called Bohemians were doping themselves with—

FREDA: But did Martin . . . ?

GORDON: Yes, he liked it, and took more and more of it!

ROBERT: But how could he get it?

GORDON: Through someone he knew in town. When he couldn't get it, he was pretty rotten.

STANTON: But didn't you try to stop him?

GORDON: Of course—but he only laughed. I don't blame him really. None of you can understand what life was like to Martin—he was so sensitive. He was one of those people who are meant to be happy.

STANTON: We're *all* those people who are meant to be happy. Martin's no exception.

ROBERT: Yes, that's true. But I know what Gordon means.

FREDA: You couldn't help knowing what he means, if you knew Martin. There was no sort of middle state, no easy jog-trot for him. Either he had to be gay—and when he was gay, he was gayer than anybody else in the world—or he was intensely miserable.

ROBERT: But what about this drug, Olwen?

OLWEN: He took some—while I was there and it had a terrible effect on him. It gave him a sort of devilish gaiety. I can see him now. His eyes were queer. Oh—he really wasn't sane.

[*She stops*]

ROBERT: What happened?

OLWEN: I've tried not to think about it. He knew I disliked him, but he was so frightfully conceited that he couldn't believe it. He seemed to think that everybody young, male or female, ought to be falling in love with him. He saw himself as a sort of Pan.

FREDA: Yes, he did. And he'd every reason to.

OLWEN: He began taunting me. He thought of me or pretended to—as a priggish spinster, full of repressions, who's never really lived. All rubbish, because I'm really not that type at all. But he pretended to think I was and kept telling me that my dislike of him showed that I was trying to repress a great fascination he had for me. And of course that all these repressions were bad for me. I'd never lived, never would live, and all the rest of it. He talked a lot about that. I ought to have run out and left him, but I felt I couldn't while he was in that state. In a way I was sorry for him, because really he was ill, sick in mind and body, and I thought perhaps I could calm him down. I might dislike him, but after all he wasn't a stranger. He was one of our own set, mixed up with most of the people I liked best in the world. I tried to stop him. But everything I said seemed to make him worse. I suppose it would when he was in that excited abnormal state. Well, he talked about my repressions, and when I pretended to laugh at him, he got more and more excited. And then he tried to show me some beastly foul drawings he had—horrible obscene things by some mad Belgian artist—

FREDA: Oh—my God—

OLWEN: [*Rises*] Oh, Freda, I'm so sorry. Please forgive me. I know how this thing must be hurting you.

FREDA: Martin. Martin.

OLWEN: Don't listen to any more. I'll stop if you like.

FREDA: Oh—he wasn't like that really. If you'd known him as I'd known him—*before*.

OLWEN: I know that. We all do. He was different. He was ill.

FREDA: [*Turns*] Go on, Olwen.

[*She moves up to window platform*]

ROBERT: Yes, Olwen. You can't stop now.

OLWEN: There isn't a lot to tell you. When I pushed his beastly drawings away and was rather indignant about them, he got still more excited, completely unbalanced, and shouted out things about my repressions. And then I found he was telling me to take my clothes off. [FREDA *sits*] I told him not to be a fool and that I was going. But then he stood between me and the door. And he had a revolver in his hand and was shouting, something about danger and terror and love. He wasn't threatening me with it or himself. He was just waving it about—being dramatic. I didn't even believe it was loaded. [*Crosses to drinks*] But by this time I'd had more than enough of him—I couldn't be sorry for him any more—and I told him to get out of the way. When he wouldn't, I tried to push him out of the way. And then we had a struggle. He tried to tear my clothes. We really fought one another. It was horrible. He wasn't any stronger than I was. I'd grabbed the hand with the revolver in it. I'd turned the revolver toward him. His finger must have been on the trigger. I must have given it a jerk. The revolver went off. Oh— Horrible— [*Sits on platform*] horrible. I've tried and tried to forget that. If he'd just been wounded, I wouldn't have left him alone. But he wasn't. He was *dead*.

ROBERT: Yes, we understand that. You needn't tell us.

OLWEN: When I realized what had happened, I rushed out and sat in my car for I don't know how long. I couldn't move a finger. There was nobody about. It was fairly late and you know how lonely that cottage was. I just sat on and on in the car, shivering, and it was so quiet in the cottage, so horribly quiet. I've gone through that over and over again.

[FREDA *rises, opens the windows*]

ROBERT: You can't be blamed, Olwen.

STANTON: Of course she can't be blamed. And there must never be a word spoken about this—not to anybody. We must all promise that.

OLWEN: Give me a cigarette, Robert.

[ROBERT *crosses to* OLWEN, *gives her a cigarette and lights it for her*]

GORDON: It's a pity we can't all be as cool and businesslike about this as you are, Stanton.

STANTON: I don't feel very cool and businesslike about it. But you see, it's not as big a surprise to me as it is to you people. I guessed long ago that something like this had happened.

ROBERT: But it looked so much like suicide that nobody bothered to suggest it wasn't. It never seemed to me to be anything else. All the evidence pointed that way. I can't think how you could have guessed even though you knew Olwen had been there.

STANTON: I told you I had a third reason. I was over fairly early next morning— The postman rang me up—and I was there before anybody but the village constable and the doctor. And I found something on the floor that they had overlooked. I've kept it ever since.

[*He brings out billfold and produces a small square of patterned silk.* OLWEN *rises and crosses to* STANTON]

OLWEN: Let me see. Yes, that's a piece of the dress I was wearing. It was torn in the struggle we had. So that's how you knew?

STANTON: Yes.

OLWEN: But why didn't you say something?

GORDON: I can tell you that. He didn't say anything because he wanted everybody to think that Martin had shot himself! You see, that meant that *Martin* must have taken the money.

[OLWEN *sits on settee*]

ROBERT: That's about it, I suppose. It falls into line with everything we've heard from him tonight.

STANTON: No, there happened to be another reason, much more important. I knew that if Olwen had had a hand in Martin's death, then something like that must have happened, and so Olwen couldn't be blamed. I knew her better than any of you—or I felt I did. And I trusted her. She's about the only person I *would* trust. She knows all about that. I've told her often enough. She's not interested, but there it is.

OLWEN: And you never even hinted to me that you knew.

STANTON: [*Turns to* OLWEN] Surprising, isn't it? What a chance I missed to capture your interest for a few minutes! But I couldn't take that line with you. I suppose even nowadays, when we're all so damned tough, there has got to be one person that you behave to always as if you were Sir Roger de Coverley, and with me you've been that person for a long time now. And I knew all along that you were saying nothing because you thought Robert had taken the money and that he was safe after everybody assumed it was Martin. And that didn't always make it any easier for me!

BETTY: [*Rises*] No? What a shame. But what a fine romantic character you are, aren't you?

ROBERT: Betty. You don't understand.

FREDA: How *could* she?

BETTY: Why do you say that—in that tone of voice?

FREDA: Why does one say anything—in any tone of voice?

OLWEN: [*To* STANTON] You know, I nearly did take you into my confidence. And that might have made a difference. But I chose a bad moment.

STANTON: Why? When was this? Tell me.

OLWEN: I told you, I sat in my car that night for some time, not able to do anything. But then, when I felt a little better, I had to tell somebody, and you were the nearest person.

STANTON: But you didn't go there—that night?

OLWEN: Yes, I did. I drove over to your cottage that very Saturday night. I got there about eleven o'clock or just afterwards. I left my car at the bottom of that tiny narrow lane and walked up to your cottage. And then—I walked back again.

STANTON: So that's when you came. After that, it was hopeless.

OLWEN: Quite hopeless. I think that added the last touch to that night. I don't think I've ever felt the same about people—not just here, but everybody, even the people who walk into the office or sit opposite one in buses and trains—since that night. I know that's stupid, but I couldn't help it. And you must all have noticed that I've been completely off country cottages.

FREDA: Yes, even Betty's noticed that.

ROBERT: Why, what's the matter, Betty?

GORDON: What a little liar you are, Betty!

BETTY: Haven't we *all* been liars?

ROBERT: But you haven't, Betty.

GORDON: Oh, don't be a fool, Robert! Of course she has. She's lied like fury.

ROBERT: What about?

FREDA: Why don't you ask her?

OLWEN: Oh, what does it matter? Leave the child alone.

BETTY: I'm not a child! That's the mistake you've *all* made.

ROBERT: Not you—and Stanton? Is that what they mean? Why don't you tell them it's ridiculous?

FREDA: How can she? Don't be absurd.

STANTON: Oh, drop this! I'm going.

ROBERT: You're *not* going!

STANTON: Don't be a fool. It's no business of yours!

FREDA: That's where you're wrong, Stanton.

ROBERT: I'm waiting for an answer, Betty.

BETTY: What do you want me to say?

ROBERT: Were you with Stanton at his cottage?

BETTY: Yes.

ROBERT: Were you his mistress?

BETTY: Yes.

ROBERT: Betty—in God's name—Stanton—how could you?

BETTY: How could I? Because I'm not a child! You *would* drag all this out and now you can damned well have it! Yes, I stayed with Stanton that night, and I've stayed with him *other* nights. And he's not in love with me and I know it, and I'm not in love with him. I wouldn't marry him if I could. But I had to make *something* happen. Gordon was driving me mad. If you want to call someone a child, then call *him* one, for that's all he is! This damned marriage of ours that you all get so sentimental about is the biggest sham there's ever been. It isn't a marriage at all. It's just nothing —pretense, pretense, pretense! Betty darling and Gordon darling, the very sight of him makes me want to scream!

FREDA: Betty, you mustn't go—

BETTY: It's not my fault! I was in love with him when we were married and I thought everything was going to be marvelous. I wouldn't have looked at anybody else if he'd been—real. But he just isn't. He can't even talk to me.

GORDON: For God's sake, keep quiet, Betty.

BETTY: I won't! They want to know the *truth* and they can have it. I don't care. I've had nothing, *nothing* out of my marriage. If I were the child you all thought me, perhaps it wouldn't have mattered. But I'm not! I'm a woman. And Stanton was the *one* person who guessed what was happening and treated me like a *woman*.

GORDON: I wouldn't have blamed you if you'd fallen in love with someone, but this was just a low sordid intrigue, a dirty little affair, not worth all your silly lies. I suppose Stanton gave you all those fine presents?

BETTY: Yes, he did. You couldn't even be generous, though you'd have given your *precious* Martin everything we'd had. I know Stanton didn't really care for me. But men who say they're in love with one woman and spend their weekends with another deserve all they get.

FREDA: [*To* STANTON] Is that why you suddenly had to have that money?

STANTON: Queer, how it works out, isn't it?

GORDON: Then Betty is responsible for all this misery, for Martin!

BETTY: *Always Martin!* If I was responsible for all that, then it's *your* fault really, Gordon. Because you're responsible for everything that happened to me. You never should have married me.

GORDON: I didn't know. It was a mistake.

[*He sits on stair platform*]

FREDA: We seem to make that kind of mistake in our family.

BETTY: I ought to have left you long before this. That was *my* mistake—staying on—trying to make the best of it—pretending to be married to one who wasn't there—simply dead!

ROBERT: [*To* BETTY] I suppose you knew how I felt about you!

BETTY: Yes. But I didn't care very much.

ROBERT: No, why should you?

BETTY: No. It isn't that. But I knew you weren't in love with me. You didn't know me. You were only worshipping somebody you'd invented, who looked like me. And that's not the same thing at all.

ROBERT: Yes, I even thought that you and Gordon were happy together—

BETTY: Yes, we put up a good show, didn't we?

ROBERT: You did.

GORDON: Yes, we did. What would have happened if we'd gone on pretending like hell to be happy together?

BETTY: Nothing.

GORDON: No. If we'd gone on pretending long enough, I believe we might have been happy together, some time. It often works out like that.

BETTY: Never.

OLWEN: Yes, it does. That's why all this is so wrong, really. The real truth is something so deep you can't get at it this way, and all this half truth does is to blow everything up. It isn't civilized.

STANTON: I agree.

ROBERT: You agree. You might as well.

STANTON: You'll get no sympathy from me.

ROBERT: Sympathy from you? I never want to set eyes on you again, Stanton. You're a thief, a liar, and a dirty seducer.

STANTON: And you're a fool. You look solid but you're not. You've a good deal in common with that cracked brother of yours. You won't face real things. You've been living in a fool's paradise, and now, having got yourself out of it by tonight's efforts—all *your* doing—you're busy building yourself a fool's hell to live in!

ROBERT: I think this was your glass, Stanton. [*He crosses to table and picks up glass. Moves up to window and throws it out*] And now take yourself after it. Get out!

STANTON: [*Starts to go, then stops*] Good-night, Olwen. I'm sorry about all this.

OLWEN: So am I. Good-night.

STANTON: Good-night, Freda.

FREDA: Good-night.

GORDON: [*As* STANTON *goes up steps*] Don't forget, Stanton, we expect your resignation.

STANTON: [*Turning*] Oh, you're going to take it that way, are you?

GORDON: Yes, I'm going to take it that way!

STANTON: Good-night. No, don't trouble. I can find my way out.

[*He exists and closes door*]

OLWEN: Don't be too hasty, Gordon. [GORDON *rises*] Whatever his faults, Stanton's a first-class man at his job. If he goes, the firm will suffer.

GORDON: I can't help it. I couldn't work with him after this. The firm will have to suffer, that's all.

ROBERT: Don't worry. It's not a case of the firm suffering. The firm's smashed to hell now.

FREDA: Nonsense.

ROBERT: Is it? I don't think so.

GORDON: Well, Betty darling, I think we'd better return to our happy little home, our dear little nest.

BETTY: Oh, don't, Gordon!

FREDA: I'll let you out.

[*Gordon exits, followed by* FREDA. BETTY *picks up coat and starts for door*]

ROBERT: [*To* BETTY, *staring at her*] Good-bye.

BETTY: [*Stops*] Why do *you* look like that?

ROBERT: I'm not saying good-bye to you. I don't know you. I never did, it seems.

[BETTY *leaves.* ROBERT *turns, crosses to drinks. As* ROBERT *pours drink,* OLWEN *rises*]

OLWEN: Robert, please don't drink any more tonight. I know how you feel, but it'll only make you worse—really it will.

ROBERT: What does it matter? I'm through, anyway.

[*He drinks*]

OLWEN: Robert, I can't bear seeing you like this. You don't know how it hurts me.

ROBERT: I'm sorry, Olwen, I really am sorry. You're the only one who's really come out of this. I know that. Strange, isn't it—that you should have been feeling like that about me all the time. I'm sorry.

OLWEN: I'm not. I mean about myself. I suppose I ought to be, but I'm not. It hurt at times but it kept me going.

ROBERT: I know. And you see, now I've stopped going. Something's broken—inside.

OLWEN: It won't seem bad tomorrow. It never does.

ROBERT: All this isn't going to seem any better tomorrow, Olwen.

OLWEN: Freda will help you. After all, Robert, she's fond of you.

ROBERT: No, not really. It isn't that she dislikes me steadily, but every now and then she hates me—and now I see why, of course. She hates me because I'm Robert and not Martin, because he's dead and I'm alive.

OLWEN: She may feel differently—after tonight.

ROBERT: She may. I doubt it. She doesn't change easily—that's the trouble. And then again, you see, I don't care any more. That's the point. Whether she changes or doesn't change I don't care now.

OLWEN: You know there's nothing I wouldn't do for you, Robert.

ROBERT: I'm terribly grateful, Olwen. But nothing happens here— inside. [FREDA *returns*] That's the damned awful cruel thing. Nothing happens. [*Sits*] All hollow, empty.

[FREDA *closes door*]

FREDA: [*On top step*] I'm sure, it's not at all the proper thing to say at such a moment, but the fact remains that I feel rather hungry. [*She comes down steps*] What about you, Olwen? You, Robert? Or have you been drinking too much?

ROBERT: Yes, I've been drinking too much.

FREDA: Well, it's very silly of you. [*She takes empty glass from* ROBERT]

ROBERT: Yes.

FREDA: And you did ask for all this.

ROBERT: I asked for it. And I got it.

FREDA: Though I doubt if you minded very much until it came to Betty.

ROBERT: That's not true. But I can understand your thinking so. You see, as more and more of this rotten stuff came out, so more and more I came to depend on my secret thoughts of Betty—as someone who seemed to me to represent some lovely quality of life.

FREDA: I've known some time, of course, that you were getting very sentimental about her. And I've known some time too all about Betty and I've often thought of telling you.

ROBERT: I'm not sorry you didn't.

FREDA: You ought to be.

ROBERT: Why?

FREDA: That kind of self-deception's rather stupid.

ROBERT: What about you and Martin?

FREDA: I didn't deceive myself. I knew everything—or nearly everything—about him. I wasn't in love with somebody I'd made up!

ROBERT: I think you were. Probably we always are.

OLWEN: Then it's not so bad. You can always build up another image for yourself to fall in love with.

ROBERT: No, you can't. That's the trouble. You lose the capacity for building. You run short of the stuff that creates beautiful illusions, just as if a gland had stopped working.

OLWEN: Then you have to learn to live without illusions.

ROBERT: Can't be done. Not for us. We started life too early for that. Possibly they're breeding people now who can live without illusions. I hope so. But I can't do it. [*Rises*] I've lived among illusions.

FREDA: You have.

ROBERT: [*Turns*] Well, what if I have? They've given me hope and courage, they've helped me to live. I suppose we ought to get all that from faith in life. But I haven't got any. No religion or anything. Just this empty damned shell to live in. And a few damn glands and secretions and nerves to do it with. But it didn't look too bad. I'd my little illusions, you see.

FREDA: Then why didn't you leave them alone, instead of clamoring for the truth all night like a fool?

ROBERT: [*Turning on* FREDA] Because I *am* a fool! Stanton was right. That's the only answer. I had to meddle, like a child, with fire. I began this evening with something to keep me going. I'd good memories of Martin. I'd a wife who didn't love me but at least seemed too good for me. I'd two partners I liked and respected. There was a girl I could idealize. And now—

OLWEN: No, Robert—please! We know.

ROBERT: But you don't know, you can't know—not as I know—or you wouldn't stand there like that, as if we'd only just had some damned silly little squabble about a hand at bridge!

OLWEN: This is mad!

ROBERT: Don't you see, we're not living in the same world now. Everything's gone. My brother was an obscene lunatic—

FREDA: [*Moving away*] Stop that!

ROBERT: [*Following* FREDA] And my wife doted on him and pestered him! [*Turns to* OLWEN] One of my partners is a liar and a cheat and a thief! The other—God knows *what* he is— [*He goes up steps. The lights begin to dim*] And the girl's a greedy little cat!

FREDA: Robert, please!

OLWEN: No, Robert. It won't be like this tomorrow!!

ROBERT: [*On platform*] Tomorrow. Tomorrow. I tell you, I'm through, I'm through! There can't be a tomorrow!

> [*He rushes out. As* ROBERT *goes through the door the lights dim out except for the moonlight and a light in hall*]

FREDA: He's got a revolver in his bedroom!

OLWEN: Stop, Robert! Stop. Stop!

> [*In the darkness,* MISS MOCKRIDGE *and* BETTY *enter and take the same positions as in the blackout in Act One.*

After a moment's pause there is the sound of a revolver shot offstage right. BETTY *gives a sharp little scream. Startled exclamations from the other three women.* FREDA *advances toward the door]*

FREDA: [*Calling*] Robert, Robert, what was that! [*Pause*] Robert!!
ROBERT'S VOICE: [*Off*] It's all right. I was showing them my gun and took a crack at a flower pot.

[FREDA *switches on the lights*]

GORDON'S VOICE: Pretty good shot. . . .
ROBERT'S VOICE: And what's more, I hit it!
STANTON'S VOICE: Pretty lucky, I'll say. . . .
ROBERT'S VOICE: We'll be in in a minute!
FREDA: I should hope so. Those idiots, firing Robert's revolver out the window!

[*The positions and movement are identical with Act One*]

BETTY: You ought to take it away from him. They nearly frightened the life out of me.
FREDA: Well, we've no hope of seeing our ghost bird *now*. If it was there, it must have cleared out pretty quickly.
BETTY: I should think so after all that racket.
OLWEN: Perhaps it will come back later.
FREDA: No, I hardly think so. I've never caught sight of it much after ten.
MISS MOCKRIDGE: I suppose you all miss your brother-in-law. He used to be up here with you too, didn't he?
FREDA: You mean Robert's brother, Martin?
MISS MOCKRIDGE: Yes.
FREDA: What made you think of Martin just then?
MISS MOCKRIDGE: Well, I don't quite know. He just came into my head, I suppose.
FREDA: It must have been the shot.
MISS MOCKRIDGE: Oh, surely not. I was away at the time and never quite understood what happened. Something rather dreadful, wasn't it? I'm sorry if I—

FREDA: No, it's all right. It was very distressing for us at the time, but it's done with now. Martin shot himself. It happened a year ago—last October, in fact—at his own cottage, about twenty miles from here.

MISS MOCKRIDGE: Oh, yes. Dreadful business, of course. I only met him twice, I think. I remember I thought him very amusing and charming. He was very handsome, wasn't he?

[STANTON *and* GORDON *enter*]

OLWEN: Yes, very handsome.

STANTON: Who's very handsome?

FREDA: Not you, Charles.

STANTON: Well, who is it? Or is it a secret?

GORDON: They must have been talking about me. Betty, why do you allow them to rave about your husband?

BETTY: Darling, I'm sure you've had too much manly gossip and old brandy. You're beginning to look purple in the face and bloated —a typical financier.

[ROBERT *enters, switching on extra light as he comes in*]

ROBERT: Why so dim? Sorry about that gun, Freda. It was stupid. I hope it didn't frighten anybody.

FREDA: As a matter of fact, it did. All of us.

MISS MOCKRIDGE: Yes, and I'd just been saying what a charming little group you've made here, all of you.

ROBERT: I'm glad you think so.

MISS MOCKRIDGE: I think you've all been lucky.

ROBERT: I agree, we have.

STANTON: It's not all luck, Miss Mockridge. You see, we all happen to be nice easy-going people.

ROBERT: Except Betty—she's terribly wild.

STANTON: That's only because Gordon doesn't beat her often enough —yet.

MISS MOCKRIDGE: You see, Miss Peel, Mr. Stanton is *still* the cynical bachelor. I'm afraid he rather spoils the picture.

GORDON: I wonder if there's any dance music on the radio tonight?

ROBERT: I hope not. Let's be quiet. What have you people been talking about?

FREDA: Olwen had been telling us about *The Sleeping Dog*.

ROBERT: *The Sleeping Dog?* Oh—that novel we're going to publish, the one she's so keen on.

STANTON: Why does he call it that?

OLWEN: Don't you know the proverb—Let Sleeping Dogs Lie?

STANTON: Where does that come into it?

FREDA: From what Olwen says, the sleeping dog represents truth.

OLWEN: Yes, and the chief character—the husband—insisted upon disturbing it.

ROBERT: Well, he was quite right to disturb it.

STANTON: Was he? I wonder. I think it a very sound idea—the truth as a sleeping dog.

MISS MOCKRIDGE: Still we do spend too much of our time telling lies and acting them.

BETTY: Oh, but one has to. I'm always fibbing. I do it all day long.

GORDON: You do, darling. You do.

BETTY: It's the secret of my charm.

MISS MOCKRIDGE: Very likely. But we meant something more serious.

ROBERT: Serious or not, I'm all for it coming out. It's healthy.

STANTON: I think telling the truth's about as healthy as skidding round a corner at sixty. What do you think, Olwen . . . you're looking terribly wise?

OLWEN: I agree with you. I think telling *everything* is dangerous. What most people mean by the truth is only half the truth.

FREDA: Well, let's talk about something else. Who wants a drink? Drinks, Robert, and cigarettes. [*She crosses to table and picks up cigarette box*] Cigarette, Miss Mockridge.

MISS MOCKRIDGE: [*Rising*] No, thanks, I'm a slave to my own brand!

FREDA: [*Crosses to* OLWEN] Cigarette, Olwen?

OLWEN: [*Taking box from* FREDA] Oh, I remember that box! It plays a tune, doesn't it? I remember the tune. [*Opens box; as it plays:*] Yes, it's the Wedding March.

ROBERT: Good, isn't it!

GORDON: [*Who has been fiddling with the radio; suddenly:*] Wait a minute. Listen to this.

[*"Can't We Talk It Over?"* *gradually fades in on the radio set*]

BETTY: [*Rising*] Oh, I adore that tune.
STANTON: What is it?
BETTY: "Can't We Talk It Over?"
MISS MOCKRIDGE: What?
GORDON: [*Starts to dance with* BETTY] "Can't We Talk It Over?"

[STANTON *crosses to* OLWEN *and they start to dance.* MISS MOCKRIDGE *takes a cigarette from her case and* FREDA *lights it for her.* ROBERT *crosses down to them and they stand talking as the curtain falls. The curtain goes up again.* OLWEN *and* STANTON *continue dancing;* GORDON *and* BETTY *continue to dance; the* GROUP *by the fireplace watch them in animated conversation*]

CURTAIN

Dracula

THE VAMPIRE PLAY

HAMILTON DEANE
JOHN L. BALDERSTON

Adapted from Bram Stoker's novel,
"Dracula"

Hamilton Deane–John L. Balderston

In 1897, while the legendary actor, Sir Henry Irving, was stalking the stage of the Lyceum Theatre (London) as the Napoleon to Ellen Terry's *Madame Sans-Gêne* in Sardou's play, the seed of one of the modern theatre's most popular and extensively performed melodramas sprouted, of all places, in the box office of his historic playhouse. That was the year that Sir Henry's devoted business manager-cum-novelist, Bram Stoker, published his fifth novel, *Dracula*, which was destined to become a classic and perhaps the most famous Gothic horror story of all time. Stoker's earlier contributions to literature are all but forgotten, yet *Dracula*, with a tenacity worthy of his vampiric heritage, has managed, through numerous transmogrifications, to survive and "jolt the marrows" of countless millions for almost three quarters of a century.

"Of monsters, famous or infamous," wrote James Nelson in his 1970 preface to the original novel when it was issued in the series of Great Illustrated Classics, "—Cyclops, Dr. Jekyll's Mr. Hyde, the Phantom of the Opera, King Kong, the Hunchback of Notre Dame, Frankenstein's monster—of them all, the one who reigns in enormity is Count Dracula. He was vampire, werewolf, bat, and man."

Admittedly, scarcely a combination of characteristics a guidance counselor would link together as a formula for durable success. But perhaps the strange hold that Stoker's creation has exercised undiminishingly through the years can best be summarized from David Zinman's perceptive commentary in his book, *50 Classic Motion Pictures*: ". . . unlike other monsters, Dracula is a man who walks among us. And he is more than that. He is an aristocrat, a titled nobleman . . . He dresses impeccably and has the cultured good manners and good taste to play the gracious host to his victims . . . In fact, an irresistible allure pervades his entire being. Where other monsters repelled their prey, Dracula's suave, gallant air, his intense, burning eyes, exerted a hypnotic charm."

Bram (Abraham) Stoker was born in Dublin on November 8, 1847, and like his compatriot, George Bernard Shaw, later "became so prominent in England that most thought him English." His exceptional diversity propelled his early career in many directions, ranging from journalism to officiating as an Inner Temple barrister. Most of his later life, however, was given over to serving as business manager for Sir Henry Irving during the latter's reign in the English theatre. He remained with Sir Henry for twenty-seven years, and on occasion, stepped out of the box office to moonlight as stage manager or even actor when an exigency arose in the company. And, of course, there were his novels.

Dracula immediately was recognized as a magnificent tale of horror, "one of the best things in the supernatural line" and "the very weirdest of weird tales." Though the author published four more novels before his death in 1912, his immortality is due to a single literary creation, Dracula.

Years passed before the famed story was adapted for the stage by Hamilton Deane (1891–1958), son of one of Stoker's childhood friends and an accomplished actor who established his own repertory company and for some twenty years ran seasons in the English provinces. His dramatization of Dracula had its London première on February 14, 1927, at the Little Theatre, with uniformed nurses in attendance to administer to the fainthearted and the "hopeful staggerers with strained faces queuing up outside the manager's office, putting on some fine performances in fond hopes of emergency brandy." The play ran for 391 performances, and for more than three years in the provinces, often with Deane in the role of Van Helsing. In 1939, Dracula returned to the West End in revival at the Winter Garden Theatre, and later was transferred, either by coincidence or design, to the Lyceum Theatre where it was the penultimate play to occupy the stage on the same site where Stoker once had command of the "front of the house."

A commercial success of such proportions was bound to attract the eye of an American impresario, and in October 1927 Dracula was brought to New York by Horace Liveright, a colorfully egocentric publisher who "used his publishing capital to back and produce plays, and his play winnings to back authors." During its transatlantic crossing, *Dracula*, somehow, acquired a collaborator, John L. Balderston, and when the melodrama opened at the Fulton Theatre he shared co-authorship billing with Deane. According to available records, this was a "slightly different version," evidence that also is sustained by a perusal of the disparate London and New York playbills.

John L. Balderston (1889–1954) was an American journalist and foreign correspondent whose variegated career caught the international spotlight in 1926 with the London première of his play *Berkeley Square*, written in collaboration with J. C. Squire. The drama's success was duplicated in New York (1929) with Leslie Howard as star, then as a film for which Mr. Balderston fashioned the screenplay. He wrote several more works for the stage (including his co-authorship of *Dracula*), but most of his subsequent professional life was dedicated to motion picture writing, and among the noted films he contributed to were: *Lives of a Bengal Lancer; Prisoner of Zenda; Smilin' Through; Gone With the Wind;* and *Gaslight*.

At the time of its Broadway opening, the press described *Dracula* as "an evening rich in horror," one that is "blithely blood-curdling" and had the "audience quaking delightedly." The play's engagement lasted for 261 performances, then took to the road where it continued to chill and "jolt" audiences for several more years.

Dracula not only had the very agreeable habit of swelling the coffers of its creators and managements, it catalytically brought lifelong fame to Bela Lugosi, an erstwhile romantic Hungarian actor who essayed the title role on Broadway and later on the screen. Lugosi was the perfect incarnation of Count Dracula, and his masterful performance, even today, is regarded as a classic of cinematic art. His total identification with the part lasted throughout his lifetime and when he died, in 1956, he was buried in Dracula's emblematic black cape. The film's extraordinary popularity signaled an entire new screen trend in vampire epics, though none ever achieved the status or prosperity of the original that emanated from the Stoker novel and the Deane-Balderston play.

Dracula was first presented by Hamilton Deane and H. L. Warburton (by arrangement with José G. Levy and Henry Millar) at the Little Theatre, London, on February 14, 1927. The cast was as follows:

COUNT DRACULA	*Raymond Huntley*
ABRAHAM VAN HELSING	*Hamilton Deane*
DOCTOR SEWARD	*Stuart Lomath*
JONATHAN HARKER	*Bernard Guest*
QUINCY P. MORRIS	*Frieda Hearn*
LORD GODALMING	*Peter Jackson*
R. M. RENFIELD	*Bernard Jukes*
THE WARDER	*Jack Howarth*
THE PARLORMAID	*Kilda Macleod*
THE HOUSEMAID	*Betty Murgatroyd*
MINA HARKER	*Dora Mary Patrick*

Directed by   Hamilton Deane

Dracula was first produced in the United States at the Fulton The-atre, New York, on October 5, 1927, by Horace Liveright. The cast was as follows:

MISS WELLS, *maid*	*Nedda Harrigan*
JOHN HARKER	*Terence Neill*
DR. SEWARD	*Herbert Bunston*
ABRAHAM VAN HELSING	*Edward Van Sloan*
R. M. RENFIELD	*Bernard Jukes*
BUTTERWORTH	*Albert Frith*
LUCY SEWARD	*Dorothy Peterson*
COUNT DRACULA	*Bela Lugosi*
Directed by	Ira Hards
Settings by	Joseph Physioc

ACT ONE

The library in Dr. Seward's Sanatorium, Purley, England. Evening.

ACT TWO

Lucy's boudoir. Evening of the following day.

ACT THREE

SCENE 1: *The library. Thirty-two hours later; shortly before sunrise.*

SCENE 2: *A vault. Just after sunrise.*

ACT ONE

The library on the ground floor of DR. SEWARD's *Sanatorium at Purley. Room is medieval, the walls are stone with vaulted ceiling supported by two stone pillars, but is comfortably furnished in modern style. Wooden paneling around walls. Tapestries hang on the wall. Medieval fireplace in wall right. Fire burning. There is a divan right center, a large armchair right. At left, a desk with armchair back of it, a small chair to right of desk. Double doors in the rear wall. Large double window across angle of room, left rear, leading out into garden. The curtains are drawn. Door downstage left. Invisible sliding panel in bookcase rear wall right.*

MAID, *an attractive young girl, enters, showing in* JOHN HARKER. HARKER *is a young man of about twenty-five, handsome in appearance; a typical Englishman of the Public School class, but in manner direct, explosive, incisive and excitable.*

HARKER: [*Agitated*] You're sure Miss Lucy is no worse?
MAID: [*Soothingly*] Just the same, sir.

[DR. SEWARD *comes in, downstage left. He is an alienist of about fifty-five, intelligent, but a typical specialist who lives in a world of textbooks and patients, not a man of action or force of character. The* MAID *exits, closing doors*]

SEWARD: Oh! John.
HARKER: [*As* SEWARD *extends hand*] Doctor Seward. What is it? Why have you sent for me?
SEWARD: My dear John. I told you in my wire there was nothing new.
HARKER: You said "no change, don't worry," but to "come at once."

SEWARD: [*Approvingly*] And you lost no time.

HARKER: I jumped in the car and burned up the road from London. Oh, Doctor, surely there must be something *more* we can do for Lucy. I'd give my life gladly if it would save her.

SEWARD: I'm sure you would, my boy. You love her with the warm blood of youth, but don't forget I love my daughter, too. She's all I have. . . . You must see that nothing medical science can suggest has been left undone.

HARKER: [*Bitterly*] Medical science couldn't do much for Mina. Poor Mina.

SEWARD: Yes, poor Mina. She died after these same incredible symptoms that my Lucy has developed.

HARKER: *My* Lucy too.

SEWARD: *Our* Lucy, then.

[*Wild, maniacal laugh is heard offstage left*]

HARKER: Good God, what was that?

SEWARD: [*Sits at desk*] Only Renfield. A patient of mine.

HARKER: But you never keep violent patients here in your sanatorium. Lucy mustn't be compelled to listen to raving madmen.

SEWARD: I quite agree, and I'm going to have him sent away. Until just lately he was always quiet. I'll be sorry to lose him.

HARKER: What!

SEWARD: An unusual case. Zoophagous.

HARKER: What's that?

SEWARD: A life-eating maniac.

HARKER: What?

SEWARD: Yes, he thinks that by absorbing lives he can prolong his own life.

HARKER: Good Lord!

SEWARD: Catches flies and eats them. And by way of change, he feeds flies to spiders. Fattens them up. Then he eats the spiders.

HARKER: Good God, how disgusting. [*Sits*] But tell me about Lucy. [*Leans over desk*] Why did you send for me?

SEWARD: Yesterday I wired to Holland for my old friend Van Helsing. He'll be here soon. The car has gone down to the station for him now. I'm going to turn Lucy's case over to him.

HARKER: Another specialist on anæmia?

SEWARD: No, my boy, whatever this may be, it's not anæmia, and this man, who speaks a dozen languages as well as his own, knows more about mysterious diseases than anyone alive.

HARKER: [*Rises*] Heaven knows it's mysterious enough, but surely the symptoms are clear.

SEWARD: So were poor Mina's. Perfectly clear. [*A dog howls at a distance. Other dogs take up the lugubrious chorus far and near.* SEWARD *rises; crosses to fireplace*] There they are, at it again, every dog for a mile around.

HARKER: [*Crosses to window*] They seem howls of terror.

SEWARD: We've heard that chorus every night since Mina fell ill.

HARKER: When I was traveling in Russia, and the dogs in the village barked like that, the natives always said wolves were prowling about.

SEWARD: [*Gets cigarette on mantel; lights it*] I hardly think you'll find wolves prowling around Purley, twenty miles from London.

HARKER: Yet your old house might be in a wilderness. [*Looks out of window*] Nothing in sight except that place Carfax that Count Dracula has taken.

SEWARD: [*Turning from fireplace*] Your friend, the Count, came in again last evening.

HARKER: He's no friend of mine.

SEWARD: Don't say that. He knows that you and I gave our blood for Lucy as well as for Mina, and he's offered to undergo transfusion himself if we need another volunteer. [*Sits on divan*]

HARKER: By Jove, that's sporting of him. I see I've misjudged him.

SEWARD: He seems genuinely interested in Lucy. If he were a young man I'd think . . .

HARKER: What!

SEWARD: But his whole attitude shows that it isn't that. We need sympathy in this house, John, and I'm grateful for it.

HARKER: So am I. Anyone who offers to help Lucy can have anything I've got.

SEWARD: Well, I think he does help Lucy. She always seems cheered up when he comes.

HARKER: That's fine. May I go to Lucy now?

SEWARD: [*Rises*] We'll go together. [*Bell rings off.* HARKER *crosses to door left.* SEWARD *puts out cigarette in ashtray*] That must be Van Helsing. You go ahead and I'll come presently.

> [HARKER *exits.* MAID *shows in* ABRAHAM VAN HELSING, *who enters briskly. Man of medium height, in the early fifties, with clean-shaven, astute face, shaggy gray eyebrows and a mass of gray hair which is brushed backward showing a high forehead. Dark, piercing eyes set far apart; nervous, alert manner; an air of resolution, clearly a man of resourceful action. Incisive speech, always to the point; raps his words out sharply and quickly.* VAN HELSING *carries small black bag*]

MAID: Professor Van Helsing.

SEWARD: [*He and* VAN HELSING *shake hands warmly as* MAID *goes out*] My dear Van Helsing, I can never repay you for this.

VAN HELSING: Were it only a patient of yours instead of your daughter, I would have come. You once rendered me a service.

SEWARD: Don't speak of that. You'd have done it for me. [*Starts to ring*] Let me give you something to eat . . . [*Stopped by* VAN HELSING'S *gesture*]

VAN HELSING: [*Places bag on table back of divan*] I dined on the boat train. I do not waste time when there is work to do.

SEWARD: Ah, Van Helsing, you cast the old spell on me. I lean on you before you have been two minutes in my house.

VAN HELSING: You wrote of your daughter's symptoms. Tell me more of the other young lady, the one who died.

SEWARD: [*Shows* VAN HELSING *to chair right of desk.* SEWARD *sits at desk*] Poor Mina Weston. She was a girl just Lucy's age. They were inseparable. She was on a visit here when she fell ill. As I wrote you, she just grew weaker, day by day she wasted away. But there were no anæmic symptoms, her blood was normal when analyzed.

VAN HELSING: You said you performed transfusion.

SEWARD: Yes, Sir William Briggs ordered that. [*Baring forearm*] You see this mark? Well, Lucy herself, and her fiancee, John Harker, gave their blood as well.

VAN HELSING: So . . . Three transfusions . . . And the effect?

SEWARD: She rallied after each. The color returned to her cheeks, but the next morning she would be pale and weak again. She complained of *bad dreams*. Ten days ago we found her in a stupor from which nothing could rouse her. She . . . died.

VAN HELSING: And . . . the other symptoms?

SEWARD: None, except those two little marks on the throat that I wrote you about.

VAN HELSING: And which perhaps brought me here so quickly. What were they like?

SEWARD: Just two little white dots with red centers. [VAN HELSING *nods grimly*] We decided she must have run a safety pin through the skin of her throat, trying in her delirium to fasten a scarf or shawl.

VAN HELSING: Perhaps. And your daughter's symptoms are the same?

SEWARD: Precisely. She too speaks of *bad dreams*. Van Helsing, you've lived in the tropics. May this not be something alien to our medical experience in England?

VAN HELSING: [*Grimly*] It may indeed, my friend.

> [*Laugh is heard from behind curtain at window.* VAN HELSING *rises, followed by* SEWARD *who crosses to window and draws curtains.* RENFIELD *is standing there. Repulsive youth, face distorted, shifty eyes, tousled hair*]

SEWARD: [*Astounded, drawing* RENFIELD *into room*] Renfield. How did you . . . ?

VAN HELSING: Who is this man?

SEWARD: [*Crosses to bell; rings*] One of my patients. This is gross carelessness.

VAN HELSING: Did you hear us talking?

RENFIELD: Words . . . words . . . words . . .

SEWARD: Come, come, Renfield, you know you mustn't wander about this way. How did you get out of your room?

RENFIELD: [*Laughs*] Wouldn't you like to know?

SEWARD: How are the flies? [*To* VAN HELSING] Mr. Renfield makes a hobby of eating flies. I'm afraid you eat spiders, too, sometimes. Don't you, Renfield?

RENFIELD: Will you walk into my parlor, said the spider to the fly. Excuse me, Doctor, you have not introduced me to your friend.

SEWARD: [*Reprovingly*] Come, come, Renfield.

VAN HELSING: Humor him.

[*Enter* MAID]

SEWARD: Tell the Attendant to come here at once.

MAID: Yes, sir. [*Exits*]

SEWARD: Oh, very well. Professor Van Helsing, Mr. Renfield, a patient of mine.

[VAN HELSING *steps toward him. They shake hands.* VAN HELSING *rubs* RENFIELD's *fingers with his thumb and* RENFIELD *jerks hand away*]

RENFIELD: Ah, who does not know of Van Helsing! Your work, sir, in investigating certain obscure diseases, not altogether unconnected with forces and powers that the ignorant herd do not believe exist, has won you a position that posterity will recognize.

[*Enter* ATTENDANT *dressed in uniform. He starts at seeing* RENFIELD, *then looks at* SEWARD *sheepishly*]

SEWARD: [*As severely as his mild nature permits*] Butterworth, you have let your patient leave his room again.

ATTENDANT: Blimme, sir, I locked the door on 'im, and I've got the key in my pocket now.

SEWARD: But this is the second time. Only last night you let him escape and he tried to break into Count Dracula's house across the grounds.

ATTENDANT: 'E didn't get out the door this time, sir, and it's a drop of thirty feet out of the windows. [*Crosses to* RENFIELD] He's just a bloomin' eel. Now you come with me. [*As they start toward door; holds* RENFIELD *by coat collar and right arm*]

SEWARD: Renfield, if this happens again you will get no more sugar to spread out for your flies.

RENFIELD: [*Drawing himself up*] What do I care for flies . . . *now?* [ATTENDANT *gives* VAN HELSING *a look*] Flies. Flies are but poor things. [*As he speaks he follows with his eyes a fly.* ATTENDANT *sees fly too; releases* RENFIELD *indulgently. With a sweep of his hand he catches fly, holds closed hand to ear as if listening to buzz of fly as he crosses a few steps, then carries it to his mouth. Then seeing them watching him, releases it quickly*] A low form of life. Beneath my notice. I don't care a pin about flies.

ATTENDANT: Oh, doncher? Any more o' yer tricks and I'll take yer new spider away.

RENFIELD: [*Babbles; on knees*] Oh, no, no! Please, dear Mr. Butterworth, please leave me my spider. He's getting so nice and fat. When he's had another dozen flies he'll be just right, just right. [*Gives little laugh. Rubs hands together, then catches fly and makes gesture of eating*]

VAN HELSING: Come, Mr. Renfield, what makes you want to eat flies?

RENFIELD: [*Rises*] The wings of a fly, my dear sir, typify the aerial powers of the psychic faculties.

SEWARD: [*To* ATTENDANT, *wearily*] Butterworth, take him away.

VAN HELSING: One moment, my friend. [*To* RENFIELD] And the spiders?

RENFIELD: [*Impressively*] Professor Van Helsing, can you tell me why that one great spider lived for centuries in the tower of the old Spanish church—and grew and grew? He never ate, but he drank, and he *drank*. He would come down and drink the oil of all the church lamps.

SEWARD: [*To* ATTENDANT] Butterworth.

RENFIELD: One moment, Doctor Seward . . . [VAN HELSING *gets wolfsbane from bag on table*] I want you to send me away, now, *tonight*, in a straight waistcoat. Chain me so I can't escape. This is a sanatorium, not a lunatic asylum. This is no place for me. My cries will disturb Miss Lucy, who is ill. They will give your daughter *bad dreams*, Doctor Seward, *bad dreams*.

SEWARD: [*Soothingly*] We'll see about all this in the morning. [*Nods to* ATTENDANT, *who moves toward* RENFIELD]

VAN HELSING: Why are you so anxious to go?

RENFIELD: [*Crosses to* VAN HELSING; *hesitates, then with gesture of decision*] I'll tell *you*. Not that fool Seward. He wouldn't understand. But you . . . [*A large bat dashes against window.* RENFIELD *turns to the window, holds out his hands and gibbers]* No, no, no, I wasn't going to say anything . . .

[ATTENDANT *crosses up; watches* RENFIELD]

SEWARD: What was that?

RENFIELD: [*Looks out window, then turns*] It was a bat, gentleman. Only a bat! Do you know that in some islands of the Eastern seas there are bats which hang on trees all night? And when the heat is stifling and sailors sleep on the deck in those harbors, in the morning *they* are found dead men . . . white, even as Miss Mina was.

SEWARD: What do you know of Miss Mina? [*Pause*] Take him to his room!

VAN HELSING: [*To* SEWARD] Please! [*To* RENFIELD] Why are you so anxious to be moved from here?

RENFIELD: To save my soul.

VAN HELSING: Yes?

RENFIELD: Oh, you'll get nothing more out of me than that. And I'm not sure I hadn't rather stay . . . After all, what is my soul good for? Is not . . . [*Turns to window*] . . . *what I am to receive worth* the loss of my soul?

SEWARD: [*Lightly*] What's got him thinking about souls? Have you the souls of those flies and spiders on your conscience?

RENFIELD: [*Puts fingers in his ears, shuts eyes, distorts face*] I forbid you to plague me about souls! I don't want their *souls*. All I want is their life. The blood is the life . . .

VAN HELSING: So?

RENFIELD: That's in the Bible. What use are souls to me? [*To* VAN HELSING] I couldn't eat them or dr . . . [*Breaks off suddenly*]

VAN HELSING: Or drink . . . [*Holding wolfsbane under his nose,* REN-FIELD's *face becomes convulsed with rage and loathing. He leaps back*]

RENFIELD: You know too much to live, Van Helsing! [*He suddenly lunges at* VAN HELSING. SEWARD *and* ATTENDANT *shout at the attack and as they drag* RENFIELD *to door he stops struggling and says clearly:*]

RENFIELD: I'll go quietly. [SEWARD *lets go of him*] I warned you to

send me away. Doctor Seward, if you don't you must answer for
my soul before the judgment seat of God!

[RENFIELD *and* ATTENDANT *exit. Wild laughter can be
heard off.* VAN HELSING *puts wolfsbane in bag as* SEWARD
closes door]

SEWARD: My friend, you're not hurt?

VAN HELSING: No.

SEWARD: My deepest apologies. You'll think my place shockingly
managed . . .

[VAN HELSING *waves apology aside with impatient gesture*]

What was your herb that excited him so?

VAN HELSING: Wolfsbane. [*A little look out of window as he crosses*]

SEWARD: Wolfsbane? What's that? I thought I knew all the drugs
in the pharmacopoeia.

VAN HELSING: One of the . . . eremophytes. Pliny the Elder mentions
the plant. It grows only in the wilds of Central Russia.

SEWARD: But why did you bring it with you?

VAN HELSING: It is a form of preventive medicine.

SEWARD: Well, we live and learn. I never heard of it.

VAN HELSING: Seward, I want you to have that lunatic securely
watched.

SEWARD: Anything you say, Professor Van Helsing, but it's my Lucy
I want you to look after first.

VAN HELSING: I want to keep this man under observation.

SEWARD: [*Annoyed and hurt*] An interesting maniac, no doubt, but
surely you'll see my daughter.

VAN HELSING: I must see the records of his case.

SEWARD: But Doctor . . .

VAN HELSING: Do you think I have forgotten why I am here?

SEWARD: [*As they start to go out left*] Forgive me. Of course I'll show
you the records, but I don't understand why you're so curious
about Renfield, because in your vast experience . . .

[*They exit. The room is empty for a few seconds; then*
LUCY *enters, supported by* HARKER. *She is a beautiful girl*

*of twenty, clad in filmy white dressing gown, her face un-
naturally pale. She walks with difficulty. Round her throat
is wound a scarf. She crosses to desk and leans on it as*
HARKER *closes door*]

HARKER: Why, I thought they were here, Lucy.

LUCY: John, do you think this new man will be any better than the others?

HARKER: [*Moving her to divan*] I'm sure he will. Anyway, Lucy, now that I'm back I'm going to stay with you till you get over this thing.

LUCY: [*Delighted*] Oh, John. But can you? Your work in town?

HARKER: [*Seating her, then sitting next to her*] You come first.

LUCY: [*A change comes over her*] I . . . don't think you'd better stay, John. [*A look about room*] Sometimes . . . I feel that I want to be alone.

HARKER: My dear. How can you say that you don't want me with you when you're so ill? You love me, don't you? [*Taking her hand*]

LUCY: [*Affectionately*] Yes, John, with all my soul.

HARKER: Just as soon as you're well enough I'm going to take you away. We'll be married next month. We won't wait till June. We'll stretch that honeymoon month to three months and the house will be ready in July.

LUCY: [*Overjoyed*] John, you think we could?

HARKER: Of course, why not? My mother wanted us to wait, but she'll understand, and I want to get you *away* . . . [*Starts to kiss her. She shudders as he does so*] Why do you shrink when I kiss you? You're so cold, Lucy, always so cold . . . now . . .

LUCY: [*With tenderness but no hint of passion*] Forgive me, dear. I am yours, all yours. [*Clings to him. He embraces her. She sinks back*] Oh, John, I'm so tired . . . so tired.

[SEWARD *and* VAN HELSING *return*]

SEWARD: Lucy dear, this is my old friend, Professor Van Helsing.

[*She sits up; extends her hand to him*]

VAN HELSING: My dear Miss Seward . . . [*He kisses* LUCY'S *hand*] . . . you don't remember poor old Van Helsing. I knew you when you were a little girl. So high . . . and now what charm, what beauty. A little pale, yes, but we will bring the roses back to the cheeks.

LUCY: You were so kind to come, Professor.

VAN HELSING: And this, no doubt, is the fortunate young man you are to marry?

SEWARD: Yes, John Harker, Professor.

HARKER: Look here, Professor. I'm not going to get in your way, but if Doctor Seward will have me I'm going to make him give me a bed here until Lucy gets over this thing. [*Turns to* SEWARD] It's absolute hell, being away in London, and of course I can't do any work.

SEWARD: You're most welcome to stay, my boy.

VAN HELSING: Indeed, yes. I should have asked you to stay. I may need you. [*Takes chair from desk to left of divan; turns to* LUCY] Now lie back, so . . . [*Examines her eyelids carefully and feels her pulse*] And now tell me when did this, this weakness first come upon you? [*Sits, after examining eyelids; looks at her gums, examines tips of fingernails, then takes out watch as he feels her pulse*]

LUCY: Two nights after poor Mina was buried I had . . . a bad dream.

VAN HELSING: [*Releases pulse, after looking at watch*] A bad dream? Tell me about it.

LUCY: I remember hearing dogs barking before I went to sleep. The air seemed oppressive. I left the reading lamp lit by my bed, but when the dream came there seemed to come a mist in the room.

VAN HELSING: Was the window open?

LUCY: Yes, I always sleep with my window open.

VAN HELSING: Oh, of course, you're English. [*Laughs*] We Continentals are not so particular about fresh air. And then . . .

LUCY: The mist seemed so thick I could just see the lamp by my bed, a tiny spark in the fog, and then . . . [*Hysterically*] I saw two red eyes staring at me and a livid white face looking down on me out of the mist. It was horrible, horrible!

[HARKER *makes move toward her.* VAN HELSING *stops him by a gesture*]

VAN HELSING: There, there . . . [*Soothingly, taking her hands from her face*] Go on, please.

LUCY: [*Gives little start when* VAN HELSING *touches her hands. Looks at* HARKER *and starts; and at* SEWARD *and starts, then at* VAN HELSING *and relaxes*] The next morning my maid could scarcely wake me. I felt weak and languid. Some part of my life seemed to have gone from me.

VAN HELSING: There have been other such dreams?

LUCY: Nearly every night since then has come the mist . . . the red eyes and that awful face.

[*She puts hands to her face again.* VAN HELSING *soothes her; ad libs, as he takes her hands from face, "There, there, now."*]

SEWARD: We've tried transfusion twice. Each time she recovered her strength.

LUCY: But then would come another dream. And now I dread the night. I know it seems absurd, Professor, but please don't laugh at me.

VAN HELSING: I'm not likely to laugh. . . .

[*Gently, without answering, he unwinds scarf from her throat. She puts hand up to stop him and cries, "No, no." A look at* HARKER *when her neck is bare. As* VAN HELSING *does so he starts, then quickly opens small black bag on table and returns with microscope; examines two small marks on throat.* LUCY *with eyes closed. Controlling himself with difficulty,* VAN HELSING *puts microscope back in bag, closes it, puts back chair by desk*]

And how long have you had these little marks on your throat?

[SEWARD *and* HARKER *start violently and come to divan. They look at each other in horror*]

LUCY: Since . . . that first morning.

HARKER: Lucy, why didn't you tell us?

DRACULA

SEWARD: Lucy, you've worn that scarf around your throat . . . to hide them!

[LUCY *makes convulsive clutch at throat*]

VAN HELSING: Do not press her. Do not excite her. [*To* LUCY] Well?

LUCY: [*Constrained; to* SEWARD *and* HARKER] I was afraid they'd worry you, for I knew that . . . Mina had them.

VAN HELSING: [*With assumed cheerfulness*] Quite right, Miss Lucy, quite right. They're nothing, and old Van Helsing will see that these . . . dreams trouble you no more.

MAID: [*Appears at door*] Count Dracula.

[DRACULA *enters. He is a tall, mysterious man of about fifty. Polished and distinguished. Continental in appearance and manner.* LUCY *registers attraction to* DRACULA]

SEWARD: Ah, good evening, Count.

DRACULA: Gentlemen . . . [*He bows to men; then goes to the divan and bows in courtly fashion*] Miss Seward, how are you? You are looking more yourself this evening.

[LUCY *registers thrill. Alternate moods of attraction and repulsion, unaccountable to herself, affect* LUCY *in* DRACULA'S *presence. But this should be suggested subtly*]

LUCY: [*Quite natural*] I feel better already, Count, now that father's old friend has come to help me.

[DRACULA *turns to* VAN HELSING. LUCY *looks up at* DRACULA, *recoils, and turns to* HARKER]

SEWARD: Count Dracula, Professor Van Helsing.

[*The two men bow*]

DRACULA: A most distinguished scientist, whose name we know even in the wilds of Transylvania. [*To* SEWARD] But I interrupt a consultation.

SEWARD: Not at all, Count. It's good of you to come, and we appreciate your motives.

HARKER: Doctor Seward has just told me of your offer, and I can't thank you enough.

DRACULA: It is nothing. I should be grateful to be permitted to help Miss Lucy in any way.

LUCY: But you do, Count. I look forward to your visits. They seem to make me better.

VAN HELSING: And so I arrive to find a rival in the field.

DRACULA: [*Crosses to* LUCY] You encourage me, Miss Seward, to make them more frequent, as I should like to.

LUCY: [*Looking at him fixedly*] I am always glad to see you.

DRACULA: Ah, but you have been lonely here. And my efforts to amuse you with our old tales will no longer have the same success, now that you have Professor Van Helsing with you, and especially now that Mr. Harker is to remain here.

HARKER: How did you know I was going to stay, Count?

DRACULA: [*Little start*] Can the gallant lover ask such a question? I inferred it, my friend.

HARKER: You're right. Nothing is going to shift me now until Lucy's as fit as a fiddle again.

DRACULA: Nothing?

LUCY: Please come as before, Count, won't you?

[DRACULA *bows to her; kisses her hand.* VAN HELSING *meanwhile has been talking to* MAID]

VAN HELSING: . . . you understand, you will not answer bells. She must not be alone for a single moment under any circumstances, you understand.

[*As* DRACULA *crosses to below desk,* LUCY *leans toward him, extends her hand, then recovers herself.* VAN HELSING *registers that he sees her look at* DRACULA]

MAID: Yes, sir.

VAN HELSING: [*To* LUCY] Good. Your maid will take you to your room. Try to rest for a little, while I talk to your father.

[MAID *comes to divan to get* LUCY. *Pause, as* LUCY *looks at* DRACULA]

SEWARD: Wells, remember, don't leave her alone for a moment.

MAID: Oh, no, sir.

[LUCY *exchanges a long look with* DRACULA *as* MAID *takes her out*]

DRACULA: Professor Van Helsing, so you have come from the land of the tulip, to cure the nervous prostration of this charming girl. I wish you all the success.

VAN HELSING: Thank you, Count.

DRACULA: Do I appear officious, Doctor Seward? I am a lonely man. You are my only neighbors when I am here at Carfax, and your trouble has touched me greatly.

SEWARD: Count, I am more grateful for your sympathy than I can say.

VAN HELSING: You, like myself, are a stranger in England, Count?

DRACULA: Yes, but I love England and the great London . . . so different from my own Transylvania, where there are so few people and so little opportunity.

VAN HELSING: Opportunity, Count?

DRACULA: For my investigations, Professor.

SEWARD: I hope you haven't regretted buying that old ruin across there?

DRACULA: Oh, Carfax is not a ruin. The dust was somewhat deep, but we are used to dust in Transylvania.

HARKER: You plan to remain in England, Count?

DRACULA: I think so, my friend. The walls of my castle are broken, and the shadows are many, and I am the last of my race.

HARKER: It's a lonely spot you've chosen . . . Carfax.

DRACULA: It is, and when I hear the dogs howling far and near I think myself back in my Castle Dracula with its broken battlements.

HARKER: Ah, the dogs howl there when there are wolves around, don't they?

DRACULA: They do, my friend. And they howl here as well, although there are no wolves. But you wish to consult the anxious father and the great specialist. . . . May I read a book in the study? I am so anxious to hear what the Professor says . . . and to learn if I can be of any help.

SEWARD: By all means, Count. [DRACULA *bows; exits.* SEWARD *watches him leave. Dogs howl offstage*] Very kind of Dracula, with his damned untimely friendliness, but now what about my daughter?

HARKER: Yes, Professor, what do you think is the matter with Lucy?

VAN HELSING: [*Crosses to window, looks out. Long pause before he speaks*] Your patient, that interesting Renfield, does not like the smell of wolfsbane.

SEWARD: Good Heavens. What has that got to do with Lucy?

VAN HELSING: Perhaps nothing.

HARKER: In God's name, Professor, is there anything unnatural or occult about this business?

SEWARD: Occult? Van Helsing! Oh . . .

VAN HELSING: Ah, Seward, let me remind you that the superstitions of today are the scientific facts of tomorrow. Science can now transmute the electron, the basis of all matter, into energy, and what is that but the dematerialization of matter? Yet dematerialization has been known and practiced in India for centuries. In Java I myself have seen things.

SEWARD: My dear old friend, you can't have filled up your fine old brain with Eastern moonshine.

VAN HELSING: Moonshine?

SEWARD: But anyway, come now, what about my daughter?

VAN HELSING: Ah! Seward, if you won't listen to what will be harder to believe than any Eastern moonshine, if you won't forget your textbooks . . . keep an open mind, then, Seward. Your daughter's life may pay for your pig-headedness.

HARKER: Go on, go on, Professor!

SEWARD: I am listening.

VAN HELSING: Then I must ask you to listen calmly to what I am going to say. Sit down. [VAN HELSING *crosses to window; closes curtains.* SEWARD *and* HARKER *exchange glances, then both look at* VAN HELSING *as they sit*] You have both heard the legends of Central Europe, about the Werewolf, the Vampires?

SEWARD: You mean ghosts, who suck the blood of the living?

VAN HELSING: If you wish to call them ghosts. I call them the undead.

HARKER: [*Quickly*] For God's sake, man, are you suggesting that Mina, and now Lucy . . .

SEWARD: [*Interrupting*] Of course, I have read these horrible folk tales of the Middle Ages, Van Helsing, but I know you better than to suppose . . .

VAN HELSING: [*Interrupting*] That I believe them? I *do* believe them.

SEWARD: [*Incredulously*] You mean to tell us that vampires actually exist and . . . and that Mina and Lucy have been attacked by one?

VAN HELSING: Your English doctors would all laugh at such a theory. Your police, your public would laugh. [*Impressively*] *The strength of the vampire is that people will not believe in him.*

SEWARD: [*Shaking head*] Is this the help you bring us?

VAN HELSING: [*Much moved*] Do not despise it.

HARKER: [*To* SEWARD] Doctor, this case has stumped all your specialists. [*To* VAN HELSING] Go on, Professor.

VAN HELSING: Vampires are rare. Nature abhors them, the forces of good combine to destroy them, but a few of these creatures have lived on for centuries.

HARKER: [*Excited*] What *is* a vampire?

VAN HELSING: A vampire, my friend, is a man or a woman who is dead and yet not dead. A thing that lives after its death by drinking the blood of the living. It must have blood or it dies. Its power lasts only from sunset to sunrise. During the hours of the day it must rest in the earth in which it was buried. But, during the night, it has the power to prey upon the living. [*Incredulous move from* SEWARD] My friend, you are thinking you will have to put me amongst your patients?

SEWARD: Van Helsing, I don't know what to think but I confess I simply can't follow you.

HARKER: What makes you think that Lucy has been attacked by such a creature?

VAN HELSING: [*From now on dominating them*] Doctor Seward's written account of these ladies' symptoms at once aroused my suspicion. Anæmia? The blood of three men was forced into the veins of Miss Mina. Yet she died from loss of blood. Where did it go? Had your specialist any answer? The vampire attacks the throat. He leaves two little wounds, white with red centers. [HARKER *rises slowly*] Seward, you wrote me of those two marks on Miss Mina's throat. An accident with a safety pin, you said. So I thought, I suspected, I did not know, but I came on the instant, and what do I find? These same wounds on Miss Lucy's throat. Another safety pin, Doctor Seward?

SEWARD: Do you mean to say that you've built up all this nightmare out of a safety pin? It's true I can't make out why she hid those marks from us.

VAN HELSING: I could tell you that.

SEWARD: [Pause] What! I don't believe it. Of course Lucy's trouble can't be *that*.

HARKER: I do believe it. This theory accounts for all the facts that nobody has been able to explain. We'll take her away where this thing can't get at her.

VAN HELSING: She will not want to go.

SEWARD: What!

VAN HELSING: If you force her, the shock may be fatal.

HARKER: But why won't she go if we tell her that her life depends on it?

VAN HELSING: Because the victim of the vampire becomes his creature, linked to him in life and after death.

SEWARD: [Incredulous, shocked; rises] Professor, this is too much!

HARKER: Lucy become an unclean thing, a demon?

VAN HELSING: Yes, Harker. Now will you help me?

HARKER: Yes, anything. Tell me what to do.

VAN HELSING: It is dangerous work. Our lives are at stake, but so is Miss Lucy's life, so is her soul. We must stamp out this monster.

HARKER: How can we stamp it out now?

VAN HELSING: This undead thing lies helpless by day in the earth or tomb in which it was buried.

SEWARD: A corpse, in a coffin?

VAN HELSING: A corpse, if you like, but a living corpse, sustained by the blood of the living. If we can find its earth home, a stake driven through the heart destroys the vampire. But this is our task. In such a case the police, all the powers of society, are as helpless as the doctors. What bars or chains can hold a creature who can turn into a wolf or a bat?

HARKER: A wolf! Doctor Seward, those dogs howling! I told you they

howl that way in Russia when wolves are about. And a bat . . .
Renfield said there was a bat.

SEWARD: Well. What of it?

VAN HELSING: [*Reflectively*] Your friend Renfield does not like the
smell of wolfsbane.

SEWARD: But what in the world has your wolfsbane to do with all
this?

VAN HELSING: A vampire cannot stand the smell of wolfsbane.

HARKER: You suspect that lunatic?

VAN HELSING: I suspect no one and everyone. . . . Tell me, who is
this Count Dracula?

SEWARD: Dracula? We really know very little about him.

HARKER: When I was in Transylvania I heard of Castle Dracula. A
famous Voivode Dracula who fought the Turks lived there centuries ago.

VAN HELSING: I will make inquiries by telegraph. No, but after all
this Thing must be English. Or at least have died here. His lair
must be near enough to this house for him to get back there before sunrise. [*To* SEWARD] Oh, my friend, I have only the old be-
liefs with which to fight this monster that has the strength of
twenty men, perhaps the accumulated wisdom and cunning of
centuries.

HARKER: This all seems a nightmare. But I'm with you, Professor.

VAN HELSING: And you, Doctor Seward?

SEWARD: It all seems preposterous to me. But everyone else has failed.
The case is in your hands at present.

VAN HELSING: [*Sternly*] I need allies, not neutrals.

SEWARD: Very well, then, do what you will.

VAN HELSING: Good. Then bring your daughter here.

SEWARD: What are you going to do?

VAN HELSING: To set a trap. Miss Lucy is the bait.

HARKER: My God, we can't let you do that!

VAN HELSING: There's no other way. I believe this Thing knows that
I plan to protect Miss Lucy. This will put it on its guard and the
first moment she is alone it will no doubt try to get at her, for a
vampire must have blood or its life in death ceases.

HARKER: No, I forbid this.

SEWARD: She's my daughter, and I consent. We'll show the Professor he's mistaken.

HARKER: You allow it only because you don't believe, and I do believe. My God, Doctor, I've heard that lunatic laugh . . . life-eating, you said he was, and you subject Lucy to that risk.

VAN HELSING: [*Interrupting harshly*] I must be master here or I can do nothing! I must know in what form this Thing comes before I can plan how to stamp it out. Bring your daughter here.

> [SEWARD *turns and sees* HARKER *looking at him; stares at* HARKER. *There is a short pause, then* HARKER *reluctantly exits.* SEWARD *follows him.* VAN HELSING *thinks a moment, then looks about noting the positions of doors, furniture, etc. He then turns out lights. The room is dark except for the firelight.* VAN HELSING *moves into firelight, looks at divan, then walks back to door and turns, looking at divan, satisfying himself that the light from the fire is sufficient to see anything that happens on the divan. Opens curtains. Suddenly, the double doors open sharply and* VAN HELSING *starts violently; the* ATTENDANT *enters*]

ATTENDANT: Beg pardon, sir. Is Doctor Seward here?

VAN HELSING: What do you want with him?

ATTENDANT: Ole Flycatcher's escaped again, sir.

VAN HELSING: Escaped, how?

ATTENDANT: Gor' blimme, out of the window. The door's still locked and I was in the corridor all the while. It's a drop of thirty feet to the stone flagging. That loonie's a bloomin' flyin' squirrel 'e is.

VAN HELSING: [*Commandingly*] Say nothing to Doctor Seward at present. Nothing, do you hear? Now go.

> [ATTENDANT *exits.* VAN HELSING *switches on lights again. Enter* LUCY, *supported by* HARKER *and* SEWARD]

LUCY: Oh! Oh!

SEWARD: Lucy, you have nothing to fear.

> [*They take her to divan*]

VAN HELSING: I want you to lie down here, my dear.

LUCY: But, Doctor . . .

VAN HELSING: You trust me, do you not? [*She smiles weakly at him; nods. They place her on divan*] I want you to lie here for just a little.

LUCY: But . . . I am so frightened.

VAN HELSING: Make your mind passive. Try not to think. Sleep if you can.

LUCY: I dare not sleep. It is when I sleep . . .

[HARKER *takes her hand*]

VAN HELSING: [*Arranging her on divan, head on pillows, soothingly*] I know, my dear. I know. I am going to cure you, with God's help.

LUCY: Oh, but, Father.

SEWARD: You must do as the Professor says. Come, Harker.

VAN HELSING: Come, Harker.

[VAN HELSING *leads* SEWARD *to the door.* SEWARD *exits.* HARKER *lingers and* VAN HELSING *calls him.* VAN HELSING *switches off lights as he and* HARKER *go out. No movement.* LUCY *closes her eyes. Low howl is heard outside . . . howl of a wolf. It is followed by a distant barking of dogs. Firelight grows dimmer.* DRACULA's *hand appears from back of couch, then his face.* LUCY *screams; swoons. When* LUCY *screams, ad libs offstage until* VAN HELSING *switches on lights*]

HARKER: Lucy! Lucy!

SEWARD: Professor, what is it?

[VAN HELSING *enters, followed by* SEWARD *and* HARKER. VAN HELSING *switches on lights. They are just in front of door as a bat flies in the room from window to center, then out of the window*]

VAN HELSING: You saw?

SEWARD: God, what was that?

HARKER: Lucy, Lucy, speak to me!

VAN HELSING: Take her to her room, Harker, quickly.

[HARKER *carries* LUCY *to door as* DRACULA *enters. He looks about, his glance taking in everyone*]

DRACULA: [*Mildly, sympathetically*] The patient is better, I hope?

[RENFIELD *gives a wild laugh offstage right.* VAN HELSING, SEWARD *and* HARKER *turn.* RENFIELD *gives a second wild laugh*]

CURTAIN

ACT TWO

LUCY's *boudoir. Window right rear, closed but curtains open. Chairs, small occasional table with toilet articles on it by window. Couch against wall up left center. Mirror on wall. Small stand, with flowers in vase, near couch. Doors, right, leading into bedroom, left, leading into hall. Arch left center.*

The next evening.

Dogs howling. As curtain rises, MAID *enters from bedroom, glances up at window over her left shoulder, takes a few steps, looks back over right shoulder, then to couch and takes newspaper. Sits on couch; reads newspaper. As she turns a page,* ATTENDANT *knocks on hall door.*

MAID: [*Starts*] Who is that?

ATTENDANT: [*Enters; smiles at her*] Excuse me, Miss. Did you 'appen to 'ave seen anything of the Guv'ner's pet looney? 'E's out again, 'e is.

MAID: [*Holding paper*] And what would he be doing here? You'll not hold your job, you won't, if you can't keep that man safe and sound. Why, he gets out every night. [*She crosses toward bedroom door*]

ATTENDANT: 'Ere, don't go, Miss.

MAID: Miss Lucy's asked for the evening paper.

[MAID *smiles as she goes off; indicates speedy return.* AT-TENDANT *looks out of window and then looks under couch.* MAID *returns. Her line comes just as* ATTENDANT *bends over, causing him to jump back, frightened*]

MAID: Well, have you found him?

ATTENDANT: No, I 'aven't. [*Confidentially*] And I'll tell you, Miss, this job is fair gettin' on my nerves.

MAID: Your nerves? And what about *my* nerves? Isn't it enough to have dogs howling every night and foreign counts bobbing up out of the floor, and Miss Lucy taking on the way she does, with everybody having their veins drained of blood for her, and this Dutch Sherlock Holmes with the X-ray eyes about, without you letting that Renfield loose?

ATTENDANT: [*Grieved*] I 'aven't let 'im loose. . . . Just now I 'ears a noise like a wolf 'owling. I opens 'is door with me key, and what do I see but 'is legs goin' through the window as though 'e was goin' to climb down that smooth wall. 'E ain't 'uman, 'e ain't.

MAID: Climb down the wall?

ATTENDANT: [*Gloomily*] I don't expect no one to believe it, but I seen it, and w'ot's more, I grabbed 'old of 'is feet, I did.

MAID: [*Laughs unbelievingly*] Climbing down, head first, like a bat?

ATTENDANT: Queer your mention of bats, for just as I got 'old of 'im, a big bat flies in the window and 'its me in the face.

MAID: [*Mysteriously*] I know where that bat came from.

ATTENDANT: [*Startled*] You do? Where?

MAID: Out of your belfry. [*Crosses to head of couch and arranges pillows, then to dresser*]

ATTENDANT: No, Miss, it's Gawd's truth I'm tellin' yer . . . [*Look from her*] . . . out that bat flies, and the looney is gone, but I 'eard 'im laugh, and Gawd, what a laugh. Blimme, but I'll catch it from the Guv'ner for this.

MAID: [*At dressing table*] If you tell the Guvernor any such tales he'll shut you up with the looney.

ATTENDANT: Lor', Miss, but you're a smart one . . . that's just what I've been thinkin', and I daren't tell 'im what I see or what I 'eard. But 'e's 'armless, this bloke.

MAID: [*Ironically*] Wouldn't hurt a fly, would he?

ATTENDANT: 'Urt a fly? Oh, no, not 'e. 'E only *eats* 'em. Why, 'e'd rather eat a few blue-bottles than a pound of the best steak, and what 'e does to spiders is a crime.

MAID: It seems to me somebody will be coming after *you* in a minute, you and your spiders.

ATTENDANT: I say, Miss. This is a queer neighborhood. [*Looking out of window*] What a drop that is to the ground. [*Turns to her*] You don't have to be afraid of burglars, do you? No way of getting up here unless they fly. . . . Don't you never feel a bit lonesome like, out there . . . [*Points to window*] . . . on your nights off?

MAID: Just lately I have a bit. [*Looks toward window*] I never noticed trees had such shadows before.

ATTENDANT: Well . . . if you feel you'd like a h'escort, Miss . . .

MAID: I'll not walk with you in your uniform. People might be taking me for one of your loonies.

ATTENDANT: [*Puts arm around her*] In mufti, then, tomorrow night.

MAID: I say, you haven't wasted much time, have you?

ATTENDANT: I've 'ad my eye on you.

MAID: Better keep that eye on your looney, or you'll be looking for a new job. [ATTENDANT *tries to kiss her. She pushes him off and slaps him*] Here, you. Buzz off. Your Guvernor will be in any minute. [*Gestures to door*] Go find your looney.

ATTENDANT: Oh, orl right, but I've got somethin' 'ere that'll tempt 'im back to 'is room.

MAID: Why, what's that?

[*He fumbles in pocket. She comes up to him*]

ATTENDANT: [*Takes white mouse by tail out of pocket; holds it in her face*] This 'ere.

MAID: [*Screams; climbs on chair; holds skirt*] Take it away! Take it away!

ATTENDANT: [*Mouse climbs up his arm to shoulder. To mouse*] Come on, Cuthbert. We ain't too popular. [*Offended, walks off left with dignity, remarking from door:*] Some people 'ave *no* sense of humor.

SEWARD: [*Enters hastily from bedroom*] What was that?

MAID: [*Puts down her skirt*] Pardon, sir. He frightened me with that . . . that animal.

SEWARD: [*Agitated*] Animal, what animal?

MAID: A white mouse, sir.

SEWARD: [*Relieved*] You mustn't scream . . . not in this house . . . now.

MAID: I'm sorry, sir, but that nasty little beast . . .

SEWARD: You alarmed Miss Lucy so. She's dreadfully upset as it is by something in the paper.

MAID: Oh, do you mean about that Hampstead Horror, sir? The lady in white who gives chocolates to little children . . .

SEWARD: [Interrupts impatiently] Never mind that, but I will not have Miss Lucy disturbed.

> [SEWARD returns to bedroom. Dogs howl. Lights go out. MAID screams. Green spot comes up on DRACULA who stands in center of room. MAID screams again as she sees him]

DRACULA: [Soothingly] Forgive me. My footfall is not heavy, and your rugs are soft.

MAID: It's all right, sir . . . but how did you come in?

DRACULA: [Smiling] The door of this room was ajar, so I did not knock. How is Miss Lucy and her nervous prostration?

MAID: I think she's better, sir.

DRACULA: Ah, good. But the strain of Miss Lucy's illness has made you also ill.

MAID: How did you know, sir? But it's only a pain in my head that runs down into the neck.

DRACULA: [Winningly] I can remove this pain.

MAID: I don't understand, sir.

DRACULA: Such pains yield readily to suggestion.

MAID: [Raises arm slightly to shield herself] Excuse me, sir, but if it's hypnotism you mean, I'd rather have the pain.

DRACULA: Ah, you think of hypnotism as an ugly waving of arms and many passes. That is not my method. [As he speaks he gestures quietly with his left hand and she stares at him, fascinated. Placing his left thumb against her forehead, he stares straight into her eyes. She makes a feeble effort to remove his hand, then remains quiescent. He now speaks coldly, imperatively; turns her face front before speaking] What is given can be taken away. From now on you have no pain. And you have no will of your own. Do you hear me?

MAID: [Murmurs] I hear you.

DRACULA: When you awake you will not remember what I say. Doctor Seward ordered you today to sleep with your mistress every night in the same bed because of her bad dreams. Is it not so?

MAID: [Murmurs] Yes, Master.

DRACULA: Your mistress is threatened by horror and by death, but I will save her. A man whose will is at cross purposes with mine has come to this house. I will crush him. Receive your orders. You hear me?

MAID: Yes, Master.

DRACULA: Hear and obey. From now on you will carry out any suggestion that reaches you from my brain instantly without question. When I will you to do a thing it shall be done. My call will reach you soon.

[Green spot dims out slowly. DRACULA exits through window. Lights come on. Dogs howl outside. MAID looks up at window as VAN HELSING enters left. She starts when door shuts]

VAN HELSING: [His face is paler. He looks drawn and weak. He carries box tied with string] You've not left your mistress alone?

MAID: Doctor Seward is with her, sir. [Sways a little]

VAN HELSING: [Looking at her keenly] What's wrong with you, my girl?

MAID: Nothing, sir.

VAN HELSING: You've just had a severe shock.

MAID: It's nothing, sir. I . . . I suddenly felt queer. [Looks toward window] That's all. I can't remember anything.

VAN HELSING: Mr. Harker has just arrived. Ask Doctor Seward to come here. Remain with Miss Lucy yourself.

MAID: Yes, sir. She's dreadfully upset, sir.

VAN HELSING: Upset over what?

MAID: It's in the evening paper, sir. About the Hampstead Horror.

[VAN HELSING motions MAID to silence] Yes, sir.

VAN HELSING: [Shaken] Oh, God, she has seen it!

[MAID goes into bedroom. HARKER enters left]

HARKER: [Worried] Everything just the same? [VAN HELSING nods.

HARKER *closes door*] When I leave this house even for a few hours I dread what I . . . I dread what I may find when I come back.

VAN HELSING: And well you may, my friend. [*He places box on table under mirror*]

HARKER: God must have sent you here to help us. Without you there'd be no hope. And this morning, Professor, when you opened your veins to revive Lucy again . . .

VAN HELSING: It was the least I could do . . . for my lack of foresight was responsible for this attack.

HARKER: Don't say that.

VAN HELSING: Her maid slept with her . . . and yet we found the wolfsbane thrown off the bed to the floor.

HARKER: She was so weak, so pale, the two little wounds opened fresh again . . .

VAN HELSING: [*With gesture to box*] I have prepared a stronger defense. But our main task is not defense, but attack. What have you found in London?

HARKER: A lot, but heaven knows what it means or whether it's any use.

VAN HELSING: I, too, have had news of which I can make nothing.

SEWARD: [*Enters*] Ah, John, back from town.

HARKER: Yes. [*Sits*]

VAN HELSING: We must try to piece together what we have learned today. [*Producing telegram of several sheets*] My colleague in Bucharest wires that the Dracula family has been extinct . . . for five hundred years.

SEWARD: Can the Count be an impostor?

VAN HELSING: [*Referring to telegram*] The castle he calls his own is a desolate ruin near the border. It was built, as you said, Harker, by the terrible Voivode Dracula, who was said to have had dealings with evil spirits. He was the last of his race. But for many generations the peasants have believed the Castle Dracula inhabited by a vampire.

HARKER: Then it must be he . . .

VAN HELSING: [*Shakes head; puts telegram back in pocket*] My friends, I am bewildered.

SEWARD: But surely this confirms your suspicions. I was incredulous till I saw that creature hovering over Lucy . . .

VAN HELSING: A vampire from Transylvania cannot be in England.

SEWARD: But why?

VAN HELSING: Because, as I have told you, the vampire must rest by day in the earth in which the corpse it inhabits was buried.

HARKER: [*Rises*] In the earth.

VAN HELSING: The vampire must return to its burial place by sunrise.

HARKER: [*Excited*] I found today that Dracula arrived at the Croydon airdrome in a three-engined German plane, on March sixth.

SEWARD: March the sixth? Three days before Mina first was taken ill.

HARKER: This plane had made a nonstop flight from Sekely in Transylvania. It left just after sunset. It arrived two hours before dawn. It carried only the Count and six packing cases.

VAN HELSING: Did you learn what was in those cases?

HARKER: He told the customs people he wanted to see whether Transylvania plants would grow in a foreign climate in their native soil.

VAN HELSING: Soil? What was in those boxes?

HARKER: Just plain dirt. He left in a lorry, with the six coffinlike boxes, before sunrise.

VAN HELSING: Oh, God, yes, before sunrise. The King of Vampires, my friends. [*Crosses between* SEWARD *and* HARKER] This creature is the terrible Voivode Dracula himself! In his satanic pride and contempt, he even uses his own name. For who could suspect? For five hundred years he has been fettered to his castle because he must sleep by day in his graveyard. Five centuries pass. The airplane is invented. His chance has come, for now he can cross Europe in a single night. He prepared six coffins filled with the earth in which he must rest by day. He leaves his castle after sunset. By dawn he is in London and safe in one of his cases—a great risk, but he has triumphed. He has reached London with its teeming millions, with its "opportunity," as he said . . .

SEWARD: God protect my Lucy!

HARKER: [*To* VAN HELSING, *new tone*] I saw the estate agent from whom he bought Carfax here and got the address of four old houses he has leased in different parts of London.

VAN HELSING: One of his coffin retreats is in each of those houses.

SEWARD: Two heavy boxes were delivered at Carfax the day after he took possession.

VAN HELSING: He has scattered them, for safety. If we can find all six, we can destroy him.

SEWARD: But how?

VAN HELSING: His native earth will no longer receive his unclean form if each box is sanctified with holy water.

HARKER: Then we must get at those boxes, tear them open one by one. If we find him, then in God's name, Professor, I demand that my hand shall drive the stake into this devil's heart and send his soul to hell!

[SEWARD *motions no noise because of* LUCY]

VAN HELSING: Your plan is too dangerous.

SEWARD: But why? These attacks on Lucy continue. Are we to delay while my child is dying?

HARKER: No, not for a moment.

VAN HELSING: Patience, my friends. This creature is more than mortal. His cunning is the growth of the ages. How if we find five of his boxes and close them against him, and cannot find the sixth?

SEWARD: Well?

VAN HELSING: Then he will bury himself in his last refuge, where we can never find him and sleep until we are all dead.

HARKER: Then Lucy will be safe.

VAN HELSING: For her life, yes . . . but his unclean kiss has claimed her for his own. When she dies she will become as he is, a foul thing of the night. The vampire can wait. No, my friends, there is only one way to save her from him . . . to destroy him.

SEWARD: You're right, as always.

VAN HELSING: We have one great advantage . . . by day he is a coffined corpse . . . of our search by day he can know nothing, if we leave no traces.

HARKER: God, this delay!

VAN HELSING: We must make the round of his houses and find all six boxes, without his knowledge, and *then* we act.

SEWARD: But what about the caretakers or servants?

VAN HELSING: All the houses will be empty. The vampire plays a lone hand.

[*Maniacal laugh heard behind curtains of window.* SEWARD *crosses quickly to window*]

SEWARD: Renfield!

[*He grabs* RENFIELD *by arm and throws him into room.* RENFIELD *laughs cunningly*]

VAN HELSING: He's been here all the time we've been talking.

SEWARD: Did you hear what we were saying, man?

RENFIELD: Yes, I heard . . . something . . . enough . . . [*With gestures to* SEWARD *and* HARKER] Be guided by what he says. [*Points to* VAN HELSING] It is your only hope. . . . It is her only hope. [*Crosses to* VAN HELSING] It is *my* only hope. [*Falls on knees before* VAN HELSING] Save my soul! Save my soul! I am weak. You are strong. I am crazy. You are sane. You are good and he is evil.

VAN HELSING: [*Impressively*] I will save you, Renfield, but you must tell me what you know. Everything.

RENFIELD: [*Rises*] Know? What should I know? I don't know anything. [*Taps head*] You say I'm mad and Doctor Seward will tell you about that. You mustn't pay any attention to anything I say.

SEWARD: We can't waste time with this fellow. I'll have him taken away. [*Crosses to bell*]

RENFIELD: [*To* SEWARD] Fool, fool, and I thought you were wise! The whole world is mad just now, and if you want help you must come to a madman to get it. [*Little laugh, cunningly*] But I'll not give it to you, I'm afraid. [*Turns to window*] A wise madman will obey him who is strong and not the weak.

VAN HELSING: [*Moves to him fiercely*] Him? Whom do you mean?

RENFIELD: Need we mention names among friends? Come, Professor, be reasonable. What have I got to gain by being on your side? The Doctor keeps me shut up all day, and if I'm good he gives me a little sugar to spread out for my flies, but on the other hand, if I serve *him* . . . [*Points to window*]

VAN HELSING: [*Sharply, taking him by coat*] The blood is the life, eh,

Renfield? [*Dragging him again*] What have you to do with Count Dracula?

RENFIELD: [*Convulsed with terror*] Dracula! [*Drawing himself up defiantly*] I never even heard the name before!

VAN HELSING: You are lying!

RENFIELD: Madmen, Professor, lack the power to discriminate between truth and falsehood . . . [*Breaks away*] . . . so I take no offense at what most men would consider an affront. [*Crosses to* SEWARD] Send me away! I asked you to before and you wouldn't. If you only knew what has happened since then. I dare not tell you more. I dare not! I should die in torment if I betrayed . . .

VAN HELSING: Doctor Seward will send you away if you speak.

SEWARD: Yes, Renfield. [RENFIELD *moans*] I offer you your soul in exchange for what you know.

RENFIELD: God will not damn a poor lunatic's soul. God knows the devil is too strong for us who have weak minds. But send me away . . . I want you to promise, Doctor Seward!

SEWARD: If you will speak.

VAN HELSING: Come, Renfield.

RENFIELD: [*Pause. Looks at* SEWARD, VAN HELSING, HARKER, *and* SEWARD *again, then speaks as a sane man*] Then I will tell you. Count Dracula is . . . [*Bat comes in window; flies out again.* RENFIELD *rushes to window with arms outstretched, screaming*] Master! Master, I didn't say anything! I told them nothing. I'm loyal to you. I am your slave.

[SEWARD *and* HARKER *rush to window*]

SEWARD: [*Looking out window*] There's a big bat flying in a circle. It's gone.

HARKER: What's that, just passing that small shrub? It looks like a big gray dog.

VAN HELSING: Are you sure it was a dog?

HARKER: Well, it might easily be a wolf. Oh, but that's nonsense. Our nerves are making us see things.

VAN HELSING: Come, Renfield. What were you about to say?

RENFIELD: Nothing, nothing.

[LUCY *comes in from bedroom with newspaper*]

LUCY: Professor . . . have you seen what's in this . . .

VAN HELSING: Miss Lucy, give it to . . .

RENFIELD: [*Crosses to her*] Are you Miss Seward?

LUCY: I am.

[SEWARD *moves closer to her; indicates* HARKER *to ring bell*]

RENFIELD: Then in the name of the merciful and compassionate God, leave this place at once!

[*She turns to him.* VAN HELSING *motions silence to others*]

LUCY: But this is my home. Nothing would induce me to leave.

RENFIELD: [*Sane*] Oh, that's true. You wouldn't go if they tried to drag you away, would you? It's too late. What a fool I am. I shall be punished for this and it can't do any good. It's too late. [*In tone of pity*] You are so young, so beautiful, so pure. Even I have decent feelings sometimes, and I must tell you, and if you don't go your soul will pay for it. You're in the power of . . . [*Bat flies in window and out.* RENFIELD *rushes to window and screams.* SEWARD *moves toward couch.* HARKER *crosses to* LUCY *to protect her*] The Master is at hand!

[RENFIELD *crosses back on knees.* ATTENDANT *appears at door*]

SEWARD: Butterworth!

[SEWARD *helps* RENFIELD *up, then* ATTENDANT *grasps him and takes him to door*]

RENFIELD: [*At door*] Goodbye, Miss Seward. Since you will not heed my warning, I pray God that I may never see your face again.

[*He exits with* ATTENDANT]

LUCY: What did he mean, Professor? What did he mean? Why did he say that?

[*She goes off into bedroom, in hysterics.* HARKER *follows her*]

SEWARD: That crazy thing in league with the devil; horrible, and Lucy already upset by something in the paper.

VAN HELSING: Go in and get that paper from her.

SEWARD: Whatever it is, she keeps on reading that article again and again.

VAN HELSING: Take it away from her, man, and come back to me. [*Places hand on forehead as if faint*]

SEWARD: Don't overdo it, Van Helsing. God knows where we should be if you went under. After a transfusion operation, at your age you really ought to be in bed . . . the loss of so much blood is serious.

VAN HELSING: I never felt more fit in my life.

SEWARD: I only ask you not to overestimate your strength now, when we lean on you. . . . [*As he exits*] Feeling fit, are you? Just look at yourself in the glass.

> [VAN HELSING, *alone, registers as tired and exhausted, and walks slowly across room, looking at his drawn face in mirror.* DRACULA, *with stealthy tread, in evening dress and cloak as before, enters from window and walks slowly to directly behind* VAN HELSING]

VAN HELSING: [*Looking at himself, touching face, shakes head*] The devil.

DRACULA: Come. [VAN HELSING *turns suddenly to him and looks back into the mirror*] Not as bad as that. [*Suave, cold, ironical*]

VAN HELSING: [*Long look in mirror, then turns to* DRACULA. *Controlling himself with difficulty*] I did not hear you, Count.

DRACULA: I am often told that I have a light footstep.

VAN HELSING: I was looking in the mirror. Its reflection covers the whole room, but I cannot see . . .

> [*Pause. He turns to mirror.* DRACULA, *face convulsed by fury, picks up small vase with flowers from stand, smashes mirror, pieces of mirror and vase tumbling to floor.* VAN HELSING *steps back; looks at* DRACULA *with loathing and terror*]

DRACULA: [*Recovering composure*] Forgive me, I dislike mirrors. They are the playthings of man's vanity. . . . And how's the fair patient?

VAN HELSING: [*Meaningly*] The diagnosis presents difficulties.

DRACULA: I feared it might, my friend.

VAN HELSING: Would you care to see what I have prescribed for my patient?

DRACULA: Anything that you prescribe for Miss Lucy has the greatest interest for me.

> [VAN HELSING *crosses to table to get box.* DRACULA *crosses, meets* VAN HELSING *coming back with box.* VAN HELSING *deliberately turns away from him, goes to small table right of arch, turns front as he opens pocketknife and, in cutting string of parcel, cuts his finger. He gives slight exclamation of pain; holds up finger covered with blood.* DRACULA *starts for* VAN HELSING *with right hand raised, then keeping control with difficulty, turns away so as not to see blood.* VAN HELSING *stares at him a moment, then walks up and sticks bleeding finger in front of him*]

VAN HELSING: The prescription is a most unusual one.

> [DRACULA, *baring teeth, makes sudden snap at finger.* VAN HELSING *turns away quickly; ties handkerchief around it.* DRACULA *again regains poise with an effort*]

DRACULA: The cut is not deep . . . I . . . looked.

VAN HELSING: [*Opening parcel*] No, but it will serve. Here is my medicine for Miss Lucy. [DRACULA *comes up to* VAN HELSING, *who quickly holds handful of wolfsbane up to his face.* DRACULA *leaps back, face distorted with rage and distress, shielding himself with cloak. Putting wolfsbane back in box*] You do not care for the smell?

DRACULA: You are a wise man, Professor . . . for one who has not lived even a single lifetime.

VAN HELSING: You flatter me, Count.

DRACULA: But not wise enough to return to Holland at once, now that you have learned what you have learned.

VAN HELSING: [*Shortly*] I preferred to remain. [*Meaningly*] Even though a certain lunatic here attempted to kill me.

DRACULA: [*Smiling*] Lunatics are difficult. They do not do what they are told. They even try to betray their benefactors. But when servants fail to obey orders, the Master must carry them out for himself.

VAN HELSING: [*Grimly*] I anticipated as much.

DRACULA: [*Gazing at him intently*] In the past five hundred years, Professor, those who have crossed my path have all died, and some not pleasantly. [*Continues to gaze at* VAN HELSING; *lifts his arm slowly; says with terrible emphasis and force*] Come . . . here. [VAN HELSING *pales, staggers, then slowly takes three steps toward* DRACULA. *Very slight pause as* VAN HELSING *attempts to regain control of himself, then takes another step toward* DRACULA; *pauses, places hand to brow, then completely regains control of himself and looks away*] Ah, your will is strong. Then I must come to you. [*Advances to* VAN HELSING, *who takes out of breast pocket small velvet bag.* DRACULA *stops*] More medicine, Professor?

VAN HELSING: More effective than wolfsbane, Count.

DRACULA: Indeed? [*Starts for* VAN HELSING's *throat.* VAN HELSING *holds bag out toward him.* DRACULA's *face becomes convulsed with terror and he retreats left before* VAN HELSING, *who follows him*] Sacrilege.

VAN HELSING: [*Continuing to advance*] I have a dispensation.

> [VAN HELSING *has cut him off from the door and remorselessly presses him toward window.* DRACULA, *livid with rage and snarling, backs out of the window. As* DRACULA *is just outside the window he spreads his cape like a bat and gives a long satirical laugh as he makes exit.* VAN HELSING *almost collapses; puts bag back in pocket; crosses himself; mops perspiration from brow with handkerchief. A shot is heard.* VAN HELSING *leaps up; rushes to window. Bat circles almost into his face. He staggers back.* SEWARD *hurries in, carrying newspaper*]

SEWARD: God, Van Helsing, what was that? [*Dropping newspaper on table*]

VAN HELSING: A revolver shot. It came as a relief. That at least is something human.

SEWARD: Who broke the mirror?

VAN HELSING: I.

[HARKER *enters*]

HARKER: Sorry if I startled you. I saw that infernal bat around this side of the house. I couldn't resist a shot.

SEWARD: Did you hit it?

HARKER: Why, I . . .

VAN HELSING: The bullet was never made, my friend, that could harm *that* bat. *My* weapons are stronger.

HARKER: What do you mean?

VAN HELSING: Dracula has been here.

SEWARD: Good God!

HARKER: How did he get in?

VAN HELSING: You ask how the Vampire King, during the hours of night, the hours that are his, comes and goes? As the wind, my friend, as he pleases. He came to kill me. . . . But I carry a power stronger than his.

HARKER: What power?

VAN HELSING: I expected an attack. I secured a dispensation from the Cardinal. I have with me . . . [*Crosses himself*] . . . the Host. [HARKER *crosses himself*] He came. I proved my case if it needed proof. The mirror does not reflect this *man that was*, who casts no shadow. See, I cut my finger, *it* leapt at the blood, but before the sacred wafer *it* fled.

SEWARD: Lucy must not know.

VAN HELSING: [*Gently, worried*] Miss Lucy knows . . . more than you think.

HARKER: How can she? If she knew, she'd tell me.

VAN HELSING: As these attacks continue she comes more and more under his power. There is a mystic link between them. [SEWARD *sighs*] Oh, it is hard to bear, but you must face it. It may be that he can already learn what passes in her mind. And so Miss Lucy must not be told that we know about earth boxes . . . for he may learn . . . whatever she knows.

[LUCY *enters*]

SEWARD: But Professor, that would mean that Lucy is in collusion with this creature. That's impossible. . . .

[LUCY *crosses to table; takes newspaper*]

VAN HELSING: No, no, Miss Lucy, you must not.
HARKER: Lucy, what's in this paper that's upset you?
LUCY: [*Hands newspaper to* HARKER] Read it, John.

[HARKER *takes newspaper; reads.* VAN HELSING *moves as if to stop him, then checks himself*]

VAN HELSING: No, Harker, no.
LUCY: Read it!

[LUCY *sits on couch. They all listen*]

HARKER: [*Reading*] "The Hampstead Horror. Further attacks on small children, committed after dark by a mysterious and beautiful woman in Hampstead, are reported today. Narratives of three small girls, all under ten years of age, tally in essential details. Each child speaks of a beautiful lady in white who gave her chocolates, enticed her to some secluded corner and there kissed and fondled her and bit her slightly in the throat." [*He looks at* SEWARD *and* LUCY]
LUCY: Go on.
HARKER: [*Reading*] "The wounds are trivial. The children suffered no other harm and do not seem to have been frightened. Indeed, one small girl told her mother she hoped she might see the beautiful lady again."

[*He turns to* LUCY. SEWARD *takes paper from* HARKER]

VAN HELSING: So soon . . . so soon.

[HARKER *and* SEWARD *look at each other*]

SEWARD: You know what has been happening, Lucy? [LUCY *nods*]

HARKER: Professor Van Helsing knows, too, Lucy, and he knows how to protect you.

LUCY: Is it not too late?

VAN HELSING: No, Miss Lucy, it is not too late.

SEWARD: These poor innocent children . . .

VAN HELSING: [To SEWARD] You think Count Dracula . . .

LUCY: [Shudders] Not that name.

VAN HELSING: You think the Werewolf has done this too?

SEWARD: Of course, in the form of a woman. Who else could it be?

VAN HELSING: It is worse. Far worse.

HARKER: Worse? What do you mean?

[LUCY is motionless, her face frozen in horror]

VAN HELSING: Miss Lucy knows.

LUCY: The woman in white . . . is Mina.

HARKER: Mina. But she's dead, Lucy.

LUCY: She has joined . . . the Master.

SEWARD: Oh, God, have pity on us all. [Drops newspaper on chair]

VAN HELSING: My dear Miss Lucy, I will not ask you how you know. After tonight no more little children will meet the woman in white. She will remain at rest . . . in the tomb where you laid her. And her soul, released from this horror, will be with God.

LUCY: How can you do this?

VAN HELSING: Do not ask me.

LUCY: [Takes hold of VAN HELSING's arm] Professor, if you can save Mina's soul after her death, can you save mine?

HARKER: Oh, Lucy! [Sitting on couch, arm around her]

VAN HELSING: [Takes her hand] I will save you. In God's name, I swear it. And He has given me a sign . . . in this room tonight.

LUCY: Then promise me one thing. Whatever you plan to do, whatever you know, do not tell me. [Turns to HARKER] Not even if I beg you to tell me, swear that you will not, now, while I am still yours, while I am myself, promise it.

HARKER: I promise it. [Takes her in his arms; tries to kiss her]

LUCY: [Breaks from him, horrified] No, no, John! You mustn't kiss me. Promise that you never will, not even if I beg you to.

HARKER: I promise.

VAN HELSING: My dear Miss Lucy, from tonight on one of us will be awake all night, here in this room, next to your bedroom, with your door open.

LUCY: [*Murmurs*] You are so good.

VAN HELSING: Yes, and I will make the room safe for you. Your maid will be with you. [HARKER *talks to* LUCY *on couch while* VAN HELSING *takes handful of wolfsbane*] Doctor, rub these over the window in the little room there. See, like this. [*He starts rubbing around edge of window*] Rub it around the sashes and especially above the lock. [SEWARD *watches* VAN HELSING *rubbing, then takes wolfsbane from* VAN HELSING *quickly, and goes out through arch.* VAN HELSING *turns, goes to table and takes out wreath of wolfsbane*] See, I have made this wreath that you must wear around your neck tonight. While you wear this those . . . dreams . . . cannot come to you. [*Hangs wolfsbane around her neck. Takes out of pocket crucifix on cord, which he also hangs around her neck*] Swear to me that you will not take these off.

LUCY: I promise.

VAN HELSING: Swear it on the cross.

LUCY: [*Kisses cross*] I swear it!

[VAN HELSING *crosses toward door*]

HARKER: Professor, surely the Host is more powerful than this wolfsbane.

VAN HELSING: Of course.

HARKER: Then leave the Host with her . . . nothing can harm her then.

VAN HELSING: No, the Host cannot be used where there has been pollution. [*Screams off left*] What is it?

[ATTENDANT *enters left.* MAID *comes in from bedroom;* SEWARD *enters from arch*]

ATTENDANT: It's Renfield, sir.

SEWARD: Why haven't you got him locked up?

ATTENDANT: Because he's barred himself in, sir. He got hold of one of the patients. He had her by the throat.

[*He exits.* LUCY *rises*]

VAN HELSING: Ah . . . human blood now! [*Starting*] Come, Seward! Come, Harker!

SEWARD: I should have had him sent away!

[MAID *crosses to* LUCY. VAN HELSING *and* SEWARD *exit.* HARKER *hesitates, then follows them off.* HARKER *ad libs during exit, "It's all right, Lucy. I'll be right back," etc.*]

LUCY: John . . . [*To* MAID] Don't you leave me, too.

MAID: Of course I won't, Miss Lucy. It's nothing but a quarrel among the patients. Mr. Harker will be back soon. [MAID *places her on couch.* LUCY *swoons.* MAID *gets smelling salts*] Here, Miss Lucy. [DRACULA'S *face appears back of tapestry on rear wall; disappears after a count of eight or nine.* MAID *steps down right, gets message, then returns. Puts salts back on dresser; crosses to* LUCY] These evil-smelling flowers have made you faint. [*Takes crucifix and wreath from around* LUCY'S *neck, throws them on floor; crosses two steps down right. Another message comes to her. Puts hand to head, turns slowly, looks at window, steps toward couch*] It is so close, Madam. A little air . . . [*Turns to window.* LUCY *moans again.* MAID *pulls back latch; opens window. As window opens, clouds of mist roll in. Steps down. Gets message. Count eight. Switches out lights, then exits into bedroom. The stage is now dark. Dogs without, far and near, howl in terror. A gauze curtain comes down and a green light dims up covering the couch and center of the stage, revealing* DRACULA *standing center with back to audience, hands outstretched to resemble a large bat. As he moves up a few steps,* LUCY *slowly rises from couch and falls into his arms. A long kiss and then, as she falls back on his right arm, he bares her throat and starts to bite her as:*]

CURTAIN

ACT THREE

SCENE 1

The library. Thirty-two hours later, shortly before sunrise.

A stake and hammer are on desk. Dogs howl. Curtains move as if someone is entering window. Then chair back of desk, which is turned upstage, moves around, facing front. After a moment, VAN HELSING *enters with* SEWARD. VAN HELSING *paces up and down;* SEWARD *sits at desk. The center doors are flung open and the* ATTENDANT *comes in.*

VAN HELSING: What is it?

ATTENDANT: [*To* VAN HELSING] Anybody w'ot wants my job, sir, can 'ave it.

[SEWARD *rouses himself*]

SEWARD: What's the matter?

ATTENDANT: I knows what I knows, and w'ot I seen I saw, and I 'ops it by the first train, and don't ask for no wages in loo of notice.

VAN HELSING: Where's Renfield?

ATTENDANT: If you asks me, I says 'e's probably payin' a little visit to 'ell.

SEWARD: You've let him escape again?

ATTENDANT: Look 'ere, sir. 'Avin', so to speak, resigned, I don't 'ave to put up with any more from any of you. [*Looks at* VAN HELSING *and* SEWARD] W'ot a man can't 'elp, 'e can't 'elp, and that's that.

[SEWARD *sinks back on desk, head in hands*]

VAN HELSING: Can't you see, man, that Doctor Seward is not well? Will you desert him when he needs all the help he can get?

ATTENDANT: Puttin' it that way, sir, I ain't the man to run under fire. But I'm sick and tired of being told off for what ain't my fault.

VAN HELSING: We don't blame you. No bolts or bars could hold Renfield.

ATTENDANT: [SEWARD *looks up at him*] Now, sir, you're talkin' sense. I 'ad 'im in a straitjacket this time. Nearly all yesterday I worked at clampin' bars across the winder. Now I finds them bars pulled apart like they was made o' cheese and 'im gone.

VAN HELSING: Then try to find him.

ATTENDANT: Find 'im, sir? Find 'im? I can't chase him up and down the wall. I ain't no bloody mountain goat! [*Exits*]

VAN HELSING: The Thing mocks us. A few hours after he finds out what we know, and what we have done, he comes here, and drags that poor creature of his to himself.

SEWARD: [*In dull, hopeless tone*] What can the vampire want with Renfield?

VAN HELSING: Renfield is serving an apprenticeship . . . to join the Vampire King after his death. We must prevent that.

SEWARD: What does Renfield matter? . . . If we are beaten, then there is no God.

VAN HELSING: [*Crosses to him*] We dare not despair, Seward.

SEWARD: To figure out in advance what anyone would do who got on his track!

VAN HELSING: I thought we had him when we broke into Carfax and found two earth boxes there and then found one box in each of his four other houses, and when I pried up the lid of the sixth box I was sure we would find him there, helpless.

SEWARD: [*Bitterly*] Empty.

VAN HELSING: An empty packing case, left as a blind.

SEWARD: He only brought six in his plane, so there can be only the one left.

VAN HELSING: Only one, but hidden where we can never find it. And now we've put him on his guard.

SEWARD: Yes. [*Chair turns back. Curtains flap out.* SEWARD *looks at wrist watch*] It's not half an hour till sunrise. [*Rises and crossing to fireplace*] Poor John has been sitting up with Lucy for nine hours. She'll be safe at dawn and he can get some sleep . . . if anyone can sleep in this house.

VAN HELSING: Whoever else sleeps or does not sleep, Miss Lucy will sleep at dawn.

SEWARD: Another horror?

VAN HELSING: Oh, you've noticed how she keeps awake all night now and sleeps by day.

SEWARD: Is that part of . . . the change?

VAN HELSING: Of course. And sometimes . . . the look that comes into her face.

SEWARD: [*Turns face away in horror*] Don't, man, for God's sake, I can't bear it!

VAN HELSING: We must face the facts, for her sake.

SEWARD: How could it have got at her with the wolfsbane and the cross around her neck? [*Pause*] Suggestion, conveyed from the Monster?

VAN HELSING: Yes. He must have impelled the maid to take away the wolfsbane and cross and open the window. I should have foreseen that.

SEWARD: Don't blame yourself. The devil is more cunning than we are. [*Sits couch*] Yet Lucy seems better. Until this last attack she's always been exhausted, but at sunset last night, when she woke up after sleeping all day . . .

VAN HELSING: There was blood in her cheeks again.

SEWARD: Yes, thank God.

VAN HELSING: [*With terrible emphasis*] My poor friend, *where does that blood come from?*

SEWARD: What do you suggest now? What fresh horror . . .

[*Door left opens a crack. Long skinny hand protrudes into room.* SEWARD *sees it first and starts in alarm. Rises.* VAN HELSING *turns quickly. Door opens slowly and* RENFIELD *slinks in*]

RENFIELD: Is not half past five in the morning a strange hour for men who aren't crazy to be up and about? [*Crosses to window*]

VAN HELSING: [*Aside to* SEWARD] We may get help from this thing that's still half-human. [*To* RENFIELD] Renfield.

RENFIELD: [*Crosses, with growing hysteria*] He's after me! He's going to kill me!

VAN HELSING: Help us, Renfield, and we'll save you.

RENFIELD: You, you poor puny man, you measure your brains against his? You don't know what you're dealing with! You, a thick-headed Dutchman and a fool of an alienist, and a young cub of a boy. Why, not all the soldiers and police in London could stop the Master from doing as he likes.

VAN HELSING: But God can stop him!

RENFIELD: God permits evil. Why does he permit evil if He is good? Tell me that.

SEWARD: How did you escape through those iron bars?

RENFIELD: [*Cunningly*] Madmen have a great strength, Doctor.

VAN HELSING: Come, Renfield, we know you didn't wrench those bars apart yourself.

RENFIELD: [*Sane*] No, I didn't. I wanted them there. I hoped they'd keep him out. He did it, then he called to me and I had to come. [*Back to insanity*] The Master is angry. He promised me eternal life and live things, live things, big ones, not flies and spiders; and blood to drink, always blood. I must obey him but I don't want to be like him. . . . I am mad, I know, and bad, too, for I've taken lives, but they were only little lives. I'm not like him. I wouldn't like a human life. [LUCY *laughs offstage and says,* "Oh, John!" *as she enters with* HARKER. LUCY *has changed; there is blood in her cheeks, she is stronger and seems full of vitality. She and* HARKER *stop in surprise at seeing* RENFIELD. *To* LUCY] And why did I seek to betray him? For you. [*She smiles*] I said I'd serve the devil, but I didn't serve him honestly. I don't like women with no blood in them. [LUCY *laughs*] And yet I warned you and made him angry, and now . . . [*Working into frenzy*] . . . perhaps he will kill me. [LUCY *laughs*] And I won't get any more live things to eat. There'll be no more blood.

> [RENFIELD *starts for* LUCY's *throat.* HARKER *grasps him by right arm,* VAN HELSING *by left arm, then* SEWARD *steps in and takes* HARKER's *place as* RENFIELD *struggles violently.* SEWARD *and* VAN HELSING *bear him away, struggling and screaming*]

HARKER: Lucy, darling, you mustn't mind that poor, crazed creature.

LUCY: [*With low laugh as before*] I don't. He amuses me.

[*She crosses to divan and sits*]

HARKER: Oh, Lucy, how can you? The poor devil! Thank God . . . it will soon be dawn now.

LUCY: Dawn. The ebb tide of life. I hate the dawn. How can people like daylight? At night I am really alive. The night was made to enjoy life, and love. . . . [HARKER *turns to her; hesitates*] Come to me, John, my own John.

[*He comes and sits next to her*]

HARKER: Lucy, I'm so happy that you are better and strong again. . . .

LUCY: I've never been so well . . . so full of vitality. I was only a poor, washed-out, pale creature. I don't know what made you love me, John. There was no reason why you should. But there is *now*.

HARKER: I worship you.

LUCY: Then tell me something, John. [HARKER *turns slightly away*] If you love me, you'll tell me. . . . Now don't turn away from me again.

HARKER: [*Wearily and sadly*] You made me promise that I wouldn't tell you . . . anything.

LUCY: Oh, but I release you from your promise. There, now. What were you and Father and the funny Professor doing all day?

HARKER: I can't tell you. I promised.

LUCY: [*Angrily*] You say you love me, but you don't trust me.

HARKER: I would trust you with my life, my soul.

LUCY: Then prove it. What were you doing . . . over there in Carfax? With the hammer and the horrible iron stake. [*He shakes his head. She registers anger. He puts his head in his hands, as though crying*] You don't think I'm asking you because . . . I'm just trying to find out whether you really love me. [HARKER *recoils from her, facing up*] So you try to hide your schemes and your plots. Afraid I'd give them away, are you? You fools. Whatever *he* wants to know, he finds out for himself. He knows what you do. He knows what you think. He knows everything.

HARKER: Lucy!

[*He puts his head in her lap and sobs.* LUCY *makes claw-like movement with both her hands, then as he sobs she changes attitude and gently strokes his head*]

LUCY: My dear, I'm sorry. Let me kiss away the tears.

[*She starts to kiss him. He quickly rises; backs away a few steps*]

HARKER: No, you mustn't kiss me! You made me promise not to let you kiss me.

LUCY: You don't know why I said that, John darling. It was because I love you so much. I was afraid of what might happen. You've always thought me cold, but I've blood in my veins, hot blood, my John. And I knew if I were to kiss you . . . but I'm not afraid now. Come, will you make me say it?

HARKER: Lucy, I don't understand you.

LUCY: [*Moves toward him*] I love you. I want you. [*Stretches out her arms to him*] Come to me, my darling. I want you.

HARKER: [*Goes to her, his resistance overcome, carried away by her ardor*] Lucy, Lucy!

[*He seizes her in his arms. Slowly she takes his head and bends it back. Slowly, triumphantly she bends her head down; her mouth hovers over his. Dogs howl outside. She bends his head further back quickly. Her mouth seeks his throat. Doors center open.* VAN HELSING *rushes in, holding crucifix*]

VAN HELSING: Harker! Harker, save yourself! [HARKER *rises, draws away. With outstretched arm,* VAN HELSING *holds crucifix between them.* LUCY's *face becomes convulsed with loathing and rage. She snarls like an animal, retreats, fainting onto divan.* VAN HELSING *follows, holds crucifix to her; strokes her forehead with left hand*] I warned you, my poor friend. [*He kneels beside* LUCY; *begins to chafe her temples. She revives slowly, looks about her, sees cross and seizes it and kisses it passionately.* VAN HELSING, *fervently:*] Thank God! Thank God!

[*Pause.* HARKER *crosses to divan*]

LUCY: [*Broken-hearted*] Don't come to me, John. I am unclean.

HARKER: [*Sits beside her*] My darling, in my eyes you are purity itself.

VAN HELSING: You love her, and in love there is truth. She is pure, and the evil thing that has entered her shall be rooted out.

LUCY: [*In weak voice as in previous acts; to* VAN HELSING] You said you could save Mina's soul.

VAN HELSING: Mina's soul is in heaven.

LUCY: [*Murmurs*] Tell me how.

> [SEWARD *enters, comes up to group in alarm, but* VAN HELSING *motions silence*]

VAN HELSING: It is your right to know . . . now. I entered her tomb. I pried open the coffin. I found her there, sleeping, but not dead . . . not truly dead. There was blood in her cheeks, a drop of blood like a red ruby on the corner of her mouth. With a stake and hammer I struck to the heart. One scream, a convulsion, and then . . . the look of peace that came to her face when, with God's help, I had made her truly dead.

LUCY: If I die, swear to me that you will do this to my body.

VAN HELSING: It shall be done.

HARKER: I swear it.

SEWARD: And I.

LUCY: My lover, my father, my dear friend, you have sworn to save my soul. And now I am done with life. I cannot live on to become . . . what you know.

VAN HELSING: No, no, Miss Lucy, by all you hold sacred, you must not even think of suicide. That would put you in his power forever.

LUCY: I cannot face this horror that I am becoming.

HARKER: [*Rises*] We will find this *Thing* that has fouled your life, destroy him and send his soul to burning hell, and it shall be by *my* hand.

LUCY: You must destroy him if you can, but with pity in your hearts, not rage and vengeance. That poor soul who has done so much evil needs our prayers more than any other. . . .

HARKER: No, you cannot ask me to forgive.

LUCY: Perhaps I, too, will need your prayers and your pity.

VAN HELSING: My dear Miss Lucy, now, while you are yourself, help me. [*Takes her hand*]

LUCY: How can I help you? Don't tell me, no, you mustn't tell me anything.

VAN HELSING: Each time the white face, the red eyes came you were pale, exhausted afterwards. But that last time . . .

LUCY: [*Shudders*] Last time he came he said I was his bride, he would seal me to him for the centuries to come.

VAN HELSING: And then?

LUCY: And then . . . [*Rises; crosses toward door*] No, no, I can't tell you. I can't. . . .

VAN HELSING: But you must.

SEWARD: You must, Lucy!

LUCY: He scratched open one of his veins. He pressed my mouth down to it. He called it a mystic sacrament . . . he made me . . . he made me drink. . . . I can't, I can't . . . go on. . . . [*LUCY rushes off hysterically.* SEWARD *follows her*]

VAN HELSING: I warned you, my poor friend. I broke in when I heard the dogs howling.

HARKER: The dogs. Then the Werewolf is about.

VAN HELSING: He is pursuing Renfield.

HARKER: God, we must do something!

VAN HELSING: And at once. I shall leave Renfield here, as I did Miss Lucy. If the *Thing* appears, we three will bar the two doors and the window.

HARKER: [*Crosses up toward window. Laughs bitterly*] Bar? Against *that*?

VAN HELSING: Even against *that*, for we shall each carry the sacred element.

HARKER: And then?

VAN HELSING: Then I do not know. It will be terrible, for we do not know his full powers. But this I know. . . . [*Looks at watch*] It is eight minutes to sunrise. The power of all evil things ceases with the coming of day. His one last earth box is his only refuge. If we can keep him here till daybreak he must collapse. And the stake and the hammer are ready. [*Dogs howl.* HARKER *crosses to window, goes out*] He is here. Quickly! [VAN HELSING *runs to window. Seizes* RENFIELD]

RENFIELD: [*As he is dragged in by* VAN HELSING] No, no!

VAN HELSING: But you must, man, and this may save your soul and your life as well.

RENFIELD: No, no, no, not alone! Don't leave me alone! [VAN HELSING *shoves him forward.* RENFIELD *falls.* VAN HELSING *hurries out, closing door and putting lights out.* RENFIELD *slowly rises; looks about him.* RENFIELD *howls in terror; crouches in firelight as far away as possible from doors and window.* DRACULA *appears, door center, in pale blue light, in evening clothes, dress and cloak as before. Red light from fireplace covers* DRACULA. *As* DRACULA *moves,* RENFIELD's *back is to audience*] Master! I didn't do it! I said nothing. I am your slave, your dog! [DRACULA *steps toward him*] Master, don't kill me! For the love of God, let me live. Punish me . . . torture me . . . I deserve it . . . but let me live! I can't face God with all those lives on my conscience, all that blood on my hands.

DRACULA: [*With deadly calm*] Did I not promise you that you should come to me at your death, and enjoy centuries of life and power over the bodies and souls of others?

RENFIELD: Yes, Master, I want lives, I want blood . . . but I didn't want human life.

DRACULA: You betrayed me. You sought to warn my destined bride against me.

RENFIELD: Mercy, mercy, mercy, don't kill me!

[DRACULA *raises right arm very slowly toward* RENFIELD, *who screams, this time in physical pain.* RENFIELD, *like a bird before a snake, drags himself to* DRACULA, *who stands motionless. As* RENFIELD *reaches* DRACULA's *feet,* DRACULA, *with swift motion, stoops, seizes him by the throat, lifts him up, his grip stifling* RENFIELD's *screams. Doors center are thrown open.* VAN HELSING *switches on lights.* DRACULA *drops* RENFIELD, *who falls into corner below couch and remains there during following scene.* DRACULA *starts toward* VAN HELSING, *who takes case containing Host out of inside breast pocket and holds it out toward* DRACULA *in his clenched right fist.* DRACULA *recoils; turns quickly to window.* HARKER *appears through window and holds cruci-*

fix toward DRACULA *in clenched fist.* DRACULA *recoils.* SEW-
ARD *enters window, holding crucifix. The three men stand
during the following scene with right arms pointing toward* DRACULA. *He turns, walks to fireplace, turns and
faces them*]

DRACULA: [*Ironically*] My friends, I regret I was not present to receive your calls at my house.

VAN HELSING: [*Looks at watch*] Four minutes until sunrise.

DRACULA: [*Looking at wrist watch*] Your watch is correct, Professor.

VAN HELSING: Your life in death has reached its end.

SEWARD: By God's mercy.

DRACULA: [HARKER *steps toward* DRACULA. DRACULA, *turning to them,
suavely*] Its end? Not yet, Professor. I have still more than three
minutes to add to my five hundred years.

HARKER: And three minutes from now you'll be in hell, where a thousand years of agony will not bring you one second nearer the end
of your punishment.

VAN HELSING: Silence, Harker. Miss Lucy forbade this. She asked for
prayer, and for pity. [*To* DRACULA] Make your peace with God,
Man-That-Was. We are not your judges . . . we know not how this
curse may have come upon you.

DRACULA: [*Furiously*] You fools! You think with your wafers, your
wolfsbane, you can destroy me . . . me, the king of my kind? You
shall see. Five of my earth boxes you have polluted. Have you
found the sixth?

VAN HELSING: You cannot reach your sixth refuge now. Take your
true form as Werewolf if you will. Your fangs may rend us, but we
have each sworn to keep you here . . . [*Looks at watch*] . . . for
two minutes and a half, when you must collapse and we can make
an end.

DRACULA: *You* keep *me*. Fools, listen and let my words ring in your
ears all your lives, and torture you on your deathbeds! I go, I go to
sleep in my box for a hundred years. You have accomplished that
much against me, Van Helsing. But in a century I shall wake, and
call my bride to my side from her tomb, my Lucy, my Queen.
[HARKER *and* SEWARD *move closer*] I have other brides of old times

who await me in their vaults in Transylvania. But I shall set *her* above them all.

HARKER: Should you escape, we know how to save Lucy's soul, if not her life.

DRACULA: [*Moving left*] Ah, the stake. Yes, but only if she dies by day. I shall see that she dies by night. She shall come to an earth box of mine at her death and await her Master. To do to her what you did to my Mina, Van Helsing, you must find her body, and that you will not.

HARKER: Then she shall die by day.

DRACULA: You will kill her? You lack the courage, you poor rat of flesh and blood!

SEWARD: Silence, John . . . he is doomed. This is his revenge. He hopes to trouble us . . . afterwards.

VAN HELSING: [*Looks at watch*] Thirty seconds.

[*They move in*]

DRACULA: [*Calmly, suavely again*] I thank you for reminding me of the time.

VAN HELSING: Harker, open the curtains. [HARKER *opens curtains. Red light of approaching dawn outside*] That is the East. The sun will rise beyond the meadow there.

[DRACULA *pulls cape over his head*]

SEWARD: [*Glancing behind, leaves wolfsbane on desk as he looks up at window*] The clouds are coloring.

HARKER: God's daybreak.

[HARKER *leaves crucifix on desk.* VAN HELSING *checks watch.* SEWARD *and* HARKER *step in*]

DRACULA: [*Coolly. Turns upstage, with back to them*] A pleasant task you have set yourself, Mr. Harker.

VAN HELSING: Ten seconds. Be ready when he collapses.

[SEWARD *crosses to hold* DRACULA's *cape on left of* DRAC-ULA. HARKER *holds cape on right of* DRACULA]

HARKER: *The sun!* The stake, Professor . . . the stake! Hold him, Doctor.

SEWARD: I've got him.

> [DRACULA, *with loud burst of mocking laughter, vanishes on the word "sun," leaving the two men holding the empty cape. A flash goes off in front of fireplace.* HARKER *backs down left, drops empty cape in front of desk. The three men look around them*]

HARKER: Up the chimney, as a bat. You heard what he said?

SEWARD: God will not permit it. What's to be done now, Van Helsing?

VAN HELSING: [*Crosses, after looking at the prostrate* RENFIELD; *motions* HARKER *and* SEWARD *to him. Whispers to them*] We'll trick Renfield into showing us! [*Then:*] Dare we leave Renfield on earth to become the slave when he dies?

SEWARD: But he's human. We can't do murder?

HARKER: I'll do it if you won't, Doctor!

VAN HELSING: [*To* SEWARD] Go to your office and get some painless drug.

RENFIELD: [*Sensing their drift without hearing their words, has been edging toward panel. Looks around room, then at panel*] They're going to kill me, Master! Save me! I am coming to you.

> [*Panel in bookcase opens,* RENFIELD *exits and panel closes*]

VAN HELSING: He has shown us the way! Where does that passage go?

SEWARD: I never knew there was a passage.

> [HARKER *hastens to desk; gets stake and hammer. They rush to panel*]

VAN HELSING: Only that devil has the combination. We'll break through somehow. Harker . . . quick, the hammer.

BLACKOUT

CURTAIN

SCENE 2

A vault.

Absolute darkness. Coffin right center and back of gauze drop. Flash of electric torch seen coming slowly downstairs center. Coffin contains body of DRACULA.

VAN HELSING'S VOICE: For God's sake, be careful, Seward.
SEWARD'S VOICE: These stairs go down forever.
VAN HELSING'S VOICE: May God protect us.
SEWARD'S VOICE: Is Harker there?
VAN HELSING'S VOICE: He's gone for a lantern.
SEWARD'S VOICE: I've got to the bottom.
VAN HELSING'S VOICE: Be careful. I'm right behind you.

[*Torch flashes around vault and they walk about slowly*]

SEWARD'S VOICE: What can this place be?
VAN HELSING'S VOICE: It seems an old vault. [*Stifled scream from* SEWARD. *Torch out. The torch is seen to jerk back*] What is it? Oh, where are you, man?
SEWARD'S VOICE: Sorry. I'm all right. A big rat ran across my foot.

[*Light seen coming downstairs.* HARKER *appears carrying lighted lantern which reaches floor; partially illuminates bare vault. He has stake and hammer in left hand*]

HARKER: Where are you? What is this place?
VAN HELSING: We can't see.

[HARKER *moves with lantern*]

HARKER: The place smells horribly of bats.
VAN HELSING: It has an animal smell, like the lair of a wolf.
HARKER: That's what it is.
SEWARD: [*Still flashing torch about*] There's absolutely nothing here.
HARKER: [*At extreme left with lantern*] Here's another passage.
VAN HELSING: [*Moving left*] I thought so. That must lead to Carfax. The sixth earth box is hidden somewhere here.

HARKER: And the monster is in it.

SEWARD: You can't be sure. [*As he speaks, light from his torch falls on* RENFIELD, *stretched on floor.* RENFIELD *screams as light falls on him; scurries off right into darkness*] Renfield!

[HARKER *and* VAN HELSING *hurry across*]

VAN HELSING: Where is he?

SEWARD: Over there somewhere. Even if Renfield knew about this place, that doesn't prove the vampire's here.

VAN HELSING: [*As* SEWARD *is speaking* VAN HELSING *moves right; seizes* RENFIELD] It is the vampire's life or yours! [*Drags* RENFIELD *into light of lantern*] Look at him, man, look at him. He knows.

RENFIELD: I know nothing. Let me go! Let me go, I say! [*Breaks away; goes right*]

VAN HELSING: He was stretched out here, but he wouldn't let me drag him back. Ah! Here it is. Quick, that stake.

[HARKER *and* VAN HELSING, *with stake, pry up stone slab and open coffin. The three men gaze in horror and triumph at coffin*]

SEWARD: What a horrible undead thing he is lying there!

HARKER: Let me drive it in deep!

[VAN HELSING *takes stake from* HARKER, *lowers it into the coffin.* RENFIELD *stands at right end of coffin*]

VAN HELSING: [*Almost in a whisper*] That's over the heart, Doctor?

SEWARD: [*Back of coffin*] Yes. [VAN HELSING *hands hammer to* HARKER. HARKER *raises hammer high over head; pounds stake with full force. Low groan. Silence. Stake remains fixed in* DRACULA'S *body.*]

VAN HELSING: See his face now . . . the look of peace.

SEWARD: He is crumbling away.

RENFIELD: Thank God, we're free!

LUCY: [*Comes down stairway and halts at bottom*] Father, Father, John!

HARKER: Lucy!

VAN HELSING: [*Takes handful of dust; scatters it over the body*] Dust to dust . . . ashes to ashes . . .

CURTAIN

[*The curtain rises again and the entire cast comes downstage before a black drop for curtain speech*]

VAN HELSING: [*To* AUDIENCE] Just a moment, Ladies and Gentlemen! Just a word before you go. We hope the memories of Dracula and Renfield won't give you bad dreams, so just a word of reassurance. When you get home tonight and the lights have been turned out and you are afraid to look behind the curtains and you dread to see a face appear at the window . . . why, just pull yourself together and remember that after all *there are such things.*

THE CURTAIN FALLS

STANLEY RICHARDS

Stanley Richards, a native New Yorker, is a man of varied experience in the theatre. He has written twenty-five plays, among them: *Through A Glass, Darkly; August Heat; Tunnel of Love; Sun Deck; O Distant Land;* and *District of Columbia.* He is also the editor of a number of play anthologies.

Twelve of his own plays have appeared in the annuals *The Best One-Act Plays* and *The Best Short Plays.* His plays have been widely performed on stage, television and radio, and most of them have been translated for production and publication abroad.

One of his most recent plays, *Journey to Bahia,* adapted from a prize-winning Brazilian play and film *O Pagador de Promessas,* had its première at The Berkshire Playhouse and later was produced in Washington, D. C. under the auspices of the Brazilian Ambassador and the Brazilian American Cultural Institute.

In addition, he has been the New York theatre critic for *Players Magazine,* and a frequent contributor to *Theatre Arts; Playbill; The Theatre; Actors' Equity Magazine;* and *The Dramatists Guild Quarterly.*

As an American theatre specialist, Mr. Richards has been awarded three successive grants by the United States Department of State's International Cultural Exchange Program to teach playwriting and directing in Chile and Brazil. He taught playwriting in Canada for ten years and in 1966 was appointed Visiting Professor of Drama at the University of Guelph, Ontario. He has produced and directed plays and has lectured extensively on theatre at universities in the United States, Canada and South America.